DEDICATION

This book is dedicated to our husbands and
children. May we continue to learn and grow together.

TEACHING TORAH

A TREASURY OF INSIGHTS AND ACTIVITIES

SOREL GOLDBERG LOEB AND
BARBARA BINDER KADDEN

A.R.E. Publishing, Inc.
Denver, Colorado

ACKNOWLEDGEMENTS

We would like to thank Rabbi Raymond A. Zwerin and Audrey Friedman Marcus for their dedication to seeing this project through from beginning to end and for their insightful contributions to the manuscript. Thanks also to Anita Wenner for her help with the Bibliography.

Thanks also to Rabbi Bruce Kadden for his support and assistance, to Donna Kemper for her editing and typing skills, and to Anita Wenner for her help with the Bibliography.

Published by:
A.R.E. Publishing, Inc.
Denver, Colorado

Library of Congress Catalog Number 97-71132
ISBN 0-86705-041-1

CONTENTS

INTRODUCTION   vii

GENESIS
Overview   1
Beresheet (1:1-6:8)   3
Noah (6:9-11:32)   11
Lech Lecha (12:1-17:27)   19
Vayera (18:1-22:24)   25
Chayay Sarah (23:1-25:18)   33
Toledot (25:19-28:9)   39
Vayaytzay (28:10-32:3)   46
Vayishlach (32:4-36:43)   52
Vayayshev (37:1-40:23)   58
Mikaytz (41:1-44:17)   65
Vayigash (44:18-47:27)   71
Vayechi (47:28-50:26)   77
Review Activities for Genesis   83

EXODUS
Overview   85
Shemot (1:1-6:1)   87
Vaera (6:2-9:35)   94
Bo (10:1-13:16)   100
Beshalach (13:17-17:16)   107
Yitro (18:1-20:23)   113
Mishpatim (21:1-24:18)   121
Terumah (25:1-27:19)   128
Tetzaveh (27:20-30:10)   134
Ki Tisa (30:11-34:35)   140
Vayakhel (35:1-38:20)   148
Pikuday (38:21-40:38)   155
Review Activities for Exodus   161

LEVITICUS
Overview   163
Vayikrah (1:1-5:26)   165
Tzav (6:1-8:36)   172
Shemini (9:1-11:47)   177
Tazria (12:1-13:59)   183

Metzora (14:1-15:33)   189
Acharay Mot (16:1-18:30)   194
Kedoshim (19:1-20:27)   201
Emor (21:1-24:23)   207
Behar (25:1-26:2)   214
Bechukotai (26:3-27:34)   220
Review Activities for Leviticus   226

NUMBERS
Overview   227
BaMidbar (1:1-4:20)   229
Naso (4:21-7:89)   235
Beha'alotecha (8:1-12:16)   242
Shelach Lecha (13:1-15:41)   248
Korach (16:1-18:32)   254
Chukat (19:1-22:1)   260
Balak (22:2-25:9)   266
Pinchas (25:10-30:1)   272
Matot (30:2-32:42)   278
Mas'ay (33:1-33:13)   284
Review Activities for Numbers   290

DEUTERONOMY
Overview   291
Devarim (1:1-3:22)   293
Va'etchanan (3:23-7:11)   299
Ekev (7:12-11:25)   304
Re'eh (11:26-16:17)   310
Shofetim (16:18-21:9)   316
Ki Taytzay (21:10-25:19)   322
Ki Tavo (26:1-29:8)   329
Nitzavim (29:9-30:20)   335
Vayaylech (31:1-30)   340
Ha'azinu (32:1-52)   345
V'zot HaBrachah (33:1-34:12)   350
Review Activities for Deuteronomy   356

**APPENDIX: COMMENTATORS/
   COMMENTARIES**   359
BIBLIOGRAPHY   367
**LIST OF AUDIOVISUAL PUBLISHERS
   & DISTRIBUTORS**   378
INDEX OF STRATEGIES   379

Introduction

Torah is at the foundation of the Jewish people. It records earliest history; it outlines fundamental laws; it models significant values and standards of behavior; it reflects basic truths about human nature; it opens us to relationship with, and wonder of, the divine. Its language is the portal to Jewish study, worship, and identity.

Because Torah is all of this and more, it has been, and remains today, the core curriculum for Jewish learning. *Teaching Torah: A Treasury of Insights and Activities* is a comprehensive resource facilitating the presentation in an engaging and educationally sound manner of the history, laws, values, and relationships embodied in Torah.

WHO CAN USE THIS BOOK

Teaching Torah is both a resource book and a teacher's guide. The material is geared to students and teachers of upper elementary school age through adult and can be used in a variety of settings. In day schools or in supplementary schools, *Teaching Torah* can become the primary tool for teaching Bible or the portion of the week. Participants in and leaders of Junior Congregations will find that the use of *Teaching Torah* will enrich the Torah service.

This is also an excellent resource for individuals preparing for Bar/Bat Mitzvah. An addition to *Teaching Torah* is the inclusion of a Bar/Bat Mitzvah project with each Torah portion. Families can use this book each week as a basis for effective Torah study, as can individuals seeking a framework for private study. Retreat and weekend study groups can organize an ongoing series around one portion utilizing a variety of the suggested Insights and Strategies. Camp, Havurah, campus, and youth group leaders will also find *Teaching Torah* a valuable resource. Substitute teachers will benefit by having ready-made teaching ideas upon which they can draw in last minute situations.

Teaching Torah is an indispensable aid for Rabbis and others who prepare sermons and lectures and lead discussions. The Synopsis can be used as the basis for a handout or guide for the congregation during worship services. The section on Insights from the Tradition can touch off a flood of ideas or associations; any one of the more than a thousand Strategies can be the kernel around which a presentation or lesson is built.

Non-Jews will also find this book valuable. The Synopses, Insights, and Strategies are applicable and/or adaptable to their needs and uses. For this audience, the material contained herein can also provide an opportunity to learn how Jews view and study Torah.

CONTENT AND ORGANIZATION

Each chapter deals with one of the 54 weekly Torah portions. The chapters are organized as follows:

Synopsis

Each Synopsis contains a precise summary of the narrative, dialogue, and laws found in the portion. While not intended to replace a careful reading of the Torah text itself, the Synopsis of each portion is included to serve as a frame of reference for the Insights and Strategies which follow it. The 1962 Jewish Publication Society translation of the Torah is used as the basis for each Synopsis.

Insights from the Tradition

Each Synopsis is followed by a section entitled Insights from the Tradition which presents a selection of interpretive and explanatory material. These Insights do not, by any means, exhaust the massive wealth of commentary and homiletic materials available. Instead, they are meant to serve as a model of how the text can be treated and as an illustration of the dynamic nature of the interaction which Jews have had with Torah through the ages. Whether dealing with a Hebrew wordplay, a *midrash,* an ethical standard, a *halachic* issue, or the use of language, the Insights shed light on the text. They help the student of Torah recognize the text as a living and challenging entity.

Following each Insight are two types of questions: those which deal directly with the Insight itself and those which bring the Insight into the world of the student. Taken together, the Insights and questions enable learners to probe some of the nuances and subtleties of Torah.

Strategies

The Strategies section consists of a large and varied collection of activities arranged under the following headings: Analyzing the Text, Extending the Text, Personalizing the Text, Other Resources, Involving the Family, and a Bar/Bat Mitzvah Project.

The activities under Analyzing the Text provide a way into the text itself. While the methods used vary, the object of this sub-section is to involve the student of Torah in textual analysis.

Extending the Text directs the student to see Torah as a source of Jewish symbols, observances, ceremonies, and liturgy. Also found here are activities (1) which compare or contrast the text under study to another text, to a *midrash,* or to another literary source and/or (2) which involve creating new *midrashim.* Thus, these activities track the text as its influence extends into Jewish history, literature, and contemporary Jewish life and thought.

As the name of the next sub-section implies, Personalizing the Text takes Torah beyond tradition and into the world of the student. These activities will elicit from students personal beliefs and opinions and a clarification of their values, thus making Torah timely for them. This sub-section also contains many art, music, and drama activities.

Additional books and media useful in teaching a given portion are listed under the title Other Resources. These include videos, art activities, creative movement, music, textbooks, and related stories. The Other Resources sub-section is not comprehensive, nor has any evaluative judgment been made regarding the materials cited here. The goal of this sub-section is simply to expand the teacher's list of options in teaching the Torah text.

Torah study belongs in the home. Parents and children learning together enrich their appreciation for each other and for Torah. The activities under Involving the Family are intended to involve an entire household in the study of Torah. For each weekly portion, one or two family activities are presented using such modalities as discussion, values clarification, social action, and art. Many of the activities in the other sub-sections of Strategies can be appropriate for families as well.

The Strategies in this sub-section are also appropriate for use by Rabbis, Havurot, or group leaders on a family Shabbaton or a retreat. Involving the Family strategies might also be presented as open-ended questions, offering possibilities for further exploration of Torah after a fixed study period.

The Bar/Bat Mitzvah project is a new section in this revised edition of *Teaching Torah*. Many congregations now require that students complete such a project as part of their preparation for Bar/Bat Mitzvah. Such projects can add a significant additional dimension to this already special time in the lives of Bar/Bat Mitzvah students.

Review Activities

A brief section of creative Review Activities is found at the conclusion of each biblical book. These are suitable for evaluating students and culminating a unit of study. With a little imagination, Review Activities from one biblical book can be adapted for use in reviewing another.

For maximum flexibility, the Strategies in this book are not designed for a specific age or grade level. The teacher can decide which are appropriate for use with a particular age group and setting. It should be noted that while some Strategies complement and expand on the material in Insights from the Tradition, others present new insights and or interpretive material.

Appendix: Commentators/Commentaries

The Appendix consists of capsule biographies of the commentators and overviews of the most significant commentaries/sources referred to in *Teaching Torah*. For further information on these, consult a Jewish encyclopedia.

Bibliography

The comprehensive Bibliography includes all references mentioned in the text, as well as a selection of other useful sources and materials all of which are currently in print. Following the Bibliography is a list, with addresses, of publishers and distributors of books and materials related to Torah and teaching Torah. There is also an Internet listing along with fax addresses for individual Torah study, plus additional information on weekly and on-line Torah study groups.

Index of Strategies

A thematic Index of Strategies has been created for subjects which appear frequently in the text (for example, Shabbat, Holidays, God, Life Cycle, Environmental Concerns). This Index will direct the teacher to all the strategies found in this book on a particular subject. It will also provide easy access to subject material for groups whose primary purpose is not the study of Torah per se, but the study of a subject that derives from, or bears on, Torah. (Note that strategies pertaining to subject areas are in the Index.)

USING THIS BOOK

The Insights and Strategies presented in *Teaching Torah* assume a familiarity with the biblical text. Each Synopsis will provide a clear and concise overview of the contents and highlights of a given portion. However, to capture the literary and linguistic flavor of Torah, the textual devices, and the rich nuances, there is no substitute for a thorough reading of the Torah itself.

Once well acquainted with the portion, the teacher may decide to teach one small segment of it. A reading of the Insights and Strategies in *Teaching Torah* can be the basis for determining which segment to choose for study or can help pinpoint material which corresponds to a segment already chosen.

Alternatively, the teacher may want to highlight for study a specific aspect of the portion or a general theme (e.g., the character of Moses, the use of irony, etc.). Here again, helpful material will be found in both the Insights and the Strategies.

Those who have only a few minutes of class time each week to devote to the portion of the week might use a single Insight and its questions as the basis for a lesson.

Those who have a longer period of time for Torah study might proceed in the following manner: (1) with students, read the Synopsis (along with the actual text) to see what the text actually says perhaps using an activity from Analyzing the Text; (2) introduce an Insight which illumines the text keeping in mind that many of the Insights are too difficult for younger children; (3) have students do another strategy which analyzes the text; (4) use a strategy or two which extends or personalizes the material; (5) make use of Other Resources as desired; (6) assign a strategy from Involving the Family to do at home. Overall, select strategies for use in one session which employ a variety of techniques so as to reach all kinds of learners and to provide a dynamic and balanced lesson. Those studying individually or privately (e.g., Bar/Bat Mitzvah students) can be guided to follow the above sequence. Each Bar/Bat Mitzvah project connects directly to its Torah portion.

When using the material in *Teaching Torah*, it is important to be sensitive to the background of each student. Subjects such as intermarriage, divorce, death, and relationships with non-Jews need to be broached and approached with sensitivity. When discussing God, for example, remember that Judaism stresses righteous action more than dogmatic belief and that there are many ways to view and understand God.

IN CONCLUSION

Torah study has been vital to Jews for centuries precisely because it lends itself to search and discovery by each new generation. The text is accessible on some level to all individuals. The teacher is, therefore, wise to act as a patient guide, allowing students to discover for themselves the meanings and messages of the Torah.

Our liturgy calls Torah a "tree of life." Trees sway to and fro in the wind, but they are firmly rooted in the ground. Trees can shelter us from rain, satisfy our senses with sweet fruit, delightful fragrance, rustling leaves, and ever-changing beauty. Similarly, a knowledge of Torah can root us firmly in Jewish tradition and keep us from being blown about by the changing currents of modern life. Torah study can satisfy our need for beauty and poetry, a sense of identity, relevance, and meaning. It is hoped that *Teaching Torah: A Treasury of Insights and Activities* will encourage teachers everywhere to discover or to reaffirm the richness of Torah study and to transmit it diligently to all their students.

OVERVIEW

Beresheet, the first book of the Torah, is known by several names including *Sefer Rishon* (First Book), *Sefer Beri'at HaOlam* (Book of the Creation of the World), and *Sefer HaYashar* (Book of the Upright). The latter refers to the narratives about the Patriarchs (Abraham, Isaac, and Jacob). *Beresheet* is the word with which the text opens and, as with other books of the Torah, this opening word became the accepted name of the entire book. In Latin, the name Genesis means "origins." Both the Hebrew and Latin titles reflect the contents of the book — the universal history of humankind and the accounts of the Patriarchs and Matriarchs and their families.

Genesis chronicles the creation of the world, its destruction by flood, and its reestablishment by a righteous man, Noah, and his family. It progresses through the establishment of a relationship between God and Abraham, Isaac, and Jacob. With each passing generation, a clearer picture of God and the mission of Israel emerges. Thus, Genesis moves from the universal to the particular, establishing the themes of the unity of humankind, the choice between good and evil given to all people, and the apparent tendency of human beings to turn to evil. Early in Genesis, Adam and Eve are made God's partners in Creation. Later, as a result of the disobedience of humanity, God chooses to raise up a people (the descendants of Abraham and Sarah) to live in accordance with God's commands.

Genesis has a great deal to teach us about the relationship of God to Creation. And here it differs significantly from creation myths of other cultures which may have elements in common with Genesis. The Creation described in Genesis is a purposeful one, not an act of whim and will by a group of gods. The God of Genesis is a single God who, though outside of Creation, establishes personal relationships based on justice and righteousness with the Patriarchs and takes an active role in human history. God is, therefore, the source of meaning for human life.

Genesis differs, too, from the other four books of the Torah. It is the only one which is virtually all narrative and which presents very little legal material. The accounts in Genesis have to do with individuals and their families, as opposed to Exodus through Deuteronomy which describe the history of a nation. Unlike the later books, in Genesis no conflict is described between the God of Abraham and the gods of the surrounding peoples. Lastly, the theme of divine revelation to the entire Jewish people is nowhere mentioned in the covenants made with the Patriarchs.

Genesis is an important prologue to the books which follow. It closes with a repetition of the members of Jacob's family who went down to Egypt as a confederation of tribes and whose descendants will, after the Exodus, constitute the Jewish nation.

BERESHEET 1:1-6:8 בראשית

SYNOPSIS

BERESHEET BEGINS WITH A DESCRIPTION of the creation of the world. Creation is described in two accounts. The first account lists the acts of creation day-by-day as follows:

First day: Day and night.
Second day: Sky, earth, and seas.
Third day: Plants, trees, vegetation.
Fourth day: Sun, moon, stars.
Fifth day: Fish, water creatures, birds.
Sixth day: Mammals, land creatures, Adam and Eve.
Seventh day: God rests, Shabbat.

In the second description of creation, Adam is created from the dust of the earth and placed by God in the Garden of Eden. The vegetation blooms, God creates the animals, and Adam names them. God commands Adam not to eat of the tree of knowledge of good and evil.

In order to create a helper for Adam, God causes him to fall into a deep sleep. Eve is created from one of his ribs.

A serpent in the garden persuades Eve to eat the fruit from the tree of the knowledge of good and evil. Eve also gives Adam the fruit to eat. As punishment, God banishes them from the Garden of Eden, proclaiming that henceforth they will get their food by hard toil and that women will bear children in pain.

Following their expulsion, Adam and Eve have two sons: Cain and Abel. Cain becomes a farmer and Abel a shepherd. The two brothers bring offerings to God. The offering of Abel is accepted, while the offering of Cain is rejected. In his anger and jealousy, Cain kills Abel. God punishes Cain by making him a ceaseless wanderer. Adam and Eve bear a third son, Seth, from whom Noah descends.

As the portion closes, God expresses dismay at the evil that humanity has perpetrated upon the earth and promises to blot out everything created. Noah, however, finds favor with God.

INSIGHTS FROM THE TRADITION

A *Beresheet* (in the beginning) recounts the creation of the world and the genesis of humanity. On the sixth and final day of creation, God creates the first human being. Chapter 1:26 reads, "And God said, 'Let us make man in our image, after our likeness.'" Why is God speaking in the plural? Rashi explains that it was plural because God consulted the angels, asking them if people should be created. The lesson of this verse, says Rashi, is to teach proper conduct and the virtue of humbleness, namely that the greater should consult with and ask permission from the lesser.

What does it mean to be created in the image of God?
Is it pretentious or boastful of us to think that we are created in the divine image?
In terms of Jewish tradition, what is problematic about referring to God in the plural?
God's actions, according to Rashi, model a democratic style of leadership. In what ways could this work in an office or factory, in a family, in a school, in an organization?

B With the creation of each component of the world, God comments on the goodness of the handiwork. Only with the creation of Adam does God withhold the comment "It is good." Why would the creation of Adam not merit this compliment? Rambam, in the *Mishneh Torah,* provides an explanation based on the concept of free will: "Free will is granted to every human being. If a man wants to follow the good path and be good, he has the power to do so; if he wants to follow the evil way and be wicked, he is free to do so . . . . The Creator does not decree that a man shall be either good or evil" (*The Book of Knowledge* 5:1-2).

To what extent do you agree with Rambam's statement?

Each of us is responsible for choosing our own behaviors. What influences those choices for you?

C The Talmud points out that in Genesis 2:7, when God formed Adam, the Hebrew word for "created" *(vayitzer)* is spelled with a double yud. When God formed the animals, *vayitzer* is spelled with only one *yud*. This is to show that people have two inclinations: the inclination to do good *(yetzer ha-tov)* and the inclination to do evil *(yetzer ha-ra)* (Berachot 61a).

What are the similarities between the *yetzer ha-tov* and one's conscience?
Of what significance to you is the whole discussion about an extra *yud*?
In what way would you be different if you did not have a *yetzer tov* and a *yetzer ra*?

D The two versions of the Creation story found in this Torah portion offer different ideas about the creation of the first woman. As told in Genesis 1:27, man and woman are created at the same time, whereas in Genesis 2:20-22, woman is created only after no fitting helper is found for Adam. According to Ellen Frankel, ". . . human wholeness depends upon an Other to complete the divine image" (*The Five Books of Miriam,* p. 6). Therefore, both stories — whether positing that the first people were both male and female, *or,* that woman emerged from man's body — teach the same lesson in different ways. Another view is that Adam, created from earth *(adamah),* represents the source of material being, while Eve/*Chavah,* the "mother of all the living," represents the source of spiritual being. Both are needed in this world.

Do you agree that males and females have different, but complimentary qualities? Do you think that individuals need other people to be complete? What would the world be like if people did not have the need to join with another of the opposite sex to reproduce?

E In this *sedra,* the goodness of God's creation is juxtaposed with the evil of humanity's deeds, e.g., the eating of the fruit of the tree of the knowledge of good and evil, Cain killing Abel, and humanity becoming corrupt in Noah's generation.

What have been some of humanity's good deeds? In what ways has humanity suffered for its evil deeds (such as wars, pollution, crime, lack of education)?

F In *Midrash Tadsheh,* the question is put forth: "Why did the Holy One of blessing ordain that [Adam] might eat of all the trees of the garden and withhold from him just one of them? So that he should continually remember his Creator and be conscious of the yoke of God who fashioned him . . . ."

What is meant by God's yoke?
Are there elements in your life that remind you daily of your relationship to God?
When do you have to exercise self-control?

G The tree in the Garden of Eden tested the self-discipline of Adam and Eve, a test which they failed. Once Adam and Eve ate of the tree, they had to accept the consequences of their actions: God decreed that Adam and Eve must leave the Garden of Eden, that women would bear children in pain yet still desire their husbands, and that men would have to provide food by hard toil.
God delivers the remedy before the curse. Adam and Eve were driven from the Garden, yet from that time on, they had the ability to procreate and share in the completion of the world (Genesis Rabbah 9:7).

Did the punishment (leaving Eden) fit the crime (disobeying God)?
Why would God want to withhold the knowledge of good and evil from people?
In light of the Eden story, how do you view God's relationship to humanity's problems?

H Several commentators have tried to pinpoint the cause of Cain and Abel's argument. A *Midrash* (*Beresheet Rabbah* 22:16) offers three possibilities:

1. Cain and Abel had divided the world between them and they argued over material possessions.
2. Each brother desired to have the Temple built in his own domain.
3. The brothers were arguing over their mother, Eve.

According to Ibn Ezra, when Cain's sacrifice was not accepted, he blamed Abel. The quarrel between the brothers resulted in murder. Rambam felt that the bloodshed was prompted by Cain's desire that the world be built up through his seed.

In one of the most familiar passages in the Bible, God asks Cain, "Where is your brother Abel?" And he says, "I do not know. Am I my brother's keeper?" Rashi points out that God, of course, knew Abel's fate, yet God entered into conversation with Cain to give him a chance to confess his guilt.

Is there any justification for what Cain did? Can there be greater and lesser sins? If so, whose sin was more severe, Cain's wrongdoing against his brother or Adam's against God?
Are there times when you ask a question to which you already know the answer? Why?

I The text tells us that God regretted creating humankind (Genesis 6:6). The Rabbis commented extensively on this verse.

Rabbi Judah said: God created man out of earthly elements, for had God created man out of heavenly elements, he would not have rebelled against God. Rabbi Nehemiah argued that had man been created out of heavenly elements, he would have incited the celestial creatures to revolt just as he has incited the terrestrial beings to revolt.

Rabbi Levi interpreted: God was pleased that man was created from earthly elements so that he will remain in the earth, mortal and subject to burial (*Genesis Rabbah* 27:1).

Do any of these Rabbis think God made a mistake creating humanity?
What do you think?

J For two and a half years, Bet Shammai and Bet Hillel disputed whether God should have created humankind (*Eruvin* 13b). Bet Shammai said it would have been better for people not to have been created, while Bet Hillel held the opposite view. Finally, they took a vote and decided it would have been better had people not been created, but since they were, each person is responsible for examining his/her past and future deeds.

The Talmud does not report the arguments that were used by Bet Shammai and Bet Hillel. What are some of the reasons that might have been used for and against the creation of humanity?

STRATEGIES

ANALYZING THE TEXT

1 Role play various scenes from *Beresheet*. This may help you understand the dilemmas and issues which faced our ancient ancestors.

a. Eve and the Serpent.
   Two participants: Eve, serpent.
   Reference: Genesis 2:25-3:6.
b. Cain and Abel.
   Three participants: Cain, Abel, God.
   Reference: Genesis 4:8-16.
c. Adam and Eve after eating the forbidden fruit.
   Three participants: Adam, Eve, God.
   Reference: Genesis 3:7-24.

General guidelines: Follow the story line as presented in the biblical text, but improvise private reactions and thoughts and share these with the audience. The leader can stop the action at crucial moments to open up group discussion and to assess the characters and their actions.

2 Compare the two accounts of the creation of human beings in Genesis 1:24-31 and Genesis 2:4-24. Identify the similarities and differences. How would you explain the fact that there are two accounts of creation? Do the two accounts answer different questions regarding (a) the nature(s) of the first human beings and/or (b) their relationship to the divine?

An excellent format for analysis and discussion of these two stories can be found in *Learning Torah* by Joel Lurie Grishaver, pp. 40-50.

3 *Beresheet* tells of humanity's beginnings in a paradise, then depicts its decline. There are four episodes which show this decline: Adam and Eve (Genesis 3), Cain and Abel (Genesis 4), Lamech (Genesis 4:23-24), humanity in general (Genesis 6:1-4). Examine each episode closely. What was the sin in each case? Which sins are most severe? How so? Why would only the wickedness detailed in Genesis 6:5 cause God to regret making people?

4 Make your own list of behaviors which would show the decline of humanity. Include the sins detailed in *Beresheet*. Rank order the sins from least to most severe. If you were God *(kevayachol)* judging your creation, which actions would cause you to regret making people? Why? (For more, see the Index: "Creation of humankind.")

5 Eve has generally been depicted by a series of negative stereotypes which are commonly applied to women. She is seen as curious, but not very bright, easily influenced, talkative, and having a sort of seductive power over Adam. What basis for this description can you find in the text? Some contemporary feminists are attempting to paint a different picture of Eve based on a modern reading of the same text. According to them, Eve is assertive, inquisitive, honest, and optimistic. Use the text to prove that Eve does or doesn't have these

positive qualities. Write your own character sketch of Eve.

EXTENDING THE TEXT

6 A famous *midrash* recounts how each letter of the Hebrew alphabet unsuccessfully begged to be the first letter of the Torah. Finally, the letter *Bet* claims the privilege because all *brachot* (blessings) begin with it. Stage a dramatic reading of this midrash using the play "Midrash of the Aleph-Bet" in *Jewish Story Theater* by Eleanor Albert. This version of the *midrash* includes only a few letters of the alphabet. A group with a good command of Hebrew could brainstorm ideas about why God also refused to begin the Torah with other Hebrew letters. This idea could also be adapted to the English alphabet. Create your own illustrations for this *midrash*.

7 Should God have made human beings? There are several sources which debate this question. One *midrash* tells how God took counsel from the angels before creating human beings. The angels of Truth and Peace opposed the creation, claiming that humanity would be full of lies or would be quarrelsome. The angels of Love and Justice spoke in favor of the creation. They pointed to humanity's loving nature and pursuit of justice. (See *Legends of the Jews* by Louis Ginzberg, Vol. I, pp. 52-54.)

Organize a forensic union to discuss the question, "Should God have made human beings?" Conduct the discussion as follows. Choose two individuals to speak from five to seven minutes for each side of the issue. After these speeches, let members of the audience physically move themselves to the side of the speaker with whom they agree. The sides should then confer for a brief time to prepare a three to five minute rebuttal which is given by the original speaker. After the rebuttal, the participants move to the side with which they now agree. A question period follows in which all the participants from both groups can question each other. After one more move, each group should draft a summary of its point of view which is read aloud. One caution: A discussion format such as this requires people to keep an open mind and allow themselves to be influenced by the speeches. (For more, see the Index: "Creation of humankind.")

8 One of the ways in which our sages dealt with questions was to present the answer(s) in a story or parable. Stories which explain how various physical phenomena came to be are called "etiological tales." Some examples can be found in *The Legends of the Jews* by Ginzberg, pp. 35-41, and "Why Man Has an Adam's Apple," retold by Barbara Rush in *The Book of Jewish Women's Tales,* p. 3. Do you ever wonder why things are the way they are? Using this format, write your own etiological tale explaining the origin of the traits of a particular animal or of people.

9 For an activity about the root word of the name Adam, see the Index: "Adam."

10 In *Beresheet* 2:4, God is called *"Adonai Elohim."* This is the first place in Torah where these two names of God are used together. Jewish tradition teaches that the name *Elohim* reflects the aspect of divine justice, while the name *Adonai* represents God's merciful qualities. God saw that both qualities are necessary to sustain the world. List those actions which you think make humanity wicked in God's eyes (see Genesis 6:4 and Genesis, *Beresheet* #3 and #4 above). If you were *Elohim (kivayachol)* judging your creation, how would you judge these actions? If you were judging your creation as *Adonai (kivayachol),* what would your verdict be? Explain why it was necessary for God to judge the world using the qualities of both mercy and justice — as *"Adonai Elohim."*

11 Read about various creation stories in *The Torah: A Modern Commentary,* edited by W. Gunther Plaut, pp. 24 and 32. Create a chart to show the commonalities and differences between these stories. During the discussion, bring out the universal questions which the ancients were attempting to answer.

12 Reading the two creation stories in sequence, the Rabbis wondered what had happened to the woman created alongside man in Genesis 1:27 that would necessitate the creation of another woman in Genesis 2:20-22. In answer, they named the first woman (of Genesis 1:27) Lilith and told the following story about her. Created at the same time and equal to Adam in every way, Lilith rebelled when Adam insisted on being in charge. She left the Garden of Eden and was punished for her impudence. A modern, feminist version of this *midrash* has been written by Judith Plaskow. (See "The Coming of Lilith" in *Four Centuries of Jewish Women's Spirituality — A Sourcebook,* edited by Ellen M. Umansky and Diane Ashton, pp. 215-216.) Why do you think feminists are especially attracted to the character of Lilith and want to retell and re-imagine her story? Write your own version of Lilith's story. What do you think Eve and Lilith can learn from each other?

PERSONALIZING THE TEXT

13 *Beresheet* 4:8 begins: "Cain said to his brother Abel . . ." and concludes with the murder of Abel. The conversation that took place between the two brothers and may have led to the murder of Abel is not reported. Imagine you are Cain. Write a diary entry in which you detail this conversation and the motive behind the murder.

14 In Elie Wiesel's book *Messengers of God: Biblical Portraits and Legends,* God speaks to Adam saying, "Look well, Adam, all this immensity was created for your sake alone; be careful, do not destroy anything, for after you there will be no one to repair what you have undone" (p. 9). What human responsibilities are implied by this *midrash*? How well has humanity fulfilled these responsibilities?

15 Invite a representative from a local conservation group such as Sierra Club, Friends of the Earth, Save the Whale, Greenpeace, or a local zoological society to discuss what humanity has done to the earth and to describe the efforts of the many people trying to repair it. After the speaker leaves, write a story in which you are Adam or Eve returning to survey the earth after all these years. What do you see? How do you feel? Resource materials may be found in current issues of environmental or geographic magazines.

16 For decades, the issue of how the world came to be has been hotly debated. Explore this topic in one or more of the following ways:
a. Read or view and discuss *Inherit the Wind* (available from local video stores).
b. Bring science textbooks to class and investigate the creation theories included in each. What biases do the books put forth? How do you recognize a biased view?
c. Create a panel to discuss creationism/evolution. Include on the panel those with traditional and liberal Jewish views. Structure the discussion so there is time for individual presentations and a question and answer period.
d. Display and discuss newspaper clippings and stories on the creationism/evolution controversy.

17 Illustrate the six days of creation and the seventh day of rest (Shabbat) in 3-D. Make seven papier-mâché balls (use inflated balloons as a base). Let the balls dry thoroughly, then paint what the world looked like on each of the subsequent days of creation.

Papier-mâché:
Cut newspaper into one-inch strips.
Cover with hot water and soak. Next day, squeeze out excess water.
Add 1 cup paste to every three cups newspaper.
Paste is 1/3 cup of flour to 1/4 cup water.
Knead together (avoid a mess by placing inside a plastic bag while kneading).

18 A *midrash* tells that the Hebrew words for man איש *(ish)* and woman אשה *(ishah)* are derived from the root word אש *(aysh)* meaning fire. In order to keep humanity from "burning out of control," the letters in God's name *yud* and *hay* were added to "fire" to make "man" and "woman." Using oil pastels, create an artistic depiction of this *midrash*. Incorporate the Hebrew words into abstract portraits of man and woman.

19 There are many prayers in our liturgy which praise the beauty and orderliness of creation. Among these are the *"Yotzer Or"* and the *"Ma'ariv Aravim."* Use a prayer book to look for and read some of these prayers. List all the beautiful aspects of creation that these prayers praise. Which are your favorites? What would you add to the list of creations to single out for praise? Write prayers of your own which reflect upon and praise some aspect of creation.

(Note: For more, see the Index: "Shabbat," "Environmental concerns," and "God.")

20 When God asks Cain about Abel after his murder, Cain replies "Am I my brother's keeper?" (Genesis 4:9). In a later era, the great Rabbi Hillel answered this question with his famous words "If I am not for myself, who will be for me? If I am only for myself, what am I?" *(Pirke Avot)*. What do you think is the answer to Cain's question?
1. Organize a debate on this subject — Resolved: Everyone is responsible only for himself/herself.

2. Over a period of several weeks, look for news articles about people's actions which relate to Cain's words. Create a poster or a bulletin board display which illustrates the quote "Am I my brother's keeper."
3. Make a list of things a sibling could do to "be his/her sibling's keeper."
4. Make a list of simple things you could do to help "keep" your brothers and sisters alive and well both locally and world-wide.

OTHER RESOURCES

21 For a craft activity related to *Beresheet,* see "And Then There was Light" in *An Artist You Don't Have to Be* by Joann Magnus with Howard Bogot.

22 View and discuss the animated film *The Big Bang and Other Creation Myths* (Pyramid Films).

23 View and discuss the episode for *Beresheet* from *Torah Toons I: The Video.*

24 Read, act out, and discuss the skit for *Beresheet* in *Sedra Scenes: Skits for Every Torah Portion* by Stan J. Beiner, pp. 1-6.

25 Complete the pages which relate to *Beresheet* in *Bible People Book One* by Joel Lurie Grishaver, pp. 7-13. Also check the accompanying Leader Guide for procedures and additional activities.

26 Learn the song "When God Made the World" from *Bible People Songs.*

27 In recent years many picture book versions of the story of Creation have been published. Read and discuss these retellings, paying attention to the tone, omissions, style, and illustrations. Is God depicted? If so, how? After a careful study of the Torah and the text of these books, write and illustrate your own version of the story of Creation.
References: *And It Was Good* by Harold Horst; *Light,* retold by Sarah Waldman; *The Creation* by Ori Sherman; *The Story of Creation* by Jane Ray.

28 For creative movement activities, see "Light from Darkness," "Fill the Earth," "First Shabbat," and "Discovery" from *Torah in Motion* by JoAnne Tucker and Susan Freeman, pp. 2-11.

29 Listen to, discuss, and sing *"Hinei Tov M'od"* from *Sounds of Creation: Genesis in Song.*

30 Read and discuss the illustrated commentary for *Bereishit* in *American Torah Toons* by Lawrence Bush.

INVOLVING THE FAMILY

31 *Beresheet* is the first portion in the Torah cycle. This portion is read right after the High Holy Day period, a time when we review our lives and resolve to start over in a new year. As a family, sit down and plan a fresh start. This might include activities you want to share, relationships/ conflicts you hope to work out, plans for holiday celebrations, etc.

32 In *Beresheet,* God refers to all created things as "good" except human beings. A *midrash* explains that this is because only human beings have the ability to choose to do good. They can also therefore choose to do evil. Maybe this explains why on Shabbat, which marks the culmination of creation, we recite special praises and blessings for members of our family. This highlights the good in each of us. (For more, see the Index: "Blessing/Curse.")

BAR/BAT MITZVAH PROJECT

33 Write letters to find out the specific work of different organizations working to care for and preserve the earth. Some groups include: Sierra Club, 85 Second Street, San Francisco, CA 94105; Friends of the Earth, 1025 Vermont Ave., N.W., Suite 300, Washington, D.C. 20005; World Wildlife Fund, 1250 24th Street, N.W., Washington, D.C. 20037; American Society for the Protection of Nature in Israel, 28 Arrandale Avenue, Great Neck, NY 11024.

1. Create a newsletter explaining what you've learned. Invite your guests to make a contribution to one of these organizations in honor of your reading *Beresheet*.
2. Choose your favorite organization and make a donation to it in honor of your celebration.

NOAH 6:9-11:32 נח

SYNOPSIS

NOAH IS A RIGHTEOUS INDIVIDUAL IN his generation. The rest of humanity, however, is corrupt and God decides to destroy it. God commands Noah to build an ark and to bring into it seven pairs (male and female) of all clean animals and one pair of all unclean animals found on earth. Noah also takes along his wife, their three sons Shem, Ham, and Japheth, and their wives. A great flood lasting 40 days and nights covers the earth, destroying all living creatures save Noah, his family, and the paired animals on the ark. Once the flood subsides, Noah and his family inhabit the earth and multiply. God's promise not to destroy the earth again becomes a covenant with people and is symbolized by the rainbow.

An incident follows in which Noah becomes drunk and disrobes. His son Ham sees his nakedness, but Shem and Japheth cover their father without looking at him. Because of Ham's sin, Noah curses Canaan, who represents the descendants of Ham. The text then lists the generations of Ham and Japheth.

Prior to the description of Shem's line, the story of the tower of Babel is told. When all the inhabitants of the earth spoke the same language, they decided to build a city and a tower which would reach to the sky in order to make a name for themselves. When God sees what one people with one language can do, God confounds their speech and scatters them all over the earth.

The genealogical narrative resumes with the names of Shem's descendants. From Shem's line, Abram (Abraham) descends.

The portion ends with Terach, his son Abram, daughter-in-law Sarai, and Abraham's nephew Lot settling in Haran.

INSIGHTS FROM THE TRADITION

A This portion describes Noah as "a righteous man; he was blameless in his age; Noah walked with God" (Genesis 6:9). This verse has been interpreted both to Noah's credit and to his discredit. In the *Tanchuma*, we are told: Righteous in his generation, but not in others. To what may this be compared? If a man places a silver coin among copper coins, then the silver appears attractive. So Noah appeared righteous in the generation of the flood. Others interpret it to his credit. How so? It may be compared to a jar of balsam placed in a grave; it gave off a goodly fragrance. Had it been in a house, how much the more so!

What are some characteristics of a righteous person in our generation?
Who are some of the righteous people in our generation?
Would a person who is considered righteous in our generation have been considered so in a past generation? In a future generation?

B The Torah provides no specific examples of Noah's behavior, yet he found favor with God. The text does say that Noah was grateful to God, that he obeyed God, and that he had faith in God.

Are faith, gratitude, and obedience enough to save a world?
When and how do you show faith, gratitude, and obedience?

C Rashi wonders: God could have saved Noah in many different ways. Why then did God burden Noah with the construction of the ark? So that the generation of the flood would see Noah working on the ark for 120 years and might ask him, "What do you need this for?" Then he could answer them, "The Holy One of Blessing is about to bring a flood upon the world." Perhaps they might repent.

Is this story telling us that God would rather have no humanity than a humanity that is wicked? Can you give some examples of individuals who are like Noah (e.g., anti-nuclear protesters)? Who is most like Noah, one who builds a bomb shelter or one who petitions and protests against nuclear weapons? Do you see yourself as a shelter builder, a protester, or neither? Explain.

D Noah's wife is not given a name in the Torah. In *Beresheet Rabbah* 23:3 she is given the name Naamah. The *midrash* asks, "Why was she called Naamah? Because her deeds were *ne'imim* — pleasing." Ellen Frankel in *The Five Books of Miriam* adds another dimension to our understanding of Naamah's deeds. She helped to save life on earth and, like Eve, she was a Mother of Life (p. 12).

What were Naamah's deeds? Does the Torah offer any explanations? What qualities would Naamah have needed to survive and even thrive on the ark? Remember her husband, three sons, their wives and all the animals were with her. Are the qualities Naamah needed any different than the qualities needed for a nurturing parent in today's world?

E After Noah, his family, and the pairs of animals have entered the ark, Genesis 7:16 states "And the Lord shut him in." Aharon Shmuel Tameret taught that not only was the ark like a city of refuge (a city which provided safety for one who accidentally committed a murder) for Noah, but also like a prison because God shut the door behind Noah, just as a jailer would lock in a prisoner. Explaining Tameret's comments, Kushner and Olitzky cite the Rabbinic opinion that "Noah

was a *tzadik im pelz* (a holy man in a fur coat), only concerned about his own welfare. They remind us that, "We diminish our righteousness in not being open to the suffering of our neighbors. If we are not sensitive to their needs, we too will be shut out, not only from them but from God as well (*Sparks Beneath the Torah* by Lawrence Kushner and Kerry Olitzky, p. 10).

Why would Noah be treated like a prisoner? Did he do anything wrong? He followed God's commands to build the ark, to save the animals and his family. Did he not do enough? Was there anything left undone? How could the Rabbis discern from the text that Noah had not done enough?

F God promises never to destroy the earth again by flood. The promise is called a covenant and it is symbolized by the rainbow. The rainbow has been given a variety of interpretations. It has been likened to God's glory, to an archer's bow pointed away from the earth (Rambam), and to a bond between heaven and earth (Hirsch). Nehama Leibowitz, in discussing the significance of the rainbow, says: ". . . we are not to look for and ferret out its symbolism in the form of the bow, its colour or physical characteristics . . . . The text simply says: 'Ye shall behold it and ye shall remember . . .'" (*Studies in Bereshit*, p. 87).

To you, which is the most meaningful interpretation of the rainbow as a symbol of God's promise? Can you think of other symbolic meanings (like the colors of the Olympic Games rings, the colors of the rainbow represent the continents of the earth, the races of humanity, etc.)?

G Prior to the flood, God had not yet established laws. Nevertheless, God punished wrongdoing and evil.

Is it possible for society to function without external laws? Are most people ethical and law abiding because they have a desire to be good (intrinsic) or because of the possible consequences (extrinsic)? How would your behavior be affected if you lived in a different environment? Such as among people from a totally different culture? Among cave dwellers? In a governor's mansion? In a space colony?

H Though non-Jews are not bound by the laws of Torah, everyone is bound by seven general laws referred to as Noachide laws. These prohibit idol worship, blasphemy, murder, adultery, robbery, eating flesh cut from a living animal, and demand that courts of law be established.

Which of these Noachide Laws are still in force in contemporary society?
Why do you think these laws have endured?

I Paradoxically, the righteous Noah becomes the Bible's first drunk. Ramban said that one reason for this was to show that intoxication can be so harmful that even the righteous Noah who saved the world was brought to curse his own grandchild.

What can alcohol and drugs do to your body? To your relationships with your family and friends? To school work, jobs, and other activities? What are some appropriate uses for alcohol and drugs?

J There are significant similarities between the accounts of Noah and his descendants and the tale of the Tower of Babel. Both provide explanations for the dispersion of humanity throughout the known world, the development of tribal groups, and the evolution of different languages.

Would it have made more sense for the Tower of Babel episode to appear in the text before the generations of Noah?
Would you prefer a world in which everyone spoke the same language?

K In Babel, everyone was a builder, but for the wrong reason, whereas in his generation only Noah was a builder, but for the right reason.

What does this tell you about making certain of goals and motives before setting out to work on or for something?

STRATEGIES

ANALYZING THE TEXT

1 Read Genesis 6:9-8:14 and answer the following questions: How many of each animal was Noah to bring into the ark? How long did it rain? When did dry land appear? How long were Noah, his family, and the animals in the ark? What was Noah's age when he boarded the ark and what was his age when he left the ark? Are the answers given for these questions consistent? Does the Torah provide more than one answer for the same question? What could be the reason for this? (See "The Two Biblical Sources of the Flood Story" in The *Torah: A Modern Commentary*, edited by W. Gunther Plaut, p. 62.)

2 Although not specifically stated, the Noachide Laws were derived from divine commands given to Adam and Noah. Compare the Noachide Laws to the Ten Commandments. What are the similarities and differences? Are there more positive or negative commandments in the Noachide Laws than in the Ten Commandments? Which set of laws has more positive commandments? Which has more negative commandments? Can you explain why?

3 Are there laws in the Ten Commandments (or later in the Torah) that seem to be expansions of some of the Noachide laws? Are there peoples in the world today who observe the Noachide laws and who could be considered "children of the covenant of Noah"? If so, what implication does this have for the Jewish view of humanity?

4 The Noachide Laws were intended for all people, while the Ten Commandments were given to Israel. Even in cases where the laws appear to be similar, non-Jews are not required to follow the law as strictly. Why do you think this is so? Which aspects of the two sets of laws illustrate different attitudes about the groups for whom they were intended? (For more, see the Index: "Ten Commandments.")
Reference: *Encyclopaedia Judaica*, Vol. 12, pp. 1189-1191 ("Noachide Laws"); Exodus 20:2-14.

5 Interesting parallels exist between Adam and Noah. Each was to be the progenitor of a new line of humanity. Because in Noah's case, human-kind was being given a second chance, there are some differences in the guidelines given to the two men. Compare and contrast the following texts from Genesis, *Beresheet* and *Noah* to highlight these parallels and differences.

Adam/Eve	Noah
1:27	9:6
1:28	9:1-2
3:17	8:22

How do these verses highlight the history of humanity between the time of Adam/Eve and Noah?

6 Study verses 1:29-30 and 9:3-4 to find the diet prescribed for Adam/Eve and Noah. Can you explain the difference between the diets? Read Isaiah's vision of the messianic age (Isaiah 56-66) to get an idea of the human diet in that future. How does this diet compare to that of Noah? To that of Adam/Eve? Explain the differences and similarities. What can you learn from this about the Jewish view of the natural order? For more information contact the following groups:
Jewish Vegetarians of North America
c/o Israel Mossman
6938 Relance Road
Federalsburg, MD 21632

The Jewish Vegetarian Society
210 Riverside Drive
New York, NY 10025

The Vegetarian Resource Group
PO Box 1463
Baltimore, MD 21203

The Baltimore group publishes a guide to vegetarian restaurants in Israel with a listing of vegetarian, environmental, and animal welfare groups in Israel. Contact them for purchasing details. (For more, see the Index: "Vegetarianism.")

7 The Jewish and Arab peoples have been called "Semites," descendants of the biblical figure Shem. Trace the family tree of Abraham back to Noah (see Genesis 11:10-26).

8 For an activity on the ark, see the Index: "Ark."

EXTENDING THE TEXT

9 Many of the stories which occur in Genesis parallel those found in other cultures. Read several of the references below. Then make a chart which documents the similarities and differences between the stories. Take the information you have gathered a step further and generate a list of universal questions which these stories sought to answer.
References: *Ancient Near Eastern Texts*, edited by James Pritchard (see "Gilgamesh"); *The Torah: A Modern Commentary*, edited by W. Gunther Plaut, pp. 56 and 64.

10 Expanding on Insight D, page 12, read the contemporary *midrash*, *Prayer for the Earth: The Story of Naamah, Noah's Wife* by Sandy Eisenberg Sasso. Discuss the following: What task was Naamah given by God? Was she able to do this? How is the story of the raven and the dove changed in this *midrash*? Was God pleased with Naamah's work? What gifts did she receive?

11 See the video *Noah's Ark* from *The Greatest Adventure Stories from the Bible* (Turner Home Entertainment). Discuss: What was added to the Noah story to make it more "interesting." Which characters are not found in the biblical text, but appear in the video? Do these additions add to your understanding of the story of Noah? If you could be a time traveler what biblical event would you like to drop into? Why?

12 God promised that a flood would never again destroy the earth. The sign of that promise (covenant/*brit*) is the rainbow. Do you remember the first time you saw a rainbow? Were you excited, impressed, full of wonder? Jewish tradition provides us with a special blessing to remember the covenant with God when we see a rainbow. Learn to read this blessing:

בָּרוּךְ אַתָּה יְיָ אֱלֹהֵינוּ מֶלֶךְ הָעוֹלָם
זוֹכֵר הַבְּרִית וְנֶאֱמָן בִּבְרִיתוֹ וְקַיָּם בְּמַאֲמָרוֹ.

Praised are you *Adonai*, our God, Sovereign of the world, who remembers the covenant, keeps the promise, and fulfills [God's] Word.

PERSONALIZING THE TEXT

13 In *Wrestling with Angels,* Naomi H. Rosenblatt and Joshua Horwitz compare the violence of Noah's time with the violence we face today. Noah was God's partner by building the ark and preserving life. You can also be God's partner by "making your own life a small ark of hope in a world awash with violence" (p. 77). Become an ark builder like Noah; design a small ark either as a drawing or model. Instead of bringing aboard a menagerie of animals, load your ark with *mitzvot*, values, ideas, and activities in which

you can be involved that take a stand against violence. Create a display of such modern day arks.

14 The rainbow is a symbol of one covenant between God and humankind. Are there other signs and symbols in Judaism which serve to remind us of events, covenants, and practices? Choose your favorite symbol and make it the basis for a "stained glass look" design. Cut a frame and an outline of your design out of dark colored construction paper. Set it aside. Stick rough torn pieces of colored tissue paper to a piece of wax paper (this should be slightly larger than the frame you cut above) by painting over them gently with liquid starch. Don't leave any wax paper uncovered. When the tissue and wax paper are dry, glue on the construction paper frame. Trim the edges. Hang in a window.

15 A *midrash* tells that it was Nimrod who was behind the building of the Tower of Babel. He was corrupted by his own power and was moved to stir up rebellion among the people. The Hebrew name Nimrod means rebellion. There are other examples in the Torah of people being led into wickedness by corrupt leaders (such as Korach and Balaam). Yet, there are also many instances of individuals who remained righteous despite the pressure they may have felt to follow the group, for example Pinchas, Noah, Caleb, and Joshua. Organize a debate on this statement: "In every generation, corruption is the responsibility of the leaders" (*Sifrei Numbers*). Use biblical and contemporary examples to support your point of view.

16 Sometimes even people who speak the same language have problems communicating. This activity and the next one explore this problem. Construct your own Tower of Babel. Unroll a long sheet of white paper (at least 10 feet long). Provide markers, crayons, pencils, glue or tape, but give no directions other than telling the group to design one big tower. Allot 15-20 minutes for constructing the tower. Display the tower and discuss the following:

a. How did the group decide on how to build the tower?
b. Was the tower made with a cooperative effort on the part of the entire group?
c. Were there any disagreements as to how the tower should be constructed?
d. What roles (e.g., leader, mediator, follower) did people take on to help get the tower built?
e. How does this activity relate to the Tower of Babel episode?

17 How well does your group work together without spoken language? Take sheets of 9" x 12" construction paper and cut each into a puzzle. Divide participants into small groups and distribute one puzzle to each group. The task for each group is to reconstruct the puzzle into a complete rectangle without talking. In the follow-up discussion, talk about (1) the difficulty of accomplishing this task, (2) how important verbal communication is, (3) what other kinds of communication were improvised, and (4) how this activity relates to the Tower of Babel episode.

18 God found Noah to be righteous in his generation. But was Noah truly righteous or simply righteous compared to others? Place yourself at the point on each values continuum which most clearly reflects your view.

By building the ark Noah was warning the people; they could see what was to happen.	Noah did not do enough; he should have warned the people.

Noah's dedication to building the ark shows he was truly a righteous man.	Noah was afraid to take his warning to the people. Though faithful, he was not truly righteous.

The ark was an effective warning to the people.	The ark was not an effective warning to the people.

The act of building the ark was the more effective warning to the people about the consequences of wickedness.	The rainbow was the more effective warning to the people about the consequences of wickedness.

19 Take a field trip to a local zoo, farm, or wildlife conservation area. Take along a good Hebrew dictionary and name as many of the animals as you can in Hebrew. Expand the activity by taking photos, labeling them in Hebrew, and setting up a display.

20 The story of Noah and the flood has been retold numerous times for children. Check your synagogue, Jewish community, and public libraries to find as many versions as possible. Assemble them and compare the text and the illustrations. Discuss how the differences and similarities color your understanding and reactions to this biblical story.
References: *Aardvarks, Disembark* by Ann Jonas; *The Ark* by Arthur Geisert; *Let's Play: Noah's Ark* by Leo Baxter; *Noah and the Flood* by Barbara Brenner; *Noah and the Rainbow* by Shoshana Lepon; *Noah's Ark* by Peter Spier; *Why Noah Chose the Dove* by Isaac Bashevis Singer.

21 Noah built an ark and took pairs of all the animals on it in order to save their species. Today there are modern day ark builders — environmentalists and conservationists who are working to preserve our world. Create a bulletin board and display pictures, poems, and stories which illustrate their work.
References: Current issues of environmental magazines and the Internet.

22 The effects of alcoholism and drug addiction can be devastating. In one brief incident, Noah curses his descendants in Ham's family. Teenage alcoholism and drug addiction is now being recognized as a serious problem. Contact a local drug and alcohol treatment center or speakers bureau to do a program for your group.

23 Make a soft sculpture or wall hanging of Noah, the ark, and the animals. Check local fabric, craft, or quilt stores for patterns, fabric and ideas.

24 A *midrash* tells that God consulted the angels about the creation of humankind. Imagine that a similar consultation took place at the time of the events in this *parashah* (including the Tower of Babel incident). Form a committee of angels to evaluate creation. Assign each angel a standard from which to judge (e.g., Truth, Love, Hope, Peace). Ask each: What is your opinion of Creation from the time of Adam and Eve to the building of the Tower of Babel? Would you advise God to continue the experiment? Why or why not?

25 There is nothing like food for a celebration. Celebrate the beauty of rainbows by making "Edible Rainbows."

Edible Rainbows

1 cup soft margarine	3 cups flour
3/4 cup white sugar	1/2 tsp. baking soda
3/4 cup brown sugar	1/2 tsp. salt
2 eggs	food coloring
1 tsp. vanilla	

Directions:
1. Mix well: margarine, sugar, eggs, and vanilla.
2. Blend together: flour, soda, salt. Then mix them into the first mixture.
3. Divide the dough into four (or more) parts. Color each part with a different color food coloring to make rainbow colors.
4. On waxed paper, pat each color of dough into a strip four inches (10 centimeters) long and 1/4 inch (1/2 cm.) thick.
5. Stack the rainbow strips on top of one another. Press down to help the strips stick together.
6. Wrap the pile in waxed paper and refrigerate overnight.
7. Slice the layered block of dough in 1/4 inch (1/2 cm.) slices. Gently curve the slice into an arch.
8. Bake on an ungreased cookie sheet at 375° for about seven minutes.

From *I Can Make a Rainbow* by Marjorie Frank. Used by permission.

26 When Noah sent the dove out of the ark, it returned with an olive branch signifying that the dry land was once again visible. Both the dove and the olive branch have become symbols of peace easily recognizable to people all over the world. Create a bulletin board display with a giant cut out dove with an olive branch in its mouth. Write the word for peace in several different languages. Use the library, local language schools, universities, and speakers of other languages to help you collect a wide variety of languages. For more, see the Index: "Olive trees/Olive oil."

27 Find out how long a cubit is. It is thought to be the distance from a person's bent elbow to the tip of his/her longest finger. Pace off an area the size of Noah's ark in the synagogue parking lot. How many people can stand in that space? Think of a building or object in your community that would be roughly the size of the ark.

OTHER RESOURCES

28 View and discuss the video *Jinja's Israeli Safari,* which provides an opportunity to learn about the animals in Tel Aviv's Safari Park.

29 Complete the pages which relate to *Noah* in *Bible People Book One* by Joel Lurie Grishaver, pp. 14-16. Also check the accompanying Leader Guide for procedures and additional activities.

30 Read, act out, and discuss the skit for the portion *Noah* in *Sedra Scenes: Skits for Every Torah Portion* by Stan J. Beiner, pp. 7-12.

31 View and discuss the *Torah Toons* episode for *Noah* from *Torah Toons I: The Video*.

32 For creative movement activities, see "Bursting of the Floodgates" and "Gibberish" from *Torah in Motion* by JoAnne Tucker and Susan Freeman, pp. 12-15.

33 Read and discuss the illustrated commentary for *Noach* in *American Torah Toons* by Lawrence Bush.

34 Listen to, discuss, and sing "The Rainbow Covenant" from *Sounds of Creation: Genesis in Song*.

INVOLVING THE FAMILY

35 It sometimes happens that one member of a family must assume the responsibility of convincing siblings and/or parents of the importance of a certain task or idea. Noah is a case in point. Although God told him to take his wife and family with him onto the ark, God communicated with Noah alone. As a family, role play the conversation during which Noah informs his family of the coming flood. Have individuals representing his family express a range of responses to this news (laughter, disbelief, trust, etc.). Take turns playing the role of Noah. Afterward, discuss how Noah's will was imposed on the family in the role play. Was Noah forced to resort to his authority as a father? Were you, as a family, able to reach an agreement that was acceptable to all? How did you feel when you assumed a role other than your own in the family (e.g., when father played son, did he feel powerless, free, rebellious)? Can you relate this role play and discussion to your daily family life?

BAR/BAT MITZVAH PROJECT

36 Incorporate Insight D and Activity 10 and develop the following project: Continue the tradition of remembering Naamah as *Aym Zerah*, Mother of Seed, by planting a garden. Add the element of *tzedakah* to this project by growing vegetables for distribution to the needy. Grow flowers, too, because we all need beauty. Utilize a local food bank or meals program to help distribute what you have grown. Additionally, you might run a campaign where you encourage synagogue members to add a row for the needy in their home gardens. Consider naming your garden project in honor of Naamah.

LECH LECHA 12:1-17:27 לך לך

SYNOPSIS

GOD TELLS ABRAM TO LEAVE HIS NATIVE land and go to a land which God will show him. God promises Abram that a special land will be set aside for him and his descendants, and that Abram will be the father of a great nation. Abram and his family, which includes his wife Sarai and his nephew Lot, travel from Haran to Canaan. On his journeys in the land, Abram sets up an altar to God in Alon Moreh between Bethel and Ai.

A famine in Canaan forces Abram to seek food in Egypt. Upon entering Egypt, Abram declares that Sarai is his sister, not his wife; she is then taken into Pharaoh's palace. Abram realizes good fortune from this deception, but God afflicts Pharaoh with plagues. Pharaoh realizes that Sarai is really Abram's wife. Pharaoh sends Abram, his wife, and their possessions out of Egypt.

Abram and his nephew Lot graze their flocks together, but the land will not support them both. Lot chooses to live on the Plain of Jordan, while Abram remains in Canaan.

During an intertribal war, Lot is carried away as a hostage. Abram and his men pursue the captors and free Lot, his possessions, and the rest of the prisoners.

God appears to Abram and again promises him progeny and land. This covenant is confirmed when Abram brings sacrifices. At this point, God foretells the Israelite bondage in Egypt.

Sarai, who has not been able to bear children, gives her handmaid Hagar to Abram as a concubine. Hagar bears Ishmael. God repeats his covenant to Abram, but now requires Abram and all the males of his household to be circumcised as a sign of the covenant. God changes Abram's name to Abraham and Sarai's name to Sarah.

INSIGHTS FROM THE TRADITION

A *Lech Lecha*, the name of this portion, has been translated and interpreted in a variety of ways. Rashi interprets the phrase to mean Abram should "get out" for his own benefit, because there (in the land to be shown to him), God will make him a great nation. Also, Abram should leave so that God may make Abram's character known throughout the world. Samson Raphael Hirsch felt that the phrase meant "to go alone, to isolate oneself." In other words, Abram had to detach himself from his previous life, and his isolation accomplished this.

Throughout history, there have been numerous individuals who sought isolation before becoming leaders. What benefit can isolation serve? Might there be a negative side to such isolation? How long could you stand to be totally alone? What would you do?

B Abram answered God's call to leave Haran. In this initial step, he was acknowledging his acceptance of one God. A *midrash* explains Abram's attitude to the multiple gods his father Terach, an idolmaker, crafted. The *midrash* states that one day Abram, left in charge of the idols, smashes every one but the largest. When Terach returns, he asks, "Who smashed the gods?" Abram replies: "The largest one." Terach responds: "Idols cannot move. They are made of clay and wood." "Then why do you worship them?" counters Abram.

Like Noah, Abram may be considered a maverick for his stand. What characteristics or qualities did Abram exhibit which set him apart from other people?
How does the worship of one God differ from the worship of idols?

C In this *sedra*, Abram is called an *Ivri* (a Hebrew). Rashi explains the term by its root letters *ayin, bet, resh,* meaning "other." He translates the phrase as: "the one who came from the other side of the river (Euphrates)." *Genesis Rabbah* uses the same translation, but interprets it as: The whole world stood on one side and "Abram the *Ivri* stood on the other," meaning that Abram's faith ran counter to what all others believed.

Does Judaism today still run counter to what others such as Moslems and Christians believe? Do you as a Jew ever feel like an "other"?

D Were Abram and Sarai the first Jews to prose-lytize? Some interpreters understand Genesis 12:5 which mentions "the persons that (Abram and Sarai) had acquired in Haran" as a reference to converts. In this connection, Ellen Frankel notes that "In this verse, the Hebrew word for 'persons' is *nefashot,* usually translated as 'souls.' And the word for 'acquired' literally means 'made' (*The Five Books of Miriam* by Ellen Frankel, p. 15). Thus Abraham and Sarah's companions on their journey might have been individuals who chose to link their fate with the first Jews, rather than be slaves who had no choice in the matter.

Why might Abram and Sarai have preferred that the members of their household join their journey freely and out of shared convictions?
What might have motivated these individuals to join them?
What journeys or events in your life have you participated in because you were made to?
Which did you choose to undertake?
How did the nature of your participation change the event or journey?

E When Abram entered Egypt, he hid the fact that Sarai was his wife. He claimed to be her brother. Because of Sarai's beauty, he feared the Egyptians would murder him in order to take her.

Are there circumstances when it is okay to lie?
Are there situations when one must lie?

F In this portion, God repeats the promise of progeny and land to Abram three times. The number three, as used in the Bible, implies completeness, for there is a beginning, a middle, and an end. In Genesis, the number three is used in

conjunction with: the family group (mother, father, child), the Covenant-between-the-Pieces (sacrificial animals are all three years old), and the Patriarchs.

What other numbers are prominent in Torah? What is their significance? (See: *Encyclopaedia Judaica,* Vol. 12, "Numbers, Typical and Important"; *The Jewish Book of Numbers* by Ronald H. Isaacs)
What numbers are of special significance to you in your life?

G Hagar was Sarai's handmaid. Where did she come from? In *Genesis Rabbah* (45:1), we learn that she was a daughter of Pharaoh. When he saw the miracles which had been performed for Sarai's sake, he said, "It is better for my daughter to be a handmaid in this man's house than a mistress in another man's house." It was a common practice for a childless woman to give her maids to her husband in order that he might still have children. Sarai did this, yet once Hagar conceived, Sarai became angry and jealous. A close reading of the text shows Sarai in a very unfavorable light. The Rabbis point out that Sarai's lifetime was short-ened because of her behavior.

Are anger and jealousy appropriate emotions for a Matriarch?
Given her actions, why was Sarai still to become a Matriarch?
Are you easily given to jealousy? Explain.

H There are many interesting parallels between the life of Hagar and the experiences of the earliest Jews. Just as Abraham banished Ishmael, later Ishmael's descendants sold Joseph into slav-ery. Just as Sarah banished Hagar the Egyptian, so the Israelites lived as strangers and then as slaves in Egypt. And just as Ishmael was saved by God from dying in the desert, later the Israelites had to cross the desert as part of God's plan to save them.

Seen in this light, the character and story of Hagar become much more significant. In what ways might Sarah's animosity toward Hagar have set in motion important pieces of Jewish history? Do you believe in fate or predestination? Explain. What can we learn from Hagar's story about how we should treat the strangers in our midst?

Before Abram became a father of both a son and a people, his name and Sarai's are changed. Everett Fox, in his commentary on Genesis, explains the significance of this. During the biblical era, a person's name reflected his/her character and future. Thus, receiving a new name meant a new phase in a person's life. Kings and popes still carry on this tradition (*The Five Books of Moses* by Everett Fox, p. 70).

While we do not usually change our names, what sort of labels do we acquire when we pass certain milestones in our lives? (Think of graduations, Confirmation, Bar/Bat Mitzvah, scouting awards, etc.)
How do these new labels "change" us?

STRATEGIES

ANALYZING THE TEXT

1 Using the *Atlas of Jewish History*, edited by Martin Gilbert, and *The Macmillan Bible Atlas*, edited by Yochanan Aharoni and Michael Avi-Yonah, create plaster of paris relief maps of Abram's journeys. Read ahead to the next *sedra* and continue mapping this Patriarch's travels.

2 In *Lech Lecha*, God makes five promises to Abram (Genesis 12:1-3, 12:7, 13:14-17, 15:1-6, 13-16, 17:1-22). Read and analyze them carefully, noting their placement in the context of the story. Why did God speak to Abraham at each of these times? What new information is added with each promise? What is omitted? How does the new

information serve to resolve questions about the narrative and help to move the story along?

3 Rambam suggested that Abram wandered from place to place proclaiming the worship of the true God." Find evidence for this in the text (see Genesis 12:5, 8-9, and 13:10).

4 Many Hebrew names contain the word "God" — אֵל (*Ayl*). Make a list of all the names mentioned in *Lech Lecha*. Where possible, find the meaning of each name from the text itself. Use a reference dictionary such as *The Complete Dictionary of English and Hebrew First Names* by Alfred Kolatch to help you. Can you find a connection between a person's name and his/her character and/or the events in his/her life? Using one of these names, write an acrostic describing that person's relationship with God.

EXTENDING THE TEXT

5 Abram's uniqueness is found in his acceptance of one God alone in the midst of a society which worshiped a multiplicity of gods. Many *midrashim* illustrate this point:

When he was born, Abram's mother abandoned him in a cave. She feared that the evil King Nimrod would slay him, because prophets had warned that he would triumph over Nimrod. Tended by the angel Gabriel, the infant Abram worshiped the stars as gods until they were obscured by the sun. Then he declared that the sun was god until it set and the moon rose in its place. Clouds covered the face of the moon, showing Abram that the moon was not god either. At last, Abram perceived that there was one supreme God guiding the forces in the universe.

As he grew older, Abram challenged the people's worship of idols. When a person would approach him to buy an idol, Abram would ask, "How old are you?" "Thirty years," a person might reply. "You are thirty years old," said Abram, "and you want to worship this idol made only today?"

Abram reached a new understanding of God. How did his understanding of the world differ from that of his neighbors? Why do the *midrashim* depict a society which felt very threatened by Abram's beliefs?

References: For other *midrashim*, see *The Midrash Rabbah*, translated by H. Freeman; *Legends of the Jews* by Louis Ginzberg, Vol. I; *Yalkut Me'am Lo'ez* by Yaakov Culi.

6 The Geneva Convention established a code of behavior for nations at war. Read through the section relating to soldiers' behavior regarding prisoners and spoils of war. Compare this to the behavior of the warring nations in this portion. You may want to extend the activity and examine news clippings dealing with current military activities.

Reference: *Encyclopedia Brittanica,* article on "Laws of War."

7 In *Lech Lecha*, Abram begins the journeys which will characterize his life both physically and spiritually. There is an old Jewish expression which says: "Changing your place changes your luck." Can you cite other instances in Jewish history when changing or moving changed a person's luck or future?

8 Pretend that you are Abram or Sarai and you are preparing to leave Ur of the Chaldees. Write a letter to a parent, close friend, or relative explaining why you are leaving.

9 Sarah is the silent partner in the stories about Abraham. There are *midrashim* which cite her piety and tell how she spread the teaching of God to the women of her time. Yet, in *Lech Lecha* and *Vayera*, her actions and speeches have a negative flavor. She distrusts the messengers of God and laughs at their promise and she mistreats Hagar. It is possible, however, to view Sarah as a dedicated and independent woman who bravely journeyed with her husband to a strange land, who faced danger in the land of Egypt, and who even gave her servant to Abraham so that he would have an offspring. Write a *midrash* explaining how Sarah came to her own strong belief and trust in one God. In your *midrash*, describe how her faith gave her the courage to face these trials.

10 Learn the lyrics and melody of the Debbie Friedman song *"Lechi Lach"* on *And You Shall Be a Blessing*. What did Friedman add to and/or change about the text in Genesis 12:1-3? What occasions or life cycle events might be appropriate for singing this song?

PERSONALIZING THE TEXT

11 Imagine that you are Abram or Sarai and you are preparing to leave Ur of the Chaldees. Bearing in mind that you will not ever return, what would you pack in your suitcase? Explain your choices.

12 The making of covenants and sealing of pacts characterizes much of the Book of Genesis and in particular this portion.
a. Plan the kind of special meal you would prepare on an auspicious occasion (possibly carry the plan through and prepare and serve it).
b. Discuss how we make covenants or pacts today.
c. Invite a lawyer or a business person to your class to give an historical or current view of how contracts evolved.

13 God commands Abraham to circumcise himself. This is the physical sign of the covenant which God has established with Abraham. This covenant, known as *Brit Milah*, become a sign for all generations of male Jews. Learn more about this important life cycle ceremony. Is it meaningful for Jews today? Why? References: *Circumcision* by Raymond Zwerin, Audrey Friedman Marcus, Leonard Kramish; *Encyclopaedia Judaica*, "Circumcision," Vol. 5, pp. 567-576; *Teaching Mitzvot* by Barbara Binder Kadden and Bruce Kadden; *Berit Mila in the Reform Context*, edited by Lewis M. Barth; *Witness to the Covenant of Circumcision: Bris Milah* by Dale Lieberman.

14 *Brit Milah* is a ceremony welcoming male children into the covenant. Until recently, no such ceremonies existed to welcome girls into the covenant. Create a *brit* ceremony for female children. Get ideas for appropriate prayers and readings by looking at the *Brit Milah* ceremony and then at some newly created ceremonies for girls. References: "Oh Boy, It's a Girl" in *The Second Jewish Catalog*, edited by Sharon Strassfeld and Michael Strassfeld, pp. 30-37; *The New Jewish Baby Book: Names, Ceremonies and Customs, A Guide for Today's Families* by Anita Diamant; *Lifecycles: Jewish Women on Life Passages and Personal Milestones*, Vol. 1, edited by Debra Orenstein.

15 Hagar is described as Sarah's handmaid. What do you think her duties were? What would be the contemporary equivalent of this role? Using Sarah and Hagar's relationship as a reference point, write a series of guidelines describing how we should treat people that we employ to help us in our own homes (housekeepers, caregivers, repairmen, etc.).

OTHER RESOURCES

16 Listen to and/or learn the song "Abraham" from *Bible People Songs*.

17 Complete the pages which relate to *Lech Lecha* in *Bible People Book One* by Joel Lurie Grishaver, pp. 20-22. Also check the accompanying Leader Guide for procedures and additional activities.

18 Read, act out, and discuss the skit for the portion *Lech Lecha* in *Sedra Scenes: Skits for Every Torah Portions* by Stan J. Beiner, pp. 13-19.

19 View and discuss the episode for *Lech Lecha* from *Torah Toons I: The Video*.

20 For creative movement activities see "Abram Go Forth" and "Sister . . . Let Me Live!" from *Torah in Motion* by JoAnne Tucker and Susan Freeman, pp. 16-19.

21 Listen to, discuss, and sing *"Vahakimoti Et B'riti"* from *Sounds of Creation: Genesis in Song*.

22 Read and discuss the illustrated commentary for *Lech Lecha* in *American Torah Toons* by Lawrence Bush.

23 Read and discuss the story "A Girl Who Had Never Heard of God" in Level Alef of *The Melton Graded Curriculum Series Holidays, Mitzvot and Prayer*, Vol. II, p. 156. Compare the story with the *midrash* about Abraham's discovery of God in #5 above.

24 Act out the play "Midrash of Abram and the Idols" from *Jewish Story Theater* by Eleanor Albert, pp. 73-75.

INVOLVING THE FAMILY

25 Abram is told, "Go forth from your native land, from your birthplace, and from your father's house" (12:1). Yet, he actually leaves his father's house first and the borders of his native land last. One commentator explains that the Torah is not describing Abram's physical journey, but rather the emotional attachments he would have to break in order to establish a new people (*Studies in Bereshit* by Nehama Leibowitz, p. 113). His country would be the easiest for him to leave. But it would be difficult and painful for Abram to cut himself off from his family. Rank the three elements in Abram's leave taking in order of their importance to you: native land, birthplace (city of birth), family home. Which of these would be hardest for you to leave? Why? Have you/your parents ever left any of these places? Which was more difficult — the physical or emotional leaving? If you had a choice, would you choose to stay in your city/country of birth? Discuss circumstances which might force you to leave. Can you suggest any ways to remain in touch with your place of origin?

BAR/BAT MITZVAH PROJECT

26 Note that in Genesis 12:1, Abraham is told to leave his father's house *not* his father. Perhaps despite the *midrashim* which tell that Abraham's father was a maker of idols, there were important ideals and values which he passed on to Abraham. Thus Abraham's departure was not a break with his family. What are some values and ideals which your family holds dear, that you will always carry with you? Have a family letter writing session during which parents write about the values they hope their children will cherish, and children affirm the important ideals they have learned from their parents.

VAYERA 18:1-22:24 וירא

SYNOPSIS

AND GOD APPEARS (VAYERA) TO Abraham. Three strangers appear to Abraham and he welcomes them with a great show of hospitality. In the midst of their stay, one of the visitors predicts the birth of a son to Abraham and Sarah. This greatly amuses Sarah who can hardly believe she is to become a mother at 90 years of age.

God appears to Abraham and foretells the destruction of Sodom and Gemorrah. A discussion ensues in which Abraham bargains for the citizens of these cities. Two angels arrive in Sodom and accept Lot's hospitality. The townspeople clamor at Lot's door demanding that the "strangers" be turned over to them. Lot offers the townspeople his two virgin daughters instead. The offer is refused. As the people press forward to break down the door, they are struck blind by a bright light.

Lot is warned by angels to flee with his family before the destruction, but his married daughters and sons-in-law refuse to heed the warning. Lot and his family are told not to look upon the annihilation of the city as they escape, but Lot's wife looks back and immediately turns into a pillar of salt. Lot and his daughters seek refuge in a cave. His daughters, believing they are the last survivors on earth, get Lot drunk and lay with him. Both daughters become pregnant and bear children who will found the nations Moab and Ammon.

While journeying in Gerar, Abraham claims that Sarah is his sister. Abimelech, King of Gerar, takes Sarah for himself, assuming she is unmarried. In a dream, God reveals Sarah's true status to Abimelech, telling him that his entire household will perish if Sarah is not restored to Abraham. Abimelech returns Sarah and questions Abraham regarding his actions. Abraham uses the same excuse that he used in *Lech Lecha* — his fear that his hosts would kill him on account of his wife. He adds that Sarah is indeed his sister — his father's daughter, but not his mother's.

Sarah finally bears Abraham a son whom they name Isaac. In time, Sarah becomes displeased when she sees Ishmael at play. She asks Abraham to cast out Hagar and Ishmael so that Ishmael will not share in the inheritance with Isaac. Although it grieves Abraham, he follows the advice of God and listens to Sarah. God promises that Ishmael will found a nation.

God tests Abraham and commands him to sacrifice his son Isaac. Abraham obeys, but as he is about to lower the knife to slay his son, an angel of the Lord calls out to stop him. Due to Abraham's obedience God, repeats the promise to make of him a great nation.

INSIGHTS FROM THE TRADITION

A Rabbi Hama the son of Hanina said: It was the third day after his (Abraham's) circumcision and the Holy One of Blessing appeared (*vayera*), and inquired after the state of his health (*Baba Metzia* 86b). From this interpretation comes the tradition of *Bikur Cholim* (visiting the sick). According to the Rabbis, a visit to the sick removed 1/60th of the illness. However, simply visiting the sick did not fulfill the *mitzvah*. Rather, the sick person had to be aided and his/her material needs satisfied by the visit.

B As *Vayera* begins, Abraham receives a divine visitation in the form of three men. According to tradition, these were the angels Michael, Gabriel, and Raphael. Each of them had been given a task. Raphael was to heal the wound (circumcision) of Abraham, Michael was to bring Sarah the news of her impending motherhood, and Gabriel was to destroy Sodom and Gomorrah. Rashi points out that Abraham sat at the entrance to his tent so that he might see passersby and invite them into his home. The *Encyclopaedia Judaica* states that *Hachnasat Orchim* (welcoming guests) was not simply a sign of good manners, "but a moral institution which grew out of the harsh desert and nomadic existence."

Hachnasat Orchim is a central value in Jewish tradition. During the Rabbinic period, Rabbi Huna publicly announced that his mealtimes were to be considered an open invitation to strangers (*Ta'anit* 20b). He had a saying which is incorporated into the Passover Haggadah: *"Kol Dichfin Yaytay v'Yaychul"* — Let all who are hungry, come and eat.

During the Middle Ages, the concept of *essen tag* (eating days) came about. Householders in the Jewish community would invite *yeshivah* students to eat a given number of meals in their homes during the week. In the Talmud we read, "one who gives hospitality to a Rabbinic student is regarded as if he had offered a daily sacrifice" (*Berachot* 10b).

Are we missing the essence of the law and its practice by allowing charitable institutions to supply meals and lodging to the poor?
In what ways do you or might you fulfill the *mitzvot* of *Bikur Cholim* and *Hachnasat Orchim*?

C Rashi identifies the lad in Genesis 18:7 as Ishmael. Thus, Abraham was teaching the concept of welcoming the stranger to his son by involving him directly in the *mitzvah*.

How do your parents transmit this and other Jewish values today?

D God informs Abraham that Sodom and Gomorrah are to be destroyed. The text (Genesis 18:17-19) reads in part: "Now the Lord had said, Shall I hide from Abraham what I am about to do? For I have singled him out, that he may instruct his children and his posterity to keep the way of the Lord by doing what is just and right . . ." Martin Buber explains this verse: "To keep the way of the Lord . . . is no metaphor. The way of God means the actual movement of God throughout the history of the world. Israel is expected, as the Torah and Prophets repeatedly

insist, to follow the Lord's footsteps on this road. The nature of the road is characterized by God, in this passage, as doing justice and righteousness" (from "Abraham the Seer" in *On the Bible: 18 Studies,* edited by Nahum Glatzer, p. 40). God wanted such actions to provide a model for Abraham and his descendants upon which to base their lives.

How did Abraham's response to the proposed destruction of Sodom and Gomorrah differ from Noah's response to the proposed destruction of the world by flood? Was Abraham foolish to challenge God's plans to destroy Sodom and Gomorrah?
How does Abraham's bargaining with God exemplify the relationship between the Jewish people and God?

E Sarah laughed when she heard she was to become a mother. "Now that I am withered, am I to have enjoyment, my husband being so old" (18:12)? In reporting this to Abraham, God says: "Why did Sarah scoff and ask: 'How can I have children old as I am?'" God changed Sarah's words so that Abraham would not be angry with her. As the commentary *Tzenah Ur'enah* states, it is from this episode that Sages learned that for the sake of *sh'lom bayit* (family harmony), a harmless lie is allowed.

When do you think it justifiable to lie?
What does the term *sh'lom bayit* imply? How is *sh'lom bayit* a responsibility of each family member?

F Abraham was subjected to a number of divine tests, three of which occur in this portion. They are detailed in *Yalkut Me'am Lo'ez* by Yaakov Culi, Vol. II, pp. 310-311.
1. When Abraham was in the land of the Philistines, Abimelech had Sarah brought to his harem by force.
2. When Isaac grew up, Sarah saw Ishmael using him as a target to practice archery. She told

Abraham to write out a will leaving everything that he owned and everything that God had promised him to Isaac, so that Ishmael would not share in the inheritance at all. God then told Abraham to drive Hagar and Ishmael away from his house. Of all the troubles that Abraham suffered, none was worse than driving away his firstborn son.

3. The third test found in this portion is the Akedah — the binding of Isaac.

Which of these tests would you have found most difficult?
Has there been a test in your life similar to those experienced by Abraham?

G Robert Alter provides us with a fascinating insight on parallels between the lives of Ishmael and Isaac. In Genesis 21, Ishmael is banished into the desert with his mother Hagar. He faces a life-threatening trial — near collapse due to thirst. This is witnessed by his anguished mother. Isaac also faces a life-threatening trial — the *Akedah* — when he is bound upon an altar prepared for sacrifice by his own father. In both cases, an angel of God calls out at a critical moment announcing that the boy will live. Alter points out that even the episode between these two events provides additional connections. Abraham secures a treaty which guarantees peace and well-being for his descendants (*The Art of Biblical Narrative*, pp. 181-182).

Can you find more connections between these events? What is the locale of each of these events? What are the feelings of the parents? Might the feelings of Ishmael and Isaac be similar? Why? Are there life threatening tests which young people face in our society today (learning to drive; registering for the draft; going to school in a tough neighborhood, etc.)?

H Abraham's nephew Lot was a resident of Sodom, yet he was not to share the fate of the rest of the Sodomites. Why would Lot escape the punishment? His righteous behavior is witnessed in the episode with the "visitors" who, it appears, are divine beings sent to destroy Sodom and Gomorrah. We see the extreme lengths to which Lot would go so as to fulfill the *mitzvah* of *Hachnasat Orchim*. He was ready to sacrifice the honor of his daughters in order to protect his guests who were strangers to him. Lot, his wife, and daughters ultimately escaped, but the text states that Lot's wife looked back and turned into a pillar of salt. Abravanel interpreted "looking back" to mean that Lot could disregard the wealth and property he was leaving behind in Sodom. His wife, unable to do this, turned back, was consumed, and turned to salt.

Abravanel's explanation removes, in part, the "miraculous" in his explanation of Lot's wife. Isaac Asimov in *Asimov's Guide to the Bible,* Vol. 1, pp. 81-83, regards the destruction as a natural phenomenon.

Do such explanations tend to reduce Torah to legends rather than history for you?
Do you think such explanations make Torah easier for a modern person to understand?
What parallels do you see between Lot and Noah?
In what ways was Lot righteous in his generation?

I Lot's wife and daughters are not named in the biblical text, but in later Rabbinic writing they are given names. Lot's wife is named Idit, the feminine equivalent to *Ayd,* meaning witness. In a *midrash* the Rabbis accuse Idit of spreading the news that Lot had guests in their home, which was definitely a breach of Sodomite custom. She went house to house, letting people know they had guests by trying to borrow salt to serve with the meal. Rabbinic tradition says she sinned through salt and thus was punished by salt.

By turning into a pillar of salt, does Idit literally serve as a witness? If so, how?
Is she also serving as a warning and if so a warning for what?

J The Torah relates that the angels had to take Lot and his family by the hands and hurry them out of Sodom for Lot had delayed and delayed. Lot's wife looked back during their escape though she had been warned not to. From the Rabbis we learn that this may be interpreted to their credit or discredit. Lot delayed because he did not want to leave his married daughters and their husbands behind, or because he was sorry to leave behind his wealth and possessions. His wife looked back to see if her married daughters were following and in compassion for her friends and neighbors, or because she was trying to see what was happening to all the possessions she and Lot had left behind.

Why didn't Lot and his wife take to heart the messages from the angels?
Which Rabbinic interpretation appeals to you most and why?

STRATEGIES

ANALYZING THE TEXT

1 Often we remember great individuals by recalling an event in their lives, an attitude they expressed, a speech or sentiment they shared. Examine this portion and the previous one and find quotes or events that best characterize Abraham and Sarah. Display these quotes along with a paragraph which explains your choice.

2 Read Genesis 18:12-13. What was Sarah's reaction when she overheard that she was to bear a child? Did God report her reaction to Abraham? Was the wording identical? If not, what was the difference? Why do you think it was handled this way?
Reference: *The Torah: A Modern Commentary*, edited by W. Gunther Plaut, p. 125.

3 The Torah tells us that Noah found favor with God because he was a righteous man who walked with God. We learn, too, of the character of Moses. However, no explanation is given as to why God chose Abraham. *Beresheet Rabbah* responds to this by noting that Abraham was tested ten times after God chose him. These tests establish Abraham as the founder of the Jewish people. Examine portions *Lech Lecha* and *Vayera* to find events that tested the character of Abraham. Explain how each event could be considered a test. Rank the tests in order of difficulty for Abraham. Which is the best proof of his worthiness to be the father of the Jewish people?

The ten tests are: (1) Nimrod casting Abraham into the fiery furnace (for the *midrash* which describes this, see: *Legends of the Jews* by Louis Ginzberg, Vol. I, pp. 198-99); (2) leaving his homeland and family; (3) the famine in Canaan; (4) when Pharaoh took Sarah; (5) the attack of the four kings; (6) when at the "Covenant-of-the-Parts" God reveals the future of the Jewish people to him; (7) circumcising himself; (8) when Abimelech took Sarah; (9) sending Hagar and Ishmael away; (10) the *Akedah*, the binding of Isaac (see *Yalkut Me'am Lo'ez* by Yaakov Culi, Vol. II, pp. 210-311).

4 The Hebrew text of the *Akedah*, Genesis 22:1-19, is one of the most remarkable narrative passages in the Torah. The account is full of tension and emotion. The language is concise and the phrases terse. Read the text carefully in Hebrew and discuss how the spoken phrases both reveal and conceal the emotions at play. What questions are written between the lines? What significant information about Abraham's relationship with God and his relationship with Isaac is hidden in the way God phrases the command to sacrifice Isaac? Why doesn't God simply say in Genesis 22:2, "Take Isaac . . . "? For *midrashim* that answer some of these questions, see *Yalkut Me'am Lo'ez* by Yaakov Culi, Vol. II, pp. 321-345, and *Legends of the Jews* by Louis Ginzberg, Vol. I, pp. 274-286.

5 When told that he must abandon Ishmael and sacrifice Isaac, Abraham did not argue with God on their behalf. Why not? How do we judge Abraham? Role play putting Abraham on trial. Have participants gather evidence from witnesses and the Torah text to decide whether or not to put Abraham on trial. If a trial ensues assign parts for the main characters and the courtroom. Dress in costume and videotape the proceedings. Use real attorneys and other professionals as resources to add authenticity to your production.

EXTENDING THE TEXT

6 When God chose to destroy Sodom and Gomorrah, Abraham debated the wisdom of God's decision. Read the "Kaddish of Rabbi Levi of Berdichev." What other events are questioned? Can you add any modern occurrences to this *Kaddish* using the style of Rabbi Levi?
Reference: *Arguing with God: A Jewish Tradition* by Anson Laytner

7 Hagar and Sarah harbored deep resentments against one another. The text never shows them having a face-to-face confrontation, nor does it reveal their feelings. Write a letter as if you are Hagar or Sarah in which you express yourself and the condition of your life. Direct this letter to a sister, friend, or other family member.

8 Expand Strategy #7 by interpreting one of the scenes involving Hagar and/or Sarah by building a diorama. (See *100+ Jewish Art Projects for Children* by Nina Streisand Sher and Margaret A. Feldman, p. 88, for procedure.)

9 The binding of Isaac has inspired many of our writers and sages. Read through some different versions of this account in the suggested references below.

a. Choosing one of the interpretations, assume you are Isaac and write a diary excerpt of the events.
b. Imagine that you are the rock upon which Isaac is to be sacrificed. You witness the event; now write a description of what happened.
References: *Legends of the Jews* by Ginzberg, Vol. I, pp. 274-286; *The Midrash Genesis*, Vol. I, Chapter LVI; *Bereshit*, Art Scroll Series, see "An Overview/ The Akedah" and commentary on the appropriate verses; *The Last Trial* by Shalom Spiegel; *GOD was in this PLACE & I, i did not know* by Lawrence Kushner, pp. 160-165.

10 Rabbi Huna announced that mealtimes at his home were to be considered an open invitation to strangers (*Ta'anit* 20b). A saying of his, "Let all who are hungry, come and eat" made its way into the Passover *Haggadah*. Create an illustrated banner on paper or fabric with this saying. If your synagogue conducts a food drive use it as part of the publicity or hang it in a local soup kitchen or food pantry.

PERSONALIZING THE TEXT

11 Set up a large tent with flaps that open on all four sides. If a tent is not available use large sheets and four poles which you can stabilize. Make original welcome signs for each of the openings. Some suggestions include: "*Hachnasat Orchim* Practiced Here," "Welcome to Our Tent," "Abraham, Sarah, and Our Class Spread the Welcome Mat for You," "*Bruchim HaBa'im*: Blessed Be Those Who Enter." Continue the activity by preparing a snack or meal to which you invite guests.

12 After the three messengers had completed their task with Abraham, they set off for Sodom. The text states in part, ". . . Abraham walking with them to see them off." From this phrase we learn the importance of sending off a traveler.

A custom developed in which those seeing off a traveler would recite particular verses. The first verse beginning with the letter *lamed,* the second with the letter *vav,* the third with the letter *yud,* and the fourth with the letter *heh.* The letters spell out *levayah,* meaning escort. A text and complete explanation can be found in *Yalkut Me'am Lo'ez* by Yaakov Culi, Vol. II, pp. 183-188.

Create a ceremony for an individual taking an important or special journey. You might direct it to someone going to Israel, a Soviet emigré, or a Jew leaving another land of oppression (a South American nation, Ethiopia, etc.), or to an individual beginning a new stage of life (college, marriage, new job, etc.).

13 Ultimately, Isaac was not sacrificed; a ram caught in a nearby thicket replaced him. On Rosh HaShanah, we retell the events of the binding of Isaac and we recall the ram sacrificed in his place. A symbol of that ram is the *shofar.* Learn to sound a *shofar* with the appropriate notes. You may even become proficient enough to do this during High Holy Day services.

14 As mentioned in #2 on page 28, God did not truthfully report Sarah's reaction to Abraham. Also in this portion, Abraham calls Sarah his sister for the second time. Regarding God's actions, the Talmud explains that God wanted to preserve family peace and not cause an argument. Abraham sought to save his own life, fearing that the Egyptians might murder him in order to take Sarah. Both of these explanations offer a justification for masking the truth. Can you cite any examples from your own life in which it might have been better to mask the truth? Give examples of other such situations in communal life.

15 The portion begins with God appearing to Abraham. The text does not explain the purpose of the visit. One *midrash* explains that this was the third day after Abraham had circumcised himself and the God was inquiring about

Abraham's health. From this we derive the *mitzvah* of *Bikur Cholim,* visiting the sick. As a group, choose one of the following activities to put this *mitzvah* into action:

a. Visit a children's hospital.
b. With permission, distribute the pulpit flowers after Shabbat to synagogue members who are in the hospital.
c. Have a fund-raiser, such as a bake sale or car wash. Use the money to create packets for hospital patients or nursing home residents which might include: note cards, pen, change for phone calls, crossword puzzle book, comb and brush, playing cards, and other items which might make them more comfortable. Distribute similar items to synagogue members or to patients who might not be able to afford these extras. Contact the hospital social worker to identify such patients.

16 Abraham welcomes his three visitors with open arms. There is a saying in Hebrew which exemplifies this attitude: ברוכים הבאים (Blessed be those who enter). Create a small mosaic with this inscription to hang by your doorway. Do this with paper cut into small pieces resembling mosaic tiles, or buy tiles and cement from a craft supply store.

17 Mount Moriah, where the *Akedah* took place, is a sacred site for Jews, Moslems, and Christians. According to tradition, the Dome of the Rock marks the location of the *Akedah.* The Al Aqsa mosque is also located on the Temple Mount. The First and Second Temples once stood on Mount Moriah, and various *midrashim* associate this mountain with the site of the creation of Adam and the resting place of Noah's ark. A number of important Christian sites are located near Mount Moriah as well — the Church of the Holy Sepulchre and the Via Dolorosa. Create a mural which illustrates all the events which tradition informs us have taken place on Mount Moriah. Reference: *Encyclopaedia Judaica,* "Jerusalem," s.v. "In Judaism," Vol. 9, p. 1549, s.v. "In Other Religions," Vol. 9, p. 1568.

18 Once God reveals to Abraham the intention of destroying Sodom and Gomorrah, Abraham is not content to sit idly by and watch the righteous die with the wicked. God has condemned all the inhabitants, but Abraham insists God should not punish all if only a few are guilty. In this case, all the inhabitants were labeled as evil. What are some labels or stereotypes you have heard which wrongly categorize all members of a particular age group, race, or religion? How do you think these labels evolved? Do you have any notions about others which might be considered stereotypes? How did you come to believe them?

19 Read Isaac Asimov's explanation of the destruction of Sodom and Gomorrah in *Asimov's Guide to the Bible,* Vol. I, pp. 81-83. Asimov suggests that the destruction could have been caused by an earthquake, a volcanic eruption, or a large meteorite striking earth. Consider these questions: Do we always need a rational explanation for events in the Bible? What lesson was the incident trying to teach? (Societies based on injustice cannot survive.) Can you give modern day examples of this lesson? What are the similarities and differences between your example and the incident of Noah and the flood?

20 In this portion and the previous one, *Lech Lecha,* Sarah forces Hagar to leave, for as the text reads, "Sarah dealt harshly with her" (Genesis 16:6). Could this occurrence be a foreshadowing of the animosity between the Arabs and the Israelis? Do you think Sarah or Hagar could have acted differently? Why or Why not?

OTHER RESOURCES

21 Learn the songs "Abraham" and "Sarah Laughed" from *Bible People Songs.*

22 Complete the pages which relate to this portion in *Bible People Book One* by Joel Lurie Grishaver, pp. 18-19 and 23-26. Also check the accompanying Leader Guide for procedures and additional activities.

23 Read, act out, and discuss the skit for *Vayera* in *Sedra Scenes: Skits for Every Torah Portion* by Stan J. Beiner, pp. 20-27.

24 View and discuss the episode for *Vayera* from *Torah Toons I: The Video.*

25 For creative movement activities see "Sarah Laughed," "Lot's Wife," "Hagar's Eyes Are Opened," and the "Binding of Isaac," from *Torah in Motion* by JoAnne Tucker and Susan Freeman, pp. 20-27.

26 Read and discuss the illustrated commentary for *Va-Yera* in *American Torah Toons* by Lawrence Bush.

27 Listen to, discuss, and sing "Sarah and Hagar" from *Sounds of Creation: Genesis in Song.*

28 Make the Purim Basket project from *Jewish Origami 2* by Florence Temko. Rename it a *Hachnasat Orchim* treat dish.

29 See "Workshop 5 The Binding of Isaac" from *Handmade Midrash* by Jo Milgrom.

30 For additional background and activities on *Bikur Cholim* and *Hachnasat Orchim,* see *Teaching Mitzvot* by Barbara Binder Kadden and Bruce Kadden.

INVOLVING THE FAMILY

31 Abraham left his family and homeland in obedience to God. He was even willing to sacrifice his son Isaac to demonstrate his belief in God. Ask every family member to think of a very strong belief he or she holds or a value to which he or she is committed. Would any of you put the belief or value above the lives of those you love? Would any of you be willing to give up certain of your possessions to demonstrate the extent of your faith? Would any of you be willing to leave your home and family because of a cherished belief or value?

32 Start a family "*Mitzvah* Project" by brainstorming ways that you can fulfill the *mitzvah* of *Bikur Cholim.* Choose one of the ideas your family generated and make it a part of your family's routine. Some suggestions: "adopt" a resident of an old age home or a chronically ill child or adult providing them with special things associated with the holidays and regularly visiting them; cook and/or do household chores for someone

confined to his/her home by reason of age or illness.

BAR/BAT MITZVAH PROJECT

33 This portion contains the biblical foundation for the *mitzvah* of *Hachnasat Orchim:* welcoming the stranger. Assemble *Hachnasat Orchim* baskets for new students who enroll in your school.
Some suggestions of items to include:
a school calendar
names, telephone numbers, E-mail addresses of their new classmates
a map of your community
T-shirt or other item with the synagogue logo
a listing with telephone numbers of local youth sports leagues
a list of age appropriate Jewish community groups and activities
name of a student buddy to team up with at school
a bag of sweets and treats!

CHAYAY SARAH 23:1-25:18 חיי שרה

SYNOPSIS

SARAH DIES AT AGE 127 IN KIRIAT-ARBA, now known as Hebron. Abraham buys a burial site there — the Cave of Machpelah — from the Hittites, inhabitants of that area.

In time, Abraham decides that a wife should be found for his son Isaac. Abraham directs his senior servant, Eliezer, to search for this wife, cautioning him not to take a Canaanite woman. The servant travels to Aram-Naharaim to the city of Nahor, the land of Abraham's kin. Upon arrival, the servant prays to God to direct him to the woman chosen for Isaac. Rebekah, the daughter of Bethuel who is the son of Nahor, Abraham's brother, comes to the well. Through her words and deeds, Eliezer knows that she is the answer to his search. The servant is welcomed into Bethuel's house and after conferring with Bethuel and his son Laban, it is agreed that Rebekah will go to Canaan to become Isaac's wife.

The next morning, Eliezer prepares to leave, but Laban and his mother request that Rebekah remain with them a while longer. The servant asks not to be delayed and the decision is put to Rebekah. She consents to leave immediately and journeys to Canaan with her maids to become Isaac's wife.

Abraham takes another wife, Keturah, who bears him six children. Before dying, he wills all his possessions to Isaac and gives gifts to his other children. When Abraham dies, Isaac and Ishmael bury him in the Cave of Machpelah beside Sarah.

The portion closes with the naming of Ishmael's twelve sons. Ishmael dies at the age of 137.

INSIGHTS FROM THE TRADITION

A *Chayay Sarah* (Sarah's lifetime) was 127 years. A *midrash* tells us that Satan brought the news of Abraham's sacrifice of Isaac to Sarah; the shock killed her. Abraham chose the Cave of Machpelah as the burial site for Sarah. Sarah was the first member of the Patriarch's immediate family to be buried there. The purchase of the Cave of Machpelah is the first example of the Jewish people's legal ownership of property in the Promised Land. In *Beresheet Rabbah* (79:7), Rabbi Yudan bar Simon said: "The Cave of Machpelah is one of three places about which the nations of the world cannot taunt Israel saying: 'these are stolen lands.' The other two are the Temple Mount bought by David, and Shechem, the burial place of Joseph."

A number of *midrashic* sources indicate that Abraham chose Machpelah because it was the burial place of Adam and Eve. Abraham had previously come upon it when chasing a runaway ox.

Abraham purchased the cave from Ephron who initially desired to give it to Abraham as a gift. Abraham may have been concerned that Ephron would later take back the gift and wish to bury Hittite dead with Sarah; therefore, he insisted on a formal sale (Abrabanel). Ephron set the price at 400 shekels of silver, an astronomical price, which Abraham promptly paid. It seems that Ephron took advantage of Abraham in his grief.

Based on *Baba Metsia* 87a, Rashi points out that the name Ephron is spelled defectively (without the *vav*). This indicated that there was something missing in Ephron (i.e., sincerity) because he promised much, but did not do even the very least. Moshe Dayan points out that Abraham was a wanderer not connected to the land in any way. In fact, the Torah makes special note of the one tree he planted: "Abraham planted a tamarisk in Beersheva" (Genesis 21:33). Note that a tamarisk bears no fruit. It is used only as a shade tree. Abraham did buy one plot of ground — for burial, not for sowing and reaping. Thus, he maintained a nomadic lifestyle (*Living with the Bible* by Moshe Dayan, p. 18).

In our transient society, how do we show our commitment to the place where we live?

Why would it be easy to take advantage of a person who is in a state of grief?

How would you feel if you wanted to give someone a gift and were rebuffed?

Why do you think Ephron offered the cave as a gift and then set a very high price for its purchase (as opposed to a low price)? Might his pride have been hurt?

B Despite their contentious past, the text tells us that Isaac and Ishmael together buried their father Abraham in the Cave of Machpelah in Hebron. To this day, the Cave of Machpelah is an important religious site for both Jews and Moslems. The city of Hebron itself has become a hotly contested place between Israelis and Palestinians. How might Isaac and Ishmael's reconciliation serve as a model for handling current and future disputes?

C The commentary *Tzenah Ur'enah* states that Abraham did not want Isaac to marry a Canaanite lest the Canaanites should say that God did not want to fulfill the promise to give the land to Abraham's descendants, who had to marry Canaanites to inherit it. Abraham forbade his son to marry a Canaanite woman because he knew that God would give him the land without this" (p. 188). W. Gunther Plaut suggests that Abraham wanted Isaac to marry within his own group, thereby remaining a stranger in Canaan (*The Torah: A Modern Commentary*, p. 161). Here are the seeds of strong feelings about mixed marriage in Judaism.

Abraham sent Eliezer to Haran to find a suitable wife. One might wonder why Abraham did not send Isaac to find his own wife. The *midrash* notes that Isaac having been an offering without blemish could not leave the land of Israel. Indeed, Isaac was the only Patriarch who never journeyed outside the land of Israel. *Yalkut Me'am Lo'ez* by Yaakov Culi (Vol. II, p. 391), quotes Abraham as saying "Since Isaac carries God's blessing, he cannot marry into an accursed family." The

Canaanites were considered cursed because they descended from Ham. (See Genesis, *Noah* 9:20-27.)

Was Abraham justified in choosing a wife for Isaac? Nachmanides maintains that Isaac would not disobey the wishes of his father regarding whom he would marry.

Can parents influence their children in their choice of spouses? Should they?

Did Isaac ever have a chance to be his own person? In what matters are you totally free to act as you choose?

D At the well, Eliezer prayed to witness certain behavior so as to be able to identify Isaac's future bride. A debate exists among the commentators as to whether Eliezer was practicing sorcery by allowing a "sign" to determine his actions (Rambam). Abrabanel and Malbim maintain that Eliezer gave a character test to determine the bride's kindness and generosity.

What qualities characterize Rebekah?

What role will those qualities play in furthering the beliefs of Abraham's descendants?

What qualities would you especially look for in a future life partner?

E A curiosity exists in the text when Rebekah introduces herself as the daughter of Bethuel. When Eliezer enters Rebekah's home and explains his mission and describes Rebekah's successful completion of the test, both her brother Laban and her father Bethuel agree that the matter stemmed from the Lord and Rebekah should become Isaac's wife. The following morning, only Laban and Rebekah's mother conclude the negotiation. What then happened to Bethuel? *Genesis Rabbah* (60:12) states that Bethuel suddenly died because he wished to hinder the marriage. The proof text for this is Proverbs 11:5, "The righteousness of the sincere shall make straight his way, but the wicked shall fall by his own wickedness." "The righteousness of the sincere" alludes to Isaac; "shall make straight his way" refers to Eliezer; "but the wicked shall fall by his own wickedness" alludes to Bethuel.

Why might Bethuel have wished to prevent the marriage between Isaac and Rebekah?
Are there traits or habits that you have which you sincerely want to change?

F Isaac brought Rebekah into his mother Sarah's tent. Rebekah not only took physical possession of the actual tent, but according to *Genesis Rabbah* (60:16) the four blessings Sarah had brought to Abraham's house returned: (1) a cloud (signifying the Divine Presence) hung over her tent; (2) the household was blessed with abundance; (3) a lamp remained lit from Friday to Friday (the Sabbath light kindled Friday afternoon would burn all week); (4) the doors were always open wide and alms were provided for the poor. Just as the Rabbis created behavioral expectations for the Patriarchs, so, too, were these established for the Matriarchs.

What purpose or role must Rebekah fulfill?
What were the Rabbis trying to teach regarding these four blessings?
What blessings characterize your home now?
What blessings do you hope will characterize your home when you are married?

G Rashi, using the *midrash* as a source, identifies Abraham's wife Keturah as Hagar. In fact, the commentary *Yalkut Me'am Lo'ez* by Yaakov Culi (Vol. II, p. 429), records that after Sarah's death, Isaac brought Hagar to Abraham.

Considering Rashi's interpretation, Abraham had an enduring love for Hagar. How does this affect your opinion of Sarah, Abraham, and Hagar?
If you were Hagar, why might you want to return to Abraham's tent?

STRATEGIES

ANALYZING THE TEXT

1 The portion opens with the death of Sarah. Retrace her footsteps filling in events that transpired, reminiscences of her journeys, and her reactions to what happened to her and to those around her.

Make an outline of a footprint and reproduce a footprint for each of the entries you have collected. Put these in chronological order and place them on a wall or on the floor for display.

2 Play a biblical version of "To Tell the Truth." Prepare statement sheets for some or all of the following figures: Abraham, Sarah, Isaac, Rebekah, and Esau. Choose three people for each round, one of whom is the "real" biblical figure. The audience or panel of contestants asks questions of the two fake and one "real" figures and then must choose, based on their answers, who they think represents the "real" character.

3 Review this portion and the previous two, *Lech Lecha* and *Vayera*. Identify those values which Abraham exemplifies and create a values mobile. Use cardboard or construction paper for the balancing pieces and on each write one of Abraham's values. Suspend from wire hangers or wooden dowels, using nylon thread or light string.

4 Every word, indeed, every letter of the Torah is thought to be present (or thought to be missing) for a specific reason. Therefore, the commentators paid close attention to words that seem to be extraneous or unnecessary. Read Genesis 23:1 carefully in Hebrew. What word seems not needed? Answer: שנה (*shanah*) year(s). How would you translate this sentence into literal English? ("Sarah's lifetime came to one hundred years . . . these were the years of Sarah's life.")

What lesson might the text be trying to teach us about Sarah? Can you connect this with the fact that the portion which tells of Sarah's death is called *Chayay Sarah,* or "Sarah's Life"? Some explanations suggested in *The Torah Anthology Yalkut Me'am Lo'ez* by Yaakov Culi (Vol. II, pp. 350-352): Sarah lived exactly as long as she was meant to; despite Sarah's righteousness, Sarah died before her time as punishment for her treatment of Hagar; Sarah was as beautiful at one hundred as she was at twenty, and as sinless at twenty as she was at seven.

EXTENDING THE TEXT

5 Both Abraham and Sarah die in this portion. Write the epitaphs for their headstones.

6 Create a newspaper edition based on this portion. Include obituaries, real estate sales (Cave of Machpelah), wedding announcements, travel agency advertisements, news stories, and an advice column. For an example, see *Chronicles: News of the Past,* Vol. I.

7 One *midrash* explains why Eliezer did not eat the food placed in front of him: An angel warned him that Bethuel was trying to poison him. Bethuel ate the poisoned food and died. While this may seem to be a fanciful explanation, it does solve some of the dilemmas in the text. Compose your own *midrash* to explain why Eliezer did not eat the food and why Bethuel is no longer mentioned in the text.

8 Recreate the conversation that took place when Isaac and Rebekah met for the first time. Stage several different conversations, choosing different students to play Isaac and Rebekah each time. Identify the issues, emotions, and information shared. Selecting the best pieces from each exchange, record or videotape a final conversation.

9 Imagine that you are Eliezer. Send a telegram reporting to Abraham that you have found a wife for Isaac. Create a telegram form a la Western Union. You might rename it "Middle East Express" or something else that is appropriate. Compare the telegrams of each participant.

10 In Genesis 24:60, Rebekah is blessed with the words, "O sister! May you grow into thousands of myriads." These words are part of the *bedeken* ceremony in a traditional wedding. For an activity on this ceremony, see the Index: "*Bedeken.*"

11 In the stories introducing Rebekah, the women of her family play unusually prominent roles: Rebekah's *grandmother* is named in her genealogy (Gen. 24:15), Rebekah is said to report the events with Abraham's servant to "her *mother's* household" (Gen. 24:28), and it is Rebekah's mother and brother (not father) who negotiate the marriage arrangement. Furthermore, Rebekah is one of the few women in the Bible to receive a special blessing, and she is the only woman to receive a blessing from her own mother. Perhaps this story reflects some aspects of women's roles in biblical times which the Torah doesn't usually reveal. Using a variety of resources, write a report on the place of women in biblical society.

12 According to Professor Carol Meyers, writing for the on-line Torah study project "Learn Torah With . . . ," "Rebekah's role as mother of nations looms larger than that of her husband and father of nations . . . especially in comparison with the other 'mothers' of Genesis. Rebekah is a much more active, autonomous individual" (p. 35, 37). Meyers has identified a number of ways in which the narratives about Rebekah parallel the stories of Abraham. Examine Genesis 24 for examples of Rebekah's activism and likeness to Abraham. Do you agree with Meyers that perhaps "we ought to replace the familiar sequence, 'Abraham, Isaac, and Jacob' with the phrase 'Abraham,

Rebekah, and Jacob' in referring to the leading figures of this period of our ancestors?

13 A close reading of *Chayay Sarah* and *Toledot* reveals Isaac as a quiet man of many virtues, most particularly as a son, husband, and father. Imagine you are Rebekah, after many years away from home, writing a letter home to your mother describing your husband Isaac. What would you say to praise him?

14 Eggs are customarily given to mourners as their first meal when they return from the funeral. Many Jewish life cycle events and holidays have special food customs associated with them. Research some of these and then write appropriate menus (with explanations) for several life cycle celebrations or holidays.
References: *The Jewish Holiday Kitchen* by Joan Nathan; articles in the *Encyclopaedia Judaica* about life cycle ceremonies and holidays; "Caring for the Dead" in *Teaching Mitzvot* by Barbara Binder Kadden and Bruce Kadden.

PERSONALIZING THE TEXT

15 Extend #3 above by creating a list of your own values. Place these on balancing pieces and attach to the same mobile as Abraham's. To distinguish between the two sets of values, choose one color for Abraham's values and another for yours.

16 Many of our contemporary burial customs trace their roots to the biblical period. Invite a guest speaker from the *Chevrah Kaddisha* (Jewish burial society) or a funeral director from a funeral home to describe Jewish funeral customs.

17 Listen to the song "Matchmaker, Match-maker" from the musical *Fiddler on the Roof*. What Jewish marriage practices are sung about in this song? Interview family members, especially older relatives, to find out how they met their spouses. Do any relatives recall arranged marriages of family members? Write lyrics to the song "Matchmaker, Matchmaker" about the matchmaking of Rebekah and Isaac.

18 Design a wedding invitation for Isaac and Rebekah. Use calligraphy pens or chisel point markers for wording. Then decorate the invitation using watercolors and/or multi-colored markers.
References for examples of invitations: "Scribal Arts" in *The First Jewish Catalog* by Richard Siegel, Michael Strassfeld, and Sharon Strassfeld, pp. 184-209; *The Jewish Wedding* by Anita Diamant.

19 *Kaddish* is the prayer recited in memory of the departed. While Abraham probably did not say *Kaddish*, the text reads: " . . . and Abraham proceeded to mourn for Sarah . . . " (Genesis 23:2). Learn the *Kaddish*. Write your own mourning prayer.

20 Examine in more detail the traditions associated with Jewish burial customs.
References: *Death, Burial and Mourning in the Jewish Tradition* by Audrey Friedman Marcus, Sherry Bissell, and Karen S. Lipschutz; *The Minhagim: The Customs and Ceremonies of Judaism, Their Origins and Rationale* by Abraham Chill, pp. 319-338; "Caring for the Dead" in *Teaching Mitzvot* by Barbara Binder Kadden and Bruce Kadden, chapter 9.

21 In the course of bargaining with Ephron the Hittite to purchase the Cave of Machpelah, the text (25:12) tells us that Abraham bowed low before *Am HaAretz*, literally, "the people of the land." In later times, this phrase came to have negative connotations, such as ignorant, illiterate, boorish. Speculate on the reasons behind this transformation in meaning. Design and illustrate a poster showing the meaning of the phrase in both its positive and negative senses.

OTHER RESOURCES

22 Read, act out, and discuss the skit for *Chayay Sarah* in *Sedra Scenes: Skits for Every Torah Portion* by Stan J. Beiner, pp. 28-31.

23 Listen to and/or learn the song "A Woman Strong and True" from *Bible People Songs*.

24 Complete the pages which relate to this portion from *Bible People Book One* by Joel Lurie Grishaver, pp. 27-38. Check the accompanying Leader Guide for procedures and additional activities.

25 Complete the worksheet on the *Kaddish* on page 44 of *The Life Cycle Workbook* by Joel Lurie Grishaver. Check the accompanying Leader Guide for procedures and additional activities.

26 View and discuss the episode for *Chayay Sarah* from *Torah Toons I: The Video*.

27 For creative movement activities see "Sarah's Lifetime" and "Rebekah's Veil" from *Torah in Motion* by JoAnne Tucker and Susan Freeman, pp. 28-31.

28 Listen to, discuss, and sing *"Hatina Chadeich"* from *Sounds of Creation: Genesis in Song*.

29 Read and discuss the illustrated commentary for *Chayyei Sarah* in *American Torah Toon* by Lawrence Bush.

INVOLVING THE FAMILY

30 As a family, discuss whether there are things children should be able to do without their parents' consent. Base your discussion on Genesis 24:57, 58 — Rebekah's decision to go with Eliezer and marry Isaac even though her family may not have approved (see Synopsis). How does the age of a child affect the answers to this question? Are there other factors involved (e.g., demonstrating responsible behavior, the ability to pay one's own way)? At what age should children be able to act completely independent of their parents? Do parents need to have the consent of their children for certain decisions and actions?

BAR/BAT MITZVAH PROJECT

31 Among the many *mitzvot* is an obligation to rejoice with bride and groom. In Jewish tradition, weddings were also seen as opportunities for the celebrants to share their joy and good fortune with the less fortunate. For examples of how the Jewish community has brought the element of *tzedakah* into the marriage celebration, read about the work of The Rabbanit Bracha Kapach or "Rachel's Table" in *Mitzvahs* by Danny Siegel (pp. 94, 101).

a. Contact The Rabbanit Bracha Kapach, 12 Lod Street, Jerusalem, Israel, and ask if it is possible to send used wedding gowns. Run a campaign to collect used and unwanted wedding gowns, then send them off to Israel.

b. After reading about Rachel's Table, institute a similar program in your community.

c. Write to MAZON, 2940 Westwood Blvd., #7, Los Angeles, CA 90064, to ask about what you can do to help feed the hungry.

TOLEDOT 25:19-28:9 תולדות

SYNOPSIS

REBEKAH IS BARREN, SO ISAAC PRAYS TO God on her behalf. God responds to Isaac's plea and Rebekah conceives twins. She experiences a difficult pregnancy. The twins have already begun a struggle within the womb which will continue for many years once they are born. The first twin to emerge is red and hairy and is named Esau; the other, born holding Esau's heel, is called Jacob. Esau is a hunter; Jacob is a quiet individual who chooses to stay in camp. Isaac favors Esau, but Rebekah loves Jacob.

One day while Jacob is cooking a stew, Esau comes in starving and demands some food. As payment, Jacob insists that Esau sell him his birthright. Esau does so without hesitation.

A famine occurs in the land. But God commands Isaac to remain in Canaan and not travel to Egypt so that Isaac may receive the blessings bestowed on his father Abraham (i.e., a great nation and land). Isaac remains in Gerar and tells the inhabitants that Rebekah is his sister. One day Abimelech, ruler of the area, sees Isaac and Rebekah being intimate together. When questioned, Isaac states that he called her his sister in order to preserve his life. Isaac becomes very wealthy in Gerar, and is ultimately asked to leave. He settles first in the wadi of Gerar, but the local herdsmen quarrel with Isaac's servants about the ownership of the water in the wells they have dug. Isaac moves to Rehovot (meaning "expansive"), so named in gratitude for its ample room to expand without complaint and quarrel from the local people. A series of wanderings ensue, but eventually Isaac settles in Beersheva and makes a peace treaty with the Philistines.

Esau takes two wives from among the Hittites. This makes Isaac and Rebekah bitter.

Isaac grows old. The time of blessing his offspring is at hand. Isaac directs Esau to hunt game and prepare a meal for him after which Isaac will

bless Esau. Rebekah overhears She convinces Jacob to deceiv putting on skins and pretending to be Esau. Jacob does so and receives Isaac's blessing for himself. Rebekah, fearing that Esau plans revenge against Jacob, tells Jacob to flee to Haran, to her brother Laban. In order to have Isaac approve of Jacob's journey, Rebekah convinces Isaac that Jacob should be sent to Laban to find a bride from among their kin. Esau sees that his brother obeys their parents regarding the choice of a bride, so he, too, chooses a bride from among their kin — Mahalath, the daughter of Ishmael.

INSIGHTS FROM THE TRADITION

A *Toledot* means "generations." This portion begins by recounting the family background of Isaac in preparation for its description of his adult life.

B When, in the previous portion, Rebekah prepared to leave her home, her mother and brother blessed her. "But the blessings did not come from the bottom of their hearts. Indeed, as a rule, the blessing of the impious is a curse, wherefore Rebekah remained barren for years" (*Legends of the Jews* by Louis Ginzberg, Vol. I, p. 296).

Yebamot 64a deals with the issue of barrenness, a condition which affected Sarah, Rebekah, and Rachel. The passage states that God longs to hear the prayers of the righteous. What does this mean? Radak explains: "Such prayers publicize the efficacy of prayer. God therefore gives them cause to pray so that [God] can miraculously fulfill their requests publicly."

Why is having children such an important theme in the Book of Genesis?
For the Matriarchs, what purpose does bareness followed by childbirth serve? (to show the working

of God in human life, that older parents are better able to pass on the tradition, to show how important each individual really is).

C Rebekah becomes pregnant, but feels a great struggling (*va'yitrotzitzu*) within her. Rashi felt this "struggling" needed a *midrashic* explanation. "Our Rabbis explain that *va'yitrotzitzu* has the meaning of running, moving quickly. Whenever Rebekah passed by the school of Shem and Eber, Jacob moved . . . to be born. But whenever she passed by the gate of a pagan temple, Esau moved . . . to be born" (*Genesis Rabbah* 63).

In what ways are you different from your brothers and sisters?
What do you think accounts for these differences?

D The text states that "Rebekah went to inquire of the Lord." Various commentators suggest that Rebekah consulted Shem, a teacher of Torah. Through divine inspiration, Shem became God's mouthpiece (*Yalkut Me'am Lo'ez* by Yaakov Culi, Vol. II, p. 455). Shem explained that Rebekah was carrying twins who were beginning a power struggle in the womb which would continue after their birth.

If you were looking for answers to very difficult questions, who would you ask?
If you had a problem which really bothered you, would you pray for help? What traditional prayer would you recite? Would you feel free to make up a prayer in your own words?

E At birth, the first twin to emerge was red and hairy and he was named Esau. Esau is a synonym for Seir, a wordplay on *sayar* — hair (Genesis 25:25). The second infant to emerge was holding the heel of Esau. He was named Jacob, a play on the word *aykev* — heel.

How are the names Esau and Jacob (given at birth) an accurate reflection of the kind of people these two became?

In what ways are you like Esau?
In what ways are you like Jacob?

F Jacob conspired to take Esau's birthright. The birthright entitled Esau to inherit first. At the moment of Esau's physical weakness, Jacob asked him to give up the rights of the firstborn. In return, Esau got some of the red pottage (stew). This also alludes to his name since the pottage was called *Adom* (red) and Esau was known as "Edom."

Can it be said that Esau let himself be cheated because he didn't want the responsibility of being a Patriarch of the Jewish people?
What would you not want to take responsibility for at this stage in your life? Do you expect this to change as you grow older? In what way might this be similar to Esau's selling of his birthright?

G A famine broke out in Canaan, but Isaac, unlike Abraham his father, was commanded by God not to go down to Egypt. Rashi provides a reason for this: "Do not go down to Egypt for you are a burnt offering without blemish and residence outside the Holy Land is not befitting you." Because Isaac followed God's command, he and his descendants would continue to merit the blessing of land and of being a great nation. Instead, Isaac goes to Gerar, then controlled by the Philistines under King Abimelech.

Isaac follows his father's example and claims Rebekah is his sister rather than his wife. The *midrash* states that Isaac was afraid of being killed if his relationship to Rebekah should be discovered.

The commentary *Tzenah Ur'enah* compares Abimelech's reaction to that of Pharaoh's: "Abimelech said, 'What have you done to us?' while Pharaoh asked, 'What have you done to me?'" (p. 135). Pharaoh took this as a personal insult for had he known, he would not have touched another man's (Abraham's) wife, yet his people might. Abimelech on the other hand said that both he and his nation were moral and no one would touch Rebekah.

Is the Torah already hinting at the immorality of Egypt?

Is this another instance of Isaac's misjudgment of character?

H Some commentators suggest that Isaac actually knew that he was blessing Jacob, but pretended to be fooled in order not to destroy his relationship with Esau. The key factor seems to be Isaac's becoming blind. It is ironic that when he had his sight, he favored Esau, and it was only with his blindness that he was able to give Jacob the blessing.

If Jacob already had the birthright, why did he have to "steal" his father's blessing?
Did Jacob do the right thing in fooling his father? Would you have done it under the circumstances?

I Fox points out the incredible use of the physical senses as Jacob receives the blessing intended for Esau. Seven times we hear of the game to be caught; six times of the delicacy or tasty dish to be prepared; three times, as Jacob draws near his father, Isaac touchs him; four times smell and hearing are brought into play; and it is around Isaac's defective sight that the story revolves. Isaac's blindness enables the ruse which leads to the blessing (*The Five Books of Moses* by Everett Fox, pp. 105-107).

There is a saying: "Love blinds the eye." How does this apply to Isaac? To Rebekah?
If an individual loses one physical sense, other senses often compensate. Why didn't this happen in Isaac's case, or did it?

J Esau is described as a red and hairy individual who becomes a hunter and a man of the outdoors. He is considered by Jewish tradition as wild and uncouth. He spurned his own birthright because of his appetite. There is nothing in the text that lets us see any other side to this person. Yet, when he learns that he has been tricked out of

his blessing, he lets out a cry of such intensity that we finally do see the human in Esau. As Norman J. Cohen says, "His very human response elicits our sympathy and we see him as a deeply moving figure, the victim of a terrible plot" (*Self, Struggle & Change* by Norman J. Cohen, pp. 108-109). Cohen then suggests that not only do we sympathize with Esau, we can also identify with him. If we are members of families with more than one child, we, too, have at times felt ignored, unloved, and unimportant.

Do you ever feel as though your sibling(s) get more than you, that your parents are unfair and show favoritism?
Do you ever feel as though you receive more than your sibling(s)?

K A logical question based on this portion is whether or not Rebecca loved Esau. If you base your response on the text, it appears that very likely she did not. Ellen Frankel in *The Five Books of Miriam* (pp. 47-48) has Rebecca speaking directly to us: "Didn't you hear me cry out when I urged Jacob into exile to escape Esau's revenge: 'Let me not lose you both in one day' (Genesis 27:45). How clearly I understood what a high price I'd pay for my actions: losing Esau's love in exchange for Jacob's blessing. From the moment that God told me the destiny awaiting my two sons . . . 'The older shall serve the younger' — I devoted myself to forcing that blessing from Isaac's lips . . . when I finally succeeded . . . I heard Isaac tell Jacob: 'Be master over your brothers, and let your mother's sons bow to you,' I'd also lost. Jacob's curse was now on me just as I'd set it up. For the next 20 years, I suffered Esau's revenge: my beloved Jacob's absence."

Could Rebekah have chosen another path, or was it divine intention that left her no other options? Is she simply the instrument through which God achieves the preordained aim of having Jacob receive the blessing?

Esau is seen as a dark character. Yet, what did he do that was so bad? He respected his parents. He went out immediately to hunt a favorite food for his father. He waited to mourn his father's death before setting out after Jacob. Despite knowing that it would not be as grand as the one received by Jacob, Esau desperately sought his father's blessing. He married a Hittite woman, but when he saw it displeased his father and mother, he took an Ishmaelite woman to wife. So what was his sin? He despised his birthright for a pot of stew. In needing that which is material, he lost that which is spiritual. He squandered the future for the desires of the present.

Have you ever wanted something so much that you would do anything or give anything for it? If so, what was it? What did you do?
Is it possible that this story contains hints of the superiority of settled folk over nomadic peoples? Explain.
What common elements can be found in this story and in the account of Cain and Abel (Genesis 4:1-15)?

STRATEGIES

ANALYZING THE TEXT

1 Review these verses: Genesis 26:34-35, 28:6-9. Examine the character of Esau. Was Esau completely wicked? Was he a victim of circumstances? How did he treat his parents? Give specific examples. Take this activity a step further and do a parallel study of Jacob. (See Genesis 25:29-34, 27:5-29; also read through the portions *Vayaytzay* and *Vayishlach* to learn more about Jacob's life.)

2 In *Toledot,* Jacob receives two blessings. The first (Genesis 27:28, 29) was the blessing intended for Esau. The second blessing (Genesis 28:3-4), given him by Isaac on his departure for Paddan-aram, was the only one meant specifically for him. Compare the two blessings. Note how the first blessing is more concerned with material well-being, whereas the second blessing is directed toward spiritual matters and the future of the Jewish people. Which son of Isaac is named in these blessings to carry out the legacy of Abraham? What does a comparison of these blessings suggest to you about Isaac's "blindness"? Can you argue on the basis of this comparison that Isaac was aware of the differences between his sons and their divergent futures?

3 *Toledot* contains three interesting examples of Hebrew wordplay. Read Genesis 26:8 and 27:36 in Hebrew to find the wordplay in each (compare the wordplay in 26:8 to the similar one in 21:9). Then explain what insight each wordplay gives about the character described and/or the speaker.

4 Organize a "Scavenger Hunt" of the portion *Toledot.* Working in two or more teams, come up with a list of 15 questions that can be answered after a careful reading of the story (for example, the name of the king of the Philistines; Isaac's age when he married Rebekah). Trade lists with the other team and have a timed race to answer the questions. If desired, do this activity utilizing Hebrew.

5 Write a thumbnail sketch of Rebecca based on your reading of this portion and Insight K. How would you describe her as a wife and mother? Consider: What was your opinion of Rebekah before you read about her? Did reading and discussion change your feelings? How much of an impact did God have on her actions?

EXTENDING THE TEXT

6 Expand Strategy #5 by doing the following: Discuss and write a different version of this portion so that the end result, Jacob getting the blessing, does not split the family apart and cause so many bad feelings.

7 Write first person accounts of the story of Jacob's deception of Isaac. Choose one or more of the following main characters and retell the story through his/her eyes: Isaac, Rebekah, Jacob, Esau.

8 Certain events in Rebekah's life invite comparison with Sarah. Both women left their families to live in strange lands with their husbands, both were able to deceive local leaders about their true relationship with their husbands, and both experienced conflict and concern over their sons and took an active role in assuring that the favored son would receive the blessings God conferred upon Abraham.

Imagine that Sarah had lived to observe how Rebekah handled these events. Write and stage a conversation between the two women that might have occurred after the departure of Jacob. Have them reminisce about their lives and evaluate their success as Matriarchs.

9 Esau plotted to avenge the wrong that Jacob had done to him. Jacob fled to Haran, but the text never states that Esau knew where his brother had gone. Imagine that you are the private detective hired to locate Jacob. Do a character analysis of Jacob based on interviews with other biblical figures. You may want to add a few fictional elements, characters, and events. Formulate a number of plausible places for Jacob to have gone.

10 Rewrite the story as if Esau had received the blessing. Speculate on how Jewish history might have been different.

11 Without question, Jacob did carry out a deception with the aid of his mother. Imagine what would have happened had Jacob been brought to trial for his wrongdoing. Arrange a mock trial for Jacob. Include judge, jury, lawyers for the defense and prosecution, court reporter, and all of the characters and spectators.

12 Throughout the Book of Genesis, the passing on of blessings to the firstborn and the content of the those blessings is clearly detailed. Research the rights of the firstborn in different cultures.
References: *Encyclopaedia Judaica*, "First Born," Vol. 6, p. 1306; in secular encyclopedias, see "Primogeniture," "Inheritance," "Intestacy," and "Law of Succession."

13 In light of Jacob and Esau's relationship, discuss these two verses from the Talmud: "Show no partiality among your sons. Treat them all alike" (*Shabbat* 10); "Honor thy father and thy mother — including, also, thine older brother" (*Ketubot* 103).

PERSONALIZING THE TEXT

14 There are several instances in this portion when lies are told. Identify these instances. Is the lying justified? There are times when telling the truth would do more harm than telling a lie. Can you describe such situations? Have you, as an individual, ever been put in that position?

15 Many commentators have suggested that Isaac was not just physically blind, but that he was also blind to the natures of his two sons. When Jacob came and stole the blessing, Isaac was unable to identify him correctly. Isaac "blindly" trusted Jacob. Test your ability to trust by participating in a "Blind Walk." Choose a partner and blindfold one of you. With the other functioning as a caring guide, take a walk outside and inside. Include some obstacles, such as climbing over an obstruction, negotiating stairs, etc. When the walk is complete, review it in discussion.

a. How did each partner feel (nervous, powerful, etc.)?

b. How did the element of trust fit in?

c. Can you now more fully appreciate Isaac's position? Explain.

16 Isaac dug a number of wells providing water for his family and herds. Isaac was not carrying out a sophisticated irrigation project, but he was in a way reclaiming the land and making it more fertile. A major project in Israel has been reclaiming desert lands and making them bloom. The work has largely been carried out by the Jewish National Fund. Contact your local J.N.F. representative for information, brochures, program materials, and films. Mount a campaign to raise funds for trees in Israel.

17 The red pottage for which Esau begged and which he received at such a dear price must certainly have been delicious. Try the following recipe:

Mujeddrah
(Rice with Lentils, Jacob Style)

1 cup brown lentils
2 teaspoons salt
1 cup long-grain rice
2 cups water
2 large onions, sliced in rings
2 tablespoons vegetable or olive oil

a. Pick over the lentils; wash and drain. Boil in water with one teaspoon salt for about 30 minutes, or until tender.

b. In another pan, bring water to a boil. Add the rice and the remaining one teaspoon salt. Turn off the heat and let sit until the lentils are ready.

c. Drain and rinse the lentils and rice. Combine. Bring about 1¹/₂ cups water to a boil. Put in the lentils and rice, cover and simmer slowly about 20 minutes, or until the rice is cooked.

d. Sauté the onions in oil until golden. Add to the cooked rice and lentils.

(From *The Jewish Holiday Kitchen* by Joan Nathan.)

18 In Genesis 26:34-35 we read that Esau's Hittite wives "were a source of bitterness to Isaac and Rebekah." As the portion goes on, however, we see that Esau continues to seek the love of his parents. View and discuss the video *Intermarriage: When Love Meets Tradition.*

OTHER RESOURCES

19 Read, act out, and discuss the skit for *Toledot* in *Sedra Scenes: Skits for Every Torah Portion* by Stan J. Beiner, pp. 32-38.

20 Complete page 48 in *Bible People Book One* by Joel Lurie Grishaver. Check the accompanying Leader Guide for procedures and additional activities.

21 View the episode for *Toledot* from *Torah Toons I: The Video.*

22 Use "Parent-Child Interchange" from *Jewish Identity Games* by Richard J. Israel.

23 Listen to, discuss, and sing "Brother on Brother" from *Sounds of Creation: Genesis in Song.*

24 Read and discuss the illustrated commentary for *Toledot* in *American Torah Toons* by Lawrence Bush.

25 Read, act out, and discuss the play "Intermarriage" in *Class Acts* by Stan J. Beiner, pp. 221-231.

26 For creative movement activities, see "Jacob Emerges" and "Jacob: One Who

Disguises" from *Torah in Motion* by JoAnne Tucker and Susan Freeman, pp. 32-35.

INVOLVING THE FAMILY

Note: When assigning Strategy #27, please be sensitive to the fact that some participants may be children of, or partners in, mixed marriages.

27 Interdating and intermarriage are extremely sensitive issues for Jewish families today. In some ways, our situation is not all that different from that of Isaac and Rebekah and their family. We, too, live surrounded by people who do not share our religion and our values. Most of us want to balance our Jewish values and the values of secular society. As a family, discuss the portion as it reflects these issues. Do you think that Esau's actions show indifference to his parents' values? Was Esau being openly defiant of Isaac and Rebekah? What options did Esau have to change the final outcome of the situation? What options did Isaac and Rebekah have?

BAR/BAT MITZVAH PROJECT

28 Preparing for a Bar/Bat Mitzvah can take its toll on a family. Work with your family

members to establish and nurture *sh'lom bayit* — a peaceful, loving home. There are several suggested activities listed here designed to get parents and children talking, sharing, and working toward understanding each other.

With your parent(s) watch the video version of one or more films which deal with family relationships. After seeing the videos, share thoughts, feelings, and reactions. Some suggested titles: *What's Eating Gilbert Grape,* rated PG13; *Miss Rose White,* NR, made for television; *Dad,* rated PG; *Family Prayers,* rated PG; *King of the Hill,* rated PG13. These videos are available at video rental stores.

Sometimes verbal communication has its drawbacks. Writing letters gives some distance so that the correspondents can fully express themselves without interruption. Have parent(s) and the upcoming Bar/Bat Mitzvah student write letters to each other explaining personal preferences and desires for the Bar/Bat Mitzvah learning process, the ceremony, and the celebration.

Read the one of the following books to gain some additional insight about the Bar/Bat Mitzvah process. Suggested titles include: *Putting God on the Guest List* by Jeffrey Salkin; *Bar/Bat Mitzvah Basics: A Practical Guide to Coming of Age Together,* edited by Helen Leneman; *A Spiritual Journey: Bar Mitzvah and Bat Mitzvah Handbook* by Seymour Rossel.

VAYAYTZAY 28:10-32:3 ויצא

SYNOPSIS

WHILE FLEEING TO HARAN, JACOB RESTS one night. In a dream, Jacob sees angels ascending and descending a ladder. God comes to Jacob, repeats the blessing given to Abraham and Isaac, and promises to protect him and return him to Canaan. Jacob vows that the Lord will be his God if God fulfills the promise.

Jacob arrives in Haran and is taken in by his uncle Laban. Laban has two daughters, Leah and Rachel. A bargain is struck. Jacob will work seven years and be given Rachel as a wife. Laban deceives Jacob on the wedding night and substitutes Leah for Rachel. To resolve Jacob's anger at what has happen, Laban offers Rachel also in exchange for Jacob's promise to work another seven years.

Leah bears Jacob four sons: Reuben, Simeon, Levi, and Judah. Rachel is barren, so she gives Jacob her maid Bilhah as a concubine. Bilhah bears two sons, Dan and Naphtali. Leah in turn gives Zilpah, her maid, to Jacob as a concubine and Zilpah bears two sons, Gad and Asher. Leah has three more children: Issachar, Zebulun, and Dinah. Finally, Rachel conceives and bears Joseph. Jacob asks Laban to allow him to return to his home in Canaan. They agree that as his wages for 20 years of service, Jacob will build himself a flock from Laban's herds. Jacob amasses a large flock [through the use of magic or genetic manipulation]. Then, unbeknownst to Laban, Jacob and his household flee. Prior to leaving, Rachel steals her father's idols. Laban pursues Jacob, but is warned by God in a dream not to take revenge. Jacob promises Laban that whoever stole his idols shall not remain alive, but the idols are not found. The portion ends with Jacob and Laban sealing a pact to end hostilities.

INSIGHTS FROM THE TRADITION

A It is difficult to visualize a steady stream of angels going up and down an ordinary ladder.

Speiser suggests it be understood as a ramp or a solid stairway similar to a Mesopotamian temple tower. These towers had flights of stairs leading to the top where the deity could visit and speak with mortals. Jacob describes the place about which he dreamed as " . . . the abode of God, and . . . the gateway to heaven." As Speiser puts it, this [dream] was a symbol of the ancients' efforts to reach out to heaven (*The Anchor Bible: Genesis,* edited by E.A. Speiser, pp. 219-20).

Can you think of other interpretations for the ladder in Jacob's dream?
Why do you think the "ancients" may have thought God dwells in heaven?
Have you ever had a dream similar to the one Jacob experienced?

B Why does the Torah tell us that angels were "ascending and descending?" One might think angels would descend first. Rashi explains: "Those angels who accompanied Jacob in the land of Israel were not permitted to leave the land; they ascended to heaven. And angels which were to minister to him outside the land descended to accompany him."

Does the idea of a guardian angel appeal to you, or do you think the idea foolish? Explain.
If we are to accept Rashi's explanation, why would angels be limited as to territory?
If angels have wings and fly, then why was there a need for a ladder?

C Jacob promises that God will be his God if God is with him — protecting him, giving him sustenance and clothing, and ensuring a peaceful return to his father's home. Some nerve that Jacob would make acceptance of God conditional on his own good fortune! One *midrash,* in explaining this, had two Rabbis disagreeing as to the word order. One Rabbi felt that Jacob had prayed and asked for God's protection and made his promises and vowed his oath. The dream and the blessings were an answer to his prayer. The other Rabbi felt that Jacob meant that if God were with him to prevent him from sinning, Jacob would be worthy of God's blessing and would be able to keep his vow and maintain a relationship with God (*Genesis Rabbah* 70:4).

How does Jacob's dream provide him reassurance on his journey?
What do you think about just before you go on a trip?
How does that compare to Jacob's dream?
How would you characterize the relationship Jacob has with God?

D Lawrence Kushner has written an extended commentary about this portion in his book, *GOD was in this PLACE & I, i did not know it.* Kushner explains Jacob's words when he awoke from his dream in various ways, among them — "God was here because I stopped being aware of myself," and "if I had known God was here, I wouldn't have gone to sleep."

Which explanation of Jacob's words do you prefer?
Have you ever had an experience which prompted you to say or feel like Jacob does? What are some places where you feel close to God?
How is God present in your ordinary places?

E Just as Jacob deceived his father, so he was deceived in turn. He works seven years to marry Rachel only to be deceived with a substitute, her older sister Leah. *Genesis Rabbah* 70:19 comments on this deception: In the evening, they led Leah into the bridal chamber and extinguished the light. The whole of that night he called her "Rachel," and she answered him. In the morning, however, "Behold, it was Leah" (29:25). Jacob said, "You are a deceiver . . . " Leah retorted "Did not your father call you 'Esau' and you answered him? So, you called me 'Rachel' and I answered you!" Jacob then asked Laban, "Why did you deceive me?" This provides an interesting parallel as Jacob's

deceit comes back to haunt him. Laban replied: "It is not the practice in our place to marry off the younger before the older." Jacob was thus reminded that the firstborn takes precedence.

Jacob deceived his father and now he, in turn, is deceived. Is this what usually happens in our world? Do people who act deceitfully usually receive the same in return?
Have you ever been tricked into accepting something you didn't want (a chore, a gift, an assignment, etc.)?
How do you feel when you don't get what you want?

F Torah says that Jacob "loved Rachel more than Leah" (Genesis 29:30). This tells us that Jacob also loved Leah. One should therefore not think that Jacob actually hated Leah. If he had hated her, he would not have lived with her. Because he did not love her as much as he did Rachel, Leah considered herself totally unloved" (*Yalkut Me'am Lo'ez* by Yaakov Culi, Vol. IIIA, pp. 62-63).

What do you think it was about Rachel that made Jacob love her more than Leah?
Have you ever felt unloved by people who you know love you?

G Rav Kook, the first chief Rabbi of Israel, explained that Jacob knew it was time to leave Laban's home when his original loathing of Laban and his devious ways was giving way to his acceptance of these same behaviors. Jacob did not want to become like Laban, so he had to depart. This realization shows us how much Jacob, who was a devious young man himself, has grown and matured during the time of his sojourn in Haran.

How can repeated or prolonged exposure to suffering or cruelty harden us?
Why is it dangerous to become accepting of, or indifferent to, unacceptable behavior?

What would your response be if you ever found yourself in such a situation?

H Upon leaving Laban, Jacob gathers his wives, children, and all his possessions. Rachel takes her father's household idols with her. Several reasons have been given for her theft:
1. She may have felt it necessary to have deities with her on the journey (*The Torah: A Modern Commentary*, edited by W. Gunther Plaut, p. 312).
2. Idols served as symbols of property rights and family status, thus possibly establishing a claim for Jacob against Laban's estate (*The Anchor Bible: Genesis*, edited by E.A. Speiser, p. 250).
3. She stole them to keep her father from idol worship (*Genesis Rabbah* 74:5).

Which answer has the most appeal to you? Explain.
If, for some reason, you had to leave your home in haste, what would you take with you? Why?

I Jacob unwittingly curses Rachel. He declares to Laban that whoever stole Laban's idols shall not remain alive. Rashi comments that because of this curse, Rachel dies enroute to Canaan (see Genesis, *Vayishlach*).

Why would Jacob react so strongly to the report that Laban's idols had been stolen? Why should he care at all about Laban's idols?
Running away appears to be a theme of Jacob's life. Is this accurate, or does Jacob have other reactions to danger?
With all of his faults, how did Jacob come to merit being one of the Patriarchs?

J The Hebrew word for ladder is *sulam*. The numerical value of the letters in that word (*samech, lamed, mem*) is 130. The numerical value of the letters in the word Sinai (*samech, yud, nun, yud*) is also 130.

In what ways is the ladder for Jacob what Sinai was for Moses?
In what ways are they very different experiences?

STRATEGIES

ANALYZING THE TEXT

1 The Matriarchs suffered from barrenness. Research and study the verses for each of the Matriarchs which deal with this issue. Using the questions below, fill in the pertinent information.

Discuss: Why do you think barrenness was such a critical issue?

Name of
Matriarch

Reaction to
Barrenness

Who interceded
for her? What
was done?

What was the
reaction of
the spouse?

2 Genesis recounts a number of incidents in which "angels" intervene in the lives of the Patriarchs. The Hebrew word for angel is *malach*, which could more properly be translated as "messenger." Look at the following passages in the Torah, each of which describes the appearance of angels, and then answer the questions which follow: Genesis 18:1ff.; 19:1ff.; 21:17-20; 22:10-14; 28:10-15; 31:10-13; 32:25-31; 37:12-17.

Under what circumstances does an angel appear? How does the angel serve as a messenger? How did the biblical characters understand the function of angels?

References: *Encyclopaedia Judaica,* "Angels and Angelology," Vol. 2, p. 956-977; *The Torah: A Modern Commentary,* edited by W. Gunther Plaut, p. 124.

3 Some commentators have contended that Laban was insincere and loath to accept responsibility. What evidence can you find in the text to support these assertions? Examine especially the scene in which Laban welcomes Jacob (24:28-31) and compare it to Laban's earlier welcome of Eliezer (29:3) and to Laban's exploration and proposed solution concerning Jacob's marriage to Leah. Use a text with commentary by Rashi for some good insights into this question. Using ideas derived from your examination, imagine you are Jacob and write a letter to your mother Rebekah describing Laban.

4 Make an illustrated map of the "places" where the Patriarchs could be said to have "come upon God" (e.g., Jacob at Bethel).

EXTENDING THE TEXT

5 In many ways, the biblical text is dominated by male accomplishments and we are left to fill in the details of the women in the Bible. Imagine you are one of the Matriarchs (Sarah, Rebekah, Leah, or Rachel) or a handmaid given to one of the Patriarchs (Hagar, Bilhah, or Zilpah) and you are being interviewed about your life. Answer the following questions which have been adapted from "What Your Grandmother Never Told You," *Ms. Magazine* (March 1983), p. 80.

Where were you born?
What do you most remember about your family?
Do you have a favorite relative?
How did you meet your husband?
What was your wedding like?
How did you feel about your husband early in the marriage?

How did you feel about him after you had been married many years?
What are your favorite memories of your children?
When and how did they leave home?
How did it affect your life when they left?
How do you spend your days?
Who are your role models?
What is your happiest memory? Your saddest memory?
What is your proudest achievement?
How would you like to be remembered?

6 Insight H, page 48, contains three reasons why Rachel stole her father's household idols. Choose one of them and expand it into a full story.

7 Using the format of the old television game show "Queen for a Day," create "Matriarch for a Day." Choose four contestants, each representing a Matriarch. Have one or two support staff from among the rest of the participants help the Matriarch prepare a statement explaining why she should be named "Matriarch for a Day." After all the Matriarchs speak, have the group vote by applause. The Matriarch receiving the loudest applause is the winner.

8 Bethel, the place of Jacob's dream, was a significant site at other times in Jewish history. Use a Jewish encyclopedia or history book to create a time line of important moments in the history of Bethel.

PERSONALIZING THE TEXT

9 The text states about Jacob, *"Ba bamakom"* — He came upon a certain place (Genesis 28:11). The Hebrew word for "place" (*makom*) became, in Rabbinical usage, a name for God. Using this translation, the verse could then read, "He came upon God." Compare this with Genesis 22:4. The Rabbis explained their use of *HaMakom* as a name for God by teaching that God is the place of the world, but the world is not God's only place (*Genesis Rabbah* 68:49). Rachel Adler, a contemporary writer, explains why *HaMakom* is her preferred name for God. She writes, "Just as the universe is the place where I meet God, so I am the place where God meets me . . . I then cannot talk about God's goodness or God's holiness without talking about mine or about yours, because your face, too, is a place in the universe where I can see God" ("I've Had Nothing Yet So I Can't Take More," *Moment*, Vol. 8, No. 8, September 1983, p. 26).

Discuss each of the following post-biblical names for God in turn to understand what insight it gives us about God: *HaMakom* (The Place), *HaKadosh Baruch Hu* (the Holy One of Blessing), *Ribbono Shel Olam* (Master of the Universe), *HaRachaman* (the Merciful One), *Avinu Sheh-ba-Shamayim* (Our Father in Heaven), *Shechinah* (Indwelling spirit). Rank order the Names from the most to least meaningful to you personally. Explain your choices.
References: *Close Encounters: Jewish Views about God* by Ronald H. Isaacs; *The Encyclopedia of Jewish Symbols* by Ellen Frankel and Betsy Platkin Teutsch; *Encyclopaedia Judaica*, "God, Names of," Vol. 7, pp. 674-678.

10 Conduct a public interview of Jacob. A public interview gives one student a chance to publicly affirm his/her stand on different values and issues. One or more volunteers sit at the front of the room and the teacher questions them about any aspect of their values or their life. Students must answer honestly, but can pass at any time. Participants should answer the interviewer's questions as if they were Jacob. After the interview, have a general discussion on Jacob's life.

11 On a sheet of paper, the teacher draws a ladder with approximately 20 rungs. On each rung of the ladder, write a Hebrew vocabulary word from this *sedra*. The students each receive a vocabulary ladder and they must translate each word, working their way up the ladder. As an alternative, the teacher distributes copies of the ladder without vocabulary. Each student fills in the rungs of the ladder with his/her own vocabulary list, possibly drawing from a master list created by the group. The lists are then traded and worked on.

12 The custom of *bedeken hakallah*, veiling the bride, resulted from Laban's deception of Jacob. Put on a mock *bedeken* ceremony to get a clearer idea of the elements which go into a traditional ceremony.
Reference: *The New Jewish Wedding* by Anita Diamant.

13 Translate the written description of Jacob's dream into a picture. Use pastels to give your work a dreamlike quality.

14 In some ways, it seems that Jacob was making his acceptance of God conditional on his own good fortune. Have you ever been in that position? Think. Did you ever promise to be really good if God let you receive an "A" on an exam? Or, did you promise to believe in God if you won a race or contest? Discuss your ideas about what is and what is not appropriate to pray for. (For more, see the Index: "God.")

15 Many contemporary congregations have taken "Beth El" as their name. What are some other common names of synagogues in your area? Imagine that you are creating a new Jewish congregation. What name would you choose for it? Why?

16 In some communities, *challot* were formed in ladder shapes for special occasions. At various times, the ladder may have symbolized Moses ascending Mount Sinai or prayers for forgiveness reaching God on high. Adapt this tradition to create a special *challah* for use on the Shabbat when this Torah portion is read. Prepare your favorite *challah* recipe. Before braiding it, set aside a small portion of dough to be shaped into a ladder and placed on top of the *challah* before baking.

OTHER RESOURCES

17 Read the description of Jacob in "The Gate of Heaven" in *The Fire Waits: Prayers and Poems for the Sabbath and Festivals* by Michael I. Hecht, pp. 27-28. What ordinary things are you involved in which serve God? What challenge is the poet presenting? What responsibilities does the poet imply that we have?

18 Listen to and/or learn the song "Jacob and Israel" from *Bible People Songs*.

19 Complete the pages which relate to this portion from *Bible People Book One* by Joel Lurie Grishaver, pp. 39-45. Check the accompanying Leader Guide for procedures and additional activities.

20 Read, act out, and discuss the skit for *Vayeytze* in *Sedra Scenes: Skits for Every Torah Portion* by Stan J. Beiner, pp. 39-43.

21 View and discuss the episode for *Vayetze* from *Torah Toons I: The Video*.

22 For creative movement activities see "Jacob's Dream," "Jacob's Journey Continues," and "Sisters: Leah and Rachel" from *Torah in Motion* by JoAnne Tucker and Susan Freeman, pp. 36-41.

23 Listen to, discuss and sing *"Ufaratsta"* from *Sounds of Creation: Genesis in Song.*

24 Read and discuss the illustrated commentary for *Va-Yetze* in *American Torah Toons* by Lawrence Bush.

INVOLVING THE FAMILY

25 In this portion, 12 of Jacob's 13 children are born. All of their names are discussed as to meaning and significance. Using *The Complete Dictionary of English and Hebrew First Names* by Alfred J. Kolatch, research the meaning of your Hebrew name. Ask your parents why you were given the names you have (both English and Hebrew). If you were to change your name, what would you change it to and why?

BAR/BAT MITZVAH PROJECT

26 According to Rashi, we learn from the words, "He came upon a certain place and stopped there for the night" (Genesis 28:11), that Jacob instituted the custom of regular evening worship. What is the worship schedule in your synagogue? Ask to attend a ritual committee meeting of your synagogue and/or interview the chair of the committee to find out what are the responsibilities and tasks of the ritual committee. Brainstorm ways to increase your participation and support of the worship services at your synagogue. For example you could serve as an usher for services on a regular basis, become a Torah reader, or ask to be a teen member of the ritual committee.

VAYISHLACH 32:4-36:43 וישלח

SYNOPSIS

ON HIS JOURNEY BACK TO CANAAN, Jacob passes through the territory controlled by Esau. Jacob seeks a reconciliation with his brother. Before he meets Esau, he sends gifts ahead hoping to fend off a hostile confrontation. He divides his family into two camps, sending them to safety. Someone comes to Jacob that night and wrestles with him until dawn. He wrenches Jacob's thigh, but Jacob will not release him. Jacob demands a blessing from the "someone." The blessing is a new name for Jacob — Israel, "for he has striven with divine beings and prevailed."

Jacob then meets Esau and they are reconciled. Esau wants Jacob and his household to travel on to Seir with him, but Jacob says that because of the frailty of the children and the flocks, he will lag behind. Jacob settles in Shechem, a city in Canaan.

One day Dinah, his daughter, goes out to the fields and is raped by Shechem, a Canaanite, who ultimately wishes to marry her. Her brothers convince the male inhabitants of Shechem to be circumcised so that marriages may take place between Jacob's household and the Canaanites. On the third day after the circumcisions, while the Canaanites are still in pain, Jacob's sons Simeon and Levi rise up in retaliation. They slaughter and plunder the Canaanites.

Jacob expresses anger, reminding his sons that they are few in number and may easily be destroyed by the rest of the inhabitants of the land. The brothers respond by saying that they were defending the honor of their sister. God tells Jacob to go to Bethel and build an altar. Jacob cleanses his household of all alien gods and departs. On the journey, Rachel goes into labor. She delivers a son, but dies in the process. Jacob names his son Benjamin.

Isaac dies at 180 years of age. Jacob and Esau bury him. The portion closes with a detailing of Esau's descendants.

INSIGHTS FROM THE TRADITION

A Jacob is told that Esau is coming to meet him and that he is bringing 400 men with him. Jacob is understandably afraid. When Jacob left Canaan 20 years earlier, Esau had vowed revenge. Jacob assumes that Esau will now make good on his promise. Jacob develops a three-fold plan in response to Esau's approaching. First, Jacob divided the people and possessions with him into two camps so that if a war occurred, one camp might escape. Next, he prayed for a favorable outcome to the meeting. Lastly, he prepared "and sent" (*vayishlach*) gifts to Esau in order to placate him (Rashi). Arama felt that the biblical text supported these contingencies, but that they should be carried out in a different order. As he writes: "This is the proper attitude for man to trust in the Lord and rely on His God, when he has done everything possible to help himself. In His providence He will then answer his prayer . . . (*Studies in Bereshit* by Nechama Leibowitz, p. 363). The text stresses personal responsibility and the importance of action.

After Jacob puts Esau's gifts in order, he apparently changes his plans. He takes his family and possessions across the river. He then returns alone to his first camp.

If you were Jacob, what would you have done to prepare for Esau?
Do Jacob's plans seem realistic to you?
Considering Jacob's plans, is there any reason to believe that the brothers' relationship has changed for the better?
What feelings might Jacob have for Esau?
Why do you think Jacob chose to spend the night alone prior to his reunion with Esau?

B Although the text states that Jacob wrestled with someone that night, all the commentators agree that it was no ordinary human being. Rambam and Ramban differ as to the exact nature of the struggle. Was it an actual event in the real world sense, or was it an internal struggle? Of more importance, what did the struggle accomplish? First, the event tested and changed Jacob. It tested his strength; he prevailed, showing the strength that would be required for future events (*The Anchor Bible: Genesis,* edited by E.A. Speiser, p. 257). Second, it changed Jacob's name; now he would be known as Israel. The name is related to two Hebrew words meaning "one who struggles with God."

Jacob insists that the "someone" bless him. Rashi interprets this to mean "admit my right to the blessings which my father gave me and to which Esau lays claim." How do you interpret the demand for a blessing?

How does Jacob's new name — Israel — reflect Jewish experience?

With what fears, feelings, or ideas do you wrestle?

C The story of Dinah is troubling for two reasons: (1) the violence carried out against a human being, and (2) the extreme retaliation against a whole community, rather than against just the guilty person. Why was Jacob silent when Hamor suggested that his son Shechem be allowed to marry Dinah? Why did he not respond when Hamor suggested further intermarriages between his people and Jacob's? Instead, Jacob's sons Simeon and Levi tell Hamor that all his men must be circumcised, or they must release Dinah and that will be the end of the matter. Jacob probably did not realize the violence Simeon and Levi planned. According to Ramban, Jacob was convinced that the Shechemites would not accept circumcision and would simply release Dinah. If they did become circumcised, then later while they were convalescing, the brothers could rescue Dinah without a fight. Simeon and Levi came with guile and deceit. Again we see the repetitive theme of Jacob's life. (For more, see the Index: "Circumcision.")

It has been said, "Some are guilty, but all are responsible." How does this relate to the incident?

What is the significance of the Dinah story for future Jewish history?

How would you or your family react to a personal tragedy?

What personal or family qualities would give you the strength to deal with great difficulties?

D We know that Dinah went out to visit the daughters of the land (Genesis 34:1). Most traditional Jewish commentaries blame Dinah for what occurred. Rashi and Maimonides fault Dinah for leaving her home and inviting trouble. Maimonides says that while every woman has the right to leave her home, her husband should only allow her to go out once or twice a month. Maimonides also said that a woman's beauty consists in her sitting in a corner of her home (*Marriage* 13:11). Contemporary women's commentary takes a very different approach to Dinah. Ellen Umansky focuses on Dinah's desire to see her friends among the Canaanites. Despite religious difference, Dinah developed friendships among these women because they lived nearby under similar patriarchal cultures (*Life Cycles,* Vol. 2, edited by Debra Orenstein and Jane Rachel Litman).

Why did Jewish tradition limit women's freedom of movement?

Why did the Rabbis condemn Dinah?

Are there any contemporary cultures which limit women's freedoms? What is the intent in doing this? What purpose does it serve?

E In the previous portion, Jacob promised Laban that whoever had stolen his household idols would not remain alive. While journeying toward Bethel after leaving Shechem, Rachel dies in childbirth. One may wonder if this is a fulfillment of Jacob's promise or if it is some sort of divine retribution for her theft of her father's idols. It has also been suggested that Rachel died at a young age because she had been disloyal to her father which, to the ancients, was a grave sin.

Do you think Rachel's death was a punishment for her disloyalty?

What is the basis for loyalty to one's parents?

Did Laban deserve Rachel's loyalty? Why or why not?

Do you feel a sense of loyalty to your parents? What is the basis for this loyalty and how do you show it?

F Rachel is the only Matriarch not buried in the Cave of Machpelah. According to a *midrash,* this is because Jacob foresaw that the Jews would pass by Ephrath (now Bethlehem — Rachel's burial place) as they were being exiled to Babylon. As they passed by, Rachel would plead to God on their behalf (*Genesis Rabbah* 82:10). The prophet Jeremiah alludes to this when he says, "A cry is heard in Ramah, wailing, bitter weeping — Rachel weeping for her children. She refuses to be comforted for her children who are gone" (Jeremiah 31:15).

If a people can weep for a land, can a land (as it were) rejoice over or weep for a people? How might this be reflected by the condition of the land of Israel at various times throughout history? What are your feelings for Israel?

STRATEGIES

ANALYZING THE TEXT

1 Jewish tradition asserts that Amalek, Israel's eternal enemy descends from Esau. Many of Israel's enemies throughout history have been identified with Amalek.

a. As a group, brainstorm some reasons why the enemies of Israel have been identified as descending from Esau. (Remember that Esau and Jacob were reconciled.)

b. Read the entry on Amalek in the *Encyclopaedia Judaica.*

(For more, see the Index: "Amalek.")

2 Genesis 33:4 reads: "Esau ran to greet him [Jacob]. He embraced him and, falling on his neck, he kissed him, and they wept." In the Torah, the Hebrew word for "and he kissed him" (*vayishakayhu*) is written with a dot over each letter. To what does the presence of these dots alert us? Rashi gives two responses: (1) Esau's kiss is insincere; (2) only at this moment was Esau finally able to feel and express the extent of his love for Jacob. Which do you think is the better explanation? For help answering this question, compare the descriptions in the Torah of other meetings to that of Jacob and Esau. Read about Jacob and Rachel (Genesis 29:11); Joseph and Benjamin (Genesis 45:14); Jacob and Joseph (Genesis 46:29); Moses and Aaron (Exodus 4:27). Which of these greetings is most affectionate? Which are suspect? Why? What answer is suggested by Jacob's actions after his meeting with Esau?

3 Esau wishes that Jacob and his family travel on to Seir with him, possibly intending that their families would be together from then on. Reread Genesis 33:1-17. Was Esau's invitation to live together ever clearly extended? Do you think Jacob wanted to settle near Esau? What excuse did Jacob offer? Did Jacob ever state clearly what he wanted or did not want to do? Do you think that Jacob retained a fear of Esau even after they reconciled? Esau did arrive with 400 armed men. Was he assuming there would be violence? He remembered Jacob as a heel grabber, a supplanter. But who does Esau meet? Is it Jacob or someone else? Consider what happened to Jacob the night before and what changes occurred both physically and personally. Read Genesis 36:1-8. Is this a different version of the same story?

EXTENDING THE TEXT

4 One of the laws of *kashrut* is derived from this Torah portion. While Jacob was wrestling,

he was injured in his hip. As a reminder of that struggle and injury, Jews were commanded not to eat meat of the thigh muscle of an animal. To learn more about the laws of *kashrut,* invite the Rabbi, a kosher butcher, or someone else knowledgeable about *kashrut* to come and talk to the group.

5 Jacob sent his family and all his possessions across the river Jabbok and returned to his original campsite alone. While the Bible tells us what happened to Jacob, there is no reference to his family. Imagine that you are one of Jacob's children. Write the dialogue (in play format) for the conversation the children might have had on that night. You might do this in small groups and present different skits.

6 Israel means "one who struggles with God." The Jewish people became known as Israelites, and ultimately the Jewish homeland adopted the name Israel at its founding in 1948. Discuss how the name "Israel" might also be valid to apply to Abraham and Moses. Can you think of other Jews whose lives reflect a struggle with God?

7 Jacob and Esau reunite peacefully. The Torah text is very clear about Jacob's anxiety, preparations, and struggle the night before their meeting. Yet, the text does not tell us Esau's thoughts, feelings, and preparations. Individually or in pairs write a *midrash* explaining what Esau thought, felt, and did prior to seeing Jacob. Include his reaction to Jacob's gifts.

8 The Hebrew word *shalom* has many meanings, one of which is completeness or wholeness. Consider that Jacob and Esau are twins and twins are thought of as two sides of the same coin. In their reuniting, their incomplete selves come together as a whole. To honor this wholeness (this *shalom*), do the art activity "Shalom (Peace) Plaster Balloons" from *An Artist You Don't Have to Be* by Joann Magnus with Howard Bogot (p. 87).

9 The death of Rachel is recorded in this portion. Rachel was considered the most beautiful of the Matriarchs and she inspired many *midrashim,* songs, and literary compositions. Jeremiah visualized her weeping in Ramah for exiled children (31:15). Her tomb in Bethlehem is still an important pilgrimage site for Jews.
a. Write a poem or a song praising Rachel's virtues.
b. Stage a version of "This Is Your Life, Rachel," in which significant characters from her life surprise Rachel with mementos and stories recalling events in which she participated.
c. Imagine you are a movie producer casting a film about the life of Rachel. Write a letter to convince a famous actress to star in this biographical film.

10 In this *sedra,* Isaac dies. Create a headstone and an epitaph for him. Use self-hardening clay to make a realistic depiction.

11 Write a newspaper-style obituary for Isaac.

12 In Genesis 35:4, Jacob buries all the idolatrous holy objects belonging to the members of his household. Plaut notes that "it seems there was an ancient taboo against destroying holy objects of any kind" (*The Torah: A Modern Commentary,* p. 232). How does this custom persist in Judaism today regarding prayer books, Torah scrolls, and any other written work which contains the name of God (*Shaymot*)? What is the explanation for it? What has been the significance of this custom for Jewish history? Research the history of the *genizah* (a place where unusable holy books and objects are stored). Write a report on the most famous *genizah* of all — the Cairo *Genizah.* (For more, see the Index: "*Genizah.*")

13 The nation Edom is said to be descended from Esau. For an activity about the name Edom, see the Index: "Adam/*Edom.*"

14 The Israeli flag consists of a white field with a blue Star of David in the center. Blue stripes run horizontally over the top and under the bottom of the star. While this is a beautiful and enduring symbol, design a new emblem for Israel which would illustrate the meaning of its name (see Strategy #6 above).

15 Design a family tree for the Patriarchs. Make it large enough for a bulletin board or display. For each of the Patriarchs, design a heraldic shield in an appropriate color, with objects, symbols, creatures, etc. Use the shields to decorate the family tree.

PERSONALIZING THE TEXT

16 Give a copy of the following activity sheet to each participant to work on individually.

Activity Sheet

Jacob is making plans to meet his brother Esau after a 20 year separation. Esau is approaching, and with him are 400 men. Imagine that you are Jacob and you are making plans for your meeting. Choose the best thing you could do in this situation. Mark your choice with an "X."

_____   Prepare to battle Esau.
_____   Assemble gifts to greet him first.
_____   Pray to God to protect you.

I feel my answer is best because:

17 Jacob and Esau are reconciled in this portion. Have students pair up: one assumes the role of Jacob, the other Esau. Each pair composes a letter to Isaac relating what happened at the reunion.

18 The theme of deception and retribution runs through Jacob's life. Review the portions and insights for *Toledot, Vayaytzay, Vayishlach,* and *Vayayshev* to find as many examples of this theme as you can. Stage the life of Jacob in the style of a medieval morality play, emphasizing both the comic and tragic sides of the deception/retribution theme. Show how Jacob gets entangled and caught in a web of trickery which he himself initiated. Don't forget to close your play by reminding the audience that, "The moral of the story is . . . . "

19 Create simple illustrations of vocabulary words you choose from this portion. Each participant receives copies, decides what the illustration represents, and writes the correct Hebrew word to go with it.

20 Dinah's silence throughout her ordeal is disturbing. In poem, picture, or *midrash*, become Dinah's vocal advocate and express what she did not say or what was not recorded in the Torah text.

Reference: *The Five Books of Miriam* by Ellen Frankel, pp. 65-71.

21 Rape, although treated differently in today's society, is still the same violent crime described in this Torah portion. For older students, invite a guest speaker from a local rape awareness group to do a presentation. To find such organizations, check the phone book, call the police department, or get in touch with local women's organizations.

22 Expand Strategy #21 by holding a women's self-defense workshop. Utilize the same resources listed there to find an instructor.

OTHER RESOURCES

23 Listen to and/or learn the song "Jacob and Israel" from *Bible People Songs*.

24 Complete pages 47 and 48 in *Bible People Book One* by Joel Lurie Grishaver. Check the accompanying Leader Guide for procedures and additional activities.

25 Read, act out, and discuss the skit for *Vayishlach* in *Sedra Scenes: Skits for Every Torah Portion* by Stan J. Beiner, pp. 44-48.

26 View and discuss the episode for *Vayishlach* from *Torah Toons I: The Video*.

27 For creative movement activities see "Jacob Wrestles," "Dinah," and "Isaac Dies" from *Torah in Motion,* by JoAnne Tucker and Susan Freeman, pp. 42-47.

28 Read and discuss the illustrated commentary for *Va-Yishlach* in *American Torah Toons* by Lawrence Bush.

29 Listen to, discuss, and sing *"Ki Sarita"* from *Sounds of Creation: Genesis in Song*.

INVOLVING THE FAMILY

30 Through much of the Book of Genesis, there are stories of siblings and families who cannot get along. Even while valuing the family, the Torah presents examples of family murders, deceit, jealousy, and treachery. As a family, do a "Proud Whip" to help you identify and share those things which make you proud to be a member of your family. Each family member takes a turn completing the statement, "I'm proud of . . . " or "I'm proud that . . . "

BAR/BAT MITZVAH PROJECTS

31 Just as Jacob and Esau made peace, add peace/*shalom* to your environment. Make a poster which lists your goals for peace and ways you believe they can be achieved. Organize a group to create art and written works that illustrate your ideas. Take all these pieces and create a display. Include sayings from Jewish tradition and songs.

32 The rape of Dinah and its resolution are troubling. It makes clear that this is an age-old crime with severe repercussions for the victim, her family, and the community. It is extremely important that we educate, protect, and prevent this type of violence. Collect pamphlets, handouts, and listings of organizations and services available in your community on this issue. Set up a distribution center for middle school and high school students. If possible, invite a guest speaker or a panel of presenters to help educate the middle school and high school students in your synagogue school about rape, date rape, and abusive relationships.

VAYAYSHEV 37:1-40:23 וישב

SYNOPSIS

JACOB MAKES AN ORNAMENTED TUNIC for Joseph, his favorite son. His other sons, seeing that Joseph is favored, are jealous. Joseph dreams two dreams in which he appears to have supremacy over his family. He relates these dreams to his family which serves to increase the brothers' anger toward him.

At Jacob's request, Joseph goes to meet his brothers in Dothan where they are grazing their father's flock. Before Joseph reaches them, they plot to kill him. Reuben asks them not to kill Joseph, but to throw him into a pit instead. Reuben plans to rescue Joseph later. The brothers cast Joseph into a pit, but take his coat. Then, unbeknownst to Reuben, they sell Joseph to some merchants who, in turn, sell him in Egypt to Potiphar, an Egyptian noble.

The *sedra* then digresses to the story of Judah and Tamar. When his eldest son Er dies, Judah gives Tamar, his daughter-in-law, to his second son Onan as a wife, in order to ensure a descendant for his dead son. Onan does not carry out his obligation to procreate with Tamar, and as divine punishment, he also dies. Tamar, now twice widowed, is promised to Judah's third son, Shelah. But Shelah is still a lad and needs time to mature. Tamar waits, but Judah reneges on his promise. Tamar, the righteous widow, dresses as a harlot and deceives Judah into having sexual relations with her. She becomes pregnant by him and bears twins, thus preserving the name of her first husband.

The portion now continues with Joseph in Egypt. Potiphar entrusts his entire house and holdings to Joseph. Potiphar's wife tries to seduce Joseph, but Joseph spurns her. In retaliation, she accuses Joseph of attempting rape. Potiphar has Joseph imprisoned. Yet, even in prison, Joseph succeeds. He is put in charge of all the prisoners.

In this prison are Pharaoh's cupbearer and baker who had committed offenses against Pharaoh. While in prison, each has a dream which Joseph interprets. As he foretells, the cupbearer is restored to his former position, while the baker is put to death. Joseph asks the cupbearer to remember him, but . . . Joseph is forgotten.

INSIGHTS FROM THE TRADITION

A *Vayayshev* means "and he [Jacob] settled." The portion begins by noting the resettlement of Jacob in the land of his father and grandfather. *Vayayshev* sets the stage for the descent of the Israelites from their homeland to Egypt as was foretold to Abraham (Genesis 15:13).

B Jacob loved Joseph over all his sons because, according to the text, Joseph was the child of Jacob's old age. The Torah does not mention another reason — Rachel was Joseph's mother. Rachel was Jacob's true love, the one for whom he had labored 14 years. As a symbol of his love, Jacob had an ornamented tunic made for Joseph. Everett Fox identifies Jacob as the primary cause of Joseph's problems. By showing Joseph preferential treatment, Jacob created a rift between the brothers. This rift was made worse by Joseph's tale bearing and by the telling of his dreams (*The Five Books of Moses*, 37:2-11).

Is it right that because Jacob favored Joseph, the brothers should hate Joseph? Why not be angry instead at Jacob?

C Jacob sent Joseph to find his brothers. On the way, Joseph got lost and a certain man appeared and sent Joseph in the right direction. Nehama Leibowitz interprets this seemingly innocent account as the essence of the Joseph story. The tale operates on two levels: the mortal and the divine. In the Covenant of the Parts (see the Synopsis of Genesis, *Lech Lecha*), God promised that Abraham's seed would sojourn in a land not their own for 400 years. This promise was now about to be realized. While on a human level,

Jacob simply sends Joseph to meet his brothers, on the divine level, "a certain man" appears to direct Joseph in finding them. This "man" set into motion the prophecy that God made to Abraham.

The brothers plot to kill Joseph as they see him approach. Reuben convinces them to throw him into a pit instead, planning to save him later. Reuben apparently leaves and then Judah convinces the brothers to reconsider their murderous plan and to sell Joseph instead. Two of Joseph's brothers have acted to prevent his death.

What do you think causes jealousy and anger? When these emotions happen within a family, they can be especially strong. Why? The brothers do not kill Joseph, but they throw him into a pit. What do they accomplish by this act? How would selling Joseph help the brothers? Fate seems to be operating in the life of Joseph. Do you believe in fate? Has fate ever manifested itself in your life?

D Genesis 37:24 reads, "The pit [into which Joseph was cast] was empty, there was no water in it." Rashi was prompted to wonder why the Torah tells us there was no water in what we already know was an empty hole. Rabbi Julie Wolkoff (in *Learn Torah With . . .* , p. 74) suggests that this additional phrase teaches us that there was nothing at all to sustain and nourish life — either physically or spiritually — in the place where Joseph's brothers cast him. His family having rejected him, Joseph was utterly alone.

What are the essential things necessary to sustain physical life? What is needed to promote emotional and spiritual well-being? How might people who are physically needy, also be needy for psychological well-being? Which elements do you think are easier to provide to people in need?

E When Jacob is shown the apparent "evidence" of Joseph's death, he is inconsolable. According to Rashi, when the brothers saw their father's grief, they said to Judah: "You told us to sell him. If you had told us to send him back to his father, we would also have obeyed you."

Do the brothers ever consider what Jacob's reaction will be? Even though the brothers witnessed their father's sorrow, they still did not reveal what they had done. Why not? The brothers try to comfort Jacob, yet they withhold the news which would be the most comforting. Do you think they are punishing Jacob? Would you have told Jacob? Why or why not?

F In the commentary *Yalkut Me'am Lo'ez* (Vol. III, p. 298), Yaakov Culi suggests these several reasons why the Joseph narrative is interrupted with the story of Tamar: (1) "God always brings the remedy before the illness" — the Messiah was to be a descendant of the union between Judah and Tamar; (2) "God always makes the punishment fit" — the brothers used a goat (its blood on Joseph's coat) to deceive their father, and Tamar used a goat to deceive Judah. In payment for sleeping with him, she was to receive a goat.

Can you identify other instances in the Torah or in history when a "remedy" appeared before the "illness"? In what instances can humanity supply the "remedy" before the "illness"?

G Many commentators, including E.A. Speiser (*The Anchor Bible: Genesis*, p. 266), feel that the story of Judah and Tamar is a complete interruption with no connection to the material which either precedes or follows it. It is to be seen, say these commentators, as a literary device which gives the sense of time passing and it builds suspense within the Joseph story.

Robert Alter sees the story of Judah and Tamar in a different light. In his view, this incident of deception amplifies many elements found within the Joseph story. Alter points out the following to support his contention: When the brothers bring the blood-spattered tunic to Jacob, they say *"chaker na"* (please recognize this). Tamar challenges Judah to *chaker na* — please recognize his seal, cord, and staff. The brothers used the blood of a kid to stain Joseph's tunic. Tamar also used a kid as a subterfuge to obtain Judah's possessions or, as Alter calls them, "his major credit cards." Jacob bemoans the fate of his son Joseph. Judah bemoans the deaths of his sons (*The Art of Biblical Narrative*, pp. 3-12).

Alter points out for us the unique qualities of the Torah. Similar themes and motifs play back and forth between characters and situations. Can you pick out other "echoes" between biblical events? What other situations contain parallels or similarities?
How does this affect your understanding of the text?
Are there parallel or recurring themes/events/conditions in your life? Explain.

H After being sold to Potiphar, Joseph made his master very successful. Things are going very well for Joseph until the appearance of Potiphar's wife. Genesis 39:6 reads in part, "Now Joseph was well built and handsome." Rashi comments that when Joseph realized his position in Potiphar's house, he began to eat, drink, and curl his hair. Joseph gave no thought to his mourning father and, in response, God set a bear (Potiphar's wife) loose against him. A *midrash* supplies another reason for the wife's behavior. "'My father was tried, and my grandfather was tried, but I am not put to the test' [Joseph thought to himself]. Said God to him; 'By thy life! I will try thee even more than them . . .'" (*Genesis Rabbah* 77:4). Thus, Joseph's imprisonment begins. Again we see two levels operating in the story: (1) the mortal —

seduction, deceit, and imprisonment, and (2) the divine — the setting of the stage for Joseph's eventual rise to a position of power.

Do you want to be tried and tested in your life or would you prefer to have everything come easy for you?
Do achievements mean more or less when you strive for them? When they come easily?

STRATEGIES

ANALYZING THE TEXT

1 Create a flow chart which plots out how Joseph got to Egypt and what then became of him. Begin with Joseph's being favored and the gift of the special coat. Include all the incidents which you feel led to Joseph's imprisonment in Pharaoh's jail.
In Genesis 15:13-14, God predicts Israel's enslavement in a foreign land. To extend the activity, prepare a parallel flow chart which plots out how Jacob and his family — and ultimately their descendants — came to be in Egypt.

2 Review Genesis 37:1-27 and discuss the following:
a. Which child did Jacob love the most?
b. What was given as a sign of that love?
c. What experiences did Joseph share with his family that angered them?
d. Did Abraham and Isaac have favored children? Did this cause problems? Explain.
e. Jacob singled out Joseph for special treatment. If you were one of the brothers, how would you have felt? What might you have done?
f. How does Jacob affect his children by his actions?

3 Joseph sees that he is a servant in the home of Potiphar. Potiphar's wife finds Joseph attractive and brings him to the brink of disaster.

Angered by her failure with Joseph, she gets revenge by disclosing the events untruthfully. Compare the way the biblical text records the event, how Potiphar's wife explains the event to the men of her household, and then later how she explains the event to her husband.
Reference: *Studies in Bereshit* by Nehama Leibowitz, pp. 417-422.

4 According to *Yalkut Me'am Lo'ez* by Yaakov Culi (Vol. IIIA), p. 247, the "man" who directed Joseph to his brothers in Genesis 37:15-17 was the archangel Gabriel. For an activity about angels and their appearance in the lives of the Patriarchs, see Genesis, *Vayaytzay*, Strategy #2.

5 Why was Joseph the favorite son of Jacob? It has been suggested that Joseph was best loved because he was the first son of Rachel, Jacob's favorite wife. Other interpreters say it was because he was born in Jacob's old age. But, Yaakov Culi suggests that Jacob favored Joseph because the two lived lives which had many common elements (p. 237). Review the births, childhoods, and adult lives of this father and son to determine what experiences they shared. Why would seeing his troubles reflected in Joseph's life cause Jacob to favor this son?

EXTENDING THE TEXT

6 Joseph gave a positive interpretation to the dream of the chief wine steward and a negative interpretation to the dream of the chief baker. Perhaps he saw in these dreams prophecies of the fate of the Israelites in Egypt. Match up the dream images with the Israelite experiences in Egypt below:

Dream Images
1. Vine with three branches.

2. Vine blossoming and ripening into grapes.

3. Grapes squeezed (into Pharaoh's cup).

4. Pharaoh's cup.

5. Spontaneous budding, flowering, and ripening of the vine.

6. Three baskets of fine pastry.

Israelite Experiences
A. Descendants of Jacob settling in Egypt.

B. Abraham, Isaac, and Jacob.

C. Troubles of Israelites in Egypt.

D. Bricks and mortar, field work, drowning of male infants (suffering the Israelites endured as slaves).

E. Sudden premature Exodus from Egypt.

F. Descendants of Abraham, Isaac, and Jacob.

ANSWERS: 1–B; 2–F; 3–A; 4–C; 5–E; 6–D.

7 Imagine that Joseph had somehow managed to smuggle a message for help out of prison. To which member of his family would he send it? Make up a secret code and devise a message. Exchange your message with another student and try to decipher each other's codes.

8 Tamar, Judah's daughter-in-law, is widowed. According to custom, Judah directed Onan (Judah's son and the brother of Tamar's deceased husband) to cohabit with Tamar. This custom became known as Levirite marriage. Older audiences can view the modern film on this theme, *I Love You, Rosa*.

9 Imagine that you come upon the scene of the crime after Joseph has been sold. You see evidence of a scuffle (which occurred when Joseph's coat was taken), and on the ground, you see a sack. As it turns out, this sack belonged to Joseph. Examine its contents. What do you find?

a. Write a description of the contents.

b. Create a facsimile of the sack and its contents.

10 There are two tales in the *Tanach* which establish the lineage of King David. The first is the account of Judah and Tamar in this portion. David is descended from their son, Perez. The second is in the Book of Ruth (4:12). Boaz, a descendant of Perez, marries Ruth. Ruth and Boaz were David's great grandparents. W. Gunther Plaut states that these two stories about surprising turns of events in the lives of two widows "show the steady, though not always readily visible, guiding hand of God who never forgets His people and their destiny" (*The Torah: A Modern Commentary*, p. 253).

Discuss the significance of King David's strange and fortuitous lineage. Draw a family tree for David using Genesis 38:14-30 and 46:12. Then skip a few generations to Ruth 4:12, 18, 22.

PERSONALIZING THE TEXT

11 The word *hineni* occurs in Genesis 22:7 and Genesis 27:18. Read the contexts in which this word is written. Identify who is speaking to whom. How are the situations alike and different? How are both situations a test? When have you ever been called upon to respond *"hineni"*? Write a poem describing situations in which you feel compelled to respond *hineni*.

12 Similar to *hineni* is the word *hinanni*. It is used as the name of a prayer from the Rosh HaShanah liturgy. It is usually recited or sung by the leader of the service. Read this prayer in Hebrew and/or English.
References: *The New Mahzor for Rosh Hashanah and Yom Kippur*, compiled and edited by Sidney Greenberg and Jonathan D. Levine, p. 608; *Gates of Repentance: The New Union Prayerbook for the Days of Awe*, pp. 18-19.

13 Create a Hebrew crossword puzzle for this portion. Instead of clues, quote a passage leaving out one word and give the chapter and verse where it appears in the Torah. To find the answer, the participants must look up the Hebrew verse according to the citation and fill in the missing word.

14 Jacob's life is filled with many ironies. Try to identify and describe them in a discussion session. For help, refer to Insights for this portion and for the previous one, *Vayishlach*. Culminate the discussion by writing a cinquain about Jacob. A cinquain is comprised of five lines, each line of a prescribed number of words as follows:
Line 1 – one word (noun)
Line 2 – two words (adjectives)
Line 3 – three words (verbs)
Line 4 – four words (adjectives)
Line 5 – one word, (noun, a synonym for the first word)

15 Draw a dream picture reflecting the dreams of the cupbearer and the baker. Overlay the images in the actual dreams with images showing their significance for the Israelites (see Strategy #6 above). Use a wet chalk technique to produce a dreamlike effect. Dip your drawing paper in water before you draw on it with colored chalk. Or, wet the chalk before you draw with it.

16 Design a coat for Joseph using collage pieces which represent important themes or ideas in Joseph's life. For example, depict one of his dreams on the multi-colored coat you design, or contrast bright and dull colors to illustrate Joseph as favored son of Jacob, and Joseph alone and abandoned in prison.

17 Create three-dimensional representations of Joseph and his family using empty wine bottles or one quart bleach bottles. Cover with papier-mâché, gluing on additional body parts from cardboard cut-outs. Build up layers of papier-mâché until the desired thickness is achieved. Let dry thoroughly. Undercoat with white latex wall paint. Let dry, then paint as desired. You might want to illustrate Joseph's dreams using this medium. Directions for papier-mâché can be found above in Genesis, *Beresheet*, Strategy #17, page 8.

OTHER RESOURCES

18 Produce the musical *Joseph and the Amazing Technicolor Dreamcoat.*

19 The brothers harbored a great deal of jealousy toward Joseph. For another story about the "green-eyed monster" of envy, see "The Peach, the Pitcher and the Fur Coat" in *Who Knows Ten?* by Molly Cone, pp. 86-92.

20 Read, act out, and discuss the skit for *Vayayshev* in *Sedra Scenes: Skits for Every Torah Portion* by Stan J. Beiner, pp. 49-55.

21 Listen to and/or learn the song "Joseph You're a Dreamer" from *Bible People Songs.*

22 Complete page 53 in *Bible People Book One* by Joel Lurie Grishaver. Also check the accompanying Leader Guide for procedures and additional activities.

23 Listen to music from the record *Joseph and His Amazing Technicolor Dreamcoat* by Tim Rice and Andrew Lloyd Webber. See also the book of the same title by the same authors.

24 Act out "Joseph and His Brothers Bible Story" found in *Jewish Story Theater* by Elaine Albert, p. 67.

25 View and discuss the episode for *Vayayshev* from *Torah Toons I: The Video.*

26 For creative movement activities, see "Joseph Dreams," "Joseph Is Cast into the Pit," and "Judah's Pledge To Tamar" from *Torah in Motion* by JoAnne Tucker and Susan Freeman, pp. 48-53.

27 Read and discuss the illustrated commentary for *Va-Yeshev* in *American Torah Toons* by Lawrence Bush.

INVOLVING THE FAMILY

28 Joseph's brothers were troubled by the preferred treatment given to Joseph. It is not unusual for brothers and sisters to feel sometimes that their parents are favoring one child over another. As a family, explore the issue of jealousy. After reading the portion, take turns speaking the emotions which you think the various characters might have felt. Brainstorm some more positive ways the brothers could have handled their anger and jealousy. Let each family member tell about a time he or she felt jealous of a sister or brother. What did he/she do about it? Would any of the positive strategies suggested by family members for Joseph's brothers have been helpful in these personal cases?

BAR/BAT MITZVAH ACTIVITY

29 Famine and other natural disasters, still plague our world. The Red Cross is an organization which attempts to meet the basic physical needs of people in times of crisis. For information on their varied activities write: American Red Cross, 431 18th Street, N.W., Washington, D.C. 20006.

There is also an organization called Magen David Adom, which is the Israeli version of the Red Cross. For information contact: American Red Magen David for Israel, 888 7th Ave., Suite 403, New York, NY 10106.

Contact your local Red Cross to find out about volunteer opportunities and take advantage of one of them, or find out by writing them what you can do for Magen David Adom. Some cities have local chapters of Magen David Adom and you may be able to work with them.

Create a poster to display what you learned about both organizations. Include photos of yourself doing your Red Cross and/or Magen David Adom work.

MIKAYTZ 41:1-44:17 מקץ

SYNOPSIS

TWO YEARS ELAPSE AND JOSEPH IS STILL a captive in Pharaoh's prison. One night, Pharaoh has two dreams which no one in his court can interpret. The cupbearer recalls that Joseph, a Hebrew prisoner, interpreted dreams correctly. Pharaoh calls upon Joseph. Joseph avers that interpretations come from God. Joseph tells Pharaoh that both dreams carry the same message — that there will be seven years of plenty followed by seven years of famine. To reward him, Pharaoh places Joseph in charge of food collection during the years of plenty and food distribution during the subsequent years of famine. Pharaoh gives Joseph an Egyptian name, *Tzaph'nat Panayach,* and a wife, Asenat.

During the years of plenty, Joseph fathers two sons: Manasseh and Ephraim.

Meanwhile, back in Canaan, Jacob is forced to send his sons to Egypt to buy grain during the famine. Jacob keeps Benjamin at home. Joseph recognizes his brothers when they arrive before him, but they do not recognize him. Hiding his identity, Joseph accuses them of being spies and decides to test them. He challenges them to return to Egypt with their youngest brother Benjamin. They are given grain, and each is secretly given back his money. Joseph keeps Simeon as a hostage until the brothers come back with Benjamin.

The brothers return to Canaan. Jacob initially refuses to send Benjamin, but soon realizes they need more grain. Benjamin now accompanies his brothers on their return to Egypt. Joseph continues the test. After placing grain in their sacks, he again returns their money secretly and has his silver goblet placed in Benjamin's bag. Joseph sends his men to pursue his brothers and to accuse them of theft. The portion closes with Joseph declaring that Benjamin must remain as his slave, but the other brothers are free to go.

INSIGHTS FROM THE TRADITION

A *Mikaytz* means "at the end of." The portion thus establishes that two years have elapsed since Joseph's dream interpretations in prison.

Is there any point to Joseph's having been kept in jail for such a long time?
Can you gain any insight into human nature from the cupbearer's forgetting Joseph for two years?

B Joseph's skill in interpreting dreams rescues him from prison. Pharaoh's wise men could not explain his dreams. Why? One account tells us that Pharaoh dreamed the interpretations, too. Until Joseph reminded him, he remembered the dreams, but not their interpretations. Another account suggests that God had caused the magicians and wizards to lose their wisdom, so that Joseph would be called upon to interpret (*Yalkut Me'am Lo'ez,* Vol. IV, by Yaakov Culi, p. 361). Joseph included advice with his dream interpretations. He counseled Pharaoh to stockpile the surplus grain during the years of plenty in order that the Egyptian people would be able to survive the years of famine.

For many years, there has been a survivalist movement in the United States. Survivalists stockpile food and supplies to be used in the event of a disaster. What are the similarities/differences between modern-day survivalists and Joseph and the Egyptians?
Does it make sense for people to make such preparations today? Explain.
Under what circumstances would you do this?

C Joseph becomes thoroughly Egyptianized. His name is changed, as is his style of dress; he takes a wife and his children are born in Egypt. Even with his important position, he does not contact his family. It seems as though Joseph has forever severed his ties to his family. According to Ramban, Joseph's silence regarding his father is a grave sin, but Abravanel excuses his behavior on grounds of political considerations.

Has Joseph's behavior changed since the previous portion? If so, how?
What does "growing up" mean to you?
What kind of political "considerations" might have kept Joseph from contacting his family? If you were Joseph, would you have contacted your family? (Remember, Joseph does not know that his father thinks he is dead.)

D Jewish tradition considered Asenat (the wife of Joseph) to be Dinah's daughter. This daughter was born as a result of the rape committed by Shechem (*Targum Jonathan; Sofrim,* chapter 21). Dinah's brothers were ashamed of this child for she was a reminder of the family's dishonor. Asenat was cast out of the house, but prior to her abandonment, Jacob placed a necklace on her which told the story of her birth. She was carried off to Egypt by traders and adopted by Potiphera and his wife.

Another tradition has Asenat abandoned under a bush then found and raised by Potiphera. In either case she grows up in luxury in Potipher's palace. Called either Potiphera or Potiphar, the tradition considers it is one and the same man who also bought Joseph. Once Joseph is released and achieves a position second only to Pharaoh, he becomes a very suitable match for Asenat.

Look at the details of Asenat's life. Is she similar in any way to any other biblical character? (Moses) What are the similarities in the stories of their births and abandonments? In their growing up? Who exiled Asenat to Egypt? Who exiled Joseph to Egypt? Who went to Egypt to secure food for Jacob's extended family? Did this connection ultimately lead to the enslavement and exile of the Israelites? Who brought an end to this slavery?

E Did Joseph seek revenge against his brothers? A surface reading of the text indicates that he did. Joseph orchestrated a series of events which greatly frightened his brothers. What purpose other than revenge was Joseph aiming at? Several commentators have stated that Joseph wished to test his brothers and allow them to repent of their actions against him. As Rambam explains (based on *Yoma* 86b): "What constitutes complete repentance? One who is confronted by the identical thing wherein he transgressed and it lies within his power to commit the transgression again, but he does not succumb out of repentance, and not out of fear or weakness."

Consider the statement: "As you do, so shall be it done to you." How does this apply to the brothers? Does this apply to any other situations with which you are familiar?
Do you think Joseph treated his brothers badly for a particular reason?
Had you been Joseph, what would you have done to your brothers?

F Joseph created a situation similar to the one in which he was sold by his brothers. He took Benjamin, his only full brother, a son of Rachel, and deeply loved by Jacob, and framed him! It was the brothers' reaction to Benjamin's trouble that Joseph wanted to see.

The *Tanchuma* relates the brothers' conversation after discovering the cup in Benjamin's sack. The brothers assumed that Benjamin had actually stolen the cup. They began beating him and saying, "You're a thief just like your mother. Your mother Rachel humiliated our father Jacob by stealing Laban's fertility gods (Genesis 31:19). Now you have embarrassed us in a similar manner."
"You have your nerve" replied Benjamin. "Assume that I did steal the chalice. Is it as bad as what you did to my brother? You hated him so much that you killed a kid and told our father that a beast devoured him."

By interpreting the dream of the cupbearer, Joseph gets out of jail and begins his rise to power. Now it is his cup put in Benjamin's sack that will soon reunite Joseph with his family.

If you were Jacob, would you have allowed Benjamin to go to Egypt? Was there any choice? Why did Jacob not go, too?

Joseph put his cup in Benjamin's sack. What object do you own that is so much identified as yours that you could have put it in the sack to frame Benjamin?

How do the recurring elements (cups, dreams, wheat, pits, coats, the number 17, etc.) in the Joseph story tie the story together and help move it along?

Are there any recurring themes or elements in your life?

STRATEGIES

ANALYZING THE TEXT

1 The fulfillment of Joseph's dreams comes about in this portion. Read aloud the initial description of the dreams (Genesis 37:5-7, 9) and compare this to how they come true.

2 Joseph is considered neither prophet nor patriarch, although he possesses qualities of both. What might Joseph be — prophet, patriarch, priest, judge? Do some research about each of these categories. Does Joseph meet the criteria for any or all of them?

3 Compare the meanings of the word *leshalom* (Genesis 44:17) and *beshalom* (Genesis 15:15). Which word is associated with life? With death? Can you suggest a better translation of Genesis 44:15 based on this distinction? What kind of outcome do Joseph's words hint at?

4 Examine the use of the word יִשָּׂא (*yisa*) in Genesis 40:13, 19, 20. How many meanings does it have? How are these meanings wordplays on each other? Suggest ways that these meanings, although not used in connection with Joseph, reflect the pattern of Joseph's life.

5 In this portion, it is again stated how the children of Rachel are favored. Specifically, Benjamin is mentioned here as being the most dear to his father. This time the brothers relate this information. How have their feelings changed? Do you think Benjamin behaved differently from Joseph? Why?

EXTENDING THE TEXT

6 Simeon was singled out as the hostage to be kept until the other brothers returned with Benjamin. A *midrash* suggests that it was Simeon who cast Joseph into the pit. Imagine that you are Simeon cast into a dungeon. What graffiti would you write on the walls of your cell? Use large cardboard boxes or tri-wall to simulate the cell. Let each participant assume the role of Simeon.

7 In *Mikaytz,* the brothers know Joseph only as an agent of the Pharaoh. Imagine you are one of the brothers. Write a character sketch of Joseph as he appears in this portion.

8 Read Genesis 41:51. What is the meaning of the name Manasseh (changed)? Do you think that Joseph really meant that he had changed or forgotten the hardship he had endured and the home he had left behind? Is there any significance to the order of Joseph's words when he states that he has forgotten? The birth of his sons seems to make Joseph wish to forget his past and to feel settled in his adopted land. But, it is only with the arrival of his brothers that these wishes can be realized.

Design two family crests for Joseph — one for the time following the birth of his sons, but before the arrival of his brothers, and the second for the period of his life after his reconciliation with his family. Use the ideas introduced by the names Manasseh and Ephraim to illustrate the change in Joseph.

9 The story of Joseph is retold in many children's books. Read, discuss, and compare these retellings, paying attention to the tone, omissions, and style of illustrations. Some suggested titles: *Joseph and His Magnificent Coat of Many Colors* by Marcia Williams; *Joseph and the King of Egypt* by Kath Mellentin; *Joseph the Dreamer* by Shoshana Lapon. Choose from these and other renditions which you are able to locate.

PERSONALIZING THE TEXT

10 One may wonder why Joseph never contacted his family. One reason was simply that for a long time, he was a prisoner. Yet, he did achieve a position of great power second only to Pharaoh himself.

Imagine that you are Joseph. You have been keeping a diary of your experiences. The first line of today's entry reads: "Even though I have become a powerful man in Egypt, I have chosen not to contact my family because . . . " Your task is to complete the diary entry. Explain in detail your reasons for isolating yourself from your family.

11 The Torah describes Joseph's unfair imprisonment. In Jewish law, the *mitzvah* of *Pidyon Shevuyim* — redeeming of the captives — remains operative to this day in the Jewish community. Throughout our history, we have worked to free Jews living under repressive governments and in countries where it is unsafe to live as Jews. This *mitzvah* has also become a value in the general population through the work of Amnesty International. This organization works with those imprisoned because of their race, religion, or beliefs. Write to: Amnesty International USA, 322 Eighth Avenue, New York, NY 10001.

Using information they provide along with traditional Jewish sources and further library and Internet research, create an information kiosk on the theme of redeeming the captive. The kiosk should be placed where congregants and other students have easy access. For more, see "Redeeming the Captive" in *Teaching Mitzvot* by Barbara Binder Kadden and Bruce Kadden.

12 Although Joseph is a stranger in the land of Egypt and is often in a precarious position, he never hesitates to proclaim his faith in God (see Genesis 39:9; 40:8; 41:15-16; 41:25-33). The climax of these affirmations is in Genesis 41:38-39 in which Pharaoh himself defers to God as the ultimate source of his dreams. Would you be as bold as Joseph in such a setting? Think of a setting in which you feel isolated and unsupported because you are Jewish. Place yourself on the continuum below to indicate how free or unfree you feel to proclaim your Jewish values in that setting.

Timid Tevya   Bold Beruriah

13 *Mikaytz* details how Joseph distributed the food to the Egyptians and to foreigners who also came to buy. Invite a representative from an emergency food organization in your community to discuss how food is allocated and distributed. Consider these questions: Where does the food come from? Is any food purchased? How is food stored? Must the recipient fit certain criteria? Are there any similarities between this allocation process and Joseph's? If Joseph was able to feed the Egyptians and the foreigners who came to buy, is it not also possible that we could feed all the hungry today? (For more, see the Index: "World hunger.")

14 Famine and its devastating effects still exist even in this age of overabundance. Many organizations exist which seek to intervene and aid in emergency areas. For information and program ideas, contact: Oxfam America, 115 Broadway, Boston, MA 02116; MAZON, 2940 Westwood Blvd., Suite 7, Los Angeles, CA 90064; American Jewish World Service, 15 West 26th St., New York, NY 10010. For more, see "Leaving the Gleanings" from *Teaching Mitzvot* by Barbara Binder Kadden and Bruce Kadden.

15 One immediate step that you can take in your own community to intervene in food crisis situations is to donate food to the local emergency food organizations. You might consider organizing a major collection program for your group or synagogue.

16 As a symbol of Joseph's authority, Pharaoh gave him a ring. Research what rings such as this are used for. Design the ring Joseph was given. If you have access to jewelry making equipment carry out your design.

17 Joseph's actions are explained by some as a test of his brothers, and not as an effort to seek revenge (see Insight E, page 66). What do you think? Have you ever been in a position where you wanted to get even with someone? What did you choose to do? How did you feel about it? How did the other person(s) react and feel?

18 Imagine you are directing a film about the life of Joseph. Create a storyboard for the events in this portion. (A storyboard is an illustrated, step-by-step version of the events as they are to be reenacted on film. It contains dialogue, sketches of costumes, and other pertinent information about setting and action, as well as suggestions to the actors.)

19 Read aloud or write on the chalk board Rambam's explanation of complete repentance (see Insight E, page 66). Discuss how this applies to the Joseph story. Create an illustrated story which exemplifies this quote. Draw on your own experiences as the basis for the story.

OTHER RESOURCES

20 Read, act out, and discuss the skit for the portion *Mikaytz* in *Sedra Scenes: Skits for Every Torah Portion* by Stan J. Beiner, pp. 56-62.

21 View and discuss the episode for *Mikaytz* from *Torah Toons I: The Video*.

22 For creative movement activities, see "Joseph in Charge" and "Joseph Names His Sons" from *Torah in Motion* by JoAnne Tucker and Susan Freeman, pp. 54-57.

23 Read and discuss the illustrated commentary for *Mi-Ketz* in *American Torah Toons* by Lawrence Bush.

24 Listen to, discuss, and sing "Forgive and Forget" from *Sounds of Creation: Genesis in Song*.

INVOLVING THE FAMILY

25 On *erev* Shabbat, parents traditionally bless their sons with the words: "May God makes you as Ephraim and Manasseh." Daughters are blessed with the words: "May God make you as Sarah, Rebekah, Rachel, and Leah." Can you suggest some reasons for choosing Ephraim and Manasseh and the Matriarchs for mention in these blessings? Which reasons for doing so are most meaningful to you and why? (For more, see the Index: "Blessing/Curse.")

BAR/BAT MITZVAH PROJECT

27 In this portion Joseph feeds the hungry of Egypt. You can emulate Joseph and help feed the hungry of your community. Volunteer to cook and/or serve at a local soup kitchen. Possibly your own synagogue is involved in a project like this and you can sign on to be a member of the team. You will also be putting a face on hunger by working face to face with the hungry and poor.

VAYIGASH 44:18-47:27 ויגש

SYNOPSIS

JUDAH BEGS JOSEPH TO ALLOW HIM TO become a prisoner in place of Benjamin. The brothers are fearful for their father Jacob's life, since he is so close to Benjamin. Joseph, unable to conceal his identity any longer, reveals himself to his brothers. They are astounded. Pharaoh learns that Joseph's brothers are in Egypt. He directs Joseph to invite Jacob and his entire household to live in Egypt. Joseph extends the invitation, sending along gifts and provisions for his father's journey, but warning his brothers not to quarrel on the return to Canaan. Jacob is told that Joseph is alive and waits to see him in Egypt. One night during the journey, God calls out to Jacob and tells him that he will prosper in Egypt and that Joseph will be present at Jacob's deathbed.

Jacob and Joseph have a tearful reunion. The family continues to work as shepherds in Egypt in the region of Goshen. The famine continues in Egypt and Joseph sells grain to the people. Eventually, the people sell all they own to Pharaoh in order to purchase grain. By the end of the famine, Pharaoh owns all of the land in Egypt save the land of the priests. At the end of the famine, Joseph gives seed to the people and directs them to repay Pharaoh with one-fifth of their harvest.

INSIGHTS FROM THE TRADITION

A The eloquent and impassioned speech of Judah, pleading for Benjamin's freedom, opens this portion. *Genesis Rabbah* 93:6 explains that Judah was ready to take three possible courses of action (based on three explanations of the word *vayigash*, "and [he] went up"):
1. to plead mercy for Benjamin.
2. to battle Joseph and his armies if he refused to release Benjamin.
3. to use his ultimate weapon, prayer. Judah would pray to God for direction.

Judah's response showed the responsibility and love the brothers had for Benjamin. In his speech, Judah states that his father Jacob's fate is tied to Benjamin's life. It seems that the brothers have come to accept the elevated status of Rachel's son. Judah did not need to go beyond his first line of action. The brothers had successfully passed Joseph's testing and, therefore, Joseph was able to reveal his identity.

Based on the text, Benjamin replaced Joseph in his father's attention and affection. Why didn't the brothers hate Benjamin as they once hated Joseph? What actions would you take to get into someone's good graces?

B Joseph tells his brothers that divine providence sent him to Egypt so that he might one day save his family. Joseph then proceeds to make plans for his father's entire household to join him in Egypt in order to survive the famine. As the brothers prepare to leave, Joseph bestows gifts upon them. Joseph gives a larger gift to his brother Benjamin. One may question the wisdom of this action, since previous preferential treatment caused so much grief. Joseph also cautions the brothers not to quarrel on their return to Canaan. According to Rashi one reason for this was that Joseph realized that the brothers were ashamed of selling him and they might quarrel as to who was originally at fault.

Joseph forgives his brothers, yet he did punish them.
Do you ever feel vengeful? When? Why?
What do you do to work out the feeling? Once wrongdoers have admitted their wrongdoing and taken responsibility for it, should one always forgive them?
Do you feel better after you confess to a wrongdoing?
Is it enough to admit a wrongdoing to yourself or must you tell the one you wronged?

C The text does not record what the brothers told their father about Joseph. Whether they confessed their role in Joseph's disappearance is a matter of conjecture. It is Ramban's opinion that the brothers never told Jacob that they had sold him. He simply thought Joseph had gotten lost in the field and had been captured and sold by those who found him. The brothers did not tell the truth, for they did not want Jacob to curse them.

Is it better or more hurtful to the person you wronged to admit your wrongdoing?
Are there times when it is better to be silent about a wrongdoing?
Considering the burden of guilt the brothers carried, would it have been better for them to clear the air and tell their father what really happened?

D On his journey to Egypt, Jacob offers sacrifices to the God of his father Isaac. Why does the text say "God of his father Isaac" when Jacob already has his own relationship with God? Nehama Leibowitz suggests (*Studies in Bereshit*, pp. 500-501) that Jacob knew his father had been commanded not to leave Canaan and he was concerned that he would be violating a command by going to Egypt. God appears to Jacob and says, "I am God, the God of your father; fear not to go down to Egypt" (Genesis 46:3). In the next verse, God promises to accompany Jacob to Egypt and back to the Promised Land. The verse may be understood in two ways: (1) that Jacob will reside in Egypt and upon his death be buried in Canaan; (2) that Jacob represents all Jews. The entire population will sojourn in Egypt, but a nation will be brought back to its homeland.

In the context of Jewish history, why was it important for Jacob and his family to settle in Egypt? Is this in any way similar to one's leaving home to go to college? To find a new job? A spouse? Explain.

E Joseph chooses to settle his family in Goshen, an area in northeastern Egypt (see *Atlas of Jewish History* by Martin Gilbert). The Egyptians worshiped sheep and thus had an aversion to shepherds. Joseph was therefore able to justify the need for physical distance between his family and the Egyptian population centers. The Netziv explained Joseph's motive differently. Regarding the settlement in Goshen, ". . . though it involved degrading his family in the eyes of Pharaoh, everything was worth sacrificing in order to ensure the preservation of Israel's sanctity." Herding sheep is an isolating life-style. By remaining isolated, according to Bachya, ". . . one has nothing to distract him from having his thoughts on God" (*Jewish Biblical Exegesis*, p. 79). Therefore, the tribes would more easily maintain and strengthen their relationship with God. Joseph did not want the household of Jacob assimilating into the Egyptian culture. He wanted to preserve them as a group so that they could become a nation.

The commentator Bachya stated that by being shepherds, our ancestors would not come to worship sheep as the Egyptians did. Do you agree with the notion that what is familiar and known can not become sacred?
Do you tend to isolate yourself when you are trying to accomplish something? Does being alone improve your concentration and/or your results? Why might a person need solitude and time alone?

F Genesis 46:15 contains the last mention of Jacob's daughter Dinah. She is named among those who went down to Egypt with Jacob, but she is not among the children that Jacob/Israel blesses in *Vayechi*, the next portion. Ellen Frankel, in *The Five Books of Miriam*, names Dinah "The Wounded One." Frankel has Dinah's character describe herself: "I speak for all those who have been silenced by violence, by neglect, by abuse, by disdain. Mine is a still, small voice, but it echoes through the ages" (p. xxii).

Do you think the victims of crimes and neglect need a stronger voice in society?

Why does Frankel assign that role to Dinah in her commentary?

How can you be a voice for those whom society has silenced?

G In Genesis 46:28, we read that Jacob had sent Judah ahead of the family "to point the way before him to Goshen." Rashi comments that the Hebrew expression *lehorot lefanav* can also be understood to mean "to establish for him a house of study from which teaching might go forth." This commentary is based on the fact that the Hebrew word *hora'ah* (teaching, instruction) and Torah are related to the verb used in Genesis. The word for parents (*horim*) is also related.

How might establishing a house of study help create a climate in which Jacob's family was discouraged from assimilating into Egyptian society? Who serves the function of a Judah for you in your life, *lehorot lefanav* (walking before you to point the way)?

H In the *Kabbalah,* Joseph is known as "the harvester." Perhaps this refers to the way Joseph saved the Egyptians from famine through management of their harvests. Maybe the name refers to the harvest Joseph reaped when he was reunited at last with his family. The name also reminds us of the harvest of wisdom which Joseph reveals when he forgives his brothers, telling them, "It was to save life that God sent me ahead of you."

Which "harvest" do you think was the most important in Joseph's life?

In what ways are you a "harvester"?

What "harvests" do you hope to reap in your life?

STRATEGIES

ANALYZING THE TEXT

1 The impassioned speech Judah gives cuts across centuries and reaches our modern ears. Give a dramatic reading of Judah's speech to Joseph (Genesis 44:18-34).

2 In Insight E, page 66, for the portion *Mikaytz,* a quote from Rambam concerning what constitutes true repentance is cited. Discuss whether or not Judah's behavior regarding Benjamin satisfies this definition. Why or why not? If not, what could Judah have done differently?

3 Review from Genesis, *Vayishlach,* Insight A, page 52, the threefold plan Jacob developed in response to his meeting Esau. Did Judah follow a similar pattern? (See Insight A, page 71.) Reread the section dealing with Jacob and Esau (Genesis 32:4-22). Create a chart listing all the parallels.

4 Each of the Patriarchs — Abraham, Isaac, and Jacob — underwent some sort of test. The sons of Jacob were also tested. Review the portions through Genesis to identify these tests. Consider the following questions in discussion.

a. How did these tests strengthen their attachment to God and belief in the covenant?

b. Were the tests appropriate to those who underwent them?

c. Although some of the tests might seem to reflect the supernatural, they all have elements of everyday life. Can you relate to any of these personally?

d. How do the Matriarchs and other women mentioned in Genesis fit into this discussion? How were they tested?

5 The division of the portions which deal with the Joseph story add to the dramatic tension of the story. For a clear example of this, read the end of the previous portion, *Mikaytz*, and then the start of this portion. Take a look at the following portions: *Vayayshev*, *Mikaytz*, and *Vayigash*. Divide them up in a way that emphasizes the dramatic tension. Remember, a good storyteller always leaves the audience wanting more.

EXTENDING THE TEXT

6 In Insight D, page 72, two explanations are given for Genesis 46:3. Review these explanations and the biblical verse. Discuss: How is Jacob a representative for all Jews?

7 Joseph warns his brothers not to be quarrelsome on the return trip to Canaan. As suggested in Insight B, page 71, Joseph was cautioning them not to fight over who was originally at fault for selling him.
a. Imagine you are one of the pack animals. Write the dialogue the brothers spoke on their way back to Canaan.
b. Choose 11 individuals to represent Jacob's sons. Role play the conversation(s) that might have taken place on their journey home.

8 In this portion, Jacob and his family leave Canaan, the land which God had promised to Abraham and his descendants. Compose a prayer such as Jacob may have recited as he began this journey away from his home and toward his son. What would have been his feelings about the journey and his hopes for the future? You may wish to use *"Tefillat HaDerech"* — the Traveler's Prayer — as a model.

9 Script and stage the reunion between Jacob and Joseph. Consider their reactions to the physical changes in each other (aging, growing up,

becoming Egyptianized), the events and feelings which they might want to share with each other, and possibly reactions of onlookers (certainly, of the brothers, and the Pharaoh) to the scene.

10 As far as the biblical account goes, Jacob's daughter Dinah went down to Egypt with her family, but there we lose track of her. There is no record of the subsequent events in her life, or of the descendants she may have left behind. Imagine you are Dinah, the only daughter in a family of many sons, the victim of a crime of violence which led to violent reprisals. Based on what you know about Dinah and her family, make five predictions about her future life in Egypt. Speculate about her role in the extended family and the kind of person she might have been (refer to Insight F above).

11 In October 1960, Pope John XXIII greeted a group of United Jewish Appeal leaders with the words, "I am your brother Joseph" (Genesis 45:4). Pope John was one of the first papal leaders to attempt to change the Catholic attitude of anti-Semitism to one of tolerance and understanding. Thus, his choice of words on this occasion was very significant. Why did Pope John choose these particular words as his greeting? What message do you think he wanted to convey? Research the life story and philosophy of this remarkable man.
References: *Encyclopaedia Judaica*, "John XXIII," Vol. 10, pp. 159-60 and "Church Councils – Vatican Councils I and II," Vol. 5, pp. 549-550; *Jewish History — Moments & Methods: An Activity Source Book for Teachers* by Sorel Loeb and Barbara Binder Kadden, p. 124.

12 Make up a *midrash* which establishes a connection between the Hebrew words for teaching and Torah (see Insight G, page 73, for Rashi's commentary on this point).

PERSONALIZING THE TEXT

13 Although the Bible records that the Egyptian people seemed satisfied to impoverish themselves for grain, to our modern ears, this seems tyrannical. Conduct a town meeting taking place among the Egyptians. Try to find a more equitable solution to the purchase of grain. A town meeting is an open forum in which you can air grievances. You may wish to invite in a "Joseph" and a "Pharaoh."

14 In this portion, all the brothers find Joseph. Create a Hebrew word search which has Joseph's name hidden in it eleven times. Use the Hebrew version of his name, "Yosef." The name can be written vertically, horizontally, and diagonally. Copy this for all the participants.

15 Genesis 45:26 reads, "And they told him, 'Joseph is still alive; yes, he is ruler over the whole land of Egypt.' His heart went numb, for he did not believe them." R. Hiyya taught: "What is the liar's fate? Even when he speaks the truth he is not believed" (*Genesis Rabbah* 94:3). "The Boy Who Cried Wolf" is a story which illustrates this idea. Read this story with the group and discuss how it illustrates this *midrashic* statement. Reference: "The Shepherd Boy and the Wolf" in *Aesop's Fables,* found in *Classics for Young People.*

16 Joseph was concerned that once his family settled in Egypt they would totally assimilate into Egyptian culture. To maintain their identity Joseph settled them in Goshen and encouraged them to continue shepherding. Forcibly ghettoizing an ethnic or religious group would now be considered discriminatory. Joseph created a workable solution for assimilation. What were the elements of his plan? Are there aspects of Joseph's plan which could be adapted today to strengthen Jewish identity and help to halt assimilation?

OTHER RESOURCES

17 Serach, the daughter of Asher, is the only female grandchild of Jacob named in the Torah. According to tradition, it was she who told Jacob that Joseph was not dead, but had survived, indeed flourished, in Egypt. Read "A Psalm of Serach" in *But God Remembered: Stories of Women from Creation To the Promised Land* by Sandy Eisenberg Sasso.

18 For an activity exploring the process of assimilation, see *Jewish History — Moments & Methods: A Source Book for Teachers* by Sorel Loeb and Barbara Binder Kadden, p. 59.

19 Listen to and/or learn the song "Joseph You're a Dreamer" from *Bible People Songs.*

20 Complete the pages which relate to *Vayigash* in *Bible People Book One* by Joel Lurie Grishaver, pp. 49-51. Also check the accompanying Leader Guide for procedures and additional activities.

21 Read, act out, and discuss the skit for the portion *Vayigash* in *Sedra Scenes: Skits for Every Torah Portion* by Stan J. Beiner, pp. 63-68.

22 View and discuss the episode for *Vayigash* from *Torah Toons I: The Video.*

23 For a creative movement activity, see "Egyptians Become Serfs" from *Torah in Motion* by JoAnne Tucker and Susan Freeman, pp. 58-59.

24 Listen to, discuss, and sing *"Vayish'lacheini Elohim"* from *Sounds of Creation: Genesis in Song.*

25 Read and discuss the illustrated commentary for *Va-Yigash* in *American Torah Toons* by Lawrence Bush.

INVOLVING THE FAMILY

26 An overriding concern which the brothers had was the effect on Jacob should Benjamin be kept as a prisoner. A value which may be derived from this is that one should always be concerned with the welfare of one's parent(s). As a family, discuss how the children show concern for the parent(s). How do the parent(s) show concern for the children? Draw up a list of ways of being more concerned for each other and post it on the refrigerator as a reminder.

BAR/BAT MITZVAH PROJECT

27 Not only does Joseph continue to provide grain to the Egyptians during the famine, he also gives them seed to replant their crops when the famine has ended. In this way, he helps the people to help themselves. In 1985, a group of Rabbis and community leaders founded The American Jewish World Service to provide Jewish aid and disaster relief to Third World countries. Among their primary projects are those that promote agricultural development. Find out about the work of AJWS by writing to them at 15 West 26th St., 9th Floor, New York, NY 10010. Use your Bar or Bat Mitzvah as an occasion to educate people about the work of this important organization.

a. Include some information and thoughts about AJWS in your *D'var Torah* or Bar/Bat Mitzvah speech.

b. Help your guests learn about the organization through table placards which you create and display.

VAYECHI 47:28-50:26 ויחי

SYNOPSIS

JACOB LIVES FOR 17 YEARS IN EGYPT. HE feels that his death is imminent. He makes Joseph swear to bury him in Canaan. Prior to his death, Jacob formally adopts Joseph's sons, Manasseh and Ephraim, and blesses them. In the blessing, he elevates the younger Ephraim over Manasseh, explaining to Joseph that Ephraim would father a larger people than Manasseh.

On his deathbed, Jacob summons his sons. He describes the character and depicts the future of each one. Jacob directs his sons to bury him in the Cave of Machpelah.

Following his death, Jacob is embalmed. A great Egyptian procession accompanies Joseph and his brothers to Canaan. When they reach Goren HaAtad, Joseph observes a seven day mourning period for his father. Joseph and his brothers return to Egypt after the burial. Although the brothers are concerned that Joseph will take revenge upon them now that Jacob is dead, Joseph tells them they have no cause for concern.

The Book of Genesis closes with Joseph's death at 110 years of age. On his deathbed, he speaks to his brothers, requesting that his bones be taken back to the land promised to Abraham, to Isaac, and to Jacob.

INSIGHTS FROM THE TRADITION

A This portion derives its name from the Hebrew for he lived — *Vayechi* — Jacob lived seventeen years in the land of Egypt.

The famine in Canaan lasted seven years. Why did Jacob and his family remain in Egypt after the famine had ended?
What is the significance of the number 17 to the entire Joseph story?

B As E.A. Speiser points out (*The Anchor Bible: Genesis*, p. 358), Joseph's eventful career in Egypt is drawing to a close and the biblical narrative must provide the link to the next generation. Therefore, Jacob on his deathbed adopts Joseph's sons and gives them a blessing elevating them to equal status with his own sons. Several commentators suggest that Jacob adopted Ephraim and Manasseh because Rachel, who died an untimely death, could possibly have lived to bear more children.

Joseph brings his two sons for Jacob to bless. Jacob responds, "Who are these?" (Genesis 48:8). Jacob saw two boys dressed as Egyptians and speaking Egyptian. The boys did not "look" like members of the Hebrew tribes (*Legends of the Jews* by Louis Ginzberg, Vol. II, p. 137).

Consider Jacob's comment about his foreign looking grandsons. Do you "look" Jewish? Do you speak a Jewish language? In what ways are you similar to the grandsons? In what ways do you see yourself as Jewish? In what ways do others see you as Jewish?
What connects you and Judaism? What will keep your descendants connected to Judaism?

C In bestowing the blessing, the younger brother, Ephraim, is placed before the elder, Manasseh. The favoring of the younger son over the elder is a repetitive pattern in Genesis. Abel's sacrifices were placed over Cain's. Isaac displaced Ishmael, and Jacob usurped the blessing from Esau.

There is no tribe of Joseph; instead, there are two tribes named for his sons Ephraim and Manasseh.

Does Jacob bless the younger child over the elder because that is what he saw in his own home and in the generation that preceded him, or is he perpetuating a very problematic family custom?
In the case of Isaac and Jacob, how did they come to receive the blessing of the firstborn? How did

Jacob determine who was to get the blessing of the firstborn?

Is Joseph honored or slighted when his younger child is placed before the elder?

D Malbim explains that Joseph did not want to swear that he would bury Jacob in Canaan. Joseph wanted to carry out Jacob's wish as a faithful son. Because he swore an oath, Joseph would not be able to take credit for fulfilling his obligations freely. As Nechama Leibowitz comments (*Studies in Bereshit,* p. 533), this helps explain the biblical and Rabbinic disapproval of vows. Even so, Jacob made Joseph take an oath which ultimately aided Joseph. Leibowitz notes that it was an Egyptian custom for a nobleman to prepare his burial site during his lifetime, and it was only there that he would be buried. In speaking to Pharaoh's court, Joseph says: "My father made me swear, saying, I am about to die. Be sure to bury me in the grave which I made ready for myself in the land of Canaan."

A vow is like a sacred promise. Are there times when, despite the negative Rabbinic view of vows, you feel they are appropriate? If so, when?
Which places more responsibility on an individual — a vow or an offer to do something freely?

E Although the words spoken by Jacob to his sons are called a blessing, upon closer examination, we see that three sons are chastised and two of them, Simeon and Levi, are actually cursed. Speiser suggests renaming this section the Testament of Jacob, rather than the Blessing of Jacob (*The Anchor Bible: Genesis,* p. 370).

The rest of Jacob's words are more of a prophecy. In his blessings, Jacob deals with his sons more as tribes than as individuals. Plaut states that the future is tied to Judah and Joseph and these he addresses directly. The others are only spoken about (*The Torah: A Modern Commentary,* edited by W. Gunther Plaut, p. 311).

How well do you think Jacob understood his sons?
Do you think Jacob ever came to love all of his sons?
Was Jacob a "successful" man? Did he accomplish his life's goals?
What do you think constitutes success?

F Once Jacob is buried in Canaan, the brothers return to Egypt and send a message to Joseph. It reads, "Before his death, your father left this instruction: So shall you say to Joseph, 'Forgive, I urge you, the offense and guilt of your brothers who treated you so harshly.' Therefore, please forgive the offense of the servants of the God of your father" (Genesis 50:15-17). Rabbi Simeon ben Gamliel taught: "Great is peace, for even the tribal ancestors resorted to a fabrication in order to make peace between Joseph and themselves" (*Genesis Rabbah* 100:8).

Did the brothers do the right thing?
What were they afraid of? Did they have cause for fear?
Was any other course of action possible?
Who is the peacemaker in your family?

G "'Where are the graves of Bilhah and Zilpah' our daughters ask" (*The Five Books of Miriam* by Ellen Frankel, p. 89). We know that Rachel is buried on the road to Ephrath and that in the Cave of Machpelah, Abraham and Sarah, Isaac and Rebecca, and Leah are buried. On his deathbed Jacob also asks to be buried there. But what of Bilhah and Zilpah, concubines to Jacob and mothers of four of his sons who are also four of the tribes? Frankel has Bilhah and Zilpah answer: "Like so many of our sisters, mothers, daughters, and countless other women in our lives we lie buried in the white spaces of the holy scroll. And like Joseph's bones, we still wait for you to carry us home from Egypt."

To what scroll do Bilhah and Zilpah refer?

What does it mean to be buried in the white spaces of the holy scroll?

Which other women in the Bible can you identify as being buried in the white spaces?

For Bilhah and Zilpah, the white spaces of the holy scroll mean the same thing as Egypt. Can you explain this connection?

Suggest ways we can carry these two home from Egypt, as well as from the white spaces of the holy scroll.

STRATEGIES

ANALYZING THE TEXT

1 In Genesis 50:26, we read: "Joseph died . . . he was embalmed and placed in a coffin in Egypt." The Hebrew word used for coffin is *aron*. This word is never again used in the Torah with this meaning. *Aron* elsewhere refers to the Ark (as in Exodus 25:10) which was used to carry the Tablets of the Law. In their wanderings through the desert, the Israelites carried both the coffin containing Joseph's remains and the Ark containing the Ten Commandments. What lessons might be derived from the double meaning of the word *aron*? What is significant about the fact that the word is used only in reference to Joseph's burial (and not to that of the Patriarchs and Matriarchs)?

2 Deuteronomy 21:15-17 warns that a man must give his firstborn son his birthright. Yet, Genesis contains several examples of a younger, favored son being given the blessings and privileges that were traditionally reserved for the firstborn. This portion has two such examples: Reuben, the oldest of Jacob's sons is seemingly usurped by Judah and by Joseph (see Genesis 49:3-9; 8-10; 48:21-22; 49:26). Joseph's son Ephraim was given preference over the firstborn (see Genesis 48:13-20). Even today, the order in which the brothers are mentioned makes it seem as if

Ephraim was the older. (See also Isaac and Ishmael, Genesis 16:15-16 and 21:1-13; Jacob and Esau, Genesis 25:23, 30-34.) Two other men who succeeded despite being younger sons are Moses and David.

What do you think is the significance of the theme of younger (weaker) sons triumphing over older (stronger) sons?

In what ways might this be a metaphor about Jewish survival?

Write a dialogue between these elder and younger brothers. What would they say to each other, what might they be thinking and feeling? Stage the dialogue as a "Face the Nation" or "Larry King Live" program.

3 W. Gunther Plaut once wrote a magazine article (*Jerusalem Report,* Jan.14, 1993) focusing on biblical numbers and the messages they contain. What follows here is a synopsis of Plaut's "numbers game." Write the following on the board leaving out the answer for Jacob. Ask the students to try and figure out the pattern.

Abraham lived to be 175 (5 squared x 7)

Isaac lived to be 180 (6 squared x 5)

Jacob lived to be 147 (7 squared x 3)

Ask the students to check through portion *Vayechi* to find out how long Joseph lived (Answer: 110 years, Genesis 50:26). Looking at the sets of numbers for the Patriarchs, is there any way to arrive at the number 110? (Add up the sums of 5 squared, 6 squared, and 7 squared.)

Joseph took the Children of Israel out of the Promised Land and Joshua brought them back. What was Joshua's age at his death? (110 years, Joshua 24:29)

Between Joseph and Joshua is Moses, who lived to be 120 years. Tradition tells us that this was considered the perfect age because it was part of the physical structure of the human body. Ask the students how one could arrive at this number based upon a part of our anatomy? (Our hands have five fingers, multiply them — 1 x 2 x 3 x 4 x 5 = 120.)

What is the meaning of these calculations? Is this simply a biblical math teaser, or does it serve a purpose? If so, what is it?

EXTENDING THE TEXT

4 Examine the blessings Jacob bestows upon Joseph (Genesis 48:21-22; 49:22-26). How do they reflect the reality of Joseph's life and his future? Imagine you are a reporter on the spot for the *Egyptian Enquirer*. Upon hearing Joseph's blessing, write a profile of Joseph for your newspaper. Use phrases from the blessing as headings under which you review his life.

5 Read Judah's blessing (Genesis 49:10). Discuss how this prophecy has been fulfilled in Jewish history. Consider the ancestry of King David (see Genesis, *Vayayshev* #10, page 62) and the fact that the word "Jewish" is derived from Judah, and the tradition that the Messiah will be a descendant of David (and therefore of Judah). Create a mural which illustrates the prophecy and aspects of its fulfillment.
Reference: *Encyclopaedia Judaica*, "Judah," Vol. 10, pp. 326-333.

6 In this portion, *Vayechi*, the sons of Jacob receive their blessings. Dinah, the only daughter, is not even mentioned in the text. Compose a blessing for Dinah. Consider her life history and how she was treated (see Genesis 34:1-31) to help determine the content of her blessing. Create a bulletin board display titled "Remembering Dinah."

7 Look at a map showing the division of the Land of Israel into tribal areas following the Exodus from Egypt. How does the allotment of land reflect the blessings of Jacob? In what instances does it conflict?
Reference: *The Macmillan Bible Atlas* by Yohanan Aharoni and Michael Avi-Yonah.

8 In his blessing, Jacob does not leave material objects to his sons. Rather, he does a character analysis and gives a future picture of the tribes. In some ways, this may be a form of an ethical will. Ethical wills are a well established part of Jewish ethical literature dating from the Middle Ages. Short and practical in nature, such wills usually took the form of a great teacher's deathbed advice to students. However, ethical wills also exist in which parents, sometimes as the time of death nears, or just before embarking on a long journey, leave moral instructions for their children.
References: *Jewish History — Moments & Methods: An Activity Source Book for Teachers* by Sorel Loeb and Barbara Binder Kadden, p. 147; *Ethical Wills: Handing Down Your Jewish Heritage* by Bruce Kadden and Barbara Binder Kadden; *So That Your Values Live On: Ethical Wills & How to Prepare Them*, edited by Jack Riemer and Nathaniel Stampfer.
a. Research and read about ethical wills (see references above).
b. Think about the kind of ethical will you would write. Imagine that you are a parent. Write an ethical will to leave for your children.
c. Joseph also dies in this portion. He instructs his family to take his bones along when they return to Canaan. He foresees a journey for his descendants. Compose an ethical will for them as if you were Joseph.

PERSONALIZING THE TEXT

9 Both Jacob and Joseph ask that they be buried in the Land of Israel (Genesis 47:29-31; 50:24-25). Burial in the Land of Israel has been the wish of many generations of Jews throughout history. One reason for this is the belief that the resurrection of the dead in Messianic times will take place in the Holy Land. Since this wish has obviously been difficult to accomplish, the custom arose of symbolizing burial in Israel by burying with the body a small sack of earth from Israel. Research Jewish beliefs and folklore about what happens after death, especially these concepts: resurrection, afterlife, and immortality of the soul. Which of these concepts hold meaning for you? Discuss answers.

References: *What Happens After I Die? Jewish Views of Life After Death* by Rifat Soncino and Daniel B. Syme; the mini-course *Death, Burial and Mourning in the Jewish Tradition* by Audrey Friedman Marcus, Sherry Bissell, and Karen S. Lipschutz, pp. 15-17; *Encyclopaedia Judaica*, "Resurrection," Vol. 14, pp. 96-103, and "Afterlife," Vol. 2, pp. 336-339, and "Soul, Immortality of," Vol. 15, pp. 174-181.

10 This portion deals with two deaths. While no mention is made of bequeathing material goods, there certainly would have been property to pass on to heirs. Invite a probate lawyer (a lawyer who deals with wills and estates) to explain what a will is, the importance of such a document, and who should have a will. Imagine what goods Joseph would have had. Create his "will" in which specific items are left to specific family members, friends, and Egyptian officials. (For more, see the Index: "Death/Burial.")

11 The meanings of names and the changing of names occur in several portions of the book of Genesis. Typically, Jewish children are given Hebrew names which are used within the Jewish community for ritual practices and often in synagogue and day schools. Construct Hebrew name pins. Materials: Hebrew *Aleph Bet* noodle letters and small balsa wood pieces or chips on which to mount them, pin findings (the clasp on the back of a brooch), sequins, and beads, all of which are available in craft stores. Use white glue to assemble the pins. If desired, paint the wood and/or letters with water color or tempera paint. Or use Fun Foam (also available at craft stores) for the base and the lettering of the name pin. It is easily cut, comes in a variety of colors, and bonds with white craft glue.

12 Design and make a felt and fabric banner which represents each of the 12 tribes. There are many Jewish fine art books and Jewish craft books which have a variety of visual interpretations of the symbols, colors and meanings of these 12 tribes. Do some library research to locate these designs. Work with them, but add original elements of your own.

Reference: *The Encyclopedia of Jewish Symbols* by Ellen Frankel and Betsy Platkin Teutsch.

13 Dinah was the only child of Jacob not to have a tribe descend from her offspring. Create a banner representing Dinah. You may also want to make banners for the other lost women of the Bible (e.g., the Matriarchs, female prophets, mothers, and servants). (For more on death/burial, see the Index: "Death/Burial.")

OTHER RESOURCES

14 View and discuss the video, *The Corridor: Death* which deals with the meaning of death and the afterlife in Judaism.

15 Complete the pages which relate to *Vayechi* in *Bible People Book One* by Joel Lurie Grishaver, pp. 54-55. Also check the accompanying Leader Guide for procedures and additional activities.

16 Read, act out, and discuss the skit for *Vayechi* in *Sedra Scenes: Skits for Every Torah Portion* by Stan J. Beiner, pp. 69-73.

17 View and discuss the episode for *Vayechi* from *Torah Toons I: The Video.*

18 For creative movement activities, see "Blessing Ephraim and Manasseh" and "Joseph Mourns His Father" from *Torah in Motion* by JoAnne Tucker and Susan Freeman, pp. 60-63.

19 Read and discuss the illustrated commentary for *Va-Yechi* in *American Torah Toons* by Lawrence Bush.

20 Listen to, discuss, and sing "May God Inspire You" from *Sounds of Creation: Genesis in Song*.

INVOLVING THE FAMILY

21 Two deaths are recorded in *Vayechi*. Our tradition reflects a number of different ideas about what happens after a person dies (see above, Strategy #9, page 80). There are many Jews who do not believe in a life after death. They believe that immortality results when others remember the deceased with love and respect and are influenced by the person's life and deeds. (See *Gates of Prayer: The New Union Prayerbook*, p. 552, for a lovely poem on this subject.)

Discuss special memories you have of family members or close friends who have died. When do you especially think of these individuals? Have each family member take a turn and tell two or three ways he/she would like to be remembered.

References on discussing death with children: *Talking about Death: A Dialogue between Parent and Child* by Earl Grollman; *A Candle for Grandpa: A Guide to the Jewish Funeral for Children and Parents* by David Techner and Judith Hirt-Manheimer.

BAR/BAT MITZVAH PROJECT

22 There are many instances of honoring parents throughout the book of Genesis. Read through Genesis to locate at least three examples. Create illustrated posters using various media of your choice: paint, chalks, charcoal, ink, along with cut-outs from fabric, pictures, magazines, decorative trims, ribbons, and buttons. Use foam core as the base for the posters. Foam core is available in various sizes and colors at craft and hobby stores.

Following this, recall times when you honored your parent(s) and create a fourth poster in the series.

Line up the four posters with the biblical instances first, followed by your contemporary one. Use decorative tape to make hinge-like attachments between the inner edges of the posters. When set up as a display it will be able to stand. Name the display: Honoring Parents — *Kibbud Av va'Aym*.

REVIEW ACTIVITIES FOR GENESIS

1 Hold a biblical "scavenger hunt" for the whole book of Genesis. Working in two or more teams, come up with a list of 50 questions that can be answered after a careful reading of the book (e.g. the name of the king of the Philistines, Isaac's age when he married Rebekah). Trade lists with another team and have a timed race to answer the questions. Try adding Hebrew questions and answers.

2 Organize a "Who Said It?" in a Spelling Bee style. Cull 50 or more significant quotes from throughout Genesis. Split the group into teams. Rotate questions among the teams asking "who said" a particular quote. Winner is determined by the team with the most points at the end of the round.

3 Assemble a family scrapbook for the Genesis families. Do illustrations, captions, etc., or dress people in biblical style clothing and have them pose for photographs. Create an actual photo album; remember to include captions.

4 Design a "Who's Who in the Book of Genesis" bulletin board or display. Include illustrations, quotes, songs, stories, etc.

5 Make a plaster of paris relief map of the region and trace the journeys of the characters in Genesis. Color code the travels of the different individuals so they are easily distinguishable.

6 Stage the Book of Genesis as installments of a soap opera. You may want to utilize the skits from *Sedra Scenes: Skits for Every Torah Portion* by Stan J. Beiner.

7 Play a fun review game based on material in Genesis. Use the game show "Family Feud" as a format. Organize teams around biblical families (for example: Adam, Eve, Cain and Abel; Noah, wife, and sons, etc.). Create questions of biblical concern and take a poll to get the top answers from a group of people other than the players.

8 Complete the review unit for Genesis in *Bible People Book One* by Joel Lurie Grishaver, pp. 56-64.

9 The creation and establishment of families is a focus of the Book of Genesis. Create a collage of your family as described in *An Artist You Don't Have To Be* by Joann Magnus with Howard Bogot, p.14.

10 Complete some or all of the pages related to the Book of Genesis in *Torah Tales Copy Pak™: Genesis* by Marji Gold-Vukson.

Note: For other concluding strategies which can be adapted, see the Review Activities in this volume for the other books of the Torah.

שמות

Exodus

OVERVIEW

In Genesis 15:13, God tells Abraham, "Know well that your offspring shall be strangers in a land not theirs, and they shall be enslaved and oppressed four hundred years." The Book of Exodus begins with the realization of this prophecy.

Although historians differ as to the exact dates and nature of the sojourn and the enslavement of the Israelites in Egypt, few doubt that these events, and the subsequent Exodus, did occur.

Rabbi J.H. Hertz refers to the theory underlying this as "the inconvenience of biblical tradition." "What people," he asks, "would invent for itself so ignoble a past? A legend of such tenacity, representing the early fortunes of a people under so unfavorable an aspect, could not have arisen save as a reflection of real occurrences" (*The Pentateuch and Haftorahs,* pp. 396ff.).

Many commentators looked for the reason behind this first major exile in Jewish history. The traditional explanation has been to see it as punishment for sin — usually the sin of assimilation. Along this line, Nehama Leibowitz notes that Genesis 47:27 tells us that Israel "acquired holdings in [Egypt]" (*Studies in Shemot,* Part I, p. 1) — very different from staying in Egypt temporarily. Exodus 1:7 ("the land was filled with them") has even been interpreted as meaning that the amphitheaters and circuses were full of them.

Leibowitz notes, however, that the Torah supplies an educational motive for the exile and slavery, using numerous instances as the reason

behind the observance of the commandments: "You shall not wrong a stranger nor oppress him, for you were strangers in the land of Egypt" (Exodus 22:20).

Whatever the reason, it is certain that the collective experience of exile and slavery molded the diverse descendants of Jacob into a "people." Indeed, the Hebrew word *"am"* is used in reference to the Israelites for the first time in the Book of Exodus (1:9).

The Book of Exodus supplies the framework for this peoplehood. It contains the most significant historical memories of the Jewish people — our liturgy enjoins us frequently to remember the Exodus from Egypt. The tale of the enslavement and subsequent redemption of the Israelites constitutes the moral underpinning of much of Jewish tradition. Exodus presents the key legal and ethical rules of the Jewish religion in the Ten Commandments, and describes the establishment of one of the earliest forms of Jewish community worship in the Tabernacle, a form which was to become the basis of the Temple service.

The Book of Exodus was originally called *Sefer Yitziat Mitzraim* — "Book of the Going out from Egypt"— which is the sense of the title by which it is known in English. The name "Exodus" is derived from the earlier Greek name *"Exodos"* — The Departure. However, the Hebrew title of the book, *Shemot,* Names, comes from its first verse, wherein the "names" of the sons of Israel who went down into Egypt are given.

SHEMOT 1:1-6:1 שמות

SYNOPSIS

THE BOOK OF EXODUS BEGINS FOUR hundred years after the end of Genesis, by recounting that the descendants of Jacob flourished and multiplied in Egypt "and the land was filled with them." Then arises a new Pharaoh in Egypt who did not remember Joseph and he perceives the numerous Israelites as a potential threat. Therefore, the Egyptians enslave the Israelites, making life bitter for them. The Pharaoh instructs midwives to kill all male children born to Israelite women. When the midwives, fearing God, do not obey, Pharaoh orders all newborn boys drowned in the Nile River.

Now a certain couple of the house of Levi bear a son and hide him for three months. When the infant can no longer be hidden, his mother sets him afloat in the Nile River in a wicker basket. Miriam, the boy's sister, is stationed to watch what will become of him. The Pharaoh's daughter finds the infant and resolves to save him. Miriam arranges for her own mother to nurse and tend him.

When the child is grown, he is brought to the Pharaoh's daughter to live in the palace as her son. She names him Moses, meaning "drawn out" of the water. When Moses is grown, he kills an Egyptian taskmaster who was beating a Hebrew slave. He is forced to flee Egypt. He goes to Midian, where he becomes a shepherd, a husband, and a father.

One day, while Moses is tending his sheep, God appears to him in a burning bush. God instructs Moses that he is to lead the Israelites out of Egypt and into the land of Canaan. When Moses protests his inadequacy for the task, God gives him signs through which he is to convince the Israelites and Pharaoh. His brother Aaron is appointed to be his spokesperson. Moses and his wife Zipporah and his sons begin to journey back to Egypt. One night, God encounters him [it is unclear whether the text refers to Moses or his son]

and seeks to kill him. Zipporah quickly circumcises her son and God leaves him alone.

Moses and Aaron go to Pharaoh demanding, in the name of God, that the Israelites be permitted to leave Egypt to worship God in the wilderness, but the Pharaoh refuses to heed them. Instead, he increases the labor of the Israelites, refusing now to provide them with the straw they need to make bricks.

INSIGHTS FROM THE TRADITION

A The *midrash* tells us that the Israelites were tricked into slavery. Pharaoh's counselors suggest building fortified cities using both Israelites and Egyptians. Initially, all the workers were offered wages in proportion to the number of bricks each produced. Unbeknownst to the Israelites, their Egyptian co-workers were told to leave. Soon the Egyptians became taskmasters, the wages disappeared, and the enslavement came upon the Israelites.

Why do you think the Egyptians changed their attitude toward the Israelites?
Did the enslavement serve any positive purpose for the Israelites?
In what ways have you been "tricked" into doing something unpleasant?

B Even during the enslavement, the Hebrew population continued to increase. In order to hold down their numbers, Pharaoh ordered the midwives to kill all newborn Israelite males. Rashi identifies Shifrah as Jocheved and Puah as Miriam. According to the commentary *Yalkut Me'am Lo'ez* by Yaacov Culi, Vol. IV, p. 28, God made Pharaoh believe the explanation of the midwives, that they were not present at the births. Due to their actions God rewarded them. Jocheved became the mother of Moses; and the descendants of Miriam include Bezalel, the builder of the Tabernacle, and King David.

From the text, why did the midwives defy Pharaoh?

How do the midwives serve as models to the enslaved Israelite population in Egypt?

Is the action of the midwives a true example of civil disobedience? Explain.

What did the midwives risk in defying Pharaoh?

How is the action of the midwives like the behavior of some non-Jews in Germany during World War II?

What would you do in a situation if someone you feared required you to do something you consider wrong?

Why do the writers of the *midrash* think that an appropriate reward for a virtuous woman is to be the mother or ancestor of a great man? Do you agree that this is a reward to be wished for?

C *Exodus Rabbah* tells us that Pharaoh's daughter went down to the Nile to cleanse herself from idol worship. Other *midrashim* suggest that God sent a great heat upon Egypt at the time of Moses' birth. Seeking relief, Pharaoh's daughter went to bathe in the Nile. It was at this time that she discovered the infant whom she named Moses. Philo, a Jewish thinker and historian, explained her actions in light of her father's decree: she was Pharaoh's only child and thus much loved. She was also childless, and when she had the opportunity to become an adoptive mother, Pharaoh could not say no (*Legends of the Jews* by Louis Ginzberg, Vol. II, p. 266).

Pharaoh's daughter is childless, just like the Matriarchs of Genesis. Is this parallel just a coincidence, or do you think the Torah might be trying to tell us something about the importance of her role in Jewish history?

How does the saying "To save one life is as if one saved the whole world" apply to Pharaoh's daughter?

Are there certain kinds of requests that you make to which your parents never say no?

D According to Ibn Ezra, Moses was raised in Pharaoh's palace so that (1) he would be an educated individual and not feel oppressed as one raised as a slave, and (2) he would be looked upon as someone set apart and thus able to gain the respect of the Israelites to lead them.

The biblical text provides very little information about Moses. Do you think there is a reason for such sketchy details about Moses' early life?

Moses is not one of the Patriarchs, nor are we to consider him on that level. How does the biblical narrative encourage this attitude? Does one have to be from a wealthy family, or a particular ethnic or religious group in order to become a leader?

E Moses alludes to the fact that he is slow of speech and slow of tongue. A *midrash* explains that, as a child, Moses grabbed Pharaoh's crown and placed it upon his own head. Concerned that this was a sign that Moses would one day replace Pharaoh, a test was arranged. A bright jewel and a hot coal were placed before Moses. Choosing the jewel would mean that Moses was a threat and must be put to death. Moses reached for the jewel, but an angel pushed his hand toward the coal. However, when Moses grabbed the coal, it burned his hand and he stuck his burning hand in his mouth. Thus, his lips and tongue were burned and his speech was affected (*Legends of the Jews* by Louis Ginzberg, Vol. II, pp. 272-274; or in *The Book of Legends: Sefer Ha-aggadah*, edited by Hayim Bialik and Yehoshua Ravnitzky, p. 60:19).

Do you believe in signs or omens that indicate the future?

Have any signs proven to be true for you? Explain.

Wouldn't it have been much easier had God simply performed a "miracle" and had the Israelites released?

When a task is too difficult, we give up. When a task is too simple, we don't appreciate the results. How does this maxim apply to the struggle to free the Israelites from bondage?

How is this saying reflected in your life?

F The humility of Moses has long been viewed as a valuable and important quality; however, there are some situations that demand self-confidence. The Torah commentary *Sparks Beneath the Surface* by Lawrence S. Kushner and Kerry M. Olitzky suggests that God's promise to Moses of a divine sign was given in order to build up Moses' confidence for the task that he was about to undertake. Moses' knowledge that God would be with him throughout the trials in Egypt would bolster his self-esteem at critical moments.

If God is with Moses, why does he need self-confidence?
Are self-confidence and humility conflicting qualities? How can you cultivate both of them? What are some situations in which you are better served by confidence than humility?

STRATEGIES

ANALYZING THE TEXT

1 The Book of Exodus picks up the tale of the Israelites some four hundred years after the events with which Genesis was concluded. Can you recall those events? To review, set up teams and outline how the Israelites came to Egypt. Begin with the story of Joseph and his brothers. The teams can take turns, each advancing the story one detail at a time. Give one point for each correct statement. When a gap in the sequence is detected, deduct five points from the team that made the omission.

2 The name of this portion is *Shemot* (Names). Read through the portion and list the names of all the people you can find. Can you identify all these people? Imagine you are a playwright beginning to write a play based on this portion. Write up a formal list of the cast of characters such as you would find in an actual script, giving a brief description of each character.

3 Compare Moses' first encounter with God (Exodus 3) with the first meetings of other prophets with God. Read Isaiah 6 and Jeremiah 1. What do all of these accounts have in common? What common characteristics do all three prophets share? Do you think these are essential qualities for a prophet? Why? Why not?

4 Acquaint yourself with some of the key Hebrew words which will be repeated throughout the next few portions of the Torah. How many times can you find the following words in *Shemot* – מצרים, מדבר, פרעה, אהרן, משה? Now how many words can you find with the root עבד? Write a brief summary of the portion with all of these Hebrew words as the focus.

5 Cite specific differences between the narrative treatment of Moses and that of the Patriarchs.

6 Read the *midrash* explaining Moses' slowness of speech in Insight E above, page 88. Why should Moses, of all people, suffer from a speech impediment? Is there a lesson for us here? Can you suggest other interpretations for the expression "slow of speech and slow of tongue?"

7 Following God's command, Moses and his family set out for Egypt. During the journey, a curious incident occurs (4:24-16). Though the commentaries differ somewhat, the issue appears to be that Moses had failed to circumcise his son Eleazar. Moses is nearly killed, but his wife Zipporah performs the circumcision and thus saves Moses. What might the circumcision incident signify? Why do you think it might be especially significant at this place in the text?

8 It is in this portion that we witness the essential struggle of the Exodus. Pharaoh recognizes only himself as a divine being. In his world, there simply isn't room for competitors. He does not see God as being able to affect him or his policies. What does Moses' struggle with Pharaoh accomplish? Does it still affect Jewish thought to this day? If so, in what ways?

9 This portion contains an unusually rich and diverse collection of active women. To illustrate and explore this, create a portrait gallery of the women in *Shemot*. Draw or create staged photographic portraits of the female characters. Beside each one, mount a fact sheet listing important biographical information — name, age at time of your portrait, personal background, best known for, personal motto, etc. Display your portrait gallery on a bulletin board or in a school hallway.

EXTENDING THE TEXT

10 It is interesting that despite the conspicuous role played by Aaron in the events of the Exodus, there is comparatively little *midrashic* and/or historical material about him. Using a variety of resources including the Book of Exodus, put together a biography of this remarkable man.

11 There is a tradition that ten things were created just before the first Shabbat (see *Pirke Avot* 5:8). These items, according to the Rabbis, came to play wondrous parts at specific times in Jewish history. Moses' staff was one such wondrous object. It became a snake in order to convince Pharaoh of God's great power. Come up with your own list of ten things from this portion or other parts of the Torah which God might have made just before the first Shabbat and which miraculously affected Jewish history.

12 Retell the events detailed in *Shemot* from another point of view. How would the members of Moses' family describe their slavery and the return of Moses to lead the people to freedom? What would be the view of Moses' father-in-law or his wife, both non-Hebrews? How would

Moses' foster mother, the princess of Egypt, have interpreted these events?

13 The purpose of many *midrashim* is to explain why events or conditions in the text are as they are. There is an abundance of such *midrashim* which relate to this portion. Review some of them (see *Legends of the Jews* by Louis Ginzberg, Vols. II and III; *Messengers of God* by Elie Wiesel; *The Book of Legends: Sefer Ha-aggadah*, edited by Hayim Bialik and Yehoshua Ravnitzky) and then study the portion to find the point at which they interface with the text. For example, the *midrash* in which Pharaoh offers Moses a choice between hot coals and royal jewels serves as one explanation of how Moses became "slow of speech and slow of tongue" (Exodus 4:10).

14 The text gives very few details about Moses' childhood and young adulthood. Yet, we must assume that he developed special qualities and characteristics which led him to be God's chosen leader. Write a *midrash* describing an incident in Moses' childhood which reveals certain of these qualities.

15 The bush which burns but is not consumed is a powerful image which has been interpreted in many ways (see, for example, *Legends of the Jews* by Louis Ginzberg, Vol. II, pp. 303-4 and *The Book of Legends: Sefer Ha-aggadah*, edited by Hayim Bialik and Yehoshua Ravnitzky, pp. 62:28-63:31 and p. 504:12). Using this image, try to come up with some analogies. You might want to think along these lines: How is the people of Israel like a burning bush? How is the word of God like a burning bush? How is the lesson of the Exodus like a burning bush? (For a follow-up activity, see Strategy #21 below, page 91.)

16 If one reads the Torah carefully, the language used in various portions recalls similar expressions in other portions. Where similar language is used, we can draw on our knowledge of those other portions to help expand our understanding of the portion at hand. *Shemot* contains several such Hebrew words or phrases:

a. The word תבה (ark) occurs in only two sections of the Torah — here (Exodus 2:3) and in the Noah story (Genesis 6:14ff.). What parallels can you draw between Noah and Moses? What parallels do you see between Noah's ark and the "ark" in which the baby Moses was placed?

b. At his birth, Moses' mother sees כי טוב הוא — "that he was good" (Exodus 2:2). A similar expression is used in Genesis 1:3 — God saw that the light "was good" — כי טוב. Rashi interprets this: "When Moses was born, the whole house became filled with light." What other interpretations can you supply?

c. Review Genesis 22 and I Samuel 3 to look for a word and a theme which connect the leadership qualities of Abraham and Samuel to those of Moses in Exodus 3. What parallels do you see? Why do you think readiness, exemplified in the use of the word *"hineni,"* is important for a leader?

17 In reading *Shemot,* it might appear that the Israelites had forgotten God. The text doesn't say that the people cried to God, but rather, "their cry . . . rose up to God" (Exodus 2:23). Later in the portion, Moses says that the people will ask him God's name. If the people *had* forgotten about God, why were they remembered by God?

18 There are several instances, in this portion, of reluctance on Moses' part. He feels inadequate to the task which God commands him to perform. Compare Moses' initial reply to God with that of Abraham in Genesis 22:1. Both men were called to a task. What impact did these respective events have on them? What was Abraham called to do? What was Moses called to do? What kinds of sacrifices would each have to make?

PERSONALIZING THE TEXT

19 Proverbs 22:1 states: "A good name is rather to be chosen than great riches." In a reference work of names, look up the meanings of the names you found in the text. Which would you choose for yourself and why? You may have to "invent" feminine versions of the names you found.
Reference: *The Complete Dictionary of English and Hebrew First Names* by Alfred J. Kolatch.

20 The phrase "Let my people go" (Exodus 5:1) makes its first appearance in *Shemot*. This expression has become the slogan for a variety of social causes. Brainstorm a list of historic and contemporary causes for which this phrase would make a good rallying cry. Create a poster which illustrates one such cause and uses the slogan "Let my people go!"

21 Summarize your interpretation of the burning bush (see Strategy #15 above, page 90) in one brief sentence, and design an art project which represents the bush in a form appropriate to your understanding. Some ideas you might want to consider — a collage, stained glass real or tissue paper technique, or "found" objects.

22 *Shemot* tells in passing about the heroic acts of a variety of women: the midwives, the mother and sister of Moses, and the Pharaoh's daughter. These characters are among the "unsung heroes" of the Exodus. Listen to the song "The Righteous Midwives" on the tape *Bible People Songs* and then write songs of your own using melodies you know to praise any of these heroic women.

23 What other great "exoduses" have there been in Jewish history? What elements do these experiences have in common with the Exodus from Egypt (e.g., assimilation, oppression, journey to a "Promised Land")? Choose one such exodus and write a brief first person account of the experience using metaphors of the Exodus from Egypt.

24 In many ways, Hitler was like Pharaoh. Compare what you know about Hitler to Pharaoh. Compare Pharaoh to other tyrants, such as Haman.

25 Create a list of 15 things you enjoy doing. Which of these would you still be able to do if you were a slave?

OTHER RESOURCES

26 Read, act out, and discuss the skit for *Shemot* in *Sedra Scenes: Skits for Every Torah Portion* by Stan J. Beiner, pp. 74-80.

27 Complete the pages which relate to *Shemot* in *Bible People Book Two* by Joel Lurie Grishaver, pp. 6-13. Also check the accompanying Leader Guide for procedures and additional activities.

28 Read and discuss the story "Moses and the Lost Lamb" in *Stories from our Living Past* by Francine Prose, pp. 76-79.

29 View and discuss the episode for *Shemot* from *Torah Toons I: The Video*.

30 For creative movement activities, see "A New Pharaoh Deals Harshly," "The Burning Bush," "Moses Stands on Holy Ground," and "Let My People Go" from *Torah in Motion* by JoAnne Tucker and Susan Freeman, pp. 68-75.

31 Listen to, discuss, and sing "Here I Am" from *Sounds of Freedom: Exodus in Song*.

32 Read and discuss the illustrated commentary from *Shemot* in *American Torah Toons* by Lawrence Bush.

33 Read and discuss the story "Bityah, Daughter of God" in *But God Remembered: Stories of Jewish Women from Creation to the Promised Land* by Sandy Eisenberg Sasso. In her story, Sasso gives Pharaoh's daughter two names — an Egyptian name and a Hebrew one.

34 Read and discuss "The Strange Story of 'Eema' and Pharaoh's Daughter" in *Mitzvahs* by Danny Siegel, p. 60.

35 Follow the directions in *An Artist You Don't Have to Be* by Joann Magnus with Howard Bogot, to create a "Moses Umbrella Puppet," p. 1.

INVOLVING THE FAMILY

36 In Genesis, there are many stories about conflicts between siblings (e.g., Cain and Abel, Jacob and Esau, Joseph and his brothers). In contrast, in the first portion of Exodus, we read about brothers and sisters cooperating — first, to save the life of the youngest, Moses, and later, to bring about the Exodus. Which pattern is more common in your family, conflict or cooperation? Together with your family, recall a time when you had a serious conflict with a brother or sister. Try telling about it from the point of view of the brother or sister. Imagine you are one of your parents watching the conflict develop. Suggest solutions. Now recall a happy time when you and a brother or sister cooperated. Tell about how your parents might have felt watching their children work together. Conclude by having each family member place himself/herself on the values continuum below. Then think of ways to move each of you toward the ideal position.

Carla Conflict   Carl Cooperation

BAR/BAT MITZVAH ACTIVITY

37 In past decades, Moses' words "Let my people go!" became the rallying cry for the campaign to free Soviet Jewry. Today, the Jews who remain in the former Soviet Union (FSU) struggle to provide the ways and means for their children to get a Jewish education. As a *mitzvah* project, collect and purchase new school supplies to be sent to the FSU. Supplies to consider: pens, pencils, markers, chalk, crayons, paper clips, and construction paper. Speak with your Rabbi or educator to find out if your congregation is twinned with a congregation in the FSU or contact one of the following:

1. World Union Task Force on Soviet Jewry, 838 Fifth Avenue, New York, NY 10021.
2. Bay Area Council for Jewish Rescue and Renewal, 106 Baden Street, San Francisco, CA 94131.
3. A local agency in your community which works with Jews in the FSU.

These organizations may also suggest additional projects you can work on and offer suggestions on what, where, and how to send supplies.

VAERA 6:2-9:35 וארא

SYNOPSIS

THIS PORTION BEGINS WITH GOD reviewing the covenant with Abraham, Isaac, and Jacob. "I have heard the cries of the Israelites," God says, "and I will now fulfill my promise to them, redeeming them from slavery and bringing them into the land which I promised to their ancestors" (6:5).

When Moses tells all this to the Israelites, they will not listen. So Moses appeals to God, claiming that if the Israelites will not heed him, how can he hope to convince Pharaoh? God tells Moses that Aaron will be the spokesperson before Pharaoh, and that though God's signs and wonders will be many, Pharaoh will, in the beginning, refuse to give in. This is because God is going to harden Pharaoh's heart.

When Pharaoh does refuse to allow the Israelites to journey into the wilderness to worship God, the plagues of blood and frogs occur. However, the magicians of Pharaoh duplicate these occurrences. When the third plague, lice, afflicts the land, the magicians become fearful and tell Pharaoh that this act is the finger of God. But it is only with the fourth plague, swarms of insects, that Pharaoh begins to show signs of softening, offering to allow the Israelites to worship God *within* the land of Egypt. Once the plague abates, however, Pharaoh changes his mind, and the fifth, sixth, and seventh plagues (cattle disease, boils, and hail) follow in swift succession.

INSIGHTS FROM THE TRADITION

A *Vaera* means "I appeared." This is the word with which God's self-revelation to Moses begins (Exodus 6:3).

What is the first thing you usually tell someone about yourself — what you do, who your parents are, where you live, etc.?

What do you not want others to know about you right away?

B The passages which open this portion pose a technical problem to the student of Torah. In 6:3 God says to Moses, "I appeared to Abraham, Isaac, and Jacob as *El Shaddai,* but I did not make myself known to them by my name YHVH." A careful reading of Genesis, however, reveals that God did indeed use this name with Abram (Genesis 15:7) and Jacob (Genesis 28:13). Whether or not we hold with certain biblical scholars who believe that these passages derive from different times and/or authors of the Torah (see notes in *The Torah: A Modern Commentary,* edited by W. Gunther Plaut, p. 424), we must still wonder about the contradiction.

As we saw in the book of Genesis, a name change often reflects an event experienced by an individual. For example, Abram to Abraham, Sarai to Sarah, Jacob to Israel. Everett Fox explains that this act is extremely important in the biblical world. A person's name reflected one's personality and fate. Getting a new name meant a new life or a new stage in life (*The Five Books of Moses,* p.70).

Perhaps the revelation of God's explicit name (YHVH) to Moses and all the Israelites marks a new life and future — not in this case for God, but for all Israelites.

Do you think God did not use this name with the Patriarchs because the generation of the Patriarchs was not ready for the fulfillment of the promises made by God?

Do you think that God has made other promises which have not yet been fulfilled? What about the messianic era? What role does humanity play regarding the time of the Messiah?

C Moses and the Israelites are to see that God remembers the covenant and *keeps* all promises. God uses four phrases regarding the coming redemption: I will free you (*v'hotzayti*), I will deliver you (*v'hitzalti*), I will redeem you (*v'ga'alti*), and I will take you (*v'lakachti*) to be my people (6:6-7).

These phrases parallel the four decrees which Pharaoh issued against the Israelites: They were forced to build Pithom and Ramses, their lives were made bitter by harsh labor, Israelite male infants were to be drowned, and no straw was provided for the bricks (1:11- 22). God was indicating that the Israelites would be rescued from all four decrees (*Yalkut Me'am Lo'ez* by Yaacov Culi, Vol. IV, p. 162).

In life, does it seem that evil wins out over good or vice versa?
Does more good than bad happen in the world? to you?

D Initially, the Israelites welcomed Moses and Aaron, but on their second visit, they are rebuffed. The conditions of slavery had worsened due to Moses' request to let the people go worship in the wilderness. Moses now tells God he feels inadequate for the task. Although there is no divine response in the biblical text, a *midrash* has God speaking to Moses and Aaron: "My children are obstinate, bad tempered, and troublesome. In assuming leadership over them, you must expect that they will curse you and even stone you" (*Exodus Rabbah* 7:3).

Why wouldn't the Israelites listen to Moses?
Should Moses and Aaron have dealt in a special way with the Israelites?
Could Moses have done a better job with Pharaoh? When have you witnessed bad temper or troubled behavior? What might cause people to behave in this way? How did others react? Was the situation resolved? How?

E The plagues pose a problem because they seem to go against the natural order of the universe. Some commentators stress the educational or legendary value of this story, and ignore the question of historicity. The release of the slaves and the subsequent triumphs of the Israelites were in themselves events so unprecedented that they may have been perceived and thus embroidered as miraculous. (For more, see the Index: "Ten Things Made before Creation.")

In Exodus 12:12, God says, ". . . I will mete out punishments to all the gods of Egypt." Thus, the plagues are symbolic of the defeat of the various gods worshiped by the Egyptians. The frogs, a very ancient Egyptian symbol of fruitfulness, and the insects, symbols of rebirth, particularly the dung-beetle or scarab, became themselves a plague on the land. The sacred bull, considered to be the god Apis, and the sacred ram, the god Amon were devastated by the fifth plague, cattle disease, and finally Ra, the supreme sun god, was defeated by the plague of darkness.

Do you think the plagues were only for the Egyptians? What might the Israelites have gained by witnessing these events?
How does this account affect your understanding of Jewish history?

STRATEGIES

ANALYZING THE TEXT

1 In *Vaera,* the family background of Moses and Aaron is traced back to the sons of Jacob (Exodus 6:14-25). Draw a family tree for Moses and Aaron based on the information given in these verses of the Bible. Add in any additional information which you may be able to derive from *Shemot.*

2 Make a list of the attributes of God based on God's words and actions in this portion.

3 Organize a *Scavenger Hunt* of the portion *Vaera.* Working in two (or more) teams, come up with a list of fifteen questions that can be answered after a careful reading of the story. For example: What is the relationship of Amram to Yocheved? What was the age of Moses at the onset of the plagues? Trade lists with the other team(s) and have a timed race to answer the questions.

4 Conduct a Hebrew version of the preceding *Scavenger Hunt*. Conclude the activity by creating a Hebrew crossword puzzle using the questions and one word answers you found.

5 Consider the Torah as a piece of literature. Are the portions *Vaera* and *Bo* divided at a reasonable place? Imagine you are a book editor. Read both portions and suggest a new way of dividing the text into "chapters." Be prepared to defend your ideas to the Editor in chief.

6 Moses repeatedly states his inability to carry out the task given him by God. Did he really lack self-confidence or was he just being modest? Write a job description for the position Moses was to take. Create a help wanted ad. Two people play Moses and a job recruiter. The job recruiter seeks to assure Moses he has the background, skills, and education for this position.

EXTENDING THE TEXT

7 The custom of drinking four cups of wine during the Passover *Seder* is derived from the phrases in Exodus 6:6-8:
I will free you . . .
I will deliver you . . .
I will redeem you . . .
I will take you . . .
I will bring you . . .

To make sure you understand the promise each verb introduces, write out the complete sentences in which these phrases occur. Rank the five promises in order of their importance to the future of the Jewish people at the time of the Exodus. When the Rabbis compiled the *Haggadah,* which of the five promises had not been fulfilled? (Answer: The fifth.) How is this handled in the *Haggadah?* (Clue: We drink only four cups of wine — where

is the fifth? Answer: It is the cup of Elijah.) What special words were added to the *Seder* to show that we hope that the fifth promise will be fulfilled? ("Next year in Jerusalem.") How have these words been changed in recent years, and why? (They have been amended since the birth of the State of Israel to read "Next Year in the rebuilt Jerusalem.") References: *A Feast of History: Passover through the Ages as a Key To Jewish Experience* by Chaim Raphael; *The Passover Anthology* by Phillip Goodman.

8 In the *Amidah* prayer, we refer to God as "our God and God of our fathers, God of Abraham, God of Isaac, and God of Jacob . . ." Martin Buber has noted that by saying the above and not "God of Abraham, Isaac, and Jacob . . . we indicate that Isaac and Jacob did not merely take over the tradition of Abraham; they themselves searched anew for God" (*Likrat Shabbat,* edited by Sidney Greenberg and D. Levine, p. 106). Since Jewish tradition has always regarded Moses as the greatest of prophets, the man most intimate with God, why is Moses not considered one of the Patriarchs and included in this prayer? Why is his name mentioned only once in the *Haggadah?* "Interview" Moses to determine *his* feelings about this.

9 As an extension to Strategy #8 above, consider that in many contemporary prayer books, the names of the Matriarchs are now included in the *Amidah.* For centuries this was not even considered. Also "interview" Sarah, Rebecca, Rachel, and Leah to see how they felt about being excluded. You might also include Miriam.

10 Many events in the Book of Exodus defy rational explanation. Is it always necessary for things to have a scientifically correct and logically understandable explanation? What would be the effect on our religious beliefs if every aspect of our history and faith was rationally provable? What if nothing was provable or even rational?

11 Why was it necessary for the Israelites to journey into the "wilderness" to worship God? Explore the answer to this question in the following ways:

a. Name a place where you might feel uncomfortable praying. Name a place where you might feel good praying. Explain the differences between the two places. How do you feel when you go out into the wilderness? How does the wilderness make you feel about God?

b. The Rabbis found it very significant that the Israelites not only wanted to worship God in the wilderness, but that the Torah was given there as well. Look at some *midrashim* which comment on this (from *The Torah: A Modern Commentary*, edited by W. Gunther Plaut, see "Into the Wilderness," pp. 443-4 and "In a Public Place," p. 529). Then make up your own *midrashim* to explain the reasons for the journey into the wilderness.

12 In *Vaera*, Moses is told God's personal name, signified in English by the letters YHVH. This name is known as the Tegragrammaton (the four letters). Among ancient peoples, it was believed that knowing the name of someone gave you a certain special understanding of or power over that someone.

a. The name YHVH has been translated as "I will be what I will be," "I am what I am," or sometimes simply as "I am." It has also been interpreted as meaning "keeping faith." What understanding do you gain about God by knowing this name? How would knowledge of this name help Moses in the task facing him? How would this name reassure the Israelites?

b. Do you think that *your* name reveals anything about you? Design the letters of your name so that they reveal some information about you, such as something about your family, a belief you value, some powers you have, or an important experience you have had.

13 In the text, we read about the effect of the plagues upon the Egyptians. The text does not tell us how the Israelites responded to these disasters. Imagine what their reactions to the plagues might have been like. In pairs have a conversation with another "Israelite." Share and discuss your responses.

14 View the film *A Woman Called Moses* (not rated, available as a video rental), which tells the story of Harriet Tubman, a freed African-American slave who helped lead other slaves to freedom. Questions to consider: What qualifications did Harriet Tubman have to take on this task? Did she feel "called" to do this work? How was she like Moses?

PERSONALIZING THE TEXT

15 According to Plaut, the Pharaoh remains "an intelligible human being, acting as one would expect a man of his tradition and position to act" (*The Torah: A Modern Commentary*, edited by W. Gunther Plaut, p. 454). Bearing this in mind, write diary entries as if you were Pharaoh describing your actions and feelings during the period of the plagues.

16 Imagine you are an Egyptian living at the time of the events detailed in the beginning of the Book of Exodus. Compose a telegram to the Pharaoh, briefly advising him on a course of action to take.

17 Illustrate a section of *Vaera* in the style of Egyptian art. Begin by exploring some books about ancient Egypt which describe the characteristics, and show examples of, this type of art. Egyptian art looks flat and one-dimensional. It is also interesting to see that the figure of Pharaoh is always portrayed larger than the figures of others. There is also a lack of perspective in the work, which means there isn't both a background and a foreground. The work is usually all in the foreground. The art work you create might take the form of carved relief or drawings. Media to consider using in carved relieve includes: copper or foil tooling, carving lines into Styrofoam pans or into wet clay. Another medium to use would be simple pen and ink line drawings with paint or marker added in using the colors you see depicted in the examples you find. Much Egyptian art has been found on clay pots and vessels. Often these paintings told a story or related information. Try to include this in your work. Consider using a flower pot or other pre-made clay container for your drawings. The clay surface will have to be sealed with a primer before it can be painted. Check with a craft or hobby store for suggestions. References: *Wanderings: Chaim Potok's History of the Jews* by Chaim Potok; *Bible Lands: Eyewitness Books* by Jonathan N. Tubb.

18 The enslavement, treatment, and eventual freedom of the children of Israel are very important parts of the Jewish experience. This makes it difficult to learn that there were Jews involved in the eighteenth and nineteenth century slave trade in the United States. There were also some Jews who actively opposed slavery and, as a result, faced unhappy consequences. Find and read some of the original documents on this subject. Then complete the following sentences: I was surprised to learn that _____, I felt ashamed when I read that _____, I felt proud to learn that _____.

Reference: *American Jewry and the Civil War* by Bertram W. Korn. For additional information on this subject contact: American Jewish Archives, 3101 Clifton Avenue, Cincinnati, OH 45220-2488. Requests need to be specific and are preferred through the mail, or e-mail them at aja@fuse.net. Also see their web page at http://home.fuse.net/aja to find out more about the American Jewish Archives and how to access information.

19 Make a list of the Ten Plagues as detailed in portions *Vaera* and *Bo*. Look at your list. Do you agree that each plague is increasingly more severe than the preceding plague? If *you* were delivering the plagues to the Egyptians, in what order would you send them? Which order would be most devastating for the land? Which would be most frightening to the people? What would be the reaction today if such a series of plagues would occur? Write a science fiction story using this idea.

20 Reread Insight B, page 94, and discuss the following: Do you have a Hebrew name? Is that a name you use all of the time or is it a name that you are generally "not known by?" Is it a name you use only in a Jewish setting (for example, in Hebrew School or during ritual occasions such as a Bar/Bat Mitzvah)? Does your Hebrew name reveal another side of you? Look up the meaning of your Hebrew name. Does the translation have any special meaning for you? How?

OTHER RESOURCES

21 Complete the pages which relate to *Vaera* in *Bible People Book Two* by Joel Lurie Grishaver, pp. 14-17. Also check the accompanying Leader Guide for procedures and additional activities.

22 Listen to and/or learn the song "The Ten Plagues" from *Bible People Songs*.

23 Read, act out, and discuss the skit for the portion *Vaera* in *Sedra Scenes: Skits for Every Torah Portion* by Stan J. Beiner, pp. 81-84.

24 View and discuss the episode for *Vaera* from *Torah Toons I: The Video*.

25 For creative movement activities see "Moses' Impediment," and "Frogs Everywhere" from *Torah in Motion* by JoAnne Tucker and Susan Freeman, pp. 76-79.

26 Listen to, discuss, and sing "The Promise" from *Sounds of Freedom: Exodus in Song*.

27 Read and discuss the illustrated commentary for *Va-Era* in *American Torah Toons* by Lawrence Bush.

INVOLVING THE FAMILY

28 The plagues God brought upon the Egyptians threatened to destroy Egyptian society. Today, we are faced with many "plagues" which make our world less secure. Some recent *Haggadot* have new readings that remind us of this fact (see *A Passover Haggadah,* edited by Herbert Bronstein, p. 49). Write your own reading about contemporary plagues to be included in your *Seder* following the section dealing with the Ten Plagues. Note: The Ten Plagues are not all detailed in *Vaera*.

The next portion, *Bo* recounts the eighth, ninth, and tenth plagues. See portion *Bo* for additional insights and strategies on the plagues.

BAR/BAT MITZVAH ACTIVITY

29 As we can see in this portion, becoming a spokesperson is challenging. Moses feels inadequate for the task and appeals to God. God announces that Aaron will now be the spokesperson. Perhaps Aaron was naturally gifted and could easily accomplish this task. For many of us, however, we have to develop skills and confidence in order to function as a spokesperson. There are many resources to help in this process. One of them is specifically for kids, and it is called *The Kid's Guide to Social Action* by Barbara A. Lewis. Use this Guide to help you create and implement a plan of action for a social or environmental cause you wish to work on.

Additional Resources: *Mitzvahs* by Danny Siegel; *It's a Mitzvah!* by Bradley Shavit Artson; *Teaching Mitzvot* by Barbara Binder Kadden and Bruce Kadden.

BO 10:1-13:16 בא

SYNOPSIS

MOSES AND AARON REBUKE PHARAOH for refusing to allow the Israelites to go and worship God. Although Pharaoh's courtiers plead with him to obey God in order to save Egypt, the Pharaoh ignores their advice, and locusts, the eighth plague, come to destroy those parts of Egypt left unharmed by the hail. The plague is lifted when Pharaoh pleads with Moses and Aaron, but God once again hardens Pharaoh's heart and the Israelites are not freed. Then the plague of darkness falls without warning — only the Israelites have light where they live.

God tells Moses that the next plague will be the last and Moses warns Pharaoh that God will triumph with the slaying of all the firstborn of Egypt.

Prior to the occurrence of the tenth plague, Moses and Aaron instruct the Israelites in the laws of Passover. On the tenth day of the first month, the people are to slaughter a lamb, smear its blood on their doorposts, and eat its roasted flesh hurriedly in remembrance of the tenth plague and their hasty Exodus from Egypt. In the future, this festival is to be a time of remembrance for the Israelites. For seven days, they are to eat only unleavened bread. Further, the people are commanded to explain these observances to their children so that the festival will be a reminder to all generations that God freed the Israelites from Egypt.

The Israelites apply lamb's blood to their doorposts as they were instructed by Moses. In the middle of the night, all the firstborn in the land of Egypt are struck down. The Pharaoh summons Moses and Aaron and bids them to depart with the Israelites. Because of their haste in leaving Egypt, the people take their dough with them before it is risen. They also take spoils from the Egyptians. The portion concludes with the note that the Israelites had lived in Egypt for 430 years and at the time of the Exodus, some 600,000 departed from Egypt plus children, livestock, and a mixed multitude of others.

INSIGHTS FROM THE TRADITION

A The name of this portion, *Bo*, comes from God's instruction to Moses to "go" once again to Pharaoh and deliver the warning of the eighth plague, locusts.

B Even before Moses returns to Egypt, God tells him, "I will stiffen [Pharaoh's] heart so that he will not let the people go" (Exodus 4:20). However, the text states, in relation to the early plagues, it was Pharaoh who hardened his own heart (Exodus 7:13, 22; 8:11, 15, 28; 9:7). After each of the later plagues, it was God who stiffened Pharaoh's will (9:12, 10:16-20, 11:1). The Rabbis were troubled by this seeming divine interference with Pharaoh's free will. If God is responsible for hardening Pharaoh's heart, they asked, how can Pharaoh be held accountable for his acts?

There are a variety of answers. Looking at this from a literary standpoint, some have held that Pharaoh's refusal to free the slaves as the plagues got progressively worse seems so abnormal that the text can explain it only as an act of God. Another literary view points out that the intent of the story is to demonstrate the supremacy of God. Therefore, God uses Pharaoh, too, as a device to increase the glory God would receive.

Rambam's interpretation however, sticks more closely to the sense of the text: "It may sometimes happen that man's offense is so grave that he is penalized by not being granted the opportunity to turn from his wickedness, so that he dies with the sin he committed . . . [Pharaoh] sinned, first of his own free will . . . until he forfeited the opportunity to repent" (*Yad, Teshuva* 6:3).

From *Yalkut Me'am Lo'ez* by Yaacov Culi we learn that in a number of instances, repentance is very difficult (Vol. V, p. 3):

1. When a person has committed many serious sins.
2. When a sin has been purposely repeated many times.
3. When one wishes to repent, but stubbornly refuses to.
4. When one sins against another human being.

Is Pharaoh's resistance logical to you?
Have you ever had an argument with a friend or a sibling and, even though you wanted to make up, you found it very difficult?
What causes a person to be stubborn?
What causes you to be stubborn?

C The plagues are unleashed upon the Egyptians to encourage Pharaoh, and perhaps his people, to change his/their attitude and behavior towards the Israelites. Yet despite the suffering the plagues produced, the Torah tells us that Pharaoh hardened his heart. Although we often find this reaction hard to understand, one approach (see Stuart Kelman, writing about *Bo* in *Learn Torah With . . .* , pp. 113-117) suggests that we consider how we respond to our contemporary plagues such as cancer, AIDS, pollution to mention just a few examples. Sometimes we, as individuals or communities, harden our hearts and refuse to respond. Sometimes we feel despair and say "but what can we do?" And perhaps our lack of appropriate reaction may lead us to a point where it is too late to alter the course of events.

What are some plagues of contemporary society which trouble you? How do you respond to them?

D The names of the holiday which commemorate the Exodus are derived from this portion. The festival which came to be known as Pesach is called in Exodus 12:17 the Feast of Unleavened Bread. The English name, Passover, is seen as a play on the Hebrew word used in Exodus 12:23 to describe how God would "pass over" the blood smeared doors of the Israelites. However, the word is first used in Exodus 12:11 to describe the paschal lamb — the Passover offering given to God. In that verse, the word has the sense of "to protect or to spare." The most concise explanation of the word Pesach and its connection to the Passover offering is attributed to Rabban Gamliel in the *Haggadah:*
"The Passover offering which our fathers ate in Temple days, what was the reason for it? It was because the Holy One of Blessing, passed over the houses of our forefathers in Egypt . . . " (*Passover Haggadah,* New Revised Edition by Nathan Goldberg, p. 21).

What elements do Passover and Chanukah have in common?
In what ways can Pharaoh be compared with Antiochus IV?
Would you have preferred to live during the days of the Exodus or of the Maccabees? Explain.

E The Israelites were commanded to place blood on the doorposts of their houses. *Yalkut Me'am Lo'ez* by Yaacov Culi (Vol. V, p. 72) points out that even if a Hebrew was in the home of an Egyptian, the Hebrew would be safe. On the contrary, an Egyptian in a Hebrew home would not be safe. The purpose of the blood was as a sign for the Hebrews.

What do you think this sign signified to the people in those days?
What lessons were the Israelites to derive from this last terrible plague?
What do you do to remind yourself that you are unique and special?

F There are differing opinions concerning Israel's behavior in Egypt: (1) The Israelites adopted Egyptian idol worship and deserved punishment, but a merciful God liberated them (*Yalkut Me'am Lo'ez* by Yaacov Culi, Vol. IV, p. 208); (2) Israel remained faithful, they did not change their names or their language, they did not participate in talebearing, and they did not commit adultery (*MeKilta de-Rabbi Ishmael,* Vol. I, p. 34).

After 430 years in Egypt, what do you think might have happened to the traditional beliefs of the Hebrews?

Do you consider yourself more closely identified with the country of origin of your relatives or with the country in which you are a citizen?

G In Exodus 12:8, the idea of *matzah* is introduced with no explanation other than that the Israelites are to eat it. Verse 12:34 then states that the Israelites left Egypt in haste before the dough had a chance to rise. In Deuteronomy 16:3, *matzah* is referred to as *lechem oni,* the bread of affliction. According to Jewish law, leavened foods are forbidden on all the days of Passover, but the commandment to eat *matzah* applied only to the first night. At the *Seder,* one must eat some *matzah.*

Nearly every Jewish holiday is associated with certain foods. With which holiday foods are you familiar?

Why do you think those foods became linked to those holidays?

Does your favorite food belong to your favorite holiday?

H A section of this portion, Exodus 12:1-20, is read in addition to the regular reading, on Shabbat HaChodesh, the last of four special Shabbatot in the spring. Shabbat HaChodesh precedes or falls on Rosh Chodesh Nisan, the month in which Passover is celebrated. Therefore, this section, which deals with the Passover observance, is particularly timely. (For more about the statement in Exodus 12:2 "This month shall mark for you the beginning of months," see Strategy #8, page 103.)

The secular year begins in the winter (January 1); the Jewish calendar begins in the Spring (1 Nisan); the Jewish spiritual new year is in the fall (1 Tishre). How do the seasons influence the attitude we bring to each of these celebrations? How do the seasons influence your attitudes and moods?

STRATEGIES

ANALYZING THE TEXT

1 Scholars have tried to analyze the plagues and to group them according to which are alike, or according to a pattern. Study the plagues in detail (include those in the previous portion, *Vaera*) to see if you can come to a greater understanding of these events. Answer the following questions (making up some more of your own) and arrange your answers in chart form so that you can compare and group the plagues:

Which plagues come without warning?

Which plagues do not affect the Israelites?

Which plagues seem to have the greatest effect on Pharaoh?

Which plagues can the magicians duplicate?

Which plagues are brought on with the use of Moses' staff?

Which plagues stop by themselves, and which does Moses ask God to stop?

In which plagues does Aaron play an important role?

What is natural/supernatural about the plagues?

List the words from this portion and the previous one, *Vaera,* that tell you the purposes of the plagues.

2 *Bo* contains the first passages thought to refer to *tefillin.* Locate these verses (Exodus 13:9 and 16) and explain how *tefillin* literally fulfill the words. How else might these verses be interpreted?

3 Play "$25,000 Pyramid" using material from the portions *Vaera* and *Bo.* Establish categories of related elements in the portions, providing an equal number of elements in each group. For example: Things that get eaten, things God did, things you do on Passover, things the Israelites did, things that happened during the plagues, things Moses and Aaron said. Play in competing teams of two partners. The team should choose a category and then work through all the elements with one partner giving clues so that the other can guess the items. Score one point for each correct guess. For example, in the category "Things you do on Passover," one element might be "eat *matzah*." Acceptable clues would be such things as "you do it to remind you of what the Israelites did," or "you get crumbs all over everything when you do it."

4 In *Bo,* we find three of the four passages from which the Four Sons/Children of the *Haggadah* are derived. The fourth passage is Deuteronomy 6:20-21. See if you can match the wise, wicked, simple, and unable-to-ask sons with the passage from which each is derived. (Answers: Exodus 12:26-27 – wicked son; Exodus 13:8 – son unable-to-ask; Exodus 13:14 – simple son; Deuteronomy 6:20-21 – wise son.)

5 Dramatize Exodus 10:1-11 using the text in Hebrew as your script. Read the verses carefully to decide how many spoken parts there are and if and how these should be divided up, exactly what actions take place, and what the setting is. Once the roles are assigned, you will have to practice the dialogue carefully until you can speak it fluently and in the right "tone." After your dramatization, analyze the relative strength of the characters: Who is controlling the course of events in this scene? How is the power of Pharaoh belittled by Moses and Aaron? By the servants? How is it heightened?

6 Tradition split on whether the Passover observance was meant only for the generation of the Exodus or for all subsequent generations. Find verses in the text which would support both views. Why do you think it evolved that all generations would observe the Passover?

EXTENDING THE TEXT

7 Be an Egyptian journalist and write a report for the *Nile News* about events leading up to the Exodus of the Hebrew slaves.

8 According to Exodus 12:2, "This month [Nisan] shall mark for you the beginning of months; it shall be the first of months of the year for you." Despite this passage, Rosh HaShanah, the Jewish New Year, is celebrated on the first of the month of Tishre. How many New Years are there? The Mishnah tells us there are four. Use the text *Learn Mishnah* by Jacob Neusner, pp. 75-84, to help you learn about these.

9 The laws of Passover are first set down in *Bo.* Over the centuries, the Rabbis expanded and explained these laws in some detail. Make a list of the original laws as you understand them from this portion. What are the main differences between this first Passover and all subsequent ones? Why do these differences exist?
Reference: *Jewish Holy Days* by Abraham Bloch; *Seasons of Our Joy: A Modern Guide to the Jewish Holidays* by Arthur Waskow; *The Jewish Holidays: A Guide and Commentary* by Michael Strassfeld.

10 Through all of Genesis and up until *parashat Bo* in Exodus, the Torah lists very few commandments. Beginning in *Bo,* however, many more prescribed practices and behaviors are found. In this portion alone are the commandments to eat *matzah,* wear *tefillin,* and reserve the firstborn for a special role. All of these commandments are preceded by a declaration of a new monthly cycle in Exodus 12:2. Why do you think commandments begin to be given at this point in the narrative? What is the significance of the information about the calendar? Create an illustrated calendar for this first month according to the information in the portion. Include the celebration of Passover and depictions of the commandments presented in *Bo*.

PERSONALIZING THE TEXT

11 Invite someone to discuss *tefillin* and to explain how they are made and demonstrate how they are worn. Go to the sanctuary or other quiet meditating space. Have each student put on *tefillin* and a *tallit*. The *tefillin* are worn on weekday mornings, Sundays through Fridays. Although this may be the first time students have worn *tefillin* and may feel odd, ask the students to try. Several activities about *tefillin* can be found in *Teaching Mitzvot* by Barbara Binder Kadden and Bruce Kadden.

12 In order to protect themselves from the tenth plague, the Israelites were instructed to slaughter lambs and put lamb's blood on their doorposts. This was an act of courage and faith in Egyptian society, as these animals were considered sacred. As Jews in a primarily Christian society, we are sometimes in the position of doing things which set us obviously apart from our neighbors. Can you give some examples? Put these items on a continuum to show which are most difficult for you to do as a Jew in a non-Jewish world and which of them are most significant to you.

13 Discuss what the phrase "hard-hearted" means as we use it today. Does this differ from its use in the first three portions of the Book of Exodus? What do you think would have happened if God *hadn't* hardened Pharaoh's heart? Is the account better with this idea, or without it? Can you think of some times when you have hardened your heart or when contemporary leaders of nations have hardened their hearts?

14 Examine different *Haggadot* and compare the presentations of the Ten Plagues. Consider the traditional explanations and *midrashim* they include or exclude, the editor's additional notes, any contemporary material they contain, and the artistic depiction of the plagues. Using a book-size format, put together your own *Haggadah* segment about the Ten Plagues. Include art work and add your own "Editor's Note" explaining your choice of materials.

15 The Ten Plagues are recounted as Psalms of Praise in Psalms 78:44-51 and 105:23-38. Using these as examples, write your own poetic account of the plagues.

16 In Exodus 13:12 we read: "You shall set apart for the Lord every first issue of the womb." The tradition of giving the firstborn animals and first fruits of a harvest to God derives from this statement. The statement draws its authority from the fact that God spared the firstborn among the Israelites when he slew the firstborn Egyptians. In pagan religions, the firstborn were preferred for sacrifice or service to the gods, but in the case of Israel, according to the priestly tradition, the Levites became the substitutes of the firstborn for Temple service. Two customs remain, however, to remind us of the special status conferred on the firstborn: *Pidyon HaBen* (Redemption of the Firstborn) and *Ta'anit Bechorim* (Fast of the Firstborn, observed on the day before Passover). To learn about the first of these special customs, plan and stage a mock *Pidyon HaBen* ceremony. References: *Teaching Jewish Life Cycle* by Bruce Kadden and Barbara Binder Kadden. For more, see the Index: "Firstborn."

17 Make *matzah*. First read the children's book *The Mouse in the Matzah Factory* by Francine Medoff for a complete picture of the process of making strictly kosher *matzah*. Follow the directions in *The First Jewish Catalog* by Richard Siegel, Michael Strassfeld, and Sharon Strassfeld, pp. 143-145. If you have a local *matzah* factory, arrange to visit it!

18 A habitual criminal is one who simply cannot stop committing crimes. How do the four instances cited above in Insight B apply to such an individual? Is there anything that individuals or societies can do to help someone go straight or repent?

19 At Passover, we are commanded to recall the events of the Exodus. Is it enough just to recount the story or is there more to do? What is it? What does Passover mean to you? How does the Passover *Seder* strengthen your ties to Judaism?

20 Why are Jewish and secular customs and traditions important? What purposes do they serve? Make a chart of those you find especially meaningful and list their purposes.

OTHER RESOURCES

21 Complete the pages which relate to *Bo* in *Bible People Book Two* by Joel Lurie Grishaver, pp. 14-17. Also check the accompanying Leader Guide for procedures and additional activities.

22 Listen to and/or learn the song "The Ten Plagues" from *Bible People Songs.*

23 Read, act out, and discuss the skit for the portion *Bo* in *Sedra Scenes: Skits for Every Torah Portion* by Stan J. Beiner, pp. 85-89.

24 For more about *Pidyon HaBen* and its place in Jewish birth customs, see *The Life Cycle Workbook* by Joel Lurie Grishaver, pp. 14-17.

25 For more insights and activities about the commandments of Passover, see *Teaching Mitzvot* by Barbara Binder Kadden and Bruce Kadden.

26 View and discuss the episode for *Bo* from *Torah Toons I: The Video.*

27 For creative movement activities, see "Darkness Descends on Egypt," "Leaving Egypt," and "Sign and Symbol of Freedom" from *Torah in Motion* by JoAnne Tucker and Susan Freeman, pp. 80-85.

28 Read and discuss the illustrated commentary for *Bo* in *American Torah Toons* by Lawrence Bush.

INVOLVING THE FAMILY

29 Note the unusual wording of Exodus 10:2. God wants the Israelites to be able to "recount in the hearing of [their] sons how [God] made a mockery of the Egyptians . . ." The verse does not continue by saying "that they (the offspring) may know that I am the Lord." Rather, it says "that you may know — you, that is, the parents" (*The Hasidic Anthology: Tales & Teachings of the Hasidim,* edited by Louis Newman, pp. 118, #4).
To whom else might the word "you" refer? Discuss the lesson of this verse and its implications for your family's Jewish activities.

Note: The Ten Plagues are not all detailed in *Bo.* The previous portion, *Vaera,* recounts the first seven plagues. See that portion for additional insights and activities on the plagues. For more, see the Index: "Ten Plagues."

BAR/BAT MITZVAH PROJECT

30 In *sedra Bo,* the law to eat unleavened bread during Passover is given. To help poor Jews obtain *matzah* and other Passover foods a special fund was established. *Ma'ot Chitim* is a Jewish community fund which provides Passover foods to needy Jews. The fund may be run by the synagogue(s), Jewish Family Service, or other agency in your community.

Begin this project by speaking with your Rabbi to find out if such a fund exists in your community, determine who to contact, and explore opportunities for your participation. Some ideas include: fund raising for the fund, packing boxes of Passover foods, helping to distribute the food boxes to selected households.

BESHALACH 13:17-17:16 בשלח

SYNOPSIS

CONCEALED IN A PILLAR OF CLOUD BY day and fire by night, God leads the Israelites out of Egypt by way of the Sea of Reeds. Moses carries with him the bones of Joseph.

For a final time, God hardens Pharaoh's heart, and the Egyptians pursue the escaping slaves. At the edge of the Sea of Reeds, the people hesitate. It is only when they go forward into the water that the sea splits so that they walk through on dry land. When the Egyptians pursue them, the sea closes and all of Pharaoh's army is drowned. Now convinced of the greatness of God, the Israelites, led by Moses and Miriam, sing songs of praise.

Traveling on through the wilderness, the Israelites are without water for three days. When they reach the bitter waters of Marah, God instructs Moses to throw a piece of wood into the water and the water becomes sweet and suitable for drinking.

Shortly afterward, the Israelites, in their hunger, begin to grumble against Moses and Aaron. God tells Moses and Aaron that the Israelites will eat flesh that evening and bread the next morning. In the evening, quail appear and cover the camp. In the morning, God sends manna to feed each according to his or her own need. But the people do not heed the instruction not to keep any of the manna overnight, and the leftover portions become infested and smelly.

On the sixth day, the Israelites gather a double portion of manna, for on Shabbat no manna is to appear. The two-day-old manna remains fresh, and the people rest on the seventh day.

When the Israelites encamp at Rephidim, they again quarrel with Moses over the lack of drinking water. Moses cries out to God about the rebelliousness of the people and God instructs him to strike a rock at Horeb from which water will flow. Moses does so in the sight of the people. The place is named Massah and Meribah (Trial and Quarrel) because the people had tried the patience of God there.

At Rephidim, the Amalekites come to attack the people. Joshua is appointed by Moses to lead the army, while Moses and Aaron and Hur go up to the top of a hill. While Moses' hands are raised up, the Israelites prevail. When Moses lowers his hands Amalek prevails, Joshua and Hur hold Moses' hands up and Amalek is defeated.

God instructs Moses to record these events and to remember Amalek as Israel's eternal enemy.

INSIGHTS FROM THE TRADITION

A The name of this portion, *Beshalach,* is taken from the second word of Exodus 13:12 — ". . . and when Pharaoh sent out." The title announces what the text will tell, namely, the events that befell the Israelites when Pharaoh "sent them out."

B In *Beshalach,* several miracles or acts seem to contradict the laws of nature. Attempts have been made to supply scientific explanations for the pillars of cloud and fire, the splitting of the Sea of Reeds, the miraculous waters of Marah and Horeb, and the provision of quail and manna. In this connection, Martin Buber has written:

"It is irrelevant whether much or little, unusual or usual, tremendous or trifling events happened; what is vital is only that what happened was experienced, while it happened, as the act of God. The people saw in whatever it was they saw 'the wondrous power which God had wielded' and 'they had faith in God.' From the biblical viewpoint, history always contains the element of wonder" (*Moses: The Revelation and the Covenant* by Martin Buber, pp. 75, 77, and 79).

What is a miracle?
Do miracles happen today?
How do you understand the miraculous events in the story of the Exodus?
Is it important to you to find a reasonable explanation for the miracles in the Bible?

What experiences have you had that might be seen as miraculous?

C That God is the controlling power of the Exodus is again demonstrated in this portion. Aside from all the wondrous events, the Torah explicitly states that God also chose the route by which the Israelites traveled to Canaan (Exodus 13:17,18).

The *midrash* adds that the inhabitants of the Promised Land were ready to battle the Israelites shortly after the departure from Egypt. Concerned that they might become fainthearted at the thought of war, God led the Israelites by another route (*Exodus Rabbah* 20:17).

Why might not the Israelites have been ready for war?
How might the slavery experience have affected their attitude toward defending themselves?
What feelings do you have at the thought of a fight?

D At the Sea of Reeds, with the Egyptians approaching, the Israelites cry out to God. They question Moses' wisdom. Moses calms the people with a promise of God's deliverance. God responds by saying that the people are responsible for taking action and saving themselves. The people are directed to "march into the sea on dry ground" (14:16). The *Midrash Exodus Rabbah* asks how this is possible. How can the people be on dry ground and in the sea at the same time? We learn from this that the sea divided only after the Israelites stepped in and the water reached their noses.

Why might Pharaoh have had a change of heart and pursued the Israelites?
How did the Israelites react when they realized Pharaoh was pursuing them?
Consider the phrase "a leap of faith." How does this apply to the Sea of Reeds event?
Why are the people continually called upon to express their faith?

Can you describe other moments in Jewish history when Jews were similarly pursued? Have you ever been forced to make a decision in an instant? Was there an element of faith in your act? Explain.

E In the Talmud we read, "All the songs in Scripture are written in the form of a half brick over a whole brick, and a whole brick over a half brick (*Megillah* 16b). *Yalkut Me'am Lo'ez* by Yaacov Culi (Vol. V, p. 244) explains this as follows: When the Song of the Sea is written, blank spaces are left in the middle of each line. It is to indicate that there are blank spaces in our knowledge of and in our praise of God. If one thinks that he/she knows how to praise God more fully, let that one come and fill in the blanks.

In what ways is praising God like constructing a building?
Are you comfortable with the words which are traditionally used to praise God?
What words are you most comfortable using to praise God?

F The Israelites express fears and doubt about their journey. This, in fact, becomes a recurrent and troublesome theme during the years of wandering. Nevertheless, an ongoing attempt is made to transform the mixed multitude of escaped slaves into a united people through the imposition of codes of behavior and observance. The first concrete lesson in the observance of divine law was given in Exodus 15:22-30. No manna would be gathered or found on Shabbat. The tradition of having two *challot* on Shabbat is derived from the double portion of manna God provided on the sixth day.

How does God respond to the Israelites' grumbling?
Why does Moses fear the people's complaints? Would these have an effect on his ability to lead them?

Can you explain why the Israelites continue to doubt and complain even after experiencing the Exodus?

Have you ever grumbled at authority exercised by parents? Synagogue? School? Did you openly rebel? Were you satisfied with the results of your complaining? Would you act in a similar way again?

G *Beshalach* introduces us to Amalek, the archetypal enemy of Israel. After the first defeat at Rephidim, Amalek is victorious against the Israelites at Hormah (Numbers 14:44-45). In I Samuel, we read of the defeat of Amalek first at the hands of King Saul (15:5ff.) and then by King David (27:8ff.). The final destruction of Amalek is by King Hezekiah (I Chronicles 4:39-43). Many enemies of the Jewish people came to be known as Amalekites. Tradition has it that Haman was descended from Amalek. Therefore, the portion in Deuteronomy (25:17-19) that recalls the actions of Amalek is read on Shabbat *Zachor,* the Shabbat before Purim.

Who were other "Amaleks" who have attacked the Jewish people?
Are there any modern day Amaleks? Who are they and why do you consider them to be like Amalek? When do you act like Amalek?

H When the Temple stood in Jerusalem, the Song at the Sea was recited by the Levites at the time of the Shabbat afternoon *Minchah* offering. After the Temple was destroyed, this song was incorporated first into the Shabbat service after the Shacharit *Pesukay d'Zimra*. Read Exodus 15:1-18, which is the Song at the Sea.

Why do you think this song has been considered so important as to be read every day as part of a worship service?
Is it more a song praising God's might, or a song recounting a remarkable event? After something remarkable happens to you, are you more likely to dote on the details of the event or on your gratitude and thankfulness to God?

I The first time Miriam is mentioned by name in the biblical text is at the shore of the sea. Everett Fox points out that the deliverance from Egypt began with a little girl guarding her baby brother as he floated down the Nile in a basket. Once the Exodus is completed, the same little girl, now a grown woman, sings and dances at the shore of the sea (*The Five Books of Moses,* p. 336-339.)

Does Miriam deserve more recognition for her role in the Exodus than the Bible provides for her?

STRATEGIES

ANALYZING THE TEXT

1 Throughout the story of the Exodus and the account of the forty years wandering in the desert, there are instances in which the Israelites rebel against Moses and God. How many examples can you find in this portion alone? In this connection, Rabbi Mordecai Katz (*Lilmod Ulelamade,* p. 70) notes that all the plagues in Egypt (and the miracles at Sinai) had two purposes: (1) to convince the Egyptians of the greatness of God, and (2) to convince the Israelites of the same thing. What proof can you find in the text for this idea (see Exodus 13:4 and 14:31).

2 According to the *Encyclopaedia Judaica* ("Exodus, Book of," Vol. 6, p. 1055), "The interval between the crossing of the sea and the arrival at Sinai is filled with episodes relating to trials and tribulations." The key Hebrew word in these instances have the root נסה, meaning to "try" or "test." How many times can you find words with that root in Exodus 15-17? List the trials and tribulations described in these verses. (Answer: It can be found in 15:25; 16:4; 17:2; 17:7.)

3 Read Chapter 15:20-21 of this portion. How is Miriam described? What role did she fulfill in just these few verses? If Miriam was described this way is it possible there were more women who also held leadership positions? Consider Pharaoh's daughter and the Hebrew midwives.

4 Generate a list of qualities that characterize leaders. Using a concordance, look up women who are in the Bible and read the verses in which they appear. Suggested names are: Eve, Sarah, Rebekah, Leah, Rachel, Miriam, Deborah (the judge), Ruth and Naomi, and Huldah. Add any other biblical women you wish to research.

As you read about these women, identify their leadership qualities and list them. Discuss. Compare the two lists of leadership qualities. Are they similar or very different? Are there new qualities you identified while researching the women that you want to add to the original list? What are those qualities?

EXTENDING THE TEXT

5 Like the rod of Moses, the manna that God provided in the desert is considered to have been one of the ten things built into the world on the eve of the Shabbat of Creation. This explanation allows for the occurrence of "miracles" which do not contradict the laws of nature. List as many events in the Bible which you would consider to be miraculous. In your opinion, which is the most significant event and why? What does miracle mean to you?

6 The Song at the Sea, which is part of the daily morning service, is not the only reference to the Exodus in the *Siddur*. Divide into teams and search the *Siddur* (or a specific section of it) for references to the Exodus in other prayers. How many did you find? What does this suggest to you about the centrality of the theme of redemption

from Egypt in Jewish tradition? List some other important themes found in the *Siddur*. Rank the themes in the order that you think shows their importance to Judaism. Where did you put the theme of the Exodus? Why?
Reference: *Teaching Tefilah: Insights and Activities on Prayer* by Bruce Kadden and Barbara Binder Kadden.

7 Miriam is one of only four women in the Bible who is referred to as a prophetess (Exodus 15:20). Do you know who the other three are? One is Deborah, the subject of the *Haftarah* for this portion (Judges 4:4-5:31). The other two are Huldah (II Kings 22:14) and Noadiah (Nehemiah 6:14). Very little is known about these women. Use this occasion to begin compiling a "Who's Who of Women in the Bible." Under each entry, include the pertinent biblical references, a brief biography, *midrashim,* and your own thoughts, stories, artwork, and poems.
Reference: *The Encyclopedia of Jewish Symbols* by Ellen Frankel and Betsy Platkin Teutsch; *The Book of Legends: Sefer Ha-aggadah,* edited by Hayim Bialik and Yehoshua Ravnizky; *Biblical Women Unbound* by Norma Rosen.

8 The Bible mentions several instances when women danced in celebration. (See Judges 5:1-31; Judges 21:19-23; I Samuel 18:6-7.) Even today, a dance tradition exists among Jewish women from Iran, Kurdistan, and Yemen. Continue this tradition by choreographing a dance that will be performed by a modern day Miriam and all the women. Use castanets as today's version of timbrels.

9 Read or sing the song *"Dayenu"* from the *Haggadah.* Except for a brief outline of some of God's further actions, why do you think the retelling of the Exodus ends in the song with the events in *Beshalach*? Add additional verses to retell completely the story of the Exodus.

PERSONALIZING THE TEXT

10 The Shabbat on which the Song at the Sea is read from the Torah is called "Shabbat *Shirah*" — the Sabbath of the Song. When the song is read, the congregation rises, a custom which we observe with only one other Torah reading — the Ten Commandments. In some communities, food was given to "nature's singers" — the birds — on Shabbat Shirah. Some sources say, too, that having men and women sit separately at services is derived from this portion, since we read that Miriam led the women (i.e., presumably separately) in song. Plan a special observance for Shabbat Shirah. You might want to include explanations of the above customs. Consider teaching some new melodies for the prayer *"Mi Chamocha,"* the words of which are taken from the Song at the Sea. Include dancing in your observance, too (see Strategy #21 below, page 112).

11 How did the manna taste? The Rabbis tell us that manna tasted different to everyone. It was a kind of magical food: to babies it tasted like milk, to young children, it tasted like bread, and to the elderly it tasted like honey. Suppose you were one of the children of Israel and you, too, gathered manna in the desert. What would you want the manna to taste like? Make up a "manna menu." As a follow-up to this activity, view and discuss the segment on manna from the video *The Sabbath.*

12 In this portion, the Israelites cry to Moses: ". . . you have brought us out into this wilderness to starve this whole congregation to death!" Imagine that you are Moses and all of the people are complaining to you. Complete the sentences below:
I wish that _____.
Why don't they understand that _____.
If only God would _____.

13 The Rabbis of the Talmud were of two views regarding how the Israelites responded as they stood at the Sea of Reeds with the Egyptian army at their backs. Rabbi Meir said, "The tribes strove with one another, each wishing to descend into the sea first." But Rabbi Judah said, ". . . each tribe was unwilling to be the first to enter the sea. Then sprang forth Nachshon, the son of Amminadab, and descended first into the sea . . ." (*Sotah* 37a). Give some reasons which would explain either version of the Israelite behavior. What kind of person do you think Nachshon was? When are you most like Nachshon? When are you most like one of the Israelites who was unwilling to enter the sea? Give some examples.

14 Benjamin Franklin suggested that the United States one dollar bill have a picture on the back showing the liberation of the Israelites (*The Torah: A Modern Commentary,* edited by W. Gunther Plaut, p. 486). Why would the theme of liberation and freedom, so central to Jewish history, have been suitable for American adoption? Design a new one dollar bill for the United States using Franklin's suggestion for the back of the bill.

15 Unroll a Torah scroll to see how the Song at the Sea is written (see Insight E, page 108). After examining the Song at the Sea create your own visual picture that repeats the long and short lines and spaces of the original. Use your own words of praise and illustrations to fill in the lines. Utilize regular and chisel point markers in a variety of colors in making your Song at the Sea.

16 The words "Who is like You, O God, among the celestials? Who is like You, majestic in holiness, awesome in splendor, working wonders!" (Exodus 15:11) have entered Jewish liturgy and song. Collect and learn many melodies for these words. Record the various versions on tape. Incorporate this *Mi Chamocha* medley into your Shabbat *Shirah* service.

OTHER RESOURCES

17 Complete the pages which relate to *Beshalach* in *Bible People Book Two* by Joel Lurie Grishaver, pp. 18-22. Also check the accompanying Leader Guide for procedures and additional activities.

18 Listen to and/or learn the song "A Song of Freedom" from *Bible People Songs*.

19 Read, act out, and discuss the skit for the portion *Beshalach* in *Sedra Scenes: Skits for Every Torah Portion* by Stan J. Beiner, pp. 90-94.

20 View and discuss the episode for *Beshalach* from *Torah Toons I: The Video*.

21 For creative movement activities, see "Crossing the Sea" and "Hands of Victory" from *Torah in Motion* by JoAnne Tucker and Susan Freeman, pp. 86-89.

22 Listen to, discuss, and sing "*Ozi V'zimrat Yah*" from *Sounds of Freedom: Exodus in Song*.

23 Read and discuss the illustrated commentary for *Be-Shallach* in *American Torah Toons* by Lawrence Bush.

INVOLVING THE FAMILY

24 A *midrash* relates that the angels began to sing when they saw the Egyptians drowning in the sea. But God chastised them saying, "The work of my hands is drowning in the sea and you desire to sing songs!" (*Megillah* 10b). To this day, we show our sorrow that others had to suffer so that we could be free by removing one drop of wine from our cups for each plague. As a family, brainstorm a list of things you could do to remind yourselves that others in the world are less fortunate than you and ways to relieve some of that suffering. Write or find a prayer or poem that includes remembering those in need as part of your Shabbat home observance. It is traditional to give *tzedakah* just before Shabbat begins. Human dignity comes from the act of consideration for others at all times.

BAR/BAT MITZVAH PROJECT

25 A traditional observance that has been "rediscovered" and is being celebrated is Rosh Chodesh. Rosh Chodesh marks the beginning of a new Jewish month and was traditionally regarded a women's holiday. Does your synagogue host a monthly Rosh Chodesh service? If yes, interview those who lead the service to find out its traditional origins, background of its being observed at your synagogue, and who helps create the service each month. Ask to attend. Join in the celebration 2-3 times and, if appropriate, ask to be a part of the planning group for a subsequent Rosh Chodesh.

YITRO 18:1-20:23 יתרו

SYNOPSIS

JETHRO, THE FATHER-IN-LAW OF MOSES, brings Moses' wife and two sons to Moses in the desert. After observing how Moses settles disputes among the Israelites, Jethro advises him to delegate chiefs to judge all except the most difficult of cases. Moses follows Jethro's advice, and Jethro returns to his own land in Midian.

On the third new moon after the Exodus, the people enter the wilderness of Sinai and encamp by Mount Sinai. God tells the people through Moses that if they will obey God's teachings, they will be for God a "kingdom of priests and a holy nation." The people respond as one, saying, "All that the Lord has spoken we will do."

After the Israelites wait a period of three days for purification, God appears to them in a cloud of smoke and fire on the mountain and proclaims the Ten Commandments.

The people fear that they will die if they hear God speak or if they speak to God themselves; so they ask Moses to be God's spokesperson in the future. God tells Moses to remind the Israelites that they themselves had heard God speak. Therefore, they are to hold fast in their resolve to worship no idols. God commands them to build an altar of earth and to bring sacrifices.

INSIGHTS FROM THE TRADITION

A Yitro, the name of this portion, is the name of Moses' father-in-law with whom the *sedra* begins. There are six portions which are titled with the name of a person: Noah, Sarah, Jethro, Korach, Pinchas, and Balak. This is the only one so titled in the Book of Exodus. Of the six, three are non-Jews.

B Although Jethro was not an Israelite, it is evident that he is wise and that he has the respect of Moses. Jethro's declaration that "God [YHVH] is greater than all gods" (Exodus 18:11), in effect, signals the final victory of God over the gods of Egypt. It sets the stage for a new dimension in the relationship between God and Israel.

What might Jethro have seen or observed that would lead him to declare the supremacy of God? What is significant about a non-Israelite declaring the greatness of the Jewish God?
What Jewish ideas are most appealing to you, and why?

C Jethro advises Moses to choose judges who are capable individuals and who fear God (18:21). Ibn Ezra points out that they are to fear God, not people.

By creating a system of judges, was Moses in danger of losing esteem and power over the Israelites?
What benefits would Israel derive by having many judges?
Has contemporary society been able to follow this advice?
If you lived in the days of Moses, would you qualify to serve as a judge?

D In Exodus 19:9-13, God tells Moses to instruct the people to prepare to receive the law. But when Moses conveys this direction in verse 15 he adds the words "do not go near a woman." The implication seems to be that for Moses, the community of Israelites that God wanted to address consisted only of the men. Indeed, *The Five Books of Miriam* (by Ellen Frankel) suggests that for Moses, holiness is only available to men in isolation from women (p. 118). While on the one hand, interpreting the Torah this way may make us feel angry, it also reflects the real experience of some women who feel excluded by parts of our tradition. But here, as in the wording of the Ten Commandments (see Strategy #4, page 116), we also have to be careful to include in our reading the parts of Torah which clearly include us all.

With whom do you relate in this story?
Are there parts of the Torah's teachings or stories in which you feel especially included? excluded? How might you explain Moses' attitude in this section?

E According to the *Mechilta de-Rabbi Ishmael,* "The Torah was given in public, openly, in a free place. For had the Torah been given in the land of Israel, the Israelites could have said to the nations of the world: You have no share in it. But since it was given in the wilderness, publicly, and in a place that is open to all, everyone wishing to accept Torah may come and accept it" (Vol. II, p. 198).

Does the notion that everyone wishing to accept the Torah is free to do so contradict the idea that Israel is God's chosen people?
What does "Torah" mean to you?
In what ways can you maintain that you accept Torah?

F There is a *midrash* which teaches that God offered the Torah to the other peoples of the world. Each of them declined to accept it, not wanting to take on the task of obeying the *mitzvot.* Only the people of Israel responded as one (Exodus 19:8) "All that the Lord has spoken we will do" (*Legends of the Jews* by Louis Ginzberg, Vol. III, pp. 80-82). This interpretation is in accord with later tradition which saw Israel's "chosenness" in contractual terms — depending on the acceptance and performance of the commandments laid out in the Torah. "Chosenness" implies the obligation to act as a "kingdom of priests and a holy nation" (Exodus 19:6). (See the Insights for Leviticus, *Kedoshim,* page 201.) This idea persists to this day in the sense that Jews see a particular duty to behave in a moral and ethical way. Indeed,

the *Haggadah* reminds us that each of us must regard ourselves as having personally made the Exodus from Egypt and as having assumed the obligation of Torah.

Therefore, while earlier in the Book of Exodus the relationship between God and Israel was primarily that of Redeemer and redeemed, with the giving of the Ten Commandments, a new element is added. Now that God's power and trustworthiness have been shown (by acting on promises made to Abraham, Isaac, and Jacob), God establishes a conditional, Ruler-subjects relationship with the people. In the earlier relationship, the people's claim to God's protection derived solely from their historic relationship with God. Now, God's protection of the Israelites is conditional upon their fulfillment of a set of obligations.

This concept of chosenness has been both a blessing and a curse for the Jewish people. Positively speaking, this relationship with God has been central to Jewish existence. It has given hope and comfort in bad times, but it has also spurred negative reactions from the non-Jewish world.

For what was Israel chosen? Was it for special privileges and benefits, or was it for duties and special obligations?
Should the Jewish people resist the use of the term "chosen people" as a description? If not, how should the term be understood and explained to the non-Jewish community?
The generation of the Exodus bound their descendants for all generations at Sinai. How do contemporary Jews fulfill the covenant? How do they ignore it?
Does God need the people of Israel? Is there an eternal purpose for a covenanted people?
In what ways do you see yourself as "chosen?"

G The people are called to the foot of Sinai with the blasting of a heavenly *shofar.* They gather waiting to hear God's words. The *midrash* tells us that each Israelite heard what was in his/her power to hear (*Exodus Rabbah* 29:1).

The *shofar* is an important feature of the High Holy Days. It calls the people to repentance. Do you see any parallels between the Sinai experience and the modern High Holy Days?
On Mount Sinai, the *shofar* was sounded for us. Today it is sounded by us. What is your reaction to this change of focus?
"Each heard what was in his/her power." Explain. Do we today have the same ability to hear and understand as the Israelites did in the desert?

H The mountain from which the Israelites were to hear the revelation is called Sinai or Horeb. Jewish tradition does not preserve its exact location.

Why do you think that Jewish tradition did not preserve the exact location of Sinai?
The fourth commandment teaches the Israelites to observe the Sabbath. A "holy time" is to be celebrated. What is the difference between celebrating a holy time and the worship of a place such as Sinai?
Do you think Jewish tradition benefits or loses from "ignoring" the place of revelation?
What does Sinai mean to you? Is it more than just a place?

I We are told in a *midrash* that when Torah was given, no bird chirped, no fowl stirred, no cow lowed, no seraph flew, no cherub whispered "*Kadosh, Kadosh,*" and no person uttered a word. Indeed, the entire universe was absolutely silent, and then God said: "*Anochi Adonai Elohecha*" — I am the Lord your God.

In what ways does this *midrash* match your vision of how nature reacted when Torah was given?
Which would be more awesome, absolute darkness or absolute silence?
What has been the quietest moment in your life?

STRATEGIES

ANALYZING THE TEXT

1 Make a detailed study of the Ten Commandments. From Exodus 20:1 to 20:14, how many commandments can you find? Are any of these not actual *commands,* but rather statements? Can you suggest any other ways these statements and commands might be combined to get ten commandments? (See *The Torah: A Modern Commentary,* edited by W. Gunther Plaut, pp. 434-435.) Try to find ways in which the commandments are related to each other. For example, list them according to whether they concern a person's relationship with God, or a person's relationship with other people. Or, group them as laws of the heart — things that affect your thought and belief, laws of the tongue — things that affect your speech, or laws of action — things that affect what you do. Each commandment can be seen as a subject heading under which related laws of conduct could be listed. Can you give examples of other *mitzvot* you know, and explain how they would fit into the way you grouped the Ten Commandments? For more, see Strategy #1 in Exodus, *Mishpatim,* page 123.

2 In Hebrew, the Ten Commandments are called עשרת הדיברות (*Aseret HaDibrot*). In earlier times they were called עשרת הדברים (*Aseret HaDevarim*), after the expression used in Exodus 20:1. What does the word דבר (*davar*) or דיבור (*dibur*) mean? How do these words differ from the following: משפטים (*Mishpatim*), חקים (*Chukim*), מצוות (*Mitzvot*)? Study the text of the Ten Commandments in Hebrew. Use either *The Pentateuch and Haftorahs* by J.H. Hertz or *The Torah: A Modern Commentary,* edited by W. Gunther Plaut. Pay special attention to the Hebrew words these commentators highlight in their notes. These words were singled out by the commentator because in Hebrew their meaning adds an extra dimension to the text. Later, edit your own commentary on the Ten Commandments with each member of your group choosing and writing a brief note about an interesting Hebrew word in the text. Set up your page of comments around the verses of the commandments in the form traditional to Jewish commentary.

3 The Ten Commandments are often grouped in two units of five: all the *mitzvot* that begin "Thou shalt not . . ." are listed together, while the first four commandments which deal in some way with our relationship with God are placed with the fifth command, to honor your parents. Can you suggest ways in which the fifth commandment is related to the four that precede it?

4 Although all the people stood together at Mount Sinai to receive the Ten Commandments, the commandments themselves use the singular form of address: *You* (singular) shall keep the Sabbath, *You* (singular) shall not murder, etc. Each person is thus individually and equally addressed and obligated. No one can argue that the laws do not include him or her. In order to experience the power of this insight, practice a personal reading of the Ten Commandments (in Hebrew or English). As you read each commandment aloud (and use a "commanding" voice!), insert your name into the words; for example, "You, *Josh,* you shall not steal." Discuss how this kind of reading affects the way you react to the Ten Commandments.

5 In *Pirke Avot* 4:1 we read, "Who is strong? One who subdues his evil impulse. Who is rich? One who is content with his lot." In your view, which of these two statements is a better interpretation of the tenth commandment? Why? Express one of the two statements in the form of a resolution and debate the question. Let the audience vote for the statement they prefer.

EXTENDING THE TEXT

6 In the Temple in Jerusalem, the Ten Commandments were recited by the priests as part of the daily service. The Talmud (*Berachot* 12a) tells us that the people wanted to continue this tradition by reciting the Ten Commandments during the synagogue service. The Rabbis forbade it, however, so that no one could claim that the Ten Commandments were the only valid or most important part of the Torah. Organize a debate on this issue. Resolved: The Ten Commandments should be recited as part of our daily worship.

7 In *Yitro* (Exodus 19:3), the Israelites are called by a new name — בֵּית יַעֲקֹב (House of Jacob). Make a list of all the names by which the Jewish people have been known; include Hebrews, Jews, Israelites, Congregation of Israel, Children of Israel, Chosen People, etc. Do you know the origin and meaning of each name? You may have to do a little research to help you find out. A good general book on Jewish history would be helpful, or prepare a list of questions and interview an educator or Rabbi. Once you have all the facts, choose the name you like best and design a crest that illustrates the meaning of the name.

8 The Ten Commandments are, above all, a guide to action. Each commandment can be seen as a subject heading under which related laws and guides to conduct will later be added. Therefore, Judaism has often been called a "doing" religion: we serve God by our deeds, rather than through merely holding the right set of beliefs. Look at some (or all) of the stories about the Ten Commandments in *Who Knows Ten?* by Molly Cone, or *God's Top Ten* by Roberta Louis Goodman, and discuss how these stories indicate that Judaism is a "doing" religion.

9 The commandments begin with the reminder to the Jewish people that God redeemed us from slavery in Egypt. Why is this emphasized rather than the point that God is our Creator or that God made a covenant with Abraham? Make a list of other important turning points for the Jewish people that were not referred to in the Ten Commandments. Rank these in order of their importance to Jewish history.

PERSONALIZING THE TEXT

10 Although, in the Torah, Shavuot is purely an agricultural festival, the Pharisees linked the holiday to history: calculations placed the revelation at Sinai on the 50th day after the Exodus, thus making Shavuot, which is 50 days after Passover, the anniversary of the giving of the Torah. For a good explanation of this, see *Seasons of Our Joy* by Arthur Waskow, pp. 188-191. On Shavuot, the story of the revelation at Sinai is the Torah reading, and it is customary for the congregation to stand while the Ten Commandments are being read. Sephardic and Yemenite Jews include in their Shavuot observance the reading of a special *ketubah* (marriage contract) between God and Israel. The *ketubah* is based on the idea that the revelation at Sinai led to an unbreakable covenant between God and Israel — a marriage. Examples of Shavuot *ketubot* can be found in *Seasons of Our Joy,* pp. 194-5. Using the texts from those examples or a version you've written yourself, create an illuminated *ketubah* to be read and displayed at your synagogue on Shavuot.

11 Jewish tradition teaches that not only the generation of the Exodus, but all future generations of the Jewish people were present at Sinai. Furthermore, even though God spoke the Ten Commandments to *all* the people, the wording in the first commandment (Exodus 20:2) suggests that each person was addressed as an individual: "I am *Adonai* your (singular) God." Write a first person account titled "I Stood at Sinai," describing what you saw, how you felt,

and the impact that witnessing the event had on your life.

12 There is a wealth of *midrashic* and interpretive material about Shabbat. Good samplings can be found in *The Torah: A Modern Commentary,* edited by W. Gunther Plaut, pp. 551-552; *A Shabbat Haggadah,* compiled by Michael Strassfeld; *The Art of Jewish Living: The Sabbath Seder* by Ron Wolfson; *The Book of Legends: Sefer Ha-aggadah,* edited by Hayim Bialik and Yehoshua Ravnitzky.

Read several selections on Jewish understandings about Shabbat. Choose one theme that most closely mirrors your own view of Shabbat. Plan a special Shabbat observance for your family and/or friends around this theme. Include a study session about Shabbat as presented in the Torah (see Exodus, *Vayakhel,* Strategy #4, page 150) or a study session about the theme you chose. Be sure to include practical, how-to advice on observing Shabbat.

13 Anthropomorphism is the assigning of human characteristics and qualities to that which is non-human. In the Song at the Sea, for example, God is called a "Warrior" (Exodus 15:3), even though we know (and Moses knew) that God is not like a man and can't really be described in quite that way. The Torah warns us (both in the second commandment and in the review of the events in the desert in Deuteronomy) not to make images of God: "For your own sake, therefore, be most careful since you saw no shape when *Adonai* your God spoke to you at Horeb out of the fire . . ." (Deuteronomy 4:15ff.). How are "word" images different from visual images? Look in a *Siddur* for examples of anthropomorphic words we use to describe God (e.g., King, Father). What do we mean by using these words? How do they help us to understand God? How do they limit our understanding of God? Since we read in Genesis 1:27 that we are created in the image of God, how can we use our ideas about God to teach us what we should be like?

References: For more on anthropomorphism, see *God: The Eternal Challenge* by Sherry Bissell with Audrey Friedman Marcus and Raymond A. Zwerin; *When Children Ask About God* by Harold S. Kushner; *When Your Child Asks: A Handbook for Jewish Parents* by Simon Glaustrom.

14 Make a chart comparing the attitudes of different branches in Judaism to such things as revelation, *halachah,* and Israel. After you have finished the chart and understand its contents, add a column to it and write in a brief statement explaining your own attitude to these concepts.
References: *One People: A Study in Comparative Judaism* by Abraham Siegel; *The Many Faces of Judaism* by Gilbert S. Rosenthal.

15 Inform the group that God is going to give them a great gift, the Torah, but first they must offer God some kind of "surety" to prove that they will observe and cherish the Torah. In small groups, discuss what kind of "surety or deposit" to give God. Have the groups present their "surety" to a member of the group acting as God's representative. Are the "sureties" acceptable to God? Why or why not? Conclude by reading the *midrash* "Who Will Be My Surety?" (retold in *Lessons From Our Living Past* by Jules Harlow, pp. 11-15 and in *Legends of the Jews* by Louis Ginzberg, Vol. III, pp. 89-90).

16 The second commandment deals with the misuse of images and the third warns against the misuse of words. Can you think of contemporary examples of each? What are the consequences of such misuses? Can you develop some personal guidelines you might follow in observing the spirit of these commandments?

17 In explaining why the fifth commandment bids us to honor first *father* and then *mother,* the Rabbis taught that children more easily honor their mothers and therefore we are first told honor their mothers and therefore we are first told to honor our fathers. The Rabbis contrast this with Leviticus 19:3 where the Torah tells us to "fear your mother and father." Here they explained that people are more likely to "fear" (or revere) their father, so we must be reminded to fear our mothers first. Do you agree with these ideas? To conclude, complete the following sentences which are applicable to you:
My parent(s) and I _____.
I was surprised to see that _____.
I wish that _____.

Do you think people have different relationships with each parent or adult caregiver in their lives? Does having different relationships with these individuals enrich your life? How?
To each of these adults dedicate a page on which you list the important aspects of your relationship with them.

18 A Rabbinic concept concerns the *Chasiday Ummot HaOlam* — righteous gentiles. Maimonides tells us that any people who desire to worship God, to know God, and to walk uprightly in God's ways are considered righteous (*Yad, Shemitah* 13:13). How does this concept apply to Jethro? Can you share other examples of righteous gentiles?

19 If all people would seriously follow the Ten Commandments, what would society be like? Would we still need a judicial system?

20 The location of Mount Sinai is not known. A film which explores archaeological efforts to find this site is *The Mountain of Moses.* View it and then discuss why some people might be interested in locating Mount Sinai. If Mount Sinai were ever found, how would it affect Jewish tradition?

(For additional strategies about God, see the Index: "God." For additional strategies about Shabbat, see the Index: "God," "Shabbat.")

OTHER RESOURCES

21 Complete the pages which relate to *Yitro* in *Bible People Book Two* by Joel Lurie Grishaver, pp. 27-36. Also check the accompanying Leader Guide for procedures and additional activities.

22 Listen to and/or learn the song "The Ten Commandments" from *Bible People Songs*.

23 Read, act out, and discuss the skit for the portion *Yitro* in *Sedra Scenes: Skits for Every Torah Portion* by Stan J. Beiner, pp. 95-99.

24 Read, discuss, and do the activities suggested in the Teacher's Guide for the stories "The Thief's Secret" (pp. 84-87) and "The Education of Alexander" (pp. 99-102) in *Lessons From Our Living Past* edited by Jules Harlow.

25 For related stories, see *Who Knows Ten?* by Molly Cone and *God's Top Ten* by Roberta Louis Goodman.

26 Read, discuss, and do the activities suggested for the story "Honor Your Father," pp. 54-56, in *Stories From Our Living Past* by Francine Prose.

27 For other insights and activities related to the Ten Commandments, see *Teaching Mitzvot* by Barbara Binder Kadden and Bruce Kadden.

28 View and discuss the episode for *Yitro* from *Torah Toons I: The Video*.

29 For creative movement activities, see "Keep the Sabbath" and "Amazement at Sinai" from *Torah in Motion* by JoAnne Tucker and Susan Freeman, pp. 90-93.

30 Listen to, discuss, and sing "Hear My Voice" from *Sounds of Freedom: Exodus in Song*.

31 Read and discuss the illustrated commentary for *Yitro* in *American Torah Toons* by Lawrence Bush.

INVOLVING THE FAMILY

32 Test your knowledge (and your family's) of the Ten Commandments. Below are listed 15 commandments. Can you pick out the real ten? Can you put them in order? Once you find the real Ten Commandments, rank them in order of importance to the Jewish people and to yourself. Decide which commandment has the least significance for you, for each member of the family, or for the family as a whole at this time in your lives. Is there a new commandment that you would add?

_____ Love your neighbor as yourself.
_____ Keep the Shabbat.
_____ Give *tzedakah*.
_____ Keep kosher.
_____ Honor your parents.
_____ I am the Lord your God who brought you out of Egypt.
_____ Do not make images of anything in the heavens or the earth.
_____ Be fruitful and multiply.
_____ Do not steal.
_____ Do not commit adultery.
_____ Do not murder.
_____ You shall have no other gods but Me.
_____ Do not covet.
_____ Do not bear false witness.

Note: The Ten Commandments are repeated in Deuteronomy 5:6-18 (*Va'etchanan*) and also in a different order in Leviticus 19:2-18 (*Kedoshim*).

See those portions for additional Insights and Strategies.

BAR/BAT MITZVAH PROJECT

33 In this portion, Jethro suggests that Moses lighten his burden of leading the Israelites by appointing judges over the people. Jethro advises Moses that by lightening his load, he will be able to endure and be there for himself and for the people (Exodus 18:1-27 in *The Five Books of Moses,* translated by Everett Fox).

Similar situations happen in our world. An individual can become so overburdened that he/she cannot endure. Many times helping hands can lighten their load. Investigate through your synagogue, the local Family Service Agency or a volunteer center in your community for a situation where you can "be there" for someone and lighten his/her load. This might be as a parent's helper after school a day or two a week; helping a physically challenged person with yard work, taking out the trash cans and cleaning sidewalks during the winter; bringing a meal to a shut-in or to someone who is ill; or becoming a mentor and tutoring a younger student.

MISHPATIM 21:1-24:18 משפטים

SYNOPSIS

IN THIS PORTION, MOSES SETS BEFORE the Israelites the following groups of rules:

1. The rules concerning slaves: The Israelites are permitted to retain slaves, but they must always bear the dignity of the slave in mind. Hebrew slaves are to be freed after six years of service, or immediately if their owner willfully injures them. A slave who does not wish to leave a master shall have an ear pierced and remain a slave for life.

2. Certain crimes are punishable by death: Among these are murder, kidnapping, and insulting one's parents.

3. The laws detailing the responsibilities incurred by the owner of an ox: The owner of an ox which is known to have previously injured or killed another person or animal is to be punished along with the animal. The owner of an ox which causes death or injury just once does not incur punishment, although the ox must be stoned or sold in restitution for its actions.

4. Rules and penalties for theft and lending.

5. Certain laws pertaining to the Israelites remaining a holy people are presented. Among these are reminders not to curse God and to dedicate to God firstborn sons and cattle and the first fruits of a tree. Other laws pertaining to holiness include prohibitions against eating flesh torn by wild beasts and against boiling a kid in its mother's milk.

6. In the Sabbatical year, the land is to lie fallow or rest. The commandment to rest on the seventh day follows.

7. The observance of the three festivals — the Feast of Unleavened Bread (Passover), The Feast of the Harvest (Shavuot), and the Feast of the Ingathering (Sukkot) — is prescribed. All males are commanded to present themselves before the God at those times.

In addition, the principle of just restitution for damages is stated (*lex talionis*, an "eye for an eye,"

etc.). The slavery of the Israelites in Egypt is recalled to remind the people not to mistreat strangers, widows, and orphans in their midst.

God tells Moses that an angel will lead the Israelites through the desert to Canaan. God promises to destroy all the peoples whose path the Israelites cross, so that the Israelites will not be tempted to worship the gods of other nations.

Moses repeats all the rules to the people and then writes them all down. Offerings are made to seal the covenant with God and the people accept the law saying, "All the things the Lord has commanded we will do."

The mountain is covered by the presence of God (the cloud) for six days. On the seventh day, God calls Moses to ascend and Moses goes up the mountain and remains there for 40 days and nights.

INSIGHTS FROM THE TRADITION

A The word *mishpatim* means judgments. Rabbinic interpretation distinguished between *mishpatim* and *chukim*. *Mishpatim* were those laws in the Torah which could be arrived at by human reason. *Chukim* were the laws which were beyond the grasp of human understanding and so had to be obeyed solely because God had so demanded. (For more about this distinction, see Insight G in Leviticus, *Acharay Mot*, page 196.)

This section of the Torah is also known as the "Book of the Covenant" because it begins the detailing of the laws and ordinances which Moses wrote down (Exodus 24:4,7). The rules contained in this section are diverse, covering virtually every aspect of human life.

Have you ever been told to follow a rule that did not make sense? Was a reason ever given for the rule? Why do you think the rule was given in the first place?

B Many of the laws given in this portion have to do with behavior and moral values. The Israelites are called upon to remember their treatment as strangers in a strange land. This admonition is repeated 36 times in the Torah. Also the Israelites must not afflict the widow or orphan because their own wives and children could become widows and orphans.

What does empathy mean? How is it different from sympathy? Is there a qualitative difference to a response given out of empathy rather than out of sympathy? Give some examples.
How do you feel when you are a stranger in a new place?
Why should strangers be treated with special consideration?
Why is the commandment not to wrong a stranger given such emphasis?
How do the experiences of an individual and a society influence their ethical and legal expectations and standards?

C In looking at the regulations in this portion, Ibn Ezra notes that they focus upon just treatment for the most vulnerable members of society — slaves, borrowers, minors, resident aliens, widows, and orphans. The Shabbat and festivals, too, are seen by Ibn Ezra in this light. The Israelites are a people whose belief may be weakened by outside influences; therefore, the festivals and Shabbat are given to reinforce the Israelite commitment to God (see *Encyclopaedia Judaica*, "Exodus," Vol. 6, "Rules and Admonitions," p. 1059).

Ahad Ha-am wrote: More than Israel has kept the Sabbath, the Sabbath has kept Israel. How does this echo the insight by Ibn Ezra?
How does the fact that the Israelites were slaves in Egypt affect their treatment of others? Does the experience of suffering sensitize one to the suffering of others? If so, why the need for laws concerning the treatment of others?

Is there such a thing as a slave mentality? If so, what is its effect on the human psyche? To what thoughts, attitudes, or habits are you enslaved? Do these add to or detract from your sense of self-worth? Explain.

D The Torah accepts the condition of slavery, yet includes stringent, humane guidelines for slave owners. These "humane" guidelines must be viewed within the historical context in which they were written. The laws given in the Torah gave a slave some limited rights in contrast to neighboring peoples who gave no rights to their slaves. The Torah states that if a slave is purposely mistreated he is released. Also, all slaves had to be released during the Jubilee (50th) year, and they are offered freedom in the Sabbatical (7th) year. A difficulty does arise for us when the Torah text states that if a slave had a wife when he was acquired as a slave, his wife leaves with him (21:3). But if his master gave the slave a wife and she had children, the wife and children belong to the master (21:4).

If the slave was offered freedom and his master had given him a wife and they had children, what kind of a choice did the slave have? It might be an easy choice if he was not attached to his wife and/or children. He could easily leave, but what if he was attached to them, what could he do?
How do you feel when the Torah presents laws that make us feel uncomfortable in today's world? What can we learn from the "humane" approach taken by the Torah?

E The principle of "an eye for an eye, a tooth for a tooth" is known in legal terms as *"talion,"* a claw. *Talion* means retribution authorized by law. It is the root of the word "retaliation." The biblical verses which describe this form of punishment have been sadly misunderstood. *Talion* evokes an image of harsh justice. Rabbinic commentaries, however, point to monetary compensation being the norm rather than actual physical retaliation. For, aside from inflicting physical pain in return for physical pain, no real lesson is learned from *talion* . . . and no real compensation has been paid.

Does the penalty of monetary compensation achieve something that physical retribution cannot?
Do you think that a physically strong person would prefer physical retribution while a weaker person would eagerly settle for a monetary settlement?
What kind of retaliation would you want if someone hurt you?

F Exodus 23:17 states: "Three times a year all your males shall appear before God." Since males are specified in the obligation to perform this *mitzvah,* this became one of the verses on which the Rabbis based the concept of exempting women from time-bound *mitzvot* (*Kiddushin* 34a-34b). The Rabbis sought to excuse women from the time-bound *mitzvot* so that they could be free to care for their families and homes.

How did this Rabbinic ruling help women? How did it hurt them?
Does your synagogue allow full participation for every individual regardless of gender?
Have the differences between the liberal and traditional branches of Judaism driven a permanent wedge between them? How can we work to overcome this divide while still honoring our differences?

G *Mishpatim* also contains the first of three identical admonitions: "You shall not boil a kid in its mother's milk" (Exodus 23:13, 34:26, and Deuteronomy 14:21). This text is the basis for the law of *kashrut,* which prohibits the mixing of dairy and meat.

What impact might the observance of *kashrut* have on an individual, a family, the non-Jewish world? Y.L. Gordon said, "Be a Jew in your tent and a man in the street." How would this dictum apply to observances such as *kashrut*?

Describe other ways in which people "publicize" their adherence to various cultural, ethnic, or religious groups.
How do you "publicize" your religious identity?

STRATEGIES

ANALYZING THE TEXT

1 To help you appreciate both the variety of laws given in *Mishpatim* and the elements these have in common, sort them into meaningful categories. Some possible categories are: laws for which the punishment is the same, laws involving the same type of crime (and/or victims), laws for which no punishment is prescribed. Compare your categories and the laws you fit into them with others in the group. Where did you agree? Disagree? Why? (For other ways of categorizing these laws, see Exodus, *Yitro* Strategy #1, page 115.)

2 Make a "fact file" on the Torah's attitude toward slavery. Compile as many references as you can to slavery in the Torah and list each on a separate index card. Some sources to consult are: Leviticus 25:39ff.; Deuteronomy 15:12-18; 23:16-17; a concordance to locate additional verses; reading through this portion, *Mishpatim;* and also Strategy #3, immediately below. Based on the statements you have found, discuss how the Torah stresses the humane treatment of slaves and guarantees them some personal dignity.

3 Use a Hebrew concordance to help you find references to slavery in the Torah. Look up the root word עֶבֶד (*eved*) and, working in groups, track down forms of the root in one of the books of the Torah. Proceed as for Strategy #2, immediately above.

4 Use the laws in *Mishpatim* to do Exodus, *Yitro* Strategy #1, page 115 — grouping each law with the one of the Ten Commandments upon which it expands.

5 At one time it was thought that the laws of *kashrut* evolved as health precautions. According to the text, what is the basis for these laws?

6 Compare Everett Fox's translation of Exodus 21:12-19 and 22:21-26 (*The Five Books of Moses*) with another translation, such as *The Torah: A Modern Commentary*, edited by W. Gunther Plaut. How does Fox's translation differ? Does the repetitive word usage add to or detract from your understanding of the text?

EXTENDING THE TEXT

7 You can learn a lot about a society by studying its laws. Study *Mishpatim* to help you answer the following questions about the society at the time the laws were given. Cite examples of the laws as proof of your answers. What occupations do people in biblical society have? Describe the typical biblical family: Who was the head? Can you describe differences in the roles of men and women? Were children treated differently from adults? Who were the "poor" and "weak" members of society? How did the society provide for the care of its weaker members? Can these laws apply to contemporary conditions in society? (For a commentary on this, see *The Torah: A Modern Commentary*, edited by W. Gunther Plaut, p. 593.)

8 The injunction not to seethe a kid in its mother's milk occurs three times in the Torah. The school of Rabbi Ishmael explained that one occurrence is a prohibition against eating it, one is a prohibition against deriving benefit from it, and one is a prohibition against cooking it (*Hullin* 115b). Which prohibition did you assume the text referred to? Explain the significance of the other two interpretations the Rabbis gave for this verse.

9 Play "This Is the Law." Divide into teams of four to six players. Have each team choose a law from *Mishpatim* and incorporate into a wordless skit a scene in which the law is being broken. Don't make it too obvious. When the skit is performed, the audience must identify the law which is being violated. Award points for correctly identifying the law.

PERSONALIZING THE TEXT

10 Complete these sentences twice. Answer once as a slave recently freed from Egypt and once as yourself, a free person alive today: "You shall not oppress a stranger" (23:9) because _____. "You must not carry false rumors" (23:1) because _____. "You shall not ill-treat any widow or orphan" (22:21) because _____.

11 The prohibition against boiling a kid in its mother's milk is presented for the first time in Exodus 23:19. (It is also found in Exodus 34:26 and Deuteronomy 14:21.) This passage became the basis of the laws of *kashrut* which prohibit the mixing of any dairy products with meat. List all the laws of *kashrut* you know which have to do with not mixing milk and meat. Do some research to help make sure your list is complete. Write a set of guidelines for keeping a kosher kitchen on the basis of these laws.

12 Some foods are considered neither meat nor dairy. These foods are known as *pareve*, or neutral. Using magazine pictures and library pockets, make a sorting game to sort the following foods into categories according to whether they are DAIRY (*Milchig*), MEAT (*Fleishig*) or NEUTRAL (*pareve*): Cottage cheese, hard-boiled eggs, french fries, hamburgers, apples, tuna, chicken soup, ice cream, steak, cheese pizza, watermelon, peanut butter, buttermilk, vinegar, yogurt, potato chips. (If you can't find or draw pictures of the above foods, use other foods.) Write the correct category on the back of the pictures so that the game will be self-checking.

13 The way *kashrut* is observed varies a great deal among Jewish people. Conduct an informal survey of your friends to get an idea of the differences. For example, do they wait between eating meat and milk and, if so, for how long? Do they have separate dishes for meat and milk? Do they wash their meat and milk dishes separately? Can you suggest some reasons why the practice of *kashrut* would be different for different people? (You might want to explore the differences between the way Ashkenazim and Sephardim observe *kashrut*.)

References for all the activities on *kashrut: The Jewish Dietary Laws* by Samuel Dresner and Seymour Siegel; *The Biblical and Historical Background of Jewish Customs and Ceremonies* by Abraham P. Bloch; *Kosher Code of the Orthodox Jew* by S.I. Levin and Edward A. Boyden.

14 Before reading the portion, present to your group some "cases" for which *Mishpatim* gives laws, and have them decide what should be the rule governing such cases. Use these as a basis for a discussion of whether a society needs laws. Would it be possible to have laws without punishment? Some good cases: What should be done to an ox that gores a person to death? If the animal is killed, how should the meat be disposed of? Should the owner of the ox be punished? What if the ox has (has not) previously injured a person? What if death doesn't result from the goring (see Exodus 21:28-32)? What should be done, if two men, while fighting, injure a pregnant woman and cause her to miscarry (Exodus 21:22-25)? What should be done if an object or animal is stolen while in the possession of someone other than its owner (Exodus 22:9-14)?

15 Read the story "Lyzer the Miser and Shrewd Todie" by I.B. Singer in *Stories for Children*. Stop at the point where the Rabbi makes a judgment. If you were the Rabbi, how would you decide to treat Todie? *Mishpatim* gives some basic rules concerning what should be done if an animal is stolen or injured while in the possession of someone other than its owner. Read the relevant section (Exodus 22:9-14) and discuss how these rules should be applied to stolen objects. Would you use such rules to decide the case of Lyzer and Todie? Did the Rabbi in the story use them? Explain.

16 In Exodus 22:20 we read, "You shall not wrong a stranger or oppress him, for you were strangers in the land of Egypt." The basis for this law is so important because of the reasoning behind it: there might be many reasons not to wrong a stranger, for example, political or economic considerations, but according to the Torah, there is only *one* valid reason — because it is hurtful to the stranger. Exodus 23:9 makes this especially clear by reminding us of *our* experience in the land of Egypt: "You shall not oppress a stranger, for you know the feeling of the stranger, having yourselves been strangers in the land of Egypt." Can you think of any experiences you have had which have taught you a lesson about how to treat other people? Write a story about the experience as though it were a chapter from your autobiography. Title it "Lessons I've Learned" or "Do Not Do Unto Others . . ."

17 Using information derived from Strategy #7 on page 124, paint a mural in a "naive" style which illustrates what the daily life of the people might have been like. Include the many types of people, animals, and objects mentioned in the portion. You may choose to divide your mural into smaller sections for one or two people to paint. If you do so, have each person or group include something definitely *not* in the portion. Can the others spot the misplaced article?

18 The law "You shall not wrong a stranger or oppress him for you were strangers . . ." (Exodus 22:20) should have special meaning not only for Jews, but also for all free people. Almost everybody's ancestors were strangers once. Write a speech on this theme for the leader of your country to deliver.

19 In *Mishpatim*, the death penalty is prescribed for the crimes of murder, kidnapping, and insulting one's parents. Later, in the Book of Exodus (Exodus 35:2), we read that "whoever does any work on Shabbat shall be put to death." Why does violation of these four laws merit such severe punishment? To find an answer, consider the idea that both human beings and Shabbat are a living testimony to the fact that God created the world. How do the acts of murder, kidnapping, insulting one's parents, and working on Shabbat violate this teaching?

(For more, see the Index: "Firstborn," "*Kashrut*," "Welcoming the Stranger.")

OTHER RESOURCES

20 Read, act out, and discuss the skit for the portion *Mishpatim* in *Sedra Scenes: Skits for Every Torah Portion* by Stan J. Beiner, pp. 100-103.

21 Complete the page which relates to *Mishpatim* in *Bible People Book Two* by Joel Lurie Grishaver, p. 30. Also check the accompanying Leader Guide for procedures and additional activities.

22 Read and discuss the stories "From His Royal Highness, the Caliph of Arab Spain," pp. 77-79 and "How the Helmites Bought a Barrel of Justice," pp. 98-98 in *Lessons From Our Living Past*, edited by Seymour Rossel and Jules Harlow. Follow the suggested activities in the Leader Guide.

23 View and discuss the episode for *Mishpatim* from *Torah Toons I: The Video*.

24 For creative movement activities, see "Helping Your Enemy" and "Against Cruelty" from *Torah in Motion* by JoAnne Tucker and Susan Freeman, pp. 94-97.

25 Listen to, discuss, and sing "*Mishpatim*" from *Sounds of Freedom: Exodus in Song*.

26 Read and discuss the illustrated commentary for *Mishpatim* in *American Torah Toons* by Lawrence Bush.

INVOLVING THE FAMILY

27 When the Israelites accepted the laws laid down in this portion, they proclaimed, "*Na'aseh v'Nishma*," which means, "We will do [first] and [then] we will listen" (24:7). The Rabbis noted this unusual word order and remarked that there are times when we must do things even if we do not necessarily understand them. Discuss with your family when and why this faithful obedience might be necessary to a certain extent at home, at school, in sports, in the business world, etc. How might this attitude be hurtful? Does this saying not allow for healthy debate and discussion on whether the "doing" is ethical and moral? Can you give historical examples that led to tragedy when doing preceded thinking?

BAR/BAT MITZVAH PROJECT

28 The purpose of this *mitzvah* project is to enhance and enrich your celebration of Shabbat. This will involve approximately eight Shabbatot. Each Shabbat will have an observance to follow. It is your choice whether or not you want to retain the observance for subsequent Shabbatot. Keep a diary log of the observances and your and your family's reaction to it.

1st Shabbat – On Friday evening light the Shabbat candles and recite the blessing.

2nd Shabbat – Bake *challah* for the family. Recite the blessing for bread. Research in Jewish cookbooks for a recipe.

3rd Shabbat – Pour wine or juice for each family member and recite *Kiddush.*

4th Shabbat – Help prepare a substantial part of Friday night dinner.

5th Shabbat – Make a donation in your *tzedakah* box before Shabbat begins. Attend Friday evening services.

6th Shabbat – Attend Saturday morning services.

7th Shabbat – Do Havdalah with your family.

8th Shabbat – Create a Shabbat observance from the activities you have done on the seven previous Shabbatot.

Be consistent and keep the diary log up to date. How did you feel about the eight week Shabbat experiment? Interview family members for their thoughts and feelings about the Shabbat experience. What observances and traditions do you and your family intend to continue? How will you implement them on a weekly basis? There are additional Shabbat observances you can also try. Obtain a book on Jewish holiday observance as a resource for ideas. A few suggested titles are: *The First Jewish Catalog* by Richard Siegel, Michael Strassfeld, and Sharon Strassfeld; *Jewish Family Celebrations: The Sabbath, Festivals, and Ceremonies* by Arlene Rossen Cardozo.

TERUMAH 25:1-27:19 תרומה

SYNOPSIS

IN THIS PORTION, GOD INSTRUCTS Moses to accept gifts from the Israelites. These are to be used in constructing a sanctuary so that God can dwell among the people. Acceptable gifts include precious metals and stones; tanned skins; blue, purple, and crimson yarns and linen; and special oils and spices.

God shows Moses the pattern according to which the Tabernacle and its contents are to be made. First to be made is an Ark of acacia wood, overlaid both inside and out with gold. The Ark is to be fitted with gold rings and gold covered poles to make it portable. The tablets of the law (which God will give Moses) are to be kept in the Ark. Two gold *cherubim* are to be placed facing each other over the cover of the Ark.

The Ark is to be housed in the innermost chamber of the Tabernacle, called the Holy of Holies.

God describes the construction of the Tabernacle to Moses in great detail. The entire structure is to be portable, with a wooden framework, and walls of richly colored fabric.

Inside the Tabernacle, next to the Holy of Holies, is to be a second room called the Holy place, which will contain a table overlaid in gold with the bread of display (shewbread) set on it, and a seven-branched *menorah* also wrought of gold work.

In the court of the Tabernacle, an altar is to be constructed with horns of copper at each corner, and the courtyard itself is to be 100 cubits long by 50 cubits wide, fenced in with fine twined linen on silver filleted poles with hooks of silver and sockets of brass.

INSIGHTS FROM THE TRADITION

A *Terumah* means "gifts" which the Israelites are to contribute to the building of the Tabernacle.

What is the best gift you ever received?
What is the most important gift you have ever given?

B In Genesis, the creation of the world is described in 34 verses; but the passage describing the building of the Tabernacle is nearly three times as long! Some commentators suggest that this difference reflects the difficulty of the human challenge to build a sanctuary within our own hearts wherein God can dwell. Another explanation has to do with the challenge of cooperation: God created the world alone, while the Tabernacle was the work of many people. A *midrash* tells us that all the people should be involved with the building of the Ark so that they would merit receiving the Torah.

Must one participate in the Jewish community in order to be considered a Jew?
How do you contribute to your synagogue?
What benefits do you and others derive because of the contributions?

C Torah is very specific about the *order* in which the work should be done. Rabbi Simcha Bunem of Przysucha learned from this that "all things must be done in the proper sequence" (Fran Elovitz in *Learn Torah With . . .* , p. 146). In Jewish tradition the importance of order is suggested by the name of the Passover meal and by what we call our prayer books (*Seder* and *Siddur* both have the same Hebrew root סדר — meaning "order"). Order helps us know what to expect and therefore helps us to focus on the meaning of the ritual or prayer. Think of how unsettling it would be to have the order of the Shabbat rituals or the prayers change every week.

Do you have routines in your daily life in which the sequence of events is important to you? How would it feel if the order was unpredictable? Why does the order of events in a construction project like building the Tabernacle matter? Can you think of areas of life where lack of order is desirable?

D The Rabbis debated the order of the events from *Terumah* to the end of the Book of Exodus. As the sequence stands, the story of the Golden Calf (in *Ki Tisa*) intrudes on four other portions which describe the Tabernacle, priestly garments, and the sanctification of the priests.

Rashi, holding with the Talmudic dictum "There is no 'earlier' or 'later' (i.e., no chronological order) to the events in the Torah" states: ". . . in fact, the incident of the Golden Calf happened a considerable time before the command regarding the work of the Tabernacle was given."

This view goes a long way toward explaining why God needed a dwelling place among the people at all, since Jewish tradition teaches that God can be found anywhere. A *midrash* explains that after God had forgiven the Israelites for their sin in worshiping the Golden Calf, Moses asked God for a visible sign which would indicate this forgiveness to the nations of the world. God then said to Moses: "As truly as thou livest, I will let my *Shechinah* (presence) dwell among [the Israelites], so that all may know that I have forgiven Israel. My sanctuary in their midst will be a testimony to My forgiveness of their sins . . ." (*Legends of the Jews* by Louis Ginzberg, Vol. III, p. 148).

Exodus 25:8 reads "Let them make Me a sanctuary that I may dwell *among them*." Why among them, as opposed to "that I may dwell *in it*"?

Rabbi Mordecai Katz (*Lilmod Ulelamade,* p. 87) sees in God's promise to dwell among the people a recognition of the limits of human understanding. The idea that God is everywhere was hard to grasp; this was demonstrated by the story of the Golden Calf. Thus, the Tabernacle is a concession to humankind, providing a visible focus for the idea of God's indwelling, a focus which the Israelites could readily understand and accept.

What is the role, function, or significance in contemporary society of the house of worship or sanctuary?
Are your needs to understand God different from the needs of the generation of the Exodus? Explain.

E Concerning the *cherubim*, alluded to in this portion, very little is known. Even the meaning of the Hebrew word *cherubim* is unclear. Some scholars trace it to the Akkadian word *karibu*, which referred to an intermediary who brought human prayers before the gods. The Rabbis in Talmudic times understood it to mean "like a child" (Hebrew *ki* [like] and Aramaic *rabbia* [child]), an explanation which probably influenced artistic portraits of *cherubim* as winged children.

Figures of *cherubim* were used decoratively in the Tabernacle, in Solomon's Temple, and in Ezekiel's vision of the rebuilt Temple (Ezekiel 41:18-20, 25). The two *cherubim* which rested on the Ark in the Tabernacle were the predecessors of two much larger such figures in the Temple.

Even the function of the *cherubim* is uncertain. They may have served as guards protecting the Ark, just as they bar the way to the Garden of Eden in Genesis 3:24. It has been suggested that they represented the love between God and Israel — facing each other at times when Israel was pleasing to God, and turning away from each other when the Israelites disobeyed God's word.

The Greeks depicted love as a child with bow and arrow. How does the idea of Cupid differ from the concept of *cherubim*?

What are some of the decorative images in your synagogue? Do you understand the meaning behind them all?

Why do we decorate our synagogues? Does God want, demand, or ask for this display? If not, why do people need it?

F The Hebrew word for "altar" is מזבח (*mizbay-ach*). The Rabbis explained the function of the altar by considering this word as an acronym: מחילה — *mechilah* (forgiveness) which can be sought by sacrificing at the altar; זכות — *zechut* (merit) which can be earned by following the sacrificial rites; ברכה — *b'rachah* (blessing) which is acquired by being true to the tradition surrounding the altar; חיים — *chayim* (life). The observance of the sacrificial rites point the way to eternal truths and thereby to everlasting life. Although we no longer have altars or practice sacrifices today, this interpretation of the purpose of the altar may be applied to prayer.

Is there a contemporary equivalent to the altar of old?

Note: *Terumah* and *Tetzaveh* are usually read as a double portion. For more about double portions, see Exodus, *Pikuday*, Insight A, page 155.

STRATEGIES

ANALYZING THE TEXT

1 In *Terumah,* the first object the Israelites are told to make is the Ark to hold the Ten Commandments. Why do you think they were told to make the Ark first? What can you learn from the fact that in this case the Torah says *"they shall make"* (Exodus 25:10), while in connection with other parts of the Tabernacle it says *"you shall make?"*

2 The verb "make" occurs 200 times in the story of the Tabernacle (*Studies in Shemot* by

Nehama Leibowitz, p. 475). How many times can you find the verb עשה or a variation of it (e.g., יעשו, תעשה, ועשה, עשו) in this portion? Can you suggest any special significance of such frequent use of this word. Think about *who* was to do the making. By what other means could the parts of the Tabernacle have been acquired? Consider the emphasis on the Tabernacle and its furnishings being made according to God's pattern (see Exodus 25:8,40; 26:30; 27:8).

EXTENDING THE TEXT

3 A *midrash* tells how the objects in the Tabernacle symbolized certain parts of creation. Match up the two lists below to learn the details of this *midrash*:

1. candlestick
2. high priest
3. *cherubim* (with wings)
4. tablets in the Ark
5. curtain before the Holy of Holies
6. wash stand and bowl
7. table with bread
8. *menorah*

a. heaven and earth – day 1
b. firmament dividing the waters – day 2
c. the great sea – day 3
d. plants to nourish human beings – day 3
e. the sun and moon – day 4
f. seven planets – day 4
g. birds – day 5
h. Adam – day 6

ANSWERS: 1–e; 2–h; 3–g; 4–a; 5–b; 6–c; 7–d; 8–f.

Note: For other symbolic interpretations of the parts of the Tabernacle, see *The Torah: A Modern Commentary,* edited by W. Gunther Plaut, p. 614.)

4 Two beautiful *midrashim* give different explanations of why the Israelites built a

Tabernacle as a dwelling for God. According to one *midrash,* the Israelites wanted to build the Tabernacle to give God the same kind of honor that is accorded to earthly kings (see *Legends of the Jews* by Louis Ginzberg, Vol. III, p. 148, and *Studies in Shemot* by Nehama Leibowitz, Vol. II, p. 153). The other *midrash* tells that God wanted the Tabernacle because, having given the Torah a new home among the Israelites, God wanted to continue to dwell with it (see Ginzberg, p. 153). Write your own elaboration of one of these two *midrashim,* detailing the conversations between God, Israel, and Moses. Where relevant, include elements from the description in *Terumah* of the Tabernacle.

5 Today we no longer have altars or practice sacrifices. Instead, however, we can apply to prayer the interpretation by the Rabbis of the purpose for the altar (see Insight F, page 130). Rewrite the explanation of the acronym מזבח (*mizbayach*) so that it is in keeping with contemporary life.

6 The second commandment states: "You shall not make for yourself a sculptured image, or any likeness of what is in the heavens above, or on the earth below, or in the waters under the earth." How then can you explain the construction of *cherubim*?

PERSONALIZING THE TEXT

7 How is this original Ark like and/or different from Arks found in synagogues today? See the video *The Synagogue,* and look at architectural design books for synagogues. (For a follow-up activity, see Strategy #9 on this page.)

8 Imagine you are a reporter for *Architectural Digest.* Write your own description of the Tabernacle based on the description in this portion, paying particular attention to the objects listed in Strategy #13, page 132. Describe how it would feel to worship God in such a setting. (For references on the Tabernacle, also see Strategy #13.)

9 The Ark for the Tabernacle was to be constructed of acacia wood, covered inside and outside by gold. Raba took this as a metaphor for human behavior, saying: "Any scholar whose inside is not like his outside is no scholar" (*Yoma* 72b). Express this as a lesson to guide general human behavior. How does this differ from the saying in *Pirke Avot* 4:25, "Do not look at the flask but at what it contains?" Which do you think is better advice for dealing with other people? Design an Ark for your synagogue. Use as a basis for your design one of the expressions included here.

10 Imagine that your congregation is about to design and construct a new building. Outline the steps that need to be taken in the process, paying special attention to the order in which all the work, from planning and financing to actual building, should occur. Afterward, review your plan with the following questions in mind: How much of the order of work is dictated by physical realities (e.g., you can't paint the inside wall until the roof is up)? How much is determined by your own priorities (e.g., which would you build first, the sanctuary or the school)? What role do you envision individual congregants and families playing in the process? As a follow-up, you may wish to invite a member of a congregation which has recently been involved in a building project to speak to your group.

11 Moses is told to "accept gifts [for God's Tabernacle] from every person whose heart so moves him" (Exodus 25:2). These "gifts of the heart" are called, in Hebrew, *terumah.* A distinction is made between *terumah* (a charitable gift given spontaneously because a cause or need stirs one) and *tzedakah.* The giving of *tzedakah* is an act of righteousness, a way of doing what is just. The Rabbis therefore saw giving *tzedakah* as a responsibility. Unlike the freewill offerings given by the Israelites toward the building of the Tabernacle, *tzedakah* is incumbent upon every individual, regardless of whether or not he/she is moved to give.

Compile a broad list of groups in our society which seek donations to support their work. One resource for finding these groups is in the book *Mitzvahs* by Danny Siegel. In small groups, decide to which of these groups we, as Jews, owe *tzedakah*. To which would we be giving contributions more in the spirit of *terumah*? Should a larger percentage of monies go to *terumah* or to *tzedakah*? Why? Imagine that you had $1000 to distribute among the groups on your list. Decide how you would allocate it, bearing in mind the above distinctions.

12 Imagine you are Moses entrusted with building the Tabernacle. Tell the Israelites in your own words what to make and how to make it. In your telling, stress the same Hebrew words that the text stresses. (This is a good way to review, in Hebrew or English, the names of the different parts of the Tabernacle.)

13 What objects in the Tabernacle can be found in our synagogues today in the same form? In similar form? What objects are missing? Learn the Hebrew words for the key objects: Which of these objects are mentioned in the description of the Temple built by Solomon (I Kings 7:48-50)?

Exodus 25: 10 (*aron*) – ארון – Ark
Exodus 25:17 (*kaporet*) – כפרת – cover
Exodus 25:23 (*shulchan*) – שלחן – table
Exodus 25:31 (*menorah*) – מנורה – lampstand
Exodus 26:31 (*parochet*) – פרכת – curtain
Exodus 27:1 (*mizbayach*) – מזבח – altar

References: *The Tabernacle: Its Structure and Utensils* by Moshe Levine; *Exploring Exodus: The Heritage of Biblical Israel* by Nahum Sarna.

14 The seven branched *menorah* is an important symbol in Jewish life. Today it is a key symbol of the State of Israel. Arrange a display on the subject of the significance of the *menorah* in Jewish life and art. Borrow *menorot* from people's homes. (Don't confuse a seven-branched *menorah* with a nine-branched *chanukiah*.) Take or obtain photographs of the *menorot* in the synagogues/museums of your city. Make slides/photos of *menorot* described in books on Jewish art and symbols. Draw a picture illustrating the *menorah* found in the Tabernacle (Exodus 25:31-39). Draw your own designs for *menorot*. Invite your friends and parents to view the display.

15 Express your most deeply held Jewish values through the *menorah*. Draw a seven branched *menorah*. On the central branch, write the Jewish idea or belief that you value most. On the other six branches, write six other Jewish ideas or values you hold and cherish. The *menorah* is also the symbol of the State of Israel. Draw a second *menorah* and fill in the values that you think are most important to the State of Israel. Compare and contrast the two *menorot*. As a class, discuss the differences and similarities each of you finds.

16 According to *Exodus Rabbah* 34:1, God told Moses that the Tabernacle, altar, and offerings were for the sake of the Israelites, as God has no need of such things. In light of this, prayer, life cycle, and holiday observances are most likely also for our sake and not for God's. Make a list of ways that our Jewish practices benefit *us*. Share your list with others. Compile a class list. Of all the benefits listed, decide which is the most important.

17 What makes a place or an object sacred? Can an ordinary thing suddenly become special or sacred? Can something sacred become ordinary? For more see the Index: "Holiness," "Shewbread," "Challah."

OTHER RESOURCES

18 Complete the pages which relate to *Terumah* in *Bible People Book Two* by Joel Lurie Grishaver, pp. 39-42. Also check the accompanying Leader Guide for procedures and additional activities.

19 Read, act out, and discuss the skit for the portion *Terumah* in *Sedra Scenes: Skits for Every Torah Portion* by Stan J. Beiner, pp. 104-107.

20 Follow the directions for "Copper Repousse" in *Fast, Clean and Cheap,* by Simon Kops, to create your own depiction of the *menorah* in the Tabernacle.

21 View and discuss the episode for *Terumah* from *Torah Toons I: The Video.*

22 For creative movement activities, see "Giving," "Winged Cherubim," and "Colored Gate" from *Torah in Motion* by JoAnne Tucker and Susan Freeman, pp. 98-103.

23 Listen to, discuss, and sing *"V'asu Li Mikdash"* from *Sounds of Freedom: Exodus in Song.*

24 Read and discuss the illustrated commentary for *Terumah* in *American Torah Toons* by Lawrence Bush.

INVOLVING THE FAMILY

25 A *midrash* tells that when Bezalel made the Tabernacle, he carved crowns on the altar, on the table, and on the Ark. The crown of the altar was for the priests and the crown on the table was for the kings who would rule in Israel. But, asked the Rabbis, "for whom was the crown on the Ark?" They answered, "Anyone who wishes to wear the crown of Torah, let that person study and take it!" (*Yoma* 72b). Working with your family, describe a program of study for a person who wishes to wear the crown of Torah.

Note: There is a great deal of overlap and related material in the portions *Terumah, Tetzaveh, Vayakhel,* and *Pikuday.* In particular, *Vayakhel* contains a repetition of the content in *Terumah.* Therefore, the Insights from the Tradition and the Strategies for all of these portions should be regarded as interchangeable.

BAR/BAT MITZVAH PROJECT

26 The Torah portion talks about the gifts that people brought to help build the Tabernacle. These gifts of the heart may be seen as each person's contribution to making a place for holiness in the world. In the *sedra Terumah,* the gifts seem to be physical objects such as jewelry and cloth, but such gifts might also have to do with personal qualities like effort and hope. What personal gifts do you bring to help repair the world and make it a place of greater holiness? Write a personal statement describing your gifts and how they will help make the world a better place. Create a poster with this personal statement. Add illustrations, calligraphy, and photos of yourself and others. Display this poster at the entry to the sanctuary for your family and guests to read. You may also want to include a statement about your Bar/Bat Mitzvah being a spiritual gift to yourself, your family, and your Jewish community.

TETZAVEH 27:20-30:10 תצוה

SYNOPSIS

IN THIS PORTION, MOSES IS FURTHER told to instruct the Israelites to bring olive oil for lighting the lamps of the Tabernacle. The lamps, which are to be the responsibility of Aaron and his sons, are to burn from evening to morning for all time. Moses is told to ordain Aaron and his sons as priests.

The priests are to be adorned in special clothes. All the priests are to wear four garments — linen breeches, tunics, sashes, and turbans. In addition to these four articles, the High Priest (Aaron) is to wear a special robe of pure blue decorated at the hem with pomegranates and golden bells. Over this robe, the *ephod* — an apron-like layer woven of gold, blue, purple, and crimson — is to be worn. The breastplate, inlaid with precious stones and the names of the twelve tribes of Israel, is to be worn by the High Priest over the *ephod*. The eighth special item in the High Priest's dress is a gold plate engraved with the words "*Kodesh LaYHVH*" (Holy to *Adonai*) that is to be tied with a blue cord to the front of his turban.

The priests are to be ordained in a special ceremony which first involves washing, dressing, and anointing them with oil, and secondly, the offering of various sacrifices. These ceremonies are to be repeated for seven days.

The priests are to bring offerings twice daily to the altar in the Tabernacle. Further, they are to burn incense on an altar to be constructed especially for that purpose.

INSIGHTS FROM THE TRADITION

A The word *tetzaveh* means to "instruct" or "command." It is used in reference to Moses' first task in this section, to command the Israelites to bring olive oil for lighting the lamps.

B *Tetzaveh* begins with the commandment to the Israelites to kindle the Tabernacle lights regularly. The Hebrew phrase נר תמיד (*ner tamid*) used in this instruction has been transposed over time to refer not to an act to be performed perpetually, but to an *object* to be perpetually present (i.e., the *ner tamid*/eternal lamp found in synagogues today). Thus, the eternal light in our synagogues is there to maintain some sense of the original command found here regarding the light in the Tabernacle. This command was later observed in the First and Second Temples in Jerusalem.

There is an expression: "Every Jew must light the *ner tamid* in his/her own heart . . ." What does this mean to you?
In Isaiah 42:6, God speaks of Israel as "a light unto the nations." What purpose do you think this phrase asks Israel to fulfill? Why is light used as a metaphor?
What feelings do you have when you see kindled lights? How do those feelings influence your attitude toward holidays and observances?

C In *Tetzaveh*, Aaron and his sons are given the clear and important role of serving God as priests. The Rabbis speculated that this was a role that Moses himself had hoped to be given. After all, who had a more intimate understanding of God than this greatest of prophets? It was therefore "in consideration of Moses' feelings" (*Legends of the Jews* by Louis Ginzberg, Vol. III, p. 168) that God let Moses be responsible for appointing and teaching the priests, rather than God doing so.

While the *midrash* presents this task as an opportunity for Moses to demonstrate his humility, the text itself furnishes an irony: This is the only portion in the last four books of the Torah in which Moses' name does not appear.

The Vilna Gaon noted, however, that the portion *Tetzaveh* is usually read on or near Adar 7, the traditional date of Moses' death (*The Torah: A Modern Commentary*, edited by W. Gunther Plaut,

p. 624). Thus, the absence of Moses' name from this portion may in some way signal or remind us of his death.

Does Moses strike you as a particularly humble person? Explain.
Do you think that not giving the honor of the priesthood or of the actual construction of the Tabernacle and its utensils to Moses was intentionally done to keep him humble?
What kind of work do you think you are most suited to do? Work with people? Work with ideas? Work with objects?
Which kind of work was Moses most suited to do?

D Ellen Frankel provides a fascinating insight on the lamps which were part of the Tabernacle. The character of the "Bubbes" explains that like Aaron and his sons who had to maintain burning lamps in the Tabernacle, Jewish women perform this same duty by kindling Shabbat and holiday candles. The "Bubbes" continue, ". . . our hearts and hands are every bit as pure as those of the priests, and our candles shine just as brightly as theirs" (*The Five Books of Miriam,* p 133-134).

Is the service of the Tabernacle (sanctuary) still in the hands of the priests? Still in male hands only?
Do only women light Shabbat and holiday candles?
Give examples of how things have changed for women and men since biblical times.

E God provides Moses with an elaborate description of the clothing and vestments for the priests. A part of the vestments for the High Priest were the *Urim* and *Tummim*. While no one knows for certain, it is likely that this device was a type of "lot" which was shaken and thrown, perhaps, or otherwise used as a guide in determining the will of God. This device passed out of use before the end of the biblical period.

Are there modern equivalents of the *Urim* and *Tummim*?

What do you suppose the Jewish attitude is toward these modern equivalents?

F Bells of gold were placed between pomegranate designs woven along the hem of the High Priest's robe. The text states the purpose of these bells: "Aaron shall wear it while officiating, so that the sound of it is heard when he comes into the sanctuary . . . and when he goes out, that he may not die" (Exodus 28:35). Why should Aaron's steps be heard? One answer may be that one should not enter a building stealthily; one should make his/her presence immediately known. The commentary *Haketav Vehakabbalah* tells us that the bells are an auditory counterpart of the *tzitzit.*

Rabbi Reuven Bulka explains that *tzitzit* are a "visual-impact" *mitzvah* which reminds Jews of their responsibilities to the commandments. The High Priest is obligated to many more *mitzvot,* so he was given an additional reminder, one that utilizes a different physical sense, that of hearing (*Torah Therapy,* p. 50).

Can you identify visual and auditory cues which remind you of your Jewish responsibilities?
Do you have a dominant sense? How do you use that sense in relationships? In carrying out responsibilities at home or work? in school? spiritually?

Note: *Tetzaveh* and *Terumah* are usually read as a double portion. For more about double portions, see Exodus, *Pikuday,* Insight A, page 155. For a note on the placement of the events of the portion in time, see the Insights C and D for Exodus, *Terumah,* pages 128 and 129.)

STRATEGIES

ANALYZING THE TEXT

1 Determine how (in the Ashkenazic tradition) the dress of a Torah is like that of the High Priest. Read the portion carefully. From your recollection of a Torah, list as many elements as you can that are similar to the dress of the High Priest including layers of clothing, color, ornaments, and names given to the various parts of dress. Why do you suppose these similarities exist? Then go and examine a Torah. Are there similarities you missed? Are there any significant differences between the dress of the Torah and that of the High Priest?

2 Reread the description of the High Priest's garments. Make those garments, using the colors called for in the text. This will take sewing skills. Look through pattern books, especially the costume section, at a local sewing shop. With some adaptations you will be able to find one or two patterns suitable for the garments you are making. Construct the garments full size. To display use a live model or a mannequin. Used mannequins are sometimes available for sale at thrift shops. A dress maker's dummy would also work, but a head would have to be added. Styrofoam heads are available at most wig and beauty supply shops.

EXTENDING THE TEXT

3 Moses instructs the Israelites to bring olive oil for kindling the lamps in the Tent of Meeting. There are numerous instances in the Tanach where the olive tree or olive oil is singled out for special mention. It is numbered among the seven species with which the land of Israel is blessed (Deuteronomy 8:7-8). Today, the olive branch is a symbol of peace (Genesis 8:11). Other references to olive trees or olive oil include Deuteronomy 6:11, 28:40; I Kings 6:31; II Kings 18:32; Judges 9:8-9; Jeremiah 11:16; Zechariah 4:3; Psalms 52:10, 128:3. How is Israel like an olive tree? Like the olive? Like olive oil? Obtain a picture of an olive tree and make an outline drawing of it. Using micrography, replace the drawn lines with words, phrases, poetry, or text. Micrography is the use of very tiny lettering which substitutes for the lines in a drawing. Compose original creative

writing or use biblical text for this activity. (For some *midrashim* which address these questions, see *The Torah: A Modern Commentary,* edited by W. Gunther Plaut, p. 624.)

4 Aaron is appointed High Priest. Several *midrashim* allude to the fact that Moses may have been hoping that this important and honored position would be his. Write a resume for Aaron detailing his experiences and qualifications for the job.

5 Read and discuss the *midrashim* concerning Moses cited in the Insights for this portion. Have one member of your group play the role of Moses. Appoint several people to interview Moses at this critical point in his life when he has just learned that he will not be the High Priest. How do the text and the *midrashim* stress the *humanness* of Moses? Incorporate this into your interview.

6 The Breastplate of Decision was to be fitted with four rows of precious stones, the total corresponding to the twelve tribes of Israel. Like the *ephod,* the Breastplate of Decision was to be engraved with the names of the sons of Jacob. What are the names of the twelve tribes? What are the symbols of each? Using the names, the symbols, or both, design and make a modern breastplate such as might be used to decorate a Torah, a stained glass window, or an Ark.

7 Compare the robes of the High Priest to what some Rabbis and Cantors wear today. Compare them also to the robes worn by Christian clergy. To what do you attribute the differences/ similarities? Is it true that "clothes make the person?" What is the function served by having special vestments for the High Priest? How would such vestments affect the priests themselves? The Israelites? God?

8 The *ner tamid* is only one Jewish light. What are some other special lights associated with

Jewish practice and observance? Create a bulletin board display on this theme.

9 *Tetzaveh* contains an initial description of the sacrificial cult. How strange it sounds to our ears! Worship is to be conducted through the means of sacrifice. How is contemporary worship conducted? Compare the worship services of the Israelites with that performed in synagogues today. Make a chart of similarities and differences.

PERSONALIZING THE TEXT

10 What is the procedure described in *Tetzaveh* for ordaining the priests? How was the priest "changed" as a result of this ordination? Imagine that you are a priest in biblical times who has just been ordained. In pairs, tell each other your feelings and explain them. The next activity provides a follow-up to this analysis. (For more, see the Index: "Ordination.")

11 How are Rabbis ordained today? Invite a Rabbi to speak to you about his/her ordination.

12 Write a report about the *ner tamid.* Research its origins, its history, and its meaning today. Collect pictures, stories, and sayings to illustrate your report. (For an activity about making a *ner tamid,* see Strategy #17, page 138.) References: *Synagogue: The Complete History of the Art and Architecture of the Synagogue* by Harold A. Meek; *Synagogue in Jewish Life* by J. Kohn.

13 Read carefully the description of the special robes for the High Priest. Using mixed media — fabric, buttons, beads, foil, etc. — make a reproduction of what the robes looked like.

14 In most synagogues today, the oil burning *ner tamid* has been replaced with a lamp lit by an electric light bulb. Stage a mock synagogue board meeting at which one individual presents a brief suggesting that the electric *ner tamid* be replaced by one that burns oil. Discuss the pros and cons of the suggestion and then decide the issue by a vote. Imagine you are the secretary/recorder at the board meeting. Write a report to the membership detailing the discussion and its conclusion.

15 Many gourmet cooks insist on cooking with olive oil. Other people are not aware that different oils have different tastes. Set up a salad bar for an oil taste test. Alongside your salad fixings, put labeled bottles of olive, sesame, peanut, and vegetable oil. If desired, add other exotic oils, too. Make available a bottle of wine vinegar and a variety of spices, including salt and pepper. Have everyone make for themselves small salads, each dressed with a different oil. Which is your favorite?

16 What is "holy" — objects, people, times, places? Make a list of things in Judaism that are holy. Include furnishings and people mentioned in this and the previous portion, *Terumah.* Can you identify characteristics that these holy things share? Do the shared characteristics have to do with the function or purpose of the holy things?

Write a cinquain describing your concept of holiness. A cinquain is a brief five line poem with the following structure:

Line 1 – one word, a noun.
Line 2 – two words, adjectives that describe the noun.
Line 3 – three words, verbs ending in "ing" that relate to the noun.
Line 4 – four words, adjectives that describe the noun.
Line 5 – one word "Punch line," a noun or synonym for the noun in line 1.
(For more, see the Index: "Holiness.")

17 Design and make a model *ner tamid*. You will need a tin can (any size), a long nail, a hammer, paper, pencils, a terry cloth towel, tape, paint, and access to a freezer. Cut a length of paper sufficient to wrap all the way around the can. Draw a design on the paper which will look nice when punched out on the can. Fill the can with water. Put it in the freezer until it is frozen solid. (This enables the nail punches to be quick and clean.) Place the frozen can (with the ice still in it) on a towel. With the can on its side, place the nail against one point of the design. Tap it quickly and hard enough with the hammer that the nail just punctures the can. Continue to puncture the can with the nail following the paper design. Remove the paper. Let the ice thaw and the can dry. (Be careful, the inside of the can will be very sharp.) Paint the outside of the can with regular or spray paint. Set a candle inside your "lamp." Light and use for a centerpiece.

18 Aaron and the priests are instructed to wear unique garments. What can a uniform or particular kind of dress tell about a person? Do uniforms help you identify people and their occupations? Give some examples? Do you belong to a group or organization which requires you to wear a uniform or special garments (i.e., scouts or a sports team)? How do these clothes set you apart from others? What information might a uniform impart to others?

Does putting on special clothing affect an individual mentally or emotionally? How might their garments have affected Aaron and the priests?

OTHER RESOURCES

19 Complete the pages which relate to *Tetzaveh* in *Bible People Book Two* by Joel Lurie Grishaver, pp. 37-38, 43. Also check the accompanying Leader Guide for procedures and additional activities.

20 Read, act out, and discuss the skit for the portion *Tetzaveh* in *Sedra Scenes: Skits for Every Torah Portion* by Stan J. Beiner, pp. 108-110.

21 View and discuss the episode for *Tetzaveh* from *Torah Toons I: The Video*.

22 For a creative movement activity, see "Anointment" from *Torah in Motion* by JoAnne Tucker and Susan Freeman, pp. 104-105.

23 Listen to, discuss, and sing "The Eternal Light" from *Sounds of Freedom: Exodus in Song*.

24 Read and discuss the illustrated commentary for *Tetzaveh* in *American Torah Toons* by Lawrence Bush.

INVOLVING THE FAMILY

25 A good leader must know how to delegate, as well as how to assume responsibility. Find examples from the Torah that demonstrate how ably Moses assigned responsibilities to others. What are the costs and/or benefits of his skill or lack of it in this area? How does the delegation and assumption of responsibility work in your home? Based on your cost/benefit analysis of Moses, can you suggest ways to improve the way your family functions?

Note: There is a great deal of overlap and related material in the portions *Terumah*, *Tetzaveh*, *Vayakhel*, and *Pikuday*. Therefore, the Insights from the Tradition and the Strategies for all these portions should be regarded as interchangeable.

BAR/BAT MITZVAH PROJECT

26 This portion describes the magnificent clothing of the High Priest and the garments for the other priests serving in the Tabernacle. Clothing like this transforms an individual. Do you remember the fairy tale of Cinderella, or the expression "clothes make the person"? For many individuals decent clothing which is warm and clean transforms them. It can raise self-esteem and self-worth.

Coordinate a general clothing drive at your synagogue. Additionally, or instead of a general clothing drive, run a special campaign to collect no longer wanted winter coats and jackets. Also include hats, caps, gloves, mittens, and boots. Arrange with a dry cleaner to have the coats and jackets cleaned. This may be very expensive, so you may want to ask the dry cleaning store to make a donation toward the cleaning, or to do the cleaning as their *tzedakah*. If this is not possible or if only a partial discount is offered, you will have to raise the additional funds.

KI TISA 30:11-34:35 כי תשא

SYNOPSIS

MOSES IS COMMANDED TO TAKE A census of the Israelites with each person paying half a *shekel* as an offering to God. The money is to be used for the service of the Tent of Meeting.

God also tells Moses to make a copper washbowl and stand for the priests to use when they enter the Tent of Meeting, and to make a special oil for anointing the Tent, the Ark, Aaron, and his sons.

Bezalel and Oholiab are made the chief artisans of the Tabernacle, the Ark, and the priestly vestments. Then Moses is told to remind the Israelites to keep the Sabbath forever as a sign of the covenant between God and the people. All this God says to Moses on Mount Sinai.

When God has finished speaking to Moses on Mount Sinai, God gives Moses the two tablets on which are inscribed the laws.

But the people waiting below have been impatient because Moses was so long in coming down from the mountain. They ask Aaron to make them a god to lead them. Aaron takes the gold jewelry of the people and casts a Golden Calf. The next day, he declares a festival and the people offer sacrifices to the calf as they dance before it.

On the mountain, God tells Moses that the Israelites have turned away from the laws and that God will destroy them and make the descendants of Moses a great nation. Moses pleads with God to remember the promise made to Abraham, Isaac, and Jacob and to spare the people. God agrees.

Then Moses descends from the mountain and, in his anger at seeing the gold idol, smashes the tablets of the law.

After the people have been punished and have repented, Moses must again plead with God not to forsake the covenant. God tells Moses to carve two new tablets of stone for God to inscribe again with the words of the law.

Moses ascends Mount Sinai with the tablets and God appears to him in a cloud and renews the covenant with the Israelites. Moses remains on the mountain for 40 days and 40 nights.

When Moses descends from Mount Sinai the second time, his face is radiant because he has spoken with God. The Israelites are frightened by the radiance. Because of this, Moses wears a veil over his face except when he is speaking to God or speaking God's words to the Israelites.

INSIGHTS FROM THE TRADITION

A *Ki Tisa* means "when you take up" and refers to the census with which the *sedra* begins. According to Exodus 38:26, the number of male Israelites counted was 603,550. This figure matches exactly the census in Numbers 1:46 and it corresponds closely to the tradition that 600,000 slaves were redeemed from Egypt.

Can you imagine so many people in one place? What kind of power exists in a very large group of people?
What was the largest group or crowd you ever saw or were ever a part of?

B The Israelites were counted indirectly by means of the half-*shekel* coin which each brought as a donation to the sanctuary. Was there no actual head count? The Rabbis taught that this method of counting identically valued coins shows us that each person has his/her own individual value, but that all individuals, rich or poor, have the same value before God. If this is so, then what significance can be attached to each person bringing only a half-*shekel* instead of a whole *shekel*? A variety of explanations has been suggested: the half-*shekel* may represent the time of day when the sin of the Golden Calf was committed (mid-day). The half-*shekel* is also equivalent to the penalty for those who disobey the Ten Commandments (ten *gerahs*), or to each brother's share of the price for which Joseph was sold into slavery.

Hence, this payment can be seen as an atonement of sorts (*Legends of the Jews* by Louis Ginzberg, Vol. III, pp. 147-8). Rabbi Mordecai Katz has suggested that the half-*shekel* payment emphasizes the fact that no individual is complete in and of himself/herself. Only within the context of a community can one be whole (*Lilmod Ulelamade*).

Why do you think a census was taken of the people at this particular time?

If a "coin census" were taken today in your country, what coin would be most appropriate to use? Explain.

In speaking of the half-*shekel* tax, the biblical text states the people were to "pay God a ransom" (Exodus 30:12). What does the word ransom mean? How might that word apply in this situation?

Every so many years, most modern countries conduct a detailed census of their population. What function does the census serve today? How might government census information be used today for the benefit of groups and individuals? To their detriment?

What information would you want to know from a census?

C What became of the pieces of the broken tablets of the commandments? According to tradition, they were saved and eventually carried and safeguarded in the Ark alongside the second, intact set of commandments. This is akin to the practice of never throwing out pages with Hebrew writing containing the name of God: worn-out prayer books, for example, are hidden away in a *genizah* or buried in the cemetery. Another lesson that may be derived from this has to do with respecting the "broken," hurt, or handicapped people among us, and the less-than-perfect pieces of our own selves. If broken tablets and worn books are accorded such respect and gentle treatment, how much the more so are people, whatever their physical and emotional states, to be honored and given their place in our community?

Who are the "broken" members of your community?

How does your community support and carry them?

Do you have parts of yourself that you feel are "broken?"

How do you deal with them?

D In a brief five verses, God describes to Moses the formula for, and the use of, incense within the Tent of Meeting. Plaut offers two explanations for its use: to ward off demonic powers and to purify the air (*The Torah: A Modern Commentary*, edited by W. Gunther Plaut, p. 636). The smell of incense also adds a sense of mystery to God's meetings with Moses. The only remnant of the use of incense is the spicebox used at the close of Shabbat. We are reminded of the sweetness of Shabbat by the fragrance of the spices.

Do you think incense should be introduced into the synagogue service?

Imagine a specific holiday or celebration. What elements go into creating visual and emotional pictures in your mind? How important is smell in defining the picture?

E Distressed by the absence of Moses and no tangible evidence of God's presence, the people want reassurance. They demand that Aaron make a visible god for them. The *midrash* tells us that Hur rose up and rebuked them saying, "You brainless fools! Have you forgotten the miracles God performed for you?" In response, the people killed Hur and then approached Aaron. Aaron gave in to their demands. However, he requested the gold rings of the people to use in the construction of the idol. One might ask how Aaron, God's High Priest, could participate in this blasphemous event. The Rabbis' concern with this issue is dealt with in the *midrash*. Moses thought that Aaron was a partner in this crime, but God knew Aaron's intention. Aaron merely hoped to placate the people until Moses' return.

Why would it frighten the people so if Moses had disappeared?

Considering their recent experiences, what surprises you about the Israelites' demand for a "tangible god"?

In the biblical text, what do the people say once the Golden Calf is made? Do they celebrate the fact that they now have a different and, therefore, better god? What purpose does the idol serve?

If you were one of the Israelites in the wilderness, could you see yourself giving rings for the calf and dancing around it? Or, would you have walked away from the camp to wait for Moses?

F God warns Moses of the people's behavior. Aware that their destruction is imminent, Moses pleads for the lives of the Israelites. A *midrash* relates that Moses reminded God of the people's good deeds. They accepted the Torah and they believed Moses' message about God while still slaves in Egypt. God replied to Moses, "*Your* people have become corrupt" (32:7). Since the Israelites were sinning, they did not merit being called the people of God. Moses asked God, "Why is it that when they are good, you call them *My* people [i.e., God's] and when they are bad, you call them *your* [i.e., Moses'] people? If they are Your people and Your inheritance, you should always call them 'My people.'"

Moses closes his argument with God by mentioning the Patriarchs and the divine promises made to them (Exodus 32:13). This concept of the special merit inherent in the Patriarchs is known as *zechut avot*. Simply put, all future generations benefit from the righteousness of the Patriarchs. Ultimately God relents and Israel is allowed to live.

Can you think of other instances in Tanach when an individual has pleaded with God to save a group of people? Was the argument successful? What was the persuasive point? (See Genesis 18:22-33.)

Have you ever stood up for a sibling or a friend when that person was accused of misbehavior?

What did you say in his/her defense? How did you feel when you spoke out?

G Moses descended the mountain to see what the people had been up to. Upon entering the camp, Moses flings down the tablets in rage. Remember that God had already told Moses what the people had done (i.e., made the Golden Calf). In *Yalkut Me'am Lo'ez* by Yaacov Culi (Vol. X, p. 59), we learn that Moses brought the tablets with him so that the Israelites could see what they had forfeited. Moses inflicted a severe punishment on the people. He gathered together those still loyal to God and then had the idolators put to death.

What new side of Moses' personality do we witness in this event? Do you think he could have handled the situation differently? Why did he choose such a drastic punishment?

Do you think that hearing about something is different from actually seeing it? Was this true for Moses in the case of the Golden Calf?

What is the worst punishment you could imagine happening to you?

Can you imagine the behavior that would result in such a punishment?

H In this portion, Moses' face is described as radiant or beaming brightly. The Hebrew expression is *"ki karan ohr panay Mosheh"* (34:35). The words *karan ohr* were incorrectly rendered into Latin as "horned skin." Thus it is that Michaelangelo's famous sculpture shows Moses with small horns on his head.

A *midrash* explains that the radiance that clung to Moses after he had written down the Torah was due to the fact that he had accidently brushed his forehead with some of the heavenly ink. The commentators explained, too, that by not eating or drinking while he was on Mount Sinai, Moses was merely following *minhag hamakom* (the tradition of the place). Since angels neither eat nor drink, Moses abstained from food while he was among them.

Another interpretation is that the radiance of Moses' face may have been the result of his brief glimpse of God's back, when God's presence was revealed to Moses. At that time, Moses proclaimed the words which have entered the liturgy:

"*Adonai! Adonai!* A God compassionate and gracious, slow to anger, abounding in kindness and faithfulness, extending kindness to the thousandth generation, forgiving iniquity, transgression, and sin . . ." (Exodus 34:6-7).

What acts or deeds might brush you with the "ink of heaven"?

Note: For a comment on the placement of the events of this portion in time, see Exodus, *Terumah*, Insight D, page 129.

STRATEGIES

ANALYZING THE TEXT

1 Use the text of *Ki Tisa* to prove that the following statements are true:
Moses loved the Children of Israel even when they committed a serious sin.
The Children of Israel had trouble believing in a God they could not see.
The Children of Israel needed Moses, their leader, to be with them constantly.

2 According to *Ki Tisa*, how was Aaron punished for his role in making the Golden Calf? Is it possible that the silence of the text on this question is an answer in itself? Perhaps the silence tells us that Aaron's remorse was so great that he, in effect, punished himself. Discuss.

3 According to the *Mekilta de-Rabbi Ishmael* (Vol. II, pp. 262-3), the arrangement of the Ten Commandments on the two tablets with the first five opposite the second five is meant to enrich our understanding of the commandments.

For example: On one tablet was written: "I am the Lord thy God." And opposite it on the other tablet was written: "Thou shalt not murder." This tells us that if one sheds blood, it is accounted to him as though he diminished the divine image.

What lessons can you derive from the juxtaposition of the following commandments?

You shall have no other gods.	You shall not commit adultery.
You shall not swear falsely.	You shall not steal.
Remember the Sabbath day.	You shall not bear false witness.
Honor your father and mother.	You shall not covet.

4 Before Moses, both Noah and Abraham were faced with God's intention to destroy wicked people. Compare Noah's actions at the time of the flood (Genesis 6:9ff.) and Abraham's intercession on behalf of Sodom and Gomorrah (Genesis 18:17ff.) with Moses' defense of the Israelites in *Ki Tisa*.

5 In the Torah scroll, several letters in this portion are written large:
a. In 34:7, the נ in the phrase נצר חסד is written large so it will not be mistaken for an ע.
b. In 34:14, the ר in the phrase לאל אחר is written large so it will not be confused with a ד.
How would the meaning of the text be changed if these words were misread?

EXTENDING THE TEXT

6 Look at the differences in the styles of leadership of Moses (M) and Aaron (A). Where would you place each on the following continua? In your opinion, where is the best place to be on each continuum? Where would you place yourself on each continuum?

denies responsibility for his followers' actions	accepts responsibility for his followers' actions
has low expectations of himself and others	has high expectations of himself and others
plays it safe: wants to be liked and accepted	is willing to risk losing the people's love
willing to compromise	unwilling to compromise
gets angry quickly and easily	is very patient
wavers, can't make decisions	acts quickly and decisively.

7 Read the play "Justice and Mercy" (in *Kings and Things: 20 Jewish Plays for Kids 8 to 18* by Meredith Shaw Patera, pp. 32-36) to help you understand the difference between the qualities of mercy and justice. Discuss how God and Moses exhibit these qualities in the story of the Golden Calf.

Which acts and statements of each would you call "just"? Which are "merciful"?
Write a new version of the Golden Calf episode in which God and Moses use only one of these two qualities to pass judgment on the Israelites. What are the final consequences? (For more, see the Index: "Justice and Mercy.")

8 Verses 34:6-7 have become part of the High Holy Day and festival liturgy. These words have received careful study. From them, scholars have distinguished 13 attributes of God. (See *The Torah: A Modern Commentary*, edited by W. Gunther Plaut, pp. 663-4 for a list and an explanation.) Several other prayers contain descriptions of God. Two of the best known are *Adon Olam* and *Yigdal*. Compare the view of God detailed in one of these two "songs" with the ideas detailed in this portion (34:6-7). Why is the description from *Ki Tisa* particularly suitable for the High Holy Days?

9 In *Ki Tisa*, when Moses asks to see God, God replies, "Man may not see Me and live" (Exodus 33:20). Review the other encounters of the Patriarchs and Moses with God. Critic Northrop Frye has noted the Torah's "strong emphasis on metaphors of the ear as compared with those of the eye" (*The Great Code: The Bible and Literature*, p. 116). Why do you think the word of God which the Patriarchs and prophets heard is so much more important than what they saw? How can we know about God without seeing God? Choose one or two passages in which encounters with God are described. Analyze the passages and tell what you can learn about God from God's *words* and actions as described therein.

10 Fill in the details that would explain the role of Aaron in the incident of the Golden Calf. Recreate in writing or through role play the conversation between Moses and Aaron beginning with the words which Moses speaks to Aaron in Exodus 32:21: "What did the people do to you that you have brought such great sin upon them?" In your conversation, explore the issues of blame, responsibility, and motivation.

11 Exodus 31:16-17 has become a regular part of the Shabbat service. Compare these verses with the introductory paragraph to the *Kiddush* for Shabbat. How similar is the language? Note how different language is used to express the same ideas. In what ways do the verses from Exodus broaden the perspective of the *Kiddush* even though they were written earlier?

12 Following the incident of the Golden Calf, Moses argues with God on behalf of the people. What arguments does Moses use to plead the case of the Israelites? What additional arguments could you add?

PERSONALIZING THE TEXT

13 During his ordination, blood was put on the earlobe, thumb, and toe of the priest. No one seems to know what is significant/symbolic about the choice of these parts of the body. What do you think? If *you* were designing a ritual for ordination, what parts of the body would you want to anoint or make symbolic reference to? Make up and act out your own ordination ceremony. Include explanations for each part of the ceremony. (For more, see the Index: "Ordination.")

14 In verse 31:16 of this portion, two different verbs are used to describe the observance of Shabbat: "The Israelite people shall keep (*v'shamru*) the Sabbath, observing (*la'asot* — some translate "to do") the Sabbath throughout the ages . . ." Is there a difference between these two expressions?

Make two lists, one showing how you "do" or "observe" Shabbat, the second detailing how you might "keep" the Shabbat throughout the ages. As you examine your lists, try to decide if one way is more active than the other. Which list is more of a challenge to you personally? How do the two aspects of Shabbat observance complement and reinforce each other? How might you change your own Shabbat observance to include elements from each list?

15 Retell the incident of the Golden Calf from the point of view of an Israelite who participated in it. Describe not only *what* but *why* it happened, and how you felt before, during, and after the entire event.

16 Where would you place yourself on each continuum in Strategy #6 on pages 143 and 144 above? How do you compare to Moses and Aaron as a leader? (Try judging some modern day leaders based on these same continua.)

17 The half-*shekel* tax collected from Jews for the upkeep of the Temple, and in later centuries for the Rabbinical academies, has long been out of force. Find out how our synagogues and other community institutions are supported today. Invite your synagogue administrator and/or membership chairperson to discuss this with you. How are dues for membership established in your synagogue? How are the monies collected and allocated?

18 Many artists have painted or sculpted their impressions of how Moses looked when he descended from Mount Sinai with the second set of Ten Commandments. Two of the most famous are those by Michaelangelo (see Insight H). Both can be found in many art books. Look at a variety of these portraits. Which one best fits your image of Moses? Why? Create your own drawing/painting/sculpture of Moses. Remember that the setting you choose, the pose Moses is in, and the objects he carries will convey as much about him as his face. If faces are difficult for you, make his face veiled as in Exodus 34:33, 35.

19 Pretend you are a news reporter for a major network. Plan and deliver a segment of the nightly newscast describing the incident of the Golden Calf. Make use of an anchor person, on site reporters, and a team of news analyzers and commentators.

20 The law was "cut" (*charute*) into the tablets (32:16). This Hebrew word can also be read as *chayrute,* meaning "freedom." In what ways does the existence of laws free, rather than restrict, people? (For more, see the Index: "Shabbat," "God," "Ten Commandments.")

OTHER RESOURCES

21 Read, act out, and discuss the skit for the portion *Ki Tisa* in *Sedra Scenes: Skits for Every Torah Portion* by Stan J. Beiner, pp. 111-115.

22 For a brief history of the role of the *shekel* tax in Jewish history, see the commentary on *Ki Tissa* by Professor Nahum M. Sarna in *Learn Torah With . . .* (pp. 154-157).

23 Create a "freeze frame" diorama of an important scene from this portion by following the directions for "You Are There! Famous Moments in History" in *An Artist You Don't Have to Be* by Joann Magnus with Howard Bogot, p. 5.

24 Make your own set of tablets by following the directions for "Clay Project #1 – Tablets of the Law" in *Fast, Clean and Cheap* by Simon Kops, p. 39.

25 View and discuss the episode for *Ki Tisa* from *Torah Toons I: The Video.*

26 For creative movement activities, see "The Lure of Gold," "Moses Sees the Golden Calf," and "God Shields Moses" from *Torah*

in Motion by JoAnne Tucker and Susan Freeman, pp. 106-111.

27 Listen to, discuss, and sing "*Adonai Adonai*" from *Sounds of Freedom: Exodus in Song.*

28 Read and discuss the illustrated commentary for *Ki Tisa* in *American Torah Toons* by Lawrence Bush.

INVOLVING THE FAMILY

29 Have a family storytelling session about Shabbat. Assign to each person one of the many *midrashim* connected with this portion to learn and tell. References: *Legends of the Jews* by Louis Ginzberg, Vol. III, pp. 116, 121, 123, 141-2; *The Book of Legends: Sefer Ha-aggadah,* edited by Hayim Bialik and Yehoshua Ravnitzky, see its Index under "Sabbath." There are also many wonderful Jewish storybooks; check your synagogue library collection.

30 Discuss the *midrash* about your people versus My people (see Insight F). According to Moses' statement, how should God understand the Israelites? Is there any similarity between this and situations in which your parents are angry with you? How so?

BAR/BAT MITZVAH PROJECT

31 The *shekalim* collected in the census went toward maintaining the Tent of Meeting. Out of this grew the practice of collecting from the members of the Jewish community a half-*shekel* yearly toward the upkeep of the Temple and later for the Rabbinical academies in Palestine and Babylonia. Messengers were sent out to collect this "tax"on the first of Adar (or, in a leap year, II Adar) and, therefore, the Shabbat immediately before Rosh Chodesh Adar (or II Adar) became known as Shabbat *Shekalim.* On that Shabbat, Exodus 30:11-16, which details the original collection of the half-*shekel,* is read in addition to the regular reading.

Given that many Jewish institutions are maintained by voluntary dues and contributions, would it be a good idea to reintroduce a tax on the Jewish population to help support these groups? What advantages/disadvantages would such a procedure entail? If every Jew in the world did donate one significant coin on Shabbat *Shekalim,* for what purpose would you designate the funds to be used?

In the months preceding your Bar/Bat Mitzvah, assess yourself a voluntary "tax," perhaps ten percent of your weekly allowance or your earnings from odd jobs, and deposit the money into a special *tzedakah* box. Since the half-*shekel* was collected to maintain the Tent of Meeting use the funds you have collected to help maintain your "Tent of Meeting," the synagogue where your Jewish community meets. Learn about the various funds which are supported by donations which help maintain your synagogue. Choose to donate to one of those, or find out what the synagogue may need that you can afford to do.

VAYAKHEL 35:1-38:20 ויקהל

SYNOPSIS

MOSES ASSEMBLES THE ISRAELITES AND reminds them of the commandment to observe the Sabbath as a day of rest. He further instructs them to kindle no light on Shabbat.

Then Moses reviews God's instructions concerning the building of the Tabernacle and calls upon the people to bring gifts to be used in its construction. He appoints Bezalel and Oholiab to be the chief artisans in the work of constructing the Tabernacle and to supervise the other skilled craftspeople who will contribute to the building.

The Israelites respond to Moses' call for gifts, bringing so many riches that Moses has to proclaim that enough material has been donated.

The skilled artisans make the cloth covering and the goat's hair tent over the Tabernacle, and they make the curtain, as well as the screen for the entrance to the Tabernacle.

Bezalel makes the gold covered Ark of acacia wood and the *cherubim* on the Ark cover. He makes the table for the bread of display and the seven branched *menorah*. Bezalel also makes the altars and the copper washbowl and stand.

INSIGHTS FROM THE TRADITION

A *Vayakhel* has the meaning of "to convoke," or "to assemble." From this word, the term used for a Jewish community (*kehillah*) is derived. The portion, in fact describes the process of the making of the Tabernacle, an act which forged the disparate Israelites into a community. The word *Vayakhel* is first used in Exodus 32:1 where the people "assemble" to make the Golden Calf. Whereas the first assembly was an act of rebellion, the assembly detailed here has the blessing of God. Thus, the use of the word *Vayakhel* to open this portion "is thematic in that it heralds the conclusion of the cycle [of events] that started with the

same word" (*The Torah: A Modern Commentary*, edited by W. Gunther Plaut, p. 666). The covenant, broken by the sin of the Golden Calf, has been renewed and the seal, as it were, is the building and erecting of the Tabernacle.

What are the similarities and differences between the assembly which created the Golden Calf and the assembly which created the Tabernacle? Which was created by community and which by an individual?
Do you have a different attitude toward that which you work on as opposed to that into which you have put no effort?

B In the biblical text, there is an immediate connection between the building of the Tabernacle and the observance of Shabbat. While carrying out the construction of the Tabernacle, Rashi tells us that the Israelites were not to violate the Shabbat. Shabbat was then imbued with complete sanctity.

The commentary *Yalkut Me'am Lo'ez* offers us an insight into Shabbat as a day of rest. The Hebrew word Shabbat can be seen as an acrostic for *shaynah b'shabbat ta'anug*, which means "sleep on the Sabbath is a delight." However, this only applies to those who study Torah all week and who, therefore, may sleep on Shabbat. In contrast, the individual who works all week has only the Shabbat in which to fulfill the obligation to learn (Yaacov Culi, Vol. X, p. 179).

How do you observe Shabbat?
From the insights provided by the commentaries, is Shabbat meant to be a release or a restriction? According to the text, is Shabbat to be a day of rest or a day for changing priorities?
Describe what an ideal Shabbat would be for you. How does this correspond to the ideal of Shabbat in Jewish tradition?

Note: For more about the connection between building the Tabernacle and the observance of Shabbat, see Strategy #1 on page 150.

C Moses called upon the people to bring donations for the construction of the Tabernacle. He couched his request by saying that "everyone whose heart is so moved" (Exodus 35:5) should make the contributions. Rashi explains that the donations should be made by those whose hearts prompt them to generosity. But another explanation may be found in *Legends of the Jews* by Louis Ginzberg, Vol. III, p. 174: Israel is a peculiar nation because they answered Moses' request for gold with the same enthusiasm they used in fetching gold for the Golden Calf. Not only did they bring wealth from their homes, but they forcibly snatched ornaments from their families for the construction of the Tabernacle. They thought that by doing so they could cancel out the sin of the Golden Calf.

Why is it important to give with a generous spirit? Isn't a donation just a donation? Why should an individual's motivation matter?
Do you think that contributing to the sanctuary atoned for Israel's sin with the Golden Calf? What more could the people have done?
What words or actions do you use in making atonement for wrongdoings?

D The biblical text describes what "pedigree" the gifts for the Tabernacle should have. They should, among other things, be from the possessions of the people (Exodus 35:23). *Yalkut Me'am Lo'ez* (Yaacov Culi, Vol. X, p. 209) explains that the donations cannot be stolen property. When an individual contributes for a sacred purpose it must be from personal property which was earned with personal labor. The donation may not have the slightest taint of swindle or theft.

Consider the case of a philanthropist who donates generously to the work of the community. The philanthropist, however, makes money as a racketeer. Should his donations be acceptable?
If you were the director of a Jewish institution, would you refuse these monies? What would your responsibility be in this situation?

E Moses encountered two disappointments: When God chose Aaron as the High Priest, and when Bezalel and Oholiab were chosen as the artists to construct the Tabernacle.

Why do you think Moses might have been passed over in both of these instances? Was he totally left out of these two processes? What was his role regarding the priesthood and regarding the construction of the Tabernacle?
Why might it have been important for Moses to share the honors in both of these processes?

F Something remarkable happens in this portion with the inclusion of women as contributors to the building to the Tabernacle. They are depicted not only as material contributors but also as highly skilled spinners. This is no small feat for the Bible. Biblical text does not often include the achievements of women.
The text from Exodus 35:25-26 reads:

And every woman wise of mind,
with their hands they spun
and brought their spinning —
the blue-violet, the purple, the worm-scarlet and the byssus [fine cloth],
and every one of the women whose mind uplifted them in practical-wisdom
spun the goats'-hair.
(from *The Five Books of Moses*, translated by Everett Fox, p. 465.)

How does this compare in form and feeling to Proverbs 13 — "A Woman of Valor"?
Give an example of something you have learned from women's wisdom.

Note: *Vayakhel* and *Pikuday* are normally read as a double portion. For more about double portions, see Exodus, *Pikuday*, Insight A, page 155. For a note about the placement in time of the events in this portion, see Exodus, *Terumah*, Insight D, page 129.

STRATEGIES

ANALYZING THE TEXT

1 The placement of the prohibition of work on Shabbat immediately before the description of the building of the Tabernacle led the Rabbis to understand "work" — מלאכה (*malachah*) to mean any activity that was needed for the construction of the Tabernacle. The Mishnah lists 39 main categories of work (called *avot*), and there are many other kinds of work which are outgrowths of these main 39 that are also forbidden. (These latter are called *toledot* — offspring. For example: sowing is in the *avot* category, therefore, the watering of plants is considered in the *toledot* class.) Based on a careful reading of *Vayakhel*, make a list of all types of work involved in building the Tabernacle. Compare your list of all the types of work involved in the building of the Tabernacle with the one that follows. How close did you come? (*Avot*: sowing, plowing, reaping, binding sheaves, threshing, winnowing, cleansing, grinding, sifting, kneading, baking, shearing wool, washing wool, beating wool, dyeing wool, spinning, weaving, making two loops, weaving two threads, tying a knot, loosening a knot, sewing two stitches, tearing so as to sew two stitches, hunting a deer, slaughtering a deer, flaying a deer, salting a deer, curing a deer, scraping a deer, cutting up a deer, writing two letters, erasing to write two letters, building, extinguishing, striking with a hammer, carrying from one domain to another.)

2 *Vayakhel* places great emphasis on how eagerly the Israelites *brought* their gifts for the construction of the Tabernacle. Note the number of times the Hebrew word (l'havi) להביא — (to bring) or a variation thereof is used (eight times in Exodus 35:21-29 alone). How are the people who brought these gifts described in the text? Contrast this information with Exodus 32:3 where the incident of the Golden Calf begins. In which case does it seem to have been easier for the people to

"bring" their contributions? Which event involved more people? Can you explain why the Talmud says in comparing these events, "Can we read [these verses] and not shudder?" (*Yerushalmi, Shekalim* 1:1)

3 Continue exploring the idea of the people giving so freely and so much to the building of the Tabernacle. See the video *Field of Dreams* (rated PG, running time 1 hour 46 mins.), which is available as a video rental. After viewing this film, answer the following questions for both the film and the verses in Exodus which talk about the Israelites' generosity (35:21-29).
The baseball field might be considered a metaphor for the _____.
Who is the leader in each of these stories?
Were these leaders initially eager to fulfill their positions?
What did each of these leaders risk in carrying out his/her tasks?
Do these leaders have any other similarities? What about their differences?
Describe the physical area in which these building projects were carried out.
Discuss what motivated each of these individuals to build.
What inspired the people to become a part of these projects?
Are there other characters in the film which seem similar to individuals in the biblical account?
What are the differences between the biblical story and the film?

4 The observance of Shabbat is mentioned several times in the Book of Exodus. Examine the references given below and answer the following questions. According to the Torah, how is Shabbat to be observed? What is the penalty for not observing Shabbat? What is the significance of Shabbat? Are there elements in contemporary Shabbat observance that are not mentioned in the Torah? (See Exodus 15:21-30, 20:8-11, 23:12, 31:13-17, 34:21, 35:2-3; see also

Deuteronomy 5:12-15. For more activities about Shabbat, see the Index: "Shabbat.")
References: *The Minhagim: The Customs and Ceremonies of Judaism, Their Origins and Rationale* by Abraham Chill; *The Biblical and Historical Background of the Jewish Holy Days* by Abraham P. Bloch; *Shabbat Seder: The Sabbath Seder* by Ron Wolfson; *Shabbat Haggadah for Celebration and Study* by Michael Strassfeld; *Jewish Family Celebrations: The Sabbath, Festivals, and Ceremonies* by Arlene Rossen Cardozo.

EXTENDING THE TEXT

5 Bearing in mind that for hundreds of years the Torah was heard rather than read, conduct a guided fantasy tour of the Tabernacle. Try to convey a sense of the beauty of the Tabernacle through the use of the voice of one reader.

6 Compare the places designated for worship at different times in Jewish history. For example, how did Abraham, Isaac, and Jacob worship God? How were the Temple and the Tabernacle service similar to and different from earlier practices? How did Jewish worship change with the destruction of the Second Temple and the gradual rise of the synagogue?
References: *To Pray as a Jew* by Hayim Donin, pp. 9-16; *Teaching Tefilah* by Bruce Kadden and Barbara Binder Kadden, pp. 2-9.

7 In Exodus 31:3 and Exodus 35:31, we read that God endowed Bezalel with חכמה (*chochmah*), תבונה (*tevunah*), דעת (*da'at*). These same Hebrew words are used in Proverbs 3:19-20 to explain how God created the world. Also in I Kings 7:14, they are used to describe Hiram, the chief artisan of Solomon's Temple. There have been many varied translations of these words. In *The Torah: A Modern Commentary*, edited by W. Gunther Plaut, they are rendered as "skill, ability, and knowledge." The 1917 Jewish Publication

Society edition of the Torah translates them as "wisdom, understanding, and knowledge." How would you define the Hebrew words? What is the significance of the use of the same three words in regard to the creation of the world, the Tabernacle, and the Temple? Write a poem about the creation of the world, Hiram, and Bezalel which makes use throughout of these three Hebrew words. (For more on the parallels between creation and the Tabernacle, see the Index: "Tabernacle, and creation.")

8 Exodus 31:3 describes Bezalel as having "a divine spirit of skill, ability, and knowledge of every kind of craft." According to tradition, Bezalel belonged to the family of Caleb. He was, therefore, among those "imbued with a different spirit [who] remained loyal to [God]" (Numbers 14:24) and who were protected from the fate of the generation that left Egypt and died in the desert. (Other *midrashim* about Bezalel can be found in *Legends of the Jews* by Louis Ginzberg, Vol. III, pp. 154-156. Also see the Insights from the Tradition for this portion.)

Rashi says that it was because of Bezalel's whole-hearted devotion to his work that the Torah gave him sole credit for making the Ark (Exodus 37:1ff.). Like many great artists, Bezalel's work became a legacy not only to his family, but to all the Israelites. Write an ethical will as though you were Bezalel, in which you detail the lessons about character and skill that he embodied in his life.
References: *So That Your Values Live On: Ethical Wills and How to Prepare Them* by Jack Riemer and Nathaniel Stampfer; *Ethical Wills* (mini-course) by Barbara Binder Kadden and Bruce Kadden.

9 The following activity is based on Insight F of this portion. Gather some women's wisdom for yourself by learning the basics of spinning. Invite a spinner to demonstrate how spinning is done and then to help each student have a try at spinning. If enough thread is spun, incorporate it into an art project.

PERSONALIZING THE TEXT

10 Look at the 39 categories of work listed in Strategy #1, page 150. Do they all seem like "work?" Add to the list any other "work" that you think should be forbidden on Shabbat. Does your understanding of the word work differ from that described in the Mishnah?

11 Many people with different kinds of skills contributed their talents to help fashion the Tabernacle. Imagine that you were able to transport yourself back in time carrying in a magic box a gift for the Tabernacle. The box can accommodate a gift of any size or a feeling, a value, a story, etc. What gift would you give? Anonymously, write a description of your gift and your reason for choosing it. Now scramble all the descriptions together and take turns reading out loud the gifts of others. (Idea adapted from *Clarifying Jewish Values* by Dov Peretz Elkins.)

12 Everett Fox (*The Five Books of Moses*) translates Exodus 38:8 as follows:

He [Betzalel] made the basin of bronze, its pedestal of bronze, with the mirrors of the women's working-force that was doing-the-work at the entrance of the Tent of Appointment.

Plaut, using the 1962 JPS translation for his commentary, uses the word copper in place of bronze, and the Tent of Meeting in place of the Tent of Appointment. There has been much controversy on the use of these mirrors in the construction of the laver. Mirrors are often used as instruments of vanity, but Judith Antonelli in her commentary writes, "The mirror, in its function of reflection, is also the quintessential symbol of women's greater *Binah*, which is an understanding based on the capacity to receive and reflect back" (*In the Image of God: A Feminist Commentary on the Torah*, page 226). Complete this statement in light of the explanations. When I look in the mirror on the surface I see ____, but when I look more closely and more deeply I see _____.

13 From the name of this portion, *Vayakhel,* comes the Hebrew word *Kehillah* — assembly or congregation. Many synagogue names are prefaced by the term *Kehillah Kedoshah* (Holy Congregation). We sometimes abbreviate this as K.K. How did the building of the Tabernacle make a united "congregation" out of the Israelites? In what ways do synagogues today help unite our communities? Find out about the different kinds of programs and activities occurring in your synagogue. Create a bulletin board around the theme *Vayakhel* — "Our Synagogue Unites Us."

14 Bezalel and Oholiab are the first Jewish artists whose names have come down to us. Throughout the ages, and particularly in the modern period, there have been many Jewish artists of note. Research and present an oral report on any one of these. (You may want to confine yourself to Jewish artists who dealt with specifically Jewish subject matter, such as Marc Chagall, Ben Shahn, Shalom of Safed, David Sharir, etc.) Reference: *Encyclopaedia Judaica,* "Art," Vol. 3, pp. 499-643 (see especially the Alphabetical List of Artists on pp. 594-614).

15 According to Dr. J.H. Hertz, "The highest artist, in the eyes of Jewish teachers of all generations, is not the greatest master in self-expression, but in self-control; he who fashions himself into a sanctuary" (*The Pentateuch and Haftorahs,* p. 376). Which do you value more, self-expression or self-control? Make two lists, one containing the names of people whose self-expression you admire and one naming those whose self-control you admire. Which quality do you think is harder to develop? Place yourself on the values continuum below. Then list under each end of the continuum the steps you might take to improve your mastery of that quality.

Shoshana   Shmuel
Self-expression   Self-control

16 Arrange a Jewish art show. Set a time and date and make arrangements to borrow pieces of art on Jewish themes from people in the congregation/community. Decide on the criteria for the display and whether to include ritual objects, art by Jewish artists that is not on Jewish themes, etc. Ask lenders to include the title, artists, date, and any other pertinent information typed on a blank index card to mount beside their works of art. (Ask them to tape their name and phone number on the back or bottom of the artwork.) Hang and display the art. Then open your show for one evening only to the lenders and invited guests. Feast your eyes! (If desired, send out invitations in advance and serve light refreshments.) Ask lenders to take their art home with them after the show.

17 Invite a local artist whose work expresses Jewish themes to talk to your group about his/her sources of ideas and inspirations and manner of working. Or, visit the artist's studio for such a discussion. (For more, see the Index: "Tabernacle.")

18 Shalom of Safed illustrates biblical stories and ideas by dividing his canvas into sections and depicting his scenes in bright colors and simple drawings. Use this style to depict the categories of work forbidden on Shabbat.
References: Examples of the work of Shalom of Safed can be seen in *Encyclopaedia Judaica,* "Art," Vol. 3, p. 635, and in *Images from the Bible: The Paintings of Shalom of Safed, The Words of Elie Wiesel.*

19 There are several art forms in which Jewish artists have excelled. Take, for example, illuminated scrolls (*Megillot, ketubot, Haggadot*) and ritual objects (*Kiddush* cups, holiday platters, *tallitot,* Torah ornaments, and synagogue interiors). Investigate Jewish ritual objects. Design a beautiful object for your own personal use.

OTHER RESOURCES

20 Complete the pages which relate to *Vayakhel* in *Bible People Book Two* by Joel Lurie Grishaver, pp. 39-42. Also check the accompanying Leader Guide for procedures and additional activities.

21 Read, act out, and discuss the skit for the portion *Vayakhel* in *Sedra Scenes: Skits for Every Torah Portion* by Stan J. Beiner, pp. 116-119.

22 View and discuss the episode for *Vayakhel* from *Torah Toons I: The Video.*

23 For creative movement activities, see "The Lure of Gold" and "Excellence for the Tabernacle" from *Torah in Motion* by JoAnne Tucker and Susan Freeman, pp. 106-107 and 112-113.

24 Listen to, discuss, and sing "Kindle No Fires" from *Sounds of Freedom: Exodus in Song.*

25 Read and discuss the illustrated commentary for *Va-Yakhel* in *American Torah Toons* by Lawrence Bush.

INVOLVING THE FAMILY

26 Have all family members rank order the statements below with #1 being the most significant reason for observing Shabbat, #2 next best, etc. Share each family member's choices. Try to come to a consensus about one main reason for your family to observe Shabbat. Decide together what "work" not to do in order to be consistent with your decision.

___ To make a distinction between Shabbat and the days of the week.

___ To reflect what God did on the seventh day.

___ To remind us that we are a separate people.

___ To provide us with the rest that we need.

___ To remind us that God alone is Creator and Sovereign of the world.

27 The description of the Tabernacle and its utensils tells of the intense beauty of these objects. List the Jewish ritual objects which can be found in your home. What Jewish objects were to be found in your parents' homes when they were growing up? As a family, decide on a Jewish ritual object that you would like to have in your home. Make a plan for shopping for the object and obtaining it.

Note: There is a great deal of overlap and repeated material in the portions *Terumah, Tetzaveh, Vayakhel,* and *Pikuday.* Therefore, the Insights and Strategies for these portions should be regarded as interchangeable.

BAR/BAT MITZVAH PROJECT

28 Have you ever heard the saying, "People need food for the body, but art for the soul?" In this portion the utensils for the Tabernacle are described in fabulous detail. These items could have been made simply and plainly, but the adornments of the Tabernacle would make it an artistically pleasing and wonderful space.

In some communities art programs for the homeless have been established. These programs give the homeless a place off the street for a few hours and an opportunity to express themselves in art. Does a program like this exist in your community? If there is one, call and find out how you can help. If a program like this does not exist, contact a day shelter in your community to see if there is interest in one. Then research to see if there is an artists' group in your community and find out if they will become a part of this project. Other issues to consider and plan for are funding, acquiring art materials, and determining the length of the project.

This Bar/Bat Mitzvah project is complex and you will need the help of classmates and adults.

PIKUDAY 38:21-40:38 פקודי

SYNOPSIS

PIKUDAY BEGINS WITH AN ACCOUNT OF the materials used in the making of the Tabernacle. Bezalel and Oholiab create robes for the priests and special vestments for Aaron: the *ephod*, the breast-plate, the robe for the *ephod*, and the frontlet, according to the pattern and the command of God to Moses.

When Moses sees that the work of the Tabernacle is complete, he blesses the congregation. Then God tells Moses to erect the Tabernacle of the Tent of Meeting on the first day of the first month and to place in it all of its specially crafted furnishings. Moses then anoints Aaron and his four sons as God commanded him.

When Moses has finished the work, the cloud of God covers the Tabernacle of the Tent of Meeting and the presence of God fills the Tabernacle. When the cloud is lifted from the Tabernacle, it is a signal to the Israelites to break camp and begin to travel. But if the cloud is not lifted, they would not set out. Throughout the journeys of the Israelites, a cloud of *Adonai* is present by day and a fire by night.

INSIGHTS FROM THE TRADITION

A *Pikuday* means "the records." It is the final weekly *sedra* of the Book of Exodus. In most years, *Pikuday* is read as a double portion with *Vayakhel*. The Jewish calendar, is based on a lunar cycle of 354 days, or 50 weeks a year. Since there are 54 weekly Torah readings, plus special readings for major holidays that fall on Shabbat, it is necessary to double seven weekly portions so that the whole cycle of Torah readings is completed in a year. In a leap year, when an extra month is added to the Jewish calendar, there are four more Shabbatot; in such years, *Vayakhel* and *Pikuday* are read as separate portions.

B Rashi explains that the "records" of this portion introduce an accounting of the metals used in the construction of the Tabernacle. A *midrash* posits that Moses overheard some Israelites speculate that he had derived financial benefit from the donations for the Tabernacle because he was the treasurer in charge. Upon the completion of the Tabernacle, Moses called for an accounting to show that he had not personally profited from the contributions of the people. Based on this *midrash,* the Rabbis derived that we must not appoint less than two people with control over the finances of a city or community (*Exodus Rabbah* 51:1). *Yalkut Me'am Lo'ez* relates two different reasons for why Moses would not have been concerned that he would be suspect regarding the donations: (1) He fully intended from the outset to give an accounting and, therefore, had scribes record each donation along with the giver's name. The donations could then be compared with the expenditures, and (2) At one point during the donation process, Moses told the people that a sufficient amount had been collected and thus further gifts would not be required. Had Moses wanted personal wealth, he would have encouraged additional gifts (Yaacov Culi, Vol. X, p. 258). Ithamar, Aaron's son, was chosen to find suitable Levites to carry out the accounting.

Why did the Rabbis feel that at least two people should be in charge of a communal treasury? What lessons about public funds may be derived from these insights?
Why would it have been particularly important for Moses to call for an accounting?
Have you ever been a treasurer or in charge of other people's money? How do you feel about such a responsibility?

C The commentators puzzled over the role of the bells on the hem of the High Priest's robe. Were they used to announce the presence of the High Priest, a use which might incline the priest to be proud or haughty? Jacob Zvi Meklenburg (see *Learn Torah With . . .,* p. 173) taught that the sound of the bells served the same purpose as the sight of *tzitzit* — to remind the individual wearing them of something specific. And what was it that the High Priest needed to be reminded of? The awesome nature of his task and his responsibilities.

Why was it important for the High Priest to be especially mindful of his role and task? Are there people in society today who similarly need to be mindful of their role and task? Give some examples.
Is there something which you need or want to be reminded of constantly?
Do you have an article of clothing or a piece of jewelry that you use in this way? How else might you remind yourself?

D Although Moses did not take part in the construction of the Tabernacle or its utensils, he was given the honor of setting everything in its place. Several commentators explain that the Tabernacle was too weighty to be set up by the Israelites or even by the chief artisans. Only Moses, with divine aid, was able to accomplish this task.

Which ritual objects described as part of the Tabernacle are still part of contemporary synagogues?
All of the Tabernacle was considered holy, yet the Holy of Holies was held to be the most sacred. What was the Holy of Holies? Why was it considered so special?
Does the modern *Aron HaKodesh* in a synagogue sanctuary have the same importance as the Holy of Holies in the Tabernacle of old?
What is your favorite space in your synagogue? When do you particularly like to be there? Why?

E In *Pesikta Rabbati* 5 and 9, we read that when Israel continually grumbled, God asked them to build the Tabernacle. Thus, they would be too busy to complain. When it was done, God exclaimed: "Woe is Me! It is finished!"

What does this say about the nature of the people? What happens to you on a rainy day when you have to stay indoors?
How do you use your spare time?

F The *midrash* tells us that with the completion of the Tabernacle, God forgave the Israelites the sin of the Golden Calf. But Moses insisted that the other nations be made aware of Israel's pardon. The *Shechinah* thus dwelt within the Tabernacle (*Exodus Rabbah* 51:4).

Although the portion reads that God's presence dwelt in the Tabernacle, we have learned that God's presence is everywhere. Tradition teaches us this from a variety of sources. A *midrash* points out that God spoke to Moses from a lowly thornbush, thus teaching that no place on earth is without the Divine Presence. In *Genesis Rabbah,* the question is asked: Why is God called *Makom* (place or space)? Because God is the all-space/every-place of the universe (68:9).

Can you support the idea that the Israelites were not prepared for an omnipresent God?
How might the cloud of the *Shechinah* be a source of reassurance to the people?
The ancient Israelites seemed to have needed a tangible God. Do you think it might be easier for people to believe in God if they witnessed some physical manifestation of God?
Is it important to you to have miraculous evidence of God's existence in order to believe in a Higher Power?
Is there "evidence" for you of God's existence?
Do you think that the Tabernacle was created as a counterbalance to the incident of the Golden Calf?

STRATEGIES
ANALYZING THE TEXT

1 How many times does the phrase כאשר צוה יי את משה (*ka'asher tzivah Adonai et Moshe*) (as the Lord commanded Moses) appear in *Pikuday*? (Answer: 18 times.) What is the effect of the almost constant repetition of this phrase? How does it affect your perception of Moses? Of the Israelites? Of the Tabernacle? Can you tell from the text what God "thought" of the completed Tabernacle? (Follow this discussion with Strategy #5 in *Vayakhel*, page 151, emphasizing the above phrase.)

2 Martin Buber discovered many ways in which the account of the construction of the Tabernacle parallels the Creation story (see Nehama Liebowitz, *Studies in Shemot*, Vol. II, pp. 479ff.). Compare the language used in the two accounts. What inferences can you draw from the similarities in these passages (see chart below)? Do you agree that there are parallels between the work of Creation and the making of the Tabernacle? In what ways is the work of the Israelites on the Tabernacle an imitation of the work of God as Creator? Can you find other instances in *Vayakhel-Pikuday* which seem to point to the imitation of God's works by human beings? (In *Vayakhel*, the prohibition against working on Shabbat reminds us that God rested on the seventh day.) What does it mean to imitate God? To be God's "partner in Creation?" (For more, see the Index: "God's Partners.")

Use of Same Word	Genesis	Exodus
finished: ותכל, ויכלו ,ויכל	2:1-2	39:21; 40:33
make/made: ויעש, ועשו	1:7,16, 25	25:8, 10, 23, 31
saw/behold: והנה, וירא	1:31	39:43
blessed: ויברך	2:3	39:43

3 Why is it natural for *Vayakhel* and *Pikuday* to be read together? What elements do they have in common?

EXTENDING THE TEXT

4 Find out about the yearly cycle of Torah readings. Why are some portions double portions? Look at a few examples of double portions (including *Vayakhel-Pikuday*). Why do you think these were chosen to be joined into one Torah reading?
References: *The Minhagim: The Customs and Ceremonies of Judaism, Their Origins and Rationale* by Abraham Chill; *Bechol Levavcha* by Harvey Fields.

5 What customs do we observe upon completing the reading of a book of the Torah in the synagogue? What do we do when we reach the end of a book of Torah in our studies? Learn about the appropriate customs as a conclusion to your study of the Book of Exodus. Then have a *siyyum* (party) to celebrate!
References: See those for Strategy #4 immediately above.

6 From *Shemot*, which tells of his defense of a Hebrew slave, to *Pikuday*, in which Moses gives an account of all the materials collected and used for the construction of the Tabernacle, the Book of Exodus gives us a detailed portrait of Moses as a leader. How would you rank his leadership abilities? Design a "report card" for Moses. List all the qualities you think are important in a leader. Grade Moses in each category according to his behavior in the Book of Exodus. Include a section for general comments at the end.

7 According to Exodus 39:43, when Moses saw that all the work on the Tabernacle had been completed as God had commanded, he blessed the people. The words of the blessing were those found in Psalms 90:17: "May it be the will of God that the *Shechinah* [Divine Presence] rest upon the work of your hands; and let the beauty of *Adonai* our God be upon us and establish Thou the work of our hands upon us" (Rashi). Another *midrash* tells that Moses said, "The Eternal God of your fathers make you a thousand times so many more as ye are, as He hath promised you" (*Legends of the Jews* by Louis Ginzberg, Vol. III, p. 187). The people then responded with the words cited by Rashi above.

Write a blessing such as you think Moses might have bestowed on the Israelites. What words would you have used for such a blessing. Are your words or ideas found in any prayers or biblical passages?

8 What ever became of the Ark, so lovingly constructed by Bezalel? The *Haftarah* to *Pikuday* traces the Ark to the Temple of Solomon (I Kings 7:51-8:21) where legend tells us it remained until the destruction of that Temple by Nebuchadnezzar in 586 B.C.E. Read II Maccabees 2:1-8 for an account of what became of the Ark at that point. Jewish tradition holds that the Ark will be found when it is time for it to be reinstalled in the Temple of the future. Write your own version of the adventures of the Ark of the Covenant. Confine your story to the period before the destruction of the Temple and the Ark's mysterious disappearance.

9 In the Torah portions describing the work of building the Tabernacle, the work of the Israelites is dedicated, not to a human master, but to God. So, too, the dress of the High Priest was intended to remind him of the special and sacred nature of his work. However, most of the work *we* do in our daily lives is to please or meet the needs of people: ourselves, our parents, perhaps teachers or employers. But not all of our most important human tasks can be directed in this way. So it is that we each must ask ourselves, for whom, or for what, do we really work?

How would you answer these questions? Make a list of all the "work" you do in your life. Beside each task, note the answer to the question, "for whom" or "for what." For example: I baby-sit for Mrs. Roth, for money; I study to please my parents and to get good grades, so I can get into college. Think carefully: what kind of "work" do you do that is directed toward honoring God, or the Jewish people, or toward making the world a better place? Rank order all the work you do from least to most important. What kinds of work would you like to do in the future, and for whom, and why?

PERSONALIZING THE TEXT

10 In *Pirke Avot*, we read: "Do not separate yourself from the community" (2:5). How did the special vestments worn by the priests contradict this teaching? How do you feel about Rabbis and/or Cantors today wearing special robes during services? Organize a debate on this subject.

11 Make a slide show illustrating the idea that we are God's partners in creation. Start with pictures that illustrate how Jewish observance at home and in the synagogue teaches us to "imitate" God. Move on to pictures showing people acting as God's partners in the creation of the real world today. (For more, see the Index: "God's partners.")

12 Visit a non-Jewish place of worship. Arrange for a person who worships there to show your group around and explain the significance of their religious objects and symbols. End with a question and answer period.

13 How does the text of *Pikuday* teach that people in public office should take great care to be honest? How does it teach us to take pride in our work? Find examples in local newspapers of these values in action.

14 Build a three-dimensional model of the Tabernacle and its furnishings.
References: *The Tabernacle: Its Structure and Utensils* by Moshe Levine; *Exploring Exodus: The Heritage of Biblical Israel* by Nahum Sarna.

15 Read the Torah portion carefully and list all the colors used in the Tabernacle. Using a colored pencil, crayon, or marker that is the richest shade of each color, create an abstract color design showing the palette used to decorate the Tabernacle. Why do you think these colors were used? What effect and/or feeling do they create? If possible, join together the abstract designs of all the students and create a large mural.

16 Imagine the joy and celebration which must have followed the erection of the Tabernacle. Plan a *Chanukat HaBayit* (Dedication) ceremony for the Tabernacle. What special observances would you include? What special foods would you serve?
References: For ideas about appropriate food, see *The Jewish Holiday Kitchen* by Joan Nathan; for material on dedicating a home, see *The First Jewish Catalog* by Richard Siegel, Michael Strassfeld, and Sharon Strassfeld, p. 15.

17 Play detective: In teams, create a facsimile of an object or article of clothing related to the Tabernacle that is detailed in the text. Trade objects with another team. Have each team try to discover the name and function of the object. Then locate the verses in the Torah which refer to the making of the object.

OTHER RESOURCES

18 Read and discuss the poem "Holy to the Lord" in *The Fire Waits* by Michael I. Hecht, pp. 59-60.

19 Read, act out, and discuss the skit for the portion *Pikuday* in *Sedra Scenes: Skits for Every Portion of the Torah* by Stan J. Beiner, pp. 120-121.

20 Complete the pages which relate to *Pikuday* in *Bible People Book Two* by Joel Lurie Grishaver, pp. 39-42. Also check the accompanying Leader Guide for procedures and additional activities.

21 View and discuss the episode for *Pikuday* from *Torah Toons I: The Video*.

22 For creative movement activities, see "Levels of Sacred Space" and "The Cloud and God's Presence" from *Torah in Motion* by JoAnne Tucker and Susan Freeman, pp. 114-117.

23 Listen to, discuss, and sing "Cloud by Day, Fire by Night" from *Sounds of Freedom: Exodus in Song*.

24 Read and discuss the illustrated commentary for *Pekuday* in *American Torah Toons* by Lawrence Bush.

INVOLVING THE FAMILY

25 The portions *Terumah, Tetzaveh, Vayakhel*, and *Pikuday* describe the furnishings of the Tabernacle. Some of these furnishings are still found in synagogues today (see Exodus, *Terumah*, Strategy #13, page 132). With your family, visit a synagogue other than your own. Compare the religious articles you see with those in your own synagogue. How are they alike? different?

Note: There is a great deal of overlap and related material in the portions *Terumah, Tetzaveh, Vayakhel*, and *Pikuday*. Therefore, the Insights from the Tradition and Strategies for all these portions should be regarded as interchangeable.

BAR/BAT MITZVAH PROJECT

26 In reading this portion, we learn that the vessels and vestments for the Tabernacle are completed. The large number of these sacred items were not made by one individual but resulted from the work of many dedicated Israelites. Today, there is an organization called Habitat for Humanity composed of volunteers, fulfilling community needs with team work, cooperation, and religious commitment. Habitat for Humanity is a non-profit Christian based group open to volunteers of all religious persuasions. Founded by former U.S. President Jimmy Carter, its goal is to build homes for needy families around the United States and throughout the world. Many Jewish groups and Jewish volunteers have worked with this organization. Contact Habitat for Humanity to find out more about its work and how you can help: Habitat for Humanity, International, 121 Habitat Street, Americus, GA 31709.

REVIEW ACTIVITIES FOR EXODUS

1 Evaluate the Book of Exodus as a story. Imagine you are a Hollywood movie director and write your analysis in the form of a critique of a script sent to you for a movie. Make notes to the producer, scriptwriter, costume designer, set builders, and directors of special effects about any significant details.

2 Evaluate the Book of Exodus as a biography of a great man. Imagine you are an editor for a major publishing house. Write a memo to the author with your impressions of the biography. What are its strong points? Where do the characters need fleshing out?

3 Evaluate the Book of Exodus as a fable. Imagine you are a teacher of young children. Choose the most important lesson the book teaches and write a lesson plan. Explain why you have chosen that section to teach to your class and how you would go about doing so.

4 Evaluate the Book of Exodus as a religious document: Imagine you are a Rabbi. Write a sermon based on what, in your opinion, is the most important idea for Jews to take to heart from the Book of Exodus.

5 Evaluate the Book of Exodus as a resource for building a museum. Using Fimo or Sculpey, fabric, wood, paint, and foil, build in miniature the story of the Exodus, the Ten Plagues, the life of Moses, the Crossing of the Sea, the Tabernacle, all of its utensils, and the clothing for the priests.

References: *The Tabernacle: Its Structure and Utensils* by Moshe Levine; *Exploring Exodus: The Heritage of Biblical Israel* by Nahum Sarna.

6 Make a list of the most important Hebrew words/concepts in the Book of Exodus. Include names of people, places, objects, and holidays. Trade lists with a friend and have your friend sort the words into meaningful categories. Based on one of the categories, design a poster illustrating and summarizing one aspect of the Book of Exodus.

7 In 1947, a ship named the "Exodus" carrying 4,515 Jewish refugees — survivors of World War II — reached Palestine only to be turned back by the British. Eventually the passengers were interned in Cyprus. Write a diary excerpt as though you were a Holocaust survivor who was a passenger on the ship. Connect your story to the Exodus of the Israelites from slavery in Egypt.

8 Present the cantata "Holy Moses" by Hazell (Novello and Co. Ltd.). Two recordings of this work are also available: Kings Singers, Argo Zoa 149 and Southbend Boys Choir, Vista VPS 1009.

9 View and discuss the film *The Ten Commandments*, available as a video rental, not rated. How does the movie differ from the Book of Exodus? If you had been asked to direct this movie, what would you have done differently?

10 Complete some or all of the pages related to the Book of Exodus in *Torah Tales Copy Pak™: Exodus & Leviticus* by Marji Gold-Vukson.

Note: For other concluding strategies which can be adapted, see the Review Activities in this volume for each of the other books of the Torah.

OVERVIEW

The third book of the Torah and its first portion, *Vayikra,* means "and He called," and refers to God's call to Moses. This is a most appropriate name, for in this book, laws, precepts, values, and consequences are communicated through Moses to all the Israelites. These initiate the chain of Jewish tradition — passing the law from one generation to the next.

The Latin name, Leviticus, derives from *Leuitikon,* the Greek word for the Levitical Book or Book of the Levites. This book has also been referred to as *"Torat Kohanim"* — the Priestly Manual, as it contains explicit directions for the priests, all of whom are members of the tribe of Levi and entrusted with carrying out the ritual of the sacrificial cult.

The Book of Leviticus interrupts the narrative flow which begins in Genesis and continues in Exodus, resuming in the Book of Numbers. Although the title of the book implies that its focus is the Levites, much information which specifically pertains to them (i.e., the transportation and protection of the Tabernacle) is presented in Numbers. Furthermore, the key theme in Leviticus is the attainment of ethical and spiritual holiness. Unlike the ritual and religious codes of other Near Eastern peoples, the bulk of the material in Leviticus is addressed to the entire Israelite people. While the Book of Exodus explains the construction of the Tabernacle, the priestly clothing, and the sacrificial utensils, it is in Leviticus that these items are put into practice. Thus, this book deals in the main with the sacrificial cult.

Even at the time of the prophets, there were major debates about the sacrifices. The prophets recognized that, initially, biblical Jews may have needed the "tangibles" in a worship experience. However, they questioned the people's motives with regard to the sacrifices. The prophets decried the corruption and disregard for ethical codes of behavior and the use of sacrifice as a means of atonement. Such ritual was surely empty, if not sacrilegious.

The debate about the sacrifices ended in 70 C.E. with the fall of the Second Temple. The sacrificial cult was then abandoned, replaced by prayer as a more appropriate, or higher level, form of worship. The sacrificial cult is but one aspect of the pursuit of holiness. Leviticus also contains some of the loftiest and most inspiring passages in the Torah. Leviticus also contains the most complete biblical account of the holidays (in the portion *Emor*), the laws of *kashrut,* and the Sabbatical and Jubilee years.

Leviticus contains nearly half of the 613 commandments. A measure of its importance can be derived from the fact that so much of the Talmud is based on it. As it had a great deal to say to previous generations of Jews, so it has much to say to us today.

VAYIKRA 1:1-5:26 ויקרא

SYNOPSIS

VAYIKRA BEGINS WITH GOD INSTRUCTING Moses to describe the various sacrifices to the Israelites. The five types of sacrifices are: a burnt offering (*olah*); the meal offering (*minchah*); the sacrifice of well-being (*zevach shelamim*); the sin offering (*chatat*); and the guilt offering (*asham*).

Olah, literally meaning "that which goes up," is characterized by burning the entire animal upon the altar except for the hide. The *minchah* offering consists of unleavened choice flour. A portion of it was to be burned on the altar and the remainder given to Aaron and his sons. All *minchah* offerings must contain salt.

An unblemished cow, sheep, or goat could serve as the offering for the sacrifice of *zevach shelamim*. An ordinance states that all the fat on the sacrificial animal belonged to God. Additionally, a prohibition against eating any fat or blood is included here.

These three types of sacrifices are voluntary and not brought for atonement. The *chatat* and the *asham* are both obligatory upon guilty individuals.

The *chatat* is to be brought by an individual or community which, unintentionally, commits a sin regarding any of the commandments. The specific offering to be brought was determined by one's economic condition. An anointed priest and the community are both directed to sacrifice unblemished bulls for the *chatat*. A chieftain sometimes referred to as a tribal chief is to bring a goat. A person from among the populace is to offer a goat or sheep.

Four additional transgressions are described as requiring a *chatat* offering: (1) failure to come forward to testify, (2) touching an unclean animal or carcass, (3) coming in contact with human uncleaness, and (4) failure to fulfill an oath. For these transgressions, the offering, depending on the financial means of the transgressor, can be: a female sheep, a goat, two birds, or choice flour.

The *asham* offering is to be brought by an individual who had sinned by committing robbery or fraud. The penalty for such a crime is to restore to the owner the item stolen, plus an additional one-fifth of its value, and then to bring a ram or its equivalent in money as a sacrifice. The *asham* also applies to the individual who has unwittingly sinned regarding God's sacred things.

The text describes the procedures for the people and the priests to follow for each of these sacrifices and the part of the sacrifice which is to go to Aaron and his sons.

INSIGHTS FROM THE TRADITION

A The first verse of this *parashah* reads: "God called to Moses and spoke to him from the Tent of Meeting, saying . . . " The Rabbis questioned the extra "saying" in the verse. Was there something to learn from this? The Talmud teaches that the double usage of the word "saying" teaches that if you say something to your neighbor, the neighbor must not "say" it again without your consent. This is *derech eretz* — the proper way to behave. All of our conversations are private and only if you give permission may your words be repeated.

Do you assume that every conversation should be considered private and confidential? Is every conversation repeatable? Has anyone ever said to you: "This is just between you and me," or "If you repeat this I will deny ever saying it"? Does the person speaking not trust you? Have you ever been asked to keep something confidential? Was it difficult? Do you, as the saying goes, ever "spill the beans"? Has anyone ever done it to you? Are there times when one must break a confidence? Do you think the Rabbis considered this? Invite your Rabbi or educator to share some thoughts and sources from Jewish tradition on this issue.

B How should we understand the sacrifices? From a casual reading of this portion, you might think that the sacrifices were a form of bribery — a way to influence God. But a basic belief of Judaism is that God is not a physical being who needs food. So what benefit could God derive from a sacrifice? The lesson is that God does not need a sacrifice, people do. *Yalkut Me'am Lo'ez*, by Yaacov Culi (Vol. XI, pp. 2-7) enumerates five different reasons for the sacrifices:

1. Sacrifice should arouse a person to examine misbehavior in light of the goodness of God's creation. This should lead to repentance — a change in behavior.

2. Sacrifices were commanded so that priests in the sanctuary would have a livelihood and not have to beg charity.

3. A sacrifice is like a fine. An individual who suffers a financial loss due to his/her sin may come to realize that sin is very expensive and thus repent and refrain from sinning.

4. By witnessing a sacrifice, a sinner sees the slaughter, the burning, and the remaining ashes of the animal. A sinner may realize that this is also the final end of all humans. This also may lead a person to repent.

5. Israel had witnessed the Egyptians worshiping idols; many of these idols were in the shape of certain animals. To prevent worshiping these animals, the Israelites were commanded to use them as sacrifices.

The bringing of sacrifice does not, in and of itself, appease God for one's wrongdoing; rather "it serves merely as a symbol and expression of man's desire to purify himself and become reconciled with God" (*Studies in Vayikra* by Nehama Leibowitz, p. 22).

State which of the five reasons given above for sacrifice seems to be the most significant to you. If a person sins and brings a sacrifice, does the sacrifice alone atone for the sin? If not, why not? What does repentance mean to you? Is it something you have done or can do? Explain.

C The essential element in repentance is the attitude of the individual. With the destruction of the Temple, the sacrifices were discontinued. The Sages then prescribed other practices to substitute for the sacrifices. The most important were prayer, Torah study, and *tzedakah*. Just as prayer, study, and *tzedakah* require wholehearted commitment and discipline, so repentance requires a wholehearted commitment to change one's ways.

What aspect of your life receives your most wholehearted attention and commitment?

D The biblical text describes each type of sacrifice in detail. Yet, underlying all the descriptions is the consideration extended to those individuals who could not afford to bring large animals for sacrifice. A person unable to bring cattle could bring sheep. One unable to bring sheep was allowed to bring birds. There was also a meal offering so that the poorest among the Israelites might have the opportunity to bring a sacrifice. Even with respect to the sacrifices, Torah preserves the dignity of the individual.

In light of this, can you explain why someone would choose to donate anonymously to charitable causes?
Would you prefer to give anonymously or have your gift recognized publicly?

E There is a special ordinance regarding the meal offering. No meal offering may be of leavened dough. There are two acceptable types of meal offering: unleavened cakes with oil mixed in or unleavened wafers spread with oil. The commentary *Yalkut Me'am Lo'ez* by Yaacov Culi suggests that leavening is synonymous with corruption (the evil urge). Leaven in Hebrew is called *chamaytz*, which means sour. Just as leaven makes dough expand and become sour, so the evil urge makes a person sin and thus be sour (Vol. XI, pp. 71-72). (See Strategies #12 and #13, pp. 169.)

What aspects of society would you classify as *chamaytz*?

How do you deal with that which is "sour" in your life?

F With the destruction of the Second Temple, the sacrificial cult and the priesthood for the Levites ended. In Exodus 19:6, we are told, ". . . but you, you shall be to me a kingdom of priests, a holy nation." Based on such verses, the Rabbis reinterpreted the Levitical priesthood as a priesthood for all Jews setting up a system of rules, behaviors, and mores which would dictate Jewish religious life and observance. The home became a *mikdash m'at*, a miniature version of the Tabernacle and the kitchen; in particular, the table upon which the family ate was regarded as the sacrificial altar. As discussed in *Lifecycles*, Vol. 2 by Debra Orenstein and Jane Rachel Litman, (p. 136), women came to see themselves as priests in regard to their household duties and the laws of family purity. A record of this comparison is seen in the *tkhines*, petitionary prayers for women. In these prayers, the kindling of the Shabbat lights, the taking of *challah* (a symbolic olive-sized piece of dough removed before baking the Sabbath bread, which represented the part reserved for the priests), and going to the *mikvah* are compared with the rituals associated with the High Priest.

Do you think society at that time (several hundred years ago) accepted and approved of this comparison? Do you think this was revolutionary thinking then?

Who now has the responsibility to maintain the priesthood and the altar? In a contemporary and egalitarian society, who can now maintain the altar and the priesthood?

Is sacred duty now seen as a shared endeavor and responsibility for both women and men? How is this validated in liberal Judaism?

STRATEGIES

ANALYZING THE TEXT

1 Learning the names of the sacrifices, what is to be sacrificed, and why something is sacrificed can be a bit confusing. Create a chart which illustrates these three elements. It might take the following form:

NAME OF SACRIFICE

WHAT IS SACRIFICED

WHY THE SACRIFICE IS BROUGHT

2 *Vayikra* prescribes different sin offerings to be brought by different categories of people or individuals who sin. Read through Leviticus 4. Who brings the most valuable *chatat* — the whole community, a common individual, a "chieftain" (ruler), or a priest? What do the relative values of these sin offerings teach about the role of these individuals in society?

3 We no longer bring sacrifices to be burnt on the altar, but there is still a need for repentance and reconciliation between one person and another and between individuals and God. Reexamine the five reasons for the sacrifices and the situations they seek to remedy (see Insight B, page 166). Write a contemporary version for each of these. In place of the sacrifice, suggest an action, behavior, or activity that would be an appropriate remedy for the situation you write about.

EXTENDING THE TEXT

4 In the days of the Temple when sacrifices were performed, there were prophets who spoke critically about them. Read some of the following passages: Amos 5:22-25; Jeremiah 6:20, 7:22; I Samuel 15:22-23; Hosea 6:6; Isaiah 1:11-13; Micah 6:6-8. What exactly are the prophets criticizing? What would be a parallel contemporary criticism? In your opinion, would such criticism be valid? Choose one of the prophetic passages above and rewrite it, using language and terms appropriate now.

5 Read through several different daily prayer books of your choice to find individual prayers that refer to sacrifices. Do all the prayer books contain such prayers? Look especially in the Musaf *Amidah* for Shabbat. Please note that Reform and Reconstructionist prayer books do not contain these prayers. Some Conservative prayer books include these prayers in Hebrew without the English translations. How can you explain these differences? Even if you personally do not believe in or wish to pray for the restoration of sacrifices, can you find some merit in prayers which refer to them?
References: *Encyclopaedia Judaica,* "Sacrifice," Vol. 14, pp. 599- 616; *To Pray as a Jew* by Hayim Donin, pp. 11-12, 117-121; *The Torah: A Modern Commentary,* edited by W. Gunter Plaut, pp. 750- 755.

6 List in Hebrew the five different kinds of sacrifice. Determine the Hebrew root of each word. Using a modern Hebrew dictionary, find modern Hebrew words that build upon these Hebrew roots. Compile lists of these words. Discuss how the modern words relate to their original meanings.

7 According to tradition, the three daily prayer services were established by Ezra the Scribe. They were intended to correspond to the three daily sacrifices offered in the Temple. Learn the Hebrew names and appropriate times of these services. Create a bulletin board display incorporating this information and title it "When a Jew Prays."

Reference: *Teaching Tefilah* by Bruce Kadden and Barbara Binder Kadden, p. 3.

8 Many traditional Jewish practices at mealtimes are based on the ceremonies surrounding the sacrifices. After reciting *HaMotzi*, we salt our bread before eating it because of the admonishment to the priests to salt all offerings (Leviticus 2:13). We wash our hands before breaking bread, as the priests did before bringing a sacrifice. The custom of covering the knife during *Birkat HaMazon* is explained by the fact that a knife, which is a sign of war, was not allowed to touch the altar, which is a sign of peace. (*The Jewish Dietary Laws: Their Meaning for Our Time* by Samuel Dresner and Seymour Siegel, pp. 39-40.)
a. Have a meal or snack with your class and learn about these customs by doing them.
b. Make puzzle cards to teach younger children these customs. On one half of a large index card, illustrate the sacrificial practice. On the other side, illustrate the related mealtime custom. Cut the two halves apart with a puzzle-shaped edge. Correctly matching the custom and its origin will lead to a completed puzzle and a correct answer.

PERSONALIZING THE TEXT

9 During the High Holy Days, there is a special prayer called the *Al Chayt*. The word *chayt* is usually translated as "sin," thus relating it to the *chatat*, or sin offering. The word *chayt*, used in connection with archery, means to "miss the mark." The implication is that we are especially sorry for those actions which are off-target — not in keeping with our moral standards.
a. Read a version of the *Al Chayt* from your synagogue's High Holy Day prayer book. Do any of the passages seem to refer especially to you? Why do you think we recite this prayer aloud as a community?

b. Come up with additional verses for this prayer or create your own version.

c. Have there been times in your life when you have "missed the mark"? How have you tried to set things right? Create a poster illustrating this meaning of "sin."

10 Of the many items described in this portion to be used in sacrificial ritual, the most exotic is the incense. Many import and gift boutiques sell incense. Purchase some and get some "scents" of the worship service our ancestors carried out in biblical times. Decide whether the incense adds to or detracts from the service and why.

11 According to this portion, an individual who was guilty of theft had to replace that which was stolen and add an additional one-fifth of its value. This concept of restitution has become a part of the criminal justice system in many places. The basic idea is for a criminal to make actual restitution to the victims. Find out if there is such a program in your community. Invite a representative of the police department or local victim rights organization to discuss this approach with the group.

12 The prohibition against sacrifices containing leaven reflects the fact that leaven — which causes bread to rise and various foods to ferment — was seen as a symbol of corruption (*The Pentateuch and Haftorahs,* edited by J.H. Hertz, p. 414). To help you understand this fermenting process, make a yeast/water/sugar mix called a sponge, which is the first step in bread making. To make a sponge, dissolve 1 teaspoon of sugar in 1/2 cup of warm water. Add 1 tablespoon (or 1 package) of yeast and gently stir in the large measuring cup or bowl. Cover the measuring cup with a small plate or a towel and let it stand for ten minutes. Uncover the bowl and observe what happened. Can you think of some metaphors for this in human life? For example, what happens if you add a little "greed" to a person's character? How does it corrupt him or her? What about jealousy or anger?

13 Leavened bread is good when fresh, but eventually becomes moldy, in other words soured and inedible, making it improper to use in sacrifice. Unleavened bread, however, lasts a long time; it does not sour and its flavor does not change, making it proper for use as a sacrifice. Use this as a metaphor to describe some part of your life.

14 Two of the sins requiring a *chatat* offering are acts which would be known only to the person who committed them — failing to fulfill an oath and failure to come forward to testify. How can the *failure* to do something be a sin? Can you think of other cases when failing to act would be sinful? It has been suggested that bringing the *chatat* offering was a way of relieving the guilt which a person might feel, even though his/her sin was known only to himself/herself. Since we no longer can bring sacrifices to show our repentance and relieve our guilty feelings, suggest some actions which might serve these same functions for us.

15 Read Leviticus 5:20-26. Note the order in which the person who has sinned through robbery or fraud is to make expiation for the wrongdoing. The Talmud explains that in such cases, restitution and not sacrifice or prayer is the first step in repentance. The victim of the wrongdoing must be repaid and apologized to before the sinner can ask God for forgiveness (*Yoma 87a*). Conect this explanation to the High Holy Days. Think of its implications for your own life. Give specific examples.

16 *Vayikra* does not limit itself to prescribing penitential offerings for common people who sin. It also addresses people in positions of power who do wrong (Leviticus 4:22-26). In making leaders give public sin offerings like everyone else, the text may be teaching us something about public accountability. This is a major issue in political life today. Find newspaper articles dealing with wrongdoing by public officials. Discuss whether and or how they admit, repent, and "pay" for their acts. In contemporary society, who do you think pays the stiffest price for wrongdoing: clergy, political leaders, individuals, or the whole community?

17 What is a contemporary meaning of the word "sacrifice"? Does it mean to give up something like time, energy, personal desires? Give some personal examples of things you consider sacrifice. How is this modern meaning alike or dissimilar to the biblical concept of sacrificing?

18 Traditionally, the Book of Leviticus is the first book of Torah studied by young children. The reason for this is that the pure (meaning young children) should study what is pure, referring to sacrifices. In your Religious School, does this apply? At what age do you think this book should be studied? Explain.

19 In this portion, we learn that an individual is obligated to testify in court when called upon. Failure to do so is a grave sin, since someone's life or financial well-being may be at stake. How far would you go to help another person? How much would you give of your efforts or of your means?

OTHER RESOURCES

20 Read, act out, and discuss the skit for *Vayikra* in *Sedra Scenes: Skits for Every Torah Portion* by Stan J. Beiner, pp. 122-125.

21 View and discuss the episode for *Vayikra* from *Torah Toons I: The Video*.

22 For creative movement activities, see "An Offering by Fire" and "Drawing Near" from *Torah in Motion* by JoAnne Tucker and Susan Freeman, pp. 122-125.

23 Read and discuss the illustrated commentary for *Va-Yikra* in *American Torah Toons* by Lawrence Bush.

INVOLVING THE FAMILY

24 Writing in *The Jewish Dietary Laws: Their Meaning for Our Time*, Samuel Dresner says: "Today we have no Temple in Jerusalem, no altar there, no sacrifices, no priests to minister. But, in their stead we have something even greater. For every home can be a Temple, every table an altar, every meal a sacrifice and every Jew a priest" (p. 40). In part, Dresner is referring to the practices described in Strategy #8, pp. 168.

As a family, discuss this idea. Think of ways to make your home a Temple, your table an altar, and yourself a priest. Choose one idea and incorporate it into your family life for a week. Follow the procedure described in Leviticus, *Kedoshim*, Strategy #27, page 206.

Note: The material in the portions *Vayikra* and *Tzav* is very similar. Therefore, many of the activities listed in *Tzav* will be useful for *Vayikra* as well.

BAR/BAT MITZVAH PROJECT

25 As you become a Bar or Bat Mitzvah, you become responsible for keeping the commandments. This project is really introspective and asks you to take a personal inventory of your behavior and the changes you may have to make to be in compliance with these Jewish laws. It is a fact of life that people like to gossip and repeat stories and conversations that they have heard. In light of Insight A, page 165, which you should reread for this project, how do you think you measure up? Are you careful about what you say and repeat? Do you listen to gossip? Do you repeat it? Do you consider yourself trustworthy? Keep a diary for a week or so in which you write down your personal observations regarding the above questions. To add another dimension to this project, examine several daily newspapers and news magazines. Identify stories and articles which do not seem to be based on facts, but rather on rumor or innuendo. It would be interesting to make a scrapbook with these articles and stories. You might also want to include photographs and captions which appear in these publications. Try to find the same story in two or more print publications which give different or conflicting accounts of the incident and answer the following: Are these publications reliable and responsible? What might motivate a publication to expand or sensationalize a story? Does it help sell papers? Does it keep people interested? Include your feelings and responses in your diary.

TZAV 6:1-8:36 צו

SYNOPSIS

TZAV REPEATS THE DESCRIPTION AND procedure for the sacrifices discussed in the previous portion. Directed to Aaron and his sons, the procedures for the sacrifices and the explanation of the priestly portions are given in detail. The priests are here commanded to keep the fire on the altar burning perpetually.

God commands Moses to prepare Aaron, the Tabernacle, and Aaron's sons for the new priesthood. This includes washing Aaron and his sons, dressing them in ritual garments, and anointing Aaron and the Tabernacle with oil. During this ordination ceremony, a sin offering and a burnt offering are brought. Then a ram of ordination is slaughtered. Some of the blood is put on the right ear, thumb, and big toe of Aaron and his sons. Then Moses dashes the blood against each side of the altar. Specified parts of the ram, along with one cake of unleavened bread, one cake of oil bread, and one wafer are placed in the palms of Aaron and of his sons. This is a wave offering, which is then burned with the burnt offering.

Moses takes the breast of the ram as a wave offering before God. Moses takes anointing oil and some blood from the altar and sprinkles it upon Aaron and his sons. He then directs Aaron and his sons to boil the flesh of the ram and eat it with the unleavened bread at the entrance to the Tent of Meeting. Moses explains that the period of ordination will last seven days and all that has been sacrificed and done that day is to be repeated on each of the following seven days.

INSIGHTS FROM THE TRADITION

A Even the menial task of removing the ashes from the altar entails the wearing of specific garments. For the initial removal of the ashes, when they are placed next to the altar, the priest is to wear special linen attire. Other less important clothing is worn to carry the ashes away from the camp. The Rabbis derived two lessons from this. The priestly vestments are worn even for this lowly task because it is a service to God in the Temple. Thus, we learn that when a person wishes to worship, he/she must wear special clothing. A second lesson relates to individuals and the tasks they perform. An individual should never excuse himself/herself from a task because he/she feels it is beneath his/her dignity to perform it (*Yalkut Me'am Lo'ez* by Yaacov Culi, Vol. XI, pp. 124-5).

Does your synagogue have policies or guidelines regarding what people should and should not wear to worship services? to Religious School? Do you think there should be a dress code? Do you behave differently when you are dressed up as opposed to when you are wearing everyday clothes? What household chores do you do? Does your attitude affect how well you carry out these tasks?

B *Tzav* details the priestly duties. The priests and, in particular, the High Priest offered the Israelites role models to emulate. The High Priest had to be sinless in order to carry out his duties. But, since no individual can be sinless, the High Priest brought a daily sacrifice. If the High Priest can bring a sacrifice, his action may motivate others to do so. The High Priest brings his sacrifice publicly without feeling ashamed. The Israelites, likewise, should not feel ashamed in bringing their sacrifices. The High Priest brings a meal offering, the same offering as that of the poorest Israelite. Thus, the poor should not feel embarrassed by their meager sacrifice. Lastly, twice daily a sacrifice is offered for the sin of the Golden Calf. The Sages felt that all the troubles in the world are related to the sin of the Golden Calf. These sacrifices protect Israel from the effects of the sin of the Golden Calf (*Yalkut Me'am Lo'ez* by Yaacov Culi, Vol. XI, pp. 134-135).

How is a Rabbi a contemporary role model for the Jewish community?

Should community leaders be held to a higher standard of behavior than the general population? Why or why not?

The priests carried out a detailed ritual which had great influence on the people. What do you do which has real significance for others?

C Different sections of the Tanach appear to express conflicting ideas about sacrifice. Despite the many detailed sections of Leviticus, for example, which deal with sacrifice, in I Samuel 15:22, we read "Does God delight in burnt offerings and sacrifices as much as in obedience to God's command? Surely, obedience is better than sacrifice . . ." Some commentators resolved this apparent conflict by understanding ". . . this is the *Torah* [in some texts translated as 'ritual'] of the burnt offering . . . " to refer to Torah *study*. Studying Torah and all the *mitzvot* (including those of sacrifice) is equal to the actual giving of sacrifice.

Do you agree that studying something can be equivalent to performing the act itself? What might be the value of studying about the sacrifices, even though we no longer offer sacrifices in this way?

D Leviticus 7:27 contains an absolute prohibition against consuming blood, and thus is the basis for the regulations and procedures regarding the preparation of kosher meat. A variety of reasons have been suggested for this prohibition: (1) it is a health measure; (2) it is a means of weaning the Israelites away from the practices of idolatrous nations (Maimonides); (3) it is a reminder of the sanctity of all life (Nachmanides).

What reasons can you think of for the prohibition against consuming blood?

What can the laws of and the observance of *kashrut* mean to you?

E The *midrash* points out that Leviticus should be the first book to be taught young Jewish children. Since young children are pure and the sacrifices are pure — "the pure should come and study the pure" (*Leviticus Rabbah* 7:3).

What would be your initial choice of material for children to study? Why?

Does what you read or watch on TV seriously affect your thoughts or attitudes? Can these influences make you less pure? Explain.

F The *midrash* points out that in the messianic age, all sacrifices will be annulled except the sacrifice of Thanksgiving and all prayers will be annulled except the prayer of Thanksgiving. Such a sacrifice or prayer would be offered by one who has experienced a miraculous deliverance, such as after a sea voyage, after travel in the wilderness, after recovery from an illness, or after release from imprisonment (Rashi).

Why do you think this one sacrifice and prayer would endure even in the end of days?

What does the American celebration of Thanksgiving commemorate? Why has this observance lasted?

For what are you thankful? How do you express that thankfulness?

STRATEGIES

ANALYZING THE TEXT

1 Read and/or listen to the description of Aaron and his sons being dressed for the priestly ordination (Leviticus 8:6-13). Compare this to the dressing of the Torah after it is read. (For more, see the Index: "Rabbis/Priests.")

2 Learn the names in Hebrew of the garments which Aaron and his sons wore. Compare them to the ornaments adorning the Torah.

3 For our biblical ancestors, sacrifice was the usual way they worshiped God. Look at the following examples of sacrifice in the Book of Genesis and then answer the questions: Cain and Abel – Genesis 4:3.4; Noah – Genesis 8:20-22; Abraham – Genesis 12:8, 13:4, 15:1-21, 22:1-19; Isaac – Genesis 26:23-25; Jacob – Genesis 31:54, 33:20, 35:7, 46:1. Who offered the sacrifice? Why was it offered (what is the stated reason, what reason can you derive from the context)? What did the sacrifice consist of (any special characteristics)? How would you fit the sacrifice into the Levitical scheme detailed in the portions *Vayikra* and *Tzav* (i.e., is it an *asham*, etc.)?

4 Make a list of the animals which were considered fit for sacrifice. What characteristics do these animals have in common? For example, would you describe them as fierce or gentle? Herbivorous or carnivorous? What general conclusions can you draw? Why do you suppose that only these types of animals were sacrificed?

EXTENDING THE TEXT

5 According to Rashi, the sacrifice of well-being would be offered for thanksgiving (7:11, 12) by a person who returned safely from a dangerous journey, by someone released from prison, by one who recovered from being seriously ill. Such people today recite a special blessing, *Birkat HaGomel*, after being called to the Torah for an *aliyah*. Invite a Rabbi or Cantor to discuss this *brachah* and teach it to you.

6 According to *Leviticus Rabbah* 9:7, even if all sacrifices and prayers were to be discontinued in the messianic age, the offerings and blessings of thanksgiving (well-being) will never stop being given and uttered. There is a whole category of *brachot* in our liturgy called *Birchot HaNehenin* — blessings for the pleasures we receive through our senses.

a. Many prayer books have a special section containing these *brachot*. Look them up and carefully read the occasions on which they are to be recited. Which are most meaningful to you? Learn them and use them!

b. Create a 3-D diorama which illustrates occasions when the *Birchot HaNehenin* should be recited. Include scenery and stick figures.

7 Find out how the various branches of Judaism have dealt with the history and tradition of sacrifice. Invite one or all of the following: Orthodox, Conservative, Reform, or Reconstructionist Rabbi to speak to your group about this topic. Ask them to share examples from their prayer books which relate to sacrifices. (For more, see the Index: "Sacrifice.")

8 Why were the ear, thumb (hand), and toe (foot) of the priests anointed with blood during ordination? It has been suggested that the ear is the symbol of hearing or understanding, the hand represents action, and the foot symbolizes a righteous path of life (*The Torah: A Modern Commentary*, edited by W. Gunther Plaut, p. 804). These parts of the body are appropriate symbols not only for the priests, but for ordinary individuals as well. Design a poster on this theme. (For more, see the Index: "Ordination.")

9 Using felt, fabric scraps, buttons, and glitter, make a small mock-up of the robe over which the *ephod* was worn by the priests. For a complete description of this robe in which Moses dressed Aaron, see Exodus 28:31-34.

PERSONALIZING THE TEXT

10 Today, there are ordination ceremonies for Rabbis and clergy of other faiths. Modern ceremonies, however, are nothing like that described in *Tzav*. Invite your Rabbi to explain his/her ordination ceremony. You might want to extend this activity and invite clergy from local churches to give presentations about their ordinations.

11 It states in this portion that one who consumes forbidden parts of an animal will be "cut off from his kin." This has been understood to mean ostracism from the community or capital punishment. Other related verses identify God as the one who cuts the sinner away, the penalty being premature death (*The Torah: A Modern Commentary*, edited by W. Gunther Plaut, p. 786). Attach contemporary significance to this concept of "cut off from his kin." What form might this take today? For an example, listen to the song "Cat's Cradle" by Harry Chapin, on the album *Verities and Balderdash*, Elektra 7ES-1012. (For more, see the Index: "*Karet*/Cut off from kin.")

12 According to a *midrash*, the eighth day of the ordination ceremonies, the day when Aaron first acted the role of priest, corresponds to the first day of the Hebrew month of Nisan. Read the selection "The Day of Ten Crowns" in *Legends of the Jews* by Louis Ginzberg, Vol. III, p. 181, to learn what other events are associated with this date. Create an appropriate observance for the first of Nisan.

13 Imagine you are Aaron. Write a speech which you will give to the people after you are ordained. Include your feelings, both negative and positive, about your new position.

14 Blood, in Leviticus, symbolizes purity. It is used to anoint the priests (see Leviticus 8:23). Blood is also a symbol of life (see Leviticus 17:11; Deuteronomy 12:23-25), and some have given this as the reason that Jews are forbidden to consume blood. Dresner notes that the expression to "spill blood" means to destroy life, to kill, whereas in medicine today, the injection of blood is often a means of saving life. The removal of blood from the meat we eat therefore teaches us to respect life (*The Jewish Dietary Laws: Their Meaning for Our Time* by Samuel Dresner and Seymour Siegel, p. 40). Invite a kosher butcher to explain to you the process by which blood is removed from meat in the process of *kashering*.

15 Due to its connection to blood, the color red has been used symbolically in many cultures. Use both a general and a Jewish encyclopedia to find out more about this. Create a poster illustrating what you learned.

16 In *Tzav*, the priests are instructed to dress in their linen garments even for the task of cleaning up the ashes left on the altar from previous sacrifices.
a. Think of some occasions when *you* get dressed up (for Shabbat, to go to the theater, or to make a special visit). How does putting on special clothes affect your feelings about what you are doing? Imagine that you got dressed up to do some very ordinary things like going to school or shopping. Did it change how you felt about what you were doing? Was the cleaning up of ashes not an "ordinary" task? Why do you think the priests had to wear special clothes for cleaning the altar?
b. Imagine you are the principal of a school which has just instituted the wearing of uniforms. Write and deliver a talk to your students explaining why this decision was made.
c. You are a Rabbi who has noticed that people come to the synagogue improperly dressed. Give a speech to your synagogue board explaining why the synagogue should establish a dress code for worship services.

17 The job of priest was a hereditary one — male descendants of Aaron (Levites) became priests and officiated in the Tabernacle and later in the Temple. With the discontinuation of the sacrificial rites, the priests gradually were replaced by Rabbis and scholars as religious leaders. There were and are no Jewish laws associated with the hereditary status and training of Rabbis and scholars as there was for the priesthood. Design a course of study for yourself as if you were going to prepare for ordination as a Rabbi. For ideas, you might want to write for catalogs from several Rabbinic seminaries: Jewish Theological Seminary,

3080 Broadway, New York, NY 10027; Hebrew Union College-Jewish Institute of Religion, 3101 Clifton Avenue, Cincinnati, OH 45220; Yeshiva University, 500 W. 185th Street, New York, NY 10033; Reconstructionist Rabbinical College, Church Road at Greenwood, Wyncote, PA 19095.

18 In *Pirke Avot* we read, "The world is sustained by three things: by Torah, by worship, and by loving deeds" (1:2). This verse has become a well-known Hebrew song "*Al Sheloshah Devarim.*" Learn to sing this song. (See *Songs and Hymns: A Musical Supplement to Gates of Prayer,* edited by Raymond Smolover and Malcolm H. Stern, p. 6.)

19 The major difference between *Tzav* and *Vayikra* is that in *Tzav*, the priests are addressed, while in *Vayikra*, the entire congregation of Israel is addressed. Why were the people spoken to first? In what ways might this order be of significance?

OTHER RESOURCES

20 Read, act out, and discuss the skit for the portion *Tzav* in *Sedra Scenes: Skits for Every Torah Portion* by Stan J. Beiner, pp. 126-128.

21 For other insights and activities about *kashrut*, see *Teaching Mitzvot* by Barbara Binder Kadden and Bruce Kadden, pp. 61-66.

22 View and discuss the episode for *Tzav* from *Torah Toons I: The Video.*

23 For creative movement activities, see "Holy on Contact" and "Blood Ritual" from *Torah in Motion* by JoAnne Tucker and Susan Freeman, pp. 126-129.

24 Read and discuss the illustrated commentary for *Tzav* in *American Torah Toons* by Lawrence Bush.

Note: For more, see the Index: *"Kashrut."*

INVOLVING THE FAMILY

25 According to *Tzav,* a person who violates the law by consuming blood shall be cut off from his kin (Leviticus 7:27). Following a common set of dietary guidelines was seen as an important way to maintain community and family. Does your family follow the laws of *kashrut*? Do you not mix milk and meat? What dietary guidelines do you follow for Passover? Are there particular foods your family associates with Shabbat and holidays? As a family, discuss the role that foods and eating play in your identity. What practices and customs would you like to explore together?

BAR/BAT MITZVAH PROJECT

26 The sacrifice of well-being was not brought because the bearer sought forgiveness or some other benefit, but to show gratitude for well-being or good fortune. As a family, come up with some possible sacrifices or gifts you might make to show gratitude for your well-being. Some suggestions include: a weekly donation to *tzedakah,* "adopting" an underprivileged child in a developing nation, or volunteering time in a soup kitchen. Choose the idea that you think best reminds you of your good fortune and act on it!

Note: The material in *Vayikra* and *Tzav* is very similar. Therefore, many of the activities listed in *Tzav* will be useful in *Vayikra* as well.

SHEMINI 9:1-11:47 שמיני

SYNOPSIS

SHEMINI BEGINS ON THE EIGHTH DAY OF the ordination ceremonies of the High Priests, Aaron and his sons. Moses directs Aaron to bring a sin offering and a burnt offering, followed by a sacrifice of well-being. At the conclusion of these sacrifices, Moses and Aaron enter the Tent of Meeting. When they come out, they bless the people and the Presence of God appears to all.

Nadab and Abihu, Aaron's sons, put fire and incense in their fire pans and offer alien fire to God. A fire comes forth from God and both die instantly. Moses explains God's actions to Aaron, saying that the deaths of Nadab and Abihu demonstrate specifically the responsibility of priests to do only that which God commanded. Aaron has no response. Moses calls on Aaron's nephews to remove the bodies, but cautions relatives and the congregation not to mourn for Nadab and Abihu.

God commands Aaron and his sons not to drink intoxicants, for they must be able to carry out their duties of sacrifice and teaching.

Moses tells Aaron and his two remaining sons, Elazar and Itamar, where the various offerings are to be eaten. Then he inquires about the goat of the sin offering and is told that it has been totally consumed by fire. It had been commanded that a portion of this offering was to be eaten by the priests. Moses is angry that Aaron and his sons had not eaten their portion of the offering, but Aaron responds that it would be unsuitable for the priests to eat the offering in view of the events of the day.

God now speaks to Moses and Aaron regarding the laws of *kashrut*. The Israelites are permitted to eat any mammal which has a split hoof and chews its cud. Swine are specifically forbidden. The Israelites may eat any fish which has both fins and scales. A list of forbidden birds is given. Four-legged insects are forbidden unless they have a pair of jointed legs with which they can leap. A

description of the laws of ritual defilement regarding animal carcasses is given.

The portion ends with an affirmation of the special relationship between God and the children of Israel.

INSIGHTS FROM THE TRADITION

A On the eighth (*shemini*) and final day of the ordination ceremonies, Aaron and his sons give instructions as to what is to be sacrificed. Several commentaries point out that Moses served as the High Priest during the seven day ordination period. Then, on the eighth day, Moses turns the priesthood over to Aaron and his sons. *Yalkut Me'am Lo'ez* by Yaacov Culi tells us that Moses lost the priesthood as punishment for hesitating to go to Pharaoh to bring the Israelites out of Egypt (Vol. XI, p. 187). This commentary also points out that God told Moses first to assemble the Israelites and then to ordain Aaron and his sons in public so that the Israelites would not say that Moses gave the priesthood to Aaron on his own.

What special characteristics should a High Priest have?
Would Moses have been suited for the role of High Priest?
What do you think it would be like to hold a position of authority and responsibility?

B Some commentators choose to link the deaths of Nadab and Abihu with the prohibition against drinking which follows that account. They suggest that Nadab and Abihu were drunk when the episode of bringing "alien fire" occurred. *Yalkut Me'am Lo'ez* by Yaacov Culi (Vol. XI, pp. 197-199) supports this interpretation and then elaborates: A drunken individual does not have a clear head and therefore is unable to serve God. A drunk loses status in the eyes of others. They laugh at him as if he were a monkey, and this is painful for his family.

How does being drunk on alcohol or high on drugs affect one's abilities?

Why does one need a "clear head" to serve God?

Our actions and choices often reflect upon our families. How does being aware of this affect your actions and choices? If you wish, share experiences you have had.

Do the possible repercussions of your actions and choices change or modify your behavior?

C Both *Sifra* and the *Biur* explain that, out of their joy of serving God, Nadab and Abihu brought an additional sacrifice. If this were so, death seems an extreme and even unjust punishment. Hertz explains that they were punished according to their elevated status and that this was a warning to future priestly generations not to innovate their own sacrifices (*The Pentateuch and Haftorahs*, Vol. III, p. 253).

Why shouldn't future priests innovate their own sacrifices? Does this mean that we should not add innovations to our own worship?

In *Pirke Avot* we read: "One who grabs too much loses all." In what way does this explain the above Insight?

Does this saying apply to you or anyone you know?

D The text reads that Moses became furious when Elazar and Itamar, the surviving sons of Aaron, did not eat the portion of the sacrifice meant for the priests. Aaron then reminds Moses of the tragic deaths of his sons. In his anger, Moses forgot the law that prior to the burial of one's dead, a mourner may not eat consecrated food. In the *midrash* Moses speaks to the entire camp of Israel and says: "I made an error in the law, and Aaron, my brother, came and set me straight" (*Leviticus Rabbah* 13:1).

Did you or someone you know ever get angry over a situation that was either misunderstood or in which some pertinent information was not communicated?

How does the phrase "his/her anger got the best of him/her" apply to Moses? How does it apply to someone you know?

Has anyone ever set you straight? How did they do it?

E *Shemini* includes a detailing of the laws of *kashrut*. These laws were classified as *chukim* — laws for which there is no rational explanation. A primary aim of the dietary laws is to help the individual attain holiness. This is clearly stated in Leviticus 11:44: "For I *Adonai* am your God: you shall sanctify yourselves and be holy, for I am holy. You shall not make yourselves unclean . . . " (For more, see the Index: "*Chukim.*")

Do you always need reasons for what you are asked to do?

What do you do just because you know it is the right or the good thing to do?

F In *The Five Books of Miriam* by Ellen Frankel (p. 162), Esther, the Hidden One, tells us that the purpose of these laws (i.e., *kashrut*) is spiritual. They are to sensitize our hearts, not our minds. Esther continues by saying that if we must kill in order to eat, we should be conscious, meticulous, and humane in the way we do it. How we go about killing and the way in which we eat has a powerful influence over many aspects of our lives.

What other Jewish laws sensitize your life?

Do you maintain personal practices which influence your spirituality?

STRATEGIES

ANALYZING THE TEXT

1 Read the incident about Nadab and Abihu carefully. Establish the facts of the story. Now try and answer these questions: In what way was the fire "strange"? What actually killed Nadab and Abihu, God or the fire? What did Moses intend to convey to Aaron by his words? What tone of voice do you think he used? (From "Beyond Bible Tales: Toward Teaching Text" by Joel Lurie Grishaver in *The New Jewish Teachers Handbook,* edited by Audrey Friedman Marcus and Raymond A. Zwerin.)

2 In Leviticus 10:3, Moses prefaces his words to Aaron with the remark, "This is what God meant when God said . . . " The Rabbis looked in the Torah for this previous speech and could not find these exact words. Rashi suggested that the text refers to Exodus 29:43; Rashbam cited Leviticus 21:10-12 as the reference. Read these two passages in conjunction with Leviticus 10:3. What connection do you see?

3 Make a fact file about *kashrut* using biblical references. Copy relevant biblical verses onto index cards. Sort the cards into categories of related regulations, for example, things considered an abomination, things permitted, and laws pertaining to blood. Some verses to consider are: Exodus 22:30, 23:19, 34:26; Leviticus 7:25-27, 11:9-12, 13-19, 20-24, 44-45, 17:10-11; Deuteronomy 12:23-25, 14:3-21. For a follow-up, see Strategy #7, page 180.

4 The biblical concept implied by the word תמא׳ (*tamay*) is a difficult one. The word is often translated as "unclean," but this is not the literal meaning. The word could be better understood as "ritually impure" or "defiled" for ritual purposes. To help you better grasp this concept, consider the following definitions of related words and phrases in modern Hebrew (defined according to *The Complete Hebrew-English Dictionary* by Reuben Alcalay, p. 874):

תמא׳ (*tamay*) — unclean ritually/morally
תמא׳ נפש (*tamay nefesh*) — unclean of heart
תמא׳ שפתים (*tamay sfatayim*) — unclean of speech, foul-mouthed

כל המחבר לתמא׳, תמא׳ (*kol hamichubar latamay, tamay*) — whoever mingles with unclean people becomes unclean — bad company corrupts a person.

Give examples of things which you would consider morally "*tamay*." What kind of individuals are meant by the phrases "unclean of heart," "unclean of speech"? The last phrase, "bad company corrupts," reflects the biblical idea that a state of "uncleanness" can be transferred by contact. In light of the above definitions and questions, what do you think of this idea? Are there contemporary examples of objects or people which we should avoid lest we become *tamay* ourselves? What kind of purification rituals would you suggest for people who have become "defiled"? (For more, see the Index: "*Tamay.*")

EXTENDING THE TEXT

5 Read through the laws of *kashrut* in this portion (11:1-47). Discuss: Do these laws keep us healthy? Will they help us to be smarter, wealthier, or wiser? Can you determine a purpose for these laws? Share Insight F with your students. Show the film *Willy Wonka and the Chocolate Factory,* available as a video rental, rated G. Direct the students' attention to each child winner and consider the following: What does each child want? How do they go about getting it? How do the parents treat the children? What results or consequences befall each? Is there any spirituality regarding food in the movie characters' behavior? What kinds of food laws do they need?

6 So little is said or done regarding the deaths of Nadab and Abihu. Moses forbids Aaron and his surviving sons to observe ritual mourning practices. There is a glaring omission: where is Aaron's wife, the mother of Nadab and Abihu? Does she just choose silence? Is she just a witness?

a bystander? In fact, is she so silent that she is neither included nor mentioned? The Torah does supply her with a name: Elisheva (Exodus 6:23). In small groups, create your own *midrashim* about Elisheva and her reaction to this situation. Include other participants in this incident from the biblical text. You might also want to put more characters in the story, such as additional women. Present your *midrash* as a radio play, live skit, or taped skit on video.

7 Throughout history, tyrants have attempted to restrict Jewish observance of the dietary laws. Read in I Maccabees 41-64 and II Maccabees 6:18-20 and 7:1ff. about how King Antiochus Epiphanes sought to impose his will upon the Jews. Why do you think the laws of sacrifice and *kashrut* attracted such attention from Antiochus? Why do you think some Jews were so steadfast in their refusal to give in? What would you have done had you lived then?

8 Find out how the biblical laws of *kashrut* (see Strategy #3, page 179) have been understood and practiced.
   a. If you have access to a Talmud in English, look up the following references: *Hullin* 27b, 60b-61a, 65a, 104a, 105a, 115b. On index cards, write a summary of what you read and add it to your fact file under the appropriate headings.
   b. Read about *kashrut* in one of the references cited below. Write a summary of the key points on index cards and add it to your fact file under the appropriate headings. Use your completed fact file to help you select an area of *kashrut* (from the category headings) and write a report about it.

References: *The First Jewish Catalog* by Richard Siegel, Michael Strassfeld, and Sharon Strassfeld; *The Jewish Dietary Laws: Their Meaning for Our Time* by Samuel Dresner and Seymour Siegel; *The Biblical and Historical Background of Jewish Customs and Ceremonies* by Abraham P. Bloch.

PERSONALIZING THE TEXT

9 Many of the laws concerning *kashrut* are given in *Shemini*. Create a "*Kashrut* Game." On a large posterboard, glue four large pockets or envelopes. Label as follows: MEAT, MILK, PAREVE, TREIF. Using index cards, write names of foods (one per card) and/or glue pictures of foods on the cards. Sort the cards into the appropriate pockets. In order for the game to be self-correcting, label the reverse side with the appropriate category.

10 Read Leviticus 11:45. This verse reminds the Israelites that they should be holy because God is holy. Participate in "The Holy Scavenger Hunt" by Bruce Kadden to help gain a clearer understanding of what is holy.

Holy Scavenger Hunt

1. The Hebrew word for holy is קָדוֹשׁ (*kadosh*). There are many other Hebrew words which are made up of the same consonant sounds k'd'sh, with different vowels, suffixes, etc. How many do you know?
a. prayer over the wine: _____
b. prayer said in memory of the dead: _____
c. word in candle blessing: _____
d. part of morning service: _____
e. name for the Jerusalem Temple: _____

2. Leviticus 19:1-19 spells out many ways to be holy. List as many as you can find.

3. You are to find three people around the Religious School and ask them what being "holy" means to them. Write down their responses.
a.
b.
c.

4. Go to the synagogue and list those objects which you would consider to be holy.

5. What does "holy" mean to you?

(For more, see the Index: "Holiness.")

11 Judaism is not the only religion which has food prohibitions. Research other faiths such as Islam, Hinduism, Buddhism, etc., in order to create a display which illustrates your food findings.

12 Using the text as your guide, explore the following possible solutions to the mysterious deaths of Nadab and Abihu:

a. *God* did it. Nadab and Abihu violated the sanctity of the Tabernacle and so God punished them.

b. *Aaron* did it. Nadab and Abihu tried to take over his job. They were doing too much exploring of the role of the High Priest, so he rigged the fire pans.

c. *Moses* did it. There was an ongoing tension between Moses and Aaron which goes back to the Golden Calf. Moses was worried that the priests were getting too powerful, so he arranged the accident as a warning.

d. The fire was an accident.

Write the story of Nadab and Abihu as the script of a TV detective series. Use one of the four solutions suggested above. Present the show live or videotape it. (From "Beyond Bible Tales: Toward Teaching Text" by Joel Lurie Grishaver in *The New Jewish Teachers Handbook,* edited by Audrey Friedman Marcus and Raymond A. Zwerin.)

13 The fate of Nadab and Abihu suggests the need to perform religious rituals strictly according to the rules (see Insight C, page XX). Can you think of parallel activities in contemporary society? For example, how important is acting "by the book" in police work? In the practice of medicine?

a. Write a story showing what happens to someone in our society who doesn't follow the guidelines of his/her job.

b. Find newspaper articles demonstrating the consequences of not following the rules for one's job.

14 After the deaths of his sons Nadab and Abihu, Aaron is silent. The text does not tell us whether his silence was due to shock, unbearable sorrow, or perhaps unspeakable anger. Another possibility is that Aaron was silent because he agreed with the judgment of God and Moses.

a. Write a diary entry for Aaron explaining his silence.

b. Have you ever responded with silence to a significant event or a remark? Explain why.

c. Society has used the format of a "moment of silence" as a sign of respect and grief and also as an opportunity for prayer. How do you feel during such a moment?

15 Our Sages wrote that Moses was led into error by his anger. This refers to Moses' reaction to Aaron and his sons not partaking of the sin offering on the day of the deaths of Nadab and Abihu. Have you ever been led into error because of anger? There is a saying "anger blinds the eye." How might this apply to Moses? To you?

OTHER RESOURCES

16 Read, act out, and discuss the skit for the portion *Shemini* in *Sedra Scenes: Skits for Every Torah Portion* by Stan J. Beiner, pp. 129-132.

17 View and discuss the episode for *Shemini* from *Torah Toons I: The Video.*

18 For a creative movement activity, see "They Saw and Shouted" from *Torah in Motion* by JoAnne Tucker and Susan Freeman, pp. 130-131.

19 Read and discuss the illustrated commentary for *Shemini* in *American Torah Toons* by Lawrence Bush.

INVOLVING THE FAMILY

20 Many reasons have been suggested for the observance of *kashrut*. Some are listed below. Which seem best to you? To your family? What positive values can you, as a family, learn from keeping kosher?

Keeping kosher is a commandment from God.
Kashrut teaches us respect for life.
Kashrut teaches us that we can't always have everything we want.
Keeping kosher keeps us aware that we're Jewish.
Keeping kosher has helped preserve the Jews as a unique and separate people throughout history.
Keeping kosher is a tradition observed by our recent ancestors. When we keep kosher, we establish a link with them.

(For more, see the Index: "*Kashrut*.")

BAR/BAT MITZVAH PROJECT

21 Read verses 10:1-9. Note that this is the only time in the book of Leviticus that God speaks directly and only to Aaron. Many commentators choose to link the deaths of Nadab and Abihu to the resulting command that God gave to Aaron. Does this make sense to you? In reading these verses do you see any other reasons(s) for their deaths? The commentators say that alcohol and the resulting drunkenness led to the deaths of Nadab and Abihu. Their drunkenness clouded their judgment and abilities so that they literally messed up the sacrifices. They paid the ultimate price for their errors.

Give some contemporary examples of poor judgment when someone is under the influence of drugs and/or alcohol.

Set up a panel of speakers on the subject of drugs and alcohol. You may want to include: police officers, rehabilitation workers, judges, families/individuals who have suffered losses due to alcohol and drugs, and people convicted of crimes related to the abuse of alcohol and drugs. Allow the speakers 5 to 10 minutes for presentations. Then follow up with questions and answers from the audience.

Many communities have established traveling drug and alcohol awareness programs available to local schools, synagogues, churches, and youth organizations. You will need to do some research to find out what is available in your community and how to implement the program. Also investigate what you and other teens can do in your community to combat teenage drug and alcohol abuse.

TAZRIA 12:1-13:59 תזריע

SYNOPSIS

GOD TELLS MOSES TO INSTRUCT THE Israelites that a woman who bears a son shall be impure for a total of 33 days, and a woman who bears a daughter for a period of 66 days. During the time of her impurity, she may not come into contact with anything or any place that is holy. When the period of impurity is over, the woman is instructed to bring an offering to the Tabernacle where the priest will make atonement on her behalf and declare her ritually pure.

Moses and Aaron are instructed in the diagnosis of *tzara'at* — an ailment which could affect human skin or clothing, rendering a person or garment ritually impure. Rashes, discolorations, and patches of the skin and clothes are examined by the priest who will determine the existence of this affliction. In cases of doubt, he is empowered to isolate the individual or article in question for a period of seven days in order to observe the progression of the ailment. At the end of such a period, the priest must pronounce the person ritually pure (*tahor*) or impure (*metzora*).

A garment which is found to be impure is to be burned.

A person who has been declared a *metzora* must tear his [her] clothes, let his [her] head covering shield his [her] upper face (as far as his [her] lip), and call out "Impure! Impure!" Such a person shall be impure as long as the ailment persists, and that person must live outside the camp.

When it is reported to the priest that the *metzora* is healed, the priest must go outside the camp to make an examination. To render the person ritually pure again, the priest shall make an offering and the individual shall shave off all hair, bathe, and wash all garments. After a waiting period of seven days, a second offering is made by the priest at the entrance to the Tabernacle. Then the person is ritually pure.

An alternate sacrifice is prescribed for a poor woman being purified after childbirth or for a poor person being cleansed after *tzara'at*.

INSIGHTS FROM THE TRADITION

A *Tazria* means "she gives birth." This *sedra* begins with a discussion of the ritual defilement of a new mother. It has been suggested that a woman in the pain of labor vows to herself that she will never go through such pain again. Such an oath is a transgression of the commandment "be fruitful and multiply." The oath renders her ritually impure. Upon seeing a new son, she immediately recants her oath, thus mitigating her period of uncleanness to seven days. Upon seeing a girl baby, the mother realizes that this new person will also someday experience the pain of childbirth, and so she remains in a state of uncleanness for two weeks.

Physical impurity was of great concern in biblical days. An impure person could make the priests and the sanctuary impure.

Who is an "impure" person in today's society? How does such a one threaten to make others impure?

B Blood is an important symbol of both life and death. Many religions developed special rituals for people who come in contact with blood. In the Torah, blood is connected with holiness. For example, the blood of sacrificed animals was spilled on the altar. People are told not to consume blood because it is the "life of the flesh" (Leviticus 17:11). Blood is also used on the doorposts of the houses in Egypt to ward off the tenth plague (death of the firstborn). Paradoxically, because blood is both connected to the holiness of life, and, could also be connected to death, it became a source of ritual contamination. Therefore, women became ritually impure after giving birth to new life and at the time of menstruation.

Some new feminist commentaries have noted that the Torah calls the blood that flows after the birth of a child a "source" or "fountain" (Leviticus 12:7 — *mekor damehah*). This positive image may help us as we struggle with these difficult texts.

Does the idea that blood is connected with holiness through its potential for life and death explain the special time set apart for a woman who has just given birth?
Do you feel that we still need special rituals concerning consumption of and contamination by blood?

C *Tazria* and the following portion, *Metzora,* go into great detail concerning the diagnosis of leprosy. The term leprosy as used here really covers a wide variety of skin diseases. Actual leprosy, now called Hansen's Disease, was once widespread throughout the Middle East. While Hansen's Disease is contagious, not all of the skin diseases in the Bible included in this broad category of leprosy were incurable or contagious. The priest's function was to diagnose the condition and determine how each person was to be treated.

The priest was concerned with protecting the Israelite community. What "leprosies" plague modern life? How does our society deal with them?
In what ways do you or can you serve to safeguard our society from its "illnesses"?

D *Yalkut Me'am Lo'ez* by Yaacov Culi provides seven reasons for the affliction of leprosy: malicious speech, bloodshed, unnecessary or vain oaths, sexual crimes, pride and haughtiness, robbery, stinginess, and avoiding charity. The commentary points out that the primary cause is malicious speech (Vol. XI, p. 297).

The Rabbis connected the Hebrew expression for slander or gossip (*motzi shaym ra*) to the word *metzora* (leper). Do we suffer physical or mental ills because of the way we behave? Do you think there is some sort of divine banking system which issues personal debits and credits according to the way in which we live our lives?
Do the "bad guys" always get what's coming to them?

E It is interesting how the commentators so easily make a transition from reading about physical affliction (leprosy) to the problems of behavior. By understanding leprosy as a metaphor for slander, not only the cause but also the punishment and/or cure becomes more accessible. The goal then becomes the transformation of *"naga"* (affliction) to *"oneg"* (joy) Both of these Hebrew words use the same three letters. (Rabbi Arthur Green in *Learn Torah With . . . ,* p. 201).

Can bad behavior be transformed into good behavior? How?
How is changing behavior a kind of healing?
In what ways are modern day doctors and/or Rabbis descendants of the priests? What kinds of healing do they do?

F The Talmud tells us that slander injures three persons — the one who speaks the slander, the one who hears the slander, and the person who is slandered (*Arakin* 15b).

When you are the recipient of gossip do you pass it on, keep it under your hat, tell the one who gossips to stop, or inform the one who is being talked about? What risks do you take with each of these courses of action?

Note: *Tazria* and *Metzora* are usually read as a double portion. For more about double portions see Exodus, *Pekuday,* Insight A, page 155.

STRATEGIES

ANALYZING THE TEXT

1 Consider the key players in the drama of the diagnosis of *tzara'at*. What is the role of the priest? In what ways is he to act as a doctor? In what ways is he not to act as a doctor? How is the priest like a judge?

2 In what ways was a *metzora* treated like one who had died? How do you account for such treatment? How is the *metzora* like the person he/she slandered? What similar emotions might his/her treatment arouse?

EXTENDING THE TEXT

3 There are several famous cases of *tzara'at* in the Tanach. Moses' sister Miriam (Numbers 12:1-16), Naaman and Gehazi (II Kings 5), and King Uzziah (II Chronicles 26) were stricken with this disease. Why did each get *tzara'at*? Were they cured? If so, how? Discuss how these stories formed the Rabbis' opinion that *tzara'at* was not simply a medical problem, but a punishment from God.

4 The *Haftarah* for *Tazria* (II Kings 5) tells the story of Naaman, an Aramean captain who was cured of leprosy by the prophet Elisha. Why was this particular *Haftarah* chosen to complement this *parashah*? Consider how the emphasis here is not on the cause or the consequences of *tzara'at*, but on the cure of the dread disease by God. As a result of his cure, Naaman becomes a Jew.

5 Consider the idea of "ritual impurity" in our times. Today, we might not think that bad deeds lead to physical ailments. However, we can still understand that improper acts may make us impure. Look at the confessional prayers in the *Siddur* or *Machzor*. Do you find some ideas in these prayers to aid in understanding the word *"tamay"*

(impure) for today? (For more, see the Index: *"Tamay."*)

PERSONALIZING THE TEXT

6 While modern people may be uncomfortable with the biblical understanding of menstruation and childbirth, perhaps we can learn and be enriched by the fact that the Torah recognizes that menstruation and childbirth are unique occurrences. Look at contemporary sources to find out what, if any, rituals they suggest for honoring these events.
References: *Miriam's Well: Rituals for Jewish Women Around the Year* by Penina V. Adelman; *Lifecycles: Jewish Women on Life Passages and Personal Milestones*, Vol. 1, edited by Debra Orenstein; *Four Centuries of Jewish Women's Spirituality: A Sourcebook,* edited by Ellen M. Umansky and Dianne Ashton.

7 Draw up your own list of thoughts and actions one should try to leave behind when entering a synagogue, which is our equivalent of the *Mikdash*. Write your own prayer to be said upon entering the synagogue on the model of the following prayer:

"May the door of this synagogue be wide enough to receive all who hunger for love, all who are lonely for fellowship . . . May the door of this synagogue be narrow enough to shut out pettiness and pride, envy and enmity . . . " (*The New Mahzor for Rosh Hashanah and Yom Kippur,* compiled and edited by Sidney Greenberg and Jonathan Levine, p. 10).

8 The story "The Gossip" in *Who Knows Ten?* by Molly Cone should help give some idea as to why the Rabbis considered *motzi shaym ra* a very serious sin. Discuss the following: Should a person who has gossiped be treated as a leper was treated? Does this suggest to you another way the Rabbi in the story could have "cured" the gossip? Make up some other ways through which the Rabbi might have taught the gossip a lesson. Choose a few to act out.

9 Use this portion as a departure point for examining the plight of the handicapped in our society. *Tzara'at* is a kind of physical handicap which, in ancient days, led to restrictions on the individual's participation in society. Are there parallels to be drawn and lessons to be learned by comparing our treatment of physically challenged people today to the treatment of the *metzora?* Older students might want to look at the book, film, or play *The Elephant Man,* available as a video rental, not rated, for an extreme example of how a man's physical deformity affected his treatment by the world. Draw up guidelines for appropriate, compassionate treatment of the physically challenged.

10 The diagnosis of *tzara'at* was taken very seriously. We know this because the priest was given the power to isolate a person suspected of leprosy and watch the way the disease changed over time. We can imagine the agony of the period between examinations when the diseased person waited for a diagnosis which would affect his or her whole life. Use a variety of media: pens, crayons, chalk, paint, paper, newspaper, wrapping paper or magazines to write the word *tzara'at* in a way which conveys the horror the word must have held for the Israelites. Try this technique with the words "gossip" and "slander." Can you convey through your art something about the nature of gossip?

11 Traditionally, *tzara'at* (afflictions of the skin, clothes, walls, pottery, etc.) was seen as resulting from gossip and evil talk. How does gossip get started? Play the game "Telephone" and see what happens. Have everyone in the group form a line. The first person makes up a statement,

writes it on a piece of paper, and then whispers it to the next person, and so on down the line. The last person then repeats out loud what he/she heard. Compare this to the original written statement. Then discuss how this happens in the students' lives.

12 Gossip often starts because of the different ways people see and understand the same event. Choose three individuals to present a skit to the group. The skit should include some element(s) of conflict: misunderstanding something that is said, an emotion that is unexpected like anger or joy. After viewing the skit, each viewer individually writes down what happened as he/she understands it. Then each viewer reads aloud his/her version. Compare and discuss the different versions. Can you recognize any areas that might lead to gossip? Have you ever been involved in a real life situation that was misunderstood, and resulted in gossip?

13 Examine a daily newspaper. Choose a story that might encourage rumors. Write a short story about a hypothetical rumor which resulted from the article you chose. At the conclusion of the story, write a response to these questions: What effects might this rumor have? Who might be hurt by the rumor? What would the rumor damage, someone's character, property, or personal life?

14 Invite a local newspaper editor to your class. Inform the editor that you are studying the topic of gossip. Ask the editor to give a presentation on gossip, libel, and slander and how a newspaper must protect itself from printing material which might come under those headings. Leave time for questions and answers. Consider the following questions: What is a newspaper's responsibility? Who is held accountable for the content of stories and articles? Is a newspaper obligated to print all the news or should some news be withheld for the public good?

15 According to Maimonides, "Evil talk kills three persons — the utterer, the listener, and the subject; the listener more than the utterer" (*Mishneh Torah*). How does evil talk "kill"? Why is listening to evil talk more destructive than uttering it? Who do you think is hurt most by evil talk, the utterer, the listener, or the subject?

16 Examine the prayer *Elohai Nitzor* which is recited at the end of the *Amidah*: "O God, keep my tongue from evil . . . "
a. Which of the three parties to evil talk (listener, utterer, subject, see Strategy #15 immediately above) is *not* addressed by the prayer? Write your own version of the prayer to remind us of the evil of talebearing, which includes all aspects of gossiping behavior.
b. Is evil talk such an easy sin to commit? Explain why this prayer is included in our worship three times a day. Think of some times when you are tempted to gossip. Complete these sentences:
Keep me from speaking evil about someone when they ____.
Keep me from speaking evil about someone when I feel ____.

17 The *metzora* was considered to have committed a serious sin. Aside from the physical affliction, part of the punishment was in the *public display* of the *tzara'at* (see Leviticus 13:45). The *metzora* was then isolated from the community until pronounced clean by a priest. How is our treatment of criminals today similar to this? How and why do they undergo public humiliation? In what ways do we isolate them from the community? How should criminals be treated?

OTHER RESOURCES

18 Read, act out, and discuss the skit for the portion *Tazria* in *Sedra Scenes: Skits for Every Torah Portion* by Stan J. Beiner, pp. 133-135.

19 For other insights and activities about gossip, see *Teaching Mitzvot* by Barbara Binder Kadden and Bruce Kadden, pp. 83-86.

20 View and discuss the episode for *Tazria* from *Torah Toons I: The Video.*

21 For creative movement activities, see "Unclean! Unclean!" and "Contaminated Fabric" from *Torah in Motion* by JoAnne Tucker and Susan Freeman, pp. 132-135.

22 Read and discuss the illustrated commentary for *Tazria* in *American Torah Toons* by Lawrence Bush.

INVOLVING THE FAMILY

23 Slander and gossip can drive a wedge between family members and between friends. What should you do if you hear a piece of gossip about someone? Does it matter whether or not it is true? What if it is a nice piece of news that is to be kept secret? Is gossip more acceptable in a closed family group? In the Apocrypha (*Ahikar* 2:54), we read "If you hear an evil matter, bury it seven fathoms underground." As a family, brainstorm strategies for using "If you hear an evil matter . . . ." Design a poster displaying your ideas and hang it where the family can see it and remember the discussion.

BAR/BAT MITZVAH PROJECT

24 A *metzora* is a person with a visible skin rash, which the High Priest diagnoses to determine whether the individual must be sent out of the camp into isolation. The High Priest does not allow the *metzora* to reenter camp until the rash clears. This might be considered sound medical procedure, to isolate the one afflicted so others will not be affected. Unfortunately, the idea of isolating someone with a physical defect has had a profound affect for millennia. Those who are able-bodied with no physical differences or disabilities often shun or avoid individuals with physical defects or disabilities. It has taken many years for society to begin accommodating the differently-abled. This attitude may be attributed to lack of knowledge or experience. They do not see the affected individual's humanity.

Begin this project by taking an informal survey. Show individuals photos of differently-abled people in circumstances in which they are found, e.g., using wheel chairs, with a guide dog, using sign language, or attached to an oxygen tank or other equipment. Ask participants what they saw in the pictures. Check off whether they responded that they saw a person or a disability.

The next step is for you to meet and talk with differently-abled adults and kids. Work with physicians, nurses, physical and occupational therapists, and teachers to help you locate people with physical challenges. Also visit classrooms that mainstream kids who are differently-abled. Interview these individuals, their families, and classmates to find out what their lives are like and how they feel about fitting in and being accepted.

Based on the work you have done, your final step is to create a public service announcement, 30 seconds to one minute in length. which educates people about the differently-abled. Film or videotape the announcement. Contact a local television station to determine if your video fits the requirement for a public service announcement. Ask if you could submit your work for consideration.

Note: *Tazria* is usually read as a double portion with *Metzora*. The two portions contain similar material. See *Metzora*, pages 189-193, for Insights and Strategies which can apply to *Tazria*.

METZORA 14:1-15:33 מצורע

SYNOPSIS

GOD SPEAKS TO MOSES AND INSTRUCTS him in the purification ritual for a leper who has been declared clean. Two clean birds are to be brought to the priest. One is ritually sacrificed, and the other bird is set free in the open country. After a week, the person to be purified shaves off all hair and bathes. This individual then brings a guilt offering and a sin offering. A rich person brings a large animal to be sacrificed; a poor person brings a small one. The procedure the priest is to follow is explained in detail.

The portion next deals with houses which appear to be affected by a plague. If, after a period of examination, it is determined that the house has a malignant eruption, the stones are replaced and the walls scraped and replastered. If the eruption does not reappear, the house is declared clean. A purification ceremony is detailed which includes the sacrifice of a bird. If the plague does reappear, the house is torn down.

Metzora concludes with a description of impurity arising from discharges from the sex organs. A man who has a discharge is unclean and this uncleanliness extends to any bedding he lies on, any object he sits on, anyone who touches his bedding or the objects on which he sat. Earthen vessels he touches are to be broken and wooden utensils are to be washed. Once the discharge is over, a period of purification follows ending with the bringing of a sin offering and a guilt offering.

If a man has an emission, he is to bathe and remains unclean until evening. If a man and a woman have sexual intercourse, they are to bathe and they remain unclean until evening.

A menstruating woman is also declared ritually impure; this impurity lasts seven days. Her uncleanliness extends to any bedding she lies on, any object on which she sits, anyone who comes in contact with her, and any objects she has touched. If a woman has a discharge other than her usual menstruation, the same laws as for menstruation apply. But in this case, she brings both a sin offering and a burnt offering.

INSIGHTS FROM THE TRADITION

A Depending on the Jewish calendar, there are years in which *Tazria* and *Metzora* are read together as one double portion. *Tazria* deals essentially with determining if an individual or object is ritually impure. *Metzora* describes the purification procedure for such cases.

As explained in the Insights from the Tradition for *Tazria*, the word *metzora* (leper) was used in a Rabbinic word play for the Hebrew *motzi shaym ra*, which translates as slander or gossip. Skin afflictions were seen as divine retribution for malicious talk.

Nowhere in the text is there a suggestion as to possible cures for leprosy. Leprosy is a disease which Jewish tradition considered inflicted by God. The responsibility for the cure is placed upon the afflicted individual. Jewish thinkers raised the following question: Is it permissible to be a physician and thereby attempt to cure diseases which are divinely caused? Exodus 21:18-19 is cited in the Talmud as giving permission to physicians to intervene and heal. This passage reads, "When men quarrel and one strikes the other with stone or fist, and he does not die, but has to take to his bed . . . the assailant shall go unpunished, except that he must pay for his cure." In Hebrew, the word "heal" occurs twice at the end of this verse. The Talmud interprets this repetition to mean that God has permitted the physician to heal (*Baba Kama* 85a).

In your view, what percentage of the cure of any illness is in the hands of the individual? the physician? up to God?

B Individuals afflicted with leprosy and those who had bodily discharges such as menstruation, nocturnal emissions, or a discharge from the skin were considered to be ritually impure. These individuals were isolated from the rest of the community so their "impurity" would not spread to others.

Expanding the definition of *metzora* to include individuals with physical deformities and diseases, how does contemporary society respond? What are typical responses to physically and mentally challenged individuals? In an ideal society would those responses change?
What do you think can be done to gain acceptance for people who do not fit the norm?

C There was much Rabbinic discussion concerning a house afflicted with a plague. A Talmudic opinion states that such a case never happened. But by quoting the words of Maimonides, we can see a warning: "Now this change in clothes and houses which the Torah calls leprosy . . . is not a natural phenomenon, but was deemed a sign and a wonder among the people of Israel to warn them against evil gossip" (*Mishneh Torah* 16).

The fate befalling a house appears to be more stringent than that befalling an individual. What does this say about the worth of property as compared to the worth of an individual? In ancient times, persons who entered an unclean house or who came into contact with a ritually unclean object were considered unclean themselves. Are there places in your community which you know you should not enter or come into contact with? Some examples include: a bar or liquor store that sells to underage people, a gang hangout, a place where illegal drugs are sold, etc.

D According to *Leviticus Rabbah* 17:2, the *tzara'at* of houses was a special punishment inflicted on a miser. When the priest determined that the house was infected, he ordered that the contents be emptied. Once the house was cleared, all that the miser owned would be publicly displayed and thus the miser's stinginess would be known.

The miser was subjected to a public exposure. Do similar situations occur in contemporary society? If so, what effect do they have on you as an observer?
Was the treatment that the miser received appropriate?

E Rashi explains that birds were used in the purification ceremony of the *metzora* because their constant chattering will be a reminder to the *metzora* of the nature of the sin. Leprosy was visited upon a person because of the sin of slander caused by a chattering tongue. Cedar wood, crimson, and hyssop (moss) were also a part of the purification ceremony. Each of these held special meaning. As a haughty person is brought low by leprosy, so the tall cedar is humbled by the crimson worm and the lowly hyssop plant (Rashi on Leviticus 14:4).

Is slander deserving of punishment? If so, how should a modern slanderer be punished?

Note: *Metzora* and *Tazria* are usually read as a double portion. For more about double portions see Exodus, *Pikuday*, Insight A, page 155.

STRATEGIES

ANALYZING THE TEXT

1 The recovered *metzora* is bidden to bring an *asham*, a guilt offering (Leviticus 14:24,25). Read Leviticus 5:14-26 to review the reasons for bringing an *asham*. Assuming that the *metzora* was guilty of slander, into which category would you fit the sin (trespassing against God, robbery, defrauding a neighbor, etc.)? Explain.

2 In verses 15:5, 15:18, 15:22, and 15:27 of this portion, individuals in an unclean state are directed to bathe in water and then, once evening comes, they are no longer considered unclean. This state of being "unclean" does not mean physical uncleanliness, but rather ritual uncleanliness. The requirement is to immerse in water. This immersion would take place in a *mikvah*.

If possible, visit a local *mikvah*. Learn about the construction of a *mikvah* and when and why it is used. Have the Rabbi, educator, or other knowledgeable individual discuss the significance of the *mikvah* and field questions.

References: *Teaching Mitzvot* by Barbara Binder Kadden and Bruce Kadden; *The Encyclopedia of Jewish Symbols* by Ellen Frankel and Betsy Plotkin Teutsch, under the heading: "Water"; *Lifecycles: Jewish Women on Life Passages and Personal Milestones,* Vol. 1, edited by Debra Orenstein.

EXTENDING THE TEXT

3 While the laws regarding an impure woman and an impure man are nearly identical, there is one major difference. If an impure man touches any wooden implement, it is to be washed and any earthen vessel is to be broken. These consequences did not apply to impure women. Why not? Could it possibly have been that because women were the food preparers, this would have been too disruptive? What do you think?

4 In the Book of Leviticus, both water and blood are used as purifying agents. According to *Sefer haChinuch*, bathing in water symbolizes "that the unclean person is recreated" at the moment of immersion, based on the fact that at creation, the world consisted entirely of water. Can you suggest other reasons why water or blood might be used for purifying the ritually impure and anointing the priests? Write a *midrash* explaining the reason for their use.

5 Nachmanides explained the *tzara'at* of individuals and houses by noting that whenever an Israelite committed a sin, he/she would suffer an affliction of skin, clothing, or house. This was a sign that God was displeased with him/her. What

do you make of this idea that the Israelites were given constant warnings and signals about their behavior? Would such signs be beneficial? If this were really true, what would it do to the concept of free will? Do you get constant warnings and signals about your behavior from parents, teachers, coaches, and society in general? Are these warning beneficial, or just nagging and unnecessary?

6 Part of the purification ritual for a *metzora* parallels the anointing of the priests: oil is put on the ear, thumb, and toe (see Leviticus 8:23 and 14:17). (For more, see the Index: "Ordination.")

7 Read more about misers and public exposure in the following: "Shrewd Todie & Lyzer the Miser," found in *Stories for Children* by Isaac Bashevis Singer; "Money from a Table" and "The Candlesticks," found in *The Adventures of Hershel of Ostropol* by Eric A. Kimmel. Discuss the following: Did you think the stories were funny? Does humor help you learn? Why? What is the difference between someone who saves money and someone who is a miser?

8 View the film *Mask*, rated PG13, or *Elephant Man*, not rated, both available as video rentals. How was the outcast in either of the films treated by society in general? From whom and why did they receive better treatment and love? What do you think can be done about society accepting people who do not fit the norm?

PERSONALIZING THE TEXT

9 Design a modern purification ritual or ceremony for an individual who has just completed a time of separation from family or friends due to illness, accident, distance, or incarceration for criminal behavior. Include aspects of a new beginning, being welcomed back into society, and hopes for the future.

10 Just as a person can become *tamay* (ritually unclean), so can a house or an object. What might be some modern examples of things which are *tamay*? Brainstorm a list. Sort the items on your list according to whether they are *tamay* because of their physical properties (e.g., poisonous pesticides) or for ethical reasons (e.g., nuclear weapons). Then write a "telegram" to a world leader urging the elimination of several of the items. (For more, see the Index: "*Tamay.*")

11 For centuries, humanity's attitude toward leprosy derived from the portions *Metzora* and *Tazria*. Modern medicine has made great strides in controlling and curing Hansen's Disease. At your public library or through the Internet, research this subject. Prepare an oral presentation for the group. Design a bulletin board in the fashion of a time line which illustrates the attitudes toward leprosy from biblical times to the present.

12 Draw a cartoon strip illustrating miserly behavior and its consequences according to Insight D, page 190.

13 Read some other biblical descriptions of slander in society — Psalm 12:2-5 and Jeremiah 9:1-5. In these passages, deceitful talk is considered a very common and disturbing aspect of life. Is this problem as prevalent in our day? Using the above readings as models, write your own poetic condemnation of gossip in contemporary society.

14 Make puppets in the forms of birds, cedar trees, crimson worms, and hyssop plants. Make a fifth puppet to represent a healed *metzora*. Write and stage a skit in which the *metzora* is called to task by these things from nature (see Insight E, page 190).
Reference: *Creative Puppetry for Jewish Kids* by Gale Solotar Warshawsky.

15 Read the explanation in Leviticus, *Tzav* Strategy #8, page 174 for anointing the ear, thumb, and toe of the priest. In *Metzora*, the recovered leper is also anointed in this way. Make a "Righteous Action Cube" based on this explanation. Paint the outside of a cardboard box. On each side of the box, glue, draw, or paint pictures and phrases appropriate to the theme of anointing the priest. (Try this activity with Leviticus, *Kedoshim*, too!)

16 The text insists that both rich and poor must bring an *asham*. If necessary, however, a poor person may substitute a lesser offering for the required large animal (Leviticus 14:21-32). What lessons can you derive from this? Which payments, dues, or donations should be reduced for those who today are impoverished?

OTHER RESOURCES

17 Read and discuss the poem "Contagion" in *The Fire Waits* by Michael Hecht, pp. 69-70.

18 Read, act out, and discuss the skit for the portion *Metzora* in *Sedra Scenes: Skits for Every Torah Portion* by Stan J. Beiner, pp. 136-7.

19 View and discuss the episode for *Metzora* from *Torah Toons I: The Video.*

20 For a creative movement activity, see "A Plague in the House" from *Torah in Motion* by JoAnne Tucker and Susan Freeman, pp. 136-137.

21 Read and discuss the illustrated commentary for *Metzora* in *American Torah Toons* by Lawrence Bush.

INVOLVING THE FAMILY

22 The idea of stones and plaster being afflicted with plague is an unusual one. While some think this refers to a simple case of mildew, others believe this affliction was a possible sign of improper behavior by members of the household. Imagine and discuss what kinds of family behavior would warrant the appearance of such a sign.

BAR/BAT MITZVAH PROJECT

23 From *The Five Books of Miriam* by Ellen Frankel (p. 167) we learn the following: "Our Mothers Add: In this era of AIDS . . . we know only too well the fear of contagion — but we have yet to figure out how to *manage* our fear . . . and how to reincorporate diseased individuals into our midst. Until we learn this, we will continue to let fear manage us."

This project is to enable you to learn more about AIDS, how to volunteer in some capacity, and also to help empower your Jewish community to commit to this issue.

Your first task is to create an information center for your synagogue. This can be set up and displayed on a kiosk or organized in an inexpensive cardboard shelving unit, for example, a cardboard mailbox system which is usually divided into 9 to 15 individual sections. Appropriately label each section of the system and fill with material and information that you have collected. Some ideas to consider for the information center:

Listing of videos relating to the issue of AIDS (include the rating of each one).
Reviews you or others have written of the videos.
AIDS organizations seeking donations and fundraising ideas.
Listing of ways to get involved within your community.
Magazines and news articles about AIDS.
Sharing ideas on Jewish holiday celebrations with individuals who have AIDS.
Pamphlets and other information about AIDS.

Write a report or keep a journal on what you did in addition to creating the information center.

Note: *Metzora* is usually read as a double portion with *Tazria,* which precedes it. The two portions contain similar material. See *Tazria* for more Insights and Strategies which apply to *Metzora.*

ACHARAY MOT 16:1-18:30 אחרי מות

SYNOPSIS

AFTER THE DEATH OF NADAB AND ABIHU, God tells Moses to instruct Aaron not to come freely into the Holy of Holies. Only once a year, on the tenth day of the seventh month, is the High Priest to enter the shrine behind the curtain. This is the day on which atonement is to be made for all the sins of the Israelites. No work is to be done on this day, and on it the Israelites are to practice self-denial.

On the Day of Atonement, when the High Priest enters the Holy of Holies, he is to wear plain linen robes and he is to make expiation for himself and for his household and then for all of the Israelites.

Then the High Priest is to take two male goats and, by lot, mark one for God and one for Azazel. He is to slaughter the goat marked for God as a sin offering and use its blood to cleanse the Tent of Meeting, the altar, and the Holy of Holies of the sins of the people. Then Aaron is to confess all the sins of the Israelites over the goat for Azazel, and the goat is to be sent off into the wilderness.

In this portion, Moses is told further to instruct the Israelites that all meat is to be slaughtered in a ritual way before the Tent of Meeting. The people are reminded not to consume blood, for blood represents life itself, and not to eat of an animal that has died or been torn by wild beasts.

Finally, Moses details for the Israelites forbidden sexual relationships. Relationships between blood relations are considered incestuous. The Israelites are told not to copy the practices of the Egyptians or the Canaanites; rather, they are to live by God's laws and rules.

INSIGHTS FROM THE TRADITION

A *Acharay Mot* means "After the death" (of Nadab and Abihu). After his sons died, Aaron's entrance into the Holy of Holies was restricted. Whether this was a direct consequence of the acts of Nadab and Abihu is unclear from the text. It could be that their deaths were intended to serve as a warning not to transgress the restrictions of entering the sanctuary. In any event, *Acharay Mot* details the coming together of the holiest person among the Israelites (the High Priest), the holiest place (the Holy of Holies), and the holiest day of the calendar year (Yom Kippur). (For more, see Strategy #14, page 198.)

What is unique and special about Yom Kippur for you?
What does holy mean to you?
We no longer have the holiest person (the High Priest) or the holiest place (the Holy of Holies). How then do we make Yom Kippur the holiest day?

B A wide variety of meanings have been applied to the goat marked for Azazel. The name Azazel may derive from a rebellious angel (known in the apocryphal writings of the Book of Enoch). Perhaps Azazel took on a demonic personification as a result of the associations of the word in this portion. Some scholars believe that Azazel is not a name at all, but a compound or contracted noun meaning "the goat that goes," a "wild goat," "dismissal," or perhaps the name for the mountain over which, in later times, the goat was thrown.

As the biblical text explains, the goat would bear the sins of the Israelites symbolized by red wool tied between its horns. The goat would be led by a specially chosen man into a desolate area. *Yalkut Me'am Lo'ez* by Yaacov Culi (Vol. XI, p. 345) translates the expression "a certain man" as "a timeless man," one who is not concerned with the change of seasons and is not bothered by rain or snow or any condition which might stop him from leading the goat. The goat was then allowed to escape into the wilderness. From this idea of the escaping goat who bears other's sins came the term "scapegoat."

In contemporary society, do we ever require "timeless individuals" to perform important tasks? Give some examples.

Were the Israelites avoiding responsibility for their wrongdoings by using the scapegoat?

How is Azazel a metaphor for the ridding of sins? Have you ever done something wrong and let someone else bear the blame? Did you ever try to blame someone for something they did not do?

C Although the observance of Yom Kippur as described in Leviticus differs markedly from our observance of the holiday today, several of our current practices derive from this portion. For example, the custom of wearing white on Yom Kippur is based on the white linen robes the priest wore on this day. As an extension of this, it is now customary to wear white *kipot*. Cantors and Rabbis often wear white robes. White covers grace the Torah and white flowers decorate the *bimah*.

What does the color white signify to you? Why do you think it was chosen to be used for this particular holiday?

The color used for burial shrouds is also white. Do you think there is any connection between burial dress and the symbolism of Yom Kippur?

D Although no details are given as to the way in which we are to "practice self-denial" (Leviticus 16:31), this has traditionlly been understood to mean fasting. In the biblical period, fasting evolved out of spiritual needs and extended not only to food and drink, but also to washing, anointing oneself, and to the wearing of shoes. The Rabbis in later times wanted Jews to understand the full significance and meaning of the fast. They used Isaiah 58:3-9 to explain their stand. The prophet Isaiah accuses the people, saying that their fast is only a symbol. True repentance is demonstrated by abandoning evil deeds, sharing bread with the hungry, bringing the poor and oppressed into their homes, clothing the naked, etc.

Does fasting on Yom Kippur — i.e., denying yourself something — help make you a better person? Explain.

E In verse 17:15, the words טרפה (*terayfah*) and נבלה (*nevaylah*) are used in reference to meat which the Israelites are forbidden to eat. These have become standard terms by which non-kosher meat is classified. *Nevaylah* is a limited term meaning an animal that has died a natural death or which has been slaughtered by any method other than that prescribed by the laws of *kashrut*. *Terayfah* originally meant an animal torn by another. However, the term came to refer to an animal which, after ritual slaughtering, was found to be defective in one of its organs. Today the words *terayfah* or *treif* are used to refer to any food which is not kosher.

How might this information support the notion that the laws of *kashrut* grew out of health precautions?

Why do you think that an animal which died a natural death would be unfit to eat?

F In *Acharay Mot*, the Torah lists a series of forbidden sexual relationships. It is as if the Torah was setting up boundaries to preserve the family and to protect women from those males with whom they would have the most contact in their daily lives. Traditional understanding of the various forbidden relationships detailed in this portion was that each in some way threatened family life and, sometimes, Jewish continuity. Today, our attitude toward some of these restrictions, particularly to homosexuality, has changed. Some contemporary commentators, reacting to the fact that the Torah bluntly describes forbidden sexual contacts, take the modern lesson of *Acharay Mot* to be that we should conduct our personal sexual relationships with love and respect.

What attitudes in contemporary society relate to the protection of family life?

How do you think we can protect and enhance family life in our Jewish communities today?

G Two Hebrew words used often in this portion are משפטים (*mishpatim*) and חקים (*chukim*). *Mishpatim* is translated as "rules" or "judgments" and *chukim* as "laws" or "ordinances." Rashi tells us that *mishpatim* are the kind of rules that make society work and that if they had not been included in the Torah, human reasoning would have created them. *Mishpatim* are applicable to all humanity. On the other hand, *chukim* do not seem to have any logical reason for their existence. This does not mean that they lack a purpose. Hertz explains that *chukim* are what makes Israel distinctive and are, therefore, only addressed to Jews (*The Pentateuch and Haftorahs*, p. 489).

David Hoffman sees a different distinction. *Mishpatim*, he says, govern relationships between people, and *chukim* are concerned with a person's conduct in private life (*Studies in Vayikra* by Nehama Leibowitz, p. 157). In Leviticus 18:4, God commands the people to follow the rules and keep the ordinances. The following verse tells us that only by observing the commandments shall a person live. This verse taught an important lesson — one must keep the commandments only when observance does not endanger life. For example, violation of Shabbat is allowed in order to protect or save someone's life. Based on this verse, the Sages taught that if a pagan forces a Jew to violate a commandment and threatens to kill him if he does not, the Jew should break the commandment and live.

Whatever the difference between *mishpatim* and *chukim*, the Torah instructs us not only to do them, but also to *keep* them. The Rabbis understood "keep them" to mean to study, understand, and "guard" them. Thus, the Israelites and succeeding generations are instructed "ללכת בהם" (*la-leh-chet bah-hem*) — to live by them. This Hebrew phrase, found in Leviticus 18:4, conveys a sense of movement and might also be translated as "to walk therein." Several important *halachic*

principles were based on the instructions to "keep" the laws and rules and to "live by them" (see Strategy #4, page 197).

Do you always understand the rules and regulations your parents expect you to follow? Can you give an example of *mishpatim* and *chukim* in your family (consider the definitions provided)? Replace the word "parents" with "society" and the word "family" with "world" and try the above questions again!

Note: *Acharay Mot* and *Kedoshim* are usually read as a double portion. For more about double portions see Exodus, *Pikuday*, Insight A, page 155.

STRATEGIES

ANALYZING THE TEXT

1 Use the definitions of *chukim* and *mishpatim* put forth by Rashi and Hertz (see Insight G on this page) as a basis for classifying the laws in *Acharay Mot* (and also in *Kedoshim*).

EXTENDING THE TEXT

2 This portion begins with the mention of the deaths of Nadab and Abihu. Their untimely demise, however, did not mean the end of the priestly line of Aaron. Create a family tree for Aaron, showing all of his sons. Review Exodus 6:20-23 and Numbers 3:1-4 for this information.

3 When William Tyndale translated the Bible into English in the early sixteenth century, he coined the term "scapegoat" to describe the goat marked for Azazel. Discuss what the word means in terms of the function of the goat for Azazel. How is the word used today? Can you explain the connection between the biblical usage and the modern usage?

4 Compare and contrast the observance of Yom Kippur as described in *Acharay Mot* with the way we observe Yom Kippur today. Make a chart so that you can arrange identical and similar or derivative practices side-by-side. What customs do we observe today that are derived from those pre-scribed in Leviticus? How has the holiday of Yom Kippur developed and changed over the centuries since the days of the Temple and the sacrificial system?
References: *Yom Kippur Anthology* by Phillip Goodman; *The Biblical and Historical Background of Jewish Customs and Ceremonies* by Abraham P. Bloch.

5 The opening verses of *Pirke Avot* ask us to "make a fence around the Torah" (1:1). This can be related to Leviticus 18:4, in which the Israelites are told to "observe" and "follow" (or keep) God's laws (see Insight G, page 196). *Leviticus Rabbah* (22:8) cites a *midrash* in the name of Rabbi Levi which helps explain this idea: The matter may be compared to the case of a king's son who thought he could do what he liked, and habitually ate the flesh of [non-kosher] animals. Said the king: "I will have him at my own table and he will automatically be hedged round." Look at the laws of *kashrut* as they have developed over time to see how the Rabbis "made a fence" or "hedged round" (or expanded upon) the rules specified in the Torah.
References: *The Jewish Dietary Laws* by Samuel Dresner and Seymour Siegel; *The Biblical and Historical Background of Jewish Customs and Ceremonies* by Abraham P. Bloch; *Kosher: A Guide for the Perplexed* by Irving Welfeld.

6 Learn more about the background, require-ments, and procedures for a Jewish marriage. See the video *Seal Upon Thy Heart.*

7 Find out what relatives are prohibited from marrying each other in your state or province. Compare these restrictions with the relationships prohibited in *Acharay Mot.* Can you find out the reasons behind both the biblical and the current prohibitions?

8 In Leviticus 16:21, three different Hebrew words are used for "sin" — חטא (*chet*), פשע (*pesha*), עון (*ahvon*). Of these, the word *chet* is most often translated as "sin." *Pesha* is trans-lated as "rebellion" or "transgression," and *ahvon* is rendered as "iniquity" or "crookedness." Read and discuss Rabbi J.H. Hertz's interpretation of these words (*The Pentateuch and Haftorahs*, p. 483). Using newspapers and magazines, find examples for each interpretation of the word sin. Set up a display and share with others, inviting them to add their own examples.

PERSONALIZING THE TEXT

9 Leviticus 18:5 states:"You shall keep My laws and My rules by the pursuit of which you shall live . . . " The Rabbis understood this to mean that should observance of any commandment of the Torah involve danger to life, the law may be disregarded. However, there are three Jewish laws which must never be broken even if it means sac-rificing one's own life to preserve them. Choose the three which you believe are the laws that cannot be violated:

a. You shall honor your father and mother.
b. You shall not commit murder.
c. You shall observe the Sabbath day, to keep it holy.
d. You shall observe the laws of *kashrut.*
e. You shall not worship false gods.
f. You shall not bear false witness.
g. You shall not have sexual relations with close family members (incest).
h. You shall not steal.

The correct answers are: b, e, g. Rank the three in order of their importance to you. Are there any laws or values which you would add to or subtract from this list of three? Explain. (*From Jewish History — Moments & Methods* by Sorel Loeb and Barbara Binder Kadden, p. 38.)

10 According to Leviticus 16:30 ". . . on this day, atonement shall be made for you to cleanse you of all your sins; you shall be clean before *Adonai*." The Rabbis understood from this passage that the rites of Yom Kippur would cleanse people only of those sins committed before God. For sins committed against other persons, forgiveness from God was not enough — it had to be preceded by forgiveness from the person wronged. Discuss the difference between sins against God and sins against people. Give examples of each of these kinds of sins. What steps would you take to correct your sins against another person? Is there someone to whom you want to apologize? Write a letter to this person. If you want, design an "I'm Sorry" card to include. Choose whether or not you want to send it.

11 Leviticus 18:3 is a warning against assimilation. What observances and practices most strengthen our Jewish identity, keep us different, and help prevent our assimilation?

12 In *Acharay Mot,* the Israelites are told not to copy the practices of the Egyptians and the Canaanites — the people who were most likely to influence their daily life. Who are the contemporary equivalents of these ancient peoples in terms of influence on the Jewish community? What practices of modern society would you like to discourage Jews from copying? Write your own version of this text (Leviticus 18:1-4), updating it and making it more explicit.

13 Although the usual garments of the High Priest were very elaborate, on Yom Kippur he was to enter the Holy of Holies wearing only a linen tunic. *Leviticus Rabbah* says this was so that no one would accuse the Jews of haughtiness saying, "The other day they made for themselves

a god of gold and today they seek to officiate in garments of gold" (21:10). Find out at what holidays and/or life cycle events we traditionally wear white, simple garments. Determine why we do this. Write your own explanation of the custom of wearing white along the lines of the *midrash* quoted above. (For more, see the Index: "Rabbis/ Priests.")
References: *The Biblical and Historical Background of Jewish Customs and Ceremonies* by Abraham P. Bloch; *The Minhagim: The Customs and Ceremonies of Judaism, Their Origins and Rationale* by Abraham Chill.

14 In *The Dybbuk* by S. Ansky, Rabbi Azriel gives a discourse in which he speaks of how the holiest elements of the world — the High Priest, the Holy of Holies, and the secret Hebrew name of God — come together on the holiest day of the year, Yom Kippur. The speech concludes as follows:

"Every spot whereon a man may stand and lift his eyes to Heaven becomes a Holy of Holies; every man whom God has created in His own image and in His likeness is a High Priest; every day of a man's life is a Day of Atonement; and every word that a man utters with his whole heart is the Name of God. Therefore, a man's every sin and every injustice brings destruction upon the world" (p. 114).

This idea is not so complex as it sounds. Try to express it in a few simple sentences. Then, using puppets, create and present some short skits that express these ideas. Remember in your version to include women.

15 Philo, a Jewish philosopher who lived in Alexandria, Egypt, in the first century B.C.E., taught that "the fast of Yom Kippur comes when it does because it is like a pause to say a blessing over a meal. The meal is the harvest — the meal of the entire year — so the pause is long"

(*Seasons of Our Joy* by Arthur Waskow, p. 43). Use this idea as your theme for writing a poetic reading for a Yom Kippur service. Consider the following: How does Yom Kippur relate to the seasonal and agricultural calendars? On Yom Kippur, what are the things we "pause" from doing? How does this pause heighten our awareness of ourselves and our world. (For sample readings, see Waskow, pp. 43-45.)

16 Make a video to teach about the history and observance of Yom Kippur (for references see Strategy #13, page 198).

17 In contemporary usage, the word "scapegoat" refers to someone who is made to bear the blame for another person's bad actions or for bad events that happen to another person. Can you think of times when a classmate or friend of yours has been made a scapegoat? Have you ever been a scapegoat?

18 One of the English synonyms for the word "sin" is "crookedness." This word calls up very vivid visual pictures of a sinful or wrongdoing person. Draw your own visual impressions of a person who is crooked.

19 The Rabbis taught that even a non-Jew who keeps the Torah is to be regarded as equal to the High Priest (*Sifra*). Explain how they derived this lesson from Leviticus 18:5.

20 *Acharay Mot* is the first portion in Leviticus in which laws specifically pertaining to moral conduct are presented. These laws deal with sexual relationships and the boundaries which were enacted. Jewish education plays a dual role in discussing laws such as these. A synagogue is an excellent location for discussions of sexuality and safe sex practices. But it is also an excellent location to talk about the Jewish values and ethics associated with sex. Arrange to have guest speakers who can present talks on sex and

sexuality. Also, invite speakers to connect Jewish values and ethics to this subject.
References: *Does God Belong in the Bedroom?* by Michael Gold; *Love, Marriage, and Family in Jewish Law and Tradition* by Michael Kaufman; *A Jewish View of Teenage Sexuality* by Roland Gittelsohn.

OTHER RESOURCES

21 Learn what the Mishnah says regarding atonement on Yom Kippur. Read, discuss, and follow the suggested activities in *Learn Mishnah* by Jacob Neusner, pp. 85-93.

22 Read, act out, and discuss the skit for the portion *Acharay Mot* in *Sedra Scenes: Skits for Every Torah Portion* by Stan J. Beiner, pp. 138-141.

23 View and discuss the episode for *Acharay Mot* from *Torah Toons I: The Video*.

24 For creative movement activities, see "Scapegoat" and "Defiling the Land" from *Torah in Motion* by JoAnne Tucker and Susan Freeman, pp. 138-141.

25 Read and discuss the illustrated commentary for *Acharay Mot* in *American Torah Toons* by Lawrence Bush.

INVOLVING THE FAMILY

26 In *Acharay Mot*, we are told not to copy the practices of Egypt or Canaan. In those places, people married very close relatives if they found each other attractive. Our tradition prohibits the marriage of close relatives. Further, we are taught that values are a better basis for a relationship than physical appearance. Along these lines, the humorist Sam Levenson wrote the following to his daughter:

My Darling Daughter:

The truly beautiful people are not necessarily in the jet set, the fashion set, the money set, or the sex set, but in the soul set. May I suggest several time-tested beauty hints.

1. For attractive lips, speak words of kindness.
2. For lovely eyes, seek out the good in people.
3. For a slim figure, share your food with the hungry.
4. For beautiful hair, let a child run fingers through it once a day.
5. For poise, walk with the knowledge that you will never walk alone.

(From *In One Era and Out the Other* by Sam Levenson, Copyright 1973 by Sam Levenson. Reprinted by permission of SIMON & SCHUSTER, Inc.)

Imagine that you are responsible for writing a "Dear Abby" column. As a family, write your own "time-tested beauty hints" for publication in newspapers across the country.

BAR/BAT MITZVAH PROJECT

27 This portion opens with the description of Yom Kippur and its observance during the biblical period. It was to be a day of sacrifice. It was also to be a day to practice self-denial, literally translated as a day to "afflict yourselves."

Jewish tradition understood this to mean fasting. Since the destruction of the Second Temple, there is no more sacrifice and prayer has become its substitute. Yom Kippur has become a day of introspection, prayer, repentance, and fasting.

This Bar/Bat Mitzvah project gives you the opportunity to enhance your introspection and silent thinking time during Yom Kippur. Obtain a three-ring binder and place in it poetry, short stories, photographs, news clippings, pictures, cartoons, and other written and visual items which help you think about the themes and ideas of Yom Kippur. Those to consider include: forgiveness, repentance, personal actions for good and for bad, and reconciliation. Also include your own writings, poetry, and pictures in the binder.

In addition to bringing your *Machzor*, also bring your binder to read and meditate on during services.

Potential resources for material: Speak with your Rabbi, Director of Education, and Religious School teacher. Use both the synagogue and public libraries. Also include lyrics to songs you find meaningful, whether Jewish or secular.

Gathering these items in a binder will make it easy to add or delete things from your collection as you grow and change. Finally, think of a title for your collection.

(For more, see the Index: "Nadab and Abihu," "Yom Kippur," and "Marriage/Relationships.")

KEDOSHIM 19:1-20:27 קדושים

SYNOPSIS

IN THIS PORTION, GOD TELLS MOSES TO instruct the entire Israelite community in the laws of holiness. The Israelites are to be holy because God is holy. Therefore, they are to observe the commandments and the laws of the sacrifices. They are to provide for the poor and the stranger, leaving the edges of the fields unharvested and the fallen fruits of their vineyards ungleaned, so that the needy can come and gather food.

The Israelites are told not to insult the deaf or place a stumbling block before the blind and to show respect for the elderly. They are to be fair in judgment and in commerce and they are not to bear a grudge. Moses tells them further to love their neighbors as themselves and to love the strangers in their midst, for the Israelites were strangers themselves in the land of Egypt.

The Israelites are not to mix different species of cattle or seed and they are not to wear clothes made from a mixture of two kinds of material.

Moses also reviews the prohibited sexual relations and the punishments for these.

All these laws the Israelites are to observe so that they may be holy to God, Who has set them apart from other peoples, freed them from slavery in Egypt, and chosen them as God's people.

INSIGHTS FROM THE TRADITION

A *Kedoshim* is the plural form of the word *kadosh,* holy. Holiness is the key which unifies the diverse laws detailed in this portion. It is through the observance of these laws that the Israelites are to be holy as God is holy.

Holy can mean many things. Among the definitions are: sacred, unique, divine, and complete. In one sense, holy can also mean to be separate from. Perhaps this is how the *midrash* understands *Kedoshim.* God says to Moses: "Tell the Israelites that just as I am separate, so you be separate; just as I am holy, so you be holy" (*Leviticus Rabbah* 24:4).

What elements within Judaism set Jews apart from the rest of the world?
Are Jews better able to maintain their identities when separated from the non-Jewish society?
What are the advantages and the disadvantages of being set apart?
What makes you special and unique and sets you apart from the crowd? Do your Jewish values and heritage figure into your "separateness"?

B Holy is understood as being morally perfect, pure, religious, set apart for sacred use. It is certain that the laws in this portion encourage a high level of moral behavior. For some, holy means to be outside of normal life. In some religions, a holy person is one who lives a separate, monastic life. But from the Torah, we learn that holiness is not to be achieved by withdrawal from daily life, but rather by active participation in it.

Martin Buber explained that like God, Israel should be a part of the nations of the world. Buber saw Israel as a nation which by its holiness could influence other nations of the world to do good.

Are Jews able to influence the behavior of other peoples? Explain.
In what ways do you influence the behavior of others?
Does Judaism influence you to do acts of loving kindness?

C The wording of Leviticus 19:2 is unusual. Moses is instructed to "speak to the whole Israelite community." The usual form is simply "speak to the Israelite people" (see, for example, Leviticus 1:2, 12:1). Scholars, therefore, point to the special importance attached to these laws — that the attainment of holiness prescribed here is not confined to a limited group, but is attainable by anyone.

According to this, can a non-Jew be holy? What do you try to do in your own life that gives you a sense of being holy?

D In many Torah passages, the word *kadosh* indicates times, objects, and places set apart for holy purposes. Shabbat is described as a holy day. Other holidays are called *Mikra'ay Kodesh* — holy seasons. The Ark (*Aron HaKodesh*) was kept in *Kodesh HaKodashim,* the "Holy of Holies."

How does the holiness of a time, place, or object differ from human holiness? How are they similar? What are your most holy times, objects, and places?

E In Leviticus 19:18, we read: "You shall not take vengeance or bear a grudge." To show what they meant, the Rabbis used the following example. "A" refuses to lend his spade to "B," "B" later refuses to lend "A" his axe — that is vengeance. But if "B" lends the axe to "A" and says, "See, I let you have it even though you wouldn't lend me your spade" — that is bearing a grudge and it also is forbidden (*Sifra*).

Can you cite examples from school or home when you acted improperly? How might you act so as not to be guilty of bearing a grudge or taking vengeance?
Why shouldn't a person seek revenge? What might happen to society if everyone sought revenge?

F Leviticus 19:28 reads, "You shall not make gashes in your flesh for the dead, or incise any marks on yourselves: I am *Adonai*." This was a prohibition against the pagan practices of cutting into one's skin, as a sign of mourning, and tattooing. Among traditional Jews this prohibition extends to ear and body piercing. The last phrase of this verse simply states "I am *Adonai*." From this we see that not only is God's stamp of authority on this law, but just as God is holy, our bodies are holy and should be treated with respect (*The Five Books of Miriam* by Ellen Frankel, p. 181).

What do you think of body piercing and tattooing? Are these practices disrespectful to God? to your parents? to society? What message is conveyed when someone has tattoos or piercings? Is it possible to grow tired of or disenchanted with piercings and tattoos? Could they affect many areas of a person's life? In what ways? Is this law trying to protect us from ourselves?

Note: *Kedoshim* and *Acharay Mot* are usually read as a double portion. For more about double portions, see Exodus, *Pikuday,* Insight A, page 155.

STRATEGIES

ANALYZING THE TEXT

1 The Ten Commandments are repeated in *Kedoshim* in a slightly different order and with a few variations in form. Read Leviticus 19:3-29 to find the commandments (see *The Torah: A Modern Commentary,* p. 894, for a correct listing). Compare them with the commandments as given in Exodus 20:1-14 or Deuteronomy 5:1-18. What differences are there? What lessons can you derive from these differences?

2 Complete the following sentences. Discuss the responses as a class.

The Torah advises us that "the wages of a laborer shall not remain with you until evening" (19:13) because ____.
The Torah advises us to "judge [our] neighbor fairly" (9:15) because ____.
I might be tempted to show "favor" in court to the poor (19:15) because ____.
I might be tempted to "show deference to the rich" because ____.
The Torah advises us not to take vengeance or bear a grudge because ____.
I might be tempted to take vengeance (19:18) because ____.

I might bear a grudge against someone because
____.

The Torah tells us not to "make gashes" in our
flesh or "incise any marks" on ourselves (19:28)
because ____.

3 Choose some key Hebrew words which
describe either negative or positive acts
enjoined upon us in *Kedoshim*. On pieces of poster
board, write a word or expression and a symbol
that represents the acts as described in *Kedoshim*.
For example, draw a gavel to go with the words
"Don't render unfair judgments." String the pieces
of cardboard together as a mobile under the heading "You shall be holy."

4 In *Gates of Repentance: The New Union Prayerbook for the Days of Awe,* the Reform *Machzor*
for the High Holy Days, the afteroon Torah reading for Yom Kippur is Leviticus 19:1-4, 9-18, 32-
37. The traditional reading for Yom Kippur afternoon is Leviticus 18, from *Acharay Mot.*

Read both portions, highlighting ideas, significant words, and events. Then create a diamante
which compares and contrasts the two portions.
Designate one passage subject one and the other
subject two. A diamante is written in the shape of
a diamond with this structure:

Line one	One word — a noun from subject one
Line two	Two words — adjectives from subject one
Line three	Three words — participles from subject one
Line four	Four words — nouns from subjects one and two
Line five	Three words — participles from subject two
Line six	Two words — adjectives from subject two
Line seven	One word — a noun from subject two

After the draft is written, write the fourth line
(which will be the longest) of the final draft first.
Place each of the other lines, centered, above or
below the fourth line.

Display the finished diamantes around the
room and use them as a basis for discussion.

EXTENDING THE TEXT

5 Everett Fox translates Leviticus 19:16 as follows: "You are not to traffic in slander among
your Kinspeople." The Rabbis found two prohibitions in this verse: do not make up gossip, and do
not repeat gossip. In Leviticus 19:18, two additional prohibitions are found: "You shall not take
vengeance or bear a grudge."

In a comic strip format, illustrate examples of
these four forbidden acts: (1) originating gossip,
(2) repeating gossip, (3) taking vengeance, (4) bearing a grudge. Indicate in the comic strip(s) the
attitude that the Torah wants us to take in these
cases. (For more, see the Index: "Leprosy/*Tzara'at.*")

6 What advice does the Torah give judges?
(See Leviticus 19:15; also Exodus 23:2ff.;
Deuteronomy 1:16ff, 16:18ff.) Stage a skit. Begin
by showing a judge deciding a case in one of the
ways described in *Kedoshim* as unfair. Have Moses
intervene and advise the judge about fairness in
judgment (as described in this portion or one of
the other passages above). Then retry the case.

7 The laws in *Kedoshim* were written so that
the Israelites would be holy because God is
holy. These laws guaranteed a high level of moral
and ethical behavior. Create a *Kedoshim* Wall of
Achievement composed of Jewish individuals who,
through their deeds, are holy and ethical.

Find pictures of these people or make your
own portraits. Give a short biography and examples of their moral and ethical behavior which
makes them a part of the *Kedoshim* Wall of
Achievement. Display your information on poster

board. Dress up the poster board with Contact paper, markers, stickers, glitter, etc.

8 Read Ruth 1:22-2:19 for an example of the application of the laws detailed in Leviticus 19:9-10. Discuss the assumptions behind such laws (amplified and repeated in Leviticus 23:22 and Deuteronomy 24:19ff.). How does this law assure the rights of the weaker members of society? Do you think it protects their pride and dignity? How could it enhance the pride and dignity of land-owners?

9 How many Hebrew words do you know which have the same root as *kadosh*? Which of these are the names of prayers? Which are nouns that reflect important Jewish values? The words *Kiddushin* (betrothal) and *Kiddush HaShem* (martyrdom) have the same root word, *kadosh,* although they relate to very different aspects of life. Discuss how the idea of holiness is bound up in each one. (For more, see the Index: "Holiness.")

PERSONALIZING THE TEXT

10 In *Kedoshim* we read: "You shall rise before the aged and show deference to the old." What do you think it is like to be elderly in our society?

a. Visit a home for senior citizens in your city. See if you can arrange to have one of the social workers speak to you about the plight of the elderly.

b. Conduct a two-week search of the media for articles and issues pertaining to the elderly. Post those you find on a bulletin board. When the time is up, make a list of all the problems of which you became aware. Brainstorm a variety of remedies. Find out what you can do about carrying them out.

11 Learn more about the Jewish deaf and blind and how you can help them get access to Jewish traditions and sources. Write: Jewish Braille Institute, 110 East 30th Street, New York, NY 10016 and National Congress of the Jewish Deaf, 9102 Edmonton Court, Greenbelt, MD 20770.
References: "The Jewish Deaf Community" by Lynn Gottlieb, p. 151, and "The Jewish Blind," edited by Naamah Kelman and Michael Levy, p. 167, both in *The Second Jewish Catalog*, edited by Michael Strassfeld and Sharon Strassfeld.

12 The Hebrew term for part of the Jewish wedding ceremony is *Kiddushin*. The word implies that the marriage partners are in some way holy (set aside, special, consecrated) for each other. Based on the general holiness laws detailed in *Kedoshim*, what characteristics of a good relationship between people can be considered holy? For example, how does fairness in judgment apply to a personal, private relationship? After listing the qualities of a couple's relationship that would make it holy in your eyes, rank them in order of importance. Then rank these qualities in order of difficulty to achieve.

13 What does holiness mean? According to *Kedoshim*, how does the word explain the relationship between God and Israel? How is holiness built into the way persons conduct themselves in their occupations? in their social relations? What is the purpose of holiness in Jewish life? Using *Kedoshim* as your starting point and bearing in mind the above questions, as a class discuss and write a Holiness Code for Jews today (refer to Strategies #7 and #9 above in this *sedra*).

14 Leviticus 19:18 reads: "Love Your Neighbor as Yourself." It is the basis of the Golden Rule which has been expressed in a variety of ways by both Jews and non-Jews:

Hillel: What is hateful to you do not do to your fellow.

Ibn Ezra: Love the good for your neighbor as you love it for yourself.

Ben Sira: Honor thy neighbor as thyself.

Eleazar ben Arach: Let the honor of thy neighbor be as dear to thee as thine own.

Matthew in the Christian Bible: All that you would wish that men should do unto you, do ye also unto them.

Jainism: In happiness and suffering, in joy and grief, we should regard all creatures as we regard our own self, and should therefore refrain from inflicting upon others such injury as would appear undesirable to us if inflicted upon ourselves.

Use a quotation dictionary (look up "Golden Rule") to help you find other ways of expressing this idea. Discuss and analyze the different expressions and then rank them in order from most general (i.e., broadest possible meaning and application) to most specific. Create a design for a T-shirt using the one expression you like best. Silk screen your T-shirt.

15 Choose a memorable verse from *Kedoshim* and make a poster illustrating it. Incorporate the verse into the poster. For an example, see the poster designed by Ben Shahn to illustrate Leviticus 19:16 — "Thou shalt not stand idly by . . ." in *Prints and Posters of Ben Shahn* (plate #40).

16 Make a "Righteous Action Cube." Follow the directions given in Leviticus, *Metzora* Strategy # 15, page 192, but incorporate values from *Kedoshim*.

17 Twice in *Kedoshim* we read about sins for which the punishment is being "cut off from [one's] kin" (19:8; 20:6). (For more, see the Index: "*Karet*/Cut off from kin.")

OTHER RESOURCES

18 Read and discuss the following stories about talebearing and gossip: "Yossel and the Tree" in *Lessons From Our Living Past* by Jules Harlow, pp. 117ff.; "The Gossip" in *Who Knows Ten?* by Molly Cone, pp. 78ff. (For more, see the Index: "Talebearing/Gossip.")

19 Read and discuss *Drugs, Sex and Integrity: What Does Judaism Say?* by Daniel F. Polish, et al.

20 Read, act out, and discuss the skit for the portion *Kedoshim* in *Sedra Scenes: Skits for Every Torah* portion by Stan J. Beiner, pp. 142-144.

21 Complete the pages which relate to *Kedoshim* in *Bible People Book Two* by Joel Lurie Grishaver, p. 43. Also check the accompanying Leader Guide for procedures and additional activities.

22 View and discuss the episode for *Kedoshim* from *Torah Toons I: The Video*.

23 For creative movement activities, see "Leave Some for the Poor," "Stumbling Blocks," and "Love the Stranger" from *Torah in Motion* by JoAnne Tucker and Susan Freeman, pp. 142-147.

24 Read and discuss the illustrated commentary for *Kedoshim* in *American Torah Toons* by Lawrence Bush.

25 Study about the elderly and Jewish attitudes toward aging using the mini-course *Aging and Judaism* by Kerry M.Olitzky and Lee H. Olitzky.

INVOLVING THE FAMILY

26 What can your family do in its daily life to increase awareness of and participation in holiness? Discuss the options and choose one to incorporate into your family's life for an experimental period. Some possibilities include adding the recitation of *brachot* and/or *Birkat HaMazon* to your meals, having a weekly family Havdalah service, deciding to observe *kashrut,* deciding to refrain from gossip. At the end of the experimental period, evaluate the impact your added activity had on your life and the life of your family. Have each member of the family take a turn completing the following sentences:

I learned ____.

I felt ____.

I am proud ____.

Then decide as a family whether to make this activity a permanent part of your family life. Study *Kedoshim* together and find other holiness behaviors to add to your lives.

BAR/BAT MITZVAH PROJECT

27 According to *Kedoshim,* how does the Torah want us to treat the disadvantaged?

The mentally or physically challenged? The elderly or strangers? What are the implications of these laws for today? Write a radio or television documentary which discusses these issues from biblical and contemporary perspectives. Gather local community experts in the fields of aging, the disadvantaged, the mentally and physically challenged. Videotape an interview, a round table discussion, profiles of community services which work with individuals dealing with these issues, highlights of progress being made, and biographical interviews of people who would be affected by the laws in *Kedoshim.*

Remember, you are the producer. You will need to decide if you will also direct, write, and organize all the pieces of this project. You may want to assemble a crew to help you make this project a reality.

Note: The Ten Commandments are repeated in Exodus 20:1-14 (*Yitro*) and Deuteronomy 5:6-18 (*Ve'etchanan*). See those portions for additional Insights and Strategies.

EMOR 21:1-24:23 אמור

SYNOPSIS

MOSES IS TO INFORM THE PRIESTS OF THE special rules which they must obey. The priests are to refrain from coming into contact with a corpse, they are not to shave smooth any parts of their heads, and they are forbidden to marry a divorced woman. The priests are to be scrupulous as they carry out their duties. Any priest who has a physical defect or is ritually unclean is forbidden to offer sacrifices to God. So, too, the Israelites are to take care to bring blemish free offerings to God. No animal less than eight days old is acceptable as a sacrifice and no animal shall be slaughtered on the same day as its young.

Then Moses speaks to all the people about the holy days in the year. Apart from the Sabbath, which occurs every seven days, the Israelites are to observe the Feast of Unleavened Bread and, seven weeks later, a celebration of the harvest.

The first day of the seventh month, the people are to mark as a sacred occasion with loud blasts and the tenth day of the same month shall be a Day of Atonement.

The fifteenth day of the seventh month is the Feast of Booths. This holiday is to be observed for seven days, and the people are to mark the eighth day with a special sacrifice. On all of these holidays, the Israelites are told not to work at their occupations, and special observances are prescribed.

Moses further reminds the Israelites to bring clear olive oil for the regular lighting of the lamps in the Tent of Meeting. He then instructs them in the baking and displaying of the twelve loaves of display bread for the altar.

The portion concludes by describing an incident wherein a man born of an Israelite woman and an Egyptian man fights with another man born of two Israelite parents. The half-Israelite blasphemes God's name in the course of a fight. God tells Moses that the man is to be stoned to death as punishment. So Moses tells the Israelites

of the penalty for blaspheming God or pronouncing God's name, and also of the rules by which restitution is to be made for crimes.

INSIGHTS FROM THE TRADITION

A "*Emor*" is the word by which God tells Moses to "speak" the laws of holiness to the priests. The portion begins with a detailed description of the laws of holiness as they pertain to the priests and to the offering of sacrifices. This section (Leviticus 21:1-22:3) is considered the logical conclusion to the Holiness Code begun in the portion *Acharay Mot* (Leviticus 16:1).

B The priests had a higher status than the rest of the Israelites because of their special duties. Essentially, these laws set the priests apart from the rest of society. The High Priest was further set apart from the regular priests. In five respects he was to be greater and better — stature, strength, wealth, intelligence, and appearance (*Yalkut Me'am Lo'ez* by Yaacov Culi, Vol. XII, p. 103).

What qualities give people status in our society today? Do these qualities deserve to be given status? What about the quiet, unsung heroes/heroines?
What important personal qualities not listed here also make a person very special? Does one have to be born with special personal qualities or can one develop them?
What are your best qualities?

C This portion reflects the idea that the status of a father or husband is affected by the character of his wife and/or daughters. In many traditional cultures, daughters are seen as part of their father's property until they marry and become part of their husband's household and property. Since the behavior of women therefore reflects upon the household, women were subject to numerous rules and restrictions governing their behavior. This idea may explain why it is the priest who is dishonored if his daughter should become a prostitute and why priests are forbidden to marry divorced women or prostitutes.

Do you agree with the idea that people who are involved in holy or important work should have family members whose conduct is beyond reproach?
Do you think that your personal conduct reflects upon your family?
In what way might your behavior bring honor or dishonor to your family?

D This portion contains the disturbing idea that no person who has any kind of physical defect may offer a sacrifice or come near the holy altar (21:16-23). The implication seems to be that physical perfection is most pleasing to God. Reading the words from a modern perspective, we might explain that they reflect an ancient fear of physical difference, illness, and death. Rachel Cowan explains, "themes or practices which at first seem primitive . . . speak powerfully of the modern human condition. This text, in fact, invites self-examination, for it reflects attitudes about human flaws and about leadership that many of us still hold today" (*Learn Torah With . . . ,* p. 230).

In our society, how important is beauty or physical wholeness?
How would you characterize our attitude toward people with deformities or disabilities? Do you think that their lack of "perfection" makes it difficult for them to participate fully in all aspects of contemporary life?
How welcoming and accessible to the disabled is your synagogue?

E Leviticus 22:28 states that "no animal from the herd or flock shall be slaughtered on the same day with its young." Two great Rabbis held divergent views on the reasoning behind this prohibition. Rambam wrote that the Torah wanted to prevent cruelty and suffering to animals. Since animals show affection for their young, killing them in the presence of each other would be very cruel. Ramban, however, states that if God had deep pity on the animals, their slaughter would be entirely forbidden. Instead, Ramban sees this commandment as helping humanity develop the quality of mercy.

How do the interpretations of these Rabbis differ? How are they the same?

F In *Leviticus Rabbah* 27:11, the prohibition noted immediately above in Insight E (Leviticus 22:28) is used to remind us of our many cruel and pitiless enemies, such as Haman, who caused letters to be sent "to betray, to slay, and to cause to perish all Jews . . . in one day" (Esther 3:13). Others who have sought to destroy us, treated us worse than animals are allowed to be treated.

Does an attitude of kindness toward animals lead to kindness toward people?
What kind acts have you performed toward animals or people lately?

G In the commentary on Leviticus in *The Torah: A Modern Commentary,* Bernard Bamberger speculates that the atonement rites of Rosh HaShanah and Yom Kippur were originally part of the harvest festival of Sukkot. These rites marked the beginning of the economic year because this was when the harvest was taken to be sold at market. Perhaps this is why the Torah does not mention the name Rosh HaShanah (which means the beginning of the year) for the new year festival, but calls it simply *Yom Teruah* (Numbers 29:1) — day of the sounding of the *shofar.* The holiday is not called Rosh HaShanah until Ezekiel 40:1, circa 593 B.C.E., and even that reference is questionable.
　　As with many other holidays mentioned in the

Torah, Rosh HaShanah evolved from the changing Jewish experience. It was not until the time of the Mishnah (circa 200 C.E.) that one particular Rosh HasShanah (there were three others — see Exodus, *Bo*, Strategy #8, page 103) assumed prominence as the anniversary of Creation and the onset of the Ten Days of Repentance.

In what ways is the Jewish New Year different from the secular New Year?
On both Rosh HaShanah and Yom Kippur, we sound the *shofar*. What is the *shofar* calling us to do?
How might the mood of Rosh HaShanah help you in improving relationships with family and friends?

H In addition to Rosh HaShanah and Yom Kippur, this portion discusses Passover, Shavuot, and Sukkot. These three agricultural festivals are known as the *Shalosh Regalim*. This name comes from the first two words in Exodus 23:14. Three times during the year in biblical days, the Israelites were to make pilgrimage to Jerusalem to offer sacrifices.

We can see a pattern in this. Ancient agricultural festivals take on new meanings as the Jewish faith develops. Passover celebrates the spring harvest and the freeing of the Hebrew slaves from Egyptian bondage. Shavuot commemorates both the harvest of first fruits and the revelation at Sinai. Sukkot observes the fall harvest and that period of time when the Israelites wandered in the desert after the Exodus from Egypt.

The question may be asked: Were these divinely ordained Jewish observances which incorporated agricultural celebrations, or were they agricultural celebrations which incorporated historical events? One commentary makes a fascinating point. In Leviticus 23:2, the Torah says, "There are special times . . . declare them." The word "them" (*otam*) is usually written in Hebrew with a

vav, but in this verse, the *vav* is missing. Thus, it could be read *atem*, in which case the verse would read as "There are sacred holidays that you shall declare." In effect, the holidays that Israel declares shall be God's holidays (*Yalkut Me'am Lo'ez* by Yaacov Culi, Vol. XII, pp. 121-2).

If the *Shalosh Regalim* had not become associated with Jewish historical events, would their observance have been lost in a non-agricultural society? Why is it important for us to make the experiences of our ancestors our own? Are there everyday occurrences in your life that your family made special for you, such as when you learned to walk, got your braces off, learned to swim, or ride a bike? Are these events still remembered? celebrated? What is the importance of ritual for you and for your family?

I *Emor* concludes with one of the few narrative passages in the Book of Leviticus — the story of the man who blasphemed God (24:10- 23). The entire passage is very brief and it is left to the reader to speculate on the nature of the argument which caused the man to "pronounce the Name of God in blasphemy" (see Strategy #3 on the next page). The story is noteworthy in that it is one of only four incidents in the Torah in which Moses is shown asking God how to decide an issue (the others are Numbers 9:6ff., 15:32ff., and 27:1ff.). Moses sought God's judgment because the punishment for blasphemy had not yet been detailed. More significant, however, is the placement of this story. It is, in effect, a cautionary tale, coming as it does on the heels of the sections demanding holiness and morality from the Israelites.

Sometimes the things we say cause real damage. What is this incident in Torah trying to tell us? Have you ever spoken things in anger that you really did not mean to say? What was the result?

STRATEGIES

ANALYZING THE TEXT

1 Organize a "Scavenger Hunt" of the portion *Emor*. Working in two or more teams, come up with a list of 15 questions that can be answered after a careful reading of the text. Ideas for questions include: knowing the penalty for murder, the number of holidays detailed in *Emor,* and specific observances for these holidays. Trade lists with another team and have a timed race to answer the questions.

2 Examine the treatment of Shavuot in *Emor*. How is its treatment different from that of the other holidays detailed here? Explain how the portion links Shavuot to Passover. What is the significance of this connection?

3 The story which concludes *Emor* is mysterious. Although the Torah tells us about the resulting punishment, it does not give us much information about who the man was or what the fight was about. There are, however, several tantalizing clues in the text. Read Leviticus 24:10-23 very carefully to find as many clues as you can. For example, the man was a "half-Israelite" who "came out." From where did he come out? Also look at the context of the story. Then write a report explaining the incident as though you were a detective who had gathered up all the clues and who had interviewed significant people involved. (For a *midrash* explaining this incident, see *Legends of the Jews* by Louis Ginzberg, Vol. III, pp. 238-242.)

4 Work is prohibited on all the holidays described in *Emor*. Find the Hebrew phrase which contains this prohibition. How many times does it occur in the portion in exactly this form? (Answer: Five times — 23:7, 23:21, 23:25, 23:35, 23:36). Compare this phrase with the prohibition of work on Yom Kippur (23:28). What does the change in language imply regarding work on Yom

Kippur? Why would we be given a commandment not to work on a holiday? Does God need us not to work? Does the Jewish community? Do our families? What can we gain by not working?

5 Three of the holidays detailed in *Emor* are known as the *Shalosh Regalim* (the three Pilgrimage Festivals). Find out what this name means and the names of the holidays to which it refers. What do these holidays have in common? How do we celebrate them?
References: "The Festivals," in *The First Jewish Catalog* by Richard Siegel, Michael Strassfeld, and Sharon Strassfeld; *Seasons of Our Joy* by Arthur Waskow; "Festivals," *Encyclopaedia Judaica*, Vol. 6, pp. 1237ff.; *Jewish Family Celebrations: The Sabbath, Festivals, and Ceremonies* by Arlene Rossen Cardozo.

6 The admonition "You shall not profane My holy Name, that I may be sanctified in the midst of the Israelite people" (Leviticus 22:32) was taken by the Rabbis as a challenge. It is the responsibility of the Jewish people to maintain God's reputation. Therefore, tradition says that moral and ethical behavior are especially incumbent upon Jews. Do you feel an obligation to behave in a moral and ethical way to preserve God's reputation and/or the reputation of the Jewish people? There is another saying that "all Jews are responsible for each other." Does this obligate you to influence other Jews to behave in a moral and ethical way? Are these obligations fair or unfair? Why?

EXTENDING THE TEXT

7 Based on the material from Insight E, page 208, stage a panel discussion between Rambam and Ramban concerning the interpretation of Leviticus 22:28: "No animal from the herd or flock shall be slaughtered on the same day with its young." (For more, see the Index: "*Tza'ar baalay chayim*/Treatment of animals.")

8 Use a Jewish calendar as a resource to locate the Hebrew month and date for each holiday mentioned in *Emor*. Then refer to the perpetual calendar in the Index to the *Encyclopaedia Judaica*. Match the Hebrew date of the holiday with its secular date for the present year and for two other years of your choice. Find out why the secular dates vary while the Hebrew dates remain the same. Use the Hebrew and secular holiday dates you looked up as examples to explain the functioning of the Jewish calendar. Find out your Hebrew birth date. Create a bulletin board with a birthday theme. Put each student's secular calendar birth date and Hebrew birth date on it. If you choose, have each child celebrate and bring treats on his/her Hebrew birth date. Learn to sing "Happy Birthday" in Hebrew.
Reference: *The Jewish Calendar* by Raymond A. Zwerin.

9 What holidays in the Jewish calendar today are not included in *Emor*? Make a "holiday-line" using string, clothespins, and colored construction paper. Write all the Jewish holidays mentioned in *Emor* on construction paper and arrange them on the line. Beside each holiday, hang other pieces of paper (use the same color for each holiday) on which you have written key values and practices associated with the holiday. Add to your "holiday-line" all the Jewish holidays *not* mentioned in *Emor*. Follow the same procedure for these holidays as you did for the biblical holidays. In the information display, give the reason why these holidays do not appear in the biblical text.

10 Verse 23:40 in *Emor* refers to the *lulav* and *etrog* we use on Sukkot. According to the *Pesikta de R. Kahana,* the *lulav* (made up of date palm, myrtle, and willow branches) and *etrog* symbolize the four types of Jews. See if you can match the symbols:

1. *etrog* (fragrance and taste)
2. willow (neither fragrance nor taste)
3. myrtle (fragrance, but no taste)
4. date palm (taste, but no fragrance)

a. A Jew with no learning, no good deeds
b. A Jew with learning, but no good deeds
c. A Jew with learning and good deeds
d. A Jew with good deeds, but no learning

ANSWERS: 1–c; 2–a; 3–b; 4–d.

Which is better, to be a knowledgeable Jew who doesn't perform good deeds, or to be a Jew who lacks knowledge but performs good deeds?

PERSONALIZING THE TEXT

11 Think about the spiritual implications of Sukkot, a holiday that requires people to leave their houses of abundance at harvest time and to go and dwell in simple, fragile booths. Pretend you are a Rabbi hoping to deepen your congregation's appreciation of Sukkot and to encourage each family to build a *sukkah*. Write a sermon for the holiday to accomplish this.
References: *The Biblical and Historical Background of the Jewish Holy Days* by Abraham P. Bloch; *The Sukkot Anthology* by Phillip Goodman; *Seasons of Our Joy: A Modern Guide to the Jewish Holidays* by Arthur Waskow; *Jewish Family Celebrations: The Sabbath, Festivals, and Ceremonies* by Arlene Rossen Cardozo.

12 Find out how the laws for the priests are applied today for Jews who are *Kohanim* or *Levi'im*. What special privileges are reserved for them in traditional synagogues? Are *Kohanim* today allowed to attend funerals? What if a Rabbi is a *Kohen*? Can a *Kohen* marry a divorced woman? If he does, and they have a child, what is the status of the child? How strictly are these laws enforced? Invite the Rabbi to speak to the class about this topic.

13 Although the light which burned in the Tent of Meeting has a parallel in contemporary synagogues, the 12 loaves (showbread) described in Leviticus 24:5-8 have no contemporary counterpart. Devise a parallel of the showbread that would be appropriate for use today. Explain the original significance of this symbol and why it should be reintroduced today. Draw or make a model of your idea for a contemporary parallel for the showbread.
Reference: "Shewbread," *Encyclopaedia Judaica*, Vol. 14, pp. 1394-1396.

14 Design posters to hang in your *sukkah* depicting the four kinds of Jews described in Strategy #10, page 210.

15 Find out the various Hebrew names of the three pilgrimage festivals (use the references in Strategy #5, page 210, and also look at the *Kiddush* for Festivals in a *Siddur*). Write the names on footprints cut out of construction paper and mount them on the floor, wall, or on a table. Use additional footprints on which are written facts and information about the holiday. Use a separate set of footprints for each holiday. Beside each set of footprints, create a small display depicting the holiday. The footprints lead to a large Jerusalem. Jerusalem may be depicted as a collage, using magazine pictures, photos, and other materials; as a painting; or as a 3-D model made of various boxes and containers, set on the floor or on a table. Invite friends and family to take a tour of your "pilgrimage holiday" display.

16 *Leviticus Rabbah* notes that "all sevenths are favorites in the world" (29:11). Among the favored seventh, the *midrash* includes Moses (the seventh Patriarch after Abraham, Isaac, Jacob, Levi, Kohath, and Amram), David (the seventh son), Asa (the seventh king of Judah), and the Sabbatical (seventh) year. How many examples of sevenths can you find in this portion? Are there other examples in the Torah? You may want to

use a concordance to help you find out. Create artistic representations for all the sevenths you find, and arrange a bulletin board display on this theme. Think about making a gigantic number seven — how about seven feet tall! All of the "sevenths" are then displayed on it.
Reference: *Encyclopaedia Judaica*, "Numbers, Typical and Important; Seven," Vol. 12, p. 1257.

OTHER RESOURCES

17 Read, act out, and discuss the skit for the portion *Emor* in *Sedra Scenes: Skits for Every Torah Portion* by Stan J. Beiner, pp. 145-148.

18 View and discuss the episode for *Emor* from *Torah Toons I: The Video*.

19 For creative movement activities, see "Etrog, Palm, Myrtle, and Willow" and "Sound the Shofar" from *Torah in Motion* by JoAnne Tucker and Susan Freeman, pp. 148-151.

20 Read and discuss the illustrated commentary for *Emor* in *American Torah Toons* by Lawrence Bush.

21 For other insights and activities about Passover, Rosh HaShanah, Yom Kippur, and Sukkot, see *Teaching Mitzvot* by Barbara Binder Kadden and Bruce Kadden.

22 For art projects related to the holidays described in *Emor*, see *An Artist You Don't Have to Be* by Joann Magnus with Howard Bogot.

INVOLVING THE FAMILY

23 With the destruction of the Temple and the dispersal of the Jewish people throughout the world, it is no longer possible or practical to observe the *Shalosh Regalim* by making a pilgrimage to "the Temple" in Jerusalem. As a family, think of some ways that the idea of Jerusalem could be incorporated into your observance of the *Shalosh Regalim.* These might include writing and/or reading special material, making and hanging posters and maps, participating in special *tzedakah* projects for Israel and Israeli foods related to each of the holidays. Plan to incorporate several of these in your next holiday celebration. For references, see Strategy #5, page 210. Also see *The Jewish Holiday Kitchen* by Joan Nathan.

BAR/BAT MITZVAH PROJECT

24 Each of the holidays described in this portion have come to be associated with particular *mitzvot.* Create a list of these *mitzvot.* Add to this list *tzedakah* ideas which will enable others,

such as the elderly, the poor, and the mentally or physically challenged also to fulfill the *mitzvot* of the holidays. Some things to consider investigating and, if possible, providing:

Large print prayer books, *Haggadot,* and synagogue newsletters.

TDD for the hearing impaired (see Deaf and Disabled Services in your local phone book).

Sign language interpreters.

Access to the *bimah.*

Extra wide doorways.

Levers instead of knobs in the sinks.

Food and other provisions for the holidays.

Gift certificates for clothing and/or food.

References: *Teaching Mitzvot* by Barbara Binder Kadden and Bruce Kadden; *The First Jewish Catalog* by Richard Siegel, Michael Strassfeld, and Sharon Strassfeld; *Seasons of Our Joy* by Arthur Waskow.

BEHAR 25:1-26:2 בהר

SYNOPSIS

MOSES SPEAKS TO THE ISRAELITES ABOUT some laws that are to take effect in the land that God will give them.

For six years, the people will be permitted to plant and harvest from their fields and vineyards. But the seventh year is to be a year of complete rest for the land. In the seventh year, the Israelites will not be permitted to work their fields, but they will be allowed to gather and to share whatever the land produces. God assures the people that in the year before the Sabbatical year, there will be a bountiful harvest so that there will be sufficient food to tide them over until the harvest of the eighth year.

The Israelites are told to count seven times seven years — a total of forty-nine — and to mark the arrival of the fiftieth year with a blast of the horn on the Day of Atonement. The fiftieth year is to be a Jubilee, a year of release for the land and all its inhabitants.

In the fiftieth year, the land is to lie fallow, property is to revert to its original owner, and all Hebrew slaves are to be freed. Houses in walled cities are exempt from this regulation — they can be redeemed for only one year after their sale. The houses of the Levites are to be redeemable forever.

The Israelites are to make special effort to redeem land or persons who have been forced to sell their holdings or bind themselves into slavery. Israelite slaves are to be treated as hired laborers and are to be freed in the Jubilee year, whereas non-Israelite slaves are seen as property — they are not subject to the laws of the Jubilee year.

The portion concludes with a reminder to the people not to set up or worship idols, but to keep God's Sabbaths.

INSIGHTS FROM THE TRADITION

A This portion is called *Behar* — on the Mount (Sinai) — the name of the location where these laws were given to Moses. *Behar* is usually read as a double portion with *Bechukotai*, which follows.

B The Sabbatical and Jubilee years are unique creations of the Torah. The laws of the Sabbatical and Jubilee years involve the release of slaves, the remission of debt (Deuteronomy 15: 1-3), the redemption of holdings, and the resting and "return" of the land to its one true owner, God. There are significant differences between the Sabbatical and Jubilee years.

The Sabbatical year, or Sabbath to *Adonai*, calls for the suspension of all agricultural activities and the cancellation of all debts. Several scholars felt that by not cultivating the fields, the Israelites were practicing an early form of soil conservation. The Rabbis, however, found moral lessons in this practice. Even though a person may "own" fields, he is not the true owner. The Sabbatical year makes a person realize that God is the ultimate owner. Secondly, this puts a wealthy person in a poor person's place. During the Sabbatical year, the rich have an opportunity to experience the needs of the poor. This, sensitizes the wealthy and encourages them to support the poor (*Yalkut Me'am Lo'ez* by Yaacov Culi, Vol. XII, pp. 245-6).

What other Jewish observances let us "relive" the experiences of other Jews?
How does this "reliving" help us grow as Jews and as human beings?
Imagine what life will be like for you in just seven years? Describe it.

C In *The Book of Legends: Sefer Ha-aggadah,* it is written that every man should strive to live in the land of Israel, even if it is in a city that has mostly heathens, and should avoid living outside the land even in a city that has mostly Jews. If one lives in the Land, that person is like one who has a God, but one who lives outside the Land is like one who has no God. The proof text cited is "To give you the land of Cannan, to be your God" (Leviticus 25:38). The *midrash* continues: "Is it possible that he who lives outside the Land has no God? No, but what Scripture means is that he who lives outside the Land is regarded as though he worshiped idols."

Not much of a Diaspora existed at the time this *midrash* was written. What kinds of circumstances might the biblical writer have been responding to?
Could this be one of those historical pieces that has had a great deal of influence on Israel/Diaspora relations for generations?

D "Why," the Rabbis asked, "does the Jubilee year begin on the tenth day of the seventh month (Yom Kippur) rather than on the New Year day itself?" They answered, "Just as the end of Yom Kippur marks a clean slate for the individual, so the Jubilee year marks a fresh start for society as a whole." Since the laws of the Jubilee year had the effect of remedying much injustice and inequality in society, the Jubilee year is an echo of creation, a time when humankind was innocent and the whole world was free from the consequences of human ownership. It is still customary among Jews to pay off any debts before Yom Kippur.

How do you make a fresh start for yourself?
Do you think the world could use a Jubilee year? Why? What kinds of laws or practices could be instituted so society could make a fresh start?

E Historical sources make clear that the Jubilee year was no longer observed by the time of the Second Temple. But the Sabbatical year remained in force at least through the Bar Kochba Revolt (*Sifra, Behar* 2:3). Several reasons have been given for non-observance of the Jubilee and Sabbatical years. As conditions worsened for the Jews because of the taxes the Romans placed on them, the Rabbis eased the restrictions. Also, once the majority of Jews were no longer living in the Promised Land, these laws could no longer be enforced.

Do you agree with the reasons stated above for giving up the practice of the Jubilee year?
If you were to leave the country in which you now live, what customs, laws, or celebrations would you have to abandon? What could you take with you?
What customs, laws and celebrations have the Jewish people been able to take with them no matter where they have gone?

F With the return of the Jews to Palestine in the late nineteenth and early twentieth centuries, the observance of the Sabbatical and Jubilee years became an issue. One of the great Rabbis of the time, Rabbi Isaac Elchanan Spektor of Kovno, advised the early farmers to "sell" their land to a non-Jew for the year so that they could continue to work the land. Today, the Chief Rabbi of Israel follows this practice on behalf of the entire State of Israel each Sabbatical year.
Here is a sampling of Sabbatical years: 5761 (2000-2001), 5768 (2007-2008), 5775 (2014-2015). What would be next in this sequence? Could you also calculate previous Sabbatical years from the first year given above?

Some occupations provide for a sabbatical — a one year leave for an employee from his/her job. If you were given a year in which to do whatever you wanted, what would you do with the time?
How might a professional person spend his/her sabbatical in a meaningful way?

G *Behar* tells us that it is a sin to demand interest on a loan and also to pay interest on a loan. This commandment regulated money transactions between Jews. Based on this teaching, many Jewish communities developed free loan associations. A few individuals would borrow a fixed amount and then repay that same amount. It is very important to note that Jews could take interest from or pay interest to non-Jews and vice-versa.

How did this interest restriction work against Jews? What image of Jews did this give to non-Jews? What would you do with an interest free loan for a year?

Note: *Behar* and *Bechukotai* are usually read as a double portion. For more about double portions, see Exodus, *Pikuday,* Insight A, page 155.

STRATEGIES

ANALYZING THE TEXT

1 In two teams, find all references in the Torah to the Sabbatical or Jubilee year (Exodus 23:10-11; Leviticus 25:1-7, 18-22; Leviticus 27:16-25; Numbers 36:4; Deuteronomy 15:1-11). Using a quiz show format, have the teams quiz each other to see how well team members have learned the details of the texts.

2 Study all the verses dealing with the Sabbatical year (see Strategy #1 immediately above) and those in the Book of Exodus relating to Shabbat (Exodus 16:21-30, 20:8-11, 23:12, 31:13-17, 34:21, 35:2-3). What parallels can you draw between the observances?

3 Compare the use of the two words עֲמִיתֶךָ (your neighbor) and אָחִיךָ (your brother) in *Behar.* How often, and in what context, is each word used? Are they intended to be understood literally? Are they interchangeable? What is the

effect and lesson of the use of each word in its context?

4 How does the Torah express concern for *both* parties in the buying and selling of land between Jubilees? How do the Sabbatical laws recognize that animals are entitled to the same treatment as human beings?

5 View "The Sabbath" from the video *Jewish Customs.* The video explains how the Sabbath is honored.

EXTENDING THE TEXT

6 On the Liberty Bell in Independence Hall in Philadelphia, are inscribed the words: "Proclaim liberty throughout the land unto all the inhabitants thereof." These words come from this portion. Locate them in the Bible. Read them in context. Do the words as used on the Liberty Bell convey an idea different from the sense of the words in their original context? Illustrate the words "Proclaim liberty throughout the land unto all the inhabitants thereof" with a symbol or design that is appropriate to the meaning and context of the words. Consider various media for your symbol or design: fabric, felt, a computer, a quick-set plaster available at craft and hobby shops, paints, markers, or another medium of your choice.

7 The laws of the Sabbatical year teach that the Land of Israel should not be "owned" in perpetuity by private individuals. Find out how this influenced the way in which the early twentieth century settlers in Palestine acquired land. Invite a speaker from Jewish National Fund (J.N.F.) to explain how it acquires land, how the land is used, and to whom it belongs.

8 *Behar* tells us twice that people are servants of God (Leviticus 25:42 and 55). In the text, these words seem to refer specifically to the treatment of slaves and servants. What are the implications of these words for our families, our friendships, our business dealings, and our relationships with people at our places of work?

9 Read Job 31:13-15. Compare Job's reasons for not ill-treating his servants with those given in *Behar* (see Leviticus 25:55). Which reason do you think would be the more effective one to persuade a person to act humanely toward servants? Why? (Adapted from *Studies in Vayikra* by Nehama Leibowitz, pp. 276-277.)

10 Invent a machine, technique, or innovation which would help the Israelites honor the Sabbath. Remember the people are not to light fire or do any kind of work. What might be most useful? Make a model of your invention, technique, or innovation and give a presentation to the group which details its function.

11 Read the *midrash* found in Insight C, page 215, before doing the following activity. *Midrash* often cites additional biblical verses to help prove the statements being made. This is called a proof text. In relation to this *midrash,* see Psalm 106:35. What is the proof text explaining? What does it mean to "learn the work of others?" Do you ever feel influenced by the "work of others?" Describe one or more situations in which this has occurred. Would you call this peer pressure? Try to find newspaper articles or information on the Internet that discusses Israel/Diaspora relations? What do you see as your role in all of this?

PERSONALIZING THE TEXT

12 This portion includes a reminder to the people not to set up and worship idols, but to keep God's Sabbaths. The people are not told simply to refrain from worshiping idols, but are reminded that they have very important tasks to do for the Sabbath. Here are a few impor-

tant tasks that you can do to help you honor the Sabbath.

a. Make a *Kiddush* cup or candlestick holders. Contact a ceramics shop to obtain bisque-ware goblets or candlestick holders and directions for completing them. Note: bisque-ware has already been fired once and is ready for painting and glazing.

b. Learn to make traditional Sabbath foods from different countries. One good reference is *The Jewish Holiday Kitchen* by Joan Nathan. Also check your family's cookbooks, and the synagogue and public libraries.

c. Participate in a Havdalah service for the close of the Sabbath.

13 The command "Do not wrong one another" is repeated twice in the portion *Behar* (Leviticus 25:14 and 25:17). According to the commentators, each statement refers to a different kind of "wrong." The first relates to all business transactions. The second warns against wrongdoing toward one another with words. In pairs, brainstorm a list of ways in which we wrong one another with words. Choose one of the examples on the list and prepare a role play to demonstrate it. Plan and act out a second role play in which the person doing wrong remembers the commandment and corrects or avoids his/her hurtful words and behavior.

14 Most Jews today do not have a life-style which would allow them to observe the Sabbatical year. How might observance of the Sabbatical year heighten our awareness of God and of creation? Prepare a creative service for the inauguration of a Sabbatical year to help contemporary Jews become aware of it and its lessons.

15 According to Henry George, who lived at the turn of the nineteenth century, "unqualified private ownership [of land] . . . [will] inevitably . . . separate the people into the very rich and the very poor" (quoted in *The Torah: A*

Modern Commentary, edited by W. Gunther Plaut, p. 951). Imagine you are Henry George advocating the adoption of the Sabbatical and Jubilee years to a nineteenth century audience. Prepare a pamphlet telling what advantages this practice has and how it would benefit humankind to observe it. Keep in mind what kinds of occupations most people had during the nineteenth century. You may need to do some library research in this area.

16 *Behar* deals with the theme of human enslavement. Today, many people are "enslaved" by their pursuit of material goods, which makes the lessons of Shabbat and the Sabbatical and Jubilee years all the more relevant. Create a collage contrasting the pursuit of material goods in our society with the values inherent in the idea of Shabbat.

17 Read Leviticus 25:23. If God is the *owner* of the earth, how would you describe our role? Are we tenants, superintendents, shareholders, managers, guests, stewards, or squatters? Look up these words in a dictionary so you have a clear understanding of what they mean. What other roles might we play? Choose the job title you think is most appropriate and write a job description for humankind.

18 Leviticus 25:23 states " . . . the land is Mine; you are but strangers resident with Me." This idea is beautifully expressed in Psalm 24:1: "The earth is the Lord's, and the fulness thereof; the world, and they that dwell in it." Write a poem expanding on this theme and create drawings in pastel chalks to illustrate it. Consider assembling everyone's poems and pictures together to make a long mural, then display it.

OTHER RESOURCES

19 Read, act out, and discuss the skit for the portion *Behar* in *Sedra Scenes: Skits for Every Torah Portion* by Stan J. Beiner, pp. 149-151.

20 View and discuss the episode for *Behar* from *Torah Toons I: The Video*.

21 For a creative movement activity, see "The Jubilee Year" from *Torah in Motion* by JoAnne Tucker and Susan Freeman, pp.152-3.

22 Read and discuss the illustrated commentary for *Be-Har* in *American Torah Toons* by Lawrence Bush.

INVOLVING THE FAMILY

23 Some occupations provide for a sabbatical — a one year leave for an employee from his or her job. This usually occurs after seven consecutive years have been worked. Imagine that your entire family was given a sabbatical year with a guaranteed income but no obligations for work or school. What does your family want to do? How would you use such a year? What goals would you set for yourselves? What activities would you plan? Hold a family round-table discussion to gather responses to these questions. Conclude by having each family member complete the following sentences:
A year of release from ____.
A year free of ____.
A year to return ____.
A year to allow ____.
A time for ____.
A time to ____.
A time with ____.
Have your family share their responses.

BAR/BAT MITZVAH PROJECT

24 In this portion there are several passages about the treatment of slaves during the Sabbatical and Jubilee years. Unfortunately, the freedom promised Israelite slaves does not extend to non-Israelites. The acceptance and promulgation of slavery among Jews is alarming if we look at it with contemporary eyes. By doing one or more of the following, you have the opportunity to do something about child labor and slavery in Asia.

a. View Ed Bradley's report which aired on *60 Minutes*. To order a tape of the April 21, 1996 show, call 1-800-848-3256.

b. Contact an organization called "Free the Children" to gather information and to become part of the effort to end child labor. Their website is: http://www.freethechildren. org.

c. Ask merchants, especially those who sell sporting goods, often made with child labor, to pressure manufacturers to end child labor.

d. Contact your government officials to help end child labor and slavery.

e. Provide financial support to schools which have been established for children freed from child labor.

f. Contact Rabbi Joel Soffin, Temple Shalom, 215 S. Hillside Ave., Succasunna, NJ 07876 or through the Internet at: soffins@aol.com for more information and for an address to send donations for the schools described above.

(Adapted from the ZIV Tzedakah Fund Annual Report of April 1, 1997.)

BECHUKOTAI 26:3-27:34 בחקתי

SYNOPSIS

BECHUKOTAI BEGINS WITH A PROMISE AND a curse. If the Israelites follow God's laws and commandments, God will bless them. Their land will be fertile and peaceful and their enemies will flee before them. But if the people do not obey, God will spurn and punish them. Their enemies will dominate them, their land will not produce, and they will live in fear. At last, those who survive the punishment will repent, and God will remember the covenant with Jacob, Isaac, and Abraham.

The Book of Leviticus concludes with a section detailing three types of gifts which might be promised to the sanctuary. The first type of gift consists of a promise to contribute a certain sum of money (specified in the text) equal to the valuation assigned to persons based on gender and age. For example, the amount to be given for a male of 60 years is 15 *shekels* and, for a female over this age, 10 *shekels*.

The second type of gift involved the giving of animals or property. Both were sold, and the proceeds went toward the maintenance of the sanctuary. Animals without blemish could be specified by the donor for use as a sacrifice. Gifts of this type are redeemable at their value as assessed by a priest, plus one-fifth.

The third type of contribution which a person dedicated to God (be it man, beast, or land) cannot be redeemed; everything thus given is totally consecrated to God.

The Book of Leviticus concludes with several verses on tithes and the redemption of tithes, and with the statement: "These are the commandments that *Adonai* gave to Moses for the Israelite people on Mount Sinai."

INSIGHTS FROM THE TRADITION

A *Bechukotai*, which means "My laws," is generally read as a double portion with the preceding portion, *Behar*.

B The final portion of the Book of Leviticus (along with a parallel portion in Deuteronomy 28) is known as the *tochechah* — a warning or reproof. Throughout Leviticus, the Israelites are admonished to be holy. In this portion, the consequences of obedience and disobedience are presented.

Many commentators have noted that the blessings that will follow observance of the commandments are described briefly in only ten verses (26:3-13), whereas the curses resulting from rejection of God's law are 28 verses long (26:14-42). Ibn Ezra tells us that the curses are spelled out in detail in order to frighten the hearers.

Would someone choose to follow the commandments because they wanted blessings and not curses, or because they or society would be better off?
Do you ever want to break the rules and not suffer the consequences? Is it possible to not suffer the consequences?
Why do you follow rules and regulations?
Do you always consider the consequences of your behavior?
What would happen to society if there were not consequences for breaking the rules?
For most people, is it the consequences that get them to follow the rules?

C A close reading of the text reveals that observance of the commandments will result in the people receiving many blessings at once, while the punishments are to be delivered in stages. This allows the people, by choosing either to repent or to continue in their disobedience, to determine the course of events.

What happens when you do something wrong for the first time?
If you repeat the behavior, does the punishment change? Should this be the case?

D Rabbi Hanina bar Papa was puzzled by the third phrase in Leviticus 26:1: "If you walk the path of My laws and guard My *mitzvot,* and *if you will do them . . .* " Logically, walking in the path of the *mitzvot* would mean that you are "doing them!" Rabbi Hanina's *midrash* explains that if we keep the same Hebrew letters in the word "*otam*" (them), but alter the vowels, we can read the word as "*atem.*" The last phrase then becomes "you shall make yourselves." In other words, he taught, if you strive to live a life full of *mitzvot,* you will be creating yourself in God's image.

Do you agree with the idea that people have the power to create themselves or their personalities in God's image?
How might striving to live a life full of *mitzvot* push you to shape your personality in a particular way?
Is it appropriate to use the *mitzvot* as a way of shaping your life, or should performance of the *mitzvot* have other purposes?

E Biblical passages such as the *tochechah* obviously cause uneasiness to those reading or hearing them. People, usually eager to be honored with an *aliyah,* were reluctant to be called to the Torah to bless the readings from this passage and from Deuteronomy 28:7-69. Therefore, the custom arose not to divide these verses into any more than one *aliyah* each, but rather to read them on their respective Sabbaths as one long *aliyah.* According to Bernard Bamberger, "This arrangement served a double purpose: the disturbing passage could be completed as quickly as possible and only one reluctant worshiper had to be persuaded to say the benedictions" (*The Torah: A Modern Commentary,* edited by W. Gunther Plaut, p. 954). Other customs evolved concerning these two *aliyot.* A person should not be called up by name for either of these *aliyot* and only a person who wants one of these *aliyot* should be called up (*Yalkut Me'am Lo'ez* by Yaacov Culi, Vol. XII, p. 304).

Why would a person be reluctant to be called up for these sections of the Torah?

Would it bother you to be called up for one of these *aliyot*? Why or why not?

F The section in *Bechukotai* describing the evils that will befall the Israelites should they spurn God's rules ends with a passage allowing for their atonement. God promises not to break the covenant with the people even while they are enduring the punishment of exile. This passage, containing as it does a reference to God's covenant with Abraham, Isaac, and Jacob, is bound up with the Talmudic idea of *zechut avot* — the merit of the fathers. According to this concept, the merit of the Patriarchs and the great love which God had for them help to "tip the balance" of God's judgment in favor of the Israelites even at times when they err severely. The fact that the Patriarchs are mentioned in reverse order in verse 26:42 is seen as a reflection of this. According to *Leviticus Rabbah* 36:5, " . . . If there were no good deeds in Jacob, then Isaac's would suffice, and if Isaac's deeds did not suffice, then Abraham's would suffice; in fact, the deeds of each one alone would suffice for the whole world to be kept suspended in its position on account of their merit."

In what respects do you benefit from the merit of your ancestors? your parents? your relatives?

G The final chapter of *Bechukotai* details gifts to the sanctuary. Some scholars think that this chapter is a later addition to the Book of Leviticus for which the *tochechah* seems the logical conclusion. Rashbam explained the placement of the *tochechah* before the final chapter because of its association with the preceding portion, *Behar.* Both portions mention the Sabbatical year. According to Hertz (*The Pentateuch and Haftorahs,* p. 547), however, the concluding chapter of Leviticus serves to round out the entire book which begins and ends with laws pertaining to gifts given for the maintenance of the sanctuary.

What gifts were these? If you could have given a gift at that time, what gift would it have been and why?

STRATEGIES

ANALYZING THE TEXT

1 How many distinct blessings are there in *Bechukotai*? How many distinct sections detailing curses can you find? (Clue: They all begin with the words "If you will not/don't obey . . . ")

2 Down one side of a page, list the blessings found in this portion. (Leave room between each blessing.) Now read through the curses and list them beside the blessing whose "flip side" they represent. Is there more than one curse to match each blessing? If so, rank order the curses from the least to most severe. Note when, according to the text, the most severe curses will be delivered, that is after how many warnings? For a follow-up activity, see Strategy #12 on the following page.

EXTENDING THE TEXT

3 According to Bernard Bamberger in the commentary to Leviticus (*The Torah: A Modern Commentary*, p. 956), the closing section of Chapter 26 of *Bechukotai* is "one of the classic passages about *teshuvah*," meaning return or repentance. From verses 39-46, the text presents three sources of hope that the people can hold to even when their survival seems entirely unlikely. Identify these three sources (verse 39 – repentance; verse 42 – the merits of the Patriarchs; verse 43 – God's covenant with Israel), and explain how these ideas have been incorporated into Jewish tradition. How is the idea of *zechut avot*, the merit of the Patriarchs, incorporated into our liturgy? What is the message of the High Holy Days regarding repentance? What does the text suggest about the nature of the covenant between God and Israel?

References: For more about repentance, see *The Rosh Hashanah Anthology* and *The Yom Kippur Anthology* by Phillip Goodman.

4 In what ways were Abraham, Isaac, and Jacob so meritorious as to be able to influence God to spare the Jewish people from punishment? Can you think of other individuals in Jewish history on whose merit the entire Jewish people might be judged? Write a prayer which recalls the memory of one of these people. References: *Jewish Heroes and Heroines of America: 101 True Stories of American Jewish Heroism* by Seymour Brody; *Jewish Heroes and Heroines: Their Unique Achievements* by Darryl Lyman.

5 *Bechukotai* specifies a number of blessings that will be bestowed on the Israelites if they obey God's laws. The Rabbis were puzzled, however, by the fact that the Torah does not mention the spiritual rewards of leading a holy life. One explanation for this is that people cannot attain happiness and peace if they are sick or hungry, or in the midst of war or other trying times. Therefore, the Torah speaks about material blessings not as the ultimate goal, but as a means of achieving the rewards of the spirit. To the section of *Bechukotai* which tells about the material blessing, write an addendum detailing the spiritual rewards for the people "If [you] follow My laws and faithfully observe My commandments" (26:3).

6 The blessings and curses of *Bechukotai* are expressed in beautiful poetic language. Read through Leviticus 26:3-38 and simplify the text. Write one or two key words to summarize the content of each blessing or curse. Using this summary as your outline, rewrite a section of *Bechukotai* in poetic language and images that would be especially meaningful to contemporary readers.

7 Leviticus 27:28-30 uses the word "*cherem*" to explain that things *set aside* for God must never be put to any other use. In later times, this word was used by the Rabbis to pronounce a ban of "excommunication" upon a person who had committed an important violation of community standards. How can we understand this word today? Answer the following questions: Are there things about yourself that you would like to "set aside" when you enter a place of worship? Think of some positive, as well as negative interpretations of this question. For example, you may want to "set aside" your contemplative side and bring it out only when you pray; you may want to "set aside" the selfish aspects of your personality when you pray. How did the use of the word "*cherem*" change from a positive meaning to a negative punishment in the explanations given above? Can you figure out how this transformation may have come about?

8 The *Haftarah* for *Bechukotai* is Jeremiah 16:19-17:14. Read verses 17:5-8. Explain why this *Haftarah* is appropriate for *Bechukotai*. Think of some other poetic metaphors for the accursed and the blessed. Illustrate them under headings taken from Jeremiah 17:5 and 17:7.

PERSONALIZING THE TEXT

9 How do you relate to the content of the portion *Bechukotai*? Write a journal entry explaining the way you feel as you read the blessings and curses. Are you fearful? Threatened? Indifferent? Explain. Do you take these passages literally or figuratively? Do you think your reaction is the same as, or different from, that of earlier generations of Jews? Do the blessings and curses depict things that have actually happened in Jewish history?

10 The last verses of *Bechukotai* concern gifts pledged toward the upkeep of the sanctuary. With the destruction of the Second Temple, these laws went out of force. Are there contemporary parallels to these vows? Could our voluntary donations to Jewish organizations be understood in this light? Invite the synagogue president or a board member to explain how modern day synagogues need and use pledged gifts for the upkeep of the synagogue.

11 The laws concerning gifts to the sanctuary were structured in such a way that even the poor could contribute. The text specifies that "if one cannot afford (the equivalent) . . . the priest shall assess him according to that which a person can afford" (27:8). Rashi explains that "[the priest shall] assess him, leaving him sufficient to live upon: a bed, mattress, cushion, and tools necessary for his trade." What would be the contemporary equivalent of "sufficient to live upon?" Make a list of the necessities of daily life today.

12 Analyze the blessings in this portion and make a series of felt banners that illustrate the blessings.

13 Find pictures in magazines which illustrate the blessings and curses described in this portion. Mount the illustrations which depict opposite conditions side-by-side with the appropriate texts written out underneath. For instance, mount Leviticus 26:4, "The earth shall yield its produce" next to Leviticus 26:20, "Your land shall not yield its produce."

14 Ibn Ezra understood the promise of "peace in the land" (Leviticus 26:6) to mean that the Israelites would have peace among themselves, though not necessarily with their neighbors. Write a series of guidelines for a national leader who wished to promote peace among the people of his/her nation. What social problems would have to be eliminated? What attitudes should be encouraged?

15 Leviticus 26:42 makes mention of Abraham, Isaac, and Jacob. God's promise to the Patriarchs and the memory of their righteousness serve as a source of hope to the desolated Israelites (see Insight F, page 221). Stage a scene in which the Patriarchs and Matriarchs plead with God to look favorably upon the Jewish people.

16 Several times in the Torah, blessings and curses are set before the Israelites (see also Exodus 23:20-33, Deuteronomy 28). Which do you think is a more effective way of eliciting good behavior — the promise of rewards to follow good behavior, or the threat of bad consequences in the case of undesirable behavior?

17 The image of God as the Judge of Israel has been expressed using a variety of metaphors. There is the image of a hand writing in a book, of a king sitting on the throne of judgment, and of a shopkeeper with a ledger. What other metaphors would express this idea? Design and make a greeting card for Rosh HaShanah on this theme. What words should be printed inside the card in keeping with the theme? What about the design and illustration of the front of the card? You may want to refer to a High Holy Day prayer book for additional ideas.

(For more, see the Index: "Blessing/Curse," "*Zechut Avot/Zechut Imahot.*")

OTHER RESOURCES

18 Read, act out, and discuss the skit for the portion *Bechukotai* in *Sedra Scenes: Skits for Every Torah Portion* by Stan J. Beiner, pp. 152-153.

19 View and discuss the episode for *Bechukotai* from *Torah Toons I: The Video.*

20 For creative movement activities, see "Reward and Punishment" and "Clearing Out the Old" from *Torah in Motion* by JoAnne Tucker and Susan Freeman, pp. 154-157.

21 Read and discuss the illustrated commentary for *Bechukotai* in *American Torah Toons* by Lawrence Bush.

INVOLVING THE FAMILY

22 Taking Leviticus 26:4-13 as your starting point, discuss the ways in which your family is blessed. Are there blessings which you have that are not mentioned in the text? Are there ways in which you consider our society blessed? Make a blessings poster to hang in a conspicuous place in your home to serve as a reminder of all the good things that have happened to your family. As more blessings are remembered and more blessings happen, add them to the poster. There is also the tradition to give *tzedakah* when good and bad things happen. Consider adding these elements to your family *tzedakah* collection.

BAR/BAT MITZVAH PROJECT

23 *Bechukotai* describes the many kinds of gifts that might be brought to the sanctuary. To this day, Jews often make donations of specific items such as art or furniture to the sanctuary. Find out what sorts of gifts people have made to the sanctuary where you will celebrate becoming a Bar or Bat Mitzvah. Interview individuals or groups who have made gifts to the sanctuary and the synagogue in general. Do not think of just material or financial gifts; include gifts of volunteer time, serving on committees, being part of the synagogue Board of Directors, and teaching in the Religious School. Consider what role(s) you would eventually like to take on within your synagogue community.

To complete this project, design and make an honor roll book of synagogue members who have contributed in all the ways described above to help in the upkeep of the synagogue. Include a page for yourself and list ways in which you support your synagogue. Challenge the other Bar/Bat Mitzvah students to add their own pages.

A further step to take would be to determine if the sanctuary was in need of any particular item. In consultation with your parents and the Rabbi, decide what gift you can make to the sanctuary in honor of your celebration.

REVIEW ACTIVITIES FOR LEVITICUS

1 Using Leviticus as your main source of information (but referring to other books of the Torah if necessary), write a pamphlet for home use about the biblical origins of the Jewish holidays.

2 Imagine you are one of the founding members of a totally new society. Set up a working panel to create a code of social legislation for your society. Use the Book of Leviticus as your chief reference, examining and discussing its laws for possible incorporation into your code.

3 Play "This is the Law." Divide into teams of 4 to 6 players. Each team chooses a law from Leviticus. With a wordless skit, dramatize a scene in which the law is being broken. Don't make it too obvious! When the skit is presented before the other groups, they must isolate the law which is being violated. (Have the audience do this in writing so that everyone can guess it once.) Award points for correctly identifying the law.

4 In earlier times, the Book of Leviticus was the first book of the Torah which children were taught. It was thought that children who were themselves "pure" should first learn laws of purity and holiness. Today, most children are first introduced to the Torah through the accounts of the Book of Genesis. Write a report to your principal advocating a return to the earlier practice. Based on what you have learned about Leviticus, explain your reasoning.

5 Design a title page for Leviticus based on your impressions of this book of the Torah.

6 Imagine you are a teacher who wants to teach the Book of Leviticus in depth to students. The principal of your school objects to spending so much time on this particular book of the Torah, citing as his/her reasons that the material in Leviticus is too difficult and that it is more important to focus on other books of the Torah. Write a letter to the principal asking him/her to reconsider. Give your reasons for wanting to teach students about the sacrifices, laws, and holidays detailed in Leviticus.

7 According to the Rabbis, Leviticus contains nearly half (247) of the 613 commandments. In groups, list as many Levitical commandments as you can remember. Make a master list by combining the lists of the various groups. How many commandments did all of you together remember? If you like, follow this up by actually searching the text of Leviticus for commandments. Compare the list obtained by searching with the list made from memory. Then compare your master list with that of the Rambam (see *Encyclopaedia Judaica*, Vol. 5, pp. 660ff.).

8 Which of the Levitical commandments is most significant for you personally? Why? Design a poster which describes and interprets that law. Make a display of all of the posters.

Note: For additional concluding activities applicable to Leviticus, see the Review Activities in this volume for the other biblical books.

OVERVIEW

Since the desert is the setting for the entire narrative of the Book of Numbers, the Hebrew name of this book is called *BaMidbar* (In the Desert). In the Talmud, however, the book is given a different name — *Chumash HaPekudim* (The Book of Those Numbered). This name corresponds closely to the English title and gives an important clue about the book's contents — lists.

There is a listing for each census, for places of encampment, for orders of the march, for gifts brought to the Tabernacle, and for priestly roles. In each list, the attention to detail is meticulous.

The giving of laws is not a particular focus in Numbers. Where laws are presented, they tend to be in the nature of "case law," i.e., a general rule derived from a specific case. Examples of this are the cases of the inheritance of the daughters of Zelophehad, and the punishment of one who breaks Sabbath rules.

In Numbers, the final material about the Tabernacle is presented. While the Book of Exodus details the construction of the Tabernacle, and Leviticus tells of its consecration, Numbers describes the arrangements necessary for moving the Tabernacle. Nachmanides suggested that, whereas in Exodus and Leviticus, Sinai as a place gives focus and direction to the people, in Numbers the Tabernacle is intended to be a sort of "mobile Sinai."

There are those who theorize that the Book of Deuteronomy is a later addition to the Torah. If this is the case, the Book of Numbers at one time marked the end of the account of the Exodus. And, indeed, Numbers does tell briefly of the Israelites arrival at the end of their journey, of Moses' impending death, and of the appointment of Joshua as the new leader (see Overview of the Book of Deuteronomy, page 291).

The events in the Book of Numbers take place after the revelation at Sinai and after most of the laws are already in place. Therefore, transgressions and lapses of faith which went unpunished according to the Book of Exodus meet with punishment here. Numbers contains the only extant material about the sojourn in Sinai. However, it is not a heroic record. One writer has referred to Numbers as the "Book of Israel's Failings" because of its constant theme of rebellion and relapse. Another author notes, however, that despite the frequency with which individuals, families, and even the larger community fail to live up to the standards set in Exodus and Leviticus, Numbers has a hopeful note of recurrent opportunity about it. After spending 40 years in the desert, the Israelite people survive to fulfill the promise of the Book of Genesis — entry into the Promised Land.

BAMIDBAR 1:1-4:20 במדבר

SYNOPSIS

ON THE FIRST DAY OF THE THIRTEENTH month following the Exodus from Egypt, God commands Moses to take a census of all the Israelite males over 20 years of age who are able to bear arms. Moses and Aaron and the heads of each tribe record the census. The total counted is 603,550.

The Levites, however, are counted in a separate census, since they are not to bear arms. Moses assigns to them specific duties for the care of the Tabernacle. They are to camp around the Tabernacle to guard it. The rest of the Israelites are told to camp in four groups of three tribes under their ancestral banners around the Tabernacle.

Originally, firstborn Israelites were consecrated to God, since they escaped the plague of the death of all firstborn in Egypt. Now, God tells Moses to appoint the Levites as priests in place of the firstborn. Twenty-two thousand male Levites over one month old are counted by Moses and Aaron. They are assigned to help Aaron and his sons Eleazar and Ithamar with the work of the Tabernacle.

Moses also counts all the firstborn males over one month old among the rest of the Israelite population — a total of 22,273. A redemption price of five *shekels* per head is collected and paid to Aaron and his sons for the 273 firstborn Israelites in excess of the male Levites.

A separate census is taken of the Kohathite clan of the Levites which is given the task of carrying the sacred objects and their furnishings on the journeys of the people. The Kohathites are cautioned not to touch any of the sacred objects or furnishings of the Tabernacle. Aaron and his sons are charged with the job of covering and inserting poles into all the objects in the Tabernacle in preparation for the Kohathite porterage.

Finally, Eleazar, the son of Aaron, is made responsible for the Tabernacle and all its furnishings.

INSIGHTS FROM THE TRADITION

A The name of this portion, which is also the Hebrew name given to the Book of Numbers, is *BaMidbar* — In the Desert. This title is particularly appropriate because the desert is the setting of this book. (See also the Overview to the Book of Numbers, page 227.)

The English title, Numbers, is a direct translation of the Greek *Arithmoi*. This name refers to the several census takings found in this book.

Israelites were to be known by the house of their fathers. Rashi explained that one whose father belongs to one tribe and whose mother to another shall take a place with the father's tribe. This custom holds to this day. One's standing as a Kohen, Levite, or Israelite derives from the father's side.

From whom did you get your last name? What is the meaning or origin of that name?
Do you or any of your acquaintances use both parents' names? What is the significance of using both parents' names?

B The Hebrew name of the Book of Numbers, *BaMidbar,* is also an apt title for the *kind* of events this book relates. *BaMidbar* is a book of rebellion, betrayal, and complaining. It is an extended story in which the Israelites lack unity and a sense of purpose, and Moses' leadership is challenged. It tells of a series of crises between times when the people were united in experience and goals: the escape from Egypt and the giving of the Torah in Exodus, and the entry into the Promised Land at the end of Deuteronomy. *BaMidbar* does not always present a flattering picture of the people, but its stories are important nonetheless. The wilderness experience helped shape the people and the laws which governed them.

What kind of life experiences would you call "wilderness" experiences?

How are such experiences important to the growth of individuals and groups?

C The Rabbis of earlier times did not question the census figures presented in *BaMidbar*. They did inquire, however, as to why the Torah presents such elaborate records of the census, recording not only the total fighting force, but also the numbers of each tribe.

One commentary tells us that God commanded the Israelites to be counted because something which is counted cannot lose identity and impact even when outnumbered a thousand to one (*Yalkut Me'am Lo'ez* by Yaacov Culi, Vol. XIII, p. 9).

Our tradition stresses the value and importance of each individual. What makes you especially valuable and important?
How can you help family members or classmates feel special and important?

D The Levites were not included in this first census found in the Book of Numbers. This census was of a military nature and it excluded women and children. The Levites, aside from Aaron, were exempt from fighting wars, for they had not participated in the incident of the Golden Calf. They had, however, been the fighting force which killed the idolators. Therefore, God singled out the tribe of Levi to serve in the Tabernacle (*The Torah: A Modern Commentary*, edited by W. Gunther Plaut, pp. 1028 and 1031).

Can you see a difference between fighting in a religious war and fighting in a national war?
Can you see yourself as a soldier? React.

E The description of the tribes, how they camped, and the way they marched under their tribal standards (flags) evokes a sense of pageantry and grand display. Based on these tribal standards, the custom of national flags developed (*Numbers Rabbah* 2:7). The Rabbis placed a great deal of importance on this passage about the standards. They felt that the Israelites knew their ancestry and their families due to this custom.

What enables you to know about your ancestors? What more would you like to know about your family history? Why?
Has your family traced its roots?
If you could choose any relative living or dead to interview, who would it be and why? What information would you want to know? What kinds of questions would you ask?

F Three significant Jewish traditions derive from this portion (see Insights G and H immediately below). Numbers 2:2 states that the Israelites were to camp at a distance from the Tent of Meeting. In Joshua 3:4, this distance is given as 2,000 cubits, approximately 3,000'. *Numbers Rabbah* 11:9 uses these sources as proof texts for the "Sabbath Walking-limit," the distance that one may walk beyond one's habitation on the Sabbath day.

If, according to Jewish law, one may only walk a distance of 3,000' beyond one's house on the Sabbath, how might that affect the size and shape of Jewish communities? What facilities have to be centrally located?
Are contemporary Jewish communities organized with an eye toward walking distances? Would such an arrangement be limiting or would it have positive effects?
What changes would you like to see in the size of your Jewish community or in the location of its agencies?

G In Numbers 2:1, we find one of the 18 times in the Torah that God addresses Moses and Aaron together. This number corresponds to the number of blessings in the *Amidah*. The *Amidah* describes a number of different roles which God fulfills. One of them is as "Redeemer" of the people Israel.

How did Moses and Aaron help God to "redeem" the people? Describe each of their different roles in the redemption process.

In another role, God is the source of "Revelation." In what way did Moses also play a role in the Revelation?

In the *Amidah,* God is described as the "Source of Peace." Aaron is associated with this attribute. Cite an example in which Aaron displayed the quality of peacemaker.

Which of the above roles would you be best at? Does being Jewish give you a special responsibility to fulfill any or all of these roles?

H When Moses takes a count of the Levites, he records "every male among them from the age of one month up" (Numbers 3:15). Our Rabbis, of blessed memory, said: Why was it necessary to number them from the age of one month and not earlier? Because an infant of one day old is not definitely viable, but one of a month old is definitely known to be viable . . . (*Numbers Rabbah* 3:8).

In Jewish tradition, if an infant dies before reaching one month old, no funeral or mourning practices are observed. It can also be noted that one month of age is the time of the *Pidyon HaBen* ceremony, the redemption of the firstborn.

Originally, all the firstborn among the Israelites were to be dedicated to God. But since the Levites came to hold an elevated position, their firstborn took the places of the Israelite firstborn.

In this portion, it was pointed out that there were 273 more Israelite firstborn than there were Levites. Each of these additional Israelite firstborn was to be redeemed by paying five coins, but from which of the 22,273 Israelites should the money be collected? A *midrash* tells us that Moses used lots — 22,000 read "A Levite has already redeemed you" and the other 273 read "Give the five *sela'im* which you owe" (*Numbers Rabbah* 4:10).

Do you think this was a fair way to resolve the situation? Would you have chosen the same method as Moses?

Can you suggest other solutions? Have you ever drawn lots or straws? What were the circumstances?

Considering modern medical technology, is it still accurate to consider an infant of less than one month not viable?

If an infant this age is not accorded a funeral or mourning rites, are the parents being denied an opportunity to grieve, or is it best that public grieving be cut short?

Who would you talk to about a loss in your life? (For more, see the Index: *"Pidyon HaBen."*)

I The Rabbis commented on the care with which the Torah assigned specific tasks to the Levites. Rabbi Eleazar thought that this was because, given a choice, the Levites would shirk the *more difficult* duties in favor of those demanding less responsibility. On the other hand, Rabbi Samuel felt that had the tasks not been carefully delineated, the easier duties might go undone in favor of those involving more responsibility and, therefore, more prestige. For this reason, Numbers 4:19 states: "Let Aaron and his sons go in and assign each of them [Levitical clans] to his duties and his porterage" (*Numbers Rabbah* 5:1).

Whose interpretation do you favor? Why?

Have you ever been part of a large group in which each person was assigned a task? Did everyone think the assignments were fair?

Is it really possible in a group situation to let people choose their own assignment? Why or why not?

Do you tend to tackle easy tasks first and leave the difficult ones for later, or do you tend to do just the opposite?

STRATEGIES

ANALYZING THE TEXT

1 The death of Aaron's sons, Nadab and Abihu, is mentioned here in *BaMidbar* (3:4), as well as in other passages of the Torah (Leviticus 10:2, 16:1; Numbers 26:61). The *midrash* explains that this is evidence that God "grieved" for them. In each instance where their death is mentioned, their offense is also cited: "They offered alien fire." The *midrash* points out that it was only for this reason that they died (*Numbers Rabbah* 2:23 and 24). (For strategies, see the Index: "Nadab and Abihu.")

2 Review the names of the 12 tribes of Israel. Use the information in this portion to draw a family tree showing how each of the princely leaders named in *BaMidbar* could trace his ancestry back to Abraham. You will have to skip the generations intervening between the prince's fathers and their tribal founders. Refer to Genesis 46:8-26 for help.

EXTENDING THE TEXT

3 American census reports are generally available at public libraries. Locate one and examine it to find out what kind of information is reported in a contemporary census. How does the census taken in *BaMidbar* compare? Obviously, the biblical census is not as detailed, but it does still provide a certain amount of information about the Israelite society. Follow this up with Strategy #10, page 233.

4 The Rabbis traced the origins of several of our liturgical traditions to our ancestors. Abraham, Isaac, and Jacob are credited with creating the three daily worship services. To Moses and Aaron, who are mentioned on equal footing 18 times in the Torah, the Rabbis attributed the custom of reciting the 18 benedictions in the central part of the worship service. In a *Siddur,* look up the *Amidah* prayer, also known as the *Shemoneh Esray* — The "Eighteen." Count the number of benedictions it contains. How many are there? Can you explain the reason for the discrepancy between the prayer's name and the actual number of blessings it contains?
References: *To Pray as a Jew* by Hayim Donin; *Teaching Tefilah* by Bruce Kadden and Barbara Binder Kadden, pp. 55-63.

5 Use the description in this portion as the basis for making a three-dimensional diorama of the Israelite camp. Read the portion carefully to determine the overall layout of the camp; see also the diagram in *The Torah: A Modern Commentary,* edited by W. Gunther Plaut, p. 1027. In constructing your miniature model, include the tents and whatever other items you think might have been part of the camp, such as storage tents, areas for the animals, place for the Tabernacle, etc.

6 The reading of *parashah BaMidbar* always occurs close to Shavuot. Can you think of any way to connect the holiday which marks the giving of the Torah with this portion? Write a *D'var Torah* exploring this connection and deliver it on Shabbat *BaMidbar.*

PERSONALIZING THE TEXT

7 Rashi was puzzled by the fact that verse 3:1 states that what follows is "the line of Aaron and Moses," when, in the following verses, only *Aaron's sons* are named. Why does the Torah state that both Aaron and Moses were the fathers of the priests? Sometimes the word "father" has more than a literal meaning. Moses was father to Aaron's sons, and they were his "line," in a special way. Are there people in your life who have "parented" you, i.e., contributed to your growth and development in important ways? To explore this idea, write a letter of thanks to one of these individuals, explaining how he/she has helped and influenced you. Choose whether or not you want to share this letter.

8 Find out how the ancient tribal and priestly divisions persist symbolically today. Invite a member of your congregation who is a *Kohen* or a *Levi* to explain to you how his/her family traces its roots back to their ancestral roles. What special privileges and responsibilities does this status confer? (See also the Insight C for Numbers, *Naso*, page 235, and Strategy #12 for Leviticus, *Emor*, page 212.)

9 Each of us is sometimes eager to choose the easier tasks and sometimes anxious to take on a more responsible role (see Insight I, page 231). Complete the following sentences:
I look for the easy way out when _____ .
I look for the easy way out because _____ .
I opt for the harder tasks when _____ .
I opt for the harder tasks because _____ .
Conclude by giving one example of a time you felt proud about a responsibility you were given and how you carried it out.

10 Based on Strategy #3, page 232, design your own census questionnaire and take a census of your school, camp, congregation, or neighborhood. Compile and collate the results, then write a report about your findings.

11 Great controversy surrounds the question "When does life begin?" The views in modern society run the gamut from those who believe that human life begins at the moment of conception to those who place the beginning of life after delivery. The traditional Jewish view discussed in Insight H, page 231, is concerned with the *viability* of human life. Modern medicine is making great strides toward assuring viability for all newborn babies, even those who are premature. Does the idea that an infant is viable only at one month of age still have significance? Examine

the following mini-course to help you formulate an answer: *Bioethics: A Jewish View* by James Simon, Raymond A. Zwerin, and Audrey Friedman Marcus.

12 The census recorded in Numbers was taken of all males able to bear arms. Since women were not allowed to fight, they were not counted. The issue of whether women should serve in combat units is still being debated today. Some say that in order for women to be truly equal to men, they must share equal responsibility for military defense. Others believe that women, being mothers of children, should take on a special role as advocates of peace. What do you think? Organize a debate on this subject.

13 According to *BaMidbar,* the Levites were not counted as part of the general census because their special role in maintaining the Tabernacle exempted them from military duty. Are there groups in society today in North America and/or in Israel who are routinely exempted from serving in the army? Are they required to serve in some other capacity? Invite a guest speaker from a local enlistment center to discuss the current policy of military service with your group (see also Deuteronomy 20:5-8).

14 Numbers 2:2 states that the Israelites encamped around the Tabernacle in tribal groups under flags or banners. Although no record detailing these banners survives, there are *midrashim* which attempt to describe them. Read some of these in *Legends of the Jews* by Louis Ginzberg, Vol. III, pp. 220ff., 237-8. Use one description as the basis for recreating the banner of one tribe. Use pieces of cut felt ornamented with such things as buttons and glitter, and put the banner together with a sewing machine. Another option would be to paint on plain cotton muslin.

15 According to *BaMidbar,* a blue cloth was to be used to cover the implements of the

Tabernacle before the Tabernacle was moved (Numbers 4:1). What do you think is the significance of the color blue? What might it symbolize? Create an artistic depiction of the different qualities of the color blue as it appears on various objects whose use the color blue recalls.

16 Make a title page for the Book of Numbers based on your first impression of the book. When you complete your study of Numbers, do a second, more representative title page (see Review Activity #5 for the Book of Numbers, page 290). Compare the two versions.

OTHER RESOURCES

17 View and discuss the episode for *BaMidbar* from *Torah Toons I: The Video*.

18 Read, act out, and discuss the skit for the portion *BaMidbar* in *Sedra Scenes: Skits for Every Torah Portion* by Stan J. Beiner, pp. 154-156.

19 For more insights and activities about *Pidyon Shivuyim*, see *Teaching Mitzvot* by Barbara Binder Kadden and Bruce Kadden, Chapter 8.

20 For a creative movement activity, see "In the Wilderness" from *Torah in Motion* by JoAnne Tucker and Susan Freeman, pp. 162-163.

21 Read and discuss the illustrated commentary for *Be-Midbar* in *American Torah Toons* by Lawrence Bush.

INVOLVING THE FAMILY

22 In *BaMidbar*, the names of the men appointed to help Moses with the census are given, along with a brief genealogy (Numbers 1:5-16). What purpose is served by giving a person's name together with his father's (parents') name? How does this practice reflect Jewish attitudes toward family and history? Find out your full Hebrew name. Create a plaque for your bedroom door bearing your Hebrew name.

BAR/BAT MITZVAH PROJECTS

23 The theme of redemption is important in Jewish tradition. The *mitzvah* of *Pidyon HaBen*, Redemption of the Firstborn, is incumbent upon Jewish families whose firstborn child is a son. *Pidyon Shivuyim*, the redemption or ransoming of the captive, is regarded by the Rabbis as an extremely important *mitzvah*. According to *halachah*, a person who is able to perform this *mitzvah* and does not do so is counted as a murderer of the person in captivity. In the last decades, the Jewish community has been involved with the redemption of the captive Jews of Ethiopia. To learn more about this work, its history, and what you can do to help today, contact: North American Conference on Ethiopian Jewry, 165 East 56th Street, New York, NY 10022.

Also see one or more of the following videos: *The Falashas, Operation Moses, Again . . . The Second Time*.

24 Another explanation given for the fact that in Numbers 3:1 both Aaron and Moses are named as fathers of the priests (see Strategy #7, page 232), is that Moses was the teacher of the priests. According to the Talmud, "one who teaches a child Torah is credited as if he or she had brought the child into the world" (*Sanhedrin* 19b). As a new Bar or Bat Mitzvah, decide what will be your commitment to teaching and learning Torah. Make a pledge not only to continue to learn, but to teach as well. Explore the possibilities for volunteering with the principal of your Religious School.

NASO 4:21-7:89   נשא

SYNOPSIS

GOD TELLS MOSES TO COUNT ALL MALES ages 30 to 50 of the Gershonite and Merarite clans of the Levites. Each clan is assigned specific porterage duties for the Tabernacle. The total number of Levites thus subject to duty and porterage for the Tabernacle is 8,580.

Moses goes on to remind the Israelites to remove any persons who are ritually unclean from the camp. He tells them that a person who wrongs another person is to make restitution for the full amount plus one-fifth.

The test for a woman accused by her husband of adultery is then described. The accused is given a mixture of earth from the Tabernacle and water and ink from a scroll of curses to drink. The priest pronounces a curse over her, declaring that if she is innocent, the water will not harm her, but if she is guilty, the water will cause her thigh to sag and her belly to distend. Thus, an innocent woman will remain unharmed, whereas an adulterous woman's guilt will be obvious.

The restrictions incumbent upon any man or woman who takes a Nazirite vow are described. Nazirites must refrain from drinking wine or alcohol. They must not cut their hair or come into contact with the dead. At the end of their vow period, Nazirites are to bring a special offering to the Tent of Meeting which the priest will offer in sacrifice.

God tells Moses to teach Aaron a special threefold blessing which he is to use when he blesses the people of Israel.

The portion goes on to tell in great detail how Moses accepts gifts from the heads of all 12 tribes when he consecrates the Tabernacle. Among the gifts given are carts and oxen for the Levites to use when they transport the Tabernacle. The Kohathite clan does not share in the gifts, however, since the sacred objects for which they are responsible could be carried only on their shoulders.

INSIGHTS FROM THE TRADITION

A *Naso* means literally "lift up." It is the Hebrew word with which God instructs Moses to "take a count" of the Gershonite clan. *Naso* is the longest portion in the Torah, having 176 verses.

B The Torah distinguishes between two groups of Levites — *Kohanim* were to be the priests who would officiate at the sacrificial worship, and *Levi'im* were subordinate to the priests and would serve as their helpers. The tribe of Levi descends from the third son of Jacob and Leah. In the Book of Numbers, these descendants are divided into three clans or families: Kohathites, Merarites, and Gershonites. Each is given a specific set of duties to be performed in service to the Tabernacle and the priests. The priesthood itself was a hereditary position, devolving on the direct descendants of Aaron, who was also a member of the tribe of Levi.

After enumerating the Levites by their clans, the text sums up all of their numbers together. They were numbered in detail and then numbered as a whole. This is like a person who owns some special treasured objects and counts them separately, and then counts them again all together simply for the pleasure of counting them many times. Likewise, God commanded that the number of Levites be recorded both in detail and as a whole, for they held a special place (*Numbers Rabbah* 6:10, 11).

Do you have objects which you treasure?
How do you show you care for them?
Do you have a listing or a description of them and what they mean to you?

C The Priestly Blessing occurs in this Torah portion. Moses teaches this blessing to Aaron. It is one of the significant reminders of past priestly rituals in today's liturgy. The Mishnah describes the blessing as given by the priests in the

Temple from an elevated platform called a "*duchan.*" Hence, today, the word "*duchanan*" means to deliver the Priestly Blessing. Before blessing the congregation, the *Kohanim* prepare themselves by washing their hands, sometimes with the help of the *Levi'im,* and then the *Kohanim* remove their shoes. The blessing is delivered with *tallit* draped over the head and with arms raised and fingers spread to form the shape of the letter *shin.*

Customarily, the *Kohanim* do not look at those they bless. Likewise, congregants look down or even turn away during the recitation of the Priestly Blessing. The *Kohanim* are thus less likely to be distracted from their task by loved ones or by people toward whom they might harbor bad feelings.

Rashi explains the content of this blessing. "Bless you" means "may your property increase." "Keep you" means "guard you from evil." "Deal kindly and graciously with you" means "grant you wisdom and kindness." "Bestow favor upon you" expresses the idea of God suppressing divine anger.

How do the special preparatory rituals help the *Kohanim* prepare themselves for what they are about to do?
In what ways do you prepare yourself for an important task or event?
What feelings do you think the Rabbi has while blessing the congregation?
Can you describe how you feel when a parent or a Rabbi blesses you personally or as a part of the congregation?

D Use of the Priestly Blessing today differs among the various branches of Judaism. Throughout most of Israel, it is recited every Shabbat during Shacharit and Musaf (the morning and the additional services). In Jerusalem, it is recited every day. In the Diaspora, customs range from limiting the use of the blessing to the High Holy Days and the three pilgrimage festivals to its more frequent use as a final blessing at weekly

services. The blessing is also used at important Jewish life cycle ceremonies.

Does a person need some special power or authority to utter a blessing over someone else, or can anyone bless others at anytime?
Has anyone ever blessed you?
Have you ever blessed someone else?

E *Naso* describes the ordeal of bitter waters (also known as *sotah*) to be undergone by a woman suspected of adultery. This ritual has parallels in other Near Eastern cultures (see *The Torah: A Modern Commentary,* edited by W. Gunther Plaut, p. 1054). It also has echoes elsewhere in the Torah. Exodus 32:20 relates that Moses made the people drink a mixture of powder and water after the incident of the Golden Calf. The Talmud explains this, too, as a type of ordeal undergone to separate the innocent from the guilty. The use of the ordeal implies that God sees into the hearts of people and will directly intervene into human affairs. Guilt or innocence is determined on the basis of some immediate sign.

A *midrash* from *Numbers Rabbah* 9:1 illustrates this view: An architect was appointed collector of fines over the city which he had built. The inhabitants of the city began to put their silver and gold in hiding places. Said the architect to them: "I built the city and I constructed the hiding places! Will you hide treasure from me?" So the Holy One . . . said to the adulterers: "Will you hide yourselves from Me? Is it not I who created the hearts . . . ? But you forget Me and falsely say of Me that I do not see and do not know your deeds."

The use of the ordeal of bitter waters was abolished by Rabbi Yochanan ben Zakkai before the destruction of the Second Temple.

What justifications do you think Yochanan ben Zakkai gave for abolishing the ordeal? Do you think there was anything wrong with such an ordeal?

Can your parents ever tell by the look on your face that you have done something wrong? Why do you suppose that is?

F There is still much controversy about the ordeal of bitter waters, even though the practice was outlawed before the destruction of the Second Temple. At first glance, one might see the ordeal as another affront against women in which men do not suffer any consequences. Some commentators feel that the ordeal of bitter waters may very well have protected women. Judith Antonelli explains that in many ancient cultures an accused wife was often killed by her husband and society did not intervene. If an Israelite woman was accused, she was granted due process. Her husband, in a fit of jealousy or ill will, was forbidden to avenge himself by murdering her. The two had to go before the priest and participate in this ritual. The woman was allowed to live, guilty or not, and death was never a penalty (*In the Image of God*, pp. 336-7). In being a part of this ritual, husbands also had the opportunity to exorcise their feelings of jealousy through the giving of a sin offering (*The Five Books of Miriam* by Ellen Frankel, p. 200).

Why do you think the Torah prescribed the ordeal only for a woman and not for a man?
Should anyone at any time be forced to drink the bitter waters?
Do you think this ritual protected Israelite women from their husbands?
Is it possible that participating in this ritual gave couples a fresh start in their marriage?
Is there a modern day counterpart to the ordeal of bitter waters?

G This portion explains the laws governing Nazirite behavior, but it does not explain the motivation for becoming a Nazir. One commentary tells us that an individual takes a Nazirite vow because of a "holy resolve to escape temptation and sin." By separating from worldly concerns, an individual is better able to come close to God

(*Yalkut Me'am Lo'ez* by Yaacov Culi, Vol. XIII, p. 129).

What religious tradition, in your opinion, embraces the idea of separating from worldly concerns in order to come closer to God?
Does it surprise you that this was a very early Jewish tradition?
Do you think there is a place for the Nazirite in contemporary Judaism?

STRATEGIES

ANALYZING THE TEXT

1 Compare the special laws for the Nazirite (Numbers 6:1-21) with the requirements for the conduct of the priests (Leviticus 21:1-15). What do the laws and the requirements have in common? How are they different? What reasons can you suggest for the commonalities and differences?

2 Create a visual summary of the portion *Naso*. Cut, draw, or construct pictures which represent significant details from the portion. Use no words. Mount these in a bulletin board display.

3 The Bible records that when King David went to bring the Ark to Jerusalem, he had it conveyed by wagon rather than on the shoulders of the Kohathites as prescribed in *Naso*. For an account of what happened and the precautions that David subsequently took, read II Samuel 6:33ff. and I Chronicles 15:11ff. Explain the events in terms of the method for carrying the Ark described in *Naso*.

4 Read Numbers 6:1-21 to find out about a Nazir's vows. Based on what you have read, you should be able to answer the following questions. What three restrictions were part of the vows for being a Nazir? Were any sacrifices required of the Nazir? Why do you think someone would choose to be a Nazir? With the destruction of the Temple, the practice of Nazir was no longer observed. Why do you think this happened?

5 It is interesting to note that concerning all our holidays, there are biblical passages which detail the offerings that should be brought for sacrifice. Although we can no longer bring those sacrifices, we still observe the holidays. Since our holidays survived the destruction of the Temple and the end of sacrifices, why do you think the practice of becoming a Nazir did not survive? What Jewish practices will survive in your life, long after your childhood is over?

6 Read about two famous Nazirites, Samson (Judges 13:1-16:31) and Samuel (I Samuel 1:1-28). How and why did they become Nazirites? What special laws did they observe? Did the fact that they were Nazirites confer on them any special status?

EXTENDING THE TEXT

7 The Priestly Blessing appears in this portion (Numbers 6:24-26).
a. Locate the Priestly Blessing in a *Siddur*. During what part of the service is it recited? Can you explain why?
b. Listen to and learn one or more of the following melodies for the Priestly Blessing: *"Yivarech'cha"* from *If Not Now, When?* by Debbie Friedman; *"Ruach Elohim"* from *Keep the Spirit* by Lisa Levine; or *"Y'varechecha"* from *Only This* by Mah Tovu.

8 Learn more about the Priestly Blessing, known in Hebrew as *Birkat Kohanim,* and how it is a part of contemporary worship. Have an "Ask the Rabbi" session to explain the special customs associated with the traditional preparation and giving of the blessing. Compare these tradi-

tions with liberal Jewish practice concerning the Priestly Blessing.
Reference: *Teaching Tefilah* by Bruce Kadden and Barbara Binder Kadden, pp. 98-99.

9 In *Alone Atop the Mountain,* an "autobiographical" novel of the life of Moses by Samuel Sandmel, Moses wonders: "Was it better to have a designated priest, or not? Was it better to have priesthood in a family, with the office to go from father to son, or to allow people to vie for the office, and possibly resort to ugly maneuvering, or even misdeed, to gain the office? On the other hand, was it not dangerous to have such an office?" (p. 167).
Arrange a town meeting on this subject such as Moses might have convened in the desert. Divide into two opposing groups with appointed spokespeople. Create appropriate placards and chants. Let individuals play the roles of Moses and perhaps of some elders, or of Miriam and/or Aaron, and of any other characters who might have a specific point of view. Chair the meeting and decide the issue after giving an impartial hearing to both sides.

10 Learn more about the Nazirite Samson by doing some or all of the following activities:
a. Read the story of Samson from the Book of Judges 13:1-16:31.
b. Read some of the contemporary versions of the story of Samson. Check your synagogue and public libraries for books about Samson.
c. Write a play or skit about Samson using either the biblical story or a storybook version. Consider dividing the story into sections and assign parts to small groups of students. Present the skits. Think about presenting the skits out of order and ask the students to give the actual order of the events.
d. Riddles were a part of Samson's life (see Judges 14:14, 14:18), as was short rhyming poetry (see Judges 15:16, 16:23-24). Write a riddle or short

rhyming poem about Samson and Delilah. Create a display with illustrations which will remind the readers of the key characters, i.e., some locks of hair, a large scissors cut out from paper, or a picture of a muscle-bound man.

e. Become editor and writers of the *Philistine Times*. Publish a first page expose of Samson, his life and times, including his encounters and his eventual downfall at the hands of Delilah. You can use exaggeration and follow the style of supermarket tabloids. Create eye-popping headlines, draw or duplicate incriminating photos and pictures, and write the stories with all the lurid details.

PERSONALIZING THE TEXT

11 There is a variety of Jewish traditions and practices associated with hair cutting and shaving. Do some research to find out about these. What do these practices suggest to you about the symbolic significance of hair? Make up song and dance routines about each of the traditions and then stage a vaudeville show entitled *Hair*. Look in the Index to the *Encyclopaedia Judaica* under "Hair" to get a list of some significant areas to research. Also, see the video of the musical *Hair* to gather more ideas. *Hair* can be rented at video stores and is rated PG.

12 One commentator has written: "The Bene Kehat — the 'family that carried the Ark' — had a challenging responsibility. They had to carry it upon their own bodies; they had to feel its weight; they could not seek means to make the burden easier. Religion, too, is a burden, and it is also a discipline. Anyone who seeks to carry a faith easily, shouldering no special tasks, making no distinctive sacrifices, will have a religion that is neither true nor helpful" (*The Voice* by M. Adler, pp. 282-3).

Do you agree with this? Make a chart with four parallel columns. In column one list all the distinc-

tive practices and tasks Judaism requires of you. Label the next three columns, (1) those practices you observe now, (2) those practices you see yourself observing at some future time, and (3) those practices you do not see yourself observing. Under those column headings, check off your answer regarding each practice and task you have listed. Do you view the observance of Jewish tradition as a responsibility? In what ways might the Jewish practices on your list be helpful to you?

13 In the section about the ordeal of bitter waters, the woman undergoing the ritual announces "Amen, amen!" after the priest administers the curse, but before she has drunk the water. What does the word "Amen" mean and how has it been used in Jewish liturgy? The *Encyclopaedia Judaica* (Vol. 2, pp. 803-4) has a concise article on the subject which includes several *midrashim* about the use of the word. Read the article and then choose one of the meanings or *midrashim* and create an illuminated AMEN. Outline the word in very large, thick letters. When you are finished, cut out the letters and mount them on cardboard. Using chalk pastels, draw a depiction of the meaning of the *midrash* inside the letters front and back. Attach fishing line to the letters and suspend them from the ceiling to form a giant mobile.

14 The Priestly Blessing includes the word "*Shalom*" (Numbers 6:23-27). What does the word mean? What are the broadest implications of being blessed with *Shalom*? What is the human role in bringing this blessing to fruition in both individual and communal terms? For some thoughts on this subject, see *The Torah: A Modern Commentary*, edited by W. Gunther Plaut, pp. 1067-8. Write a poem on the subject of *Shalom* and copy it neatly onto a piece of plain paper. Surround your poem with a collage which illustrates your ideas.

15 Practice reading the Priestly Blessing until you can do so fluently. Then, using a melody you know or one you've composed, set the blessing to music. Discuss when you think it would be suitable to use this prayer and melody.

16 Use the traditional way fingers are spread for the Priestly Blessing, in the form of the Hebrew letter *shin,* as the basis for a "stained glass" window design. Outline the design in black ink or marker on drawing paper (you can trace around your fingers). Color in the spaces with crayons, and then rub cooking oil on the back of the paper to make it transparent. Frame the "stained glass" in black construction paper and hang it in a window. There are simple faux stained glass kits available for purchase in craft and hobby shops. The kits utilize sheets of plastic and acrylic paints.

17 Although the Nazirite is forbidden to consume alcohol, the Jewish attitude toward wine is a positive one. According to the Talmud, wine consumed in moderation "sustains and makes glad" (*Berachot* 35b). Wine is drunk as part of the traditional observance of Shabbat, the festivals, and certain life cycle ceremonies. Unlike other juices of fruit or vegetables, over which we recite the blessing *Shehakol,* a special blessing is recited over wine. Make yourself a wine cup to use on appropriate Jewish occasions and learn the *Kiddush,* which is the special blessing over wine. To make a lasting *Kiddush* cup, purchase bisqueware from a ceramics shop and obtain the directions for painting, glazing, and firing to finish the project.

18 The Rabbis explained that the close detail with which the princes and their gifts are recorded teaches the importance of each individual. Imagine you could give any gift to the Jewish people — an object of any size, a feeling, an idea, etc. What would you give? Why? Answer this question individually. Then, compile all the answers in a format similar to the one used in this portion, stressing both the equality and importance of each individual and each gift.

19 Imagine that you are Samson imprisoned by the Philistines. During this time as a prisoner, you have the opportunity to do a *cheshbon ha-nefesh* — an accounting of your soul. As Dov Peretz Elkins explains, *cheshbon ha-nefesh* has been an important practice in Jewish moral (and spiritual) growth (*Jewish Guided Imagery,* p. 160). Using a page from an accounting ledger, make an account of Samson's soul, remembering that in this activity you are Samson. Think of these questions as you write: Did I treasure my role as a Jewish leader? How did I behave during my lifetime? Do I have any regrets about my life? What could I have done differently? How did I choose to die? I wonder if my strength returned because my hair grew back, or was there another reason?

OTHER RESOURCES

20 Read, act out, and discuss the skit for the portion *Naso* in *Sedra Scenes: Skits for Every Torah Portion* by Stan J. Beiner, pp. 157-160.

21 View and discuss the episode for *Naso* from *Torah Toons I: The Video.*

22 For creative movement activities, see "Blessing of Peace" and "Shouldering the Sacred" from *Torah in Motion* by JoAnne Tucker and Susan Freeman, pp. 164-167.

23 Read and discuss the illustrated commentary for *Naso* in *American Torah Toons* by Lawrence Bush.

INVOLVING THE FAMILY

24 It is a Jewish custom for parents to bless their children on *erev* Shabbat. The traditional blessing for sons is: "May God make you like Ephraim and Manasseh." For daughters it is: "May

God make you like Sarah, Rebekah, Rachel, and Leah." For another example of a Shabbat blessing, listen to the song "Sabbath Prayer" from *Fiddler on the Roof*. Discuss the biblical figures named in these blessings. What qualities did they have that your parents might wish for you? With what would your parents wish you to be blessed? With what would you wish to be blessed? Write a Shabbat blessing expressing your wishes for members of your family. Use it on Shabbat! (For more, see the Index: "Blessing/Curse.")

BAR/BAT MITZVAH PROJECT

25 For a more positive angle on haircuts, as opposed to the haircut Samson receives at the hands of Delilah, organize a Cut-a-thon. Seek the services of trained beauticians to give free haircuts to the homeless and indigent. Looking better makes one feel better and helps raise an individual's self-esteem. If someone is homeless or indigent, he/she often does not have the money to get a haircut. This can be your *mitzvah*. You may have to do some fund-raising to help pay for the beauticians' supplies. Contact a local shelter to recruit clients wishing a haircut.

BEHA'ALOTECHA 8:1-12:16 בהעלתך

SYNOPSIS

As the portion begins, Aaron prepares the lamps of the *menorah* as God had commanded Moses. Moses purifies the Levites, and then Aaron ordains them in the sight of all the Israelites.

The text then recounts the observance of Passover as commanded by God on the fourteenth day of the first month of the second year after the Exodus. For those members of the community who are unclean and therefore unable to offer the Passover sacrifice, God ordains a substitute Passover to be observed on the 14th day of the second month.

The presence of God hovering over the Tabernacle as a cloud by day and a fire by night is described. God tells Moses to have two silver trumpets made. These are to be sounded by the priests to summon the people to assemble and to signal the time to break camp. The trumpets are also to be blown at times of war and on joyous occasions, festivals, and new moons as a reminder of God and God's acts of deliverance.

After Passover, the Israelites break camp and march a distance of three days from the mountain of God. The people complain before God, and God causes a fire to break out and destroy the outskirts of the camp. The fire dies down when Moses prays to God.

Again the people weep before Moses, contrasting the meat and their varied diet in Egypt with the manna of Sinai. Moses is upset by the complaints of the Israelites and cries to God that he cannot cope with such a people by himself.

God tells Moses to gather 70 elders to aid him in leading the people. The appointed leaders are told to advise the people that God will give them meat to eat for a whole month — until it becomes loathsome to them.

Two of the 70, Eldad and Medad, begin to prophesy in the camp. Joshua advises Moses to restrain them, but Moses rebukes Joshua for his concern saying, "Would that all the people of

Adonai were Prophets, [and] that *Adonai* would set the divine spirit upon them!" (Numbers 11:29).

While the quail meat sent by God is still fresh, God strikes the people with a plague. The setting of these events is named Kivrot HaTa'avah (graves of craving) because the Israelites who craved meat died and were buried there.

At Hazayrot, Miriam and Aaron speak ill of Moses on account of the Cushite woman he had married. They declare themselves to be prophets of equal stature with Moses. God rebukes Aaron and Miriam, reminding them that Moses is the only prophet to whom God speaks plainly, rather than through dreams or visions. As punishment for her slander, Miriam is stricken with leprosy.

Aaron pleads with Moses to intercede with God on behalf of Miriam. Moses does so, and God agrees to limit her punishment to seven days only. The Israelites do not leave Hazayrot until Miriam is readmitted to the camp. They next set up camp in the wilderness of Paran.

INSIGHTS FROM THE TRADITION

A *Beha'alotecha* takes its name from the key word in Numbers 8:2, wherein Aaron is told to light the *menorah* in the Tabernacle.

This portion details the dedication ceremony for the Levites. Here we read that they begin to serve in the Temple at 25 years of age, but in *BaMidbar*, the minimum age is set at 30 years. To resolve this contradiction, Rashi tells us that at 25, a Levite begins studying the laws pertaining to the sacrifices and at age 30, he begins to serve.

This is also the biblical source for the Talmudic principle that a pupil who makes no progress after five years of study will never succeed (*Chullin* 24a).

Is any particular significance attached to the ages chosen for Levites to serve?
Why do you think 25 or 30 was considered a good age for the Levites to begin their service?

Why are minimum ages set for the performance of certain tasks such as driving, voting, or marriage? Do you agree with the ages legislated for these tasks by your country, state, or province?

B *Beha'alotecha* contains the date on which God told Moses to instruct the people about the observance of Passover — the first new moon of the second year following the Exodus (Numbers 9:1). The Book of Numbers, however, opens "on the first day of the second month of the second year" (Numbers 1:1) — a full month later. This seeming contradiction was resolved by the Rabbinic principle that there is no chronological order in the Torah (*Pesachim* 6b). This general principle is applied to help resolve other such textual problems. (See, for example, Insight D, Exodus, *Terumah*, page 129.)

C Moses' response (9:6-13) to the people who inquired about a second Passover provides an important lesson. It teaches that a judge should not be ashamed to say, "That is a law with which I am unfamiliar. Wait and I will ask a higher authority or one with more knowledge." Moses, not knowing the answer, turned to God.

What sort of insight does this provide into Moses' character?
Is it sometimes difficult for you to admit that you don't know something? Explain.
Has a teacher or parent ever admitted to you that he or she did not know something?

D The Rabbis were puzzled by the passage in Numbers 10:35-36: "When the Ark was to set out, Moses would say: 'Advance, O *Adonai*' . . . And when it halted, he would say: 'Return, O *Adonai!*'" These verses contradict the sense of Numbers 9:18: "On a sign from *Adonai*, the Israelites broke camp, and on a sign from *Adonai*, they made camp . . . " How can it be that the signal to travel came both directly from God and from Moses?

According to a *midrash,* these verses point out the degree of closeness between Moses and God and their "complete identity of aim" (*Studies in BaMidbar* by Nehama Leibowitz, p. 90). The uniqueness of the relationship between God and Moses is emphasized later in this portion, too, when God rebukes Miriam and Aaron for slandering Moses.

Could Israel have developed as a nation both physically and spiritually without a leader such as Moses?
If you could sit next to Moses at lunch, what would you talk to him about?

E Despite God's praise of Moses to his brother and sister, the Torah does not portray Moses as a flawless human being. In *Beha'alotecha*, the text begins to reveal an aging Moses, a man who is now quick to anger and even quicker to ask God for help with the unruly Israelites.
Even so, in this portion Moses emerges as a man of great humility and integrity. A *midrash* tells us that the appointment of the 70 Elders to help Moses lead was a test of Moses. Would he feel threatened by their strength or envious of their power to prophesy? Others have found evidence in the text that Moses more than rose above such feelings. When Moses received the report that Eldad and Medad were prophesying in the camp (Numbers 11:29), he said, "Would that all the people of *Adonai* were prophets . . ."
Moses was not asking that the prophecizing of Medad and Eldad be an aberration, but that this be a common condition.

Why would Moses have welcomed the help of others? With what do you most need help?
Can you see yourself as a prophet?

F Miriam and Aaron publicly criticize Moses, apparently because of the woman he married. They label her a Cushite. Isaac Asimov explains that Cushite simply meant foreigner, and Miriam and Aaron's complaint was that Moses had not chosen to marry an Israelite (*Asimov's Guide to the Bible* by Isaac Asimov, Vol. One, pp. 167-8).

A good case can be made for labeling this incident one of sibling rivalry. Miriam and Aaron never attained the status of Moses. They may have felt overlooked by God and by the Israelites.

Rashi provides a very interesting and complex interpretation of this event. He identifies Moses' wife as Zipporah, and states that Cushite means beautiful. To Miriam, Zipporah had revealed that she was separated from Moses because he had to remain clean in order to hear revelation. Miriam and Aaron attempted to bait her by stating that they had not separated from their spouses, yet they still heard revelation. Rashi explains that Moses had to be ready at all times to speak with God mouth to mouth, while Miriam and Aaron received prophecy at appointed times through dreams and visions. For her rebellious behavior, Miriam is covered with leprosy and exiled from the camp. Aaron, in turn, must beg Moses to entreat God to cure her.

Do the punishments of Miriam and Aaron fit their "crime?"
What makes your siblings (or classmates) jealous of you?
When are you most likely to be jealous of others?

G In many ways, *Beha'alotecha* emphasizes the senses of sound and sight. The cloud of God hovering over the Tabernacle is complemented by the cry of Moses, "Advance, O *Adonai*" and by the call of the silver trumpets. The slanderous words of Miriam and Aaron are punished by the appearance on Miriam of snow white leprosy. Some see this as an example of dramatic irony: Miriam criticized Moses on account of his Cushite (presumably black) wife and was afflicted by a disease of white skin.

In what way is Judaism a religion of the senses?
Which sense is called upon most often in Jewish ritual?

STRATEGIES

ANALYZING THE TEXT

1 Contrast Moses' attitude toward leadership and prophecy to that of Miriam and Aaron as demonstrated in this portion.

2 A casual reading of Numbers 12:1-16 leaves the impression that only Miriam (not Aaron) was punished for speaking against Moses. Rabbi W. Gunther Plaut has suggested that while Miriam was punished *physically*, Aaron was punished *mentally* — with guilt caused by seeing the pain of his sister and with the humiliation of being forced to plead with his younger brother Moses (*The Torah: A Modern Commentary*, pp. 1101-2). Reread this section very carefully to see if you can find any clues about the nature of Aaron's punishment either in the text or in what was omitted.

3 Compare the passage in Numbers 11:4-15 in which the people complain to Moses about food with the similar event recounted in Exodus 16:2-35. How are the situations similar? different? What accounts for the different reactions of Moses and God in these two cases?

4 The Rabbis explained that in *Beha'alotecha*, the discontent of the people is shown spreading — from the few to the many, from the ordinary people to an elite group, and from inward to outward rebellion. Examine Numbers 11:1-10 for proof of this. Write your own account of the rebelliousness of the people which makes this pattern clear.

EXTENDING THE TEXT

5 Write a profile of the "Leaders of the Israelites" as though you were a journalist for the *Sinai Star*.

6 Write an entry for Aaron's diary describing his feelings in the aftermath of Miriam's punishment and his plea on her behalf.

7 In verse 12:7 God says "My servant Moses . . . is trusted throughout My household." How do you understand the phrase "My household"? Does it refer to the "house of Israel," or to some other aspect of God's creation? What would it mean in contemporary terms to be trusted throughout the "household" of God? Create a poster illustrating this idea.

8 In *Beha'alotecha*, God instructs Moses that at each new moon, the silver trumpets are to be sounded. When the people settled in the Promised Land, it was more difficult to inform the widespread populace that the new month had begun. For an account of how the new moon was observed and the new month proclaimed, and for activities, see *Teaching Mitzvot* by Barbara Binder Kadden and Bruce Kadden, pp. 27-31. (For more, see the Index: "Rosh Chodesh/New moon.")

9 In this portion, Miriam and Aaron are reminded of how God communicates with prophets other than Moses. Read some other biblical accounts of God's communication with the Patriarchs or the prophets. Is the statement in Numbers 12:6-8 strictly true? What else could it mean? With which prophets did God communicate most directly? What can you infer about the status of each prophet based on this? References: Abraham – Genesis 15:1ff, 17:1ff, 18:1ff; Jacob – Genesis 28:10ff., 32:23ff.; Samuel – I Samuel 3; Isaiah – Isaiah 1:1 and 6; Jeremiah – Jeremiah 1:1ff.

10 What verses of the Tanach are used in the Torah Service? What is their original context and why are they appropriate for the places where they are used? Write explanatory notes about the prayers in the Torah Service and include them at appropriate points in your services for several weeks so that everyone can learn about the Torah service.

References: *Bechol Levavcha: With All Your Heart* by Harvey Fields, pp. 105-138; *To Pray as a Jew* by Hayim Donin, pp. 235-241; *Teaching Tefilah* by Bruce Kadden and Barbara Binder Kadden, pp. 65-68.

11 *Beha'alotecha* describes a variety of incidents in the sojourn of the Israelites in the desert. Create graffiti walls. Mark off and label sections with key words for each of the incidents you choose from this portion. Imagine that such walls were set up in the Israelite camp for the people (i.e., you) to give expression to their (i.e., your) opinions and feelings concerning what they (i.e., you) have been through. Don't neglect the artistic aspects of graffiti!

12 Invite an educator, Rabbi, or Cantor to teach you how to sound the *shofar*. Learn to distinguish between the different calls. Learn their Hebrew names. How does hearing and/or sounding the *shofar* make you feel? Look at a High Holy Day *Machzor* for examples of poetry or readings describing the impact of the sounds of the *shofar*. Write a poem of your own on this theme.

PERSONALIZING THE TEXT

13 *Beha'alotecha* and the portions which follow depict the Israelites complaining and rebelling and fondly recalling their lives in Egypt. How could the people claim that they were given fish free in Egypt (Numbers 11:5) when they were not even provided with the straw required to make bricks? Rashi explains that "free" means "free of the obligation to keep the *mitzvot*." In other words, with freedom from slavery came certain responsibilities — to themselves, to their people, and to God. Make a list of our obligations as Jews to ourselves, to our people, and to God. Then arrange a values auction. Each group receives a fixed sum of money and bids for the values it thinks are most central to Jewish life, deciding carefully how to apportion its money (perhaps establishing a spending limit for each value). Remember, you can only spend your money once!

14 In *Beha'alotecha,* God ordains the observance of a second Passover for those who were unable to celebrate the first. Can you think of any contemporary problems for which this idea might serve as an example of a solution? Write an imaginary letter about such a situation to a Rabbi. Then compose the Rabbi's response.

15 A *midrash* explains why the Israelites did not march on until Miriam had recovered from leprosy and was readmitted to the camp. This was a reward for the kind deed Miriam had done when the child Moses was placed in a basket and put into the water. At that time, Miriam walked up and down along the shore to await the child's fate. For this reason, the people now waited for her. They did not move on until she had recovered (*Legends of the Jews* by Louis Ginzberg, Vol. III, p. 261).

Read more about Miriam in *Legends of the Jews,* Vol. III, pp. 36, 50-54, 255-260, and 326. Then write the chapter headings for a biography of Miriam. Design a book jacket that would be appropriate for this biography.

16 Rewrite the incident in which Miriam and Aaron confront Moses so that it has a different ending. How would your new ending affect the rest of the Israelites' sojourn in the desert?

17 How were the 70 Elders who were to help Moses chosen? Set up a "hiring committee" composed of Moses, Aaron, Joshua, and Miriam. Invite would-be Elders to be interviewed by the committee. What type of questions should be asked? What type of person would make the best Elder?

18 Imagine you are Moses. Write a speech to deliver to the 70 Elders in which you describe their job and their responsibilities as leaders of the Israelites.

19 Find out about Passover customs observed by different groups of Jews. Try acting out some of the unique customs you find out about and preparing some of the special foods. Prepare a handbook for home use to enrich the family *Sedarim.* In it, describe the customs and foods that you liked best and explain how families can incorporate these ideas into their own *Sedarim.* References: *The Passover Anthology* by Phillip Goodman; *The Jewish Holiday Kitchen* by Joan Nathan.

20 Miriam and Aaron's slander of Moses on account of the Cushite woman he had married (Numbers 12:1) appears to be the first reference in Jewish history to an intermarriage (or perhaps to an interracial marriage). What is the Jewish attitude toward such relationships? View the video *This Great Difference,* a 13-minute discussion trigger for teenagers and adults. Invite parents to participate with their teenagers in viewing and discussing the video. (For more, see the Index: "Marriage/Relationships.")

21 According to Saadia Gaon, there are ten reasons for sounding the *shofar* on *Rosh HaShanah.* Read these reasons in *Days of Awe* by S.Y. Agnon, pp. 70-71. Use one of these reasons as the basis for designing a *Rosh HaShanah* greeting card.

22 Create a mural illustrating occasions on which the silver trumpets were to be blown. In the center of your mural, put large trumpets made of tin foil. Show that the trumpets are sounded on joyous and grievous occasions by surrounding them with appropriate pictures. (For more, see the Index: "Menorah.")

OTHER RESOURCES

23 View and discuss the episode for *Beha'alotecha* from *Torah Toons I: The Video*.

24 Read, act out, and discuss the skit for the portion *Beha'alotecha* in *Sedra Scenes: Skits for Every Torah Portion* by Stan J. Beiner, pp. 161-165.

25 For creative movement activities, see "The Wave" and "Miriam Stricken" from *Torah in Motion* by JoAnne Tucker and Susan Freeman, pp. 168-171.

26 Read and discuss the illustrated commentary for *Be-Haalotecha* in *American Torah Toons* by Lawrence Bush.

27 For more information and activities about hearing the *shofar* and sanctifying the new moon, see *Teaching Mitzvot* by Barbara Binder Kadden and Bruce Kadden, Chapters 6 and 7.

INVOLVING THE FAMILY

28 It has been said (*The Torah: A Modern Commentary*, edited by W. Gunther Plaut, p. 1086) that the key word of Judaism is not *re-eh* (see) but *shema* (hear). What do you think of this idea? List specific examples of the use of both senses in Judaism. Consider the senses of taste, touch, and smell, too. Which senses are the most involved in practicing Judaism? Examine all of the ritual objects you use in your home as you consider this question. How do these objects involve your senses? Plan a Shabbat observance with special use of objects, music, and food to appeal to all your senses.
Reference: *Using Our Senses: Hands-on Activities for the Jewish Classroom* by Marilyn Holman.

BAR/BAT MITZVAH PROJECT

29 In this portion, Moses prays for Miriam to be healed (12:13) Prayer is only one way in which we can heal the sick.

a. Explore what volunteer opportunities are available in your local hospital so that you can participate in the *mitzvah* of healing the sick.

b. Find out about the work of the Jewish Healing Center, 9 East 69th Street, New York, NY 10021. Among other things, they have liturgy and suggestions for incorporating healing rituals into the holidays. Share what you have learned with your synagogue's Ritual Committee.

SHELACH LECHA 13:1-15:41 שלח לך

SYNOPSIS

GOD TELLS MOSES TO SEND TWELVE MEN to scout the land of Canaan. Among the scouts are Caleb from the tribe of Judah and Hosea son of Nun from the tribe of Ephraim. Moses changes the name of Hosea to Joshua and he instructs the scouts to investigate the natural properties of the land and to evaluate the strength of its people.

After 40 days, the scouts return, bearing a branch with a single cluster of grapes so heavy that it must be carried by two men. They report that the land is indeed bountiful, but that its inhabitants are large and powerful.

In the face of the fearsome report of the majority of the scouts and the weeping of the people, Caleb and Joshua argue that if the people have faith in God and God's promise to their ancestors, they will surely overcome the inhabitants of Canaan. As the Israelites converge to stone Caleb and Joshua, the presence of God appears to all.

Moses is told that God will destroy the Israelites because of their lack of faith and make a great nation of the descendants of Moses. But Moses urges God to act with forbearance and mercy and to save the Israelites. He tells God that if the Israelites are destroyed, the Egyptians will say that God was powerless to bring them into the Promised Land.

God forgives the people, but consigns them to wander 40 years in the desert. With the exception of Caleb and Joshua, none of the generation that was redeemed from Egypt will survive to enter the Promised Land.

The Israelites hear this and repent. They set out in the morning for the Land. The Amalekites and Canaanites do battle with them and the Israelites are defeated at Hormah.

The portion goes on to detail the sacrifices that are to be given in the Land. The people are permitted to eat of the bread of the Land, but are bidden to set aside some of it as a gift for God.

The sacrifices and offerings to be made in instances of inadvertent sin are described. A person who purposely sins against God, however, is to be cut off from the people.

In the wilderness, the Israelites come across a man gathering wood on Shabbat. The man is brought before the whole community and stoned to death as God commands Moses.

Finally, God tells Moses to instruct the Israelites to tie fringes on the corners of their garments as a reminder of God and the commandments.

INSIGHTS FROM THE TRADITION

A The opening event of this portion involves the sending of men to spy out the Promised Land. Numbers 13:2 states that God instructed Moses to send the spies, but Deuteronomy 1:22 relates that it was at the *people's* urging that the spies were sent. Rashi harmonizes these two accounts by interpreting that in Numbers, God gave *permission* for the spies to be sent.

The Talmud explains the motivation for God's permission: "By the lives of the Israelites! I swear that I will give them the opportunity to make a mistake because of the spies' reports so that they will not merit possession of the land" (*Sota* 34b). In effect, God wanted a reason to deny that generation access to the Promised Land!

Why might the people want to send spies to the Promised Land?
In what ways did this generation of Israelites show their unworthiness for the Promised Land?
In what ways do you show that you are or are not ready to accept certain responsibilities or privileges?

B One spy was chosen from each tribe, with the exception of the tribe of Levi. This tribe was not to receive a portion in the Promised Land. Only those tribes which were to possess land were called upon to send spies (*Yalkut Me'am Lo'ez* by

Yaacov Culi, Vol. XIII, p. 341). The Israelites were punished for their behavior in this incident of the spies, but the Levites did not share their fate. For when God announced the punishment, the age of those labeled guilty was specified as from 20 years up (Numbers 14:29). But, when the Levite census was taken they were numbered (Numbers 3:40) from one month of age (Rashi). Therefore, they were not a part of those who were punished.

What other exemption did the Levites receive based on their status? (see Numbers, *BaMidbar*, Insight D and Strategy #13; Korach, Strategy #4.) What effect might these privileges have had on others?

C The decree that "none of the men who have seen My presence and the signs that I have performed in Egypt and in the wilderness . . . shall see the land" (Numbers 14:22-23) was said to have been spoken on the ninth day of the Hebrew month of Av. God's judgment against the slave generation of Israelites thus becomes the first of the tragic events associated with that date. Among the others are the destructions of the First and Second Temples.

Is there a date in the secular calendar which is associated with evil occurrences or disasters? Do you have a lucky or unlucky day? What makes it so?

D Note the curious historic twist: the number of spies who delivered the evil report about the Land is the same as the number of adults required for prayer — a *minyan*. In *Shelach Lecha*, the ten spies are called an *Edah* — which is the term used for a congregation or community of worshipers. *Megillot* 23b claims that the number in a *minyan* comes from the verse in Numbers 14:27. Others attribute the origin of the number ten in a *minyan* to Genesis 18:32 — Abraham's plea to spare Sodom if ten righteous men are found there.

What number beside ten has significance in Jewish custom and practice?
What number(s) have special significance for you? Explain.

E The portion switches abruptly from the Israelite wanderings in the desert to a variety of laws which the people are to obey. One of these is the precept concerning *challah* (15:18ff) — the offering set aside from kneaded bread dough. *Challah* was to be given to the priests. According to biblical law, this rule applied only to the land of Israel and only if a majority of the Israelites were living there. The Rabbis, seeking to preserve this commandment, created a symbolic observance. A small portion of each batch of dough is to be twisted off and burned in an open flame. From this act of twisting a piece of the batch comes the custom of braiding the Sabbath loaf as a reminder that *challah* was taken. Hence, also, its name. This became one of the three time-bound positive *mitzvot* which women were obligated to fulfill. The other two are the lighting of Shabbat candles, and the observance of *niddah* (family purity).

Have you ever baked *challah*? Have you "taken" *challah* from your bread dough?
What family customs do you most enjoy?

F The portion closes with God commanding the Israelites regarding the wearing of *tzitzit*. These fringes are a reminder of all the commandments in Torah and serve to underscore the need to observe them. The *midrash* illustrates this with a story: A person is thrown from a boat into the water. The captain stretches out a rope and tells him to take firm hold of it, for his life depends on it. The rope is like the *tzitzit*, the drowning person is like Israel, and the captain is like God. The *tzitzit* provides a lifeline, for adherence to the commandments is life itself.

What are your "lifelines" to Judaism?

G In the *Haftarah* portion, Joshua sends spies to the city of Jericho. Their mission is successful. There are important differences between Joshua's spies and the ones Moses sent. Ten of Moses' spies were prominent tribal chieftans, while Joshua sent two anonymous fellows. These two were experts at their profession, while 10 of the 12 that Moses sent had no previous experience at spying and are not even referred to as spies. The 12 embark on their mission with fanfare. When they return, they report to the entire people in public. The two that Joshua sent go secretly out on their mission and report back only to their leader. Is it any wonder why the one mission failed and the other succeeded?

"If you don't know what you're looking for, it's very hard to find it." How does that statement apply to the account of the 12 spies? How does the statement apply to a business? a sports team? a student? to you?

STRATEGIES

ANALYZING THE TEXT

1 Compare the arguments Moses uses to dissuade God from destroying the Israelites in Numbers 14:13-19 with those he uses after the incident of the Golden Calf in Exodus 32:11-13. In Exodus, Moses uses three arguments. What are they? Which of these does he stress in Numbers? What new ones are introduced? How are the Israelites referred to in each case? Can the different situations explain these differences? How does contrasting the two texts show that here in *Shelach Lecha*, Moses is disheartened?

2 What connections can you see between the following apparently unrelated events detailed in *Shelach Lecha*? (1) The tale of the spies and the command to wear fringes and (2) the description of the sin offering and the incident of the Sabbath breaker.

3 Verse 14:22 literally reads "none of the men . . . who have tried Me these *ten times*. . ." The Talmud lists the ten instances when the Israelites tried the patience and love of God (*Arachin* 15a). Can you enumerate them? (Answer: Twice at the Reed Sea, two complaints each about water, manna, and quail, the incident of the Golden Calf, and once in the wilderness of Paran.) On a long narrow scroll-like piece of paper, illustrate these ten instances in the order of their occurrence.

EXTENDING THE TEXT

4 *Shelach Lecha* relates that the spies were gone a total of 40 days. In consequence of their faithlessness, the Israelites were condemned to wander for a generation — 40 years — in the desert. What other examples of the use of the number 40 can you find in the Torah? You may want to use a Concordance to help you. See also *Encyclopaedia Judaica*, "Numbers, Typical and Important," Vol. 12, p. 1258. Produce a mural illustrating the examples you find.

5 A *midrash* tells that the spies were resting in what they believed was a cave, when they felt themselves being thrown through the air. They discovered that the "cave" was a pomegranate rind which had been thrown out by one of the inhabitants of the land — a giant. Make up your own *midrash* explaining how the spies came to the conclusion that the people in the land were *Niphilim* — giants (Numbers 13:33).
References: The *Minhagim: The Customs and Ceremonies of Judaism, Their Origins and Rationale* by Abraham Chill; *The Biblical and Historical Background of Jewish Customs and Ceremonies* by Abraham P. Bloch.

6 Learn the blessing to be recited when putting on a *tallit*. Use a daily prayer book as a source for this blessing.

7 Examine the section of *Shelach Lecha* that deals with the *mitzvah* of *tzitzit* (15:37-41). This passage has entered the liturgy as the third paragraph of the *Shema*. The Talmud explains the purpose of *tzitzit* as follows: "That ye may look upon it and remember . . . and do them." Looking [upon them] leads to remembering [the commandments] and remembering leads to doing them (*Menachot* 43b).

Looking at *tzitzit* causes us to remember the commandments because of the special numerical significance built into their design. Examine a *tallit* and solve the following:

a. Add the number of threads in one *tzitzit* (8) to the number of double knots in one *tzitzit* (5) to the numerical value of the Hebrew word ציצית (*tzitzit*) (600). The total is 613. Explain how this reminds us to look at the *tzitzit* and recall all of God's commandments. (Answer: See Numbers 15:39.)

b. Count the number of times the *tzitzit* is wrapped between each double knot. (Answer: 7, 8, 11, and 13; 7 + 8 + 11 = 26.) What is the numerical value of the letters in God's Hebrew name (*yod, hey, vav, hey*)? (Answer: 26.) How does this correspond to the first three wrappings?

What is the numerical value of the Hebrew word for One — אחד (*Echad*)? (Answer: 13.) How does this correspond to the last wrapping?
Explain how the number of wrappings reminds us that "God is One."
References: *The Minhagim: The Customs and Ceremonies of Judaism, Their Origins and Rationale* by Abraham Chill; *The Biblical and Historical Background of Jewish Customs and Ceremonies* by Abraham P. Bloch.

8 The Levites did not send spies to inspect the Promised Land and, therefore, they were not among those punished in the incident of the spies. Why didn't the Levites participate in this affair? (See Insight B, page 248.) Imagine you are a member of the tribe of Levi. A friend of yours from one of the other tribes has called upon you to explain why your tribe chose not to send a spy. Stage a conversation explaining and justifying the Levite position.

PERSONALIZING THE TEXT

9 Numbers 15:20 states "as the first yield of your baking, you shall set aside a loaf as a gift." The setting aside of *challah* (a "thick loaf") as a gift for the priest is one of the positive *mitzvot* which women are obliged to fulfill despite its time-bound nature. After the Temple was destroyed and there were no more priests, the *challah* was set aside and thrown into a fire to be consumed. When *challah* is baked for Shabbat (related to Exodus 25:30 and Exodus 16:22), a portion is set aside in observance of this commandment. To learn exactly how this commandment is observed, make and "take" *challah* following the directions in *The First Jewish Catalog* edited by Richard Siegel, Michael Strassfeld, and Sharon Strassfeld, pp. 35ff.

10 Anyone can make a *tallit* and correctly tie *tzitzit* onto it. Before planning and making your *tallit*, do some basic research into the specific laws of *tallit* and *tzitzit*. To help you make your *tallit*, follow the directions in the *The First Jewish Catalog* edited by Richard Siegel, Michael Strassfeld, and Sharon Strassfeld, pp. 51ff.
References: *The Minhagim: The Customs and Ceremonies of Judaism, Their Origins and Rationale* by Abraham Chill, pp. 11-24; *The Biblical and Historical Background of Jewish Customs and Ceremonies* by Abraham P. Bloch, pp. 77-78 and 81-82.

11 Traditionally, only adult males can be counted in a *minyan*. Women are exempt from time-bound *mitzvot*, of which daily prayer is one. Since they do not have the obligation to pray daily, they need not fulfill the *mitzvah*. Today, the liberal movements of Judaism count women for a *minyan*. Many contempory women witnessed this transformation. Invite individuals who will share first-hand accounts of their experiences. Ask them to highlight the first time they saw a woman have an *aliyah*, how it felt when they were called to the *bimah* for the first time, their reaction the first time they met a woman Rabbi or Cantor, their feelings when they participated in a service led by a woman Rabbi or Cantor. Ask them to include the reactions of males to all these changes.

12 Arrange for a guest speaker or panel discussion on the punishment of being "cut off" from one's kin, known in Hebrew as *karet*. Invite a psychologist, a Rabbi, an attorney, a judge and/or a law inforcement officer who deals with incarcerated prisoners to discuss what they think are the meanings and implications of such punishment. (For more, see the Index: "*Karet.*")

13 View one of the many travelogues about modern Israel which are available from your public or synagogue libraries, the Israel Aliyah Office, Ergo Media, or Alden Films. Then write a report as though you were a scout sent to survey the land for a group of potential settlers. For a twist on this, write a similar report based on current newspaper reports about Israel.

14 Write a first person account of the events detailed in *Shelach Lecha*. What did you see, hear, and feel regarding the report of the spies?

15 Put on a "This is Your Life" TV show using as your honoree an ordinary Israelite who began life as a slave in Egypt and was among those destined to die in the desert. Invite significant individuals from the Israelite's life to describe or act out important memories. Give the honoree gag gifts reminiscent of his/her life experiences.

16 Prepare a report on contemporary Israel for a television or radio program entitled "Channel 613 Investigates." Imagine that this report is part of a series on "Jewish Communities around the World," designed to help Jews choose places where they might like to settle. What would you have to say about Jewish life in Israel?

17 The land of Canaan is described as a land of milk and honey. Learn the well-known Hebrew song on this theme, "*Eretz Zavat Halav*" (see *Shirei NFTY, Songs NFTY Sings: The New NFTY Songbook*, edited by Daniel Friedlander, et al).

18 According to *Numbers Rabbah* (16:23), even those Israelites who disagreed with the majority in the incident of the spies were to die in the desert. Their attitude may have been correct, but their silence condemned them. How good are you at expressing your opinion if it goes against the majority opinion? Place yourself on the values continuum below.

Vocal Vickie   Silent Saul

19 Make a maze with the Israelites trapped in the center (the desert). Trace paths through the maze back to Egypt, the Reed Sea, Mount Sinai, and forward to the Promised Land. Trade mazes with a friend. Can your friend get the Israelites out of the desert and into the Promised Land?

20 *Shelach Lecha* describes how the spies returned from the Promised Land bearing one special symbol of its bounty — a huge bunch of grapes. Use the bunch of grapes as a motif for block printing on white paper napkins or tablecloths to be used on Shabbat. Slice a potato in half lengthwise. Using a sharp blade, either draw or cut out your design. Dip the cut surface into thinly spread paint. Shake off any excess. Press the image gently down onto the surface of the napkin. Let the napkin dry.

21 Design two travel brochures such as might have been distributed by the spies to the Israelites after their trip to scout the land. One brochure should depict the land as seen by Joshua and Caleb, the other as seen by the rest of the spies.

OTHER RESOURCES

22 Read, act out, and discuss the skit for *Shelach Lecha* in *Sedra Scenes: Skits for Every Torah Portion* by Stan J. Beiner, pp. 166-169.

23 Complete the pages which relate to *Shelach Lecha* in *Bible People Book Two* by Joel Lurie Grishaver, pp. 44-48. Also check the accompanying Leader Guide for procedures and additional activities.

24 For a creative movement activity, see "Fringed Reminder" from *Torah in Motion* by JoAnne Tucker and Susan Freeman, pp. 172-173.

25 Read and discuss the illustrated commentary for *Shelach Lecha* in *American Torah Toons* by Lawrence Bush.

INVOLVING THE FAMILY

26 *Yehoshua,* the Hebrew name for Joshua, means savior or redeemer. This symbolizes Joshua's future role as leader of the Israelites. Find out with your parents what your Hebrew name means and why it was chosen for you. What effect does this knowledge have on you? You may want to follow this up with Numbers, *BaMidbar,* Strategy #2, page 232.

27 Do Strategy # 9, page 251, as a family activity.

BAR/BAT MITZVAH PROJECT

28 Following the directions in Strategy #10, page 251, make your own *tallit.* Also complete Strategy #7, page 251 and Insight F, page 249. Keep a journal in which you record your thoughts as you make the *tallit* and work through the Strategy and the Insight. Additionally, have photos taken of you during the process of making your *tallit.* Insert these photos into your journal.

KORACH 16:1-18:32 קרח

SYNOPSIS

KORACH, A LEVITE, AND TWO MEMBERS of the tribe of Reuben — Dathan and Abiram — lead a rebellion against Moses and Aaron. They accuse Moses and Aaron of raising themselves above the community of Israelites, all of whom are holy. In return, Moses chides Korach for aspiring to privileges above those reserved for the Levites. He tells Korach that God will choose who is holy by accepting or rejecting an incense offering.

When Moses sends for Dathan and Abiram they refuse to come.

In the morning, each of the rebels, together with Moses and Aaron, offer incense in a fire pan to God before the Tent of Meeting. The presence of God appears and threatens to destroy the entire community, but Moses intercedes and the Israelites are told to withdraw from the dwellings of Korach, Dathan, and Abiram. Moses tells the people that if the rebels die an unnatural death, that will be a sign that Moses is God's chosen leader. The ground opens and all of Korach's people are swallowed up. A fire destroys the 250 rebels in his party. Their fire pans are declared sacred, collected by Eleazar the priest, and hammered into plating for the altar.

But the people then protest that Moses and Aaron bear responsibility for the deaths of the rebels. As God prepares to annihilate the Israelites, Moses tells Aaron to make expiation for them. Those who Aaron reaches are saved from the plague, but a total of 14,700 Israelites perish.

God tells Moses to collect the staffs of the chieftains of each tribe and to leave them in the Tent of Meeting. The staff of the man chosen by God will be made to bloom as a further lesson to the rebels. Overnight, Aaron's staff sprouts almond blossoms.

Then God speaks to Aaron telling him that he and his sons are directly responsible for the Tabernacle; the Levites are to serve under the priests and are to take care not to touch any of the sacred furnishings on pain of death.

All sacrifices and offerings, first fruits and first-born animals, and the redemption price of the firstborn — gifts to God — are given to the priests for all time. The Levites are given the tithes of the Israelites in return for their service in the Tabernacle, but are to receive no share of the land. One tenth of the tithes and the best part of the gifts are to be given by the Levites to God as their donation.

INSIGHTS FROM THE TRADITION

A This portion describes the rebellion against Moses led by Korach — the namesake of this portion. There are six Torah portions named after individuals: *Noah, Chayay Sarah, Yitro, Korach, Balak,* and *Pinchas.*

B Korach had two co-conspirators, Dathan and Abiram. They issued this challenge to the Israelites: Why should Moses and Aaron be placed above you, for the entire congregation is holy? *The Interpreter's Bible* (Vol. 2, pp. 220-222) sees this as a revolt against what some Israelites felt was the political and economic dictatorship of Moses. This commentary counsels a more tolerant approach to Korach, for his motive was to achieve religious and political democracy for the people. While this may have been a noble goal, the people were not yet sophisticated enough to handle this responsibility.

Traditional Jewish commentaries see Korach as a villian, power hungry and desiring only to elevate himself into a position of high authority. Ultimately, Korach could not be successful, for our sages tell us that "envy, passion, and the pursuit of honor drive a person out of this world" (*Yalkut Me'am Lo'ez* by Yaacov Culi, Vol. XIV, p. 10).

Do you think Korach's charge against Moses and Aaron is justified?

If we are still a "Kingdom of priests and a holy people," what functions do Rabbis and Cantors serve?

Can someone be a leader and still be a part of the common people?

Are you envious of someone?

How does your envy differ from that of Korach?

C During the course of the Korach rebellion, Moses attempts conciliation with the rebels. Rashi points out three such instances: (1) "Moses sent for Dathan and Abiram" for he wished to speak to them, but they refused (Numbers 16:12); (2) Moses delayed God's judgment: "Come morning, *Adonai* will make known . . . ," for Moses hoped that the people would have had a chance to "cool-off" and repent by then (Numbers 16:5); (3) "Moses rose and went to Dathan and Abiram" for he still believed that they would show respect to him if he personally appealed to them (Numbers 15:25).

Does admitting that you wish to reconcile weaken your position when it comes to settling an argument?

Did the attempt at reconciliation help or hinder Moses in any way?

When you have a misunderstanding or argument with someone, how do you go about reconciling with him/her?

D Even though the rebels were killed for their part in bringing the incense offering, their fire pans were considered holy. For this reason, the fire pans were incorporated into a covering for the altar. Rashi explains that this was to serve as a reminder and a deterrent for future generations.

What serves to remind and deter you from doing what is wrong?

In what way might the following monuments or places serve you as reminders and deterrents:

Statue of Liberty, Lincoln Memorial, Yad VaShem, Tomb of the Unknown Soldier, the Vietnam Memorial?

E No sooner had Korach and his cohorts been swallowed by the earth, than the Israelites began to complain again (17:6). The *midrash* reinforces the theme of the authority of both Moses and Aaron. The people thought that God had put down the rebellion for the sake of Moses alone, yet here we see Aaron's position reinforced. We are told that Moses cut fresh staffs for each of the tribal princes so that they could all start out on equal footing with Aaron. However, only Aaron's staff sent forth buds, thus proving that he was entitled to his position (*Numbers Rabbah* 18:23, pp. 743-4).

This same staff, we are told, became the royal sceptre — the mark of authority — of the Kings of Israel. It was hidden away when the Temple was destroyed, but will someday reappear to be held in the hand of Messiah ben David.

Did the people learn their lesson when they saw Korach's fate?

What symbols of authority do you see in everyday life, including in school, at home, and on television?

F By now the Israelites see a pattern emerging: they rebel, evidence is brought against them, they are punished by plague or by defeat in battle or by natural disaster. All these punishments were considered acts of God. The Tabernacle, representative of God, thus became a source of fear. The Israelites feared disastrous consequences for errors made in the sacrificial service. Rashbam tells us, therefore, that it was to allay their anxieties that they were given a preventative law: no non-priest shall come near the service (Numbers 18:4).

What places in our society are off-limits for the common person?

What places do you know you must avoid or stay out of?

G In Numbers 18:19, the sacred gifts of the Israelites are referred to as "an everlasting covenant of salt." A *midrash* explains the use of salt in sacrifices as follows: On the second day of creation, when God split the waters above and below, the lower waters complained that they wanted to be closer to God. In response, God promised them that salt (from the seas) would be used on the sacrifices (*Korbanim* — with the root meaning to "draw near").

In studying this portion, Rashi connected the word "everlasting" (*chak-olam*) to the use of salt as a preservative, and Nachmanides expanded on this metaphor. He explained that salt can be a helpful agent — preserving or seasoning food, but it can also be destructive — preventing plants from growing and acting as a corrosive. In the same way, sacrifices and gifts to God can be used for positive or negative reasons.

How might giving a gift to God be a negative act? What other things can you think of that can be put to either a positive or negative use?

H The Tabernacle became off-limits for the common Israelite. It was the duty of the Levites to guard against trespassers. The Talmud informs us that both the trespasser and the guard were subject to the death penalty (*Arachin* 116).

Is it fair that the guard should be punished with severity equal to the trespasser?
Should the guard be punished at all for someone else's wrongdoing?
When and in what ways are you a guard with responsibility for someone else's behavior?

STRATEGIES

ANALYZING THE TEXT

1 Contrast Moses' reaction to the crisis described in the previous portion regarding the report of the spies with his reaction to the rebellion of Korach. In which case does he exhibit better leadership abilities? List these positive qualities. Then, see if you can find Moses behaving in the opposite way elsewhere in the Torah. Why does the Torah take care to emphasize the human qualities of Moses?

2 Organize a "Scavenger Hunt" of the portion *Korach*. Working in two or more teams, come up with a list of 15 questions that can be answered after a careful reading of the story. Some sample questions: To what branch of the Levites did Korach belong? What was the number of rebels in Korach's party? Trade lists with the other team and have a timed race to answer the questions.

3 Examine the common language used in Moses' quarrel with the rebels. Look specifically at these phrases:

רב לכם (*rav lachem*) – You have gone too far! (16:3, 16:7)
המעט (*hame'at*) – Is it not enough? (16:9, 16:13)

How does the repetition of the same phrase by opposite parties heighten the tension and the irony of the situation? Act out the situation (Numbers 16:3-14) with particular attention to the language used.

4 Why do you think the Levites were not to be given any land of their own, but were to derive their income from the gifts of the Israelites?

EXTENDING THE TEXT

5 There is a tradition that the mouth of the earth which swallowed Korach was one of the ten things made just before the first Shabbat of creation. The preexistence of certain objects in nature which acted in wondrous ways was used by the Rabbis to explain miracles which seemed to go against the laws of nature. If, for example, the mouth of the earth had been created during the six days of creation, then opening up as it did in this portion could be said to be part of the natural order. Come up with your own list of ten things from the Torah which God might have made just before Shabbat. Give reasons for your choices. (For a list of the ten things, see *Pirke Avot* 5:8.) Illustrate some or all of the ten things you thought of from the Torah which God might have made.

6 Dathan and Abiram refuse to come before Moses. They say "לֹא נַעֲלֶה" (*lo na'aleh*) — we will not come up (Numbers 16:12,14). This expression shows some measure of regard for Moses despite their contempt for him, since, in Hebrew, the idea of "going up" usually refers to holy places or acts. For example, participants in the Torah service are given an *aliyah* and going to settle in Israel is called *aliyah*. By contrast, those who leave Israel are called *yordim* — those who "go down." For other examples of the use of the root word עלה, see the *The Complete Hebrew-English Dictionary* by Reuben Alcalay.

Design a series of posters illustrating the various meanings of this root.

7 Read Numbers 16:30-34 which describes the earthquake that destroyed Korach and his household. Note the language used. How is the earth compared to a mouth? What is the implied metaphor? According to Plaut, "It was as if the earth itself spoke in judgment" (*The Torah: A Modern Commentary*, edited by W. Gunther Plaut, p. 1129). Write a poetic account of the judgment of Korach, incorporating the idea that the earth itself spoke in judgment.

8 Numbers 18:15 states that all the firstborn, including humans, belong to God, but that the firstborn of man is to be redeemed. The custom of *Pidyon HaBen* (Redemption of the Firstborn) is derived from this concept. In Jewish tradition,

a firstborn son has both religious responsibilities and benefits. He must fast on the day before the first *Seder* of Passover, he must say *Kaddish* on behalf of his parents, and he inherits a double portion of his parent's property. Debate the pros and cons of being a firstborn son. Why were daughters excluded from the responsibilities and the benefits?
References: *Encyclopaedia Judaica*, Vol. 6, pp. 1306ff.; *Teaching Mitzvot* by Barbara Binder Kadden and Bruce Kadden, pp. 39-42. (For more, see the Index: "Firstborn.")

9 What is the effect of supernatural occurrences in the biblical text? Do you think they improve or weaken the story? What other more natural end might Korach have met? Rewrite the story, incorporating a different means of punishing Korach. Compare your version with the Torah portion.

10 Retell the events in this portion and perhaps those leading up to this portion from Korach's point of view.

11 Numbers 18:19 refers to "an everlasting covenant of salt." In the past, all sacrifices were salted, and today salt is used to "*kasher*" meat. How else is salt used in Judaism? (salt water at Pesach, salting *challah* after reciting the blessing over bread, bringing salt and bread to a new home). Research the history and use of salt. Imagine you work in the field of advertising. Using any media you would like, create an ad campaign to sell the Jewish people on the importance of salt.

PERSONALIZING THE TEXT

12 The issue of Rabbinic authority is a complicated one. On the one hand, the Rabbis are seen as the direct descendants of Moses and the Elders of Israel. On the other hand, a

Rabbi is basically a learned Jew. There are few, if any, functions in Judaism which must be performed by a Rabbi as opposed to a layperson. What areas of Jewish life do you think should be regulated by Rabbinic authority? Should the authority of a Rabbi over Jewish life be limited in any way? Invite your Rabbi and/or the head of your synagogue's Ritual Committee to discuss these issues with you.

13 Stage a mock trial of Korach and his rebels. Appoint a jury and an impartial judge to decide whether Korach's actions are treasonous and what punishment is merited.

14 Stage a "Town Meeting" of Korach and his followers during which they set forth their complaints against Moses. Appoint one member of the group to be secretary and record the discussion. Write up the complaints in the form of a petition to be delivered to Moses and Aaron.

15 *Pirke Avot* 5:23 distinguishes between two types of controversy — those which are "for the sake of heaven" (i.e., God) and those "which are not for the sake of heaven." For the Rabbis, the quarrel which Korach and his associates provoked is the archetypical example of a controversy which is not for the sake of heaven. Use this teaching as the basis for developing a series of guidelines for healthy, "holy," arguments. Consider both the content and style of such discussions. Is there any way that Korach's argument could have been transformed into a controversy for the sake of heaven? As a follow-up, you might want to analyze relevant current events according to this standard.

16 Draw and caption an editorial cartoon commenting on the events described in the portion *Korach*.

17 Design stationery or memo paper for Aaron to use, incorporating the motif of the sprouting staff (Numbers 17:21-24).

18 Rods and staffs have both commonplace and authoritative uses. The rod of the shepherd is a symbol of the simple, pastoral life, whereas the sceptre of a ruler symbolizes power. Other examples include the baton of a symphony conductor, the mallet of a judge, the staff with which Moses initiated the plagues. Based on the *midrash* cited in Insight E, page 255, that the rod of Aaron became the sceptre of the Kings of Israel, create a three-dimensional representation of this important symbol.

19 Korach said: "All the community are holy, all of them, and God is in their midst. Why then do you raise yourselves above God's congregation?" (Numbers 16:3). It is hard to disagree with this. Yet, Korach was defeated by Moses. How would Judaism be different today if Korach and his rebels had prevailed over Moses and Aaron?

20 Referring to Numbers 16:26 wherein Dathan and Abiram are called "wicked men," the Rabbis defined four kinds of wickedness:
a. A person who even thinks about doing violence to someone else.
b. A person who borrows something, but does not pay it back or return it.
c. A person who does not respect his/her elders or superiors.
d. A person who causes strife.
Into which category of wickedness would you put Dathan and Abiram? Korach? Expain why. Rank these wicked persons from the least to most wicked. If you wish, eliminate one or two kinds of wickedness from the list and add some others of your own.

21 The rebellions described in *Korach* divided the Israelites into many camps. Make "cause buttons" that might have been worn by various groups of Israelites to express their points of view about the rebellion of Korach.

22 Imagine that Korach and his cohorts escaped from the Israelite camp when it became clear that their rebellion was not going to be successful. Design a "Wanted" poster such as might have been displayed in an attempt to identify and capture Korach.

OTHER RESOURCES

23 Read, act out, and discuss the skit for the portion *Korach* in *Sedra Scenes: Skits for Every Torah Portion* by Stan J. Beiner, pp. 170-173.

24 For a creative movement activity, see "Moses Hears and Falls" from *Torah in Motion* by JoAnne Tucker and Susan Freeman, pp. 174-175.

25 Read and discuss the illustrated commentary for *Korach* in *American Torah Toons* by Lawrence Bush.

INVOLVING THE FAMILY

26 Maimonides taught that it is permissible to disagree with those in authority and to express your disagreement. It is not permissible to act contrary to the decision of the authority. How does this apply to the incidents described in this portion? What is the significance of this idea for family life? Do you think it is permissible to challenge your parents' authority? To what extent? Discuss this issue with your parents.

BAR/BAT MITZVAH PROJECT

27 In this portion, the *mitzvot* having to do with tithing (*ma'aser*) are given. Review these carefully to see what the *tzedakah* implications of these rules are. As a Bar/Bat Mitzvah celebrant, decide how you will "tithe" yourself and donate a portion of the gifts you recieve to *tzedakah*. For an excellent discussion and exercise about allocating tzedakah money, see *Zot ha-Torah: This Is the Torah: A Guided Exploration of the Mitzvot Found in the Weekly Torah Portion* by Jane Golub, with Joel Lurie Grishaver, pp. 184-185; *Teaching Mitzvot* by Barbara Binder Kadden and Bruce Kadden, pp. 91-94.

CHUKAT 19:1-22:1 חקת

SYNOPSIS

GOD INSTRUCTS MOSES AND AARON IN the slaughtering and preparation of a red heifer. Its ashes are to be mixed with water and used for purifying the Israelites and resident strangers who come into contact with a corpse. The law also specifies that those people who are already pure and who touch the mixture in the process of purifying another shall be considered unclean until nightfall. An unclean person who refuses to purify himself shall be cut off from the congregation.

Miriam dies and is buried at Kadesh.

Once again, the people are without water, and they rail against Moses and Aaron. God tells Moses and Aaron to take the rod and order the rock to yield water in the eyes of the people. Moses, however, strikes the rock twice. Water comes forth, but God declares that the actions of Moses and Aaron demonstrate a lack of faith. Therefore, they will not be permitted to enter the Promised Land. The place is called Meribah — the waters of strife.

At Mount Hor, on the boundaries of the land of Edom, Aaron dies. The Israelites mourn his death for 30 days. Eleazar, Aaron's son, succeeds him as High Priest.

The Israelites wage battle and defeat Arad at Hormah. On the journey around Edom, the people again protest against God and the leadership of Moses. God sends a plague of *seraphim* (serpents) upon the Israelites. Many die. Moses intercedes for them. He makes a bronze *seraph* figure, which promotes healing when looked at. The plague abates.

The Israelites do battle with Sihon, King of the Amorites, who refuses to grant passage through his land. The Israelites take all the Amorite towns and settle in them.

Og, the King of Bashan, engages Israel in battle and is defeated. The Israelites take possession of his country before marching on to Moab, across the Jordan from Jericho.

INSIGHTS FROM THE TRADITION

A In addition to being read during the regular cycle of weekly Torah portions, the chapter on the red heifer is also read on one of the four special Shabbatot preceding Passover (Shabbat *Parah*).

B The law of the red heifer is introduced to us in the Torah as a *chukat haTorah* (thus the name of this portion), a law whose purpose and origin are unclear. Indeed, the law of the red heifer is considered to be one of the most mysterious laws of the Torah. The Rabbis simply could not explain how the ashes of this heifer could make the unclean pure while also making the pure unclean. A law such as this tests the obedience of the people, for they are asked to observe a commandment which seems to have no rational basis.

Can you think of other *chukim* — laws whose origin and purpose are unclear?
Are there laws at home, at school, in society, or in Jewish life that you must follow in your daily life which seem unclear or without reason?

C The purification rites described in *Chukat* do not involve sacrifices, since no "sin" is involved. They are intended to restore individuals who come into contact with a corpse back to their "holy" status. The Talmud offers a unique way of understanding the law of the red heifer. It is not the heifer itself which is central to the discussion, but the prohibition of coming into contact with a corpse. A corpse was labeled unclean so that people would not come to treat the body with disrespect (*Hullin* 122a). The ashes of a red heifer were quite costly, thus reflecting the seriousness which was placed on coming into contact with a corpse.

Are there laws within general society which govern how a corpse is to be handled and treated? Why do you think the biblical laws evolved? Do you think that the laws which society in general developed had the same purpose?

Does the idea of "ritual purity" have relevance for you? Explain.

D The portion *Chukat* encompasses a period of 38 years — the time between the return of the spies and the deaths of Miriam and Aaron. According to Numbers 33:38, Aaron died 40 years after leaving Egypt. The earlier chapters of Numbers tell of the events in the second year following the Exodus. Thus, we may assume that by the time of this portion, the slave generation of Egypt has died and been succeeded by a new generation, one ready at last to enter the Promised Land.

Why was a new generation required in order for the Israelites to enter the Land?

What characteristics and attitudes did the generation of the Exodus have that could not be a part of those entering the Land?

E Following the death of Miriam, the community was again without water. A *midrash* explains that a well had been provided to the Israelites based on the good deeds of this prophetess. As this gift had been limited to the time of the march through the desert, Miriam had to die shortly before the entrance into the Promised Land (*Legends of the Jews* by Louis Ginzberg, Vol. III, p. 308).

Miriam's well was one of the ten things said to have been created on the eve of the first Shabbat which occurred at the end of the week of creation (*Pirke Avot* 5:9). In Ellen Frankel's work *The Five Books of Miriam*, Miriam mentions those deeds which merited the appearance of the well — "my powers of prophecy, my protection of my baby brother Moses, my skillful midwifery among the Hebrew slaves, and my victory song at the Sea of Reeds" (p. 226).

Can you cite any examples of special gifts society has been given based on the merit of one individual and upon the individual's death, the gift ceased?

What is the feminine equivalent of *Zechut Avot*? Do you think it would have been possible to have turned to this concept and prayed to have the well restored based on Miriam's merit? How might the story have changed if the people had done this instead of complaining to Moses about the lack of water?

F The focus of the incident at the waters of Meribah is the divine decree that neither Moses nor Aaron shall live to enter the Promised Land. Striking a rock rather than speaking to it does not seem a justifiable reason for Moses to be excluded from the land. Some commentators point to earlier sins as the real cause. Aaron's cardinal sin was the construction of the Golden Calf. Three significant sins were attached to Moses: the slaying of the Egyptian taskmaster, the sending of the spies, and the breaking of the first set of tablets. Ramban finds an answer in Numbers 20:10 wherein Moses says, "Shall *we* get you water out of this rock?" Moses credited himself and Aaron rather than God for producing water from the rock. Ramban understood from this that Moses and Aaron forgot that they were to serve as role models for the Israelites. So, when Moses and Aaron showed anger at Meribah, they misled the people into believing that uncontrolled anger is allowed in a leader. Yet, God did not show anger at the people's need for water. Because of Moses' behavior, the Israelites might imagine God as an angry diety, devoid of compassion for the people (*Studies in Bamidbar* by Nehama Leibowitz, p. 246).

Four times the Torah identifies this incident as the cause of Moses and Aaron's exclusion from the Promised Land (Numbers 20:12, 20:24, 27:14, and Deuteronomy 32:51).

Does leadership demand a higher degree of righteousness and self-control than is required from the rest of society?

Do the current government leaders in your country exhibit these traits?

What do you do when you get very angry?

Can you think of some constructive ways to let people know what made/makes you angry?

STRATEGIES

ANALYZING THE TEXT

1 Compare the two biblical accounts of the Israelites' complaining at Meribah (Numbers 20:2-13 and Exodus 17:1-7). Dramatize the two stories to show how Moses has aged in the intervening years and how his leadership has weakened.

2 Read the sections of Deuteronomy which detail the laws of war (Deuteronomy 7:16ff., 20:1ff.) and discuss in what ways and to what degree the wars of the Israelites described in *Chukat* conform to these laws.

3 Read Numbers 21:21-25 and locate the places mentioned on a map. What is the significance of these places to the present day debate in Israel about the borders of the country? References: *The Torah: A Modern Commentary*, edited by W. Gunther Plaut, p. 1165; *The Macmillan Bible Atlas* by Yohanan Aharoni and Michael Avi-Yonah, Map #52.

4 The Rabbis never fully understood the rationale behind the red heifer. They also cited three other instances of Torah law whose basis was also not understood. Look up the following: Deuteronomy 25:5; Deuteronomy 22:1; and Leviticus 6:26, 34. Based on what you read, identify the other three instances. If you were called

upon to give a rationale for them what would you say? All four cases of these Torah laws were treated in the same manner. Read *Numbers Rabbah* 14:5 in which an explanation was given for the red heifer. This explanation was also applied to the other three laws (see *Numbers Rabbah* 14:8).

5 The deaths of Miriam and Aaron are both recorded in this portion. How does the biblical account of Miriam's death and burial differ from Aaron's death and burial? Read Numbers 20:1 and Numbers 20:22-29 and discuss these accounts.

6 Why do you think the Israelites were especially cautioned not to destroy Edom, although they were told to destroy certain other enemy nations? See Strategy #10, page 263, for an explanation about the word "Edom." Based on this information, posit some theories for the caution about not destroying them.

EXTENDING THE TEXT

7 Referring to Strategy #5 above, create a burial and mourning ritual for Miriam.

8 Write a short paragraph entitled "Five Things I Would Have Liked to Ask Miriam." As you write about these five things, add your reasons for them.

9 Role play Jewish scholars who are discussing the explanations about the sin of Moses and Aaron which led to their exclusion from the Promised Land (see Insight E, page 261). Set up a panel discussion with these scholars. Have a moderator introduce these scholars with a brief, but fictional, biography. Each panel member explains his or her understanding of the sins and/or reasons for excluding Moses and Aaron from the Land. End with a question and answer period.

10 Jewish tradition identifies Edom with the descendants of Esau. According to Genesis 25:30, "Esau said to Jacob, 'Give me some of that red stuff [a stew which Jacob was cooking] to gulp down, for I am famished' which is why he was called Edom." The Root letters of *Edom* are אדם. This root has a wide variety of applications in both biblical and modern Hebrew. Find out how to say the following words in Hebrew and explain the connection between them: Adam, human being, earth, red, ruby, measles, mars, to blush, and, of course, Edom.
Reference: *The Complete English-Hebrew Dictionary* by Reuben Alcalay.

11 In the Talmud, the Romans are sometimes called "Edom." Can you explain why? Refer to Strategy #10 immediately above for help.

PERSONALIZING THE TEXT

12 As insight D (page 261) explained, portion *Chukat* encompasses a period of 38 years. It was during these 38 years that the Israelites trekked through the desert. Imagine that you are one of these trekking Israelites, and do one or more of the activities described below:

a. On long trips many families play car games, such as identifying license plates for every state, singing songs, making up stories, etc. Create a variety of desert trekker games, share these, and play.

b. On rocks and stones, either real or fake, write desert graffiti as evidence that you walked through an area.

c. To keep up the pace of marching in the armed services, song-like verses based on a one-two beat were made up to keep everyone marching in time. Do the same for the desert trekkers.

d. It is your task to create a summer camp experience for the children on this 38-year journey through the desert. Brainstorm the following

for this camp: name, logo, activities, camp/tribal clan cheer, menus for meals, T-shirt designs, etc. Also add any other camp related item or activity which you want included.

e. Finish the following sentences:
The desert is as hot as _____.
The desert is as empty as _____.
My feet are as tired as _____.

13 Write a character sketch of the Israelites based on their behavior in Numbers, from *Beha'alotecha* through *Chukat*. Describe them as if they were a single individual. What is the greatest weakness of this individual? The redeeming qualities?

14 In *Alone Atop the Mountain*, a novel about the life of Moses, the author, Samuel Sandmel, has Moses say: "To be a leader is to be always potentially angry, especially if the leader cares about what happens, cares even beyond the thwarting of his personal will. For a leader to disguise his anger is often useful, but for him to control it is even more urgent. And for him to restrict his anger, whether it is concealed or not, so that it is never out of proportion to what has made him angry, is the heaviest obligation of all" (p. 118).

Based on what you now know about Moses, write entries in Moses' "Journal of a Leader," with specific advice to others about how a leader should conduct himself/herself.

15 Write an obituary for Miriam that might have appeared in a "newspaper" of the time.

16 Hillel said: "Be of the disciples of Aaron, loving peace and pursuing peace; be one who loves others and draws them near to the Torah" (*Pirke Avot* 1:12). Based on this profile of Aaron, write an ethical will that Aaron might have left for his descendants.

17 The attribution of healing powers to a serpent is not unique. In Greek culture, Aesculapius (the god of healing) took the form of a serpent. Today the caduceus — a common medical symbol — features two serpents entwined around a winged rod. Imagine you have been commissioned by the American Medical Association to redesign the symbol of the medical profession. You are instructed to base your design on Numbers 21:8-9. Arrange to present your sketches of both the front and the back of the symbol to your group with an explanation of your design.

18 Songs related to water occur twice in the tale of the Exodus from Egypt: the "Song of the Sea" (Exodus 15:1ff.) and the "Song at the Well" in this portion (Numbers 21:16-18). Many other biblical stories center around water. Think of how many wives were found for Patriarchs at wells, how many incidents there are of the Israelites complaining about lack of water. Use a Concordance to look up the words "water," "well," and "sea," and locate some examples of biblical narratives involving these. Choose one such story and write a song about it, as if the water itself were describing the events taking place. Use a song that you already know and substitute your words.

19 You are Miriam, reviewing the events of your life. Compile a scrapbook of items you might have collected during your life. Fill it with mementos, photographs real or drawn, newspaper clippings, invitations, announcements, etc.

20 Design a book jacket for a biography of Aaron.

21 Imagine that you are the rock which Moses hit to draw water. Retell the incidents in this portion from your point of view as the rock.

22 Arrange to visit a Jewish funeral home to learn about the rites of Jewish burial.

Does your synagogue or community have a *Chevra Kaddishah* — a burial society? If so, perhaps one of the members would accompany you on your visit and help answer your questions.

(For more, see the Index: *"Karet*/Cut off from kin," "Death/Burial.")

OTHER RESOURCES

23 Read, act out, and discuss the skit for the portion *Chukat* in *Sedra Scenes: Skits for Every Torah Portion* by Stan J. Beiner, pp. 174-178.

24 For creative movement avctivities, see "Striking the Rock" and "Copper Serpent" from *Torah in Motion* by JoAnne Tucker and Susan Freeman, pp. 176179.

25 Read and discuss the illustrated commentary for *Chukat* in *American Torah Toons* by Lawrence Bush.

26 Numbers 20:29 relates that the mourning period observed for Aaron was 30 days. According to Deuteronomy 34:8, Moses was mourned for the same length of time. The 30-day mourning period is still important in Judaism. See the mini-course *Death, Burial and Mourning in the Jewish Tradition* by Audrey Friedman Marcus, Sherry Bissell, and Karen Lipschutz for activities and ideas.

INVOLVING THE FAMILY

27 Imagine that your family is a production team charged with making a commercial to promote a television movie about the life of Miriam or Aaron. Plan and stage a 60-second ad showing the key moments in the lives of one of the two.

BAR/BAT MITZVAH PROJECT

28 After the death of Miriam, recorded in this portion, the well which had provided water for the people disappears. The Israelites bewail their situation and again anger Moses. In this project, you will be able to prepare yourself better for a water crisis. The goal is to work at enhancing the beauty and environmental quality of a local natural area. In many places people have joined together to "adopt" local streams, lakes, beaches, or wetlands in order to do a cleanup. In some places the state Department of Environmental Conservation or its equivalent sponsors the formal adoption of these kinds of waterways. Such agencies may invite you to do a clean up and/or other tasks, such as helping with surveys of water and air temperatures, of water and soil pH, and of wildlife. Also you might be asked to help build or enhance habitats and nesting shelters. Decide if you want to do this individually or if you want to form a group to carry out this *mitzvah*. Remember to take before/during/after pictures of your adopted area. Be sure to record and describe the tasks and activities you become involved with in this project. (Adapted from *To Till and to Tend: A Guide to Jewish Environmental Study and Action,* pp. 8-9 in section IV, written under the auspices of The Coalition on the Environment and Jewish Life, 443 Park Avenue South, 11th floor, New York, NY 10016.)

BALAK 22:2-25:9 בלק
SYNOPSIS

WHEN BALAK, KING OF MOAB, SEES THE victory of the Israelites over the Amorites, he becomes alarmed. Fearing that the Israelites are too powerful to defeat in battle, Balak sends messengers to summon the prophet Balaam. He is to come to Moab and curse the Israelites so that the Moabites can defeat them.

Balaam sends the messengers back with the reply that God has told him not to curse the Israelites, for they are a blessed people. Once again, Balak sends dignitaries to plead with Balaam. This time, God agrees to let Balaam return to Moab with the understanding that he is to obey God's commands once he is there.

The next morning, as Balaam is on his way to Moab, his donkey sees an angel of God barring the way. Each time the donkey balks at moving forward, Balaam beats her, until finally God gives her a voice with which to rebuke Balaam. Balaam is then made to see the angel, who reiterates that Balaam is to prophesy only that which is told to him by God.

In Moab, Balak builds seven altars. Balaam sacrifices a ram and a bull upon each one. After consulting God, Balaam proceeds to speak God's words in blessing of Israel. Balak is enraged by this. He takes Balaam to a different place, hoping that Balaam will curse the Israelites from there. At each place, however, Balaam speaks the words of God, blessing the Israelites.

Finally, Balak dismisses Balaam. Before returning to his home, Balaam prophesies the destruction of Moab and the neighboring countries.

At Shittim, the Israelites sin by worshiping the local diety. God orders the leaders of the people to be slain. Pinchas, the son of Eleazar the priest, slays an Israelite man and a Midianite woman who were cavorting in the sight of Moses and the community. This ended the plague that had broken out, killing 24,000 of the Israelites.

INSIGHTS FROM THE TRADITION

A *Balak,* after whom this portion is named, is the King of Moab. He instigates the plan to fend off the Israelites. This plan involves first making peace with his old enemy, the Midianites. This is like two dogs who were growling and snarling at each other. Suddenly a wolf attacked one of them. The other dog thought: If I don't help that dog, eventually the wolf will attack me. For the time being, it is better that we forget our differences and make peace with each other.

How is this like the alliances between many of the nations in the Middle East today? What about in other parts of the world?

B As the next step in his plan, Balak sent for Balaam. According to the *midrash,* Balaam was one of the great pagan prophets who, along with Jethro and Job, were descended from Abraham's brother, Nahor (*The Legends of the Jews* by Louis Ginsberg, Vol.III, p. 356). Balak thought that Balaam could force the hand of fate by cursing the Israelites, thus perhaps weakening or destroying them.

The Rabbis had differing opinions of Balaam. Some saw him as a villain. Others saw him as a prophet equal to Moses.

What was the intent of Balaam's prophecy?
Was his prophecy for good or for evil?
How was Balaam then different from Moses?

C Balaam is approached by the messengers of Balak. Rashi remarks on Balaam's subsequent behavior. Since Balaam was only able to receive prophecy at night, Balaam invited the messengers to stay the night so that they would not think he was subservient to God. Balaam informed the messengers that perhaps they might not be worthy enough to warrant Balaam's presence. In the text, God asks Balaam,"What do these people (i.e.,

Balak's messergers) want of you?" so as to make Balaam think that God was not fully aware of what transpires in the world. Balaam drew the conclusion that since God did not know the intent of the messengers, Balaam would go ahead and curse the Israelites unbeknownst to God. Ultimately, God instructed Balaam not to accompany these messengers.

Why would God ask a question the answer to which is already known?
Has God ever done anything like this before (see Genesis 4:8-11)?
Do your parents ever ask you a question to which they already know the answer?
Do you ever ask your parents questions to which you know the answer? Why?

D Balak sends a second set of messengers to entreat Balaam, promising to reward him richly for his services. Balaam's statement, "Though Balak were to give me his house full of silver and gold, I could not do anything, big or little, contrary to the command of the *Adonai* my God" (Numbers 22:18), reveals him as a haughty and a greedy man.

Isaac Asimov relates that Balaam served for hire and bestowed his blessing and curses not necessarily as inspired to do so by God, but by the fees he was offered. Balaam and his thirst for wealth gave rise to the term "Balaamite," which refers to someone who uses religion as a money making scheme (*Asimov's Guide to the Bible*, Vol. One, p. 184).

Can you identify any "Balaamites" in contemporary society? Describe them.

E Several times, Balaam attempts to curse the Israelites, but each time he utters blessings. The verses introducing his last attempt, "How fair are your tents, O Jacob . . . " (Numbers 24:5) became part of the introductory prayers of the morning worship service. This prayer, known as

the *Mah Tovu*, is recited upon entering the synagogue. The second verse, which comes from Psalms 5:8, contains ten words in the Hebrew and has been used as a counting device to ascertain if a *minyan* of worshipers was present (*Teaching Tefilah* by Bruce Kadden and Barbara Binder Kadden, p. 31). There is a Jewish aversion to counting people by number. This is based upon a superstition that by numbering people we have singled them out and helped the angel of death find them. This is circumvented by using the words as a counting device for determining if a *minyan* is present.

What else could one use in place of numbers when trying to determine how many people are present?
Even though Balaam kept trying to curse the Israelites, he was unable to do so. God had predetermined what would come out of Balaam's mouth. Why was Balaam unable to force God to allow him to speak his curses?
Can anyone force God's hand, so to speak?
If you pray to pass a test, to receive a certain gift, or to have something special happen, do these prayers work?

F The Talmud provides an additional reason for Balaam's inability to curse Israel. ". . . Balaam looked up and saw Israel encamped tribe by tribe" (Numbers 24:2). He saw that the tribes were set apart from each other and that the tent openings did not face each other. No one could see into the tent of any one else (*The Book of Legends: Sefer Ha-aggadah*, edited by Hayim Bialik and Yehoshua Ravnitzky, 628:160). This became the source for the ruling that one may not build a door directly opposite the door of a neighbor, or make a window in line with a neighbor's window. This ensures privacy and respect of personal dignity and is in keeping with the value of modesty in behavior (*Baba Batra* 60a).

Why might this Israelite practice/value deter Balaam from cursing the Israelites?

How is privacy assured for each family member in your home?

Everyone needs his/her "own space." Is your "space" found in a special place or is it a certain time of day? Without betraying your own dignity, modesty, or privacy, can you share what that "space" is and what it means to you?

G At the end of the long story which this portion tells, there is a brief description of an incident in which the Israelites sin. What is the connection between the two seemingly separate, stories? Balaam describes the Israelites as "a people who dwells apart" (23:9), but the final incident of the portion describes something that happened when the Moabites invited the Israelites to "the sacrifices for their god" (25:2). In effect, the description/blessing of Balaam is flipped here and the reverse point is made, i.e., when the Israelites mingle with others, they sin.

Considering this final incident, we might ask ourselves, how effective are blessings?

What is our role in helping realize the contents of a blessing?

What is the lesson about contact with other groups which seems to be implied when both stories in this portion are read together? Do you agree with this lesson?

H The text points out that Zimri, who was slain by Pinchas, was a prince of the tribe of Simeon. By naming the guilty party, Torah teaches an important lesson: if a person stains his/her reputation, the reputation of his/her family is also affected (*Numbers Rabbah* 21:3).

In what ways does your behavior reflect on your family?

Does such knowledge influence how you act?

STRATEGIES

ANALYZING THE TEXT

1 Examine and compare the first three blessings delivered by Balaam. Rewrite each blessing in your own words. How is Balak treated by Balaam before each blessing? What good qualities of the Israelite people does Balaam point out?

2 Review the blessings delivered by Balaam, as found in Numbers 23:7-10, 23:18-24, 24:3-9, 24:15-24, paying particular attention to their poetic imagery. Write each blessing out in the form of poetry, deciding where one line should end and a new line begin, how many lines in a stanza, etc. Practice reading the blessings so that the poetry they contain can be appreciated. For Shabbat *Balak*, plan to present a dramatic reading of the blessings. For a beautiful and appropriate backdrop, make a mural as in Strategy #14, page 269.

3 Some Rabbis placed Balaam in the same category as Haman and Amalek. Some called him a prophet on a par with Moses. How can you explain these two very different views? Is there evidence of both very evil and very good in Balaam? Find it within the biblical text.

4 How does this portion illustrate the expression "Man rides, but God holds the reins" (*The Five Books of Miriam* by Ellen Frankel, p. 228)? Give other examples which depict the meaning of this saying. Additionally, draw an editorial cartoon or a comic strip depicting Balaam on his donkey. Use the expression "Man rides, but God holds the reins" as the caption of your cartoon.

EXTENDING THE TEXT

5 There is a tradition that the talking donkey was one of the ten things created just before the first Shabbat of creation. The preexistence of certain objects in nature which acted in wondrous ways was used by the Rabbis to explain miracles when the laws of nature seemed to be contravened. If, for example, the talking donkey was created during the period of the creation, then its behavior could be said to be part of the natural order. Try to come up with your own list of ten things from the Torah the miraculous behavior of which would be explained by this approach. (For a list of the traditional ten things, see *Pirke Avot* 5:8.)

6 Pretend you are Balak. Place an ad in the *Midianite Meteor* advertising in the "Help Wanted" section for a prophet who specializes in curses. Or, pretend you are Balaam and advertise for employment. What other ideas for ads can you derive from this portion (e.g., "Donkey for Sale")? (Adapted from *The Jewish Experiential Book* by Bernard Reisman.)

7 Consider the biblical tale of Balaam as a piece of literature. List examples of irony, humor, and repetition. Consider, for example, the incident in which the donkey is able to see the angel of God while Balaam cannot. Select either irony, humor, or repetition and rewrite a portion of the story using one of these literary devices.

8 What kind of man was Balaam? Was he truly a prophet or was he a sorcerer (see Insights B, C, D, pages 266-7, and Joshua 13:22). To help you answer this question, compare the way the prophets of Israel and Balaam received the word of God. Compare the following sources with the details of Balaam's prophecy in the portion *Balak*. Jeremiah 1:4; Ezekiel 1:3; Hosea 1:1; Joel 1:1. Who was more eager for prophecy — Balaam or the Hebrew prophets? How did the word of God come to Balaam? to the other prophets? Which prophets seem to have more freedom regarding prophecy? (For more, see the Index: "Prophecy.")

9 Write a character sketch of Balaam. For help, use the biblical text and the *Midrashim* cited in the Insights for this portion. See also Strategy #8 immediately above.

10 Is *"Balak"* an appropriate name for this portion? Imagine you are the author of this text. Defend to your editor your choice of title.

11 In mime, act out the beginning of the story told in *Balak*. Use bold but simple props to convey the tale. Try depicting two different images of Balaam — the villain and the fool.

12 There are only two instances of animals speaking in the Torah. The first is the snake which spoke to Eve in Genesis 3:1. The second is Balaam's donkey in Numbers 22:21ff. Write and stage a puppet show for younger children about these two characters.

13 Retell the story contained in this portion in a cartoon strip. Draw the action in boxes. Write captions (in Hebrew if possible), quoting from the text where appropriate.

PERSONALIZING THE TEXT

14 Choose one of the four blessings delivered by Balak and paint a large mural depicting some of its imagery. See Strategy #2, page 268, to identify the four blessings.

15 Which of Balaam's sayings comes closest to your idea of a blessing? Why? (For a follow-up, see Strategy #2, page 268).

16 In Numbers 23:9, Balaam describes the Israelites as "a people that dwells apart, not reckoned among the nations." In what ways is this true in past Jewish history? today? Do the Jews want to be a nation apart? Do non-Jews want the Jews to be a nation apart? Is it good for the Jews to be a nation apart? Arrange a forensic union on this theme: Resolved: The Jewish people should remain "a people that dwells apart." (For details about how to conduct a forensic union, see Genesis, *Beresheet*, Strategy #7, page 6.)

17 In *The Torah: A Modern Commentary* (p. 1193), we read that the name Pinchas ("Phinehas") is of Egyptian origin. It means "black skinned." Use this opportunity to learn about the existence and unique problems of black Ethiopian Jews. See one or all of the following videos: *The Falashas, Operation Moses: A Documentary, Again . . . The Second Time.* Also contact: North American Conference on Ethiopian Jewry, 165 East 56th Street, New York, NY 10022.

18 The opening words for the prayer *Mah Tovu* come from the portion *Balak* (Numbers 24:5). This prayer is often used to begin morning worship services. Collect as many different melodies for *Mah Tovu* as you can, then incorporate a *Mah Tovu* songfest into your morning worship service. Good sources for melodies are tapes and CDs, Cantors, song leaders, music teachers, and friends!

19 There is a *midrash* which tells that Balaam was unable to curse the Israelites because he witnessed the Israelite children studying the laws of peace and justice contained in the Torah. The *midrash* concludes, "Those who wish to destroy Israel shall not succeed . . . Israel will perish when her children cease to study" (*Echah Rabbati P'sichta*). In other words, the survival of our people depends on what we do, not on what others say. Organize a task force to review and make recommendations concerning Jewish education in your community. As a community, review the task force's report and how best to use the recommendations they have given.

20 Stage a session of "Meet the Press" using the characters in this portion. Have individuals role playing television journalists interview individuals acting the parts of Balak, Balaam, and perhaps Moses. Study the text in advance to learn about the characters and to develop appropriate questions to ask them.

21 Have a storytelling session. Choose a part of the portion Balak and tell it to your friends as though it were a tall tale. What degree of incredulity is built into the story? How much can you elaborate on the story and still retain a kernel of truth?

OTHER RESOURCES

22 Read, act out, and discuss the skit for the portion *Balak* in *Sedra Scenes: Skits for Every Torah Portion* by Stan J. Beiner, pp. 179-183.

23 Complete the pages which relate to *Balak* in *Bible People Book Two* by Joel Lurie Grishaver, p. 49-53. Also check the accompanying Leader Guide for procedures and additional activities.

24 For more insights and activities about the treatment of animals, see *Teaching Mitzvot* by Barbara Binder Kadden and Bruce Kadden, Chapter 22.

25 For creative movement activities, see "Balaam Blesses" and "Flaunting Leads to Death" from *Torah in Motion* by JoAnne Tucker and Susan Freeman, pp. 180-183.

26 Read and discuss the illustrated commentary for *Balak* in *American Torah Toons* by Lawrence Bush.

INVOLVING THE FAMILY

27 The donkey in this portion speaks to Balaam. What would a pet in your household want to say? If you had the chance to ask questions of your pet, what would they be? Design a list of ten such questions with your family, then imagine together how your pet might respond.

BAR/BAT MITZVAH PROJECT

28 It is debatable whether or not Balaam ever realized the wonder of his talking donkey. In this project, you will have the opportunity to learn more about animals and people. Humans and animals interact in a variety of complex ways. In recent years, therapists have discovered that, in addition to bringing pleasure, contact with animals can help relieve the stress of all kinds of illnesses and of old age. Many towns and cities have programs in which animals are brought to visit hospitals and other kinds of care facilities. Find out if your town has such a program by calling the local Humane Society. Also contact: Linda Hines, c/o Delta Society, 289 Perimeter Rd. East, Renton, WA 98055. This organization has excellent resources including videos and publications on the subject of animals as companions. (Adapted from the Annual Report of the Ziv Tzedakah Fund, Inc., April 1, 1997.)

PINCHAS 25:10-30:1 פנחס

SYNOPSIS

PINCHAS IS THE SON OF THE PRIEST Eleazar. Because of his zeal in slaying the Israelite man and the Midianite woman (see Numbers *Balak*), Pinchas receives a special reward. The high priesthood becomes the possession of his descendants for all time.

At the border of Moab near Jericho, Moses and Eleazar take a census of all male Israelites over 20 years of age, considered able to bear arms. The total is 601,730. Also counted are 23,000 Levite males from the age of one month. They are counted separately; since they are not eligible for military service; nor are they to receive land. Of those counted, only Joshua, Caleb, and Moses had been counted in the first census in the wilderness of Sinai. All adults who had been a part of the first census after the Exodus died in the desert as decreed by God.

God tells Moses that the land is to be divided among the tribes according to the census. Each section of land, however, is to be assigned by lot.

Five daughters of Zelophehad protest the injustice that land was not given to their family solely because their father had no sons. God advises Moses that the plea of the daughters is just. Moses proclaims a general rule that property is to be inherited in the following order: sons are to inherit first, but if there are no sons, property is to be assigned to daughters. In cases where there are no children, the property of a man is to pass to his brothers, and if there are no brothers, the nearest relative shall inherit.

God tells Moses to ascend the mountains of Avarim to see the land given to the Israelites. Moses is to prepare to die there. Because of his act of disobedience at the waters of Meribat-Kadaysh, he is not to enter the Promised Land. Moses asks God to appoint a new leader over the community. He is told to ordain Joshua the son of Nun in the sight of Eleazar and the whole Israelite community.

The portion concludes with a detailing of the daily, Sabbath, monthly, and festival sacrifices to be brought before God.

INSIGHTS FROM THE TRADITION

A Pinchas receives "the Lord's Covenant of Peace" also translated as "Pact of Friendship" for his zealous act in slaying Zimri and Cozbi. The *midrash* praises the gift of peace, for peace maintains the world (*Numbers Rabbah* 21:1). Pinchas was rewarded for risking his life for God's honor and because his actions reestablished peace between God and Israel (Rashi). There is a tradition which identifies Pinchas with Elijah the prophet. Both were distinguished by their zeal and their efforts at peacemaking and were therefore given the privilege of heralding the arrival of the Messiah.

What does zeal mean?
Is zealous behavior always good? Explain.
When do you act with zeal?

B Once the plague abated, which happened in portion *Balak,* God instructed Moses and Eleazer to count the Israelites. Three reasons are given for this new census: (1) to see how many survived; (2) the time of Moses' death was approaching and, as a shepherd would, he counted his flock before turning them over to a new shepherd; and (3) to serve as proof that the Israelites had kept their family lines pure. Those tribes which had behaved immorally in the desert would face divine punishment and would ultimately become extinct (*Yalkut Me'am Lo'ez* by Yaacov Culi, Vol. XIV, pp. 231-232). Nachmanides adds that the land had to be apportioned family by family. Therefore, this was a census of family groups, rather than of individuals.

What other jobs or tasks involve "census taking" at the start of a shift or a workday?

In what ways are you "counted" each day, month, and year?

C Zelophehad is specifically mentioned in the census as having died leaving behind only daughters. Since nothing in the Torah is superfluous, the account of Zelophehad foreshadows the issue of females as heirs. *Sifrei* tells us that this law had long been established, but that Moses was unable to perceive it.

Rashi explains that the daughters, due to their merit, had a clearer perception than Moses and thus brought forth their claim. Most ancient law allows only sons and male relatives to inherit. Allowing a woman (or in this case, women) to inherit was an innovation in biblical society.

Ellen Frankel, in her work *The Five Books of Miriam,* includes several teachings about this incident (pp. 235-236). The Rabbis teach that God does not prefer males over females, but God extends divine love and compassion to women as well as to men. Contemporary sages say that the story justifies why women were permitted to inherit land within a patriarchal system. Beruriah, the scholar, has the last word, stating that this story has important lessons for all of us. It teaches that Jewish law has the flexibility to expand and embrace women, giving women more rights and a fairer share of the Jewish legacy.

This initial biblical text regarding inheritance is seen as extremely innovative. What lesson can we learn from its flexibility and attitude?
What approach did the daughters of Zelophehad use to solve their dilemma? How can contemporary society use this approach?

D Moses is informed here of his impending death. In the biblical text itself, Moses does not bemoan his fate. He seems to accept it calmly and even begins the process of disposing of his earthly responsibilities. Moses asks God to appoint a new leader for the Israelites. A Hasidic commentary tells us that Moses asked that the new leader be "a man among men; a man, not a superman; a man, not a burning zealot like Pinchas" (*Al HaTorah* by Mordechai Hacohen, quoted in *The Torah: A Modern Commentary,* edited by W. Gunther Plaut, p. 1207).

Why would Pinchas not be a good choice as the leader of the Israelites?
Would you want a Pinchas-type person as leader of your country?

F Joshua ben Nun is chosen by God to be Moses' successor. God instructs Moses to bring Joshua before Eleazar the priest and the entire community to publicly transfer leadership from Moses to Joshua. Moses was to signify the transfer of authority to Joshua by placing his hand upon him (Numbers 27:18). Rashi points out that Moses placed both hands upon Joshua's head (Numbers 27:23), making Joshua the recipient of a generous helping of the wisdom of Moses. *Numbers Rabbah* 21:15 tells us that this physical transfer of authority is like one candle lighting another. The first candle loses no light in this process; there is just more light.

Joshua now is to be the keeper of Torah. This *midrash* illustrates this with a verse from Proverbs 27:18: "Whoso keepeth the fig tree shall eat the fruit thereof." Why is Torah compared to a fig tree? Because the fruits of most trees are gathered all at once, while the fruit of the fig tree is gathered little by little. This is like Torah. One gathers a little knowledge today and more tomorrow, for it cannot be learned in a year or even in two.

How does this *midrash* explain Judaism's attachment to lifelong learning?
Can you think of things other than candle lighting and Torah which grow and spread without the original source being diminished?

STRATEGIES

ANALYZING THE TEXT

1 Selected verses from *Pinchas* which describe the sacrifices to be given on each festival and on the new moon are read as the *Maftir* portion on those holidays. Therefore, verses from *Pinchas* are read more frequently than those from any other *parashiyot*. Following is a listing of the verses read on various holidays. Your task is to identify the holidays which fit with the Torah verses (Answers are given in the parentheses).

Numbers 29:1-6	(Rosh HaShanah)
Numbers 29:7-11	(Yom Kippur)
Numbers 29:12-16	(Sukkot)
Numbers 29:35-39	(Shemini Atzeret and Simchat Torah)
Numbers 28:16-25	(1st and 2nd day of Passover)
Numbers 28:19-25	(last day of Passover)
Numbers 28:26-31	(1st day of Shavuot)
Numbers 28:9-15	(Rosh Chodesh — the New Moon)

2 Read Numbers 27:15-17. How do you understand the words "who shall go out before them and come in before them?" Individually, write your own explanation of the qualities Moses sought in his successor. Copy the text neatly onto the center of a large piece of poster board. Have individuals write their explanations around the text. Then study the text together with your own *midrashim*.

3 The Book of Joshua is the first book of the Prophets. It tells how Joshua led the Israelites in their conquest of Canaan. Read the first chapter of the Book of Joshua to learn how Joshua assumed the mantle of leadership after the death of Moses. Is the message Joshua receives from God similar to the words of the Israelites? Are there any identical phrases? Compare Joshua 1:9 and 1:18. What other comparisons can you make?

Joshua never questioned God. If you were Joshua, could you have remained so silent? Write a response to God's words.

EXTENDING THE TEXT

4 Write a job description for the new leader of the Israelites which expands the poetic metaphor given by Moses in Numbers 27:17. Take into consideration the history of the Israelite people since the Exodus from Egypt. Also read the first chapter of the Book of Joshua. What tasks does God remind Joshua to do? What further instructions does God give Joshua?

5 Research the various covenants in the Torah. See the Index to this book under the heading "Covenant" to locate the covenants found in the Torah. Also make use of a biblical Concordance to aid in the search.

Using the information, make a *Covenant Match-up* card game. For each example of a covenant, make two cards. On one card, write and draw the person or people with whom the covenant was made. On the other, write and illustrate the specific nature of the covenant.

Play as you would *Concentration*. Place all cards face down on a playing surface and take turns flipping two cards over per turn trying to find matching pairs. The game ends when all the matches have been made. The player with the most pairs wins.

6 On Shabbat, an extra sacrifice was to be brought (Numbers 28:9-10). This offering was called the *"Musaf."* In the synagogue, an additional service — Musaf — replaces this offering. Examine the Musaf service for Shabbat in a traditional prayer book. What prayers are part of this service? Find and read the particular prayer which refers to the *Musaf* offering.

7 The sections from *Pinchas* pertaining to holy day sacrifices (Numbers 28:9-15) are read on Rosh Chodesh, which is observed at each new moon to celebrate the beginning of a new Jewish month. The celebration of Rosh Chodesh is seeing a renaissance in contemporary Judaism. There are several excellent resources available for you to examine and study. This information will lay the foundation for you to create a Rosh Chodesh observance. In Jewish tradition, Rosh Chodesh is seen as a semi-holiday for women. This observance may also be used to help develop a group that wishes to continue with monthly observances for the new moon.
Resources: *Miriam's Well: Rituals for Jewish Women Around the World* by Penina V. Adelman; *Celebrating the New Moon: A Rosh Chodesh Anthology* by Susan Berrin; *Seasons of Our Joy: A Handbook of Jewish Festivals* by Arthur Waskow; *The Rosh Hodesh Table: Foods at the New Moon* by Judith Y. Solomon.

8 The text does not tell us what Moses planned to bequeath to his children upon his death. Write an ethical will for Moses in which he reminds his family of the values he held dear and the lessons by which he wishes to be remembered. Reference: The mini-course *Ethical Wills: Handing Down Our Jewish Heritage* by Barbara Binder Kadden and Bruce Kadden.

PERSONALIZING THE TEXT

9 As discussed in Strategy #8 immediately above, when Moses was preparing an ethical will he may also have given some thought to a will of inheritance. Invite an attorney to speak to your group about the necessity of preparing a will of inheritance. Also ask the guest speaker to talk about the legal requirements for a will and discuss the usual contents of a will.

10 Write a resume as though you were Joshua applying for the job described in Strategy #4, page 274. Detail your qualifications to be the new leader of the Israelites.

11 Imagine you are Moses ascending the mountain and seeing the land which you will never enter. Write a soliloquy, such as Moses might deliver in a play, about this moment of his life. Choose appropriate music and set the stage for this scene.

12 The census recounted in *Pinchas* gives the family trees of the original Israelites — Jacob's sons. Why do you think the list of descendants begins with them, rather than with Jacob or even Abraham? Trace your own family tree back to a member who did something which significantly affected *your* life. Explain your choice.

13 Create a large wall chart illustrating the Jewish laws of inheritance as laid down in Numbers 27:8-11. Read about inheritance in a secular encyclopedia and/or invite a lawyer to explain the laws to you. (Draw another chart depicting the distribution of property upon death in your country today.) Compare the two charts. What differences do you see? How can you explain the reasons for these differences?

14 In this portion, God rewards Pinchas with a "pact of friendship" for his zealous behavior recorded at the end of the previous portion, *Balak*. What do you think of when you hear the phrase "pact of friendship?" When you make a friend, while a "pact" is generally not spelled out, there are basic qualities and characteristics of friendship which are generally assumed. What do you think those qualities and characteristics are?

To help facilitate a discussion, listen to some of the golden oldies listed below, which are on the theme of friendship. As part of the discussion, talk about the meaning and influence friendship has on our lives.

Some examples of songs about friendship: "Bridge Over Troubled Water" and "Old Friends" by Simon and Garfunkel; "You've Got a Friend" by Carole King, also recorded by James Taylor. Add contemporary songs about friendship. As a part of the discussion, also compare the older songs with the newer songs. Are the messages of the songs the same or different? What other comparisons can you make?

15 Although both Aaron and Pinchas performed deeds which stopped plagues (see *Korach* for Aaron and *Balak* for Pinchas), only Pinchas was given a pact of friendship. Why? A Hasidic *midrash* states: "Aaron used incense, and that was available only in the days of the Temple. But Pinchas used prayer, which may be utilized even today" (*The Hasidic Anthology* by Louis Newman, p. 3429, #133.4). Many other Hasidic stories make the same point: prayer from the heart has the power to move God. Make up your own story illustrating this idea.

16 The commentary *Al HaTorah* states that Pinchas exemplified Hillel's saying "In a place where there are no men, strive to be a man." Discuss how this applies to Pinchas and his treatment of the Israelite man and the Midianite woman (in the portion *Balak*).

Modern translators have rendered Hillel's saying somewhat differently: "In a place where no one behaves like a human being, each of us must strive to be human" (*Pirke Avot* 2:6). Does the difference in translation affect your understanding of it? In what way? Does the saying in its new form still apply to Pinchas?

Make a collage which shows what it means to be a "human being" in a place where people are acting less kindly and righteously than they should.

Suggested media for the collage: magazines and newspaper clippings and photos mounted on construction paper or poster board.

17 In *Alone Atop the Mountain* by Samuel Sandmel (p. 221), Moses describes his

meeting with Pinchas after the slaying of Zimri and Cozbi: ". . . Phinehas came to me proudly, to tell me of his achievement. He spoke as if sure I would praise him. I said, "How did you dare?" "How did I dare? I do not understand!" "How did you dare on your own to kill these people?" "But they were doing an abominable thing!" "We have our laws. There are legal procedures." "This was urgent. This was a flagrant violation." "And so was yours, Phinehas; I do not praise you. In my judgment, your trespass is even worse than the Simeonites."

Discuss Moses' judgment of Pinchas. Arrange a mock trial for Pinchas in which Moses prosecutes him for violating the law of Israel. For witnesses, select someone aided by Pinchas' deed, God, the High Priest, the individuals appointed to help Moses judge the people, and perhaps some later Rabbinic commentators.

18 In this portion, *Pinchas,* the Israelites have been in the desert for 38 years. What must life have been like in the sprawling Israelite camp? Plan and present a market bazaar full of shops and booths that might have been part of Israelite life during their stay in the desert. You could stage this as a celebration of the end of the desert exile and the start of life in the Promised Land.

19 The explanation for the long desert sojourn was that God did not want any of the adults from the generation of the Exodus from Egypt to survive and enter the Land. Write an obituary for that generation of Israelites who died in the desert.

OTHER RESOURCES

20 Read, act out, and discuss the skit for the portion *Pinchas* in *Sedra Scenes: Skits for Every Torah Portion* by Stan J. Beiner, pp.184-187.

21 Complete the pages which relate to *Pinchas* in *Bible People Book Two* by Joel Lurie Grishaver, pp. 54-56. Also check the accompanying Leader Guide for procedures and additional activities.

22 For creative movement activities, see "Daughters of Zelophehad" and "New Moons" from *Torah in Motion* by JoAnne Tucker and Susan Freeman, pp. 184-187.

23 Read and discuss the illustrated commentary for *Pinchas* in *American Torah Toons* by Lawrence Bush.

24 Since this portion contains a great deal of information on the festivals and on the observance of the new moon it would be an excellent time to learn about the Jewish calendar. Use the mini-course *The Jewish Calendar* by Raymond A. Zwerin.

INVOLVING THE FAMILY

25 In the portion *Pinchas,* a new generation is being readied to enter the Promised Land. An important part of this preparation is a review of their Israelite history, which is repeated in the Book of Deuteronomy. Plan a quiz for family members to review Israelite history through this portion. Children can then prepare questions for their parents and parents can make up questions for their children. These questions can be put into a game show format, which can entertain the entire family.

BAR/BAT MITZVAH PROJECT

26 We are taught that during the 38-year trek through the desert, neither the clothing nor shoes of the people wore out. This may have been the Israelite experience thousands of years ago, but today the reality is that clothing wears out and so do shoes. An amazing woman, Ranya Kelly of Denver, Colorado, one day accidently discovered several hundred pairs of brand new but discarded shoes. She took some of the shoes to a local shelter and once she saw the need for these shoes, she decided to continue looking for more. Ultimately, shoe stores began donating shoes to her project and continue to do so. The project, now called The Redistribution Center, has expanded to include clothing, food, toys, and building materials. Ranya takes no salary for her work, but she does need donations for a warehouse, truckers and trucks, and a full-time assistant. She also wants people to establish redistribution centers in other parts of the country. To find out how you can be a part of this project, contact: Ranya Kelly, The Redistribution Center, 7736 Hoyt Circle, Arvada, CO 80005. (Adapted from the Annual Report of the Ziv Tzedakah Fund, Inc., April 1, 1997.)

MATOT 30:2-32:42 מטות

SYNOPSIS

THE SPECIAL RULES CONCERNING WOMEN'S vows are given. Whereas a man may not break a vow or an oath which he makes to God, a woman's vow may be annulled by her father or husband on the day it is made. Vows made by widowed or divorced women, however, are binding.

God commands Moses to take revenge upon the Midianite people. One thousand men are picked from each tribe to battle the Midianites under the leadership of Pinchas. All the male Midianites are slain in the campaign, including the five kings of the region and the prophet Balaam. Their women and children are taken captive, the towns and encampments are burned, and all the booty is brought to Moses and Eleazar at Moab near Jericho.

Moses is angry with the leaders of the battle for sparing the women who were responsible for drawing the Israelites into sin at Shittim (see Numbers, *Balak*). He orders them slain together with every male child. Eleazar instructs the troops concerning cleansing themselves and concerning distribution of the booty collected. After cleansing, the booty is divided equally among the troops and the rest of the Israelites, with a share being withheld as an offering to God.

The tribes of Reuben and Gad speak to Moses. They desire to settle east of the Jordan River in the lands of Jazar and Gilead, as these lands are suitable for their cattle. Moses permits them to establish their homes there, provided that all the men then join the rest of the Israelites in the battles to be waged west of the Jordan. So the Reubenites, Gadites, and the half tribe of Manasseh establish fortified cities on the east side of the Jordan river.

INSIGHTS FROM THE TRADITION

A *Matot* means tribes or divisions. The portion begins in an unusual manner with Moses speaking only to the "heads" of the Israelite tribes about vows. Nachmanides suggested that this was done so as not to encourage the practice of making vows among the populace.

A vow is similar to a promise. It could be considered a promise to God. What does a promise mean to you?
Have you ever made a promise?
Has anyone ever broken a promise they made to you?
What do you think about the making of promises?

B A vow may also be understood as a pledge made to God in which one promises to dedicate oneself to an act, service, or way of life. The third of the Ten Commandments warns us not to take God's name in vain. If one failed to fulfill a vow, then God's wrath would be provoked.

Biblical tradition stated that a man's vows were inviolable. However, women's vows could under certain circumstances be annulled by a father or a husband. In biblical society, married women or women dependent on their fathers did not have any personal or economic power. A woman could not give away what was not hers. It is interesting to note that vows made by widows and divorcees were binding.

What was different in the status of dependent daughters and wives in relation to widows and divorcees? Why do you think the Jewish law allowed for the annulment of vows made by dependent daughters and wives as opposed to the vows made by widows and divorcees?

C Moses is told that his death will occur right after the war with the Midianites. When the Israelites heard that Moses' death was linked to the war against Midian, they refused to participate. It became necessary to draft them against their will. This shows that the Israelites truly loved Moses. Throughout his period of leadership, the Israelites gave Moses no peace, but now on the eve of his death, they showed their true feelings for him (*Yalkut Me'am Lo'ez* by Yaacov Culi, Vol. XIV, p. 344).

How might knowing the time of one's death affect an individual?

Why would the Israelites hide their true feelings about Moses? Were they so concerned about themselves that there was literally "no room" to think consciously about or express their true feelings regarding Moses?

Do you ever hide your true feelings about someone or something?

How do you prove your loyalty to another person?

D Moses did not lead his people in their battle of vengeance against the Midianites. Why? Because Moses had found refuge in Midian when he fled from Egypt. Bearing in mind the proverb "Cast no stone into the well from which thou hast drawn water," he did not wish to make war upon the Midianites. Moses relinquished his authority to Pinchas, for "he that beginneth a good deed shall also complete it." It was Pinchas who had begun God's war against the Midianites by slaying the princess Cozbi, Zimri's mistress (*Legends of the Jews* by Louis Ginzberg, Vol. III, pp. 408-9).

Do you agree that one who begins a task should have the opportunity to finish it?

What about the saying: "You are not required to complete the work, but neither are you at liberty to abstain from it" (*Pirke Avot* 2:21)?

Into what "well" would you not cast stones?

E This portion provides us with some significant information — Balaam was the cause of the Israelites sinning with the women (Numbers 31:16). Why is the account of Balaam's inducing the Israelites to sin recorded only here, in the portion in which his death is also noted (Numbers 31:8)? When the event was originally recorded, the text says, "the people profaned *themselves*" (Numbers 25:1). Balaam's role is not mentioned there. The Rabbis understood this as teaching that, although Balaam instigated the sinning, the Israelites themselves were responsible for their conduct.

"Someone else made me do it!" When was the last time you used that as an excuse? How do you really feel when you use it? How do you react when someone identifies you as the instigator? Does blaming someone else for your mistake really help you learn what to do and what not to do?

F It is interesting to note that Moses is commanded to retaliate against the Midianites and not vex Moab. In the original story (Numbers 25:1-5), blame is laid on the Moabites for the incident at Shittim. The *midrash* provides several explanations for this, while the Moabites hated them, the Midianites outdid the Moabites in their level of hatred against Israel. And, although the Moabites wanted to kill Israel, the Midianites wanted to tempt them to sin which is considered much worse than death. Moses waged war immediately against the Midianites. Retaliation against the Moabites did not occur until the time of David. The *midrash* explains that the delay in punishing Moab was part of God's plan, for Ruth, the Moabite, was to become the mother of the dynasty of David. "God said to Israel: 'Wait yet a while in this matter of the war against the Moabites: I have lost something valuable among them. As soon as I have found it, you shall avenge yourselves of them'" (*The Legends of the Jews* by Louis Ginsberg, Vol. III, pp. 405-406).

Explain the second *midrash* about Ruth and the Moabites.

G The tribes of Reuben, Gad, and the half-tribe of Manasseh approach Moses with their desire to settle east of the Jordan River, outside the Promised Land. Moses unleashes a chastisement against them, comparing their requests with the behavior of their parents. He lets them know that they are abandoning the divine mission of the chosen people. However, they express their preference for this land because it would be good for their cattle. Rashi tells us that they were more concerned about their property than their children, since they spoke of their cattle before speaking of their families. Rashi interprets that Moses said, "Make the chief thing the chief thing and what is subordinate subordinate. First, build cities for your little ones and afterward folds for your flocks."

Nehama Leibowitz relates contemporary Jewish life to the request of these tribes. She sees this as a choice between career advancement, working for personal gain, and the fulfillment of a higher mission.

The first use of the word *chalutzim* (armed men) refers to the two and a half tribes who agreed to help the rest of the Israelites conquer the land. This term is now a part of everyday usage and has come to represent those pioneers who chose to forsake personal gain in order to participate in the building of *Eretz Yisrael* (*Studies in Bamidbar, Matot,* Chapter 2).

Why do you think these tribes lost sight of the mission of the Israelites?
Can one be a builder of *Eretz Yisrael* without residing there?
What is your responsibility to the Promised Land?
Is there still a mission for Jews in the world today? If yes, what is it?

Note: The portion *Matot* is usually read as a double portion with *Mas'ay* which follows. For more about double portions, see Exodus, *Pikuday*, Insight A, page 155.

STRATEGIES

ANALYZING THE TEXT

1 Based on a careful reading of *Matot*, what can you infer about the status of women in biblical times? Write a short paragraph to present your findings. If you wish, add another paragraph expressing your feelings about these biblical ideas and attitudes in relation to contemporary Judaism.

2 Read the sections of Deuteronomy which detail the laws of war (Deuteronomy 7:16ff. and 20:1ff.). Discuss in what ways and to what degree the war on the Midianites, described in *Matot*, conforms to these laws.

3 In this portion, the prophet Balaam is slain. Read about Balaam in portion *Balak*, Numbers 22:2-24:25. Briefly summarize Balaam's story. At the end of this encounter where did Balaam go? Where was his home? When we turn to portion *Matot*, it seems that Balaam has turned up again. Read Numbers 31:8 in this portion. What do you learn here? What is his fate? Based upon your reading of Numbers 22:2-24:25, did Balaam deserve to die at the hands of the Israelites? To get some answers, read Numbers 31:13-16 in this portion followed by Numbers 25:1-5. (For more about Balaam, see portion *Balak*.)

4 In Exodus 20:7 and Leviticus 19:12, we are told not to swear falsely by the name of God. What is meant by swearing falsely? Why is swearing falsely considered a profanation of the Name of God?

EXTENDING THE TEXT

5 A study of Numbers 32:16-24 reveals that Moses and the tribes of Reuben and Gad had a very different perspective about their responsibilities. Compare and contrast the tribes' request of Moses (Numbers 32:16-19) with Moses' reply to them (Numbers 32:20-24). How does Moses emphasize what *he* sees as the Reubenites' and Gadites' responsibilities? How does he emphasize their dependence on God? How does Moses' reply subtly rebuke these tribes for valuing their material possessions above all else? Flesh out and dramatize this part of the text, highlighting the above points.

6 In *Matot,* land is given to Reuben and Gad on the condition that they fulfill their obligations. This became the basis for the Jewish law of conditional contracts (called *tennaim*). Read "Halachah on Conditional Contracts" in *The Torah: A Modern Commentary,* edited by W. Gunther Plaut, p. 1232.

To demonstrate the four principles of a conditional contract, dramatize the incident of the Reubenites and the Gadites asking for and receiving permission to settle in Jazer and Gilead. Have placards denoting each step. Carry them silently across the stage at the appropriate moments.

7 The specific rules pertaining to *kashering* utensils are derived from Numbers 31:21-23. Read the Orthodox guidelines on *kashrut* and explain how they are derived in their most basic form from this text.
Reference: *Kosher Code of the Orthodox Jews* by S.I. Levin and Edward A. Boyden.

8 Look at some of the examples of the making of vows in the Bible (Genesis 28:20-22, Judges 11:30-31, I Samuel 1:11, II Samuel 15:8, Jonah 1:16). Dramatize the incidents surrounding the making of these vows. Demonstrate the emotions of each person at the time of undertaking the vow.

Read Deuteronomy 23:22-24 for other biblical provisions concerning vows. Discuss whether the vows in the examples above conform to the standards set out in Deuteronomy. (For more, see the Index: "Vows.")

9 It is certainly true that any person, whether male or female, might make a rash or foolish vow, which he or she might later regret. The Book of Judges, for example, tells the story of Jephthah and an unfortunate vow he made. Read this story in Judges, Chapter 11. The text seems to be warning us about two practices. Can you identify them? (The making of vows and sacrificing human beings.) Pinchas, who was the High Priest at this time, did nothing to stop Jephthah. Stage a short dramatic reading of this incident. Stop at moments of high tension and allow the audience to get involved and call out advice to the characters. In a summary discussion, talk about how this tragedy could have been avoided.

10 Study the sections of the Mishnah detailing the annullment of vows.
Reference: *Learn Mishnah* by Jacob Neusner, pp. 64-74.

11 The Jordan river valley is one of the great natural treasures of the land of Israel. Many sights of historic and geographic interest lie along the river. Imagine you are a tour operator planning to guide a group on a tour of this area. Research the places you would want to take your group to see. Create a travel brochure which includes a map of your route and the historic and geographic highlights which are part of the trip.

PERSONALIZING THE TEXT

12 *Kol Nidre,* which is sung at the beginning of Yom Kippur, is a special declaration annulling vows. Read the prayer in a *Machzor.* What kinds of vows does this prayer annul?

Investigate when this prayer was written in order to explain it's origin and contents. Why do we annul all our vows at the New Year as we review our past deeds and think about the future? Write a letter to yourself about the person you are striving to be in the coming year. Seal the letter into an envelope to be opened in one year. When you reread the letter after a year has passed, use it as a kind of yardstick to measure how well you've done.

References: *Teaching Mitzvot* by Barbara Binder Kadden and Bruce Kadden, pp. 75-78; *Teaching Tefilah* by Bruce Kadden and Barbara Binder Kadden, pp. 98-103; *Encyclopedia Judaica* "Oath More Judaico" Vol.12, pp. 1302-1304.

13 Using the verses listed below, make a fact file about women in the Torah. Summarize each verse you use on individual index cards. Then group related cards together under appropriate headings such as: vows, inheritance, marriage and divorce, motherhood. Choose one category and write a short account comparing and contrasting the position of women in society today with that of biblical women.

References: Genesis 3:16; Exodus 20:12, 21:7, 22-26, 28-31, 23:17, 35:22-29, 38:8; Leviticus 11, 12:2-59, 15:1ff, 19:29, 20:10; Numbers 6:2ff., 30:4-16; Deuteronomy 5:16, 17:2,5, 22:5, 24:1-4, 29:17-18. (For more, see the Index: "Women.")

14 Moses advised the Reubenites and the Gadites that they would "be clear before God" (Numbers 32:22) if their warriors joined with the other Israelites in the fight to subdue the land of Canaan. The phrase "clear before the Lord" is the basis for the Rabbinic idea of *Mareet Ayin* — literally, "appearances").

Rabbi J.H. Hertz asserts that one should be clear not only before God, but also in the eyes of others. It is not enough that one's conscience is pure. One must strive to make even one's outward actions irreproachable and above suspicion. One should avoid doing things that appear wrong (*The Pentateuch and Haftorahs*, p. 709). Write a story illustrating the problems that can arise when a person, doing good, gives the impression of acting wrongly.

15 The word *chalutz*, which appears in Numbers 32:21 (and also in Joshua 6:13). has been translated variously as "shock-troops," "warrior," "armed," or "drafted." In contemporary Hebrew, the word means "pioneer." The biblical "*chalutzim*" formed the vanguard that led the army in its advance on the land. Explain the connection between the biblical and modern uses of the word. Design a stamp to honor either the biblical or modern "*chalutzim.*"

16 Imagine you are a journalist reporting on the Israelite war against the Midianites. Write three brief reports: one presenting a view biased in favor of the Midianites, one expressing a view favoring the Israelites, and one containing no bias. What are the characteristics of each report? Examine current reporting about Israel in a variety of sources to see if you can detect biases.

17 The Rabbis discouraged the making of vows unless a person is like Abraham, Joseph, and Job — individuals who truly feared God. Why do you think the Rabbis took this position? What characteristics did Abraham, Joseph, and Job possess that exempted them from this advice?

18 Make a jigsaw puzzle depicting the area where the tribes of Reuben and Gad wanted to settle. Draw and illustrate your map on heavy cardboard. When you are finished, cut it into jigsaw pieces using a razor blade or scissors. Put all the pieces in an envelope. Exchange puzzles with a friend. Can you assemble each other's puzzle?

OTHER RESOURCES

19 Read and discuss the poem "But Not the Children" in *The Fire Waits* by Michael Hecht, pp. 97-98. Review the sources cited by the author. Can you explain how he arrived at his thesis?

20 Read, act out, and discuss the skit for the portion *Matot* in *Sedra Scenes: Skits for Every Torah Portion* by Stan J. Beiner, pp. 188-191.

21 For a creative movement activity, see "Limits of Women's Vows" from *Torah in Motion* by JoAnne Tucker and Susan Freeman, pp. 188-189.

22 Read and discuss the illustrated commentary for *Matot* in *American Torah Toons* by Lawrence Bush.

INVOLVING THE FAMILY

23 When the Reubenites and the Gadites asked Moses for permission to settle in the lands of Jazer and Gilead, they first made mention of their cattle and then referred to their children (Numbers 31:16). Moses subtly rebukes them by reversing this order when permission is given (Numbers 32:24). As a family, discuss how your priorities are expressed. Do you sometimes seem to put things before people? Why? Make a plan to help you act on some of your priorities. List the things which are most important to you in your daily life and list some longer term goals. Decide how you can organize your time to do the things that are really important to you. This can be done either individually or as a family. In either case, share the results as a family and work together to help each other fulfill these goals.

BAR/BAT MITZVAH PROJECT

24 In *Matot,* the tribes of Reuben and Gad are given permission to settle east of the Jordan River, provided they recognize their obligation to help the rest of the Israelites conquer and settle the land of Canaan. Do you think that Jews living outside the land of Israel today continue to have an obligation to help those who are building the modern state of Israel? Find out about an organization devoted to supporting grassroots *tzedakah* groups in Israel. Write to The New Israel Fund, 1101 15th St., NW, Washington, D.C. 20005 for information about its work and the particular groups its funds. Decorate a *tzedakah* box to illustrate what you have learned and add the regular giving of small change for *tzedakah* to your home Shabbat observance. When your *tzedakah* box is full, send a contribution to The New Israel Fund.

MAS'AY 33:1-36:13 מסעי

SYNOPSIS

THE ROUTE TAKEN BY THE ISRAELITES FROM Egypt to the steppes of Moab and the major events that occurred along the way are recounted. At Moab, God tells Moses to instruct the Israelites about settling the land across the Jordan. They are to dispossess all its inhabitants, destroy their gods, and apportion the land among the tribes by lot.

The boundaries of the land are: Edom to the south, the Mediterranean Sea to the west, along a line drawn from Mount Hor to Hazar-enan in the north, and from Hazar-enan to Shepham, and then inward to the Jordan River and the Dead Sea on the east.

The Israelites are to assign, out of their holdings, towns and pasture lands to the Levites. There are to be a total of 48 towns, six of which to be cities of refuge to which a person who has killed another unintentionally may flee. It is the responsibility of the next of kin, literally the "blood-avenger," to put a deliberate murderer to death.

Laws are given citing the circumstances and manner in which murder (both intentional and unintentional) is to be judged and punished.

The descendants of Manasseh appeal to Moses and the Elders concerning the case of the daughters of Zelophehad (see Numbers, *Pinchas*). They allege that if the daughters marry persons from another tribe, their land holdings will be added to those of the tribe into which they marry, thus diminishing the size of the lands of Manasseh. Moses, therefore, rules that the daughters of Zelophehad must marry within their father's tribe. This is based on the general statement that no tribe's inheritance may pass to another tribe.

The Book of Numbers concludes with the statement: "These are the commandments and regulations that the Lord enjoined upon the Israelites, through Moses, on the steppes of Moab, at the Jordan near Jericho" (Numbers 36:13).

INSIGHTS FROM THE TRADITION

A *Mas'ay* (marches) begins with a description of the route the Israelites followed in their 40 years in the desert. Many commentators were puzzled by this dry recital of place names in the Torah. Maimonides stated that, as a general principle, there is good reason for every passage in Torah, even if we cannot see it (*Guide of the Perplexed*, p. 384). He explained that the list of names was necessary because of the passage "Moses recorded the . . . marches as *directed by Adonai*" (Numbers 33:2). According to Maimonides, God wanted the record given so that no other nation could claim that the Israelites wandered in the desert for 40 years because they were lost.

Rashi, on the other hand, explained that the places are recorded to remind the Israelites of the misery of their journey so that they might better appreciate their lives in the Promised Land.

Have you ever gone on a vacation and kept a travel diary or taken pictures? Why were you motivated to do this? When you look at these travel mementos, what kinds of memories do you have? Have your grandparents or other relatives experienced unusual events which they shared with you? How does learning about their past influence you?

B Mordecai Hacohen (*Al haTorah*) notes the curious omission of the revelation at Sinai in the account of the journeys. The reason for the omission, Hacohen posits, is that once the Torah was given, it became timeless and cut loose from any one place; every moment is its moment and every place is its place (quoted in *The Torah: A Modern Commentary*, edited by W. Gunther Plaut, p. 1240).

What memory or value or gift do you take with you wherever you go, whatever you do?

C The command to dispossess all the inhabitants of the Land and to destroy all remnants of their idol worship seems harsh and unduly cruel. A Hasidic *midrash* provides justification for this command. The Israelites were entering Canaan and their mission was to lead a holy life. The land would be sanctified by the observance of the *mitzvot*. Without Torah, Israel is like any other land (*Maayanah Shel Torah*, Vol. IV, p. 461). With idol worshipers in their midst, the Israelites might be attracted to their practices.

The goal of driving out the pagan inhabitants is to establish a land imbued with Torah. The Israelites will have to use brute force to attain this goal. Does this damage their cause? Why doesn't/can't God drive out the pagan inhabitants? Why is it the Israelites' responsibility?
Does life in a secular society weaken Judaism? Does secular society weaken all religious groups? In what ways does it affect your religious practices and observances?

D If the Israelites do not clear the land of its pagan inhabitants, they are warned that these inhabitants will be "stings in your eyes and thorns in your sides, and they shall harass you in the land in which you live" (Numbers 33:55). Rashi explains that these pagan peoples would become a barrier that hedges in the Israelites, enclosing and imprisoning them so they would not have free movement.

Does this in any way parallel the current Middle East situation?
What "pagan practices" do you see today which you wish would disappear?

E *Mas'ay* contains provisions for the establishment of the 48 Levitical cities, of which six were to be cities of refuge. Although the Torah states that the Levites were not to be apportioned land, some provision was necessary for them and their families. The Levite priesthood was not monastic and they needed land for their homes and families. Elsewhere in the Torah, the holdings of the Levites are given special protection — their land cannot be sold and, unlike the dwellings of other Israelites, their land can be redeemed forever (Leviticus 25:31-34).

The text points out that the cities of the Levites should be fairly apportioned in each tribal area; thus the burden of maintaining the Levites would then be equally shared among the tribes.

Are there people in society today who enjoy special privileges because of their jobs or economic level? Are there special privileges that you enjoy? How did they become available to you?

F The institution of the cities of refuge and the other laws pertaining to murder in this portion mark a significant advance over other Middle Eastern societies. Today, a court is assigned to resolve cases of murder, thus ending the custom of the family of a murdered person taking justice into its own hands. Similarly, only the murderer can be punished for his or her crime, as opposed to the former custom in which any member of the murderer's family could be killed to exact justice. Furthermore, this law extends to strangers in the land; all are to have equal protection under the law.

Only an individual who had *unintentionally* killed another, as determined by the court, could seek shelter in a city of refuge. A *midrash* explains that Moses was particularly sensitive to this issue. Having "unintentionally killed an Egyptian" (see Exodus, *Shemot*), "he knew the feelings of a pursued man" (*The Rabbis' Bible*, p. 188).

Numbers Rabbah 23:13 equates the establishment of the cities of refuge with God's treatment of Adam and Eve after they had eaten the forbidden fruit. Although the Torah says, "for as soon as you eat of it, you shall die" (Genesis 2:17), Adam and Eve were punished by banishment only. In like manner, a person who committed an unintentional murder deserves God's mercy.

What is mercy? How do you show it? Can you cite some contemporary examples of individuals who exercise mercy?

Why can't we let people who are wronged seek out their own justice?

Have you ever received a lighter punishment for a misdeed when you were previously told that you would face stiffer penalties? Describe what happened and how you reacted.

G The person banished to a city of refuge is not permitted to leave the city until the death of the High Priest. The fact that freedom of movement is limited makes the person conscious of having taken a human life, even if accidentally.

This release upon the death of the High Priest has been compared to the amnesties which are sometimes granted today when new leadership takes over a country. Plaut explains that even in cases of unintentional murder, a death was needed to compensate for the lost life — a role which the High Priest's death symbolically fulfilled (*The Torah: A Modern Commentary*, edited by W. Gunther Plaut, p. 1249). Maimonides, on the other hand, explains that by the High Priest's death, the relative of the slain person becomes reconciled. It is natural, he claims, to find consolation in our misfortune when the same misfortune or a greater one befalls another person. Among us, no death causes more grief than that of the High Priest (*Guide of the Perplexed*, p. 343).

Have you ever felt sad when someone you admired but didn't know died (e.g., a movie star, politician, or sports figure)? What did that person represent to you? What did you "lose" by their death? Can this be compared to the feelings of the people when they heard of the death of the High Priest?

H In Numbers, *Pinchas*, the five daughters of Zelophehad requested and were granted the right to inherit their father's portion of land. This decision affected not only these five women, but — because of them — all Israelite women were granted this privilege. Subsequently, in this Torah portion, the men of the tribe of Manasseh raised a concern. They spoke with Moses and said that if Zelophehad's daughters were to marry into another tribe the inherited land would pass to the husband's tribe. This would diminish the ancestral portion originally assigned to the tribe. Moses then issued a second ruling stating that women without brothers may inherit land from their father's, but they must marry within their father's tribe and family.

Did the second ruling negate the first?

How did this ruling affect the concept of freedom of choice?

What was the reaction of the daughters of Zelophehad?

Was the complaint of the men of the tribe of Manasseh based on economic or social issues?

STRATEGIES

ANALYZING THE TEXT

1 Draw and label a map tracing the route of the Israelites as described in *Mas'ay*. Along with place names, draw a picture including a caption, depicting the events that occurred at each place. Include the revelation at Sinai, even though the text in *Mas'ay* omits it.
References: *The Torah: A Modern Commentary*, edited by W. Gunther Plaut, p. 378, 1165; *The Macmillan Bible Atlas* by Yohanan Aharoni and Michael Avi-Yonah, Maps #48, #50, #52.

2 Imagine you are a sociologist from a Middle Eastern country close to Canaan. You have been sent on a fact-finding mission. Your task is to find out what Israelite society has done to prevent families from avenging the murder of their relatives. Write a brief report to be submitted to the ruler of your country based on the laws outlined in *Mas'ay*.

3 As discussed in Insight H, page 286, the story of the daughters of Zelophehad is told in two Torah portions — *Pinchas* and *Mas'ay*. Dramatize (1) the complaint of the daughters, (2) the response of the descendants of Manasseh, and (3) the way that Moses resolved the issue. Set your dramatization at a meeting of Moses and the leaders. Show the controversial nature of this issue by the characters' responses. Bear in mind that until the time of the daughters of Zelophehad, it was unheard of for women to inherit.

4 The Rabbis counted four instances in the Torah in which Moses did not know how to decide an issue. Read these four cases: Leviticus 24:10ff; Numbers 9:6-8; 15:32ff.; 27:1ff/35:1ff. The last two references relate to the daughters of Zelophehad and are considered one example. Imagine that you are writing a commentary on the Torah. Write a paragraph telling what these incidents teach us about Moses and about judges in general.

EXTENDING THE TEXT

5 The Shabbat walking limit of 2000 cubits outside one's habitation (approximately one half mile) comes from Numbers 35:5 (see also Insight F, *BaMidbar,* page 230). This limit caused practical difficulties, so a legal device called an *eruv* was created to extend the limit. Invite a Rabbi to explain to you how an *eruv* functions. If an *eruv* exists in your community, ask the Rabbi to show it to you and explain how it was established. (For more, see the Index: "*Shabbat.*")

6 God names the men through whom Moses is to apportion the land. Caleb son of Jephunneh is named from the tribe of Judah. Along with Joshua, Caleb was the only adult male member of the slave generation who was to live to see the Promised Land. He, along with Joshua, were the only spies to deliver a positive report about the Land. Write your own *midrash* explaining why Caleb was worthy of representing his tribe in the apportionment of the Land.

7 For an account of how the allocation of the cities of refuge was carried out, read Chapter 20 in the Book of Joshua. Also refer to maps #71, #72, and #73 in *The Macmillan Bible Atlas* by Yohanan Aharoni and Michael Avi-Yonah.

8 As a group, design and build a city of refuge. Consult the maps listed in Strategy #7 immediately above to determine where your city will be placed. Be mindful of making the city easy to get to, easy to find, with affordable housing and opportunities to find work. Also plan an advertising campaign to inform the Israelite population about the existence of this city of refuge. And don't forget to give your city a name.

9 How do the laws pertaining to the manslayer in Joshua 20 differ from those found in this portion *Mas'ay*? Can you explain the differences?

10 Read the definition of a wise person in *Pirke Avot* 5:9. Discuss how Moses' behavior, when he didn't know how to decide an issue, illustrates that he was a wise man. For the specific passages relating to these incidences, see Strategy #4 on this page.

PERSONALIZING THE TEXT

11 Make a video depicting the journeys of the Israelites. You may want to make several short, 3 to 5 minute episodes, soap opera style, to show the ups and downs the Israelites faced.

12 Invite a lawyer to discuss with your group the definitions of murder in the law code today. Keep in mind the following questions: What is the difference between murder and manslaughter? between first, second, and third degree murder? What constitutes legitimate self-defense in the eyes of the law? How does this compare with the attitude toward murder found in *Mas'ay*?

13 Draw and label a map showing the borders of the land God promised to the Israelites in *Mas'ay*. Compare this map with a map of modern Israel. What does this comparison reveal? How do you feel about the argument presented by certain groups within Judaism that Israel's contemporary borders should be those described in this portion? Is this just? The issue of a permanent settlement in the Middle East is tied to this issue of borders. Discuss ideas and strategies on this issue.
References: *The Macmillan Bible Atlas* by Yohanan Aharoni and Michael Avi-Yonah, Maps #50, #52; *The Torah: A Modern Commentary,* edited by W. Gunther Plaut, pp. 1165ff.

14 Imagine you are one of the daughters of Zelophehad. Write a diary for the events involving your family and tribe as described in the portions *Pinchas* and *Mas'ay*. In your diary, record your feelings about the issue of women inheriting and the resolution of this issue by Moses.

15 Imagine the daughters of Zelophehad as biblical political activists. You might compare them to the suffrage movement which worked to give women the vote. The word suffrage means the right to vote, especially in political matters; another word for suffrage is franchise. Suffragists was the nickname used for those who fought for the right of women to vote. The daughters of Zelophehad were "fighting" for the right to inherit. Create an appropriate name for their right-to-inherit movement and a nickname to know them by.
   Research at your public library for an illustrated history of the suffrage movement in your country.

You will see that suffragists wore banners or badges, carried slogans on signs, and held marches and rallies. Broaden your Daughters of Zelophehad project into a campaign which includes these elements.

16 Design a full-page magazine advertisement to inform the Israelites of the laws of inheritance as set forth in this portion.

OTHER RESOURCES

17 Read and discuss the poem "You Will Remember the Places" in *The Fire Waits* by Michael Hecht, pp. 99-100.

18 Read, act out, and discuss the skit for the portion *Mas'ay* in *Sedra Scenes: Skits for Evezy Torah Portion* by Stan J. Beiner, pp. 192-195.

19 Complete the pages which relate to *Mas'ay* in *Bible People Book Two* by Joel Lurie Grishaver, pp. 54-56. Also check the accompanying Leader Guide for procedures and additional activities.

20 For a creative movement activity, see "Cities of Refuge" from *Torah in Motion* by JoAnne Tucker and Susan Freeman, pp. 190-191.

21 Read and discuss the illustrated commentary for *Masei* in *American Torah Toons* by Lawrence Bush.

INVOLVING THE FAMILY

22 According to *Numbers Rabbah* 33:7, the blessing "for the land and for the food," which constitutes the second paragraph of the *Birkat HaMazon,* was added by Joshua when the

Israelites entered the Land. Prior to that time they recited only the first paragraph of the *Birkat HaMazon* (". . . who feedeth all"). Take this opportunity to learn and study the *Birkat HaMazon* as a family.

References: *Teaching Mitzvot* by Barbara Binder Kadden and Bruce Kadden, pp. 49-52; *To Pray as a Jew* by Hayim Donin, pp. 284-304.

BAR/BAT MITZVAH PROJECT

23 This project will give you an opportunity to apply what you have learned about the cities of refuge to current refugee needs around the world. Read newspapers, listen to news reports and stories on televison or radio (try "Morning Edition" or "All Things Considered," which are carried on public radio stations), and gather information from your public library and from the Internet in order to learn about refugee issues and crises around the world. Also, look for people to talk to about this topic.

After studying these materials, choose a country, area, or issue on which you want to work. Your task will be to learn more about what you have chosen, to seek out individuals and organizations which are also working on this issue, and to find a way to get involved. You may find yourself doing anything from holding a fund-raiser or writing letters to government and elected officials to working on awareness campaigns to educate others.

Choose a format to display what you have learned and what you are doing regarding the topic you have chosen.

REVIEW ACTIVITIES FOR NUMBERS

1 Stage a talk show and invite important characters from the Book of Numbers to be interviewed. Make sure everyone prepares for his/her role in advance.

2 In teams, review the portions in Numbers and choose two or three obscure bits of information from each. Make up a question for each. When play begins, let the teams alternately ask each other a question. Award a fixed number of points for each correct answer. The team with the most points at the end is the winner.

3 Arrange an auction based on the Book of Numbers. Beforehand, let each participant choose a secret identity as a character from the Book of Numbers. Each then chooses an item that is significant to that Bible character to be auctioned off (for example, Aaron might auction the flowering rod, Balaam might auction a donkey, an Israelite might auction quail or manna). Make appropriate props and costumes. Give each individual a fixed amount of paper money to spend at the auction. Instruct each participant to buy and sell at auction specific items that would help others guess his/her identity. In the course of the auction, participants try to guess each other's identity. Award ten points for each correct guess. At the end of the auction, the individual with the most points is declared a winner. Any participants who went unidentified might also be awarded prizes.

4 Along with Joshua, Caleb son of Jephunneh was a member of the slave generation who lived to see the Promised Land. Write a series of diary entries for Caleb describing the events that take place in the Book of Numbers.

5 Make a title page for the Book of Numbers based on your impressions of the book. If you did Strategy #16, page 234, in Numbers, *BaMidbar*, compare your two title pages. Which would be more appealing to readers who didn't know anything about the book?

6 Plan a dinner party to which you will invite all the significant characters in the Book of Numbers. Make placemats and place cards appropriate to each character. Draw a sketch of your seating plan. Who should sit next to whom? Why? Set up the table as a display for others to view.

7 Play *Biblical Charades*. Form two groups. Each group meets for 15-20 minutes and decides which biblical accounts, characters, or quotations to depict. The two groups come back together. While one group pantomimes the account/character/quotation, the other guesses who or what it is. Groups then reverse roles.

8 Complete some or all of the pages related to the Book of Numbers in *Torah Tales Copy Pak™: Numbers & Deuteronomy* by Marji Gold-Vukson.

Note: For other concluding strategies which can be adapted, see the Review Activities in this volume for each of the other books of the Torah.

OVERVIEW

Deuteronomy is the last of the five books of the Torah. The Hebrew name of the book, *Devarim*, means words. The name "Deuteronomy" comes from the Greek translation of the phrase "*mishneh Torah*" (Deuteronomy 17:18) meaning a copy of, or the repeated, law. Much narrative and legal material which first appears elsewhere in the Torah is repeated here: Deuteronomy is cast as Moses' farewell address to the Israelites and, in the course of his exhortation, Moses reviews both the history of the people and such important segments of law as the Ten Commandments.

Historically, Deuteronomy depicts a crucial moment in Israel's development. The people are about to enter the Land first promised to Abraham as part of the covenant. The creation of a nation is the fulfillment of this promise. Deuteronomy also details the laws by which Israel is to govern itself. The text records the challenge presented to the Israelites: by choosing to keep the law, they will merit untold blessing. But, if they choose to ignore the law and disobey, a long series of retributions is described as their fate.

In Deuteronomy, God's special relationship with Israel is stressed. The people are continually reminded that they are no more virtuous than other nations of the earth — rather, it is through their possession of the Land and their following of the Torah that their unique role in the world will come about. Therefore, idolatry, false prophets, and magic are continually denounced in Deuteronomy. Another key theme is the centralization of

the sacrificial cult.

One unusual feature of Deuteronomy lies in its presentation of Moses. Despite the lack of narrative, Moses is shown through his speeches as a stirring orator whose words reveal his deep disappointment and frustration with the people he has led for 40 years. For the first time in the Torah, Moses stresses his own role as leader of the people and as their intermediary before God. Deuteronomy concludes with several moving chapters leading up to and describing Moses' death.

A number of explanations have been given as to the origin of the Book of Deuteronomy. Within the text itself, Deuteronomy is referred to as the Book of Teaching. It is interesting to note that in II Kings 22:8, Hilkiah (High Priest during the reign of King Josiah) reports finding a book which he calls the Book of Teaching. Numerous theories have evolved suggesting that Deuteronomy and Hilkiah's find are one and the same. Some scholars have suggested that Deuteronomy may have been authored during Hilkiah's time when King Josiah was attempting to strengthen Israel and its religion. Whatever the case may be, the text of Deuteronomy presents a crystallization of Israel's mission. The historical context in which the book was transmitted — whether it was when Israel stood for the second time at the threshhold of the Promised Land or at another point in Israel's development — is irrelevant. The intent of this last book of the Torah was, and still is, to strengthen the children of Israel.

DEVARIM 1:1-3:22   דברים

SYNOPSIS

THE ISRAELITES NOW STAND READY TO enter Canaan. Moses begins to recount the events of Israel's journey from Horeb (Sinai) to the Promised Land. He also discusses the difficulty he had in governing the people. They had grown too numerous for him to administrate, necessitating the creation of a system of tribal chiefs. These chiefs were to function as judges, but if a matter was too difficult for them, Moses would intervene.

Moses continues describing the Israelite's behavior as they approached Canaan. He relates how he instructed them to take possession of the Land. The people insisted that spies be sent ahead to see what the land and people were like. The report, while favorable about the Land itself, still dismayed the people and they lost faith in God. God heard their complaint and swore that no one of that generation would live to enter the Promised Land. God was angry at Moses also and decreed that Moses, too, would not enter Canaan. Of that generation, only Caleb, who had given an encouraging report of the Land, and Joshua, who was to be the next leader, will live to enter Canaan.

Ashamed because of their attitude, the Israelites decided to go up and take the Land. Warned that God was not with them, they went ahead anyway and suffered a cruel defeat at the hands of the Amorites.

Moses continues the retelling of the journeys of the Israelites and begins summarizing the 40 years of wandering. The narrative continues with the Israelites preparing once again to enter the Promised Land. This time they successfully engage in battle with Sihon, King of the Amorites, and Og, King of Bashan. The lands east of the Jordan which the Israelites captured were divided between the tribes of Reuben, Gad, and the half-tribe of Manasseh.

The portion closes with Moses naming Joshua as his successor.

INSIGHTS FROM THE TRADITION

A *Devarim,* meaning "words" or "discourse," is the Hebrew name for the fifth book of the Bible and the name of its first portion. Much of Deuteronomy castigates Israel for its behavior, but as Rashi states, "Moses spoke as he did because he knew himself to be near death, for otherwise a leader ought not reprove and reprove, again and again."

Why should a leader "not reprove and reprove, again and again?"
Is there someone you know who behaves as Moses does in Deuteronomy? What effect does this person have? Why?
Why do you think Moses spoke as he did? If you were not going to see a loved one for a long time, by what words or thoughts would you want to be remembered?

B Much of the Book of Deuteronomy recounts the laws and ordinances which the people of Israel are to obey. *Deuteronomy Rabbah* (1:6) gives the following description for the words of Torah: "Just as the honey of the bee is sweet and its sting sharp, so, too, are the words of the Torah . . . "

Have you had any life experiences which reflect this saying? Explain.

C *Deuteronomy Rabbah* on this portion (1:15-17) poses the question: "What is the reward of one who is zealous in his or her observance of the duty of honoring father and mother?" One might question what this *halachic* issue has to do with this Torah portion.

In *Devarim,* we are reminded that the Israelites were commanded not to battle Edom, the descendants of Esau. The biblical text does not explain this ruling, but this *midrash* does. The Rabbis made a play on the words הר (*har*) meaning mountain and הורה (*horo*) meaning his parent. Deuteronomy

1:6 reads: You have stayed long enough at the mountain (*har*). Esau was very attentive, he stayed with Isaac, his parent (*horo*).

The *midrash* tells us that God planned to reward Esau for this behavior. The *midrash* also reminds us, that Esau reconciled with Jacob and did not accept Jacob's possessions as a gift. As reward for these two actions, the Israelites were forbidden to engage in battle with Edom in the process of their conquest of the Promised Land.

What was your impression of Esau before reading this *midrash*? Did your impression of him change after reading this *midrash*?
Has your opinion of a person you know ever dramatically changed because you learned more about that person? Describe.

D This portion recounts several instances in which the Israelites rebelled. Moses admonishes the people to learn from the mistakes of this previous generation. It has been pointed out that the difficulties of the people were rooted in their lack of faith and trust.

Once before, the people were at the threshold of the Promised Land. The people forfeited that initial opportunity to enter the Land because they did not then believe in God's promise. Moses exhorts this new generation to put their faith in God. They are to be the fulfillment of the promise made to the Patriarchs, and they are to be remembered in future generations as were their ancestors (*The Torah: A Modern Commentary*, edited by W. Gunther Plaut, p. 1323).

Have you ever been very close to getting something you really wanted and then acted in such a way as to lose out on getting it? Describe your experience.

E In *The Five Books of Miriam*, author Ellen Frankel portrays God as a nurse to the Israelites and also as a loving parent. Frankel has Miriam the prophet point out that Moses (knowing he would not be able to accompany the people into the Land) reminds the Israelites that God "will fight for you, just as [God] did for you in Egypt before your very eyes" (1:30). Then Frankel follows with Mother Rachel describing what Moses said in 1:31, "You saw how *Adonai,* your God, carried you, as a man carries his son, all the way that you traveled until you came to this place (p. 247).

Have you ever seen parents act as God is portrayed — as a nurse? Think of additional incidents in the Torah in which God acted as a nurse or loving parent. What was Moses' role at those times? Have you ever been faced with a challenge that your parent(s) helped you through? Discuss.

STRATEGIES

ANALYZING THE TEXT

1 There are several instances in this portion in which the text appears to contradict material found elsewhere in the Torah. Make your own comparison of the following verses by placing the two texts side-by-side:
Spies: Numbers 13:1-3 and Deuteronomy 1:20-25.
Entering the Land: Numbers 14:6-7, 24 and Deuteronomy 1:35-36.
Moses not able to enter Canaan: Numbers 20:2-13 and Deuteronomy 1:35-37.
Judicial system: Exodus 18:8-27 and Deuteronomy 1:9-18.
Continue this activity by discussing the following: Are the comparative verses written identically in both places? Do you learn anything different in the two versions? How can we understand these contradictions? Relate these kinds of comparisons to the following: Did you ever have an argument with a sibling or a friend? When it came time to tell a parent what happened, did you each have a different version of the same story? Do mood changes affect how you see events? If the same thing happened to a friend and to a stranger,

would you be likely to describe the events in the same way, with the same words and the same feelings?

2 God's stiffening of the will of Sihon, the King of Heshbon (Deuteronomy 2:30), parallels God's hardening of Pharaoh's heart (Exodus 7:13, 22; 8:11, 15, 28; 9:7). The commentators say that such actions are intended to demonstrate that God's power extends beyond the Israelite people. Read Deuteronomy 2:2-3:21. How does *Devarim* demonstrate this point? Give specific examples. Have you ever "hardened" your heart against someone? Why?

3 Rashi points out that Moses reproves the Israelites over and over again (see Insight A, page 293). The function of a prophet is to show the people their wrongdoings and set them on the right path. Read one of the books of the minor prophets, e.g., Amos, Micah, etc. What message was the prophet bringing the people? Was this at all similar to Moses' message?
Reference: *Our Sacred Texts: Discovering the Jewish Classics* by Ellen Singer with Bernard M. Zlotowitz, pp. 58-76.

4 Read the speculations about the origins of the Book of Deuteronomy in the Overview for Deuteronomy, page 291. For more about this, you might want to read II Kings 22 and 23:1-3. As you study the Book of Deuteronomy, consider how the theory that King Josiah was attempting to strengthen Israel and its religion is reflected in the text.
References: *The Torah: A Modern Commentary*, edited by W. Gunther Plaut, pp. 1290-1293; *Encyclopaedia Judaica*, "Deuteronomy, The Discovery of the Book of the Law," Vol. 5, pp. 1577-1578.

EXTENDING THE TEXT

5 Read Deuteronomy 1:19-45. Since the people who lived through the events being described

are dead, explain why Moses speaks to his audience using the word "you," implying that *they* had actually experienced these events. When the *Haggadah* is read, we are told to remember that we were slaves in the land of Egypt. Jewish tradition also places all Jews at the Mount Sinai experience. Why was this done? How do you think this has affected the Jewish people and Judaism? Do you feel conected to Jewish historical events?

6 Create a salt and flour map of ancient Israel (see below for recipe). Remember to include mountains, trees, lakes, and other topographical details. As you proceed in your study of the Book of Deuteronomy, add cities and tribal boundaries. Reference: *The Macmillan Bible Atlas* by Yohanan Aharoni and Michael Avi-Yonah.

Recipe

4 cups flour
1 1/3 cups salt
2 cups water

Mix these ingredients together. Store unused portions in refrigerator in airtight containers. To prevent hands from drying out, rub with salad oil before working with the dough. Once the map is complete, let it air dry. Another option for map making would be to use markers and poster board. Create a three-dimensional effect using folded paper, small artificial trees, aluminum foil for water ways, etc.

7 Recreate the historical conversation between Caleb and the other spies. Caleb argued that the people should obey God and occupy the Land. The spies, concerned about the conditions in the Land, counsel against this move. Refer to the following verses to gather background information: Numbers 14:6-7 and 14:24.

8 You work for a professional job placement service and your current assignment is to write a resumé of experience and qualifications for Joshua. He is applying to succeed Moses as leader of the Israelites. Use a Bible Concordance to read all the entries about Joshua in the Torah, and investigate fully his qualifications before preparing the resumé.

9 *Devarim* retells the incident of the spies. In many ways, the people's reaction was natural. They wanted to know what lay before them. Imagine that you are a spy sent to a country to explore Jewish life. Choose any time in the past or in the future for your spying adventure. If you choose a previous era, do some additional research on the time period so that the facts will be accurate, but if you choose a future time, the facts are all up to you. Present the information to classmates in an oral or written report or as part of a newscast, press conference, or as a movie or videotape.

10 The *midrash* cited in Insight B (page 293) — "Just as the honey of the bee is sweet and its sting sharp, so, too, are the words of the Torah . . ." makes a very interesting comparison. Do you think that the Torah is like a bee? Explain. Then follow up by doing one or more of the following activities:
a. Illustrate the quote.
b. Make a recipe that includes honey in the ingredients.
c. Make a simple cookie dough recipe, either one that is for cut-out cookies or cookies that can be hand-shaped. Make the dough into Hebrew letter cookies which you dip in honey before eating. This is a variation on the Jewish custom of placing a drop of honey on each Hebrew letter written on a child's chalk slate on the first day they attend school.
d. Invite a beekeeper to class to explain about bees or take a field trip to a bee farm. This might be especially interesting to do before Rosh HaShanah when we are ready to wish each other a sweet New Year, or before

Simchat Torah when we begin again the yearly cycle of Torah reading.

PERSONALIZING THE TEXT

11 The Book of Deuteronomy consists, for the most part, of farewell addresses given by Moses prior to his death. Other great leaders have prepared their followers with what might be considered farewell addresses. Do some library research to locate farewell speeches of well-known people. A few suggested individuals are: Martin Luther King ("I Have a Dream"), Mahatma Gandhi, Yitzhak Rabin (his final speech and song before being assassinated). It will take library research to locate these speeches. Discuss the thoughts and ideas expressed by the individuals you choose to study. Do any of the speakers have similar ideas? Identify these. What messages were each of these leaders trying to impart?

12 Instead of reading *actual* farewell addresses as in #11 above, create a ficticious one for a famous Jewish leader or personality. Read a biography about this individual. Try to get a sense of his or her value system, approach to life, and accomplishments. Dress up as the person whose farewell address you are giving, and present the speech. Videotape the presentations if at all possible.
Resources: *Jewish Heroes Jewish Values* by Barry L. Schwartz; *Women of Valor* by Sheila Segal.

13 Even though the generation of those who wandered in the desert had died, Moses continually reminded the people of their history. He wanted them to remember the slavery experience in Egypt so that they could more fully appreciate the freedoms in their own land. In fact, according to Jewish tradition, we should all identify as having been personally redeemed from Egypt.

a. To emphasize this concept, write an account of standing at Sinai as described in Exodus, *Yitro*, Strategy #11, page 117.

b. Become a part of Jewish history by using *The Do-It-Yourself Jewish Adventure Series* by Kenneth Roseman. The author has created a series of interactive Jewish history books in which the reader actually becomes a part of the event and learns how personal choice affected the lives of Jews through out history.

14 In this portion, the judicial system of Israel is described. Create a chart which visually details this system. On another chart, depict the judicial system in your state. Begin at the lowest level and trace it to the highest court. It may help to follow how a case would track through the court system. Determine why different levels of the court were created. Is there a relationship between the biblical judicial system and the one in your state? Invite a judge or an attorney to help you work through this activity.

15 Have someone read this portion, *Devarim*, aloud to a group which is equipped with blank paper and colored crayons. The group should try to "listen between the lines" and use the crayons to capture on paper the emotions that Moses exhibits in his speech. Later, each individual can read again the section of the text which particularly struck him or her and then add more to their crayoned sketch of the emotions of Moses. Display and discuss the drawings, the content, and the feelings of Moses.

16 In Deuteronomy 3:18, the Hebrew word *chalutzim* is used to name the warriors of the tribes of Reuben, Gad, and Manasseh. In modern Hebrew the word means "pioneers." Utilize the services of the Cantor or other music resource person to find a variety of songs sung by the *chalutzim* of pre-state Israel and songs which also contain the word *chalutzim*. On the Shabbat of this Torah portion, include these songs as part of the worship service. (For more, see the Index: "*Chalutzim.*")

17 In *Devarim* (1:5), the Pentateuch is referred to as התורה (HaTorah) — the Teaching. Look up this word in a Hebrew-English Dictionary to find other meanings, as well as a list of expressions in which it is used. Choose a favorite meaning and design a poster illustrating it.
Reference: *The Complete Hebrew-English Dictionary* by Reuben Alcalay, pp. 2767-2769.

18 Two major bodies of water are referred to in *Devarim* — the Sea of Reeds, also known as the Red Sea (2:1), and the Dead Sea (3:17). Can you locate these on a map? What are the unique characteristics of each body of water? Write a speech as though you were either the Dead Sea or the Sea of Reeds, explaining how you arrived at your present condition or what your role has been in Jewish history.

19 In this *sedra*, Moses blames the Israelites for God's refusal to let him enter the Promised Land. Moses says, "Because of you . . ." (1:37). Read the complete verse, then review Numbers 20 wherein God's refusal is first stated. Do you agree with Moses' interpretation of the events as recorded here? Discuss times when *you* have used the phrase "because of you!" What emotions were you feeling when you did this?

20 In Deuteronomy 1:10, Moses tells the Israelites ". . . God has multiplied you until you are today as numerous as the stars in the sky." This is a fulfillment of God's promise to Abraham (Genesis 22:17): "I will . . . make your descendants as numerous as the stars of heaven . . ."

a. Make this image as the basis of a collage. Use magazine pictures, cut-up or torn construction paper, decorative paper, written words and phrases, fabric scraps, greeting cards, and postcards.

b. Attach glow-in-the-dark stars to the ceiling of a room. Make Havdalah under the stars, using the quote from Genesis 22:17 as a theme for the service.

21 Make a video presentation reviewing the history Moses summarizes in this portion.

OTHER RESOURCES

22 Read, act out, and discuss the skit for *Devarim* in *Sedra Scenes: Skits for Every Torah Portion* by Stan J. Beiner, pp. 196-199.

23 For a creative movement activity, see "Moses' Final Address" from *Torah in Motion* by JoAnne Tucker and Susan Freeman, pp. 196-197.

24 Read and discuss the illustrated commentary for *Devarim* in *American Torah Toons* by Lawrence Bush.

25 Do the activities related to this portion in *Bible People Book Two* by Joel Lurie Grishaver, pp. 25 and 26.

26 The events recounted in this portion are first detailed in Exodus, *Yitro* and Numbers, *Shelach Lecha*. Refer to those portions for more Insights and Strategies.

INVOLVING THE FAMILY

27 In his farewell addresses, Moses gives advice, passes on history, seeks blessings, and gives parting words. Gather your family together and write down family stories and anecdotes, label pictures to be placed in albums, and preserve memories for future generations to share.

BAR/BAT MITZVAH PROJECT

28 One of the purposes of the Book of Deuteronomy is to recount the history of the Israelites and preserve it. Generate a list of historical events, particularly those of Jewish significance which have happened within the last 100 years. This will require research either in the library and/or through the Internet. Next find individuals who have direct experience with one or more of these events and interview them. Use your synagogue newsletter, groups in your community which work with the elderly, the Rabbi, and others who may be helpful in locating people to interview.

Create an interview outline which includes: the name of the person you are interviewing; the event(s) this person witnessed; a discription of the event(s); the effect the event had on the person, on his/her family, and on the community. List as many questions as are appropriate, then conduct the interviews.

Also, contact one or more of the following archival organizations for more information about gathering data, for details about historical events under study, as well as for brochures and other appropriate materials.

American Jewish Archives, 3101 Clifton Avenue, Cincinnati, OH 45220; YIVO Institute for Jewish Research, 555 West 57th Street, 11th Floor, New York, NY 10019; American Jewish Historical Society, 2 Thorton Road., Waltham, MA 02154; U.S. Holocaust Memorial Council, 100 Raoul Wallenberg Place, SW, Washington, DC 20024-2150. Include any other Jewish museums or organizations which are located near you.

Assemble a display of your interviews, with photos you have taken and/or with photos provided by the individuals you have interviewed, copies of news articles of those events, and any other items you may locate. Include the information you have gathered from the organizations you contacted.

VA'ETCHANAN 3:23-7:11 ואתחנן
SYNOPSIS

VA'ETCHANAN OPENS WITH MOSES reminding the people how he had pleaded with God to be allowed to see the Promised Land. God relented and allowed Moses to view the Land of Canaan, but in so doing, God reminded Moses to prepare Joshua to be the new leader of the people in their new Land.

Moses continues in his speech to the people, exhorting them to observe the laws and rules given them so that they may enter and occupy the Promised Land. The people are specifically cautioned to follow the entire law. They must not add to or delete from that which God has commanded them.

Moses details the very special relationship that God has with the people Israel and emphasizes that this unique connection should in no way be jeopardized. Moses intersperses his warnings to the people with descriptions of various statutes and commandments. These include:
The cities of refuge — cities which are set aside to protect individuals who accidentally kill someone.
A repetition of the Ten Commandments.
The first paragraph of the *Shema*.
The prohibition against intermarriage between the Israelites and the nations slated to be dislodged from the Promised Land.

INSIGHTS FROM THE TRADITION

A Moses begins this portion by reminding the people that he had "pleaded" with God to be allowed to enter the Land, but God was wrathful with Moses on account of the people and Moses was denied physical entry into the Land. *Va'etchanan* means "And I pleaded."

Is Moses blaming the people for not being allowed to enter the Land?

For what reasons was Moses denied physical entry into the Land?
What did God allow Moses to do?
Has it ever been difficult for you to accept responsibility for something you have done?

B According to Nachmanides, *Va'etchanan* introduces the real concern of the Book of Deuteronomy — the laws and precepts of Judaism. Rabbi Abba Hillel Silver points out that Deuteronomy was to serve as a complete code of all the laws for all the people of Israel with the authority of Moses conferred upon it (*Moses and the Original Torah*, p. 112). Deuteronomy was also to be the final version of the laws: "Do not add on or diminish from what is commanded you" (Deuteronomy 4:2 and 13:1). Deuteronomy puts into effect the life-style Moses taught to the Israelites. The people's relationship with the Patriarchs Abraham, Isaac, and Jacob is totally overshadowed by the experiences of the Exodus and the revelation at Sinai. These two experiences were to be treasured by the newly freed people and were to shape and color the historical and ethnic identity of their descendants.

What, in your opinion, is the most significant moment in Jewish history? for the Jewish people? Why?
What has been the most significant Jewish moment in the history of your family?
What, for you personally, has been the most significant Jewish moment?

C In *Va'etchanan*, the timeless quality of Torah is stressed. Moses commands the people to teach their children the laws (see 6:4-9). In Deuteronomy 4:9, this concept is extended "to teach your children and your children's children." Maimonides' interpretation is: "Every Jew is required to study Torah, whether poor or rich, healthy or ailing, young or old and feeble" (*Mishneh Torah*).

Why is study a religious obligation for every Jew? How does your Jewish community ensure the continuation of Jewish learning?

What do you do to improve your knowledge of our Jewish heritage?

D One of the statutes described in this portion discusses the cities of refuge. Why would this issue, while important, be included with the *Shema,* Ten Commandments, and the laws against intermarriage, all of which can be seen as essential to Jewish survival? From *Tanna Debei Eliyahu* we learn: The Levites were given 48 cities in which to live (Numbers 35:7). Six of these were to be the cities of refuge. A significant duty of the Levites was to instruct the people in Torah. Thus, the cities of refuge may be regarded as centers of Jewish learning (ER82). Study of Torah is as essential an element for Jewish survival as the *Shema,* the Ten Commandments, and Jewish family life.

How do the *Shema,* Ten Commandments, and the laws against intermarriage ensure Jewish survival? Which do you consider to be most important? What, in your opinion, are the most important centers of Jewish learning today? Where do *you* learn most about Judaism?

E The *Shema,* which appears in this portion, is a statement of belief in one God and a commandment that the people love God. Gerhard von Rad comments: "The covenant-relationship established by God had always allowed for a variety of feelings, and not for one alone . . . stress is [now] laid on love for God as the only feeling worthy of God . . . it is important that the experience of God's love for Israel had already preceded this demand" (*Deuteronomy,* pp. 63-64).

Can love (or any emotion) be commanded? What experiences had Israel had that would lead them to love God?

Why was it important for Israel to be told to love God before being told to obey the commandments?

What might lead you to love another person? to love God?

STRATEGIES

ANALYZING THE TEXT

1 Unroll a Torah scroll to this portion. Find the *Shema.* What is unusual about the *ayin* and *dalet?* Put the *ayin* and the *dalet* together. Does it spell a word in Hebrew? Look up the *ayin* and *dalet* as a word עד (*ayd*) in a Hebrew dictionary. What does it mean? Why is it appropriate to the *Shema?* Suggest reasons why the *ayin* and *dalet* are enlarged in the Torah text.

2 The Rabbis taught that nothing in the Torah is repeated without a reason. Bearing this in mind, compare the two versions of the commandment regarding Shabbat as they appear in Exodus 20:8-11 and Deuteronomy 5:12-15. What differences can you find? What lessons can you draw from these differences?

3 The speech with which *Va'etchanan* begins is a powerful and moving one. Review Deuteronomy 4:1-40 until you can read it (in Hebrew or English) smoothly. Give a dramatic reading of this passage.

4 God denied Moses access to the Promised Land. Moses was not to experience the final reward of his labors, even though he toiled long and hard, struggling with a difficult people, helping them mature to the point where they could inhabit the Land. Moses, it seems, could not have it all. It was by his authority that laws and ordinances came to Israel. He established the priesthood and the judicial body. But his leadership could not extend to the Promised Land. Moses would see the Land, but he would not set foot in it. In Insight A, page 299, Moses pleaded to be allowed to enter the Land. He was denied this request. On whom did he blame this situation? Was it the people's fault that Moses was not able to enter the Land? Is it possible that Moses denied his own behavior, that he was not taking responsibilty for his own actions? Why would that be a negative trait for a leader?

What, then, might be the danger of allowing Moses to enter Canaan?

EXTENDING THE TEXT

5 The *Ve'ahavta* is found in this portion (Deuteronomy 6:5-9). Determine, and then make symbols representing, the ideas in this prayer. For example, for *Ve'ahavta* — "you shall love," make a red heart for the word love. Make a large wall hanging of this passage substituting appropriate symbols for as many words as possible. Words which have no symbol can be written on the wall hanging. You may want to assemble this hanging out of paper or fabric.

6 Develop a series of skits about the Ten Commandments. Think of a brief story line for each commandment and use that as a basis for the skits.
Reference: *Who Knows Ten?* by Molly Cone,

7 The concept that every Jew stood at Sinai makes the covenant binding on all Jews in every generation. Read "Israel Prepares for the Revelation" in *Legends of the Jews* by Louis Ginzberg, Vol. III, pp. 88-90. Write a first person account of your experiences as *you* stood at Sinai, or prepare a live news broadcast as the events at Mount Sinai unfold.

8 The purpose of the cities of refuge was to provide a haven for those who accidently committed murder. Also, as explained in Insight D, page 300, the cities of refuge were to be considered centers of Jewish learning. Create a poster which advertises the upcoming courses to be offered in Torah and Judaica for the cities of refuge. (For more, see the Index: "Cities of Refuge.")

9 The words in Deuteronomy 4:39 have entered Jewish liturgy as part of the *Alaynu*. This prayer thanks God for making us a unique people and expresses the hope that one day all people will know God.

The *Alaynu* has a fascinating history. Originally it contained the line "For they bow down to vanity and emptiness and pray to a god that cannot save." This verse, which was considered anti-Christian as far back as the Inquisition, was removed from the prayer by a Prussian government censor in the eighteenth century.

Discuss the following: What is a censor? Is censorship allowed in the United States? Are there any current cases or issues of censorship now being discussed? Invite a librarian or journalist to discuss censorship and its effects on society.
Reference: *Teaching Tefilah* by Bruce Kadden and Barbara Binder Kadden, pp. 74-79.

10 Read Deuteronomy 6:20-24. Where have you heard those lines before? After a brief discussion, pass out *Haggadot* to all the participants and ask them to find this passage. In groups, have the students create a more complete biography of one of the four children. Direct them to create a fictional character with a few brief stories which demonstrate the child's personality and attitude. Share the stories and display.

11 Read Deuteronomy 4:44 in Hebrew and in English. Do these words sound familiar? Examine the Torah service in a prayer book. Can you find this verse? Note that in Ashkenazic prayer books it occurs after the Torah reading, but in the Sephardic tradition it is found prior to the reading of the Torah. Also read Numbers 4:37. How are the two verses connected? Ask the Cantor or music resource person to teach you the melody of this phrase and the traditions regarding lifting and showing the text to the congregation.

PERSONALIZING THE TEXT

12 Moses pleads: "Let me, I pray, cross over and see the good Land on the other side of the Jordan, that good hill country, and the Lebanon" (3:25). The fondest hope of Jews for many centuries has been to see the Promised Land. Each year we include in the Passover *Seder* the words, "Next year in Jerusalem." Take this opportunity to invite a recent visitor to Israel to share with you stories, pictures, mementos, and experiences from his or her trip.

13 The Shabbat on which this portion is read is called Shabbat *Nachamu* (Shabbat of Comfort). The name is derived from the *Haftarah* for this week, Isaiah 40:1-26. The first line reads: "Comfort, oh, be comforted, My people." This portion, *Va'etchanan*, with this *Haftarah*, is read on the Shabbat following Tishah B'Av, the ninth day of Av, the day on which, according to tradition, both the First and Second Temples in Jerusalem were destroyed. Today we observe Tishah B'Av by fasting, praying, and reading from the Book of Lamentations. It is a day on which we recall the destruction of our holy places. The *Haftarah* attempts to console the Jewish people for all they have endured. Although the Temple has not been rebuilt, the city of Jerusalem has been.

Create felt banners depicting scenes and buildings in Jerusalem. Use simple geometric shapes such as squares and rectangles for the buildings, with triangles or dome shapes for the roofs. Make templates of these shapes in a variety of sizes for the students to use as patterns. These shapes may be cut out from felt or fabric. Also collect pictures of Jerusalem from magazines, visit your synagogue and public libraries to find books with pictures of Jerusalem for ideas to incorporate into the banners. Use white glue or fabric glue to apply the cut-out felt and fabric shapes to the banners.

14 In this portion Moses pleads to be able to enter the Land. This plea is denied, but Moses is given the opportunity to go up on Mount Pisgah to see the Land. Imagine what Moses might have seen. Create pictures of views you imagine Moses was able to see.

15 This portion deals extensively with God's relationship to the Jewish people. Read the portion through together, identifying and discussing elements of this relationship, including students' thoughts about their relationship with God.
References: *God: The Eternal Challenge* by Sherry Bissel with Raymond A. Zwerin and Audrey Friedman Marcus; *Partners with God* and *Living as Partners with God,* both by Gila Gevirtz.

16 In Deuteronomy 6:20-23, the command to retell the story of the Exodus from Egypt is stated. We do this at the Passover *Seder* each year. We also "retell" other events in Jewish history when we read the *Megillah,* light the *chanukiah,* build a *sukkah,* etc. Assemble readings, liturgy, and rituals to expand our tradition by retelling some other Jewish events in modern history. Do some research to choose dates and events to commemorate.

17 This portion contains the *Shema* and *Ve'ahavta.* These verses have entered into our liturgy and emphasize the basic Jewish belief in one God.
a. The *mezuzah* scroll contains the *Shema* and *Ve'ahavta.* Try your hand at calligraphy. Use chisel point markers or an actual pen and ink set. Write a *"mezuzah* scroll." Use an already made *mezuzah* scroll as your guide. (The teacher should modify the amount the students write according to their abilities.)
b. Make *mezuzah* cases using Fimo or Sculpey. This material is easy to manipulate and form, and a variety of colors may be used in the designs. Follow the package directions for baking and drying. Remember to poke small nail holes in the top and bottom of the *mezuzah* holder before baking in order to be able later to affix it on a doorpost.

c. A variety of tunes have been composed for the *Shema* and *Ve'ahavta*. Ask the Cantor or music specialist to teach a number of these to the students. Request that the background, country of origin, and/or the composer is also shared with them. (For more, see the Index: "God.")

18 Play "What's My Line," using the Ten Commandments as guests. This television game show introduced individuals whose occupation was unknown, and the guest panel had to question this person attempting to identify what the occupation might be. In this variation, choose one participant to represent a commandment. The guest panel questions him or her to determine which commandment he or she represents. Continue in this manner for all the Ten Commandments or for those you wish to present. (For more, see the Index: "Ten Commandments.")

OTHER RESOURCES

19 The *Ve'ahavta* contains references to *tefillin* and *mezuzot*. To learn more about these two symbols, see *Teaching Mitzvot* by Barbara Binder Kadden and Bruce Kadden, *Mezuzah*, pp. 53-56; *Tefillin*, pp. 57-60.

20 Read, act out, and discuss the skit for the portion *Va'etchanan* in *Sedra Scenes: Skits for Every Torah Portion* by Stan J. Beiner, pp. 200-203.

21 For creative movement activities, see "Honor Father and Mother," "Hear, O Israel," and "Teach With All Your Heart" from *Torah in Motion* by JoAnne Tucker and Susan Freeman, pp. 198-203.

22 Read and discuss the illustrated commentary for *Va-Etchanan* in *American Torah Toons* by Lawrence Bush.

Note: Many of the events and information recounted in this portion are first presented in the following portions: Numbers, *Pinchas* and *Mas'ay*, and Exodus, *Yitro*. Refer to those portions for more Insights and Strategies, pages 284-289 and 113-120.

INVOLVING THE FAMILY

23 Deuteronomy 4:9 reads "But take utmost care and watch yourselves scrupulously, so that you do not forget the things you saw with your own eyes and so that they do not fade from your mind as long as you live. And make them known to your children and your children's children." With your family, take turns playing the role of an individual who was present when Moses spoke these words. Create a character and recount your life experiences to your "children" and "your children's children." What did you see? What do you remember? What information do you want your descendants to know?

BAR/BAT MITZVAH PROJECT

24 As mentioned in Strategy #13, page 302, this portion, *Va'etchanan*, is read on Shabbat *Nachamu*, the Sabbath of Consolation, which occurs just after Tishah B'Av. This day commemorates the destruction of both Temples in Jerusalem, as well as other tragic moments in Jewish history. After the destruction of each Temple, many of the Jewish people were carried off into exile. There, they felt abandoned.

There is a group in contemporary society that often feels abandoned and forgotten as if in exile, i.e., the elderly who live in old-age homes. Adopt a home for the aged and make visits on a regular basis. It may change your life and the lives of the residents.

EKEV 7:12-11:25 עקב

SYNOPSIS

BY FOLLOWING ALL THE RULES ESTABLISHED by God, Israel will experience great blessings — health, abundant produce, and fertility. All the enemies of Israel will be vanquished with God's help, and Israel is to destroy all signs of their enemies' idolatrous worship.

A second admonition to obey God's laws is followed by a brief description of Israel's wanderings in the desert. Despite the 40 years of hardship, their clothing did not wear out, neither did their feet swell. Manna was provided for food. God disciplined the Israelites, as a father would discipline his son, in order to teach them to keep God's commandments. Now that Israel is to enter a bountiful Land, the people are cautioned to maintain their faith in God. Moses reminds them to give thanks continually to God for the abundance provided. The people should never assume that it is by their own hand that they enjoy the fruits of the Land — all that they have is from God.

By not following God's commandments, Israel would doom itself.

Moses recounts to the Israelites all their acts of defiance: the making of the Golden Calf, complaining about the food and the water, and the incident of the spies. He reminds the people how he interceded with God on their behalf. Because of these pleadings, Israel is still able to enter Canaan.

Moses tells the people that all God wants is that Israel remain faithful to God's laws, worship God, and behave appropriately toward orphans, widows, and strangers. Such acts will result in blessings and prosperity.

INSIGHTS FROM THE TRADITION

A The trials which Israel faced in the desert were called יסורין של אהבה (*yisurin shel ahavah*). This phrase is translated as "chastisements of love." The Hebrew word *yisurin* has the dual meaning of chastisement and instruction. In his work *Concepts and Values,* Solomon Colodner states that these chastisements of love were God's way of disciplining the Jews (p. 117). Traditional sources say that just as a parent suffers when a child receives punishment, i.e., a chastisement of love, God also suffers when the Jews must receive punishment. Such punishments were intended for the betterment of the people.

Does one have to suffer in order to be a better person? A better Jew?
How is your parent "affected" when he or she has to discipline you?

B *Ekev* reviews the experiences of the Israelites in the desert and characterizes them as a "test" (8:2). However, the description of the "tests" includes not only the hardships of the journey, but also its blessings — the manna, the fact that the people's clothing and shoes did not wear out over 40 years, and, of course, their ultimate arrival at a bountiful land. The implication of the text is that both hardships and, in some way, blessings, are a kind of "test" of our faith in God. Each kind of experience demands its own response.

What have been some of the hardships in your life? The blessings?
How should we respond to the "test" or opportunity that the blessings in our lives present?

C Deuteronomy 8:10 lays the foundation for *Birkat HaMazon* — the Blessing after Meals: "When you have eaten your fill, give thanks to *Adonai* your God for the good Land which God has given you." *Birkat HaMazon* contains three blessings:
1. Blessed are You, *Adonai*, who feeds everyone.
2. Blessed are You, *Adonai*, for the Land and for the food.

3. Blessed are You, *Adonai,* who in Your mercy will rebuild Jerusalem.

Blessing God for feeding everyone is a constant reminder of the manna with which God fed the people in the desert (8:16). Blessing God for having given us the Promised Land and for the food which the Land produces, relates to 8:10 "... give thanks to *Adonai* your God for the good Land which God has given you." Mention of Jerusalem does not refer only to the physical Jerusalem. It is also a hint of the promise of the spiritual ideal — *Yerushalayim shel Ma'alah.* With these three blessings, the Grace after Meals functions to link us to the past, root us in the present, and elevate our thoughts from the merely physical now to the spiritually exalted future.

What, to you, is the significance of blessing God after eating a meal?

D The children of Israel are reminded by Moses of their misdeeds and rebellions. He stresses to the people that, in spite of their behavior, God has maintained a special relationship with them. The people are reminded of how Moses responded in anger to the sin of the Golden Calf by hurling down the Tablets of the Law. A *midrash* tells us that God asked Moses, "Weren't the Tablets entrusted to you? You broke them and now you must replace them." To this Moses responded, "The Israelites sinned and yet You blame me?" (*Deuteronomy Rabbah* 3:15)

Can you define the expression "righteous indignation"? How might it apply to Moses' reaction at seeing the Golden Calf?
Was Moses' reaction justified? Explain.
Have you ever acted out of righteous anger? What happened?

E *Deuteronomy Rabbah* 3:15 discusses Moses' anger. What if both God and Moses were angry at Israel at the same time? The Israelites could not endure. Therefore, God counseled

Moses, "When you see Me boiling with rage, you calm Me, and when you see Me being calm, you boil with anger."

How were God and Moses going to solve this problem of anger?
How was anger being used by God and Moses to move the people in the right direction?
What are some constructive ways to let out your anger?
Do you have a reciprocal relationship with someone who tempers your anger and vice versa?

F In this portion, Moses first recounts to the people the numerous times he interceded on their behalf. Then he tells the people, "You are about to cross the Jordan ... " (8:1). Moses left himself out, for he was not to join the people in the Promised Land. In reminding the people of his pleas on their behalf, perhaps he felt they would now plead for him. Rabbi Tanhuma says that Moses gave them the opportunity to pray for him, but they did not grasp it (*Deuteronomy Rabbah* 3:2).

Why do you think the people would not aid Moses in his desire to cross the Jordan?
We hear pleas all around us and we do not always respond to them. What stops us? What type of plea might make you respond?
Would you have responded on behalf of Moses? Explain.

G In Deuteronomy 10:15, Moses reminds the Israelites that God *chose them,* from among all people. This idea is reflected in the prayer book in the blessing we recite before reading the Torah: God "chose us from among all peoples and gave us the Torah." Many Jews are not comfortable with the idea of being chosen, and have suggested new, more limited interpretations of this idea. Some prayer books even translate this prayer as "God chose us from among all peoples by giving us the Torah" or "... Who brings us near to God's service" (*The Five Books of Miriam* by Ellen Frankel, pp. 259-260).

Why might some people be uncomfortable with the idea that God chose us?

How do these newer translations change the idea of the prayer and of the verse from Deuteronomy? Which translation do you prefer? Why?

H Moses continues his discourse to the people by emphasizing that they are required to revere God. In Hebrew, the word used is ירא (yirah). This word is usually translated as fear. The combined emotions of fear and love are seen as the best basis for a relationship with God. Nachmanides tells us that it is not for God's good that we are commanded to revere, rather, it is for our own good. Love and fear motivate an individual to do God's will. Fear is the nudge that makes a person "behave," so to speak.

To love God is to be commanded to do godly deeds (mitzvot), which will ensure Israel's ability to love the Lover of Israel (The Torah: A Modern Commentary, edited by W. Gunther Plaut, pp. 1370-71).

Can one be required to love or to revere?
How does love for parents and other family members come into being?
How might love of God evolve?

seriousness from your own point of view, from the point of view of Moses, from the point of view of an ordinary Israelite, and as God judged them. Explain your ranking in each case.

3 In Deuteronomy 7:22, Moses tells the Israelites that God will help them conquer Canaan "little by little" (see also Exodus 23:29-30). In the Book of Judges, several reasons are given for a gradual rather than a quick and easy conquest. Read Judges 2:1-3, 21-23, and 3:2. What reasons are given? Which do you think is best? Why?

4 Read Deuteronomy 8:3. Discuss how the giving of manna teaches the lesson that the verse states? Can you think of other events the Israelites experienced which also teach the lesson that "man may live on that which God decrees?"

5 The basis for the *Birkat HaMazon* is found in *Ekev*. Learn to read this blessing and find within its text the three key concepts mentioned in Insight C, page 304.
References: *To Pray as a Jew* by Hayim Donin, pp. 284-304; *Encyclopaedia Judaica*, "Grace after Meals," Vol. 7, pp. 838-841; *Teaching Mitzvot* by Barbara Binder Kadden and Bruce Kadden, pp. 49-52.

STRATEGIES

ANALYZING THE TEXT

1 Deuteronomy 10:22 mentions that 70 persons went down to Egypt. Who were they? From memory, try to name them. Then consult Genesis 46:27 and Exodus 1:5. Play this memory game another way by creating a word search which contains the 70 names. Give each participant a copy and see who finishes first.

2 In *Ekev*, Moses recounts to the Israelites their acts of defiance. Read through the portion and list these acts. Then rank them in order of

EXTENDING THE TEXT

6 In Deuteronomy 8:2, the 40-year journey through the wilderness is described as a "test . . . by hardships" by which God would learn the true nature of the people. Throughout the Torah, there are incidents in which people are tested. What stories suggest to you that God "tests" the human character? Do you believe this idea is true today?
a. Write anonymously about a personal test of character that you have undergone. Pass out the stories your group has written to others in the group. Have the recipient of each

story write what the test and its resolution reveal about the nature of the person whose story it is.

b. Make a list of significant trials the Jewish people have undergone in your lifetime. What can you learn about the nature of our people from the fact that we have not only survived, but thrived, despite the tests?

7 Deuteronomy 8:10 is considered the foundation for *Birkat HaMazon,* the Grace after Meals.

a. Create an illustrated version of *Birkat HaMazon.* Read through this blessing carefully and pick out major themes and ideas. Choose one and sketch a simple illustration of it on burlap. Using colored yarn, stitch along your sketched lines with a simple running stitch. Glue your stitchery to a cardboard frame.

b. Make a TV commercial promoting the recitation of *Birkat HaMazon.*

c. Locate someone who can sign all or part of *Birkat HaMazon* and is able to teach the signing to you.

8 In Deuteronomy 9:20, Moses tells of God's intention to destroy Aaron for his role in making the Golden Calf. This entire aspect of the Golden Calf account is omitted when the story is first told in Exodus 32:1-35. Write and stage the dialogue in which Moses pleads with God to spare Aaron. (For more, see the Index: "Golden Calf.")

9 The second paragraph of the *Shema* is contained in this portion (Deuteronomy 11:13-21). Create a fill-in-the blanks puzzle to help you learn the key Hebrew vocabulary. Write out the key verses/concepts from the prayer in your own words, leaving a blank space to be filled in with a missing word from the text. Exchange pages with a friend and fill in the blanks. If you like, you can complicate this puzzle by scrambling the order of the sentences. The solution would then also require that the sentences be numbered according to their appearance in the text.

10 The people are reminded in *Ekev* to remember that they do not create wealth (8:18). It is God who gives them the power to obtain wealth. As Jewish traditions developed, blessings evolved for nearly every human activity. Using the *Motzi* as a basis, create a series of sequential illustrations detailing the step-by-step process by which bread is created. Start with the seed stage. Identify divine influence in this process. What is the human role in the process?

11 Within the second paragraph of the *Shema,* we find the basis for *tefillin,* or phylacteries. Learn about this ritual object. Look up *tefillin* in a Jewish encyclopedia. Using pen and ink, draw an illustrated explanation of the design, purpose, and use of *tefillin.*
Reference: *Teaching Tefilah,* pp. 114-115, and *Teaching Mitzvot,* pp. 57-60, both by Barbara Binder Kadden and Bruce Kadden.

12 Invite a knowledgeable person to demonstrate the use of *tefillin* to your group. Perhaps you can obtain *tefillin* that can be opened so that you can actually see the parchment and verses kept inside.

13 In *Ekev,* Moses twice reminds the people that it was not because of their virtue that they will settle Canaan, but because of the merits of the Patriarchs (9:5, 27). This concept is known as *zechut avot.* Consider the concept of *zechut imahot* meaning the merit of the Matriarchs. Generate a list of the virtues, qualities, and actions of the Matriarchs upon whom we also depend. (For more, see the Index: "*Zechut Avot/Zechut Imahot.*")

PERSONALIZING THE TEXT

14 The first and second paragraphs of the *Shema* tell us to "bind them as a sign." Taking this concept literally, locate someone in the deaf community who will sign this portion of the *Shema* for your class. How is the information conveyed? If you do not know sign language, could you still understand the *Shema* or parts of it? Invite the guest to sign other prayers to observe whether or not you can identify and understand them.

15 As described in the biblical text, God provided the Israelites with water and manna in the desert. Taking this as an inspiration, generate as many plans as possible to feed the hungry. (For ideas, see *Gym Shoes and Irises*, Book II, by Danny Siegel, "Feeding the Hungry," pp. 112-125.)

16 "We Cannot Merely Pray to You" is the name of a creative prayer which deals with the issue of the hungry. It is found in the prayerbook *Likrat Shabbat*, compiled by Sidney Greenberg. Read this prayer and write your own original prayer dealing with hunger.

17 In *Ekev*, it states that human beings do not live by bread alone (Deuteronomy 8:3). Illustrate this idea by creating a series of posters which show by what else we human beings live. Think about things like music, dance, literature, sports, recreation, and fun. The posters can contain pictures, statements, poetry, or prose. Use poster paints to create vivid images.

18 The biblical verse cited in #17 immediately above, that we do not live by bread alone, comes from Deuteronomy 8:3. The second half of the verse, which is often overlooked, completely changes the meaning. Compare the implications of the complete verse with the more popular partial verse expression. Which do you like better? Why?

19 Use the description of the Promised Land found in Deuteronomy 8:7-9 and 11:11,12 as the basis for an artistic depiction of the Land

that the Israelites settled. For a textured effect, use natural objects (e.g., sand, leaves, grass, pebbles) on heavy posterboard.

20 Assign a verse or group of verses for each individual to illustrate which describes an incident during the Israelite sojourn in the desert. (Refer back to Exodus or Numbers for more detailed accounts.) Do a mural style on a roll of white butcher paper. Attach dowels at either end to make it like a Torah scroll. Then use these illustrations to help review the Israelite experience in the desert. Ask each illustrator to describe aloud for the group the event which he or she drew.

21 In the portion *Ekev*, as Moses recounts the events of the desert years, he emphasizes his own roles as the leader of the people and as their intermediary before God. In doing so, he reveals the frustrations and emotions he felt at the time. Choose one of the incidents described in *Ekev* and write a diary entry for Moses describing the event from his point of view, his role in its resolution, and his feelings at the time.

(For more, see the Index: "*Tefillin.*")

OTHER RESOURCES

22 Read, act out, and discuss the skit for the portion *Ekev* in *Sedra Scenes: Skits for Every Torah Portion* by Stan J. Beiner, pp. 204-207.

23 For creative movement activities, see "The Hornets" and "Open Your Heart" from *Torah in Motion* by JoAnne Tucker and Susan Freeman, pp. 204-207.

24 Read and discuss the illustrated commentary for *Ekev* in *American Torah Toons* by Lawrence Bush.

INVOLVING THE FAMILY

25 Imagine that you had an important value and you wanted to ensure that your descendants would share that value. With your family, brainstorm a variety of ways you could convey that value across time to your descendants. Both the *Ve'ahavta,* found in the previous portion, *Ve'etchanan,* and the *Vehaya Im Shamo'a* (Deuteronomy 11:13-21) contain statements of key Jewish values and a method for guaranteeing the survival of them. Read these two prayers and explain how survival is assured. Compare the method given in the two prayers with the method you have devised. Discuss.

BAR/BAT MITZVAH PROJECT

26 In *Ekev,* the people are commanded to "befriend the stranger" (Deuteronomy 10:19). This injunction is found repeatedly throughout the Torah. Find out how your Jewish community formally welcomes new Jewish families moving into your area. Does your synagogue have a program for welcoming new members? Find out what role you can play to help an already established program or:

a.   Generate plans for such a program and implement one or more of the ideas.

b.   Create a Jewish "Welcome Wagon" to provide families with information about the Jewish aspects of their new community.

c.   Let your Rabbi know that you would be willing to become a "buddy" to a child or teenager of your age who is just entering your community. Your role would be to make an initial welcoming phone call, invite the new person to attend certain events with you (e.g., Youth Group programs), and generally acquaint him/her with your synagogue.

27 This portion teaches us the importance of thanking God for the food we have eaten. Is this *mitzvah* observed in your synagogue? Approach the Rabbi, educator, and/or ritual committee to find out how the synagogue could begin the observance of this *mitzvah* and what role you can play in its adoption. Suggestions: help with publicity to encourage the congregation to accept this *mitzvah,* work on a literacy campaign to help teach *Birkat HaMazon,* and make sure the blessing is set out when meals are eaten at the synagogue.

28 MAZON: A Jewish Response to Hunger, is an organization which encourages Jews to donate 3% of the cost of food served at joyous celebrations to help feed hungry people throughout the world. Write to them at 12401 Wilshire Blvd., Suite 303, Los Angeles, CA 90025-1015 to learn how you can participate in their work.

RE'EH 11:26-16:17 ראה

SYNOPSIS

MOSES TELLS THE PEOPLE THAT HE HAS set before them a blessing and a curse — a blessing if they obey God's commandments and a curse if they choose disobedience. The choice is given to Israel. In order to possess the Land, the people must follow the laws established by God.

Moses continues his speech to the people detailing all the laws the people must observe. First, they must destroy the worship sites of foreign gods. The Israelites must then establish a permanent and central worship site. They may slaughter and consume meat in their settlements, but they are not to eat of the tithes set aside for the sacrifice.

The people are twice commanded in this portion to consume no blood of the animals they slaughter.

Moses admonishes the people to be wary of false prophets who might try to lure them into worshiping other gods. The penalty for such worship is death.

Moses reiterates the laws of *kashrut* to the people.

Moses instructs the people to put aside a tenth part of what they harvest and the firstlings of their herds and flocks as tithes. These are to be consumed at the central sanctuary. If the people live too far away from the sanctuary, money equal to the tithe is to be brought there in place of the actual harvest. They must then purchase food and provisions for a celebration before God.

A portion of the tithes brought by the Israelites is to be used to support the Levites, the orphaned, and the widowed. Israel is to observe a Sabbatical year every seventh year. Laws concerning Hebrew slaves are repeated.

The portion closes with Moses detailing the observance of the three pilgrimage festivals: Feast of Unleavened Bread — Passover; Feast of Weeks — Shavuot; and Feast of Booths — Sukkot.

INSIGHTS FROM THE TRADITION

A "See, I have set before you blessing and curse . . . " (Deuteronomy 11:26). This is the opening phrase of the portion. Nehama Leibowitz identifies this as the basis for the Jewish understanding of free will. In *Re'eh,* we read of blessings promised to those who obey the law and curses to those who disobey. The individual is offered a free choice, but the path chosen has inherent consequences.

The prophet Isaiah amplifies this concept: "If you are willing and obedient, you shall eat the good of the land; but if you refuse and rebel, you shall be devoured with the sword . . . " (1:19).

Are you totally free to choose how you will act in all circumstances?
Do you always know or consider the consequences of your behavior?
What might be the results of being overly cautious in our choices? of making quick or rash decisions?

B A number of biblical scholars have suggested that Deuteronomy might be a late addition to the Bible. Its contents are compatible with the religious ideas of Josiah, King of Judah (640-608 B.C.E.), who carried out an extensive Israelite religious reformation. Josiah's activities are chronicled in II Kings 22 and 23. Both Josiah and the Book of Deuteronomy mandated the idea that sacrifice is acceptable only at one central sanctuary and not at the many previously established worship sites. Eventually, Jerusalem became the approved location for the offering of sacrifice.

One Christian commentator, Gerhard von Rad, saw the Book of Deuteronomy, particularly that section dealing with the sacrifice, as a way of getting the Israelites back on track. He felt that they had obviously been influenced by other nations whose worship habits did not coincide with the Israelite belief system (*Deuteronomy,* pp. 88-94).

Consider the issues and topics with which the Book of Deuteronomy is concerned. How might this book have rejuvenated Judaism and the Jewish people in the seventh century B.C.E.?
Do you think contemporary Jews need a religious reformation? What form might this take?
What would you change about your Judaism?
What do you want Judaism to change in you?

C Sacrifices are of central concern in this portion. As mentioned in the previous Insight, a central sanctuary for the sacrifice of animals was established. Many of the laws of *shechitah* or ritual slaughter derive from the rules governing the sacrifices. Maimonides tells us these laws were set down so that we would not become accustomed to kill freely and to inflict pain, without concern, upon helpless animals. The intent of the laws was to encourage kindness and mercy (*Guide of the Perplexed* 17:17). Also, the laws of *kashrut* served to separate Israel from the surrounding nations. *Kashrut* was another way of assuring that Israel would maintain a unique attachment to certain moral values.

Are there other examples of Jewish laws which encourage or teach great human values?
The laws of *kashrut* teach us that we cannot consume everything which is available. We must control our appetites. How does this value relate to you and your life?

D This portion details what the Israelite attitude is to be regarding other nations and their religions. Deuteronomy 12:30 warns the people not to be lured into pagan habits. Simply inquiring about other gods may open the door to idolatry. Additionally, when the people settle in the Promised Land, they are to drive out the idolaters and utterly destroy their worship sites. Such rulings helped reinforce the religious system of the Israelites, foreign influences were simply not allowed.

This stance regarding faiths outside of Judaism still holds sway among many Jews. W. Gunther

Plaut points out that in some Orthodox communities, access to non-Orthodox writings, both Jewish and non-Jewish, is restricted (*The Torah: A Modern Commentary,* p. 1426). There are Jewish individuals who will not enter a church so as not to violate Deuteronomy 12:30, "Do not inquire about their gods."

In *The Five Books of Miriam* by Ellen Frankel, the Daughters ask, "What leads someone to abandon one spiritual path and take up an another? Our Mothers reply: Practicing a new faith usually precedes believing in its gods . . . Moses warns them not to follow the idolaters' ways . . . for Moses understands that the concreteness of doing wins converts more readily than the abstraction of doctrine" (p. 262).

Referring to the Frankel quote above, is studying about other faith traditions the same as practicing them?
How are our relationships with adherents to other faiths strengthened when we learn about their religious practices?
What can others learn about Jews when they learn about Judaism?
In what ways do we strengthen our own religious faith and commitment when we participate in interfaith programming?
Does interfaith programming strengthen or weaken society? Explain.

E *Re'eh* raises the issue of false prophets within Israelite society. These were Jewish individuals who sought to change Judaism from within by changing the law and by usurping power and divinity. In biblical times, the appearance of a false prophet was seen as a divine test of the people's loyalty to God. These false prophets might try to establish their validity through signs and wonders, but Rabbi Joshua, a sage from the Rabbinic period, asserted "Miracles in themselves cannot be invoked as decisive in matters of reason and law" (*The Pentateuch and Haftorahs* by J. H. Hertz, p. 806).

Are there false prophets today?

If so, are these individuals harmless or destructive to society?

Would you consider the leaders of cult groups false prophets?

F The Torah states that there will be no needy among you because the land is good and will provide for everyone's needs (Deuteronomy 15:4). W. Gunther Plaut explains that this verse is meant as an exhortation, implying: "There shouldn't really be any needy among you." The Torah never doubted that poverty would continue to exist and thus it also states: ". . . I command you: open your hand to the poor and needy . . . in your land" (*The Torah: A Modern Commentary*, pp. 1440-41). The Torah presents this as a moral imperative. *Tzedakah* was then, and is now, obligatory. Every person has the right to live a decent life, and those who are able to ensure this for others must do so.

Do the two quotes from Deuteronomy apply to society today?

Do we as a nation have a duty to do *tzedakah*? Explain.

What is your obligation to the poor in your family? in your synagogue? in your community?

Is it possible to wipe out hunger and poverty in your community? in the world?

What would you be willing to give up in order to provide food for others?

STRATEGIES

ANALYZING THE TEXT

1 Create a visual summary of *Re'eh* by constructing a mobile. Use cardboard or construction paper, cut into a variety of shapes and sizes for the balancing pieces, and on each write the concepts, short descriptions, quotes, character names and traits you have found in this portion.

Suspend from wire hangers or wooden dowels, using nylon thread or light thread.

2 Read Deuteronomy 13:2-6 and 18:20-22. According to the text, what distinguishes a true prophet from a false one? Do you agree with this distinction? Are there people in society today who you might call true prophets? Are there also false prophets which you can identify? What characteristics do they have that lead you to either conclusion? Does the criteria in Deuteronomy apply to them? Did it help in identifying them as either true or false prophets?

3 Revise the laws pertaining to Hebrew slaves in Deuteronomy 15:12-18. Draw a political cartoon depicting one of the situations described in the text. (For more, see the Index: "Slavery.")

4 Read *Re'eh* carefully. Choose several values explicit or implicit in the text which you think would be important to the average Israelite. Design a coat of arms for that individual based on those values. The coat of arms may be made in the shape of a star of David, illustrating the values you have chosen in each of the spaces in the star, or make an outline drawing of a shield and divide into six spaces and use those for your illustrations.

EXTENDING THE TEXT

5 Deuteronomy 13:17 describes a *tel olam* as an everlasting ruin. What is a *tel*? Research this term in the *Encyclopaedia Judaica*. Obtain a detailed map of place names in Israel. Do you find many sites with the word *Tel* in the name?

Now, build a *tel*. Divide into two groups. Groups A and B, working separately and without sharing what they are making, construct a number of objects and artifacts significant to a present-day Jewish community. Once these items are ready, they are buried in sand that is gradually built up into the shape of a *tel*. Use either a playground sand area or use small plastic swimming pools and fill them with sand. The two groups exchange places and "excavate" the *tel* that was prepared for them.

Conclude the activity by writing and presenting accounts of contemporary Jewish life based on what was discovered in the *tel*.

6 This portion provides the proof texts for the rules of *mohayk*, meaning "erasing." Read Deuteronomy 12:3-4. Verse 3 commands that all evidence of alien worship must be obliterated. In contrast, verse 4 instructs that God, and thus God's Name, should not be treated in this way. This led to the law that any book containing God's name is not to be destroyed, but stored away and eventually buried. Additionally, God's name must never be erased. What does your synagogue do with worn-out Bibles, prayer books, and other written materials which contain God's Name? Invite the Rabbi or head of the ritual committee at your synagogue to explain how your congregation handles this issue.

7 Seven divine names come under this ruling of *mohayk*. Find the seven divine names in the *Shulchan Aruch, Yoreh De'ah* 276:9, or in *The Torah: A Modern Commentary,* edited by W. Gunther Plaut, p. 1427, "*Halachah*." What does each name mean? Does it refer to any special attributes of God? What sort of concept of God emerges from these names?
References: *Encyclopaedia Judaica,* "God, Names of," Vol. 7, pp. 674-685.

8 Set up a quiz game to test knowledge of the *Shalosh Regalim,* the three Pilgrimage Festivals. Assign each of three teams the task of making up 20 questions about one of the festivals, Sukkot, Passover, and Shavuot. Each team will question the other two teams. Points are given for each correct answer. If a team stumps another with a question, the asking team receives bonus points. Play in rounds, a round consists of answering one question from each team and asking one question of each team. At the end of three rounds, the team with the most points wins.

9 In *Re'eh,* Moses warns the people not to be taken in by false prophets. One of the most famous false prophets was Shabbatai Zvi. Read about him in *The Jew in the Medieval World* by Jacob R. Marcus, pp. 261-269, or in the *Encyclopaedia Judaica,* Vol. 14, pp. 1219-1254. Could Shabbatai Zvi's contemporaries have known him as a false prophet if they had used the criteria given in *Re'eh* 13:1-12 and *Shofetim* 18:21-22?

10 Expand your research on the topic of false prophets within Judaism. Learn more about individuals who were uncovered as false prophets. Cover such questions as: what societal conditions led people to follow a false prophet, what kinds of promises did false prophets make and how were these false prophets eventually found out?

11 *Re'eh* contains the prohibition against eating blood (Deuteronomy 12:16). Even meat which is slaughtered according to the laws of *kashrut* must have the blood removed. An unfortunate lie evolved about Judaism. This falsehood was called the "Blood Libel," and it was very destructive to the Jewish people. The blood libel accuses Jews of using the blood of Christian children in the making of *matzah*. It is clear from our tradition that we are expressly prohibited from consuming any type of animal blood. Research this topic to find out when and where the idea of Blood Libel started and how it was perpetuated. Also look for and read fiction and non-fiction accounts of the blood libel.

PERSONALIZING THE TEXT

12 Design table setting displays which depict the three Pilgrimage Festivals. Include

traditional holiday foods, religious objects, and explanation cards to accompany each display. Use this as a basis for an interfaith activity in which you explain Jewish customs and celebrations.
References: *The Jewish Holiday Kitchen* by Joan Nathan; *The First Jewish Catalog* by Richard Siegel, Michael Strassfeld, and Sharon Strassfeld; *Jewish Family Celebrations: The Sabbath, Festivals, and Ceremonies* by Arlene Rossen Cardozo.

13 Take a close look at a kosher kitchen either in your synagogue, in your home, or in the home of someone in the community. You will need to interview the kitchen's owner(s). In what ways does it differ from a non-kosher kitchen?
References: *Teaching Mitzvot* by Barbara Binder Kadden and Bruce Kadden, pp.61-65. *Kosher Code of the Orthodox Jews* by S.I. Levin and Edward A. Boyden.

14 This portion repeats the information on the treatment of slaves in Israelite society. The issue of slavery was one of the central factors in the American Civil War. Slavery not only divided America, it also divided the American Jewish community. This was a difficult but fascinating period of Jewish life in America. Read and discuss the editorials, speeches, and sermons revolving around this issue at that time. (For more, see the Index: "Slavery.")
Reference: *American Jewry and the Civil War* by Bertram Korn.

15 In this portion, Moses admonishes the Israelites not to follow false prophets. In recent years there has been a great deal of publicity about cults and the individuals who lead them. Concern has been voiced over the legitimacy of certain cult leaders. A number of publications and resources have been devoted to this troubling phenomenon. Investigate one or more of the following to gather information: Visit your synagogue and public libraries to research this topic,

contact a local Jewish Federation to see what is available on this issue through them, and obtain *A Jewish Response to Cults* by Zari Weiss, with Elise Kahn and Gary Bretton-Granatoor.

16 In *Re'eh*, the Israelites are instructed to "open your hand to the needy" (15:8). *Tzedakah* (righteous or charitable deeds) has always been an important precept in Judaism. In the twelfth century, Moses Maimonides enumerated eight ways of giving charity. Each one of these was more praiseworthy than the one that preceded it. Read and discuss the eight degrees of charity in one of the sources listed below. Then choose one of the degrees and write a story depicting it. Try to show through your story what is and is not praiseworthy about giving charity with the degree of *tzedakah* about which you chose to write.
Resources: *Tzedakah, Gemilut Chasadim and Ahavah* by Joel Lurie Grishaver and Beth Huppin; *Encyclopaedia Judaica*, "Charity," Vol. 5, p. 343.

17 Make a *tzedakah* box for your "tithes." Visit a local crafts store to find pre-made plaster of paris, wooden or cardboard banks. Decorate per suggestions of the staff utilizing Jewish symbols, themes, and ideas.

18 In this portion, the people are instructed to establish a central and permanent worship site. Learn more about the development of your place of worship. When and how was your synagogue founded and built. Extend this activity by assembling a bulletin board display with the information you obtained. You may want to examine old synagogue records, interview knowledgeable congregants and the local historical society if the synagogue was founded long ago.

19 As previously stated in this portion, Moses warns the Israelites not to heed false prophets. View and discuss *Ticket to Heaven*, a compelling film about cults (available as a video rental, rated PG, 107 minutes) or *Leap of Faith,* the story of a traveling evangelist and his entourage (available as a video rental, rated PG-13, 110 minutes).

20 In this portion, the concept of putting aside 10 per cent for tithing is repeated. Try saving 10 per cent of the money you make through allowance, gifts, and jobs for one month. As you accumulate this money, think about and discuss the following: Is it difficult to put this money aside? Is it hard to not use the money if or when your finances get tight? Choose a cause, organization, or individual to give your money to. Conclude with a summary discussion and decide if you can continue this 10 per cent tithing.

21 Design and produce an information booklet to be distributed to the Israelites when they settle in Canaan. The booklet should contain the key laws Moses wanted them to live by as presented in *Re'eh*. If you wish, include the laws which are found in portions *Shofetim* and *Ki Taytzay*.

(For more, see the Index: "*Shalosh Regalim*," "*Kashrut*," "*Tzedakah*," "God," "False prophets.")

OTHER RESOURCES

22 Read, act out, and discuss the skit for the portion *Re'eh* in *Sedra Scenes: Skits for Every Torah Portion* by Stan J. Beiner, pp. 208-211.

23 For creative movement activities, see "Path to the Appointed Site" and "Sweep Out Evil" from *Torah in Motion* by JoAnne Tucker and Susan Freeman, pp. 208-211.

24 Read and discuss the illustrated commentary for *Re'eh* in *American Torah Toons* by Lawrence Bush.

INVOLVING THE FAMILY

25 The three pilgrimage holidays are discussed in this portion. With your family, choose a new *mitzvah*, a ritual, or a tradition for each of these holidays and observe it during the coming year. If possible take photos showing what your family chose to do. Take notes and record stories on family reactions to this new *mitzvah*. Use these as a basis for a Jewish family journal or scrapbook. Consider adding a *mitzvah*, ritual, or tradition to all the Jewish holidays throughout the year. References: See the references cited in Strategies #12 and #13, pages 313 and 314.

BAR/BAT MITZVAH PROJECT

26 The questions following Insight D, page 311, really challenge the precept given about foreign gods. The Israelites were simply not to inquire about them because this could lead to worshiping them. Yet, people of all different ethnic, cultural, and faith backgrounds share space on this planet. The more we know about one another the more it will help us break down the barriers that keep us apart. The more tolerant and accepting we become the more we will be able to appreciate and celebrate our diversity.

Your job in this Bar/Bat Mitzvah project is to be a bridge builder. Your task is to create (with adult help) an interfaith program for junior high school students, approximately ages 12-14.

An excellent group to help you do this is the National Conference of Christians and Jews (NCCJ). This long established organization works to build bridges of understanding and cooperation between people of different religious faiths. Contact your local NCCJ to see how they can help. Also work with your Rabbi and teachers.

Keep a record of what you have done and why. Speak about your project during your *D'var Torah* on the day of your Bar/Bat Mitzvah or at another appropriate time.

SHOFETIM 16:18-21:9 שופטים

SYNOPSIS

UPON ENTERING THE LAND, THE ISRAELITES are commanded to establish courts of law within their settlements. Judges are told to be fair and impartial, never accepting bribes or favoring anyone.

Again, Moses warns the people against idolatrous worship. An individual accused of establishing alien worship is declared guilty only upon the testimony of two or more witnesses. The penalty is death.

A case too difficult for a judge to decide is brought before the Levitical priests or magistrates for a ruling.

Should the people choose to establish a monarchy after they take possession of the Land, Moses provides them with a framework for how this is to be done. The king must be an Israelite. He should not have numerous wives or acquire great wealth. The teaching (Torah law) is to guide him at all times.

Moses instructs the people not to become involved in soothsaying or sorcery, for these are idolatrous practices of other nations.

Moses warns the people against false prophets and tells them how to identify a true prophet. Moses continues his discourse by describing the cities of refuge — three cities on each side of the Jordan set aside for individuals who accidentally kill someone. Moses further instructs the people to increase the number of refuge cities as their territory increases.

As the portion concludes, Moses discusses the rules by which Israel is to conduct its wars, exempt individuals from wars, and deal with unsolved murders.

INSIGHTS FROM THE TRADITION

A *Shofetim* means "judges." This portion deals extensively with the issue of how Israel is to be governed. The underlying theme is: Who will have authority over the people?

Authority may also be understood as responsibility. For what are you now responsible?
Have your responsibilities changed as you have gotten older? Explain.

B *Shofetim* opens with a description of how justice is to be carried out. The judges are warned not to judge unfairly. All litigants are to be treated equally no matter their social or financial position. The Talmud explains this to mean "that one should not stand and the other sit; one speak to his heart's content and the other be told, 'Be brief!'" (*Shevuot* 30a). The injunction to create a judicial system is not considered to be unique to Israel. From the Noahide laws the sages derived the establishment of courts of law as incumbent upon all nations.

Do you know of any societies today which do not have fair courts of law?
How would your life be different if there was no dependable justice in your society?

C This portion also discusses the establishment of a supreme court which would adjudicate cases too difficult for the local courts to decide. In later times, this supreme court became known as the Sanhedrin. The word "Sanhedrin" derives from the Greek word *synadrion*, meaning assembly. The Talmud describes two types of Sanhedrin: The Great Sanhedrin of 71 members which convened at the Temple in Jerusalem and the smaller Sanhedrin of 23 members which met in Jerusalem and other places in the Land of Israel. The Great Sanhedrin functioned as a high court and also as a legislature. The smaller Sanhedrin was empowered to handle specific serious cases which could involve capital punishment. Knowledge of Jewish law and good character were the qualifications for membership in the Sanhedrin.

What is the benefit of going to different people for help in solving different kinds of problems? What would be the reasoning for a court to travel to where the people are, rather than the people traveling to the court?

If you have difficulty deciding on an issue or problem, to whom do you turn for advice?

D While studying the texts about judges, Rashi took special note of the phrase "the magistrate who will be in charge at the time" in Deuteronomy 17:9. While we may look back with longing to a time when we think our judges or our leaders were wiser or more learned, Rashi reminds us that we have no one else to judge and lead us but those who live in our own days. This teaching is important because it validates the contemporary leadership of any period of time, including our own.

Why might people be tempted to look back at the leaders of other periods and think they were greater or wiser than our own leaders?
What dangers do you see in this practice?
How can we apply Rashi's teaching to contemporary Jewish life?

E Israel was cautioned in the previous portion not to add to or detract from the law. As if to underline this concept, we learn from *Pirke Avot:* "One is to build a hedge around the Torah." The Sages enacted legislation which would help assure that a person would not violate a law, therefore helping to preserve the laws themselves. Whereas the Torah consisted of precepts positive and negative, "the hedge" was like an early warning system which kept one far away from transgressing the law itself.

The laws of *kashrut* on Passover are an example of this hedge around the Torah. These laws enjoin one not to eat *chamaytz* (leaven) during that holiday period. The prohibition of *chamaytz* originally applied to five kinds of grain: wheat, barley, oats, rye, and spelt. In time, the Rabbis forbade eating

other grains, such as corn, rice, and legumes (peas and beans). It was thought to be difficult for a person to distinguish certain dishes made with permitted grains and legumes from those made with the five forbidden grains. To prevent this error, the Rabbis extended the prohibition to include these foods, too, thereby creating a hedge around the law of *chamaytz.*

Are there any "hedges" in your own life?
Are there any family "hedges?"

F The concept of an Israelite monarchy has its roots in this portion. Sources within the tradition criticize Israel for the establishment of the monarchy. They assert that a king would be a tyrant, would not be loyal to God, and would lead the people astray. Commentators such as Rashi, Abravanel, and Rabbi Eliezer ben Yose posit that God sensed that the people would desire a king because they would want to be like other nations. Anticipating this desire, a series of guidelines was established in advance of any monarchy. There has been much scholarly debate as to whether a monarchy was a divine command. Abravanel interprets Deuteronomy 17:15 to mean that the people should not elect a king; rather, the king would be chosen by God.

Throughout history, peoples have chosen to believe either that their kings were gods or that they were chosen by the gods. This idea allowed kings to act as they wished. It also kept rulership in the hands of a few families or houses. In what ways would this idea be preferable to elected officials as we have in our country today? In what ways would the divine right of kings be unworkable today?
If you were an absolute ruler, how would you use your power?

G Deuteronomy 20:19-20 tells warring Israelites not to destroy fruit bearing trees. Trees which produce no fruit, however, may be cut down and utilized for other purposes. From this the Rabbis derived the dictum against wastefulness (*Bal Tashchit*). While in Genesis 1:28 humanity is told to make use of God's creations and utilize nature's resources, it is also clear from a Rabbinic standpoint that it is forbidden to destroy wantonly anything that benefits humanity. The fruit tree was a grand example of this. Maimonides extends this prohibition of *Bal Tashchit* to include the breaking of utensils, tearing of garments, demolishing a building, stopping up a well, and the destruction of food (*Mishneh Torah, Melachim* 6; 8; 10). This commandment requires an individual to have self-control, to work at being a builder rather than a destroyer, and to have respect for all creation.

How do anti-litter laws reflect the principle of *Bal Tashchit*?

In what ways does your room at home (at school) reflect the principle of *Bal Tashchit*?

What have you done lately in keeping with this principle?

STRATEGIES

Analyzing the Text

1 Two famous quotes are found in this portion: "Justice, justice shall you pursue" (Deuteronomy 16:20), and "An eye for an eye, a tooth for a tooth" (19:21). Choose one of these quotes, find it in the original Hebrew, and memorize it. Make a rebus for one of these quotes.

2 In *Shofetim*, the Israelites are instructed "Justice, justice shall you pursue" (Deuteronomy 16:20). Read the portion carefully. How do the details of *Shofetim* bear out this maxim? Can you think of other means of pursuing justice? Make a bulletin board display on this theme.

EXTENDING THE TEXT

3 Read about the kings of Israel and Judah. Did they fit the criteria established by God through Moses (Deuteronomy 17:14-20)? Why or why not?

References: I and II Samuel, I and II Kings.

4 Saul, David, and Solomon were not the only kings of Israel. There were actually many generations of kings. At one point, Israel split into two kingdoms — Israel and Judah. Create an illustrated time line which names the kings in order. Draw a picture or write a character sketch which explains something about each king.

5 How was the first king of Israel chosen? Read the description of how Saul became king (I Samuel 8-10). Rewrite the narrative as if you are a television reporter, magazine writer, or radio announcer. Videotape or broadcast your report.

6 Deuteronomy 18:13 says "You must be wholehearted with *Adonai* your God." The Hebrew word for "wholehearted" is "*Tamim*," and in the Torah scroll, the first letter of this word (the *tav*) is written large. Explore the meaning of this word by looking at its use elsewhere in the Torah. What is the meaning and implication of the word as it is used in Genesis 6:9 to describe Noah, and in Genesis 17:1 in which God instructs Abram and uses this word? (Also, in the Passover *Hagaddah*, the Hebrew word for the simple child is "*tam*." See also Psalm 119:1.) After reviewing the other texts, write your own commentary on the verse in Deuteronomy, explaining what being "wholehearted" with God means to you.

7 According to *Deuteronomy Rabbah* (5:13), the reason for the law given in Deuteronomy 20:10 ("When you approach a town to attack it, you shall offer it terms of peace") can be traced to

Numbers 21:21-25. In those passages, Moses offered peace to Sihon, King of the Amorites, before putting Sihon's country to the sword. Choose another of the injunctions in *Shofetim* and write a story describing an event which led to formulation of the law you chose.

8 According to the concept of *Bal Tashchit*, "It is forbidden to destroy or injure anything capable of being useful to people" (*Shulchan Aruch* of Rav, *Hilchot Guf Vanefesh*, 14). This principle derives specifically from Deuteronomy 20:19-20. Since God is the Creator and Owner of all the earth (Leviticus 25:23), any act which causes destruction of the world is seen as an act against God. Write a series of contemporary guidelines for Jews concerned with the principle of *Bal Tashchit*.

Divide the guidelines into two sections. In the first section, detail acts which an individual should/should not do in his/her personal life in keeping with *Bal Tashchit*. In the second section, suggest strategies for dealing with issues of *Bal Tashchit* that extend beyond the action of individuals (e.g., environmental pollution by large companies).

9 The Talmud distinguishes between two kinds of war. An obligatory war (*milchemet mitzvah*) is defensive in nature and fought in self-defense for survival. This category also includes the wars fought to settle the land of Canaan. The second kind of war is *milchemet reshut* — voluntary. All wars which are not obligatory are classed as voluntary (*Sotah* 44b). Review the wars fought by the State of Israel since 1947. Discuss whether each was an obligatory or voluntary war.

PERSONALIZING THE TEXT

10 The biblical attitude toward trees is explained in this portion. The Jewish National Fund is an organization which reclaims the Land of Israel by planting trees. Learn about the contemporary Jewish attitude toward trees by contacting this organization for information and program materials. If there is no local affiliate in your community, contact The Jewish National Fund, 42 East 69th Street, New York, NY 10021.

11 Deuteronomy 20:19 asks, "Are trees of the field human . . . ?" *Sifra* to Deuteronomy (203) understood this to imply that trees and humans have much in common. Jewish teachings and tradition contain a wealth of allusions to trees. The Torah is called a "tree of life" (Proverbs 3:18), and there is a custom that when an infant is born, a tree is planted (a cedar for a girl and a cypress for a boy). When that child grows up and marries, branches of the tree are used to support the *chupah*. Choose one of these ideas and design a poster to illustrate it.

12 "Are trees of the field human to withdraw before you into the besieged city?" Draw up two lists — one detailing how trees are like humans, one noting the differences between the two. Use one of your two lists as the basis for a creative poem about trees to be read on Shabbat *Shofetim*.

13 Much of *Shofetim* deals with punishment fitting particular crimes. Compare the crimes and punishments in this portion with local ordinances. Invite a lawyer, policeman, or judge as a guest speaker. Compile questions in advance so you are prepared for the speaker.

14 In discussing the obligations of a future king, Deuteronomy says that the ruler "shall have a copy of this Teaching written for him on a scroll . . . Let it remain with him and let him read it all his life" (17:18-19). What would be the implications of this teaching if we were to take it seriously in our public and private lives today?
a. Imagine that you are an advisor to the President of your country. Write a memo reflecting

this teaching for the President to consider as he/she makes plans for a new administration.

b. Decide on ten key teachings from the Torah which you would like to remember all your life and record them in a personal journal entry. In your writing explore how you might keep the commandment to "let [them] remain with you . . . and read [them] all [your] life."

15 Find newspaper and magazine articles which reflect the quotation "Justice, justice shall you pursue." Discuss how the article(s) you chose reflect the quote. Display the articles with this quote as the caption.

16 Why do you think the Torah expresses such concern that there be *two* witnesses in order to prove a person guilty (Deuteronomy 19:15)? Play "Detective." Arrange for several people to dress up in funny costumes and to stage a tableau for 10-15 seconds. Have members of the audience describe in writing what they saw. Compare their accounts. Does this exercise help you answer the above question?

17 The Hebrew word for justice is צדק (*tzedek*). Many words are derived from this root, including צדקה (*tzedakah*) righteous action or charity. The title צדיק (*tzaddik*) is given to one whose life exemplifies the values of *tzedek* and *tzedakah*. Write a character sketch of a *tzaddik*, describing the outlook and actions of such a person.

18 The circumstances under which an individual was exempt from battle are in this portion. There is no mention here of conscientiously objecting to war. Why do you think that was left out of the text? Within the Jewish community, some young people have refused to serve in the armed forces because they were opposed to fighting in a war. Contact your Rabbi to speak to the class about the Jewish attitude toward conscientious objection.

19 Moses warned the people to be wary of false prophets and he provided them ways to identify false prophets. There are those who say that today false prophets exist as leaders of cults. View and discuss the video *You Can Go Home Again*. (For more, see the Index: "False prophets.")

20 Moses warned the people to be wary of false prophets and to avoid soothsayers, diviners, and sorcerers. He told the Israelites that these false prophets can be identified because they speak in the name of God, but their words do not come true (Deuteronomy 18:22). What do you think are the contemporary equivalents of false prophets, soothsayers, diviners, and sorcerers of old? Write a series of guidelines for young people to use to help them identify and avoid these dangerous "false prophets."

21 The statue of a blindfolded woman holding a scale represents justice. Based on this portion, why is this representation appropriate? Create your own artistic representation of justice.

22 Although astrology was prohibited by Jewish law, the *mazalot* (astrological signs) were used as a motif in many early synagogues. A fine example of this is the floor of the Bet Alpha synagogue in Israel. The floor of this sixth century synagogue is composed of mosaic tiles featuring the signs of the zodiac. Read about this synagogue in *Encyclopaedia Judaica*, Vol. 4, pp. 710-713.

Out of cut paper or ceramic tile, create a mosaic that might have been displayed in an ancient synagogue.

OTHER RESOURCES

23 Read, act out, and discuss the skit for the portion *Shofetim* in *Sedra Scenes: Skits for Every Torah Portion* by Stan J. Beiner, pp. 212-214.

24 For creative movement activites, see "Do Not Deviate" and "Protecting Trees During War" from *Torah in Motion* by JoAnne Tucker and Susan Freeman, pp. 212-215.

25 Read and discuss the illustrated commentary for *Shofetim* in *American Torah Toons* by Lawrence Bush.

INVOLVING THE FAMILY

26 According to the Talmud, the order in which exemptions from military service are treated (Deuteronomy 20:5-9) is also the order in which a person should live (*Sotah* 44a): first one should build a house, then plant a vineyard, and finally marry. Of course, expectations about the course of life have changed since biblical times. Discuss this with your parents. What are your expectations about your adult life? What did your parents expect from adult life? How have their expectations about life been fulfilled? In what instances have their expectations been changed?

BAR/BAT MITZVAH PROJECT

27 In keeping with the teachings in *Shofetim* which encourage us to be sensitive to protecting the environment, consider how your Bar/Bat Mitzvah celebration can be designed to reflect sound environmental principles. Everything from paper for invitations, to the plates we eat on, to the decorations we use, has an impact on the environment, both when it is manufactured and when we dispose of it. Together with your family, make a list of ideas for making your celebration "earth friendly." Some ideas include printing your invitations on recycled paper, and making sure your table decorations are biodegradable or recyclable (e.g., use flowers which can later be donated or planted, instead of balloons). For suggestions, write to The Eco-Kosher Project, 7318 Germantown Avenue, Philadelphia, PA, 19119.

KI TAYTZAY 21:10-25:19   כי תצא

SYNOPSIS

MOSES CONTINUES THE REPETITION OF the laws by which Israel must live. These laws deal with a variety of topics, but most are concerned with moral values. A brief summary of the moral laws follows.

Ethical Principles and Communal Norms

1. Marital and family relationships:
   a. Women who are taken captive by the Israelites due to war must be treated humanely.
   b. Men with two wives must treat all their wives' children equally.
   c. Defiant sons are to be disciplined by their parents. The community intercedes if the parents are not successful.
2. If an individual is put to death for a capital offense, his corpse must still be treated with respect.
3. Relationships with others:
   a. Return all lost property.
   b. Help care for your neighbor's fallen animals.
4. Men and women must wear clothing appropriate to their gender.
5. Do not take a mother bird along with its young.
6. When building a house, follow safety precautions and construct a parapet for the roof.
7. The following are considered unnatural mixes and are forbidden:
   a. Ploughing with two different types of animals.
   b. Wearing cloth which mixes wool and linen.
8. The Israelites are commanded to wear *tzitzit* on the four corners of their clothing.

Civil and Criminal Matters

1. Marital Relationships:
   a. After marriage, a man who falsely claims that his wife was not a virgin, shall be flogged and fined 100 *shekels* of silver payable to his wife's father. He is never allowed to divorce this woman. If the charges are true, the woman is stoned to death.
   b. Adulterers shall be put to death.
   c. If an engaged woman is raped within town and she does not cry out for help, both she and the rapist are stoned to death. If the rape occurs in the open country, only the rapist is guilty, as there was no one to hear the woman cry out.
   d. If a virgin is raped, the rapist must pay her father 50 *shekels* of silver. He must marry her and is never allowed to divorce her.
   e. A man may not marry his father's former wife.
2. The following are not to be part of the congregation of God:
   a. A man whose sexual organ is damaged.
   b. Illegitimate children and their descendants.
   c. Amorites and Moabites.
3. Third generation descendants of Edomites and Egyptians are permitted to become part of the congregation of God.
4. A runaway slave shall not be returned to his master and may freely choose where to live.
5. No Israelite woman or man shall live as a cultic prostitute.
6. Israelites must never take interest from each other on money lent, but they may take interest from a foreigner.
7. One may partake of a neighbor's harvest while standing in his field, but one may not fill a vessel and take its contents.
8. A man, during his first year of marriage, is exempt from army service.
9. A twice divorced and once widowed woman may not remarry her first husband.
10. Kidnappers are to be put to death.
11. An Israelite who lends money shall not harass his debtors.
12. Workers shall be paid on a daily basis.
13. Each individual is responsible only for the crime(s) he or she personally commits.

14. The community is responsible for the needs of the stranger, the orphan, and the widow. These three groups are permitted to gather the leftovers of the harvest in order to provide for their needs.

15. In court judgments, the guilty party may be flogged up to 40 lashes, but no more.

16. An ox must not be muzzled when it threshes grain.

17. A widow who has no children shall marry her husband's brother in order to bear a child. If the brother refuses, a formal ceremony is carried out releasing him. The widow is then free to marry anyone else.

18. The Israelites must be honest in business dealings; all weights and measures are to be reliable.

This portion closes with a reminder to the Israelites that they are never to forget their enemy Amalek.

INSIGHTS FROM THE TRADITION

A In the introduction to the *Mishneh Torah*, Maimonides states that the total number of precepts in the Torah is 613. Two hundred forty-eight of them are positive, and equal to the number of bones in the human body. The remaining 365 commandments are negative, and equal to the number of days in a solar year. Maimonides traces this information to Rabbi Simlai, a Palestinian teacher of the Rabbinic period. According to Maimonides, *Ki Taytzay* contains some 72 of these positive and negative *mitzvot*. The first laws which this portion addresses deal with the taking of hostages as a result of war. *Ki Taytzay* means, "when you go out" (to battle).

B Throughout history, Jewish teachers and scholars have sought the underlying rationale for the observance of the commandments. *Devarim Rabbah* 6:3 provides an insight on this issue.

Rabbi Pinchas b. Hama said: Wherever you go and whatever you do, pious deeds will accompany you. When you build a new house, "make a parapet for your roof" (Deuteronomy 22:8). When you make a door, "write [the commandments] upon the doorposts" (Deuteronomy 6:9). When you put on new garments, don't "wear cloth combining wool and linen" (Deuteronomy 22:1 1). When you cut your hair, don't "round the corners of your head" (Leviticus 19:27). When you plough your field, do not "plough with an ox and an ass together" (Deuteronomy 22:20). "When you reap your harvest, and have forgotten a sheaf, don't pick it up. Leave it for the stranger, the fatherless, and the widow" (Deuteronomy 24:19). God said: "Even if you are not engaged in any particular work but are merely journeying on the road, the precepts accompany you." If a bird's nest is before you on the road, "do not take the mother with her young" (Deuteronomy 22:6-7).

The commandments seek to imbue every human action with a sense of holiness. They take our every day actions and give them new meaning. Is there a difference between doing an action that you were commanded to do and doing the same action by your own initiative?
Are there *mitzvot* that you carry out which change the quality of your life?
Have you ever done a good deed unknowingly and then found out that you have fulfilled a *mitzvah*? Did your action take on new meaning for you once you found this out?

C Within the various branches of Judaism, the observance of *mitzvot* has been hotly debated. In 1976, the Central Conference of American Rabbis (Reform) adopted a "Centenary Perspective" which considered the issue of observance. It read in part: "Within each area of Jewish observance, Reform Jews are called upon to confront the claims of Jewish tradition, however differently perceived, and to exercise their individual autonomy, choosing and creating on the basis of commitment and knowledge." Essentially then, the observance of *mitzvot* is left to the discretion of the individual.

Forty years ago, Dr. Louis Finkelstein, the Chancellor of the Jewish Theological Seminary (Conservative), issued this statement regarding *halachah* and its observance: "Jewish law must be preserved but . . . it is subject to interpretation by those who have mastered it . . . " Thus, while the observance of *mitzvot* is still left to the individual, Conservative Rabbinical authorities are responsible for interpreting the law with respect to present-day realities.

How does an individual make informed choices regarding the *mitzvot* according to the Conservative movement? the Reform movement? What about within the framework of traditional Judaism?
What or who influences you most in your religious observance? Family? Friends? Teachers? Rabbis?

D The subject of returning lost property appears in this portion and also in Exodus 23:4. Both versions tell us to return lost property, whether it belongs to a person who is an enemy or a friend. Nehama Leibowitz points out that not only must one protect a lost object until the owner claims it, but one must also actively safeguard a lost possession so as to return it in good condition (*Studies in Devarim*, pp. 212ff.).

Have you ever found a valuable object? What steps did you take to find its owner?
What are some methods a person might use to either find or restore lost property?

E Deuteronomy 24:16 reads, "Parents shall not be put to death for children, nor children be put to death for parents: a person shall be put to death only for his own crime." This verse states the principle of individual responsibility. This contrasts with a phrase from Deuteronomy 5:9: ". . . visiting the guilt of the fathers upon the children, unto the third and fourth generations." What does "visiting the guilt" mean? Ellen Frankel interprets through the "Mothers," who say that

"behavior modeled by parents usually repeats in the next several generations . . . [this includes] parents' beliefs, their family myths, and their emotional responses to the world." Deuteronomy 24:16 is a warning not to legislate intergenerational guilt (*The Five Books of Miriam*, pp. 283-284). Every generation and every individual in any generation is only responsible for the actions in which he or she engages.

Rashi, offering a different interpretation, states that Deuteronomy 24:16 means that fathers shall not be put to death on the testimony of their children, nor children put to death on the testimony of their fathers. Jewish law extended this to include all relatives of an accused criminal.

Have you ever read accounts of families in which several generations are involved in the same business, activities, or hobbies?
Are there traditions in your family which have existed for generations?
There are also families who for generations have engaged in criminal activities. If a member of such a family chooses a different and law-abiding path, how does it reflect the verses cited above?

STRATEGIES

ANALYZING THE TEXT

1 Many of the commandments in *Ki Taytzay* deal with the status of women. Using the information in this portion, do one of the following:
a. Make a display or bulletin board of these laws. Include a graffiti space to record contemporary reaction to these laws.
b. Write a short story which includes one of these laws.

2 According to Maimonides, this portion contains 72 positive and negative *mitzvot*. Read through *Ki Taytzay* and list under the headings "positive" and "negative" all the *mitzvot* you find. Did you find all 72?

3 Discuss how the laws presented in *Ki Taytzay* reflect the admonition from *Shofetim*, "Justice, justice shall you pursue" (Deuteronomy 16:20).

4 What unnatural mixes are forbidden in the portion *Ki Taytzay*? Can you suggest reasons for the prohibition of these combinations? What does the existence of these laws teach us about the Jewish view of what is natural? Are there (other) combinations which you consider unnatural? Why?

5 The law given in Deuteronomy 22:6-7 about a mother bird and her young exemplifies the Torah's attitude toward the treatment of animals. Jewish tradition bases the law of kindness to animals on the notion that living things feel pain. These laws legislate the Jewish value of *tza'ar baalay chayim*, which translates as the "suffering of living beings." Read the following verses and suggest some of the laws which are part of this concept: Leviticus 22:28; Numbers 22:32; Deuteronomy 5:14; 22:6-7,10; 25:4. (For more, see the Index: "*Tza'ar baalay chayim/Treatment of animals.*") Reference: *Teaching Mitzvot* by Barbara Binder Kadden and Bruce Kadden, pp. 99-103.

EXTENDING THE TEXT

6 Invite a guest speaker from your synagogue's burial society or a Rabbi, educator, or Jewish funeral director to relate how the laws concerning the sight of unburied bodies and prompt burial are reflected in Jewish funeral practices (Deuteronomy 21:22-23) .

How do these Jewish practices show the deep respect for the human body alive or dead? References: *Teaching Jewish Life Cycle*, pp. 101-120,

and *Teaching Mitzvot,* pp. 43-47, both by Bruce Kadden and Barbara Binder Kadden.

7 *Ki Taytzay* warns that the rights of the firstborn son may not be disregarded (Deuteronomy 21:15-17). Review the relationships between the Abraham, Isaac, and Jacob and their sons. Discuss how each Patriarch violated the law stated here. What affect did the violation have on the unloved wife and/or the unfavored child? Summarize the activity by stating why such a law was needed. (For more, see the Index: "Firstborn.")

8 For an example of the application of the law given in Deuteronomy 24:19, read the following in the Book of Ruth 1:22-2:9. Discuss how well the laws designed to protect widows functioned in Ruth's situation.

9 Commemorate Ruth and her gleaning in the fields by drawing or painting the scene from her life as described in Ruth 1:22-2:9.

PERSONALIZING THE TEXT

10 Amalek is singled out in this portion as the eternal enemy of the Jewish people. Shabbat *Zachor*, which is the Shabbat preceding Purim, is a time set aside for remembering the enemies of Israel. Compose a reading for Shabbat *Zachor* based on the theme "Remember Amalek."

11 The ceremony of *chalitzah* as described in *Ki Taytzay* (25:5-10) does not portray the intense emotion which accompanies this ceremony. For a depiction of this observance, see *I Love You Rosa* (available as a video rental, not rated, but recommended for high school age and above, running time 90 minutes, dubbed into English).

12 See the film *Hester Street,* which chronicles the dissolution of a Jewish marriage and includes the traditional process of writing and delivering a *get.* It is available as a video rental and is rated PG. The film is about Jewish immigrants to America in the early 1900s.
Reference: *Teaching Jewish Life Cycle* by Barbara Binder Kadden and Bruce Kadden, pp. 69-70.

13 The characterization of the Jew as money-lender has often been used in literature to present a negative image of the Jewish people. Assign parts and read aloud *The Merchant of Venice* by William Shakespeare. Do this in the style of a reader's theater.

Once the reading is completed, discuss the play and in particular Shylock and his daughter Jessica. How did Shakespeare portray them? Were Jews living in England at the time that Shakespeare was writing? Investigate and find out. How, where, and why do you think the non-Jewish world of Shakespeare's time formed their perceptions of Jewish people?

14 Deuteronomy 22:8 instructs the builder of a new home to construct a parapet on the roof to prevent someone from falling off. Here we see the seeds of building safety codes. With the group, brainstorm regulations by which you think builders should abide. Extend the activity and invite an architect or safety inspector to evaluate and discuss your regulations in light of government standards.
References and activity suggestions: *Teaching Mitzvot* by Barbara Binder Kadden and Bruce Kadden, pp. 147-150.

15 Deuteronomy 23:16 states: "You shall not turn over to his master a slave who seeks refuge with you . . . " The issue of slavery is dealt with often in the Bible. A spiritual about slavery titled "Let My People Go" is often part of the Passover *Seder.* Learn this song. Search for other songs about slavery by asking the Cantor or music specialist or by going to the public library. Learn one or more of these songs and incorporate them into your Passover *Seder.* (For more, see the Index: "Slavery.")

16 Complete the following statements by supplying your own reasons for the laws:
Deuteronomy 22:8 – "When you build a new house, you shall make a parapet for your roof" because _____ .
Deuteronomy 22:10 – "You shall not plow with an ox and an ass together" because _____ .
Deuteronomy 23:16 – "You shall not turn over to his master a slave who seeks refuge with you" because _____ .
Deuteronomy 24:15 – "You must pay a [laborer] his/her wages on the same day" because _____ .
Deuteronomy 25:15 – "You must have completely honest weights and completely honest measures" because _____ .

17 *Ki Taytzay* ends with the admonition, "You shall blot out the memory of Amalek from under heaven" (Deuteronomy 25:19). This idea is so deeply rooted in Jewish tradition that many notorious enemies of the Jewish people came to be identified as "Amalekites." One of the most famous of these is Haman. Draw an editorial cartoon for the *Persian Press* depicting Haman in light of this tradition. (For more, see the Index: "Amalek.")

18 Deuteronomy 22:3 reads: "You shall do the same with his donkey; you shall do the same with his garment; and so, too, shall you do with anything that your fellow loses and you find: you must not remain indifferent." At the heart of it, the Torah is telling you to get involved, that you cannot stand by when your neighbor loses an item. By extension, the Torah is also saying that you need to be involved with your neighbor, with your society, and with your world. Using magazines and/or newspapers, have each participant find an article or a photograph which discusses or depicts an event about which he or she cannot remain indifferent. Everyone shares the articles and photos. Discuss these events and issues. Conclude by having group members suggest possible courses of action for the events and issues presented.

(For more, see the Index: *"Tallit," "Tefillin," "Death/Burial," "Environmental concerns."*)

OTHER RESOURCES

19 Read, act out, and discuss the skit for the portion *Ki Taytzay* in *Sedra Scenes: Skits for Every Torah Portion* by Stan J. Beiner, pp. 215-218.

20 For a creative movement activity, see "Regard for Animals" from *Torah in Motion* by JoAnne Tucker and Susan Freeman, pp. 216-217.

21 Read and discuss the illustrated commentary for *Ki Taytzay* in *American Torah Toons* by Lawrence Bush.

INVOLVING THE FAMILY

22 Many of the *mitzvot* presented in this portion were meant to help establish a strong foundation for family life. With your family read over those *mitzvot* from this portion. Discuss and create a set of guidelines based on what you have read which have particular meaning to your family and would strengthen your family life.

23 Although Deuteronomy 21:18-21 prescribes the death penalty for defiant children, the Talmud asserts that such events as would lead to the death penalty "never occurred and never will occur" (*Sanhedrin* 71a). Nevertheless, the presence of this law points to the importance of parental authority. With your family, look up "parents" and "children" in a quotation dictionary. Discuss the quotes you find. Which do you like best? least? Design posters illustrating your choices.

BAR/BAT MITZVAH PROJECT

24 This project involves the Jewish value of *tza'ar ba'alay chayim*, which means the suffering of living beings. The Torah teaches us to prevent and alleviate the suffering of animals.
Task #1: Read through this portion and take note of each law that involves animals.
Task #2: Suggest remedies for each of the situations the Torah presents.
Task #3: Put this *mitzvah* into action.

Suggestions for *mitzvah* actions:
a. Contact the local SPCA or animal shelter. They often look for volunteers to help in the care of their animals. This also may include a training class.
b. Contact The Horse Protection League, which rescues, rehabilitates, and finds homes for abused horses. How can you be involved? Write: The Horse Protection League, 5305 Eldridge, Arvada, CO 80002.
c. Start a *mitzvah* dog-walking service for physically challenged individuals who, because of their physical restrictions, are not able to walk, exercise, or easily play with their pets. Contact a local veterinarian for advice and leads on potential clients. Also advertise your services in the synagogue bulletin.
d. Are you interested in birds? Contact The Birds of Prey Foundation. This organization rehabilitates eagles, falcons, hawks, and other injured birds. Able birds are released back into the wild. Other birds, who will not fully recover, live out their lives at the Foundation. The Birds of

Prey Foundation, 2290 South 104th Street, Broomfield, CO 80020. (From the Annual Report of the Ziv Tzedakah Fund, Inc., April 1, 1997.)

KI TAVO 26:1-29:8   כי תבוא

SYNOPSIS

MOSES CONTINUES HIS REVIEW OF THE Law begun in the previous portion, *Ki Taytzay*. He tells the people that when they enter the Land and settle it, they are to bring the first fruits as sacrifices. The ceremony for bringing this sacrifice is detailed. As part of this ritual, the priest recites a brief history of the Israelites — Abraham's/Jacob's wanderings, the experience of slavery in Egypt, the Exodus, and ultimately the occupation and possession of the Promised Land.

Moses concludes his review of the Law with instructions about tithing. An individual's tithe is one-tenth of the harvest. This tenth part is divided and distributed among the Levites, the strangers, the orphaned, and the widowed.

Moses gives his final instructions to the people. Upon crossing the Jordan, the people are to set up 12 stones on Mount Ebal. The stones are to be covered with plaster and inscribed with the laws which Israel is to obey.

Ki Tavo concludes with a dramatic description of the recitation of the blessings and curses. The tribes are divided into two groups with Simeon, Levi, Judah, Issachar, Joseph, and Benjamin on Mt. Gerizim reciting "Amen" after blessings are pronounced, while the Reuben, Gad, Asher, Zebulun, Dan, and Naphtali tribes on Mt. Ebal respond "Amen" after each curse.

INSIGHTS FROM THE TRADITION

A Throughout the biblical period, prayer was largely unstructured, with each individual using his/her own language and style. In *Ki Tavo*, which means "when you enter [the Promised Land]," there is, for the first time, a specific structure and context given for a worship experience. The Israelite who brought first fruits of the harvest would recite a prescribed account of history (Deuteronomy 26:3-10). The sacrifice would follow. An assurance that the offering was a true tithe (Deuteronomy 26:13-15) would close the ceremony.

Why did such an observance evolve? Sacrifices represented material plenty. Bringing them was the only way to thank God for good fortune. Israelite history represented the divinely inspired process by which the free nation was formed. Reciting that history was a way of identifying with that history and of thanking God for the blessing of living in one's own land.

Are you comfortable with unstructured personal prayer, or do you prefer the structure of worship found in a service led by a Rabbi, Cantor, or *Shaliach Tzibur*?
If you could choose any place for prayer, where would it be? Why?
For what do you pray?

B The recitation of history described in *Ki Tavo* formed the basis of the Passover *Haggadah*. At the *Seder*, we thank God for liberation from Egyptian bondage. Just as all Jews stood at Sinai, so, too, all Jews were redeemed from slavery. The Mishnah reads, "In every generation, one must look upon himself as if he personally had come forth out of Egypt . . . "

Why do you think Passover is so important?
How do we reenact the experiences of slavery and the Exodus?
Describe customs associated with other holidays which help give you the feeling of having "been there."

C In *Sefas Emes*, Yehudah Aryeh Leib of Ger wonders about Deuteronomy 26:13, in which we are told to declare, "[I have done] just as You commanded me: I have neither transgressed nor forgotten [some translations read "neglected"] any of Your commandments."

Shouldn't it be clear that anyone who has obeyed (and not transgressed) has also not forgotten? These extra words serve to remind us to pay attention to the *mitzvot* while we are performing them. After all, many of us do things in a routine way; even while fulfilling an important *mitzvah,* our minds are elsewhere. "Don't forget," the Torah says, act with intent.

Give some personal examples of times in your life when you have done something without paying attention.
Why does Yehudah Aryeh Leib think it is important for us to pay attention while we are doing *mitzvot?*
What do you think we should be remembering?

D In this portion, the awesome pronouncement of the blessings and curses occurs. Gerhard Von Rad calls Deuteronomy 27:15-26 the Dodecalogue of Shechem. He felt that these 12 verses were the most ancient series of prohibitions in the Bible, and that they reflect the spirit and liturgical form of early Judaism. He also discusses the significance of the people responding with "Amen" after each curse is pronounced. This "Amen" was more than a signal of agreement. By it, the people were assenting to God's will. Von Rad further explains that the force of these curses was provided by the community itself, as they would then totally disassociate from the lawbreakers. Left without a community, the fate of a lawbreaker would certainly be bleak (*Deuteronomy,* p. 167).

It should be pointed out that while blessings and curses were to have been spoken, only curses are found in this section. W. Gunther Plaut speculates that the blessings may have been simply the opposite formulation of the curses. The people, in responding "Amen" to the curses, were called upon to enforce the effect of the curses (*The Torah: A Modern Commentary,* p. 1516).

In what ways are you called upon to enforce rules?
How does this role affect you?
To what in life do you say "Amen"?

E Chapter 28 of the Book of Deuteronomy is known as the "*Tochechah*" — warning. It describes the punishment which Israel would face for disobedience of God's law. The *Tochechah* begins with a list of six blessings, but is followed by a vivid detailing of numerous curses and consequences of law breaking. Why did Israel need this warning? David Hoffman explains that all the signs and wonders shown Israel did not lead them to belief in God. It was the 40 years of wandering in the desert and all the trials Israel endured which led them to belief (*Studies in Devarim* by Nehama Leibowitz, p. 289).

What are some of the things that happened in the 40 years of wandering that especially led the people to belief in God?
From Hoffman's comment, it seems that people learn better from difficulties rather than from easy experiences. What do you think this says about human nature?
With what are you especially blessed? cursed?
With what is society blessed? cursed?

F Near the end of this portion, Moses speaks to the people telling them that even with all the signs and wonders, God still had not given them a mind to understand or eyes to see or ears to hear. Nehama Leibowitz suggested that in truth it was not God who had prevented the people from comprehending what was going on, but something within the people themselves. She continues with an excellent sketch of Moses at this moment: ". . . perhaps we may detect a note of bitter irony and deep regret in Moses' tone . . . . He who had invested so much blood, sweat, and toil in leading [the Israelites] out of bondage to freedom and acceptance of Torah had not succeeded in changing them. He had not been able to influence them to exercise their free choice and choose life" (*Studies in Devarim,* p. 293).

Did Moses try to do too much? Did God ever ask Moses to change the people? Did Moses assume a task which was not required? Would Moses have become too powerful if he had influenced the people to a great degree?

Is it possible for one person to change the feelings and attitudes of a group? Can you give historic examples?

What extra special talent would you want to have? How would that talent enable you to be better able to relate to other individuals or to groups?

STRATEGIES

ANALYZING THE TEXT

1 Review the first group of curses in *Ki Tavo* (Deuteronomy 27:15- 26). Compare them to the Ten Commandments (Exodus 20:1-14 or Deuteronomy 5:1-18). What relationship do you see? Are there any curses which bear no relationship to the Ten Commandments?

2 Examine the curses in *Ki Tavo*. Which would have an effect on the physical lives of the people? Which are more psychological in nature? Which curse would be the worst for an individual? for the people as a whole?

3 The commentators disagreed as to the exact meaning of the words in Deuteronomy 26:5: ארמי אבד אבי (*Arami oved avi*). Rashi understood *oved* to mean destroyer, and he thought the Aramean referred to here was Laban. His translation would then be, "An Aramean — Laban — sought to destroy my father." Translating the passage as "My father was a wandering Aramean," Rashbam thought the person referred to was Abraham, who was born and raised in Aram. Ibn Ezra thought it referred to Jacob, who "went down to Egypt." Review Deuteronomy 26:5 carefully. Who do you think is meant by the word "Aramean"? Why? (See *The Torah: A Modern Commentary*, edited by W. Gunther Plaut, p. 1512, for a discussion of this.)

EXTENDING THE TEXT

4 Deuteronomy 26:3-19 became a significant portion of the Passover *Haggadah*. Examine various *Haggadot* to find how these Torah verses are used. Compare the *Haggadah* version of these verses with the biblical text. Also read any additional commentary the *Haggadah* contains. Lastly, learn to read these verses in Hebrew.

5 Writing in *Learn Torah With . . . (1994-1995 Torah Annual)*, p. 383, Daniel Leifer describes the verses from Deuteronomy (26:5-8) which made their way into the *Haggadah* as a "this is who I am text." When we read these words at our Passover *Seder,* we are telling ourselves our own personal history. Write your own brief "this is who I am text," beginning with our first ancestors and whatever you consider to be the key events in forming the Jewish people. Then skip to the generations before you were born and add details to bring your "text" up-to-date with your life. Include what you've written in your Passover *Seder* (or in a Bar/Bat Mitzvah *D'var Torah!*).

6 Israel is described as the land of milk and honey (26:9). Learn the Hebrew song *"Eretz Zavat Chalav U'devash."*
Reference: *Songs NFTY Sings Songbook,* edited by Daniel Freelander et al.

7 In Exodus 19:6, Israel is called a holy people — *goy kadosh*. At the end of the desert wanderings, Israel is called *am kadosh,* which also means "holy people" (Deuteronomy 28:9). But there is a difference. In *The Torah: A Modern Commentary,* W. Gunther Plaut states, "In forty years they had progressed from *goy,* a nation like other nations, to *am,* a people with a spiritual purpose" (p. 1530). Based on your studies, what is the "spiritual purpose" of the Jews? Has this purpose been a burden or a privilege?

8 Deuteronomy 27:15-26 enumerates the curses spoken to the Israelites on Mount Ebal. No reciprocal blessings are found in the portion. Compose those blessings. Try your hand at calligraphy using chisel point markers, or decorate scrolls and copy your blessings.

9 In Deuteronomy 27:15-26, the Israelites say אָמֵן (Amen) after every curse is pronounced. The word means "So be it," but it is related to the Hebrew word for faith — אֱמוּנָה (emunah). The use of the word "Amen" is governed by a simple set of *halachic* rules, and its meaning has been interpreted in a number of *midrashim*. Do some research to learn more about this interesting word. Then choose one fact you have learned and write it out in a secret code. Exchange codes with a friend and decipher!
References: *To Pray as a Jew* by Hayim Donin, pp. 227-228; *Encyclopaedia Judaica*, "Amen," Vol. 2, pp. 803-804.

10 The first fruits which Deuteronomy 26:1-11 commands the Israelites to bring were called *bikkurim* (see Exodus 23:19 and Numbers 18:13). Mishnah, *Bikkurim* 3, describes how they were brought to the Temple in Jerusalem with great pomp and ceremony. Read this Mishnah, as well as the references below. Then, stage a model *bikkurim* pageant. Have each individual or family bring to the synagogue a gift of fine fruit and produce in a beautifully decorated basket. Read the appropriate passages from the Torah and find or write other readings. Arrange a formal procession for laying the *bikkurim* on the *bimah*. After the pageant, donate the *bikkurim* to a local food distribution center or a hospital.
References: *Seasons of Our Joy* by Arthur Waskow, pp. 185-205; *Encyclopaedia Judaica*, "Shavuot," Vol. 14, pp. 1319-1322.

PERSONALIZING THE TEXT

11 Choose a law from Deuteronomy. Write a 60 second television commercial in which you introduce and teach a Jewish law. Create a set and costumes to add to the effect. If possible, videotape your commercial.

12 The description of the recitation of the blessings and curses evokes a powerfully emotional scene. Stage this event. Even though you won't have the crowds of people, try to achieve the drama of this situation.

13 The Torah makes it clear that we have an obligation to support the poor. How does your synagogue meet this obligation? Ask the Rabbi, synagogue president, or social action chairperson to speak on this issue. What can you do as individuals to help your synagogue fulfill this *mitzvah*?

14 By separating out the tithe, the Israelites were able to support the orphaned, the widowed, the Levite, and the stranger. The revenues aided the needy. Your parents pay taxes. Why? Where does the money go? What body established the budget? How are taxes assessed? Who decides the amount each individual must pay, and what criteria are used? Invite a city or state official or an accountant to speak to these issues. Are taxes today essentially the same thing as the tithe was in biblical times? Are synagogue dues today like a biblical tithe?

15 What if there was no system of collecting taxes? What might the effects be on our lives? What if there had been no system of tithing in biblical times? How might that have affected Jewish values and ethics?

16 Make papier mâché stones and paint them white. From *Ki Taytzay* and *Ki Tavo*, choose one or two laws which you feel reflect those values you most cherish. Paint them onto your "rock." Then design a felt banner illustrating what you have written. Create a display with explanation. (See Strategy #17, page 8, for a description of how to make papier mâché.)

17 Write your own capsule history of the Jewish people. Include especially those events which you feel have shaped contemporary Jewish life. Compare this with the biblical capsule history in Deuteronomy 26:3-10.

18 In *Ki Tavo*, the Israelites are told that if they follow the teachings of the Torah, God will make them "the head not the tail . . . the top [not] the bottom" (Deuteronomy 28:13,44). Express this idea using metaphors of your own. Choose one of your metaphors and use it as the basis for an illustration for a Jewish greeting card. For what holidays and occasions would such a card be appropriate?

19 The first group of curses in *Ki Tavo* (Deuteronomy 27:16-26) has been understood to be concerned with private sins which could be committed without anyone's knowledge. Examine the text and discuss this interpretation. The Rabbis taught that even private sins are important. What one does in his/her own life can have an effect on others. They told the following story to illustrate: A person seated in a small boat began to drill a hole in the boat under his seat. When the other passengers complained of the danger of his act, he declared, "Why should it bother you? The hole is under my seat." (*Da'at Z'kenim*, Deuteronomy 27:15).

a. Dramatize this story adding an answer to the final question and an ending.

b. Make up a skit of your own showing how our private acts can affect the lives of others.

c. Design a poster showing the earth as a lifeboat for which we are all responsible.

20 Deuteronomy 26:5-6 has entered the Passover *Haggadah* at the beginning of the section which recounts the story of the Exodus. These words are also to be spoken when *bikkurim* (first fruits) are brought (Deuteronomy 26:5-11). What is the significance of the use of this passage at a time of thanksgiving? W. Gunther Plaut notes that when we come to the sanctuary, we must identify ourselves historically (*The Torah: A Modern Commentary*, p. 1512). How do you identify yourself historically? When you refer to your ancestors, do you speak of a noble past or of a poor beginning?

21 W. Gunther Plaut comments in relation to the preponderance of curses over blessings that "in general, it is more usual to create codes of forbidden behavior than of desirable behavior" (*The Torah: A Modern Commentary*, p. 1520). Do you agree with him? Give examples that either prove or disprove the point. In small groups, try your hand at creating a code of "desirable behavior." Share your efforts with the larger group. Discuss the challenges your group faced in creating this code.

22 In Deuteronomy 28:47, the Torah adds an interesting requirement to our pursuit of righteous action. We are told that it is important to serve God "in joy and gladness." Do you think it is possible to demand that a certain set of feelings accompany worship or the performance of commandments? Can you defend the idea that it doesn't matter in which spirit Jews worship and celebrate? Organize a debate on this subject: Resolved: It is important to live Jewish life in a spirit of joy and gladness.

OTHER RESOURCES

23 Read, act out, and discuss the skit for the portion *Ki Tavo* in *Sedra Scenes: Skits for Every Torah Portion* by Stan J. Beiner, pp. 219-222.

24 Read and discuss the modern *midrash* "God's Mailbox" by Marc Gellman in *Learn Torah With . . . (1994-1995 Torah Annual),* edited by Stuart Kelman and Joel Lurie Grishaver, pp. 377-381.

25 For creative movement activities, see "Land of Milk and Honey" and "A Holy People" from *Torah in Motion* by JoAnne Tucker and Susan Freeman, pp. 218-221.

26 Read and discuss the illustrated commentary for *Ki Tavo* in *American Torah Toons* by Lawrence Bush.

Note: The bestowing of blessings and curses is a major theme in Leviticus, *Bechukotai.* See that portion for several additional Insights and Strategies, pages 220-225.

INVOLVING THE FAMILY

27 The verse "Blessed be you in the city" (Deuteronomy 28:3) led the Rabbis of the Talmud to teach that one should be a member of a community and live near a synagogue (*Baba Metzia* 107a). Why do you think the Rabbis considered this so important? With your family, obtain copies of your local Jewish newspaper and/or local synagogue bulletins. Read them to learn about all the resources and activities available to you in your Jewish community. Find an activity you can do as a family, perhaps attending a concert, reading a reviewed book, or cooking a given recipe, and do it! How about trying this on a monthly basis?

BAR/BAT MITZVAH PROJECT

28 *Ki Tavo* reminds us again of our obligation to care for "the stranger, the fatherless, and the widow" (Deuteronomy 26:12). Find out how the needs of orphaned and abused children are being met in Israel today. Neve Michael is a village for children who have been removed from their homes due to parental neglect or abuse. Close to two hundred children live in family units in the village, where they also attend school and receive many support services. To learn more about this important facility and how you can help, write to Neve Michael Children's Home, Attention Ms. Hava Levine, Pardes Hanna 37000, Israel.

NITZAVIM 29:9-30:20   נצבים
SYNOPSIS

MOSES CONTINUES HIS FAREWELL TO THE people. He tells them that this day they stand before God concluding their covenant. Moses informs the people that the covenant is not only made with them, but also with those not present. All Israel past, present, and future is bound to the covenant for all time.

Moses foretells of a future rebellion against God's covenant and describes the evils that will then befall the Israelites. After a time, the people will repent and God will restore them back to the Land in blessing.

The portion closes with Moses telling the people that they have a choice between life and prosperity or death and adversity. In choosing to obey God's commandments, the people choose life and will be able to enjoy the land that God promised to Abraham, Isaac, and Jacob.

INSIGHTS FROM THE TRADITION

A *Nitzavim*, which means "you are standing," opens with Moses telling the people that God is today concluding the covenant with them. The covenant is made not just with those then present, but with all of Israel — past, present, and future. On this concept the following *midrash* is based:

When Israel stood to receive the Torah, the Holy One of Blessing said to them: "I am giving you my Torah. Bring me good guarantors that you will guard it." First, the people said, "Our Patriarchs — Abraham, Isaac, and Jacob — are our guarantors." This was not acceptable. Next, they said: "Our prophets are our guarantors." These, too, were unacceptable. But when the people pledged, "Our children are our guarantors," the Holy One of Blessing accepted them immediately. "For their sake I give the Torah to you" (*Song of Songs Rabbah* 1:24).

How have you been a good guarantor? What do you expect of your descendants? How should a good guarantor behave in terms of Jewish life and traditions? How can you help others to be worthy guarantors?

B Deuteronomy 30:11-14 tells us that the law which all are to know and observe is not beyond reach. Everyone is capable of studying and understanding it. A Mishnah states that the study of Torah outweighs all the other commandments because study leads to observance (*Peah* 1:1). To aid all the people in learning the Law, the Levites were assigned to be the teachers of Torah throughout the Land. This tradition of learning has been passed down from biblical times to our day.

How do you learn about Jewish tradition? Does Religious School provide you with all the skills and knowledge you need to live as a Jew? How will you continue to learn about Judaism after you finish your Religious School education?

C It is interesting to note that the Hebrew root שוב (*shin, vav, bet*), meaning "turn," or "return," occurs seven times in the first ten verses of chapter 30. Elul is considered a time of preparation for the High Holy Days; a time of תשובה (*teshuvah*) — repentance. This portion (Deuteronomy 29:9-14; 30:11-20) has been adopted as the Torah reading for Yom Kippur morning by most congregations of the Reform Movement. The traditional Torah reading is Leviticus 16.

How do you prepare for the High Holy Days? What do the High Holy Days mean to you?

D God loves us! Deuteronomy 30:2-3 reads, "and [if] you return to *Adonai* your God, and you and your children heed God's command with all your heart and soul, just as I enjoin upon you this day, then will God restore your fortunes and take you back in love" (*The Five Books of Miriam* by Ellen Frankel, p. 293).

Have you ever thought about this as a Jewish idea? Where can we find additional evidence of God's love for the Jewish people?

What do we have to do to merit God's love?

E Deuteronomy 30:11 reads: "Surely, this instruction which I enjoin upon you this day is not too baffling for you, nor is it beyond reach." The people are told that they can attain and know the law. The *midrash* weaves a story around this verse. A fool went to the synagogue and asked how one might begin to learn the law. The Rabbis answered that study begins with . . . the Book of Law, then the Prophets, followed by the Writings. After the Scriptures, one learns Talmud, then *halachah,* ending with *aggadot.* The fool thinks, how can I do all this, and turns to leave. But one who is wise learns one chapter every day until he completes the task (*Deuteronomy Rabbah* 8:3).

How does the saying that the hardest part of a long journey is the first step apply to this *midrash?* to human nature?

Do you play a musical instrument or have another skill you worked hard to develop? How did you feel the first time you sat down to learn Hebrew? What gave you the determination to practice? Was it difficult to accomplish this task or was it fairly easy?

Note: *Nitzavim* is often read as a double portion with *Vayaylech.* For more about double portions see Exodus, *Pekuday,* Insight A, page 155.

STRATEGIES

ANALYZING THE TEXT

1 In Hebrew, read verses 1-10 in Deuteronomy 30. Find the seven words which have the root *shin, vav, bet.* Now look these words up in a dictionary. What do they mean? What is their intent?

Can you think of any reason why this word root was used so many times in so few verses?

2 There are several interesting things to notice about Deuteronomy 29:28:

a. According to J.H. Hertz, the text can be read and understood in two ways: first, according to a straight reading, and secondly, as it is read according to the musical markings [known as] trope (*The Pentateuch and Haftorahs,* p. 880). In the second case, the text reads "Concealed acts concern the Lord our God and overt acts; it is for us and our children ever to apply all the provisions of this teaching." Compare the two ways of reading the text. Which do you like better? Why?

b. Dots are placed above each letter in the words לָנוּ וּלְבָנֵינוּ עַד (*lanu u'levanaynu ahd* — . . . for us and our children ever . . .). Hertz explains that this is to draw our attention to these words (p. 880). What is so significant about these words?

3 *Nitzavim* is a very dramatic and moving review of the Israelite past and future. Practice reading the text (in Hebrew or English) until you can read it fluently. Then stage the reading of parts of this portion as a dramatic monologue complete with costumes, lighting, and sound effects.

EXTENDING THE TEXT

4 Listen to the song "Tradition" from the musical *Fiddler on the Roof.* What traditions rooted in the Bible were observed by Tevye and his generation and are still observed by Jewish people today? Discuss the ways traditions maintain a people.

5 Invite a Rabbi to explain to your group why this portion was selected by the Reform Movement as the reading for the Yom Kippur morning service.

6 In *Nitzavim,* Moses states "It [Torah] is not in the heavens" (Deuteronomy 30:12). The Rabbis of the Mishnah used this statement as support for explaining and expounding on Jewish law. For a fascinating account of their justification for doing so, see *Meet Our Sages* by Jacob Neusner, pp. 77-88.

7 How can an obligation undertaken by our ancient ancestors be binding on us today? Abravanel answered this question with the analogy of a loan, payment of which is incumbent upon the descendants of the borrower should he or she die before paying. In comparison, what is the loan in this portion? What is our debt, our obligation to God in regard to this loan? Do you think this is a good analogy? Why or why not? Create other analogies which might also "answer" the question of this enduring obligation.

8 Make a visual *midrash* in which God's love for humanity is expressed. Obtain a posterboard and white craft glue or glue stick. Look through magazines, newspapers, and other print media and collect pictures and words which fit the theme of God's love for humanity. Assemble your visual *midrash* and display.

PERSONALIZING THE TEXT

9 In order to maintain the covenant, Jews were given many laws and traditions to follow. These can be thought of as possessions. Listed below are 14 such possessions. In small groups or individually, rank order these in terms of their importance to you. Next rank order them in terms of their importance to Jewish survival. Share and discuss both rank orders with the whole group.
Israel
Torah
Tzedakah
Prayer

God
Jewish Education
Family
Shabbat
Holidays
Hebrew
Bar/Bat Mitzvah
Brit/Naming
Rabbinic Literature (Talmud, *Midrash, Shulchan Aruch*)

10 According to *Nitzavim,* God made the covenant with all Jews — past, present, and future. Try to imagine the thoughts, feelings, and emotions you might have had if you had heard this speech by Moses. Create a mood poster which reflects how you might have felt had you been present at significant points in Jewish history. Events to consider: the Covenants with the Patriarchs, the Exodus, Crossing the Reed Sea, Manna in the Desert, the Golden Calf, the Years of Wandering, etc.

Directions for the Mood Poster:
Decorate the posterboard with designs, sketches, and pictures which bring to mind the biblical events you wish to include. Then on the mood strips write verses, sayings, words, or ideas which would reflect how you "felt" about a particular event. Attach velcro to the posterboard and to the mood strips. As each event is discussed, place the appropriate mood strip on the posterboard. Remember to attach the spiny part of the velcro to the posterboard and the fuzzy side to the mood strips.

11 Read aloud the *midrash* on guarantors in Insight A, page 335. You are considered a guarantor. What obligation does this place on you? Express your thoughts and feelings in a haiku, a Japanese form of poetry containing a total of 17 syllables. You can also find this *midrash* in *Lessons From Our Living Past,* edited by Jules Harlow, pp. 11-15.

12 In this portion, the choices facing the Israelites are clearly stated. They may choose to follow God's law and experience many good things, or they may choose disobedience and suffer severe consequences. Do you think they were *really* given a choice? Relate this to contemporary life. What sorts of choices do you face? What are the possible consequences? How do the consequences influence your behavior? Have a family or group discussion.

13 In *Nitzavim*, the opposites "moist and dry" are used (Deuteronomy 29:18). According to Plaut, the use of opposites is a signal that "everything" is meant (*The Torah: A Modern Commentary*, p. 1539). Thus, "moist and dry" might refer to Jews with opposite characteristics. Think of other adjectives and their opposites (e.g., smooth and rough, sweet and sour). What kind of Jew would each describe? What pair of adjectives best describes the kind of Jew you are?

14 As we learned from Strategy #13 immediately above, when opposite words are used, it is a device for expressing the concept of "everything." The Hebrew song *"David Melech Yisrael"* concludes with one group singing a Hebrew word and a second group responding with its opposite. Learn this song and a variety of Hebrew opposites to sing with it.
Reference: *Songs of the Chassidim,* edited by Velvel Pasternak.

15 Insight B, page 335, reminds us that the Levites were assigned to be the teachers of Torah throughout the Land. Who are today's Levites? Who teaches Torah? Interview your synagogue school teachers to find out how and why they started teaching, what motivates them to continue, and what they still want to learn about Judaism. You may want to collect all the answers and make a bulletin board display. Include pictures and material from the interviews. Think about

including a section titled "A Look To the Future" which lists the reasons some of the students give for their plans to teach in Religious and Hebrew Schools.

16 Stage a conversation between you and a distant ancestor who was actually present when the events in *Nitzavim* took place. Begin by challenging his/her right to accept an obligation which would be binding on all future generations (Deuteronomy 29:13-14). On what basis can your ancestor justify his/her actions?

17 Design a formal, illuminated contract which lists and illustrates our obligations as Jews according to this portion. Include the reciprocal promises made by God.

18 This portion emphasizes the theme of repentance and is connected to the High Holy Day period. Try your hand at writing a High Holy Day sermon. Many congregations have youth services on the High Holy Days. Use the sermon you have written at one of these services. The sermon does not need to more than 5 to 7 minutes long.

19 *Nitzavim* is read near the High Holy Day period. Cut out a large paper *shofar*. On it, color the names of all those things which help make you a better person. Your creation will serve as a *shofar* — a reminder. (From *There is a Season: A Values Clarification Approach to Jewish Holidays,* edited by Audrey Marcus, et al.)

20 As stated in Strategy #19 immediately above, this portion is read near the High Holy Days, or depending on the calendar, it may be read on the Shabbat in between Rosh HaShanah and Yom Kippur. Considering the contents of this portion, how might hearing *Netzavim* affect your personal preparations for this time of repentance?

OTHER RESOURCES

21 Read, act out, and discuss the skit for the portion *Nitzavim* in *Sedra Scenes: Skits for Every Torah Portion* by Stan J. Beiner, pp. 223-225.

22 For a creative movement activity, see "Return to God" from *Torah in Motion* by JoAnne Tucker and Susan Freeman, pp. 222-223.

23 Read and discuss the illustrated commentary for *Nitzavim* in *American Torah Toons* by Lawrence Bush.

Note: For additional activities relating to this portion, see the following portion, *Vayaylech*.

INVOLVING THE FAMILY

24 Read the *midrash* about guarantors found in Insight A, page 335. Have a family discussion on those things parents do which ensure that their children will be good guarantors. What specifically does your family do? What do you do which makes you a worthy guarantor? What additional observances or activites would you and/or your family like to incorporate into family life to help strenghten your role as a guarantor? How do you as a Jewish family reaffirm the covenant?

BAR/BAT MITZVAH PROJECT

25 In this portion, we were reminded that the Levites were given the task to be teachers of Torah to the people. We also know that the people were responsible for the financial sustenance of the Levites serving in the Temple in Jerusalem. Combine those two commandments in supporting Jewish education in Russia. There is a special program sponsored jointly by the Soviet Jewry Task Forces of the Union of American Hebrew Congregations and the World Union for Progressive Judaism which matches a Bar or Bat Mitzvah student with a Russian Jewish student. For a donation of $100 or so, you will be helping to equip Russian Jewish Religious Schools with basic classroom supplies. These basics include pens, markers, tape, paints, scissors, notebooks, and posters. Additionally, funds will be used to purchase tape recorders, songbooks, and musical instruments. In return, you will receive the name and address of a Russian Jewish child with whom you can correspond, a certificate of your participation, and a personal thank you letter for your contribution from the World Union's Director in Moscow.

Task #1: Contact the sponsoring organization: Bar/Bat Mitzvah Matching Program, World Union for Progressive Judaism, 838 Fifth Avenue, New York, NY 10021.

Task #2: Raise the $100. Easy ways to do this are spend your gift money on this, or ask your parents to do it for you, or better yet raise the money yourself. Ideas: bake sales, car washes, babysitting, hiring out to do chores for others, getting sponsors for a read-a-thon, a walk, bowl, or run-a-thon, or any other "a-thon" you can think of. Good Luck!

Task #3: Correspond with your Russian partner.

VAYAYLECH 31:1-30 וילך

SYNOPSIS

MOSES EXPLAINS TO THE PEOPLE THAT HE is old and is no longer able to be an active leader. He appoints Joshua to be the next leader of Israel.

Moses completes the writing of the Teaching. He gives it to the Levites, who carried the Ark, and to all the elders of Israel. He charges them to read this Teaching every seventh year at the Feast of Booths.

God tells Moses and Joshua that the people will rebel shortly after Moses' death. God instructs Moses to write down a poem that will serve as a witness, warning the people.

The portion closes as Moses prepares to recite the poem to the whole congregation of Israel.

INSIGHTS FROM THE TRADITION

A *Vayaylech* means "and he went." Moses went before the people and spoke of his impending death. He was preparing the people for that moment when he would no longer be their leader. Nachmanides comments on the verse, "The Lord your God . . . will cross over at your head . . . " (31:3). He says that the end of Moses' leadership should not upset the people, for God will be with them and Joshua will assume leadership (*Ramban: Commentary on the Torah* [Deuteronomy] by Charles B. Chavel, pp. 344-345).

B The continuity of Judaism is not dependent upon any one individual. Moses established a chain of tradition, as it says in *Pirke Avot* 1:1: "Moses received Torah from Sinai and delivered it to Joshua, and Joshua to the Elders, and the Elders to the Prophets, and the Prophets delivered it to the Men of the Great Assembly."

Upon what *does* the continuity of Judaism depend?

What is your responsibility in this chain of tradition?

Why should Moses' message to the people not upset them? Why might it even be comforting?

C According to the text, Moses spoke to the people saying, "I am now one hundred and twenty years old . . . " (31:2). The number 120 has become associated with longevity in Jewish tradition. Although it is not possible to prove this age of Moses, the essential idea was that he had lived to a good age (Sforno). The traditional Jewish birthday wish did evolve from this verse: "May you live to 120 years!"

Why do you think Moses' age of 120 years was chosen as ideal rather than the age of one of the Patriarchs? (See Strategy #4, page 342.)

D It is interesting to see the difference in the way Christian tradition and Jewish tradition diverged in discussing Moses' reaction to his impending death. In *The Interpreter's Bible*, a Christian commentary, we read, "Knowing that his usefulness was at an end, and that God willed him not to cross the Jordan, Moses suppressed his personal longings and accepted the inevitable with complete confidence in God" (pp. 511-512). No argument, no debate, just simple acceptance.

Jewish tradition, on the other hand, shows us a Moses who is upset and who questions God's judgment. Two examples from *Devarim Rabbah* illustrate this. Moses said to God (9:4): "Master of the Universe, must I die after having seen all Your glory and power?" God replied: "What man can live and not die?" (Psalms 89:49). But Moses did not want to die. When Joshua was invested, Moses went with him into the Tabernacle. The cloud separated them. God spoke only to Joshua. Afterward, Moses asked, "What did [God] say to you?" Joshua replied: "When God spoke with you, did you tell me what was spoken?" Immediately, Moses turned to God and said that he was ready to die. "Better to die a hundred times than to experience even one moment of envy" (9:9).

Do these *midrashim* help you understand Moses? How so?
Of what was Moses envious? Loss of power? Loss of personal relationship with God? Loss of status? Explain.
Do you ever feel envious? How do you deal with this feeling? In what way is your method of coping similar to or different from that of Moses?

E God is preparing Moses to deliver one last tongue-lashing to the people. God tells Moses that there will be a future rebellion (31:16). Rashi points out that while there will be a rebellion, still the Torah will never be completely forgotten by the descendants of this generation. Rashi bases his comment on Deuteronomy 31:21, ". . . it will never be lost from the mouth of their offspring." In fact, there was no corruption of Jewish practice in that generation which entered the Land.

Judges 2:7 reads: "And the people served God all the days of Joshua." Moses was referring to a future rebellion after the days of Joshua.

Why would Moses warn that generation, when the rebellion would not stem from them? What would the responsibility of that generation be regarding future generations?
Do you have any personal responsibilities toward future generations? What about Jewish responsibilities?

F In verse 31:18 God warns the people that if they go astray, "I will keep My countenance hidden on that day . . . " The concept of the Divine Presence hiding from us is called *"hester panim"* (the hidden face). Commentators noted the similarity between this term and the name of the heroine of the Purim story — Esther. They explained the connection as follows: Esther hid her Jewishness from the king while she was in the

palace, but her presence there saved the Jewish people from destruction. By the same token, perhaps even when God hides the Divine Presence from us, it is still available to save and help us.

Another interpretation of *"hester panim"* derives from these specific verses in Deuteronomy: When people say "our God is not in our midst" and do not seek God (Deuteronomy 31:17), the result is that God is hidden even more.

This teaching seems to imply that people have some influence over the Divine Presence. How might our awareness of God heighten our sense of God's nearness? How might the reverse be true?

G This portion ends abruptly at 31:30 with the phrase: "Then Moses recited the words of this poem to the very end, in the hearing of the whole congregation of Israel." The poem, however, begins in the next portion.

Why do you think the portion was divided this way? Have you ever watched a TV series that had continuing stories from one episode to the next? How did the segments end? Did you want to watch the following week? Why? Might the division of the portion be analogous to a TV series? Would you have divided the portion this way? Why or why not?

Note: *Vayaylech* is usually read as a double portion with *Nitzavim*. For more about double portions, see Exodus, *Pekuday,* Insight A, page 155.

STRATEGIES

ANALYZING THE TEXT

1 Read Deuteronomy 31:1-8. Pretend this is a newspaper story and compose an appropriate headline. Be brief, concise, and accurate. Remember, you want to grab the reader's attention.

2 This Torah portion contains the last two commandments found in the Torah. Before reading the portion, decide what you think the final commandments in the Torah should appropriately be. Then read through the text carefully. Can you identify the last two *mitzvot*?

They are: to gather the people together for a special reading of the Torah (Deuteronomy 31:10-13), and the *mitzvah* of writing a Torah (Deuteronomy 31:19). The command to write a Torah is written in the plural, as if it were addressed to all the people. In what way is the placement of these commandments toward the end of the Torah significant? Using a long sheet of paper which you have rolled inward from each side so that it looks like a partially open Torah scroll, create a Torah mural depicting these commandments.

EXTENDING THE TEXT

3 *"Hakhayl,"* the name given to the special ceremony of gathering the people to hear the Torah read (Deuteronomy 31:10-13), was to take place on Sukkot. From this verb, *hakhayl* (gather), comes the word used today for congregation, *"kahal"* or *"kehillah."* What is the full Hebrew name of your congregation? (Many congregations precede their name with the term *"Kehillah Kedoshah"* (Holy Congregation), often abbreviated as "K.K.") Is the idea of gathering, or the idea of assembling to hear Torah, reflected in the name? Design a logo for your congregation which both lists its name and depicts its meaning.

4 In *Vayaylech,* God commands Moses to write a poem to be read to the people (31:17). Review the text to determine the purpose of the poem. Then write an outline of the poem that you would deliver if you were Moses. What would you say in his place? You may want to compare your outline to the actual poem which is found in the next portion.

5 In *Vayaylech,* Moses predicts that after his death the Israelites will become even more defiant of God. He begins his prediction with the words, "Well I know . . . " (Deuteronomy 31:27). Imagine you are a young Israelite who heard these words and decided to challenge them. Write or stage a conversation between yourself and Moses in which he explains how he knows that the people will continue being defiant.

6 Below is a list of the lifespans of several significant biblical personalities. Do you think that the length of these people's lives indicates something about their relative importance in Jewish history? How do you explain the fact that Isaac was the longest lived? What can you learn from the fact that Joseph and Joshua each lived 110 years? How would you rank these personalities in terms of their importance to Jewish history?
Isaac – 180 years
Abraham – 175 years
Jacob – 147 years
Moses – 120 years
Joseph – 110 years
Joshua – 110 years

7 Deuteronomy 31:19 reads: ". . . write down this poem." It was written in the plural, and from that the Talmud derived the lesson that every Jew is obligated to write a *Sefer Torah* or have one written for him/her in his/her lifetime (*Sanhedrin* 21b). Obviously, this would be financially impossible. Jewish tradition has modified this obligation, allowing individuals to fulfill the spirit of the obligation. Many individuals can group together to pay a *sofer* to write a Torah. There are many instances in which a congregation has collected funds from members to have a Torah written for congregational use. Do one or more of the following:
a. Visit with a *sofer* (scribe) to learn how a Torah scroll is written.
b. View and discuss the film *For Out of Zion,* which is about the role of Torah in Jewish life and how it is written and put together.

8 In *Vayaylech,* Moses instructs the people to read the entire Teaching once every seven years when the people gather to observe Sukkot. Do some research and find out how the present pattern of reading the entire Torah once a year came about.
References: *Bechol Levavcha* by Harvey Fields, pp. 106-108; *Jewish Worship* by Jacob Millgram, pp. 111-114,182-183; *Encyclopaedia Judaica,* "Torah, Reading of," Vol. 15, pp. 1246-1255.

9 In *Vayaylech,* Moses calls upon Joshua to "Be strong and resolute" (31:7). If you were Moses, what would you advise Joshua to be? Write a four word statement in the form above (Be _____ and _____) and follow it up with a letter of advice to Joshua explaining why you chose those particular words.

PERSONALIZING THE TEXT

10 Read the two *midrashim* about Moses found in Insight C, page 340. As if you were Moses, write a diary entry in which you discuss the events described there. Share diary entries, by reading each one aloud.

11 Help Moses warn the people. Print up a telegram form. The first line of your message begins "I urge _____." Suggest how the Israelites should behave in order to keep possession of the Land.

12 Imagine you are Caleb, one of the two survivors from the generation which rebelled and was forced to wander in the desert. Joshua, the other survivor, has been appointed the new leader of the Israelites. You were passed over. React! Complete the following sentences:
I wish Moses had _____.
Joshua is _____.
I feel like _____.

The Israelites should _____.
I now must _____.

13 In *Vayaylech,* Moses publicly proclaims Joshua his successor. Why is it important for leadership to change hands publicly? Examine how political leaders in this country today assume office. Who is present at their "swearing-in"? What symbolic acts take place?

14 Jewish tradition considers 120 years to be an ideal life span. Can you explain why? What do you consider the ideal life span? Write a short poem describing yourself as you expect to be at any ages you think are significant.

15 Depending on the Jewish calendar, the portion *Vayaylech* is read either on Shabbat *Shuva,* the Shabbat between Rosh HaShanah and Yom Kippur, or else on the Shabbat before Rosh HaShanah. As you review the text, consider: Is there anything in it that has special meaning for me at this time of year? How are the words of the portion like the call of the *shofar,* admonishing us to "wake up" and take heed of the themes of the season? Prepare for the High Holy Days by learning to sound a *shofar.*

16 Sukkot, the Feast of Booths, is mentioned in this portion. *Vayaylech* is often read as a double portion with *Nitzavim* on the Shabbat before the High Holy Days or on the Shabbat between Rosh HaShanah and Yom Kippur. Tradition makes a connection between Yom Kippur and Sukkot. It is customary to begin building one's *sukkah* just before breaking the fast of Yom Kippur. As a group, plan and prepare the decorations for this year's *sukkah.*

17 During the High Holy Days, we are encouraged to review the year just completed and to resolve to make changes for the good. Make three columns. Label them "Errors," "Like to Change," and "Steps to Remove Obstacles." In the "Errors" column, list ten things you have done during the past year which you feel were not right. Now put three items into the "Like to Change" column. Then, in the "Steps to Remove Obstacles" column, list two specific steps you could take to change your behavior.

18 It has become customary to send cards at the High Holy Days to wish family and friends a happy and sweet New Year. Read about the origins of New Year cards and then design and produce your own version.
Reference: *Rosh Hashanah Anthology* by Phillip Goodman.

19 The Hasidim have a saying that God dwells wherever people let God in. When do you let God into your life? When do you shut God out? Share with your classmates.

OTHER RESOURCES

20 Read, act out, and discuss the skit for the portion *Vayaylech* in *Sedra Scenes: Skits for Every Torah Portion* by Stan J. Beiner, pp. 226-228.

21 For a creative movement activity, see "God's Hidden Countenance" from *Torah in Motion* by JoAnne Tucker and Susan Freeman, pp. 224-225.

22 Read and discuss the illustrated commentary for *Va-Yelech* in *American Torah Toons* by Lawrence Bush.

INVOLVING THE FAMILY

23 What will you be like when you reach your end of days? Write a prediction of what you will have accomplished. Share this in a discussion with your family. Ask your parents what they thought they wanted to accomplish when they were your age. Do they think that their achievements have matched those early desires? What are their goals now and why?

BAR/BAT MITZVAH PROJECT

24 The final commandment in the Torah is considered to be Deuteronomy 31:19: "Write down this poem and teach it to the people of Israel." "Poem" here is understood to be the Torah. And since the command is given in the plural form (*keytvoo*), the Rabbis understood it to be a *mitzvah* for all people to participate in the writing of a Torah scroll. How might you, as a Bar or Bat Mitzvah, participate symbolically in this commandment? Brainstorm some ideas with your family and Rabbi. Perhaps you might make a contribution of Jewish books to the synagogue library, or assume the role of a teacher of Torah in some way. Or, arrange for a *sofer* to come and check the synagogue Torah scrolls. The *sofer* will determine if any repairs need to be made and will then be able to make these repairs. It will be your task to figure out how the *sofer* will be paid. Think about doing a fund-raiser.

HA'AZINU 32:1-52   האזינו

SYNOPSIS

THE POEM INTRODUCED IN THE LAST LINE of the previous portion is recited by Moses at the start of *Ha'azinu.* Moses calls upon heaven and earth to witness his words.

Moses begins by praising God and describing the special care God has given Israel. In response, the people have spurned God and God's laws. Because of Israel's unfaithfulness, they will suffer God's wrath. Ultimately, God will show mercy to the Israelites and deliver them from their enemies.

Moses tells the people to take the warning he has recited very seriously. Israel's observance of God's laws is no trifling matter. These laws are the essence of their lives.

The portion closes with God directing Moses to ascend Mount Nebo and to look at the Land promised to the Israelites. Moses is told that he will die on the mountain.

INSIGHTS FROM THE TRADITION

A *Ha'azinu,* the opening word of this portion, means "give ear." Moses calls upon heaven and earth to give ear to these words. In Hebrew, the word for song and poem is שיר (*shir*). Thus, in discussion, the words "song" and "poem" are used interchangeably.

Why did Moses call upon heaven and earth? *Devarim Rabbah* 10:4 gives us several possibilities. One of them implies that it was actually Israel who was called to witness, since God had compared Israel to the stars of heaven (Genesis 15:5) and to the dust of the earth (Genesis 28:14). Nachmanides cites Ibn Ezra's explanation that according to the plain meaning of the text, the Bible calls on those things which exist and endure, that is heaven and earth, to witness this song of Moses (*Ramban: Commentary on the Torah* (Deuteronomy) by Charles B. Chavel, p. 352).

Read the last line of the previous portion, Deuteronomy, 31:30. Who is to hear the poem? Who are the witnesses? Why couldn't the Israelites serve as the witnesses?

B This is the second time that Moses has utilized a poetic structure to communicate with the Israelites. The first time was after Israel's rescue at the Reed Sea (Exodus 15) at the *start* of the years of wandering in the desert. Here, Moses uses poetry again in speaking to the Israelites at the *conclusion* of their wandering. The first poem praised and thanked God for delivering the people from Pharaoh's hand. As Plaut states, "At the sea, the physical existence of the nation was assured, but the forty years that followed put its spiritual future in doubt" (*The Torah: A Modern Commentary,* p. 1555). The content of the second poem forewarned the people of their impending rebellion. It spelled out the retribution God would exact and the fact that the people would be ultimately redeemed.

Was using poetry an effective way to reach people in biblical times? What if it were sung? Would this work today? How do we usually or most effectively capture the attention of others? Explain why such methods work.
Is physical survival truly possible without spiritual survival?

C Deuteronomy 32:7 reads in part, ". . . Ask your father, he will inform you, your elders, they will tell you." This became the proof text or basis for the command to kindle the Chanukah lights. Your father and teachers will tell you of God's miracles and thus obligate you to carry out the lighting of the Chanukah candles (*Shabbat* 23a).

What other Jewish obligations have been given to us? Which observances do you personally carry out?
What observances do you hope future generations will maintain?

D This portion has another connection to the holiday of Chanukah. Six times in this portion God is called *HaTzur* — The Rock. In 32:15, the phrase *Tzur Yeshuati* or "Rock of my support," is used. This expression was incorporated into the Chanukah hymn *"Ma'oz Tzur Yeshuati,"* known in English as "Rock of Ages." This popular hymn, sung by Ashkenazic Jews, was thought to have been composed in the thirteenth century by someone named Mordecai. His name is spelled out in a Hebrew acrostic in the first five stanzas. *"Ma'oz Tzur"* praises God for Israel's redemption from both Egyptian slavery and Babylonian exile, for the deliverance of the Persian Jews from wicked Haman, and for the victory of the Maccabees over Antiochus Epiphanes. A sixth stanza, which called for retribution against those nations which had persecuted the Jews, was often omitted "for the sake of peace." The hymn also includes a hope of redemption for all Jews.

What symbolism do you see in calling God *HaTzur* — The Rock?
Can you suggest other such names for God which might help explain or describe divine attributes?

E Near the outset of this poem, Moses declares that all the ways of God are just and righteous (Deuteronomy 32:4). Solomon Colodner tells us that this means that all things which stem from God, including suffering and death, must be accepted as demonstrations of God's righteousness (*Concepts and Values*, p. 133). The traditional Jewish burial service includes a prayer called *Tzidduk HaDin* — justification of the divine decree. Maurice Lamm calls this "a magnificent and moving prayer recited immediately before or after the body is buried when the reality of the grave confronts the mourners" (*The Jewish Way in Death and Mourning*, p. 62). This prayer has a three-fold purpose: (1) it tells us that we cannot know God's ways, but God's ways are justified; (2) it tells us that God's decrees must be accepted; and (3) the prayer asks God's mercy on the survivors.

Read this prayer from the traditional Jewish burial service. How might you see this prayer serve to give strength or comfort to the mourner?

F In the midst of castigating Israel and describing the misfortunes the people will endure, God suddenly begins to revile the enemies of Israel (32:27). God says: I would have destroyed Israel, but I was afraid that Israel's enemies would take credit for their victory and not credit it to Me. "From the overthrow of Israel they will conclude that they themselves are strong; they do not know that God has abandoned Israel to them" (*Deuteronomy* by Gerhard von Rad, p. 199). Nehama Leibowitz points out a very daring anthromorphism in this passage, when God speaks of fearing the enemy. Nowhere else in the Torah is such a statement found. To understand this statement, Leibowitz points out God's ultimate purpose as found in the *Alaynu* prayer: "All the inhabitants of the world will acknowledge and know that it is to Thee every knee must bend, and by Thee every tongue must swear." If God took vengeance on Israel, then this ultimate purpose could not be realized.

Even the Rabbis had difficulty using anthropomorphisms, i.e., giving God human characteristics. When they did describe God in these ways, they used the word *kiveyachol*. Its literal meaning is "as if it were possible," but figuratively, it means something like "we really cannot use these words about God, but if we could, this is what we would say."

Does it make sense to talk about an all-powerful God as being fearful?
Of what are you most fearful?
What is your greatest personal strength?
How might that strength, used correctly, help you overcome fear?

STRATEGIES

ANALYZING THE TEXT

1 Examine this portion in a Torah scroll. Does it look different from other sections of the Torah? If possible, look at Exodus 15 in the scroll. Deuteronomy 32 is called "The Song of Moses" and Exodus 15 is referred to as "The Song at the Sea." What conclusions can you draw from the titles and the line arrangements of these two sections of the Torah?

2 Read and compare the two poems delivered by Moses to the Israelites Exodus 15 and Deuteronomy 32:1-43. According to W. Gunther Plaut, "both deal with Israel's survival" (*The Torah: A Modern Commentary*, p. 1555). How is this so? How does each song warn, instruct, and give hope to the people? Consider the use of anthropomorphism in each song.

3 Ask the Cantor to chant this portion for you. Ask the Cantor if the trope in any way reflects what the words are saying? Is special emphasis given to certain words? What about the tone? Could this be chanted in English? What tune or trope would be used?

4 Why would God never completely destroy the people of Israel? Find the answer in this portion.

5 In Deuteronomy 32:15 (and also 33:5), Israel is called by a new name, "Jeshurun." According to Ibn Ezra, the name is one of praise. It derives from the Hebrew word *yashar,* meaning "right" or "straight." The name is used in the text as a warning against pride; when Israel becomes "Jeshurun" and grows too proud and haughty, the fate described in Deuteronomy 32:15-27 will befall them. What is this fate? In *Ha'azinu,* Israel is also called "Jacob." Explain the significance of these two names. Which do you prefer? Why?

EXTENDING THE TEXT

6 Deuteronomy 32:3 is part of the Torah service. With the other members of the group, hold a practical workshop in which you learn the Torah service. Resource people to help with this activity are the Rabbi, Cantor, Director of Education, or a teacher.

7 Insight D, page 346, reminds us that God is called *HaTzur* (The Rock) six times in this portion. The Insight then connects the Chanukah hymn *"Ma'oz Tzur Yeshuati"* ("Rock of Ages") to the phrase *Tzur Yeshuati* (Rock of my support), found in Deuteronomy 32:15.

How does the hymn *"Ma'oz Tzur"* reflect some of the material found in this portion? What other modern day miracles or deliverances would you think warrant a stanza in *"Ma'oz Tzur?"* Write a new stanza for the *"Ma'oz Tzur,"* celebrating a modern day deliverence or miracle.

8 In the "Song of Moses," God is called *HaTzur* — The Rock (32:4,18,30,31). God is also called "Father" (32:6). Play a word association game to help you understand what we mean by using these names for God. Say the word "rock" aloud. Write down all the things you think of when you hear that word. Which of these might apply to your idea of God? Do the same with the word "father" (or substitute the word "parent"). If time allows use both "father" and "parent." Are the lists for these two words the same or do they evoke different reponses? Why or why not? Do the words we use to describe God limit or expand our ideas about God? When you are finished, complete the following sentence: "I believe that God _____ ." Collect all the sentences and share them aloud with the group. The group may want to keep these anonymous.

9 Several times in Deuteronomy, we find the image of God as a parent. Look at Deuteronomy 1:31; 8:5; 32:5-7,11. In what ways is God like our Parent? In the style of Moses, compose a poem expressing this idea.

10 In Deuteronomy 32:10, God is depicted creating the Jewish people out of *tohu* — "a howling waste." This word is used in Genesis 1:2 to describe the primeval "chaos" out of which God created the world. What can you learn from the use of this same word in such different contexts? In what ways can Israel be said to have been created out of chaos? At what point in Jewish history does this idea best apply? Can you apply it to the creation of the State of Israel after the Holocaust?

11 Why is the letter ה (*hay*), which begins Deuteronomy 32:6, written large? According to the *Tanchuma* (*Ha'azinu* 5), this ה is the last letter of Moses' hidden signature in his song. Calculate the following "*gematria*" to show how this is so. What is the total numerical value of the first letters of verses 1-6, in chapter 32? What is the numerical value of the Hebrew name משה? Could you create a story or poem which contains a "hidden" message or word? Give it a try.

PERSONALIZING THE TEXT

12 Moses delivers a warning to the people in the form of a poem. In what format would you choose to deliver this message? Using the method of your choice, recreate the warning and deliver it.

13 Create a picture which symbolizes this Torah portion. Summarize its message in a drawing or painting.

14 Choose a significant word from the portion *Ha'azinu*, such as wrath, warning, consider, or future. Write its letters vertically down a page. Using each letter as the start of a line,

summarize in an acrostic the warning Moses gave to the Israelites.

15 In *Ha'azinu*, Moses calls upon heaven and earth to witness his song (32:1). Why were two witnesses required? Why do you think he chose these two witnesses? Imagine you are heaven or earth. Tell about the events described in this portion from your point of view.

16 In Deuteronomy 32:13-14, the agricultural produce of ancient Israel is described. Plan and carry out a thanksgiving banquet such as might have been held by the Israelites after they had settled in the Land. Incorporate the foods mentioned in this portion. Remember to keep the setting authentic.

17 *Ha'azinu* warns the people that while they will rebel and ignore God's laws, there will always be a remnant holding fast to tradition. It is your job to pack a bag of Jewish values to help maintain Judaism. You can fit only seven of these values in your suitcase. Choose carefully. Compare your choices with those of the other participants. Be prepared to explain your choices.

18 Derive a lesson or moral from this portion that has meaning for your life. Is this the message Moses wanted the people to hear and take to heart?

19 Israel faced many difficult situations and did not always prosper in the Land. Yet, Israel still endures. There have been many songs written to express this endurance of the Jewish people. One of the best known is "*Ani Ma'amin.*" Learn this song.
Reference: *Songs of the Chassidim* II, edited by Velvel Pasternak.

(For more, see the Index: "God.")

OTHER RESOURCES

20 Read and discuss the poem "Without Having Walked the Promised Land" in *The Fire Waits* by Michael Hecht, pp. 119-120.

21 Read, act out, and discuss the skit for the portion *Ha'azinu* in *Sedra Scenes: Skits for Every Torah Portion* by Stan J. Beiner, pp. 229-231.

22 For creative movement activities, see "Like an Eagle" and "Israel: Fat and Kicked" from *Torah in Motion* by JoAnne Tucker and Susan Freeman, pp. 226-229.

23 Read and discuss the illustrated commentary for *Haazinu* in *American Torah Toons* by Lawrence Bush.

INVOLVING THE FAMILY

24 There is a tradition in Judaism which holds parents responsible for educating their children and informing them of the wonders God performed. Read Deuteronomy 32:7. The Talmud states that this verse was the proof text for the command to kindle the Chanukah lights (*Sabbath* 23a). How is this so? The answer is found within the text, which states that the parent will tell the children about God's miracles in the days of old. Can your family identify which of God's miracles from the days of old have been mentioned, taught, or discussed within the family? As a family, talk about these miracles from days of old. Follow up with a discussion about the responsibilities of Jewish parents and children to learn about these miracles.

BAR/BAT MITZVAH PROJECT

25 *Ha'azinu* means to "give ear." Moses requests heaven and earth to "give ear" — literally, to be witnesses to the words he was about to speak to the Israelites. In this project you will have the opportunity to "give ear" to those who witness the words not of Moses, but of the Rabbi and the participants in your synagogue's worship services. Many individuals are hard of hearing, but because this is often a hidden physical challenge, it frequently does not receive the attention it needs. Your task is to find out if your congregation has individual amplifier sets with a remote connect to the sound system in the sanctuary. These sets, often made as headphones, enable the hard of hearing to amplify the sound so that they are able to hear what is going on and can fully participate in the worship service or in a lecture or presentation. If the congregation does not own such a device or has only a limited supply, your job is to purchase one or more of these sets. You will need to determine cost, availability, and compatibility with the synagogue sound system. You will need the help and advice of the synagogue professionals, individuals with expertise in the needs of the hard of hearing, and people who sell the devices you will be looking for. Don't forget, you will need to figure out how to raise the necessary funds. Be creative, and good luck!

V'ZOT HABRACHAH 33:1-34:12
וזאת הברכה

SYNOPSIS

V'ZOT HABRACHAH IS THE FINAL PORTION of the Torah. It contains Moses' last words to the people prior to his death. Moses gives a blessing to each of the tribes:

Reuben – Moses prays for this tribe's safety and life.

Judah – With God's help, Judah will lead the other tribes.

Levi – The Levites will guard the Ark and the priestly apparel. Levi will also be the teacher of Torah to Israel.

Benjamin – God will protect this tribe.

Joseph – Consisting of the tribes of Ephraim and Manasseh, they will enjoy great prosperity.

Zebulun – This tribe is told to rejoice in its journeys.

Issachar – Residing in the mountains, Issachar will also enjoy prosperity.

Gad – Gad will live by the sword, ever ready to meet its enemies.

Dan – This tribe is compared to a lion's whelp.

Naphtali – It will enjoy God's blessing.

Asher – This tribe should be considered most blessed and the favorite of its brothers.

There is a closing blessing for all the tribes in which Moses reminds them of the abundance they are to enjoy and the goodness which God has bestowed upon them. Moses then ascends Mount Nebo and God shows him the entire Promised Land. Moses dies at the age of 120. His burial place is unknown. The Israelites observe a 30 day mourning period. Joshua now assumes the leadership position over Israel.

The portion, as well as the entire Torah, closes with the statement that never again could a prophet arise like Moses, who knew God face-to-face.

INSIGHTS FROM THE TRADITION

A "This is the blessing" (*V'zot HaBrachah*) which Moses delivered to the tribes of Israel just before his death on Mount Nebo. The people came to Moses and said that the hour of his death was approaching. In reply, Moses said, "Wait until I bless Israel. All my life, they have had no pleasant experiences with me, for I constantly rebuked them and admonished them to fear God and fulfill the commandments. I do not wish to leave this world before I have blessed them" (*Legends of the Jews* by Louis Ginzberg, Vol. III, p. 452).

In what light do you view Moses? Do you have a sense of his being a hard and unrelenting leader or someone who dealt fairly and lovingly with the Israelite people? Is he a composite of those two images? Explain.

Take some time out for personal evaluation: How do you think other people see you? What do you want people to think of you? What pleases you most about yourself?

B Deuteronomy 33:4 reads, "When Moses charged us with the Teaching, as a heritage of the congregation of Jacob . . . " The Hebrew word used for heritage is מורשה (*morashah*). This term implies that the heritage is of a spiritual nature and it is the kind of heritage which endures forever (*Concepts and Values* by Solomon Colodner, p. 135).

If the Teaching is the spiritual heritage, what is the physical heritage?

What legacy would you like to leave to future generations?

C Ramban points out that the text says the "congregation" of Jacob, not the "house" of

Jacob, or the seed of Jacob. This suggests that many strangers would join Israel and that the Torah would always be an inheritance of Jacob and all those who congregate with his people. Ramban cites two proof texts for his interpretations: "Also the aliens that join themselves to the Eternal to minister unto God" (Isaiah 56:6); ". . . and they shall cleave to the house of Jacob" (Isaiah 14:1). Ramban leaves us with the final thought that all who join the house of Jacob will be called "God's congregation" (*Ramban: Commentary on the Torah* [Deuteronomy] by Charles B. Chavel, Deuteronomy 33:4, p. 376).

Ramban teaches us that those who choose Judaism have equal status with those born into Judaism. There is a tradition which holds that once a person has chosen Judaism, his or her conversion is not to be mentioned again, so as not to stigmatize the convert or to encourage the community to see the convert as different from those who are born into the Jewish heritage.

In recent years, there has been a trend to develop special support groups for Jews by Choice. Does this help or hinder their integration into the Jewish community?
If you were a Jew by Choice, how would you want to be seen as a member of the House of Jacob?

D Compare the order in which each son/tribe is blessed:

Jacob's Blessing – Genesis 49
Reuben
Simeon
Levi
Judah
Zebulun
Issachar
Dan
Gad
Asher
Naphtali
Joseph

Benjamin
Moses' Blessing – Deuteronomy 33
Reuben
Judah
Levi
Benjamin
Joseph (Ephraim and Manasseh)
Zebulun
Issachar
Gad
Dan
Naphtali
Asher

Nachmanides comments: "The order of their blessings was, by Holy Inspiration, in keeping with their future settlement. First came Reuben, because this was also the first tribe to settle (Joshua 13:15-23). Moreover, Reuben was the firstborn, and Moses prayed, let Reuben live, that he may not become altogether extinguished on account of his sin (Genesis 35:22). Therefore, Moses granted Reuben, in his blessing, the precedence of primogeniture. Next, he blessed Judah who was the first tribe to settle in the Land proper (Joshua 15, Judges 1:2). Then followed Levi, whose mainstay was Jerusalem, in the Judean area. Then he mentioned Benjamin, who bordered with Judah, sharing with him the site of Jerusalem, and in whose province the Sanctuary was located; thus Levi was actually settled between Judah and Benjamin. Now he blessed Joseph, whose allotment borders on Benjamin. Then he concluded with the blessing for Leah's sons, giving priority to Zebulun, as Jacob had also blessed Zebulun before Issachar, and in this order, too, they settled the Land (Joshua 19:10-17). The blessings of the handmaid's sons, Dan, Naphtali, Gad, and Asher, proceeded in genealogical order. Gad is mentioned first in this group, as also with regard to the camp formation (Numbers 2:14), because he joined Reuben in the camp, as well as in settling Transjordan" (Numbers 32) (*Ramban: Commentary on the Torah* (Deuteronomy) by Charles B. Chavel, pp. 382-384).

In the blessing given by Moses, the tribe of Simeon is missing. In the Book of Genesis, Simeon and Levi are cursed by Jacob because of the retribution they sought against Shechem who had raped their sister Dinah. At the incident of the Golden Calf, the sons of Levi remained loyal to God. As the *Sifre* comments; Levi paid back for what it had done. Simeon had not. For this reason, Simeon was omitted.

Ramban has a different understanding of Simeon's absence from the blessing. The tribes are always considered to number 12. When Jacob blessed his sons, he considered Joseph to be one tribe; Moses considered Joseph to be two tribes, Ephraim and Manasseh. Simeon was omitted so that the tribal number would remain at 12. Also, Simeon was the logical choice to be omitted, for that tribe was small and became scattered throughout the other tribes, and thus they, too, were blessed through the blessing of the rest of the tribes (*Ramban: Commentary on the Torah* (Deuteronomy) by Charles B. Chavel, p. 382).

If you were a tribe, what might Moses have said about you?
If you were Moses, what might you have said in blessing your best friend? your favorite teacher?

E Once the blessings were completed, Moses ascended Mount Nebo. Based on the *midrash*, Moses was still not reconciled to his fate. He argued with God regarding the divine decree, mentioning the many times God was merciful with the Israelites. Moses desired this same consideration of mercy now. But, in light of six sins which Moses committed, God refused. Moses refused to deliver the Israelites (Exodus 4:13); Moses accused God of making conditions bad for Israel and for not delivering the people (Exodus 5:23); Moses tested God twice during Korach's rebellion (Numbers 16:29, 30); Moses slandered the people twice (Numbers 20:10 and 32:14) (*Petirat Mosheh Rabbenu* as found in *The Torah: A Modern Commentary*, edited by W. Gunther Plaut, p. 1585).

Moses was arguing for his life. What are the things you love about your life that would cause you to argue with God for its continuation?

F The text informs us that God buried Moses so that no individual would know the location of his burial site. Gersonides explains that God buried Moses so that in future generations people would not come to venerate the site and worship Moses as a deity.

Why do you think Jewish tradition discourages veneration or worship of Jewish leaders and scholars?
Does this attitude strengthen Judaism? Explain.

STRATEGIES

ANALYZING THE TEXT

1 Deuteronomy 34:10-12 describes the unique role of Moses in Jewish history. Read and discuss the verses. Do you agree with them? Memorize these verses in Hebrew and/or English.

2 There are three instances in the Bible in which the tribes of Israel are described and their fate predicted. Prepare a comparison chart. Down the left side of the paper, list the tribe and its geographical location. Then, in three parallel columns, list the descriptions given in Genesis 49, Deuteronomy 33, and Judges 5.
Reference: *The Torah: A Modern Commentary*, edited by W. Gunther Plaut, pp. 1574-1575.

EXTENDING THE TEXT

3 The word *"ayshdat"* in Deuteronomy 33:2 puzzled the commentators. Though some think the word is a place name, the tradition rules that this one word should be read as though it were two — *aysh dat* — which may be understood as the "fire of faith/knowledge." The verse then teaches us that from God's "right hand" the fire of the Torah came to the people. Coupled with the phrases which begin this verse, there is the image of the light of Torah shining upon the people. Illustrate this idea in the art medium of your choice.

4 In this portion, Moses refers to himself simply as "the man of God" (33:1); and in the closing statement of Deuteronomy he is called a prophet (34:10). Jewish tradition, however, has honored Moses with the title *Moshe Rabbenu* — Moses our teacher. Which description do you think best sums up the man? Why?

5 Many *midrashim* elaborate on the sparse text describing the death of Moses. Read some of these from the sources below. Discuss how the *midrashim* emphasize the human qualities of Moses. Why do you think the creators of the *midrashim* wanted to teach people that Moses was a person like any other?
References: *Legends of the Jews* by Louis Ginzberg, Vol. III, pp. 417-481; *Messengers of God* by Eli Wiesel, pp. 155-186; *The Torah: A Modern Commentary,* edited by W. Gunther Plaut, pp. 1585-1588; *The Book of Legends,* edited by Hayim Bialik and Yehoshua Ravnitzky.

6 What do you think: Why were the bones of Moses left in an unmarked place on Mount Nebo instead of being carried into the Promised Land as were Joseph's (Exodus 13:19)? What is meant by the expression that God knew Moses "face-to-face?" Compare with Numbers 12:8. Write your own *midrash* answering one or more of these questions.

7 The anniversary of a death is called a *yahrzeit.* According to Jewish tradition, Moses' *yahrzeit* is on the seventh day of the month of Adar.

a. Find out how a *yahrzeit* is recorded and observed in Judaism.
b. Find out what special practices have arisen regarding the *yahrzeit* of Moses. Plan a special service commemorating his *yahrzeit.*
c. Discuss: How do you think a *yahrzeit* should be observed? What customs and practices might you observe publicly and/or privately to mark the death of someone you loved?
References: *Encyclopaedia Judaica,* "Yahrzeit," Vol. 16, pp. 702-703; "Adar, the Seventh of," Vol. 2, pp. 252-253; *Teaching Jewish Life Cycle* by Barbara Binder Kadden and Bruce Kadden, p.108.

8 The 30-day mourning period which the Israelites observed for both Moses and Aaron (see Numbers 20:29) has remained a significant part of Jewish mourning practices. (For more, see the Index: "Death/Burial.")

9 Assign individuals or small groups one of the tribes. Their task is to design and make a banner, sculpture, picture, or creative reading to illustrate the blessing their tribe received. Consider using one or more of the following media: clay, metal, fabric, felt, or paints.

10 Imagine that you are Joshua, the new leader of the people. It is your task to write a eulogy remembering Moses. Use a Concordance to find those instances in the Torah when Joshua is mentioned in connection with Moses. Check under references to Joshua. In the eulogy, mention those events during and after which you, Joshua, were influenced and affected by Moses.

11 Joshua is now the new leader of the Israelites. Using the format of the television show "Meet the Press," interview Joshua. Set up a panel of questioners and choose a Joshua.

You might rotate the roles throughout the group so that everyone can participate. Have the "Joshua" participants prepare by reading ahead into the Book of Joshua to learn more about this individual.

PERSONALIZING THE TEXT

12 Moses has delivered his blessings for the tribes. You are a member of one of the tribes, choose whichever one you wish. Within the group, try to have all the tribes represented. Write your reaction to Moses' message on a postcard to a friend in a neighboring Israelite tribe. Design the picture side of the card to reflect your feelings. Display and share the results.

13 Look at the images of God that Moses uses in the concluding verse of his final blessing (Deuteronomy 33:27-30). God is described both as refuge with embracing "arms," and at the same time as a shield and sword. Which image do you prefer? If you were Moses, getting ready to leave the people you had shepherded for 40 years, what ideas about God would you want the people to have learned from your common experience? Explore this idea by writing a further blessing from Moses to the Israelites, beginning with his words "O Jeshurun, there is none like God . . . "

14 When Moses died, his grave was left unmarked. Create an inscription which you think would be appropriate for his headstone.

15 As Moses gazed out over the Land, the clouds shifted, revealing the good Land which the Israelites would enjoy. Capture in art the view which you believe Moses might have seen from atop Mount Nebo. If desired, use pastel chalk and include "clouds" made of fluffy cotton balls to add a dream-like quality to your scene.

16 After a vacation or journey, many people organize scrapbooks to remind them of their travels. They share these with friends and pass them on to later generations. Pretend you were a servant of Moses or of his wife. Compile a scrapbook about your life with Moses or Zipporah.

17 In his book *Moses and Monotheism*, Sigmund Freud wrote: "It was one man, the man Moses, who created the Jews." Organize a debate on this subject.

18 Imagine, what would have happened had Moses lived to lead the people into the Promised Land?
a. Write a "new ending" for the Torah based on this premise.
b. Read and then "rewrite" the first chapter of the Book of Joshua based on this idea. Don't forget to change the title of the biblical book!
c. Would our appreciation of Moses as a leader, as a "man of God," and as a human being be changed if Moses had not died when he did? Write a "scholarly" assessment of Moses based on this idea.

19 Before his death, Moses spoke publicly to all the Israelites and then delivered his blessing to each tribe. We do not know what messages or teachings he left to members of his own family. Write an ethical will for Moses in which you detail the values and ethics he wanted to will to his family.

20 Design a commemorative stamp to honor the life and achievements of Moses.

21 Plan advertising for a movie on the life of Moses. Create a poster for the movie for display in theaters.

22 Use the complete Hebrew Torah text to find out the first Hebrew letter in the Torah (*bet*). What is the last Hebrew letter (*lamed*)?

Together these two letters spell "*layv*" which means "heart." Write your own *Midrash* exploring the significance of this teaching.

OTHER RESOURCES

23 Read, act out, and discuss the skit for the portion *V'zot HaBrachah* in *Sedra Scenes: Skits for Every Torah* Portion by Stan J. Beiner, pp. 232-234.

24 For creative movement activities, see "God's Everlasting Arms" and "Moses Sees the Promised Land" from *Torah in Motion* by JoAnne Tucker and Susan Freeman, pp. 230-233.

25 Read and discuss the illustrated commentary for *Ve-Zot Ha-Berachah* in *American Torah Toons* by Lawrence Bush.

INVOLVING THE FAMILY

26 The words "When Moses charged us with the Teaching as the heritage of the Congregation of Jacob" (Deuteronomy 33:4) are part of a child's morning prayer in the Ashkenazic liturgy. Read this prayer in a traditional *Siddur* (see *Ha-Siddur Ha-Shalem* by Philip Birnbaum, p. 2). Why did the composer of this prayer want to include these words? Write your own version of a morning prayer for children. Include themes and actual verses that *you* think are important for children to know and repeat each day.

BAR/BAT MITZVAH PROJECT

27 On the holiday of Simchat Torah, we celebrate the cycle of Torah reading as we read both the end of the Torah (from this Torah portion) and then immediately begin again with *Beresheet*. Ask your Rabbi how you can participate in your synagogue's Simchat Torah observance. Since you have prepared a reading from this portion, you can read it during the celebration.

REVIEW ACTIVITIES FOR DEUTERONOMY

1 Together as a class, read the following poem:

Spiral

Again we have reached the end of the story.
Again we have begun at the beginning.
The tale comes full circle once a year —
But it is not a circle, rather a spiral
Coming back upon itself ever higher.
Each year we understand something more.
Each year the Torah illumines
Parts of our life we never knew were there.
God, make us wiser year by year.
May we draw ever more strength from your word.
Grant us the joy of this day of completion
And beginning.
May our faith spiral upward . . . .

(From *The Fire Waits* by Michael I. Hecht.
Hartmore House, 1363 Fairfield Avenue,
Bridgeport, CT 06605. Reprinted with permission.)

Discuss:
What is meant by the first two lines of the poem?
How is Torah like a spiral?

2 Read the poem "Spiral" at the Simchat Torah celebration.

3 Think of something very important to you. Share it with the group and explain the reasons for its importance. Then think of three reasons that the Torah is important to the Jews and share these. Try to come to a class consensus.

4 When asked by a non-Jew to summarize the Torah, Hillel replied: "Do not do unto others what is hateful to you. The rest is commentary. Go and study." Write your own summary statement of the Torah.

5 Make up a story in which the Torah can talk to you. What would the Torah say? What would you reply in return?

6 Make a video which summarizes some or all of the events in the Book of Deuteronomy.

7 Imagine . . . In your travels across Israel you discover a time capsule left by the generation entering Canaan with Joshua. What do you find inside it? As a group, create and collect those items. Include notes, messages, religious articles, household tools, and everyday objects.

8 It is traditional at the conclusion of the study of a Jewish text to hold a festive celebration — a *siyyum*. Once you have finished Deuteronomy, hold a *siyyum*. Plan to serve foods mentioned in the Bible. Invite parents and other classes to the *siyyum*.

a. Conduct a "Deuteronomy Quiz-a-thon." Divide the group into teams, have a prepared list of quiz questions, and conduct the quiz like a spelling bee.

b. In small groups, stage tableaus of various scenes from Deuteronomy. Have the rest of the group guess what is being depicted.

9 Your consulting firm has been asked by Joshua to meet with representatives of each tribe. You are to help them decide the area of Canaan in which they would like to settle. Read through Genesis 49, Deuteronomy 33, and Judges 5. Determine each tribe's strengths and the geographical areas appropriate for them. Assign a liaison from your company to deliver a presentation explaining your proposals. Then have each tribe vote. Conclude the activity by determining if the tribes chose the same locations as the ancient tribes of Israel did.
Reference: *MacMillan Bible Atlas* by Yohanan Aharoni and Michael Avi-Yonah.

10 Complete some or all of the pages related to the Book of Deuteronomy in *Torah Tales Copy Pak™: Numbers & Deuteronomy* by Marji Gold-Vukson.

Note: For additional concluding activities, see the Review Activities in this volume at the conclusion of the other Books of the Torah.

חזק חזק ונתחזק

Chazak, Chazak, v'Nitchazayk

APPENDIX

COMMENTATORS/COMMENTARIES

ABRAVANEL, ISAAC (Isaac ben Judah, 1437-1508): Finance Minister to the kings of Portugal, Spain, and Naples who settled in Venice after the expulsion of 1492. He wrote important commentaries to the Bible, the *Haggadah,* and to Rambam's* *Guide of the Perplexed.*

AKEDAT YITZHAK: A commentary to the Torah by Isaac Arama*.

ALBO, JOSEPH (c. 1380-1434): Spanish philosopher who wrote a book on the essentials of Jewish faith called *Sefer Haikkarim (Book of Principles).*

ALSHEKH, MOSES BEN CHAIM (1508-1600): Born in Adrianopolis, Alshikh spent most of his life in Safed where he was a student of Joseph Caro (author of the *Shulchan Aruch*). He was a prominent *halachic* authority, whose Shabbat sermons became the basis of a well-known commentary to the Torah.

ARAMA, ISAAC BEN MOSES (c. 1420-1494): A Spanish Rabbi who wrote an influential commentary to the Torah and to the *Megillot* called *Akedat Yitzhak* (Binding of Isaac). Arama, who was also involved in several religious disputations with Christian scholars, settled in Naples after the Expulsion from Spain in 1492.

ASHKENAZI, ELIEZER BEN ELIYAHU, THE PHYSICIAN (1513-1586): A Rabbi and doctor who wrote a commentary to the Torah called *Maaseh Ha-Shem* (The Acts of God). He lived in many of the important Jewish cultural centers of the sixteenth century, including Cairo, Venice, and Prague.

BACHYA BEN JOSEPH IBN PAKUDA (11th century C.E.): Spanish thinker and writer of liturgical poems. His most famous work, *Chovot HaLevavot* (Duties of the Heart), defines the ethical and ritual obligations incumbent upon the religious person.

BAMBERGER, BERNARD JACOB (1904-1980): An American Reform Rabbi and biblical scholar, Bamberger was a member of the committee which produced the 1962 Jewish Publication Society translation of the Torah. He authored the commentary to Leviticus in *The Torah: A Modern Commentary*.

BAMIDBAR RABBAH: A collection of *midrashim** on the Book of Numbers, part of which is believed to be the work of Moses ha-Darshan of Narbonne (eleventh century). Scholars believe that *BaMidbar Rabbah* comprises two different collections, one from the ninth century and the other from the eleventh century. The two collections were probably joined together by a scribe in the twelfth or thirteenth century.

BAR KAPPARA (Eleazar ben Eleazar HaKappara): A third century C.E. Palestinian scholar who authored a collection of *halachot* known as the *Mishnah of Bar Kappara,* which was a supplement to the Mishnah* of Judah HaNasi. Following a disagreement with Judah, Bar Kappara founded an academy in Ceasarea.

BEN ZAKKAI, YOHANAN (first century C.E.): A teacher of Torah and head of the Sanhedrin, ben Zakkai was an important force in the creation of a Jewish center at Yavneh following the destruction of the Second Temple. Called Rabban, many of his

*Denotes a cross-reference in this Appendix.

teachings and *halachic* enactments are preserved in the Mishnah* and Talmud*.

BERACHOT: A tractate of the Talmud*.

BERESHEET RABBAH: One of the earliest of the *midrashic* collections, this collection on the Book of Genesis is believed to date back to the sixth century.

BIUR: A valuable German translation and commentary to the Torah written by Moses Mendelsohn, Solomon Dubno, Naftali Herz Wessely (see Wiesel*), Aaron Yaroslav, and H. Homberg in 1783. The *Biur* was a work of great significance for the period of Enlightment.

BUBER, MARTIN (1878-1965): A Jewish philosopher whose ideas about the relationship between humanity and God had an important impact, particularly on Christian theologians. Buber also wrote a variety of interpretations of biblical texts and did significant work collecting and interpreting Hasidic thought.

CARO, JOSEPH: See *Shulchan Aruch**.

GAMALIEL II, RABBAN: An important Rabbinic authority after the destruction of the Second Temple, he worked to strengthen the new Jewish center at Yavneh. His teachings became the foundation for many current practices, including the formulation of parts of the *Haggadah* and the *Amidah* prayer.

GEMARA: see Talmud*.

GENESIS RABBAH: see *Beresheet Rabbah**.

GINZBERG, LOUIS (1873-1953): A professor at the Jewish Theological Seminary, Ginzberg played a crucial role in the formation of the Conservative movement. His most important work was the

seven volume *Legends of the Jews* (1909-1938), a retelling of hundreds of *midrashim* about the people and events of the Bible.

GUIDE OF THE PERPLEXED: see Rambam*.

HACOHEN, MORDECAI BEN HILLEL (1856-1936): Author of *Al HaTorah*, Hacohen was a Hebrew writer who, in 1897, became the first person to address the First Zionist Congress in the Hebrew language. He settled in Palestine in 1907, was a founder of Tel Aviv, and was active in promoting the use of Hebrew.

HAKETAV VEHAKABBALAH (1839): Compiled by Jacob Zvi Mecklenburg (1785-1865), Chief Rabbi of Konigsberg, this is one of the first comprehensive commentaries to the Pentateuch that was aimed at demonstrating how the oral tradition (*Kabbalah*) could be read into the written text (*HaKetav*).

HALLO, WILLIAM W.: A professor at Yale University who authored the introductory essays to each of the five books in *The Torah: A Modern Commentary**.

HERTZ, JOSEPH HERMAN (1872-1946): Hertz was the first graduate of the Jewish Theological Seminary of America (1894). He went on to become the Chief Rabbi of the United Hebrew Congregations of the British Commonwealth. His commentary on the Pentateuch (1929-1936) is one of the standard texts used in synagogues today.

HESCHEL, ABRAHAM JOSHUA (1907-1972): Heschel was a professor at the Hebrew Union College and at the Jewish Theological Seminary. He wrote a number of books exploring Jewish tradition and philosophy and became an important influence on both Jewish and Christian theologians.

HILLEL I – THE ELDER (c. 75 B.C.E. - beginning of the first century C.E.): Hillel was a sage who headed the Sanhedrin (approximately 10 B.C.E- 10 C.E.) at the end of the reign of Herod. His disagreements with the sage Shammai are reported in many sources, but gradually Hillel's views became the more widely accepted. His teachings have been preserved mainly in a series of aphorisms recorded in the Mishnah*.

HIRSCH, SAMSON RAPHAEL (1808-1888): One of the founders of the modern Orthodox movement in nineteenth century Germany, his thoughts are expressed in his works — *Nineteen Letters of Ben Uzziel* and *Horeb*. Hirsch translated the Pentateuch into German and wrote a commentary on it (1867-1878).

HOFFMAN, DAVID ZEVI (1843-1921): A German Rabbinic authority who became rector of the Hildesheimer Rabbinical Seminary in Berlin. He was a prolific scholar who authored *Responsa**, Talmudic criticism, and biblical commentary.

IBN EZRA, ABRAHAM (1089-1164): A Jew of Spanish origin who traveled throughout Europe and North Africa and was famous for his poems and scholarship. Ibn Ezra is best known for his commentary on the Bible, which makes extensive use of grammatical and etymological interpretation.

JOSEPHUS, FLAVIUS (c. 38 C.E.- after 100 C.E.): Josephus served as commander of the Galilee in the first Jewish revolt against the Romans (66-70 C.E.). He eventually surrendered to the Romans and was taken in chains to Rome where he gained the favor of the emperor Vespasian. He was the author of *The Jewish War,* the main source detailing the history of the Jews in the first centuries B.C.E. and C.E. and the origin of the war between the Jews and Rome.

KATZ, MORDECAI (1951-): Rabbi, author, and compiler of *Lilmod Ulelamade: From the Teachings of Our Sages,* a collection of teachings and interpretations of the weekly Torah portions.

KOOK, ABRAHAM ISAAC (1865-1935): Rabbi Kook was the first Chief Rabbi of Israel after the Balfour Declaration (1917). An ardent Zionist, he was a prolific writer who authored works on the Talmud* and on Jewish thought.

LEIBOWITZ, NEHAMA (1905-1997): A distinguished professor of Bible at Tel Aviv University, Leibowitz authored the series *Studies in . . . ,* consisting of one or two volumes for each book of the Torah. Her studies, which were originally printed in Hebrew, have been translated into English, French, Spanish, and other languages.

LEVI ("BERABBI"): A sage of the late third century C.E. (perhaps the Levi ben Lahma mentioned in the Talmud*), he was a lecturer (apparently unordained) at the academy of Yohanan ben Zakkai*. To him is attributed the statement: "If Israel would keep but one Sabbath properly, the son of David the Messiah would immediately come."

LEVITICUS RABBAH: See *Vayikra Rabbah**.

LUZZATTO, SAMUEL DAVID (1800-1865): Also known by the acronym SHaDaL, Luzzatto was an Italian scholar who wrote clear and simple commentaries in Hebrew to the Torah and to certain of the Prophets and Writings.

MAIMONIDES: see Rambam*.

MALBIM (an acronym for Meir Leibush ben Yehiel Michel, 1809-1879): A Rabbi of Russian origin who was a staunch opponent of the early Reform Movement. His mastery extended to languages, logic, philosophy, and *Kabbalah,* and he was well versed in the science of his day. He combined all of this in his popular commentary on the Bible, *HaTorah VehaMitzvah.*

MEGILLOT: A tractate of the Talmud*.

MECHILTA DE-RABBI ISHMAEL: *Midrashim** on the Book of Exodus produced by the school of Rabbi Ishmael, a sage who lived in the first half of the second century C.E. *Mechilta* — an Aramaic word meaning "a measure" and understood as "collection" — was first printed in 1515 in Constantinople.

MESHECH CHOCHMAH (1927): A commentary on the Torah written by Rabbi Meir Simha Hacohen (1845-1926).

MIDRASH: The word *"midrash"* is derived from the Hebrew root דרש (*drash*), which means "to search" or "to seek." *Midrashim* (plural) are explanations and interpretations of biblical texts. Most *midrashic* material (there are dozens of collections) originated in Palestine and date from the third to the tenth centuries C.E.

MIDRASH HAGADOL: A collection of *midrashim** on the Torah compiled by the Yemenite scholar David ben Amram Adini in the thirteenth century. The work is important because it contains the only known record of many teachings of the Tannaim (the sages of the first and second centuries C.E.).

MIDRASH TADSHEH: A late work, so named from its opening word. Known also as Baraita of Rabbi Pinchas ben Yair (second century C.E.), it contains much material on the symbolism of numbers.

MIDRASH YELAMDENU: See Tanhuma*.

MISHNAH: The core of the oral law, this collection of legal material is presented in six "orders" (divisions). The Mishnah was edited by Rabbi Judah

HaNasi at the end of the second century C.E. in Palestine. Mishnah, together with Gemara, form the Talmud*. The word *"Mishnah"* comes from the Hebrew root שנה (*shanah*), meaning "to repeat," and refers to the learning of the oral law.

MISHNEH TORAH: See Rambam*.

MOSES BEN JACOB OF COUCY: (Also known as Moses haDarshan, not to be confused with Moshe haDarshan of Narbonne.) A thirteenth century itinerant Rabbi whose preaching apparently led to an improvement in the observance of several of the positive *mitzvot.* His *Sefer Mitzvot Gadol* (1480), based on the *Mishneh Torah* of Maimonides (Rambam*), became one of the standard *halachic* references for later generations.

NACHMANIDES: See Ramban*.

NETZIV (Naphtali Tzvi Judah Berlin, 1817-1893): A Talmudic scholar, the Netziv was head of the Yeshivah at Volozhin for 40 years. He was an executive member of Hibbat Zion, and urged Russian Jews to support the settlement of Jews in Palestine. Among his writing are many *Responsa** and a commentary on the Torah called *Haamek Davar* (Vilna, 1879-80).

NUMBERS RABBAH: See *BaMidbar Rabbah**.

PETRIE, SIR WILLIAM FLINDERS (1853-1942): A British archaeologist who, while excavating sites in Egypt and Palestine, developed the method of dating by strata.

PHINEHAS BEN HAMA HA-KOHEN: A sage of the mid-fourth century. The maxims of Phinehas are quoted in the Jerusalem Talmud* and in *Beresheet Rabbah**.

PLAUT, W. GUNTHER (1912-): A prominent Reform Rabbi and scholar, a president of the Central Conference of American Rabbis, Plaut is the main author and editor of the *The Torah: A Modern Commentary**.

RABBAN: See Ben Zakkai, Yohanan*.

RAD, GERHARD VON (1901-1971): German Bible scholar and professor concerned with the theological aspects of certain books of the Bible and with Wisdom Literature. Among his major works are: *Biblical Interpretation in Preaching, God at Work in Israel,* and *Message of the Prophets.*

RADAK (An acronym for Rabbi David Kimchi, 1160-1235): Grammarian and translator who lived in Spain and France. Radak's commentary to the Bible is clear and straightforward. It was especially used by those who translated the Bible into Romance languages.

RAMBAM (An acronym for Rabbi Moses ben Maimon, also known as Maimonides, 1135-1204): Rambam was one of the most important Jewish authorities of the post-Talmudic period. A physician as well as a Jewish scholar, Rambam wrote the *Siraj,* a widely accepted commentary on the Mishnah; a work of philosophy, *Guide of the Perplexed;* and the *Mishneh Torah,* a 14 volume code of Jewish law. He also authored several important *Responsa**. Of Rambam it is written: "From Moses to Moses, there never arose one such as Moses."

RAMBAN (An acronym for Rabbi Moses ben Nachman, also known as Nachmanides, 1194-1270): One of the leading scholars of the Middle Ages after Rambam*, Ramban is known for his participation in the disputation at Barcelona in 1263 against the apostate Pablo Christiani. He was a prolific writer whose work was influenced by Rashi*, Ibn Ezra*, and Rambam*, but his most important works are a commentary on the Torah and his writings on *halachah.* Ramban emigrated to Palestine in 1267 and played a vital role in reestablishing the Jewish community of Jerusalem.

RASHBAM (An acronym for the Tosaphist Rabbi Samuel ben Meir, c. 1080-1158): A grandson of Rashi*, Rashbam is known for his commentary on the Torah which stresses the plain meaning of the text. He also wrote a commentary on the Talmud*.

RASHI (An acronym for Rabbi Shlomo Yitzhaki/ Solomon ben Isaac, 1040-1105): A very prominent French commentator. Rashi's explanations, which are noted for their clarity, are included in most editions of the Bible and the Talmud* alongside the text.

RESPONSA: The written answers (*teshuvot*) given by qualified authorities to questions (*she'aylot*) on all manner of Jewish law. There have been tens of thousands of such *Responsa* written since post-Talmudic times.

SANHEDRIN: A tractate of the Mishnah*.

SFORNO, OBADIAH BEN JACOB (c. 1470-1550): Sforno was an Italian biblical commentator and physician. He is the author of many Responsa*, as well as a noteworthy commentary on the Torah.

SHULCHAN ARUCH (THE PREPARED TABLE): A succinct code of Jewish law written (1565) by the Sephardic Rabbi Joseph Caro (1488-1575). Together with the commentary *HaMappah (The Tablecloth)* by Ashkenazic Rabbi Moses Isserles (1525-1572), the *Shulchan Aruch* came to be accepted as the definitive code of Jewish law.

SIFRA: A *midrash** on the Book of Leviticus dated sometime after the completion of the Jerusalem Talmud* (end of the fourth century C.E.). Scholars attribute *Sifra* to the school of Rabbi Akiva.

SIFREI: A work comprising two distinct collections of *midrashim**, one to the Book of Numbers, the other to Deuteronomy. The *Sifrei* was probably compiled in Palestine shortly after the completion of the Talmud* (end of the fifth century C.E.).

SIMLAI RABBI: A scholar who lived in the second half of the third century C.E. To Simlai is attributed the statement that the 613 *mitzvot* mentioned in the Torah are comprised of 248 positive commandments — equaling the number of organs in the body — and 365 negative commandments — equaling the number of days in the solar year.

SOTAH: A tractate of the Talmud*.

SPEISER, EPHRAIM AVIGDOR (1902-1965): An American archaeologist, Speiser was a professor of Semitic languages for most of his life. He was a member of the committee that produced the 1962 Jewish Publication Society translation of the Torah. He is also author of the commentary on Genesis in *The Anchor Bible*.

SPEKTOR, ISAAC ELCHANAN (1817-1896): A Lithuanian Rabbi who was an important authority and served as head of a *yeshivah* in Kovno, Spektor is the author of numerous *Responsa**. He was a Zionist who acted in a variety of ways to shore up the Jewish community of Eastern Europe, in particular defending Jewish rights to observe *kashrut*. (The Isaac Elchanan Seminary at Yeshiva University is named after him.)

TALMUD: A body of law and lore developed in the academies of Babylonia (the Babylonian Talmud, second to fifth centuries C.E.) and Jerusalem (the Jerusalem/Yerushalmi Talmud, second to fourth centuries C.E.). The Talmud consists of Mishnah* and Gemara*. The Rabbis whose teachings are contained in the Gemara are known as Amoraim. The titles of the tractates of the Talmud are taken from those orders of Mishnah on which they are based.

TANACH (תנ״ך): The Hebrew word for Bible, it is an acronym of the first letters of the words תורה (Torah), נביאים (Prophets), כתובים (Writings).

TANHUMA: Also known as the *Tanhuma Midrash Yelamdenu*. This is a collection of *midrashim** on the Torah ascribed to Rabbi Tanhuma*. Many of the *midrashim* are introduced with a special formula from which the second name is derived — *Yelamdenu Rabbenu* ("May our teacher instruct us").

TANHUMA, BAR ABBA: An Amora (see Talmud*) of the fifth century in Palestine, who is so frequently quoted in the *midrashic** collection *Tanhuma** that it is named after him.

TARGUM ONKELOS: A translation of the Torah into Aramaic. Said to have been written by the proselyte Aquila (first century C.E.?), this translation of the Torah has been read in synagogues throughout the centuries alongside the Hebrew text.

THE TORAH: A MODERN COMMENTARY: Published in 1981 by the Union of American Hebrew Congregations, this is the first liberal commentary on the Torah in more than 100 years of American Reform Judaism. The book consists of the Five Books of Moses in Hebrew and English with commentary, notes, and explanations by Rabbi W. Gunther Plaut (Genesis, Exodus, Numbers, and Deuteronomy) and Rabbi Bernard J. Bamberger (Leviticus).

TZENAH U'RENAH: Meaning "go forth and see," this Yiddish language paraphrase of the Torah for women by Jacob ben Isaac Ashkenazi of Yanof appeared in 1618. It contained the portion of the week, prayers, and folk tales. It was the first resource that enabled women to educate themselves.

VAYIKRA RABBAH: A *midrash** on the Book of Leviticus containing material from the Palestinian Amoraim (see Talmud*) and from the Mishnah*. *Vayikra Rabbah* is considered one of the oldest collections of *midrashim,* probably dating to the fifth century C.E.

VILNA GAON (Elijah ben Solomon Zalman, HaGRA, 1720-1797): A Jewish leader and *halachic* authority who, as head of the *Mitnagdim,* played an important role in the controversies surrounding the rise of Hasidism.

WIESEL, NAFTALI HERTZ (Also known as Naftali Herz Wessely, 1725-1805): Author of a commentary to Leviticus (1782) included in the *Biur*.* Wiesel was a Hebrew poet of the Enlightenment who based many of his poems on biblical stories and *midrashim*.*

YALKUT ME'AM LO'EZ: A popular Sephardic commentary on the Bible written in Ladino and dating from the eighteenth century. The work was begun by Yaakov Culi in 1730 with the intention of giving people who didn't know Hebrew access to traditional material. Culi died in 1732, and the work was completed by a number of other writers.

ZEIDAH LA-DEREKH (1623): A commentary on the commentary of Rashi by Rabbi Issachar Baer Eilenburg (1550-1623) of Prague.

NEW VOICES IN TORAH COMMENTARY

ANTONELLI, JUDITH S.: She is the author of *In The Image Of God: A Feminist Commentary on the Torah.* This work has been described as a blend of traditional Judaism and radical feminism.

FRANKEL, ELLEN: She is the author of *The Five Books of Miriam: A Woman's Commentary on the Torah.* Described as a folklorist, writer, and scholar, she has created a unique work which gives voice to ancient and modern stories by and about women. Frankel is also the Editor in chief of the Jewish Publication Society.

FOX, EVERETT: He wrote the translation, commentary, and notes for *The Five Books of Moses (The Schocken Bible: Volume I).* This translation is based on principles developed by Martin Buber and Franz Rosenzweig which restored the poetics of the original Hebrew text.

ROSENBLATT, NAOMI, AND JOSHUA HORWITZ: They are the co-authors of *Wrestling with Angels.* This special book examines the families of Genesis in light of contemporary psychological understandings of individuals and families.

ZORNBERG, AVIVAH GOTTLIEB: Zornberg has a Ph.D in English Literature from Cambridge University. Since 1981 she has been a teacher of Torah, *Midrash,* and the weekly Torah portion. She is the author of *Genesis: The Beginning of Desire.*

BIBLIOGRAPHY

Books

Adelman, Penina V. *Miriam's Well: Rituals for Jewish Women Around the Year.* 2d. ed. New York: Biblio Press, 1990.

Agnon, S.Y., ed. *Days of Awe: A Treasury of Jewish Wisdom for Reflection, Repentence & Renewal on the High Holy Days.* New York: Schocken Books, 1995.

Aharoni, Yohanan, and Michael Avi-Yonah. *The Macmillan Bible Atlas.* rev. ed. New York: Macmillan Publishing Co., 1993.

Albert, Eleanor. *Jewish Story Theater.* Los Angeles: Torah Aura Productions, 1996.

Alter, Robert. *The Art of Biblical Narrative.* New York: Basic Books, 1983.

————. *Genesis.* New York: W.W. Norton, 1996.

————. *The World of Biblical Literature.* New York: Basic Books, 1992.

Ansky, S. *The Dybbuk.* S. Morris Engel, trans. Washington, DC: Regnery Publishing, Inc., 1979.

Antonelli, Judith S. *In the Image of God: A Feminist Commentary on the Torah.* Northvale, NJ: Jason Aronson Inc., 1995.

Artson, Bradley Shavit. *It's a Mitzvah! Step-by-Step To Jewish Living.* West Orange, NJ: Behrman House and New York: The Rabbinical Assembly, 1995.

Aronson, Sara. *The Seven Days of Creation.* Brooklyn, NY: Sepher Hermon Press, Inc., 1985.

Asimov, Isaac. *Asimov's Guide to the Bible.* Vol. One: Old Testament. New York: Avon, 1976.

Barth, Lewis M., ed. *Berit Mila in the Reform Context.* Los Angeles: Berit Mila Board of Reform Judaism, 1990.

Beiner, Stan J. *Sedra Scenes: Skits for Every Torah Portion.* Denver, CO: A.R.E. Publishing, Inc., 1982.

————. *Bible Scenes: Joshua to Solomon.* Denver, CO: A.R.E. Publishing, Inc., 1988.

Berman, Melanie, and Joel Lurie Grishaver. *My Weekly Sidrah.* Los Angeles, CA: Torah Aura Productions, 1988.

Berrin, Susan. *Celebrating the New Moon: A Rosh Chodesh Anthology.* Northvale, NJ: Jason Aronson Inc., 1995.

Bialik, Hayim Nahman, and Yehoshua H. Ravnitzky, eds. William G. Braude, trans. *The Book of Legends (Sefer Ha-aggadah) Legends from the Talmud and Midrash.* New York: Schocken Books, 1992.

Birnbaum, Philip, trans. *Daily Prayer Book: Ha-Siddur Ha-Shalem.* New York: Hebrew Publishing Company, 1949.

Bissell, Sherry, with Audrey Friedman Marcus and Raymond A. Zwerin. *God: the Eternal Challenge.* Denver, Co: A.R.E. Publishing, Inc., 1980.

Bloch, Abraham P. *The Biblical and Historical Background of Jewish Customs and Ceremonies.* Hoboken, NJ: KTAV Publishing House, Inc., 1980.

Bloch, Abraham P. *A Book of Jewish Ethical Concepts: Biblical and Postbiblical*. New York: KTAV Publishing House, Inc., 1984.

Brody, Seymour. *Jewish Heroes and Heroines of America: 101 True Stories of American Jewish Heroism*. Hollywood, FL: LIFETIME, 1996.

Buber, Martin. *Moses: The Revelation and the Covenant*. Atlanta, GA: Humanities, 1988.

Bulka, Reuben P. *More Torah Therapy: Further Reflections on the Weekly Sedra and Special Occasions*. Hoboken, NJ: KTAV Publishing House, Inc., 1993.

Bush, Lawrence. *American Torah Toons*. Northvale, NJ: Jason Aronson Inc., 1997.

Bush, Lawrence, and Jeffrey Dekro. *Jews, Money and Social Responsibility: Developing a "Torah of Money" for Contemporary Life*. Philadelphia: The Shefa Fund, 1993.

Cardozo, Arlene Rossen. *Jewish Family Celebrations: The Sabbath, Festivals, and Ceremonies*. New York: St. Martin's Press, 1982.

Cassaway, Esta. *The Five Books of Moses for Young People*. Northvale, NJ: Jason Aronson Inc., 1992.

Chaikin, Miriam. *Children's Bible Stories from Genesis to Daniel*. New York: Dial Books for Young Readers, 1993.

Chavel, Charles B., trans. *Ramban (Nachmanides): Commentary on the Torah*. New York: Shilo Publishing House, Inc., 1974.

Chiel, Arthur, A. *Guide Through the Sidrot and Haftoras*. Hoboken, NJ: KTAV Publishing House, Inc., 1971.

Chill, Abraham. *The Minhagim: The Customs and Ceremonies of Judaism, Their Origins and Rationale*. Brooklyn, NY: Sepher-Hermon Press, 1980.

Chubara, Yona; Miriam P. Feinberg; and Rena Rotenberg. *Torah Talk: An Early Childhood Teaching Guide*. Denver, CO: A.R.E. Publishing, Inc., 1989.

Cohen, Norman J. *Self, Struggle and Change: Family Conflict Stories in Genesis and Their Healing Insights for Our Lives*. Woodstock, VT: Jewish Lights Publishing, 1995.

Cohn-Sherbok, Daniel, ed. *Torah and Revelation*. Lewiston, NJ: Edwin Mellon Press, 1993.

Colodner, Solomon. *Concepts and Values*. New York: Shengold Publishers, Inc., 1969, o.p.

Cone, Molly. *Who Knows Ten? Children's Tales of the Ten Commandments*. New York: UAHC Press, 1971.

Culi, Yaakov. *Yalkut Me'am Lo'ez*. Aryeh Kaplan, trans. New York: Maznaim Publishing Corp., 1977.

Deen, Edith. *All of the Women of the Bible*. San Francisco, CA: Harper and Brothers, 1988.

Diamant, Anita. *The New Jewish Baby Book: Names, Ceremonies, Customs — A Guide for Today's Families*. Woodstock, VT: Jewish Lights Publishing, 1993.

Donin, Hayim H. *To Pray as a Jew*. New York: Basic Books, 1991.

Dresner, Samuel, and Seymour Siegel. *The Jewish Dietary Laws*. New York: United Synagogue Book Service, 1982.

Elkins, Dov Peretz. *Jewish Guided Imagery: A How-To Book for Rabbis, Educators and Group Leaders.* Princeton, NJ: Growth Associates, 1996.

Encyclopaedia Judaica. Jerusalem: Keter Publishing House Jerusalem, Ltd., 1972.

Epstein, I., ed. and trans. *The Babylonian Talmud.* London: Soncino Press, 1982.

Falk, Aaron. *Torah for Children.* Brooklyn, NY: Judaica Press, 1993.

Fields, Harvey J. *Bechol Levavcha: With All Your Heart.* New York: UAHC Press, 1976.

———. *A Torah Commentary for Our Times, Vol. 1: Genesis.* New York:UAHC Press, 1990.

———. *A Torah Commentary for Our Times, Vol. 2: Exodus/Leviticus.* New York: UAHC Press, 1991.

———. *A Torah Commentary for Our Times. Vol. 3: Numbers/Deuteronomy.* New York: UAHC Press, 1993.

Finkel, Avraham Yaakov. *The Great Torah Commentators.* Northvale, NJ: Jason Aronson Inc., 1990.

Fox, Everett. *The Five Books of Moses: Genesis, Exodus, Leviticus, Numbers, Deuteronomy: A New Translation with Introductions, Commentary and Notes* (Schocken Bible: Vol. 1). New York: Schocken Books, 1995.

Frankel, Ellen, and Betsy Platkin Teutsch. *The Encyclopedia of Jewish Symbols.* Northvale, NJ: Jason Aronson, Inc., 1992.

Frankel, Ellen. *The Five Books of Miriam: A Women's Commentary on the Torah.* New York: G.P. Putnam & Sons, 1996.

Freud, Sigmund. *Moses and Monotheism.* New York: Random House, 1955.

Frye, Northrop. *The Great Code: The Bible as Literature.* San Diego CA: HarBrace, 1983.

Gaer, Joseph. *Torah for Family Reading.* Northvale, NJ: Jason Aronson Inc., 1992.

Gaines, M.C., ed. *Picture Stories from the Bible: The Old Testament in Full Color Comic-Strip Form.* New York: Scarf Press, 1989.

Gellman, Marc. *Does God Have A Big Toe? Stories about Stories in the Bible.* New York: HarperCollins Children's Books, 1989.

Gevirtz, Gila. *Partners with God.* West Orange, NJ: Behrman House, 1995.

———. *Living as Partners with God.* West Orange, NJ: Behrman House, 1997.

Ginzberg, Louis. *Legends of the Jews.* Philadelphia, PA: The Jewish Publication Society, 1992. Reprint.

Gittelsohn, Roland B. *Love In Your Life: A Jewish View of Teenage Sexuality.* New York: UAHC Press, 1991.

Glatzer, Nahum N., ed. *On the Bible: Eighteen Studies by Martin Buber.* New York: Schocken Books, 1982, o.p.

Glaustrom, Simon. *When Your Child Asks: A Handbook for Jewish Parents.* New York: Bloch Publishing Co., 1991.

Gold, Michael. *Does God Belong in the Bedroom?* Northvale, NJ: Jason Aronson Inc., 1992.

Goldberg, Nathan. *Passover Haggadah.* Hoboken, NJ: KTAV Publishing House, Inc., n.d.

Goldin, Barbara Diamond. *The Family Book of Midrash.* Northvale, NJ: Jason Aronson Inc., 1990.

Gold-Vukson, Marji. *Torah Tales Copy Pak™: Genesis (Grades 2-5)*. Denver, CO: A.R.E. Publishing, Inc., 1994.

———. *Torah Tales Copy Pak™: Exodus & Leviticus (Grades 2-5)*. Denver, CO: A.R.E. Publishing, Inc., 1995.

———. *Torah Tales Copy Pak™: Numbers & Deuteronomy (Grades 2-5)*. Denver, CO: A.R.E. Publishing, Inc., 1996.

Golub, Jane, with Joel Lurie Grishaver. *Zot ha-Torah: This Is the Torah*. Los Angeles, CA: Torah Aura Productions, 1994.

Goodman, Phillip. *The Passover Anthology*. Philadelphia: The Jewish Publication Society, 1993.

———. *The Rosh HaShanah Anthology*. Philadelphia: The Jewish Publication Society, 1992.

———. *The Sukkot-Simhat Torah Anthology*. Philadelphia: The Jewish Publication Society, 1992.

———. *The Yom Kippur Anthology*. Philadelphia: The Jewish Publication Society, 1992.

Goodman, Roberta Louis. *God's Top Ten: The Meaning of the Ten Commandments*. Los Angeles, CA: Torah Aura Productions, 1992.

Greenberg, Sidney, and Jonathan D. Levine, eds. *Likrat Shabbat: Worship, Study, and Song for Sabbath and Festivals and for the Home*. Bridgeport, CT: The Prayer Book Press, 1973.

———. *Mahzor Hadash: The Mahzor for Rosh Hashanah and Yom Kippur*. Bridgeport, CT: The Prayer Book Press, 1978.

Greenspahn, Frederick E. *When Brothers Dwell Together: The Preeminence of Younger Siblings in the Hebrew Bible*. New York: Oxford University Press, 1994.

Grishaver, Joel Lurie. *Being Torah*. Los Angeles, CA: Torah Aura Productions, 1985.

———. *Bible People Book One* (Genesis). Denver, CO: A.R.E. Publishing, Inc., 1980.

———. *Bible People Book Two* (Exodus-Deuteronomy). Denver, CO: A.R.E. Publishing, Inc., 1981.

———. *Bible People Book Three* (Prophets and Writings). Denver, CO: A.R.E. Publishing, Inc., 1982.

———. *Chapter and Verse*. Los Angeles, CA: Torah Aura Productions. (Instant Lesson)

———. *Learning Torah: A Self-Guided Journey through the Layers of Jewish Learning*. New York: UAHC Press, 1991.

Grishaver, Joel Lurie, and Beth Huppin. *Tzedakah, Gemilut Chasadim and Ahavah*. Denver, CO: A.R.E. Publishing, Inc., 1983.

Gunn, David M., and Donna Nolan Fewell. *Narrative in the Hebrew Bible*. New York: Oxford University Press, 1993.

Hecht, Michael I. *The Fire Waits*. Bridgeport, CT: Hartmore House, 1972.

Hertz, Joseph H., ed. *The Pentateuch and Haftorahs*. London: Soncino Press, 1960.

Hertz, Joseph H. trans. *Pirke Aboth: The Sayings of the Fathers*. Michael Muchnik, illus. West Orange: NJ: Behrman House, 1994.

Heschel, Abraham J. *The Prophets.* 2 vols. San Diego, CA: Harcourt Brace & Co., Vol I: 1969, Vol. 2: 1971.

Hirsch, Samson Raphael. *Pentateuch, T'rumath Tzvi: Hebrew Text, English Translation & Commentary Digest.* Gertrude Hirschler, trans. Brooklyn, NY: The Judaica Press, Inc., 1986.

Holman, Marilyn. *Using Our Senses: Hands-on Activities for the Jewish Classroom.* Denver, CO: A.R.E. Publishing, Inc., 1984.

Hutton, Warwick. *Adam and Eve: The Bible Story.* Old Tappan, NJ: Simon & Schuster Childrens, 1987.

———. *Moses in the Bulrushes.* Old Tappan, NJ: Simon & Schuster Childrens, 1987.

Images from the Bible: The Paintings of Shalom of Safed, The Words of Elie Wiesel. New York: Overlook Press, 1980.

The Interpreter's Bible. 12 vol. Nashville, TN: Abingdon, 1951-57.

Kadden, Bruce, and Barbara Binder Kadden. *Ethical Wills: Handing Down Your Jewish Heritage.* Denver, CO: A.R.E. Publishing. Inc., 1990.

———. *Teaching Jewish Life Cycle: Traditions and Activities.* Denver, CO: A.R.E. Publishing, Inc., 1997.

———. *Teaching Mitzvot: Concepts, Values, and Activities.* rev. ed. Denver, CO: A.R.E. Publishing, Inc., 1988.

———. *Teaching Tefilah: Insights and Activites on Prayer.* Denver, CO: A.R.E. Publishing, Inc., 1994.

Katz, Mordechai. *Lilmod Ulelamade.* Spring Valley, NY: Phillipp Feldheim, Inc., 1986.

Kaufman, Michael. *Love, Marriage, and Family in Jewish Law and Tradition.* Northvale, NJ: Jason Aronson Inc., 1992.

Keller, Werner. *The Bible as History.* New York: Bantam Books, Inc., 1983.

Kelman, Stuart, and Joel Lurie Grishaver, eds. *Learn Torah With . . . (5755 Torah Annual).* Los Angeles, CA: Alef Design Group, 1996.

Kimmel, Eric A. *The Adventures of Hershel of Ostropol.* New York: Holiday House, Inc., 1995.

Kohn, J. *Synagogue in Jewish Life.* Hoboken, NJ: KTAV Publishing House, Inc., 1988.

Kolatch, Alfred J. *The Complete Dictionary of English and Hebrew First Names.* New York: Jonathan David Publishers, Inc., 1984.

Kops, Simon. *Fast, Clean, and Cheap: Or Everything the Jewish Teacher and Parent Needs to Know about Art.* Los Angeles, CA: Torah Aura Productions, 1989.

Korn, Bertram. *American Jewry and the Civil War.* Philadelphia: The Jewish Publication Society, 1994.

Kushner, Lawrence. *GOD was in this PLACE & I, i did not know.* Woodstock, VT: Jewish Lights Publishing, 1991.

Kushner, Lawrence S., and Kerry M. Olitzky. *Sparks Beneath the Surface: A Spiritual Commentary on the Torah.* Northvale, NJ: Jason Aronson Inc., 1994.

Lamm, Maurice. *The Jewish Way in Death and Mourning.* rev. ed. Middle Village, NY: Jonathan David Publishers, Inc., 1972.

Landesman, David. *A Practical Guide to Torah Learning.* Northvale, NJ: Jason Aronson Inc., 1995.

Leibowitz, Nahama. *Studies in Bereshit.* Jerusalem, Israel: World Zionist Organization, 1980.

————. *Studies in Shemot.* Jerusalem, Israel: World Zionist Organization, 1980.

————. *Studies in Vayikra.* Jerusalem, Israel: World Zionist Organization, 1980.

————. *Studies in Bamidbar.* Jerusalem, Israel: World Zionist Organization, 1980.

————. *Studies in Devarim.* Jerusalem, Israel: World Zionist Organization, 1980.

Lepon, Shoshana. *Joseph the Dreamer.* Brooklyn, NY: Judaica Press, 1991.

Levin, S.I., and Edward A. Boyden. *Kosher Code of the Orthodox Jews.* New York: Fawcett Book Group, 1987.

Levine, Moshe. *The Tabernacle: Its Structure and Utensils.* London: Soncino Press, 1969.

Lewis, Barbara A. *The Kid's Guide to Social Action.* Minneapolis: Free Spirit Publishing, Inc., 1991.

Lieberman, Dale. *Witness to the Covenant of Circumcision: Bris Milah.* Northvale, NJ: Jason Aronson Inc., 1997.

Loeb, Sorel, and Barbara Binder Kadden. *Jewish History — Moments & Methods: An Activity Source Book for Teachers.* Denver, CO: A.R.E. Publishing, Inc., 1982.

Lyman, Jonathan. *Jewish Heroes and Heroines: Their Unique Achievements.* New York: Jonathan David Publishers, Inc., 1996.

Maimonides, Moses. *The Book of Knowledge: Mishneh Torah.* Moses Hyamson, trans. New York: Phillipp Feldheim, Inc., 1981.

————. *Guide of the Perplexed.* Leo Strauss, trans. Chicago: The University of Chicago Press, 1974.

————. *Mishneh Torah.* Philip Birnbaum, trans. Rockaway Beach, NY: Hebrew Publishing Co., 1944.

Magnus, Joann, with Howard I. Bogot. *An Artist You Don't Have to Be!: A Jewish Arts and Crafts Book.* New York: UAHC Press, 1990.

Mann, Thomas W.; David L. Bartlett; and Patrick D. Miller, eds.; Dorothea Barton, commentary and trans. *Deuteronomy.* Philadelphia: The Westminster Press, 1995.

Marcus, Audrey Friedman; Sherry Bissell; and Karen S. Lipshutz. *Death, Burial and Mourning in the Jewish Tradition.* Denver, CO: A.R.E. Publishing Inc., 1976.

Marcus, Audrey Friedman, and Raymond A. Zwerin, eds. *The New Jewish Teachers Handbook.* Denver, CO: A.R.E. Publishing, Inc., 1994.

Marcus, J.R. *The Jew in the Medieval World: A Source Book 315-1791.* New York: Greenwood Press, 1975.

McDonough, Yona Zeldis. *Eve and Her Sisters: Women of the Old Testament.* New York: Greenwillow Books, 1994.

Meek, Harold A. *Synagogue: The Complete History of the Art and Architecture of the Synagogue.* San Francisco, CA: Chronicle Books, 1995.

Meeks, Wayne A., ed. *Harper Collins Study Bible: New Revised Standard Version, with the Apocryphal/Deuterocanonical Books.* San Francisco, CA: HarperSanFrancisco, 1993.

Midrash Beresheith Rabba: Genesis Rabba, Hebrew and English. Brooklyn, NY: P. Shalom Publishing, n.d.

Milgrom, Jo. *Handmade Midrash.* Philadelphia: The Jewish Publication Society, 1992.

Moyers, Bill D., and Betty Sue Flowers, eds. Judith Davidson Moyers, exec. ed. *Genesis: A Living Conversation.* New York: Doubleday, 1996.

Nachshoni, Yehudah. *Studies in the Weekly Parashah. Bereishis Vol. I.* Brooklyn, NY: Mesorah Publications, Ltd., 1988.

———. *Studies in the Weekly Parashah. Sh'mos Vol. II.* Brooklyn, NY: Mesorah Publications, Ltd., 1988.

———. *Studies in the Weekly Parashah. Vayikra Vol. III.* Brooklyn, NY: Mesorah Publications, Ltd., 1989.

———. *Studies in the Weekly Parashah. Bamidbar Vol. IV.* Brooklyn, NY: Mesorah Publications, Ltd., 1989.

———. *Studies in the Weekly Parashah. Devarim Vol. V.* Brooklyn, NY: Mesorah Publications, Ltd., 1989.

Nathan, Joan. *The Jewish Holiday Kitchen.* New York: Schocken Books, 1988.

Neusner, Jacob. *Learn Mishnah.* West Orange, NJ: Behrman House, 1978.

———. *Meet Our Sages.* West Orange, NJ: Behrman House, 1980.

Newman, Louis. *The Hasidic Anthology: Tales and Teachings of the Hasidim.* Northvale, NJ: Jason Aronson Inc., 1987.

Olitzky, Kerry M., and Lee H. Olitzky. *Aging and Judaism.* Denver, CO: A.R.E. Publishing, Inc., 1980.

Orenstein, Debra, ed. *Lifecycles: Jewish Women on Life Passages and Personal Milestones, Vol. I.* Woodstock, VT: Jewish Lights Publishing, 1994.

Orenstein, Debra, and Jane Rachel Litman, eds. *Lifecycles: Jewish Women on Biblical Themes in Contemporary Life, Vol. 2.* Woodstock, VT: Jewish Lights Publishing, 1997.

Patera, Meridith Shaw. *Kings and Things: 20 Jewish Plays for Kids 8 to 18.* Denver, CO: A.R.E. Publishing, Inc., 1996.

Pelcovitz, Raphael, trans. *Sforno: Commentary on the Torah.* Brooklyn, NY: Mesorah Publications, Ltd., 1989.

Pitzele, Peter. *Our Father's Wells: A Personal Encounter with the Myths of Genesis.* New York: HarperCollins, 1995.

Plaut, W. Gunther, ed. *The Torah: A Modern Commentary.* New York: UAHC Press, 1981.

———. *The Haftorah Commentary.* Chaim Stern, trans. New York: UAHC Press, 1995.

Podwal, Mark. *The Book of Tens.* New York: Greenwillow Books, 1994.

Polish, Daniel F.; Daniel B. Syme; and Bernard M. Zlotowitz. *Drugs, Sex, and Integrity: What Does Judaism Say?* New York: UAHC Press, 1991.

Potok, Chaim. *Wanderings: Chaim Potok's History of the Jews.* New York: Fawcett Book Group, 1987.

Pritchard, James B., ed. *Ancient Near Eastern Texts Relating to the Old Testament. 3d ed.* Princeton, NJ: Princeton University Press, 1969.

Prose, Francine. *Stories from Our Living Past.* West Orange, NJ: Behrman House, 1972.

Rabinowitz, J., trans. *Midrash Rabbah.* London: The Soncino Press, 1961.

Rad, Gerhard von. *Deuteronomy.* Philadelphia: The Westminster Press, 1966, o.p.

Raphael, Chaim. *A Feast of History: The Drama of Passover.* Washington D.C.: B'nai B'rith International, 1993. Reprint edition.

Reisman, Bernard. *The Jewish Experiential Book: The Quest for Jewish Identity.* New York: KTAV Publishing House, Inc., 1979, o.p.

Rice, Tim, and Andrew Lloyd Webber. *Joseph and the Amazing Technicolor Dream Coat.* North Pomfret, VT: Trafalger Square, 1993.

Roseman, Kenneth. *The Cardinal's Snuffbox.* New York: UAHC Press, 1982.

——. *Escape from the Holocaust.* New York: UAHC Press, 1985.

——. *The Melting Pot.* New York: UAHC Press, 1984.

——. *The Other Side of the Hudson.* New York: UAHC Press, 1993.

——. *The 10th of Av.* New York: UAHC Press, 1988.

Rosenberg, David, ed. *Communion: Contemporary Writers reveal the Bible in Their Lives.* New York: Anchor Books, 1997.

——. *Genesis: As it is written.* San Francisco, CA: HarperSanFrancisco, 1996.

Rosen, Norma. *Biblical Women Unbound.* Philadelphia: The Jewish Publication Society, 1996.

Rosenblatt, Naomi, with Joshua Horwitz. *Wrestling with Angels.* New York: Delacorte Press, 1995.

Rosenthal, Gilbert S. *The Many Faces of Judaism: Orthodox, Conservative, Reconstructionist, and Reform.* West Orange, NJ: Behrman House, 1979.

Rosman, Steven M. *The Bird of Paradise and Other Sabbath Stories.* New York: UAHC Press, 1994.

Rossel, Seymour, et. al. *Lessons from Our Living Past.* West Orange, NJ: Behrman House, 1996.

Rossel, Seymour. *Lessons from the Torah: A Child's Bible Gamebook.* West Orange, NJ: Behrman House, 1997.

——. *A Spiritual Journey: The Bar Mitzvah & Bat Mitzvah Handbook.* West Orange, NJ: Behrman House, 1993.

Rush, Barbara. *The Book of Jewish Women's Tales.* Northvale, NJ: Jason Aronson Inc., 1994.

Salkin, Jeffrey K. *Putting God on the Guest List: How to Reclaim the Spiritual Meaning of Your Child's Bar or Bat Mitzvah.* Woodstock, VT: Jewish Lights Publishing, 1992.

Sandmel, Samuel. *Alone Atop the Mountain: A Novel About Moses and the Exodus.* New York: Doubleday, 1973, o.p.

Sarna, Nahum M. *Understanding Genesis: The Heritage of Biblical Israel.* New York: Schocken Books, 1970.

———. *Exploring Exodus: The Heritage of Biblical Israel.* New York: Schocken Books, 1986.

Sasso, Sandy Eisenberg. *But God Remembered: Stories of Women from Creation To the Promised Land.* Woodstock, VT: Jewish Lights Publishing, 1995.

———. *A Prayer for the Earth: The Story of Naamah, Noah's Wife.* Woodstock, VT: Jewish Lights Publishing, 1996.

Segal, Sheila. *Women of Valor.* West Orange, NJ: Behrman House, 1996.

Sher, Nina Streisand, and Margaret A. Feldman. *100+ Jewish Art Projects for Children.* Denver, CO: A.R.E. Publishing, Inc., 1996.

Scherman, Nasson, ed. *The Stone Edition of the Chumash.* Brooklyn: Mesorah Publications, Ltd., 1996.

———, ed. *The Stone Edition of the Tanach.* Brooklyn: Mesorah Publications, Ltd., 1995.

Siegel, Danny. *Mitzvahs.* Pittsboro, NC: The Town House Press. 1995.

Siegel, Richard; Michael Strassfeld; and Sharon Strassfeld. *The First Jewish Catalog.* Philadelphia: The Jewish Publication Society, 1973.

Silberman, A.M., and M. Rosenbaum, eds. *Pentateuch with Rashi Commentary.* Spring Valley, NY: Phillipp Feldheim, Inc., 1973.

Silver, Abba Hillel. *Moses and the Original Torah.* New York: The MacMillan Company, 1961, o.p.

Simon, James; Raymond A. Zwerin; and Audrey Friedman Marcus. *Bioethics: A Jewish View.* Denver, CO: A.R.E. Publishing, Inc., 1984.

Simon, Solomon, and David Bial Morrison. *The Rabbi's Bible.* 3 vols. West Orange, NJ: Behrman House, 1966.

Singer, Ellen, and Bernard M. Zlotowitz. *Our Sacred Texts: Discovering the Jewish Classics.* New York: UAHC Press, 1992.

Singer, Isaac Bashevis. *Stories for Children.* New York: Farrar/Straus/Giroux, 1985.

Smith, Judy Gattis. *26 Ways to Use Drama in Teaching the Bible.* Nashville, TN: Abingdon, 1988.

Sonsino, Rifat, and Daniel B. Syme. *What Happens After I Die? Jewish Views of Life after Death.* New York: UAHC Press, 1990.

Speiser, E.A. ed. *The Anchor Bible: Genesis.* New York: Doubleday and Co., Inc., 1964.

Spiegel, Shalom. *The Last Trial: On the Legends and Lore of the Command to Abraham to Offer Isaac as a Sacrifice: The Akedah.* Woodstock, VT: Jewish Lights Publishing, 1993.

Spier, Peter. *Noah's Ark.* New York: Doubleday and Co., Inc., 1977.

Steinbock, Steven E. *Torah: The Growing Gift.* New York: UAHC Press, 1994.

Stern, Chaim, ed. *On the Doorposts of Your House: Prayers and Ceremonies for the Jewish Home.* New York: CCAR Press, 1994.

Strassfeld, Michael. *A Shabbat Haggadah for Cele-bration and Study.* New York: American Jewish Committee, 1981.

———. *The Jewish Holidays: A Guide & Commentary.* New York: Harper & Row, Publishers, 1985.

Strassfeld, Sharon, and Michael Strassfeld, eds. *The Second Jewish Catalog: Sources and Resources.* Philadelphia: The Jewish Publication Society, 1976.

TANAKH: The Holy Scriptures: The New JPS transla-tion According to the Traditional Hebrew Text. Philadelphia: The Jewish Publication Society, 1985.

Temko, Florence. *Jewish Origami 2.* Torrance, CA: Heian International, 1992.

Tubb, Jonathan N. *Bible Lands.* New York: Alfred A. Knopf, 1991.

Tucker, JoAnne, and Susan Freeman. *Torah in Motion: Creative Dance Midrash.* Denver, CO: A.R.E. Publishing, Inc., 1990.

Umansky, Ellen M., and Dianne Ashton, eds. *Four Centuries of Jewish Women's Spirtuality: A Source-book.* Boston: Beacon Press, 1992.

Visotzky, Burton. *The Genesis of Ethics.* New York: Crown Publishing Group, 1996.

———. *Reading the Book: Making the Bible a Timeless Text.* New York: Anchor Books, 1991.

Warshawsky, Gale Solotar. *Creative Puppetry for Jewish Kids.* Denver, CO: A.R.E. Publishing, Inc., 1985.

Waskow, Arthur I. *Seasons of Our Joy: A Modern Guide to the Jewish Holidays.* Boston: Beacon Press, 1991.

Weiss, Zari, with Elise Kahn and Gary Bretton-Granatoor. *A Jewish Response To Cults.* New York: UAHC Press, 1997.

Welfeld, Irving. *Kosher: A Guide for the Perplexed.* Northvale, NJ: Jason Aronson Inc., 1996.

Wolfson, Ron. *Shabbat Seder.* Woodstock, VT: Jewish Lights Publishing, 1996.

Wisel, Elie. *Messengers of God: Biblical Portraits and Legends.* New York: Simon & Schuster, Inc., 1985.

Zlotowitz, Bernard M., and Abraham Segal, eds. *One People: A Study in Comparative Judaism.* New York: UAHC Press, 1983.

Zones, Jane Sprague. *Taking the Fruit: Modern Women's Tales of the Bible.* 2d ed. La Jolla, CA: Woman's Institute for Continuing Jewish Education, 1993.

Zornberg, Avivah Gottlieb. *The Beginning of Desire: Reflections on Genesis.* Philadelphia: The Jewish Publication Society, 1995.

Zwerin, Raymond. *The Jewish Calendar.* Denver, CO: A.R.E. Publishing, Inc., 1975.

Zwerin, Raymond A.; Audrey Friedman Marcus; and Leonard Kramish. *Circumcision.* Denver, CO: A.R.E. Publishing, Inc., 1983.

Audiovisual

Again . . . The Second Time. Ergo Media Inc. Video-cassette.

Bible People Songs. A.R.E. Publishing, Inc. Audio-cassette.

The Big Bang and Other Creation Myths. Pyramid Films. Videocassette.

The Corridor: Death. Ergo Media Inc. Videocassette.

Dad. Videocassette. (Available in video stores)

Elephant Man. Videocassette. (Available in video stores)

The Falashas. Ergo Media Inc. Videocassette.

Family Prayers. Videocassette. (Available in video stores)

Fiddler on the Roof. Audiocassette.

Fiddler on the Roof. Videocassette. (Available in video stores)

Field of Dreams. Videocassette. (Available in video stores)

For Out of Zion. Ergo Media Inc. Videocassette.

Friedman, Debbie. *And You Shall Be a Blessing.* Available from A.R.E. Publishing, Inc. Audiocassette.

————. *If Not Now, When?* Available from A.R.E. Publishing, Inc. Audiocassette.

This Great Difference. Direct Cinema Ltd. Videocassette.

Hair. Videocassette. (Available in video stores)

Hester Street. Videocassette. (Available in video stores)

Holy Moses. Novello & Co., Ltd. Videocassette.

I Love You, Rosa. Videocassette. (Available in video stores)

In the Synagogue. UAHC-RJ Media. Videocassette.

Intermarriage: When Love Meets Tradition. Direct Cinema Ltd. Videocassette.

Jinja's Israeli Safari. Ergo Media Inc. Videocassette.

Joseph and the Amazing Technicolor Dreamcoat. Audiocassette.

Jewish Customs. KTAV Publishing House, Inc. Videocassette.

King of the Hill. Videocassette. (Available in video stores)

Leap of Faith. Videocassette. (Available in video stores)

Levine, Lisa. *Keep the Spirit.* Sounds Write Productions, Inc. Audiocassette.

Mah Tovu. *Only This.* Available from A.R.E. Publishing, Inc. Audiocassette.

Mask. Videocassette. (Available in video stores)

Miss Rose White. Videocassette. (Available in video stores)

The Mountain of Moses. Audio Brandon Films. Videocassette.

Noah's Ark from *The Greatest Adventure Stories from the Bible.* Turner Home Entertainment. Videocassette. (Available in video stores)

Noah's Park. Ergo Media Inc. Videocassette.

NFTY Chordster and Supplement. UAHC Youth Division Resources. Songbook.

Operation Moses: A Documentary. Ergo Media Inc. Videocassette.

Seal Upon Thy Heart. Ergo Media Inc. Videocassette.

Songs NFTY Sings #1. UAHC Youth Division Resources. Audiocassette.

Sounds of Creation: Genesis in Song. Available from A.R.E. Publishing, Inc. Audiocassette.

Sounds of Freedom: Exodus in Song. Available from A.R.E. Publishing, Inc. Audiocassette.

The Ten Commandments. Videocassette. (Available in video stores)

This Great Difference. Direct Cinema Ltd. Video-cassette.

Ticket to Heaven. Videocassette. (Available in video stores)

Torah Toons I: The Video. Torah Aura Productions. Videocassette.

What's Eating Gilbert Grape? Videocassette. (Available in video stores)

Willie Wonka and the Chocolate Factory. (Available in video stores)

A Woman Called Moses. Videocassette. (Available in video stores)

You Can Go Home Again. UAHC-RJ Media. Video-cassette.

List of Audiovisual Publishers and Distributors

ALDEN FILMS
Box 449
Clarksburg, NY 08510

A.R.E. PUBLISHING, INC.
3945 South Oneida Street
Denver, CO 80237

AUDIO BRANDON FILMS
34 MacQuesten Parkway South
Mt. Vernon, NY 10550

DIRECT CINEMA LTD.
P.O. Box 10003
Santa Monica, CA 90410

ERGO MEDIA INC.
Box 2037
Teaneck, NJ 07666

KTAV PUBLISHING HOUSE, INC.
Box 6249
Hoboken, NJ 07030

NOVELLO & CO., LTD.
145 Palisade Street
Dobbs Ferry, NY 10522

PYRAMID FILMS
Box 1048
Santa Monica, CA 90406

TORAH AURA PRODUCTIONS
4423 Fruitland Avenue
Los Angeles, CA 90058

TRANSCONTINENTAL MUSIC PUBLICATIONS
838 Fifth Avenue
New York, NY 10021

UAHC PRESS & RJ MEDIA
838 Fifth Avenue
New York, NY 10021

UAHC YOUTH DIVISION RESOURCES
P.O. Box 443
Bowen Road
Warwick, NY 10990

INDEX OF STRATEGIES

Adam/*Edom*
  Numbers:
      Chukat #10, #11

Amalek
  Genesis:
      Vayishlach #1
  Exodus:
      Shemot #25
  Leviticus:
      Balak #3
  Deuteronomy:
      Ki Taytzay #10, #17

Ark/*Aron HaKodesh*
  Genesis:
      Noah #8
      Vayechi #1
  Exodus:
      Terumah #1, #7
      Pikuday #8
  Numbers:
      Naso #3, #12

Ark of Noah
  Genesis:
      Noah #8, #11, #13, #18, #20, #21, #23, #27, #35
  Exodus:
      Shemot #16a

Bedeken
  Genesis:
      Vayaytzay #12

Blessing/Curse
  Genesis:
      Vayechi #4, #5, #6, #8
  Exodus:
      Pikuday #7
  Leviticus:
      Tzav #5, #6

      Bechukotai #1, #2, #5, #6, #8, #9, #12, #13, #16, #22
  Numbers:
      Naso #8, #15, #16, #24
      Balak #2, #14, #15
      Mas'ay #22
  Deuteronomy:
      Ekev #5, #7
      Ki Tavo #8, #27
      V'zot HaBrachah #12, #13

Calendar
  Exodus:
      Bo #8
      Beshalach #25
  Leviticus:
      Emor #8, #9
      Pinchas #24

Challah
  Genesis:
      Vayaytzay #16
  Exodus:
      Terumah #3
  Leviticus:
      Emor #13
  Numbers:
      Shelach Lecha #9

Chalutzim
  Numbers:
      Matot #15
  Deuteronomy:
      Devarim #16

Circumcision
  Genesis:
      Lech Lecha #12, #13 (ceremony for girls), #15
  Exodus:
      Shemot #7

Cities of refuge
    Numbers:
        Mas'ay #2, #7, #8, #20
    Deuteronomy:
        Va'etchanan #8

Covenant
    Genesis:
        Noah #12, #14
        Lech Lecha #12
    Exodus:
        Yitro #9
    Leviticus:
        Bechukotai #3
    Numbers:
        Pinchas #5
    Deuteronomy:
        Va'etchanan #7
        Nitzavim #6, #10, #11, #12, #24

Creation/Humankind
    Genesis:
        Beresheet #2, #3, #4, #7, #16,#17, #18, #19
        Noah #5, #9, #24
    Deuteronomy:
        Ha'azinu #10

Death/Burial
    Genesis:
        Chayay Sarah #4, #5, #16, #19, #20, #21
        Vayishlach #9, #10, #11
        Vayechi #1, #8, #9, #10, #14, #21
    Exodus:
        Beshalach #24
    Leviticus:
        Shemini #6
    Numbers:
        Chukat #5, #7, #15, #22, #24
        Pinchas #8, #9, #11, #19
    Deuteronomy:
        Ki Taytzay #6
        V'zot HaBrachah #5, #6, #7, #8, #14, #19

Environmental concerns
    Genesis:
        Beresheet #14, #15, #33
        Noah #10, #21, #28, #36
        Toledot #16
    Exodus:
        Vaera #28
    Leviticus:
        Behar #17, #18
    Numbers:
        Chukat #26
    Deuteronomy:
        Shofetim #8, #10, #11, #12, #27
        Ki Taytzay #5

False prophets
    Deuteronomy:
        Re'eh #2, #9, #10, #15, #19
        Shofetim #19, #20

Firstborn
    Genesis:
        Vayera #5, #7
        Toledot #1, #2, #8, #9, #12, #13
        Vayishlach #2, #3, #7, #8, #17
        Vayeshev #2, #5, #19, #28
        Mikaytz #5, #6, #24
        Vayechi #2
    Exodus:
        Bo #16
    Numbers:
        Korach #8
    Deuteronomy:
        Ki Taytzay #7

God
    Genesis:
        Beresheet #7, #10, #26
        Noah #24
        Lech Lecha #2, #3, #4, #5
        Vayera #3, #4, #5, #6, #18, #31
        Vayaytzay #9, #14
        Vayigash #25

Exodus:
  Shemot #3, #17
  Vaera #2
  Beshalach #16
  Yitro #13
  Terumah #4, #16
  Ki Tisa #8, #9
  Pikuday #11
Leviticus:
  Bechukotai #17
Numbers:
  BaMidbar #1
  Beha'alotecha #7, #9, #10, #13
  Shelach Lecha #1, #3
  Balak #4
  Pinchas #3, #15
  Matot #4
Deuteronomy:
  Devarim #2
  Va'etchanan #14
  Ekev #4, #6
  Re'eh #6, #7
  Nitzavim #8
  Vayaylech #17
  Ha'azinu #4, #7, #8, #9

God's partners
  Genesis:
    Noah #13
  Exodus:
    Pikuday #2, #11
  Leviticus:
    Emor #6
  Numbers:
    Balak #4
  Deuteronomy:
    Devarim #15
    Shofetim #6
    Ki Tavo #22

Golden Calf
  Exodus:
    Ki Tisa #2, #4, #6, #7, #10, #12, #15, #19, #26

Leviticus:
  Shemini #12a
Numbers:
  Shelach Lecha #1
Deuteronomy:
  Ekev #8

High Holy Days
  Genesis:
    Beresheet #31
    Vayera #13
    Vayayshev #12
  Exodus:
    Bo #8
    Ki Tisa #8
  Leviticus:
    Vayikra #9
    Acharay Mot #4, #10, #13, #15, #16, #27
    Kedoshim #4
    Emor #4
    Bechukotai #3, #17
  Numbers:
    Beha'alotecha #21
    Matot #12
  Deuteronomy:
    Nitzavim #5, #18, #19, #20
    Vayaylech #15, #16, #17, #18

Holiness
  Exodus:
    Terumah #17, #26
    Tetzaveh #16
  Leviticus:
    Shemini #10
    Kedoshim #7, #9, #12, #13, #26
  Numbers:
    Korach #15

Justice and mercy
  Exodus:
    Ki Tisa #7
  Deuteronomy:
    Devarim #14
    Shofetim #1, #2, #15, #21
    Ki Taytzay #3

Karet/Cut off from kin
    Leviticus:
        Tzav #11
        Bechukotai #17
    Numbers:
        Shelach Lecha #12

Kashrut
    Genesis:
        Noah #6
        Vayishlach #4
    Exodus:
        Mishpatim #5, #8, #11, #12, #13
    Leviticus:
        Vayikra #24
        Tzav #14, #25
        Shemini #3, #5, #7, #8, #9, #20
        Acharay Mot #5
    Numbers:
        Matot #7
    Deuteronomy:
        Re'eh #13

Leprosy/*Tzara'at*
    Leviticus:
        Tazria #1, #2, #3, #4, #5, #8, #9, #10, #11,
        #17, #24
        Metzora #5, #8, #11, #14, #22, #23
        Kedoshim #5
    Numbers:
        Beha'alotecha #15, #26, #29

Liturgy and prayer
    Genesis:
        Beresheet #19
        Chayay Sarah #19
        Vayaytzay #26
        Vayayshev #12
        Vayigash #8
    Exodus:
        Vaera #8, #9, #11
        Bo #15
        Beshalach #6, #10, #15, #16
        Terumah #5
        Tetzaveh #9

    Leviticus:
        Vayikra #5, #7
        Tzav #5, #6
        Tazria #7, #16
        Bechukotai #3
    Numbers:
        BaMidbar #4
        Naso #7, #8, #13, #15, #24
        Korach #8
        Balak #18
        Pinchas #1, #6, #15
        Matot #12
        Mas'ay #20
    Deuteronomy:
        Va'etchanan #1, #5, #9, #11
        Ekev #9, #14, #16, #25
        Ki Tavo #8
        V'zot HaBrachah #26

Marriage/Relationships
    Genesis:
        Beresheet #18
        Lech Lecha #9
        Vayera #1, #2, #14
        Chayay Sarah #8, #9, #13, #17, #18, #31
        Toledot #8, #18, #23, #27
        Vayaytzay #3, #12
        Vayayshev #8
    Leviticus:
        Acharay Mot #6, #7, #20
        Kedoshim #12
    Numbers:
        Beha'alotecha #20
    Deuteronomy:
        Ki Taytzay #12, #13

Menorah
    Exodus:
        Terumah #14, #15

Mezuzah
    Deuteronomy:
        Va'etchanan #16, #18

Minyan
    Numbers:
        Shelach Lecha #11

Nadab and Abihu
    Leviticus:
        Tzav #1, #2
        Shemini #6, #12, #13, #14, #15, #21
    Numbers:
        BaMidbar #1

Ner Tamid
    Exodus:
        Tetzaveh #10, #12, #14, #17

Olive tree/Olive oil
    Genesis:
        Noah #26
    Exodus:
        Tetzaveh #3, #14, #15

Ordination
    Exodus:
        Tetzaveh #10, #11
        Ki Tisa #13
    Leviticus:
        Tzav #1, #8, #10, #12, #13

Passover
    Exodus:
        Vaera #7
        Bo #3, #4, #6, #9, #19
        Beshalach #9
    Numbers:
        Beha'alotecha #14
    Deuteronomy:
        Va'etchanan #10
        Ki Tavo #4, #5

Prophecy/Prophets
    Genesis:
        Mikaytz #1, #2
    Exodus:
        Shemot #3
        Beshalach #7

    Leviticus:
        Vayikra #4
    Numbers:
        Beha'alotecha #1, #9, #16, #19
        Balak #6, #8
    Deuteronomy:
        Devarim #3
        V'zot HaBrachah #4

Rabbis/Priests
    Exodus:
        Tetzaveh #7
        Pikuday #10
    Leviticus:
        Tzav #16, #17
        Emor #12
        Acharay Mot #13
    Numbers:
        BaMidbar #8
        Korach #11

Rosh Chodesh/New moon
    Exodus:
        Beshalach #25
        Beha'alotecha #8
        Pinchas #7, #24

Sacrifice
    Genesis:
        Vayera #4, #5, #9, #13, #16, #17, #31
    Exodus:
        Terumah #5
    Leviticus:
        Vayikra #1, #2, #3, #4, #5, #6, #7, #8, #10, #12, #14, #17, #24
        Tzav #3, #4, #5, #7
    Numbers:
        Pinchas #1, #6, #7

Shabbat
    Genesis:
        Beresheet #17
        Mikaytz #25

Exodus:
Shemot #11
Beshalach #10, #11
Yitro #12
Mishpatim #19, #28
Ki Tisa #11, #14, #29
Vayakhel #1, #4, #10, #26
Leviticus:
Behar #10,#12
Numbers:
BaMidbar #7
Naso #24
Pinchas #6
Mas'ay #5
Deuteronomy:
Va'etchanan #13

Shalosh Regalim (also see Passover, Shavuot, Sukkot)
Leviticus:
Emor #5, #15, #23
Deuteronomy:
Re'eh #8, #12, #25

Shavuot
Exodus:
Yitro #10
Leviticus:
Emor #2
Numbers:
BaMidbar #6
Deuteronomy:
Ki Tavo #10

Shewbread (showbread)
Exodus:
Terumah #3
Leviticus:
Vayikra #12, #13
Emor #13
Numbers:
Shelach Lecha #9

Shofar
Genesis:
Vayera #13

Numbers:
Beha'alotecha #12, #21
Slavery
Exodus:
Vaera #14, #18
Bo #7
Yitro #9
Mishpatim #2, #3, #10
Leviticus:
Behar #8, #9, #16, #24
Numbers:
Shelach Lecha #15
Deuteronomy:
Devarim #13
Re'eh #3, #14
Ki Taytzay #15

Sukkot
Leviticus:
Emor #10, #11, #14
Deuteronomy:
Vayaylech #8, #16

Synagogue
Exodus:
Terumah #7, #10, #13
Ki Tisa #17
Vayakhel #6, #13
Pikuday #25
Leviticus:
Tazria #7
Bechukotai #10
Deuteronomy:
Re'eh #18

Tabernacle
Exodus:
Terumah #3, #4, #8, #9, #12, #13
Vayakhel #1, #3, #5, #11
Pikuday #2, #14, #15, #16

Tallit/Tzitzit
Exodus:
Bo #11

Numbers:
  Shelach Lecha #6, #7, #10

Tamay
  Leviticus:
    Shemini #4
    Tazria #5
    Metzora #2, #3, #4, #9, #10

Tefillin
  Exodus:
    Bo #2, #10, #11
  Deuteronomy:
    Va'etchanan #18
    Ekev #11, #12

Ten Commandments
  Genesis:
    Noah #2, #3, #4
  Exodus:
    Yitro #1, #2, #3, #4, #6, #8, #9, #10, #11, #16, #17, #19, #32
    Mishpatim #4
    Terumah #1
    Ki Tisa #3, #18
  Leviticus:
    Acharay Mot #9
    Kedoshim #1
  Deuteronomy:
    Va'etchanan #6, #17
    Ki Tavo #1

Ten Plagues
  Exodus:
    Vaera #10, #13, #22, #28
    Bo #1, #12, #14, #15, #22, #28
    Beshalach #1, #24

Tishah B'av
  Deuteronomy:
    Va'etchanan #13

Torah/Torah service
  Exodus:
    Beshalach #10, #15

Yitro #10, #15
Mishpatim #16
Terumah #4
Tetzaveh #1, #6
Ki Tisa #5
Pikuday #4, #5
Leviticus:
  Tzav #2
Numbers:
  Beha'alotecha #10
Deuteronomy:
  Devarim #10, #17
  Va'etchanan #1, #2, #11
  Nitzavim #6
  Vayaylech #2, #3, #7
  Ha'azinu #1, #6
  V'zot HaBrachah #22

Tza'ar baalay chayim/Treatment of animals
  Genesis:
    Noah #6, #19, #21, #28
  Leviticus:
    Emor #7
  Numbers:
    Balak #27, #28
  Deuteronomy:
    Ki Taytzay #5, #18, #20, #24

Tzedakah
  Exodus:
    Terumah #11
  Leviticus:
    Tzav #26
    Bechukotai #10, #22
  Numbers:
    Naso #18
    Korach #27
  Deuteronomy:
    Re'eh #16, #17, #20
    Shofetim #17
    Ki Tavo #13, #14, #15

Vegetarianism
  Genesis:
    Noah #6, #36

Leviticus:

> *Shemini* #8

Welcoming the stranger/*Hachnasat Orchim*
Genesis:

> *Vayera* #10, #11, #12, #16, #30, #33
> *Vayeshev* #29
> *Mikaytz* #27

Exodus:

> *Mishpatim* #16, #18

Leviticus:

> *Tzav* #26

Numbers:

> *Balak* #17

Deuteronomy:

> *Ekev* #26

Women
Genesis:

> *Beresheet* #5, #12
> *Noah* #10, #36
> *Lech Lecha* #9, #10, #15
> *Vayera* #2, #7, #8, #20
> *Chayay Sarah* #1, #4, #11, #12
> *Toledot* #5, #8
> *Vayaytzay* #1, #5, #7
> *Vayishlach* #9, #20, #21, #22
> *Vayigash* #10, #17
> *Vayechi* #13

Exodus:

> *Shemot* #9, #23, #34
> *Vaera* #9
> *Beshalach* #3, #4, #7, #8, #25
> *Vayakhel* #9

Leviticus:

> *Shemini* #6

Numbers:

> *Naso* #13
> *Shelach Lecha* #11
> *Chukat* #15, #19
> *Matot* #1, #13
> *Mas'ay* #3, #14, #15

Deuteronomy:

> *Ekev* #13
> *Ki Taytzay* #1, #11, #13

Zechut Avot/Zechut Imahot
Exodus:

> *Vaera* #8, #9

Leviticus:

> *Bechukotai* #3, #4, #15

Numbers:

> *Naso* #24

Deuteronomy:

> *Ekev* #13